ÉE NESTLÉ

COMPLET

TS EN BAS AGE

CHIMISTE A VEVEY

embre 1875.

Nestlé

125 Years

1866–1991

Nestlé

125 Years

1866–1991

Jean Heer

PUBLISHED BY NESTLÉ S.A.

Nestlé

125 Years

☐ Nestlé is celebrating the 125th anniversary of its foundation in the same year as Switzerland, the country in which the company was founded, celebrates the 700th anniversary of the Swiss Confederation. This is a lucky coincidence, which provides us with an opportunity to reiterate everything the Nestlé Company of Vevey owes to its Swiss origins. Given the small size of Switzerland and the influence of certain aspects of the Swiss mentality, Nestlé was forced to expand abroad very quickly; yet it left each locally based Nestlé Company with a wide area for independent action.

Relating the history of a company also provides an opportunity to describe the ideas, feelings, and jobs of the persons who influenced the company's development. It also means tracing company growth within a changing socio-historic context, for a firm must constantly strive to integrate itself with its human, economic, technological, and even political surroundings in order to thrive. This explains why we decided to discuss certain events taking place in the world while the company was expanding. Updating the manuscript he wrote in 1966 (published for Nestlé's centennial), our former employee Jean Heer, now retired, has added an account of the past twenty-five years to the present book.

A company expands as a result of the work of all its employees, at every level of the firm, who contribute to its growth. This book is dedicated to them.

Helmut Maucher
Chairman of the board
and chief executive of Nestlé S.A.

NESTLÉ
A 125-YEAR-OLD FIRM

The Nestlé Company bears the name of a real man: Henri Nestlé. Nestlé was born in Frankfort on the Main, Germany, and had been living in Vevey, Switzerland, for twenty-three years when, early in the last third of the nineteenth century, he set about manufacturing a product he had invented: *farine lactée,* a special food product for infants composed of cereals and milk. The modest company Henri Nestlé created profited from its founder's painstaking work, as well as from that of his successors after it was incorporated in 1875. Subsequently, the firm expanded through its own efforts and through acquisitions. Over the course of one hundred and twenty-five years, Henri Nestlé's firm became what it is today: one of the foremost food companies in the world.

Placing the development of the Nestlé Company in its historical context is not exactly the same as writing history. Outlining in a book the major world events forming a backdrop for the ups and downs in the life of an international corporation is rather like relating a trip through time. This book's modest aim is to provide the reader with an idea of the way in which the history of the company meshed with that of the world.

The company's management and employees have made notable efforts to help the firm expand. In addition, it has benefited from alliances formed and acquisitions made in the course of its existence, which explains why this work is divided into chapters corresponding to the principal mergers that stand out as milestones in Nestlé's history. Moreover, the great historical events that accompanied the development of the largest Swiss company are reflected therein.

Over the years, the company name has changed, and yet one name has been retained throughout each metamorphosis. And that name is: Nestlé.

For this reason, the author has chosen to begin with the history of Henri Nestlé's small business at Vevey, which by 1867 had already made a name for itself beyond Swiss borders. The company's official origins date back to the founding of the Anglo-Swiss Condensed Milk Company, its first annual report being published in 1866. However, as we shall see later, it was not until 1905 that Anglo-Swiss actually merged with Nestlé. This was the first of many mergers, which have always played an important role in Nestlé's history. While Henri Nestlé did not launch his "milk food" until 1867, he had been toying with the idea for quite some time. [Translator's note: Although milk food is the name under which the product was first sold in England, this food product represented a real innovation insofar as Nestlé's *farine lactée* consisted of ground cereals as well as milk. And thus "infant cereal" is actually a more accurate translation and will be employed hereafter.] As he was the sole owner, Nestlé had no reason to publish reports on his firm's activity; nonetheless, these were published following the purchase of the company by a group of individuals in Vevey, who transformed it into a corporation.

Like the work published in 1966 for the Nestlé centennial, the present one also evokes both socio-economic and political developments throughout the world (printed in italics) as well as the actual history of Nestlé (in roman type). This will hopefully enable the reader to better understand the global socio-economic and political context in which the firm at Vevey has grown and developed.

Each period discussed consists of a section dealing with the global context and another describing the companies with which Nestlé merged. In addition, the author will attempt to provide a general idea of Nestlé's own situation at the moment of each merger.

Surely it would be pretentious to attempt to trace the growth of a particular business concern in terms of world history. While certain events, such as World War I and II, for instance, did have a direct effect on Nestlé's development, others—by far the majority—are no more than points of reference enabling the reader to orient himself as he follows the story of the company's activity.

In-depth research would be required in order to place this story against a proper historical backdrop. And so, the present writer is really more of a discoverer, who has made extensive use of books to help him in his navigation through world history. Indeed, this work is based to a great extent on that of the men and women of Nestlé. Fortunately, studies by Walter Preiswerk, Fernand Gysler, and especially Michel Liais have already amply paved the way for the portions of this work dealing with the origins of the company. Former chief executive officers Maurice Paternot, André Perrochet, Enrico Bignami, and Jean-Constant Corthésy, as well as Pierre

Liotard-Vogt—who was also chairman—were kind enough to facilitate this study. The current chairman and chief executive officer, Helmut Maucher, is also to be thanked for his support of the author's efforts. The brevity of this preface prevents the writer from expressing his indebtedness to all of these men. But without their help and that of many others (whom it has not been possible to name here), this book could never have been published in its present form. The author also wishes to thank those who cooperated closely in the creation of this work: Edy Aubry, Anne-Françoise Meckenstock, and Marthe Bachmann, who helped with research on the company's activity during its first hundred years of existence, as well as Abel Triponez and Catherine Steinmann for their participation in tracing its entire history.

Jean Heer

CHAPTER I

1867

In the Aftermath of the Battle of Sadowa, a New Industry Is Born in Vevey

ECONOMIC LIBERALISM — AT ITS APOGEE — DOMINATED THROUGHOUT A MIGHTY EUROPE...

1867: After the Battle of Sadowa (1866)

☐ *In 1867, a year after its defeat on July 3, 1866, of Austrian troops at Sadowa, Prussia emerged as a European power. Until that time, England, France, Austria-Hungary, and Russia had dominated Europe, whose influence was felt the world over. The United States, though beginning its political ascension, had not yet asserted itself as a world power. China was already in decline, and Japan was barely emerging from feudalism.*

Economic liberalism prevailed in this early nineteenth-century Europe. Great Britain, where the Industrial Revolution had begun in the early eighteenth century, ruled the world's oceans through its fleet and was a leading coal and steel producer renowned for its manufactured goods. Although it would take electricity and oil another twenty years to come into their own, steam and steel were already thriving. Western Europe was characterized during this period by steady economic growth and technological development, which began with the textile industry and then spread from one country to another. Large-scale manufacturing was born, railway networks grew, and steamships gradually replaced sailing vessels.

The first noticeable consequence of Prussia's victory at Sadowa was its increased sense of power—and it was soon to pose a threat to France. It also caused Russia to turn toward Asia rather than Europe, while encouraging the "splendid isolation" of Great Britain and its maritime empire.

The United Kingdom was not particularly unhappy to watch the development of these geopolitical events, while at the same time participating in the silent and irreversible rivalry that was building up between the great economic powers (a rivalry that Britain had in fact helped to initiate). The Industrial Revolution can be attributed to the efforts of a group of energetic, hard-working individuals from both the lower and middle classes. For them, work was not unpleasant and degrading, as it had been perceived in classical times; nor was it considered a form of penance, as in the Middle Ages; nor did it represent a religious act, whose purpose was not to make a profit, but to ensure one's livelihood, as it had been for Luther. For these people, work was a means of fighting poverty. They believed that creating a way for the poor to provide for themselves was infinitely more productive than engaging in charity. This new social group rejected aristocratic and middle-class wealth, while strongly encouraging industrial growth which could provide consumer goods for the masses. Working to the advantage of this new movement was Great Britain's firmly established banking system—already more than a hundred years old—which made possible the granting of loans at a low rate of interest.

Technical advances in agriculture had been made during the previous century. With the growth of cities came a growing demand for food, which motivated wealthy British landowners to find ways of increasing production and improving methods of cultivation. Areas of land were regrouped, which required the fencing off of plots. The high cost of these operations indirectly caused the small farmer, who exploited a very small area, to limit his cultivation to tiny plots of land that did not even yield enough crops to feed one family. Artisans and peasants who owned no property and who, in former times, had been protected by a law allowing each family to permit one cow to graze on community property, suddenly found themselves forced either to supplement their meager income by taking up manual labor in the textile industry, such as carding or spinning wool, or—and this was the unfortunate plight of many—to leave their towns for the city, in search of better pay and greater opportunity. This exodus from the countryside to the city accelerated after the Napoleonic Wars.

Transportation changed with the construction of new roads and waterways throughout the country, which, in turn, facilitated the transport of goods and raw materials—in particular, coal. In 1825, the first railway system in the world was inaugurated in Great Britain; and by 1830, Stephenson's great engine was capable of pulling 12-ton cargo at almost 15 miles per hour.

Strictly speaking, the Industrial Revolution began in two areas: the cotton and steel industries. Very early on, the cotton-based textile industry was faced with competition from the local wool industry, which obtained an embargo on the import of cotton fabric from the Indies. Cotton factories sprang up soon thereafter throughout Great Britain. It was not long, however, before two factors began to threaten this new industry: the fluctuating and thus unpredictable cost of raw materials and a scarcity of skilled labor. The industry was forced to make better use of its

IN WHICH GREAT BRITAIN WAS AT THE FOREFRONT, OWING TO ITS INDUSTRIAL REVOLUTION ORIGINATING IN THE COTTON AND STEEL INDUSTRY...

IN SPITE OF SOCIAL UNREST, DIRE POVERTY CAUSED WORKERS TO BAND TOGETHER, WHILE BRITAIN CONTINUED TO RULE THE SEAS.

human resources and mechanize its production methods. Machines soon began replacing human labor, and one invention followed another. Advances in spinning techniques, however, occurred at a faster pace than advances in textile production, leading to the accumulation of an overabundance of spun items, which resulted in the periodic lay-off of spinners. Similar problems were soon to arise in the wool industry.

The steel industry became mechanized during the first quarter of the nineteenth century. Britain, with little forest land, began mining coal, which, thanks to a series of inventions, was eventually to become useful in the production of iron. With its abundant mineral resources, Great Britain began building big steamships from steel and iron. And it was not long before these ships were to dominate the seas — some, thanks to weapons and speed, others owing to the sea routes they forged, thus allowing the United Kingdom to deposit its export shipments of coal at major ports throughout the world and to bring home raw materials and products acquired cheaply abroad.

Great Britain's rise to economic supremacy did not protect it from domestic problems, however. Landowners accused the burgeoning middle class of enjoying its newly acquired wealth at the expense of poorer workers. The middle class, in turn, blamed poverty on the high price of grain and demanded the repeal of the Corn Laws. In 1846, the latter won their case. Cereal production declined precipitously, and in the countryside farmers turned to cattle breeding. The United Kingdom began importing most of its foodstuffs, which were financed through the export of textiles, coal, and tools.

Throughout the nineteenth century, London remained the banking capital of the world. In 1867, even in those parts of the world not under British sovereignty, English merchants were predominant.

Britain asserted itself in other ways as well. In the first thirty years of the century, Great Britain's population shot from 10,000,000 to 17,000,000. And the more adventurous souls, unable to find work, emigrated to the United States or to other countries of the British Empire—the emigration rate soon averaging 100,000 persons per year.

Although production increased at a proportionately more rapid pace than population growth, the standard of living of British industrial workers remained much the same for two-thirds of the century. In rural areas, the situation was perhaps no more acute than before, but it was quite evident in the cities, where the steady influx of new arrivals from towns and villages converged to form great impoverished masses. A concentration of capital in the major cities produced a growing number of factories, which, in turn, encouraged the influx of an ever-increasing number of new workers. And this ultimately led to the creation of dire poverty. The widening gap between the privileged and those in need, between increasingly wealthy and increasingly poor social classes led thinkers like Marx and Engels to develop their ideas on revolutionary social change.

Toward the end of the century, the working class was aware of such social inequality and of the need for solidarity. The structure they created functioned both on the political level and at the work place; from then on, socialism and trade unionism were to work hand in hand, with each reinforcing the other. By putting pressure both on government and on industry, workers were to gradually bring about changes in the capitalist system. But the process was a slow one and was fraught with conflict, despite the fact that Great Britain had taken the lead in industry and was also the first to have a large and politically conscious proletariat. It was in Great Britain that a non-revolutionary labor movement came into being, albeit at the end of the century and with an improvement in the status of workers.

Thus, following Sadowa, two principal factors had begun to influence world affairs: first, British supremacy at sea, in world trade, and in the area of social development; and second, the emergence of Prussia as the foremost political power on the European continent. Indeed, Bismarck's style was to influence the course of events in that part of the world for the next quarter of a century.

At this time, France was still savoring the glories of the Second Empire. The Congress of Paris of 1856 marked the official end of the Crimean War and Russia's expansion was stopped at the Dardanelles. The czarist empire began expanding, however, into Asia, and after seizing the Caucasus and Turkestan, reached Vladivostok on the Pacific Ocean around 1860.

Nationalist sentiment was a burning issue during this period. To Austria's consternation, Napoleon III came out in defense of minority groups; after supporting the independence of Montenegro, Serbia, and Romania, in 1858 he agreed to guarantee Italy's reunification. A year

FRANCE WAS IN THE MIDST OF THE SECOND EMPIRE, AS RUSSIA TURNED ITS ATTENTION TOWARD ASIA. NAPOLEON III DEFENDED THE RIGHTS OF MINORITIES...

BUT WAS UNAWARE OF PRUSSIA'S GROWING STRENGTH. FRENCH INDUSTRY MADE GREAT STRIDES...

later, following the costly victories of Magenta and Solferino, a peace treaty was signed in Zurich which ended centuries of Austrian occupation of Lombardy, while leaving Venetia under the former's control.

A French expedition to Mexico, undertaken with the British in 1864, ended tragically in 1867, with the execution by the Mexicans of Maximilian, the emperor of Austrian descent whom the French had imposed upon them. This incident marked the end of Europe's attempts to interfere in Latin American political affairs.

In 1867, Napoleon III did not yet realize that Prussia, with its highly modern army prepared for war, was about to turn against him. France's industrial revolution had begun fifteen years earlier; progress was slower in France than in Britain, as coal was scarcer and the Revolution of 1789 had abolished the privileges of landowners and redistributed land in small parcels to the peasantry (after abolishing seigniorial rights). Above all, the credit system in France at the time was not particularly sophisticated, and the French preferred the hoarding of gold. It was the financially cautious bourgeoisie, confident in their form of savings and having no need for credit, that took the lead in industrial development. Another hindrance to industrial growth was the continual strife—with the wars of the Republic and of the Empire, as well as the revolutions of 1830 and 1848—that kept the work force deeply enmeshed in bloody combat. Finally, the French fleet, defeated at Trafalgar, still consisted largely of sailing vessels, whereas the British had been using steamships for twenty years.

Before 1852—i.e., prior to the Second Empire—France had few factories. Those that did exist were family enterprises, generally involved in the manufacture of textiles. The first steel factories had been financed by British capital and planned by British specialists. The new regime, at first authoritarian but subsequently liberal, allowed domestic industry to flourish. This was a period of great projects, among them Baron Haussmann's design and execution of the great boulevards of Paris. Railroad networks were rapidly laid out, and by 1867, the steel industry was using French coal and had grown to three times its original size in just twenty years.

Large stores, which had appeared around 1850, were by now well-established; these, too, had initially been family-run enterprises which had evolved into limited partnerships and later into corporations. The food industry developed along similar lines, growing as much because of the advent of commercial capitalism as because of the tremendous concentration of workers dwelling in the cities. These workers could no longer devote the time required to preparing traditional meals and consequently relied on more basic foodstuffs, which, in turn, led to increased food production. While most foodstuffs were perishable and expensive, the food industry set out to market affordable products that were as easy to prepare as they were to store. This trend was not unique to nineteenth-century France; indeed, it is a common one in many countries undergoing industrialization.

WHILE PRUSSIA OVERWHELMED AUSTRIA'S ARMY...

Germany was divided into four large kingdoms during this period, three free cities, several large duchies and many principalities. At the start of the nineteenth century, German society was predominantly agricultural in nature, with small peasant holdings to the west and large estates owned by military aristocracy to the east. In the center was Berlin, a city of soldiers and civil servants.

Although large-scale industry made its modest appearance around 1830, cottage industry predominated until about 1860. Between 1825 and 1850, coal production tripled, copper production quadrupled, and, in terms of horsepower, there was a five-fold increase in the energy harnessed for industrial use. The introduction of steam barges on the Rhine caused the volume of goods to double between 1836 and 1846.

Thus, by 1867, Germany had embarked on a period of large-scale economic expansion. Prussia was attempting to unify the country, a goal the Frankfurt National Assembly had not succeeded in achieving. In that same year, Prussia began the gradual unification of the country by establishing the Zollverein, *a customs union of most German states (with the exception of Austria), which was a first step toward the formation of an economic confederation. An agreement was reached with protectionist Austria whereby that country and the common market of German states established a sort of free trade area. When, in 1862, Prussia negotiated, on behalf of the* Zollverein, *a significantly greater reduction of customs duties for France than for Austria, the latter asked to become a full-fledged member of the* Zollverein. *Bismarck's government was opposed to negotiating with Vienna, however, and an economic war ensued. It was not long before a full-blown military conflict followed over the issue of the duchies—in particular, the Duchy of Holstein.*

IN THE UNITED STATES, AFTER ITS CIVIL WAR RESULTING FROM A DISPUTE BETWEEN THE NORTH AND SOUTH...

Bismarck ordered military occupation of this territory despite the 1865 accords which had provided for the establishment of an Austro-Prussian condominium to control the territory, seized from Denmark in 1864.

Although the Austro-Prussian conflict lasted only a few weeks, Prussia's victory at Sadowa had far-reaching consequences: it served to awaken Europe, indirectly to facilitate Venetia's absorption by Italy, and enable Prussia to take possession of Hanover, Hessen, Nassau, and Frankfurt. The same year, 1867, marked the second anniversary of the end of the Civil War in the United States. Following the Mexican War of 1846–48, that young country had nearly attained its present size, extending over an area roughly three quarters that of Europe. In addition, the California Gold Rush in the 1840s had attracted large numbers of new settlers.

Unlike Europe, this young country was not weighed down by burdensome social or political traditions. Exports played only a secondary role in the U.S. economy, as goods were needed to build up the domestic infrastructure. The 1848 revolution, as well as numerous wars, brought to America a new wave of European immigrants and with them an ample supply of labor. The South, however, watched with displeasure as many of these newcomers settled in the North. This became a source of growing concern, exacerbated by the fact that these new immigrants would often head west, stopping on their way only long enough to clear a plot of land, plant a few crops, and put cattle to graze. They would then sell their property to a second wave of settlers before moving yet further west, where they would prepare new lands for farming. The second wave of settlers would build sturdier houses, expand arable land, and introduce more sophisticated methods of cultivation; and then they, in turn, would also move further west, selling the land to a third wave of settlers. In this way, cities sprang up in areas where the land had cost the original settlers nothing. This led to the creation of new states which threatened the South's predominant political position during the early years of the American republic.

When the federal government, which owned millions of acres of land, voted to grant 160 acres to every pioneer settling on uncultivated land in the West, the situation deteriorated yet further. The delicate issue of slavery brought to a head the rivalry between North and South. In the North, where mainly industry and small farming prevailed, there was no need for black workers; in the South, on the other hand, where there were huge estates devoted mainly to the production of cotton, landowners could not begin to imagine forgoing slave labor and dreaded an increase in the number of states opposed to slavery.

The crisis worsened after the creation of the anti- slavery Republican party, especially when its leader, Abraham Lincoln, won the 1860 presidential election. First, South Carolina, then ten other states, seceded from the union. These formed their own separate union, the Confederate States of America and declared Richmond, Virginia, to be its capital. In 1861, a war broke out whose consequences were disastrous. More than one hundred battles were fought and these required vast financial resources. Eventually, the North won, thanks to the deployment of warships and the expansion of railways, which had made their appearance in the United States in 1840. Fortunately, America was a rich nation, its businessmen highly dynamic, and the victory of the North decisive enough to ensure political stability. From 1867 on, economic expansion accelerated at an even more rapid pace than before.

ECONOMIC EXPANSION ACCELERATED AS NEVER BEFORE. IN EUROPE, SOCIAL THEORIES ABOUNDED, PARTICULARLY THOSE OF MARX AND ENGELS.

In addition to these swift and significant changes, the nineteenth century—truly an extraordinary period in world history—witnessed the birth of new social theories, which, in the next century, were to shake the world. In England, philosophers such as Bentham and O'Connor espoused their ideas; in Russia, Bakunin was advocating his theory of anarchy; in France, Proudhon his socialist theory. In Germany, Lassalle was developing his program for the workers; while during this same time, Marx and Engels were patiently working out their revolutionary doctrine.

Let us pause for a moment and take a closer look at the ideas of Marx, who was working on the first volume of Das Kapital *in 1864. Marx had already set forth his ideas in his famous manifesto published in the wake of the meeting in London at which the First International was created. In September, 1866, the first meeting of the International Workers' Association convened in Geneva, and although Marx was not present, his ideas were a subject of heated debate. These eventually gained wide acceptance at the Hague Congress of 1872, which preceded the organization's move to the United States. By this time, Marx had eliminated all serious challengers, whom he judged to be too soft in their approach, and won the day with his ideas as set forth in the original 1864 manifesto.*

IN SWITZERLAND, WHICH ACHIEVED ITS POLITICAL UNITY A HALF CENTURY EARLIER . . .

In his famous inaugural address at the First International, Marx had taken as an example social conditions in England, portraying to his audience the dramatic situation of increasing poverty for the masses, contrasting it with increasing wealth for a small group of property owners. He pointed out the inherent contradictions of capitalism, with a view to demonstrating the need to go beyond mere reform or such partial solutions as cooperative enterprise and ultimately transfer all power to the working class. Marx argued that in Great Britain, which he termed the "European leader in trade and industry," the working class, by virtue of its "admirable perseverance," had taken advantage of a "temporary dispute between owners of the land and owners of capital" to push the Ten Hours Bill through Parliament. This victory, in Marx's view, was a milestone in the history of the workers, for it represented the introduction of a certain moral principle in the "great struggle between the blind law of supply and demand—which characterizes the political economy of the middle class—and a form of production which takes into account the needs of the workers—characterizing the political economy of the working class." And, after launching into a violent attack on "that barbarian power whose leader sits in St. Petersburg and who has a finger in each European cabinet," Marx reiterated his 1848 slogan: "Workers of the world, unite!:" a call to action that continued to ring out in radio broadcasts throughout the Marxist world a century later.

It was in the midst of—and yet far removed from—this whirlwind of political events, of extraordinary scientific and technological advances, of rapid industrial expansion in Europe and the United States, of radically new theories in politics, literature and the fine arts, that Henri Nestlé founded his firm near the shores of Lake Geneva, in Vevey, Switzerland.

In 1867, Switzerland—a small country located in the heart of Europe—watched the events taking place around it with considerable interest. The war between Austria and Prussia in early July, 1866, short as it was, had nonetheless prompted the Swiss Confederation to reaffirm its neutrality, while mobilizing its troops, fearful that the discord of Bismarck's making might touch off a full-scale European conflict.

The borders of the Swiss Confederation had taken on their final form fifty-two years earlier, when Neuchâtel became the last Swiss canton. Nevertheless, as recently as ten years earlier, Prussia had threatened to invade Switzerland; at that time, Berlin had backed the Neuchâtel royalists, who, discontent with the proclamation of the republic in 1848, had rebelled during the night of September 2–3, 1856, with the aim of restoring the region's dual status of Swiss canton and principality.

THE TEXTILE AND MACHINE INDUSTRY WERE FIRST TO DEVELOP.

When supporters of Frederick William IV were imprisoned by Swiss republicans, the prince demanded their release and that he be allowed to remain suzerain. Support from foreign powers and Napoleon III's intervention were necessary to settle the dispute. Napoleon III—who as a youth in the castle of Arenenberg had been made an honorary citizen of the canton of Thurgau and had even become a captain in the Swiss Army—was less obliging, however, when it came to the Savoy issue in 1860. Savoy was eventually returned to France, in exchange for Napoleon III's aid to Victor Emmanuel of Sardinia. The Swiss government, in possession of a petition signed by 12,000 Savoyards who wished to become Swiss, protested the return of the territory. However, its efforts were in vain. The issue was resolved in 1866, with Savoy becoming French, Victor Emmanuel ruling Italy from his seat in Florence, and Rome remaining papal.

In 1864, the Geneva Convention had chosen the distinctive emblem of the Red Cross by inverting the colors of the Swiss flag (consisting of a white cross on a red field). During this period, cholera still posed a threat to Europe, and the 1865 ascent of the Matterhorn by Whymper was much acclaimed.

In the second half of the 1860s, there were a number of cotton mills in the Swiss cantons of Zurich, Aargau, Thurgau, Glarus, and Saint Gall, and power looms had been introduced in the eastern part of the country. Cotton cloth printed in Glarus was much sought after throughout Asia, and Saint Gall embroidery and lace were particularly popular in England and the United States. Silk weaving from Basel, Bern, Aargau, Thurgau, Appenzell, and Zurich was exported in great quantities to the United States; and silkworm farms flourished in the Ticino region. The weaving of linen was becoming mechanized. And the techniques of carding, spinning, and weaving wool benefited in Switzerland, as they did in Britain, from advances in the manufacture of cotton. By this time, the Swiss textile industry had its own machinery. In addition, engines, locomotives, freight cars, and boilers for steamships were also being produced in Switzerland. The iron industry, which a mere sixty

WHILE WATCHMAKING AND TECHNICAL TRAINING SOON FOLLOWED SUIT. LEGISLATION KEPT PACE WITH PROGRESS, AND THE CHEMICAL INDUSTRY WAS BORN.

years earlier had obtained raw materials exclusively from the Jura and the Gonzen region on the Rhine, could now use scrap and foreign ore shipped into the country by rail. Indeed, the rail system had been growing steadily since 1847, when the first train plied between Zurich and Baden.

While factories producing textiles and machines and iron works began to become widespread throughout the Swiss-German cantons, watchmaking was a growing industry in such French-speaking cantons as Vaud, where Vevey is located. Many watchmakers worked at home; others were employed in the many factories built during the course of the century. The Swiss watch conquered foreign markets: first those of Europe, later those of the Far East, and finally, the most important of these: that of the U.S.

It was necessary for technical training schools throughout the country to keep up with this dynamic pace of developments. The Ecole Polytechnique Fédérale was founded in 1855, the Neuchâtel Observatory in 1859, and the Chaux-de-Fonds School of Watchmaking in 1865. These and other regional technical schools founded around the same time, are still in existence.

In 1848, a law passed by the canton of Glarus was the first to restrict the exploitation of child factory workers by prohibiting the employment of children below the age of twelve and limiting a child's workday to fourteen hours. Later, the Landsgemeinde, *or People's Assembly, of Glarus passed the first Swiss legislative measure (the second in Europe) to limit the workday of an adult factory worker to twelve hours per day. But it was not before 1877 that all of the Swiss cantons were to adopt a law establishing an eleven-hour workday, requiring that factory workers be at least fourteen years of age, and prohibiting night shifts in most circumstances.*

As for the chemical industry, which began to grow as of 1860, it had not yet made much of a name for itself, despite the 1856 invention, by the Englishman Perkin, of mauvine, the first synthetic dye. In 1866, in Basel, Alexandre Clavel began developing this on a larger scale, unaware that he was helping to lay the foundations of an important industry to come.

Merchants played an important role in making Swiss products, ranging from textiles to machines and watches, known the world over.

Customs barriers between the cantons had been done away with, and the banking system was improving steadily, with a single currency instituted for all twenty-two cantons of the Swiss Confederation.

HOWEVER, THE COUNTRY REMAINED LARGELY RURAL.

Swiss industrialization did not stifle agriculture or trade, however. Indeed, most of the Swiss remained small farmers, and the government depended on their support. These men devoted themselves to the task of improving their rough mountainous land and to tending their cattle, which at that time numbered nearly 1,000,000 head.

Such was the general situation in Switzerland and that of the world following the battle of Sadowa, when Henri Nestlé began to exploit the industrial potential of his invention.

Chapter I – Nestlé

Henri Nestlé Begins His Conquest of Europe's Markets

AT VEVEY, HENRI NESTLÉ'S FIRM BEGAN TO EXPAND AS EARLY AS 1867,

☐ The man who was to give his name to one of world's biggest food companies started out by himself in his field like any small craftsman passionately interested in pursuing work he hoped one day would benefit society. Henri Nestlé was modest, hard-working, and persuaded that his activities would be of value in the future. Born in Frankfort on the Main in 1814, Henri Nestlé moved to Vevey in 1843. On his arrival in that pretty little lakeside town in the canton of Vaud, Nestlé wished to be known as a mere "merchant." Before 1867, Nestlé could not have imagined that the product he had invented (and from which young children of the area were already benefiting) would one day be sold all over Europe. However, he was convinced that his product was good and had a promising future. For Nestlé had a strong will and a high degree of optimism, along with great ambition as an inventor and merchant—and in this he was a man of his time. He had foresight; he was always alert and on the lookout for new inventions and a way of providing his fellow citizens with products that technological progress had transformed from luxuries into indispensible items.

The era was indeed one of new ideas, not only in industry but also in the social and humanitarian fields. In 1864, for example, the Swiss Jean-Henri Dunant succeeded in convincing many nations to become signatories to the first Geneva Convention (protecting soldiers, the sick, or wounded as a result of armed conflict), which eventually led to the founding of the International Red Cross. People had also become concerned about the poor living conditions of the masses. In France, the Academy of Medicine was studying infant feeding, as the mortality rate for this group was high everywhere in the world. (In Switzerland, one child in five died before the age of one.) This situation no doubt influenced Nestlé and prompted him to concentrate his efforts on the preparation of food for young children. He decided to manufacture a product based on "wholesome cow's milk" that could be used in the first months of an infant's life if a mother should be unable to breast-feed her child. Nestlé's research in this area was soon to be crowned with success. Nestlé was quite enthusiastic about his discovery and stated proudly: "The basis of my baby food is wholesome Swiss milk, which is concentrated by an air pump at low temperature, thus ensuring that it remains as fresh as milk straight from the cow's udder. The cereal component is baked by a special process of my invention. The two are then mixed in the proper proportions, which results in the perfect food product." Prior to 1867, Nestlé's discovery had already proven to be an excellent food for young

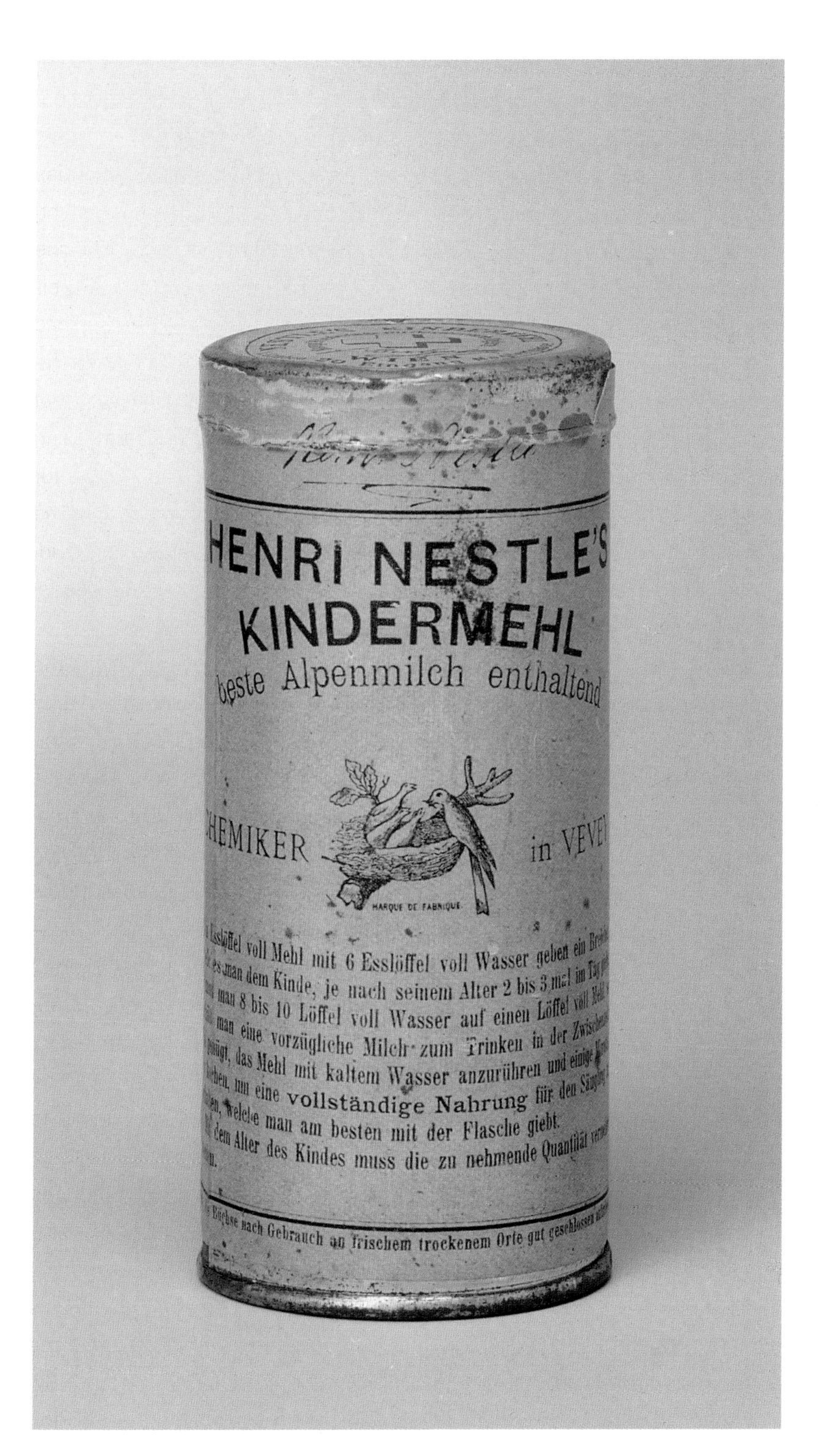

One of the first cans of Henri Nestlé's infant cereal

AFTER HE HAD TESTED HIS SPECIAL FOOD PRODUCT ON AN INFANT STRUGGLING TO LIVE.

children. However, it had never been given to newborn infants. This would soon be done with complete success.

Here is how Nestlé himself described that evening in September, 1867, when he first tested his new food product for infants, a product that was quickly to become famous on five continents. Nestlé wrote: "When I made my discovery, I had in mind babies a few months old. But it soon became clear that the preparation was perfectly suitable for even the youngest of infants. Mrs. Wanner was seriously ill, and her child was born a month too early. He was a sickly infant, who refused not only his mother's milk, but all other types of food as well. He was convulsive, and there seemed to be little hope for him. My friend Professor Schnetzler reported the case to me and asked if he might try my food product on the infant, who was then fifteen days old. Since that time, the child has been fed exclusively with my special infant cereal. He has never been ill, and he is now a 'tough' seven-month-old boy, who can sit up all by himself." Nestlé was not the type of individual intent on peddling his new and potentially lucrative product. But, he was not one to shy away from testing his discovery at a friend's request either. Until the success of his experiment on the Wanner infant, Nestlé had not realized that he had made a truly revolutionary discovery, which could be used as an effective tool in the fight against infant mortality.

The people of Vevey held Nestlé in high esteem, not only for being an authority on pharmaceutical products or for his interest in progress, but also for being a fine businessman. He had hardly moved into his house in the En Rouvenaz section of Vevey, when, like any shrewd craftsman of the period, he installed a "water pipe 0.4 inches in diameter." Later, he sold mustard, seed, and very soon, as he was industrious and understood consumer needs, oil lamps. In 1857, he set up a small company with the help of associates in Vevey to manufacture fertilizer and liquid gas. (Nestlé chose to keep his improved liquid-gas formula secret.) From 1858 to 1863, Nestlé supplied the fuel for twelve of Vevey's gaslights. But this born inventor, with his passion for chemistry, was not content with these activities alone. Indeed, Nestlé's success in saving the

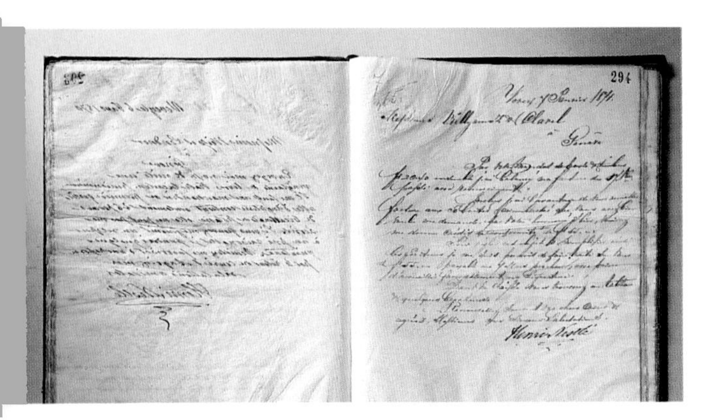

Henri Nestlé's letter of January 7, 1871

Wanner child helped convince him that he would soon be able to market his special baby food. This marked the beginning of the Nestlé adventure, which would completely transform his existence.

NESTLÉ WAS A HIGHLY ACTIVE INVENTOR, WHO FIRMLY BELIEVED IN THE QUALITY OF HIS PRODUCT.

In 1867, Nestlé's fellow citizens were still somewhat sceptical, refusing to give him credit for a mere "sack of flour." However, the greater the obstacles confronting him, the more confident Nestlé became. Convinced of the potential value of his new product, Nestlé wrote: "My discovery has a tremendous future, for there is not another food comparable to my baby food." And he added: "I have the approval of all of the physicians who have tested it. Moreover, all the mothers who have tried it just once, come back for more of my product." Nestlé's correspondence and the testimony of friends show him to be an intelligent, straightforward individual who valued simplicity and conciseness. Thus, his enthusiasm was no mere public-relations stunt. During the years he ran his small business, Nestlé always proved to be a strong-willed man of action. Having entered the food business through the back door, as it were, he went about finding ways of helping his small firm to expand and prosper. Given the high quality of his product and his enterprising nature, Nestlé immediately decided to market his product on an international scale, thereby contributing to transforming milk—"the basis of Nestlé's products"—into a much more widely used foodstuff. Moreover, Nestlé is one of those pioneers whose work formed the cornerstone for advances in public health throughout the world.

Chapter II

1866–1905
The Belle Epoque *and the Rise of Cham's Wealthy Partner: the Anglo-Swiss Condensed Milk Company*

WORLD POWER WAS DIVIDED AMONG BRITAIN, FRANCE, GERMANY, THE UNITED STATES, AND JAPAN. FRANCE WAS WEAKENED BY THE FRANCO-PRUSSIAN WAR...

1905: The Belle Epoque *in Europe*

☐ *In 1905, the year the Nestlé Company merged with Cham—a milk producer from central Switzerland—to form the Anglo-Swiss Condensed Milk Company, world power was divided among Great Britain, Germany, and France—in Europe—the United States, and Japan. The economic influence of these five powers had allowed them to develop in both the political and military spheres. Their growth, since 1867, had been accompanied by important changes: new factories had sprung up, entire armies and naval fleets were born, and wars and military conflicts were commonplace. 1905 was above all a period of European prosperity, despite the devastating effects of the Franco-Prussian War of 1870–71.*

The battle of Sadowa had foreshadowed that war, which was preceded by a diplomatic battle between Paris and Berlin to which the rest of Europe remained largely indifferent. On the eve of that war, the French emperor still clung to the illusion that he might mediate in European affairs. In fact, France was politically isolated. Napoleon had allowed Prussia to gain power at Austria's expense and could, therefore, no longer depend on the latter's support. Furthermore, when Garibaldi's troops, marching toward Rome, were defeated at Mentana in 1867 by a French division assisting the Pope's army, Napoleon lost the sympathy of Italy and the French anticlerical parties. After that, the Hohenzollerns were able to put an end to French supremacy with little difficulty.

The situation in Spain became a pretext for war. The revolution of 1868 had forced Isabella II to abdicate, and Bismark proposed installing a Hohenzollern prince in her place. France protested. It was at that moment that, in the famous Ems telegram, the Prussian chancellor misrepresented an interview between the King of Prussia and the French ambassador. Taking offense, France declared war on Prussia in 1870, thus falling into a trap set by Bismarck, whose army was already mobilized.

Following the loss of Sedan, Napoleon III, aging and unwell, surrendered. The republic was proclaimed, followed shortly thereafter by the Siege of Paris, as the rest of Europe stood by, unmoved. Italy took advantage of this unstable situation to seize Rome. On January 18, 1871, William I was crowned emperor of Germany at Versailles. Shortly after this, France was obliged to give up Alsace-Lorraine to German victors and to pay Fr. 5,000,000,000 in reparations. No sooner did Paris recover from the siege than it was shaken once again by the Commune. This revolutionary government, born of the insurrection of March, 1871—which was itself due to the activities of the socialists and to the reaction of Parisians to surrender—gave way a few months later to domination by the army of the Thiers government. German hegemony was firmly established and was to remain so throughout Bismarck's reign.

WHILE GERMANY SOUGHT AN ALLIANCE WITH AUSTRIA. FRANCE TURNED ITS ATTENTION TO ITS COLONIES...

From 1871 on, the great European empires continued to extend their influence. The new German Empire sought to form an alliance with Austria. The emperors of those two nations concentrated their attention exclusively on Europe, while Great Britain continued to remain isolated within its maritime empire. By the end of the century, the United States and Japan entered the "club" of global economic and military powers. The discord that characterized this club was due to the struggle for markets engendered by rapid industrial expansion.

After paying off its Fr. 5,000,000,000 war debt, France could do little more than lick its wounds. Without the textile and steel industries of Alsace-Lorraine, France could only hope to begin economic recovery by embarking on development in the field of agriculture. French wine growers began replanting many of their disease-ravaged vineyards with heartier American species of plants. The arrival in Europe of American and Canadian wheat, grown on large, highly mechanized farms and transported by an ever-increasing number of steamships at low cost had already compelled Denmark and the Netherlands to replace grain production by cattle breeding, the herds of these countries being fed on cheap imported cereals. France opted to protect its farmers by raising customs duties. But French farmers, protected by this artificial barrier, began to fall dangerously behind in agricultural production. At the same time, the birthrate began to decline. These factors, combined with heavy losses sustained in the war, caused France's population to fall below that of Germany and, shortly thereafter, of Great Britain as well. The country became increasingly protectionist, and from 1875 on, the growth of its exports and of its industry remained inferior to that of other large industrialized countries of the world.

Isolated from the rest of Europe, France turned its attention to Africa and Indochina. There had been a French presence in Algeria ever since 1830; in 1881, French troops also moved into Tunisia. Two years later

AS GERMANY CONCENTRATED ON BUILDING UP ITS INDUSTRIES.

came the Tonkin campaigns, then the conquest of Madagascar. French capital, though considerable, was unable to keep pace with colonial expansion. While lagging behind the other European powers, France did manage to improve the working and living conditions of its population beginning around 1875. After the fall of Marshal MacMahon, in 1879, came the rise to power of a small republican middle class which, while decrying large-scale capitalism and defending the interests of craftsmen and small farmers, was not opposed to the nationalization of several key areas of the economy.

The economic isolation to which Bismarck hoped to condemn France was short-lived. In 1875, Russia and Great Britain informed Berlin that they had no desire for France to remain the sick man of Europe. And indeed, around 1905, it had once again recovered its position among the great European powers.

The German Empire, formed in 1870, had drawn considerable strength from its unification process. The government began pursuing a ruthless but subtle European policy, backed by a distinct brand of industrial expansion, characterized by close ties between an authoritarian regime and a relatively small number of industrialists. The latter received the backing of commercial banks and were quick to realize the importance of scientific research. They helped to establish research centers and laboratories. In contrast to Great Britain, where the efforts of independent businessmen had gradually contributed to creating an industrial boom, in Germany large-scale industrialization was the result of close cooperation between science, industry and finance. By including bank representatives on their board of directors, large industries were able to improve their financial position. Likewise, in order to further promote their industrial and scientific activities, firms soon began organizing themselves into cartels from which they derived collective economic advantages without forgoing their individual identity. In this way, they were able to limit competition and to concentrate on growth, without having to give up the advantages of their legal status, as in the case of America's large trusts.

Before long, these large concerns had replaced traditional family businesses. Naturally, such intensive industrialization—often characterized by collusion between the producers of raw materials, manufacturers, and sales organizations—improved trade. And since the state had established protective tariff barriers as early as 1880, reciprocal arrangements often allowed it to gain a degree of control over certain firms.

Thus, the pace of German economic expansion was quite rapid, with its coal production tripling between 1871 and 1905. In the 1870s, Germany had already overtaken France in the production of steel; by the turn of the century, it had outstripped Great Britain. Banks offered special terms for the export of industrial goods, and the conquest of world markets was facilitated by the fact that the cartels were able to maintain high prices within Germany while selling the same goods more cheaply on foreign markets—in particular in Europe and Latin America.

Germany was now in a position to envisage colonial expansion and was to follow the unstable situation in the Balkans with keen interest. German forces were soon to enter South-West Africa and to claim the Cameroons and Togo as German protectorates.

As certain historians have pointed out, the Balkan states during this period were a veritable powder keg. And while Austria and Hungary were in perfect harmony once again in 1867, it must be admitted that they had been oscillating between latent and open hostility ever since 1848. Nationalist feeling was stifled under Turkish rule. From 1875 on, events began to snowball. An uprising took place in Herzegovina and in Bulgaria; there was harsh repression on the part of the sultan; in 1875, the Serbs and Montenegrins declared war on Constantinople. Austria-Hungary, Germany's ally, sought to eliminate Turkish domination while at the same time attempting to check Russian influence in the Balkan peninsula. Britain limited itself to preventing Russian access to the Straits. In 1877, following Russia's declaration of war on Turkey, Romania proclaimed its independence, and Russia obtained a favorable armistice at San Stefano. Bismarck offered his good services as "honest agent" at the Berlin Congress of 1878. In accordance with the agreements reached there, Russia was required to give up a certain number of its territorial gains; Austria received a mandate over Bosnia and Herzegovina (at the expense of European Turkey); while Great Britain was handed control of Cyprus.

Faced with Russian dissatisfaction at the close of the Berlin Congress, Bismarck concentrated on negotiating an alliance with Austria, soon

THE BALKANS WERE EUROPE'S POWDER KEG. WITH AUSTRIA-HUNGARY'S HELP, BISMARCK TRIED UNSUCCESSFULLY TO DIVIDE FRANCE AND RUSSIA AND WAS REMOVED FROM POWER.

BRITANNIA RULED THE WAVES AS WELL AS THE LAND. BRITISH TRADE AND BANKING ENSURED...

joined by Italy. At the same time, he sought to secure what he referred to as the "reassurance" of Russian neutrality. Bismark's goal was to separate Russia and France, while forging close links between Germany and the countries of Central Europe. But, in 1890, William II dismissed Bismarck and reversed the latter's policy of good relations with Russia. The principal result of this change in German politics was the creation of a new alliance between France and Russia.

Throughout this period, England remained the uncontested maritime power, and this status brought with it the right to have a voice in settling international disputes. The Royal Navy held strategic naval positions throughout the world, and British merchant vessels conveyed goods from one continent to another. Britain's coal production was still unsurpassed in Europe, and considerable amounts of coal, as well as textiles and machinery, were exported by that country. All this contributed to the fact that, despite its system of free trade and its abolition of customs duties on grain (which caused it to be dependent on North America), Britain's balance of trade remained enviable until the end of the nineteenth century.

A true pax Britannica *existed throughout the British Empire, which comprised one fifth of the world. The City of London controlled international trade and the movement of the world's capital. As a defender of free trade, England allowed its foreign debtors to reimburse their debts by selling their agricultural or manufactured goods on the British market. At the same time, Britain reinvested its trade surplus in developing countries such as the United States and in its own territories abroad: Canada, Australia, and New Zealand, as well as in Latin American countries such as Argentina, with wheat and cattle; Chili, with nitrate and copper mines; Mexico, a land of great potential; and Brazil, the foremost coffee producer in the world. The goal of British liberalism was to maintain that country's economic superiority, while at the same time avoiding involvement in a war on the European continent. 1905 marked the end, then, of the great era of Victorian prosperity, with its many extraordinary historical figures—Gladstone, Disraeli, Salisbury, or Balfour. Upon the death of Queen Victoria in 1901, Edward VII became emperor of India.*

While the British government's chief concern remained that of maintaining a certain balance between Germany, France, and Russia,

British financiers and merchants were preoccupied with finding new markets for their nation's goods. Since 1876, when Queen Victoria was crowned empress of India, the route to India passed through the Suez Canal, built in 1869 by the Frenchman Ferdinand de Lesseps. Britain bought shares in the canal from the bankrupt khedive of Egypt and occupied it militarily in 1882. In 1898, British forces seized the Sudan from the dervishes, who had driven them out in 1885.

ITS DOMINANT POSITION AROUND THE WORLD UNTIL THE BOER WAR.

The Belle Epoque *was also the era of the European invasion of Africa, which had been carved up among the great European powers during the Berlin Congress of 1884–85. With the exception of North Africa, the entire African continent—a continent racked by tribal wars—was rendered totally helpless in the face of this invasion. It thus formed a perfect target for France, which sought to extend its influence abroad, and for Britain, whose primary interest was to increase foreign trade by setting up trading posts at its major ports.*

The British approach to colonization did not require a highly developed army. And military weakness was especially evident in South Africa. The British had settled in Natal and the Cape of Good Hope early in the century, driving Dutch colonials further north, where they established the Boer Republic in the Transvaal and the Orange Free State. Soon thereafter, a large number of Europeans (mostly Britons), attracted by the lure of gold mines, settled in these independent territories. The Boers were anxious; in 1899, they issued an ultimatum to the British government. But it was of no avail. And a war soon broke out with Britain which would last three years. This bloody conflict underscored both the weakness of the British Army, as well as the true designs of Germany, which wished to take advantage of Britain's merchant fleet being busy with the transport of troops to hoist the German flag in distant ports and, at the same time, to constitute the second most powerful navy in the world.

It was then that anti-German sentiment first appeared in England and that it was forced to abandon its isolationist policy, signing a treaty with Japan and negotiating the famous "Entente Cordiale" with France in 1904.

In 1905, in northern Europe, Norway peacefully became independent from Sweden by choosing a king of Danish descent.

ACROSS THE OCEAN, THE UNITED STATES EXPERIENCED AN EXTRAORDINARY ECONOMIC BOOM...

During the early years of the twentieth century, Europe was at the height of its influence around the world. During the same period, across the seas, two countries—the United States and Japan—which had experienced phenomenal rates of industrialization, were preparing to emerge from isolation.

Until 1897, the lion's share of political and economic energy in the United States was deployed in the domestic sphere. Among the most pressing problems in America were: reconstructing the South politically and economically, settling the huge national debt, ensuring civil rights for blacks, exploiting the country's natural resources, transforming the American territories into states, and deciding upon a general policy of economic expansion.

The American North and West developed with astounding speed. By the turn of the century, the population of the United States—concentrated largely in the North—surpassed 70,000,000. With the completion of a national railway system linking the Atlantic and Pacific coasts in 1869, a new wave of pioneers rushed westward. The number of farms grew from 2,000,000 to 6,000,000 between 1860 and 1890. More than a third of the U.S. population lived in cities of more than 4,000 inhabitants. The population of New York and Brooklyn together totaled more than 2,500,000; while Chicago and Philadelphia each had more than 1,000,000 souls.

Industrialization began to accelerate at a particularly rapid pace around the turn of the century. Industrialists from the East used their substantial capital to invest in both rail and maritime transport, in the expansion of factories, in research into ways of exploiting new natural resources, and in the construction of industrial complexes. These advances were further hastened by such new inventions as: the gasoline engine, the electric battery, the electric cable, the telephone, the airplane, and refrigeration.

With the growth of the oil industry, the South, too, began profiting from economic expansion, though to a lesser degree than the North. (Industrial development in the South was more concentrated and specialized.) The development of the frontier territories from the Mississippi to the Pacific Ocean resulted in advances in large-scale cattle breeding, wheat, corn, and timber production, as well as the extraction of ore from America's mineral-rich soil.

In 1905, the country's major railway companies concluded an agreement on establishing rates and timetables. It was also during this period that the first great trusts were formed—a phenomenon resulting from the accumulation of the capital needed to construct big factories, intense competition (which quickly eliminated the weaker companies), and the huge profits of industrialists (who either reinvested capital in their own firms or acquired an interest in other companies). Soon, powerful industrialists like Andrew Carnegie or John D. Rockefeller were to be involved in ten to fifteen fields, simultaneously directing oil, steel, railway, and merchant shipping companies, as well as a variety of others. Along with the industrialists were the financiers, who, having already amassed large sums in the field of banking, also began to set up huge trusts, after the manner of John Pierpont Morgan. Soon, judicial power was to become centralized, which further stimulated the growth of industry. Beginning in 1888, this was accompanied by the growth of labor unions, which grouped together to form the American Federation of Labor, which was opposed to an exacerbation of the class struggle.

POWERFUL TRUSTS WERE FORMED, AND IT GRADUALLY BECAME AN IMPERIALIST POWER AS WELL...

These extraordinary transformations in the economic and social spheres were not without certain disadvantages, however. Among these were: financial scandals, economic crises, corruption in politics, unemployment, difficulties for small farmers, not to mention miserable working-class living conditions in the larger cities—teeming with millions of mainly uneducated immigrants who had arrived from Eastern Europe around the turn of the century.

In American political life, this was the age of presidents many of whom were former military men. Indeed, from 1868 to 1900, seven out of eight presidents (all Republicans) had been former high-ranking officers in the American Civil War. The sole Democrat—a civilian—was Grover Cleveland, who was elected to two terms of office. During this period of intense competition between Republicans and Democrats, customs duties on imports were modified five times, usually being raised. Though these protectionist tendencies, generally benefited industrialists, the federal government nevertheless promulgated important laws restricting hikes in rail rates and prohibiting the creation of monopolies.

By 1897, the continental United States had reached its present size, and its territory was being fully exploited. As seen earlier, during this same period, the European powers were experiencing an acute crisis of

REACHING OUT BEYOND ITS BORDERS AS FAR AS CHINA.

imperialism, with the buildup of naval fleets and armies, colonial expansion into Africa and Asia, extraordinary or secret alliances being formed, and subtle diplomatic manoeuvres being pursued. American politicians such as Theodore Roosevelt were seriously considering how the United States might take part in this global trend. His objective was an economic one: to target new markets for U.S. agricultural products, thus giving the economy an economic boost, and, at the same time, to reduce U.S. unemployment, which was already becoming something of a problem.

With the seizure of Cuba from the Spanish, America signaled its entrance into the arena of imperialism. This former Spanish colony had been the site of continual unrest and turmoil for some time when early in 1898, the battleship "Maine" exploded while in the port of Havana. Washington seized upon this opportunity to send American troops swarming onto the island, to invade Puerto Rico, and to destroy the Spanish fleet in the port of Manilla with the aid of the U.S. Navy. Subsequently, Cuba became independent; Puerto Rico and Guam fell under American control, and the Philippines were purchased by the U.S. for $20,000,000. In July, 1898, Hawaii was annexed by the United States.

Moreover, in 1900, the United States participated in its first act of overseas aggression, when, along with Japan, Russia, Britain, France, and Germany, it quelled the Boxer Rebellion in China. The Boxers, a secret group of Chinese nationalists, had vowed to systematically exterminate all foreigners, who had become objects of contempt for the indigenous population.

Theodore Roosevelt became president in 1901, following the assassination of President McKinley, and soon embarked on an aggressive policy of foreign intervention. In 1903, for example, the U.S. government helped facilitate the secession of Panama from Colombia and resumed the Panama Canal project. Soon thereafter, he installed an American customs official in Santo Domingo, struggling to come to terms with its debts to European creditors. American politicians began questioning the competence of international legal authorities and—justifying their actions under the Monroe Doctrine—repeatedly intervened in the Antilles, soon extending their sphere of influence over the whole of Latin America. By 1905, the United States was on the way to becoming the world's number one economic power.

On the other side of the Pacific, Japan was just completing a twenty-five year transformation that had taken Europe centuries to accomplish. This country, with its volcanic terrain (only 16 percent of which was arable), consisting of four large islands and a myriad of smaller ones scattered over a wide area, completed its industrial revolution virtually unassisted from the outside. As late as 1868, Japan was still a feudal state ruled by the world's most ancient dynasty.

JAPAN EMERGED FROM CENTURIES OF FEUDALISM, AND SPEEDED TOWARD INDUSTRIALIZATION IN RECORD TIME, ENTIRELY ON ITS OWN...

By this time, nearly all the islands of the Pacific Ocean had been colonized. While the first British colonists settled in Australia as early as 1788, engaging for the most part in wheat production and the raising of sheep, the discovery of gold in 1851 drew an influx of immigrants from all over Europe, which gave Australia's economy an enormous boost.

Some 1,000 miles to the southeast of Australia, New Zealand, also the new home of many European immigrants, was undergoing rapid economic change as well. Indonesia, rich in coffee, sugar, rice, indigo, tobacco, and tea, began filling the coffers of Dutch merchants and planters around 1830. The English had seized the north of Borneo in 1841, while the central and southern territories remained under Dutch control. Thousands of European islands were fair game for greedy European powers. Britain swallowed up Fiji, the Ellice Islands, Tonga, the Phoenix Islands, the Cook Archipelago, and New Guinea; while the French laid claim to the Marquesas, Tahiti, the Tuamotu Archipelago, the Gambier and Wallis Islands, and New Caledonia. The Germans took possession of Samoa and part of New Guinea; while Spain's presence had been felt in the Philippines and Portugal's in Timor for several centuries. On the Asian continent, China was powerless in the face of European demands. Siberia and Manchuria had been taken by Russia; India, Burma, and the peninsula of Malacca were British possessions; and Indochina French. Persia, Afghanistan, and Thailand escaped colonization; on the other hand, they failed to enjoy the fruits of industrialization.

Japan managed to avoid domination by the great European powers, while profiting from European technology, revolutionizing its farming methods, instituting compulsory education in 1871, streamlining its administration, and developing its industrial potential to the point that, by 1905, Japan already possessed both a formidable army and navy. Japan's political and economic reconstruction was accomplished first by

ADAPTING EUROPEAN METHODS TO ITS PARTICULAR NEEDS AND ULTIMATELY BECOMING AN IMPERIALIST POWER.

restoring the emperor's spiritual as well as temporal authority, which had been weakened during seven centuries of shogun rule. (In the Shintoist view, the emperor was both divine and omnipotent.) With the rise to power of the young Mikado Mutsuhito in 1868, the shoguns were replaced by the samurai and merchants, thus marking the start of the period known as the Enlightened Age of the Meiji.

The speed of Japan's industrial revolution was also increased by its decision to replace traditional seigniorial rights with a property tax payable in cash to the state. This generated revenues equivalent to 33 percent of the farmer's harvest, regardless of his yield for a particular season. Great amounts of these revenues were invested by the government in industry. Moreover, to compensate feudal lords for losses suffered due to the abolition of feudal law—according to which Japanese peasants (66 percent of the population) were required to pay to their daimyo, or feudal lord, 50 percent of their rice harvest—landowners now received government securities convertible into commercial bank shares. In this way, former feudal lords were transformed overnight into capitalists. As for the 2,000,000 samurai, descendants of peasants turned warrior-lords and vassals of the daimyos, they became either administrators of the great landowners or civil servants. Together with rich merchants, who had profited greatly (unlike the peasants, who, hard hit by the property tax, had had to seek financial aid from tradesmen), the samurai now helped to bring about an industrial revolution orchestrated by the state.

Although it was the government which initiated Japan's rapid pace of industrial development, it soon found itself unable to sustain that pace. In its search for fresh capital, the state was forced to sell off some of its industries to private entrepreneurs. Here the traditional family system asserted itself once again. As the middle class was still small, and the peasants poor, a few powerful families active in business joined forces with the bureaucracy to buy up state-run factories and form large industrial complexes known as zaibatsu.

The development of heavy industry and the blossoming of thousands of small factories ensued, thus serving to concentrate financial power in the hands of a few individuals. Having instituted compulsory military service in 1872, Japan was determined to show the world just how powerful it had become. Its army and navy were well-prepared; its ports and railways were of the highest standards. The training of military personnel and of the national guard was excellent. Indeed, the entire nation was organized according to the most modern principles, while retaining its respect for tradition. And, in 1895, Japan joined the club of imperialist nations. Russia's thrust toward the Pacific coupled with the weakness of China provided the Japanese with their first opportunity for expansion beyond their island. Their target was the Ming dynasty. As the European powers had already established themselves commercially in twelve of the largest Chinese ports, this served virtually to relegate that country to the role of a colonial trading center. Japan seized Formosa, southern Manchuria, and—most important—Korea. This aggressive policy resulted in inevitable conflict with czarist Russia, which had already begun the construction of the Trans-Siberian Railway, was studying the feasibility of a railway in eastern China, and had obtained a concession on Port Arthur and the surrounding territory from the Celestial Empire. On February 8, 1904, Japan invaded Port Arthur. And within one year, it had won a land battle at Mukden and a naval battle at Tsushima. In 1905, the Treaty of Portsmouth ensured Japan's status as a world power, while at the same time, it marked the decline of czarist Russia, whose ruinous defeat was to be followed by continual revolutionary turmoil.

JAPAN CHALLENGED RUSSIA IN 1905.

Situated in geographic proximity to the scene of the Franco-Prussian war, yet thousands of miles from the battles of Asia and the Americas, Switzerland meanwhile continued to develop its industrial infrastructure. One of the many important industrial mergers that took place at this time—and one that would have a considerable influence on the life of Vevey for years to come—was that of the Nestlé Company with the Anglo-Swiss Condensed Milk Company.

FARINE LACTÉE NESTLÉ
FARINE LACTÉE NESTLÉ
ALIMENT COMPLET
POUR LES ENFANTS EN BAS AGE
NESTLÉ
CHIMISTE
MODE D'EMPLOI
16, Rue du Parc Royal,
PARIS
MAISON
HENRI NESTLÉ
CHRISTEN FRÈRES
16, Rue du Parc Royal, PARIS.

Chapter II – Nestlé

1867–1905

Henri Nestlé and His Earliest Successors

NESTLÉ'S SALES SKYROCKETED.

☐ Henri Nestlé, whose political opinions were clear-cut, made no attempt to hide his pro-French sentiment during the Franco-Prussian War. In the previous chapter, we saw him in 1867, at work in Vevey and full of optimism. The results of laboratory tests convinced him of the quality of his product. He now needed only to market it on a large scale.

In 1868, Nestlé's infant cereal went on sale simultaneously in Switzerland (Vevey and Lausanne) and Germany (Frankfort on the Main). The results of initial promotion were quite promising. Demand for his product from other countries soon convinced Nestlé to launch it on other markets. He set up a sales organization in France, took on an agent in Paris, and used his brother Georges (an employee of the Crédit Lyonnais bank in Lyons) as a distributor.

The reputation of Nestlé's baby food had spread across the Atlantic as early as 1868. At the end of that year, Nestlé accepted an offer to open a sales branch in London. Nestlé wrote in this connection: "Believe me, it's no small matter to market an invention in four countries simultaneously." A fact that no one versed in business will doubt, given Nestlé's limited resources at the time.

Nestlé's business did not enjoy immediate success; indeed, in the early years he had to write his own letters, maintain his own accounting, and supervise production—in short, Nestlé was required to be a kind of one-man band. Though indefatigable, Nestlé lacked financing, which restricted rapid growth. In vain, he sought financial backing with a view to expanding operations. As if it might be a consolation to him, he wrote: "I have a waterfall that generates energy equivalent to 12 horsepower, and my house is situated in the perfect location for my industry. . . ."

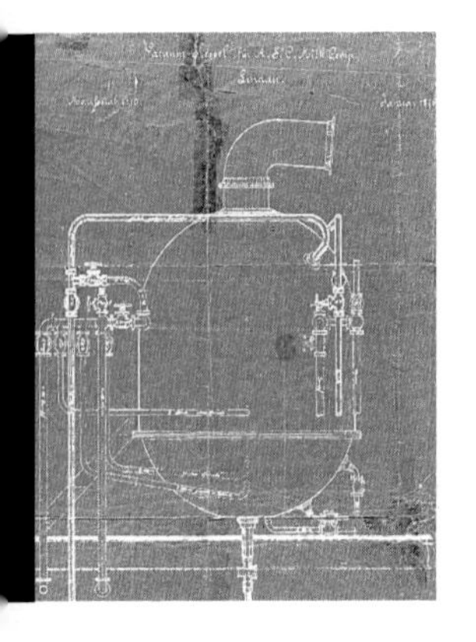

Blueprint for the first vacuum pump

In any case, by the end of 1869, Nestlé's production capacity was already over half a ton per day, although construction of additional space, remodeling, and opening of his plant brought their share of problems. Henri Nestlé worked day and night during this period: preparing plans, discussing blueprints, and personally directing execution of the work. As long as his budget permitted, Nestlé purchased new machines as the need arose. He ordered "a magnificent vacuum pump" (which still exists today), had crushing and grinding machines installed, and a boiler replaced. He did everything in his power to fill the veritable "avalanche of orders" that now came pouring in. It is no wonder then that Nestlé should begin to feel that the burden of work was too great to bear alone.

As daring as he was in terms of inventiveness, Nestlé was cautious in business matters. His natural enthusiasm and credulity made him susceptible to a certain degree of disappointment, particularly when it came to judging people and situations on appearance alone. Nevertheless, by today's standards, his sales policy and advertising programs were generally tasteful and intelligent. Nestlé aimed at low price and high sales volume. As he said: "It's not the moneybags who buy the most from us; we must try to bring the price of our baby food to within everyone's reach. It is better to sell two cans at SFr. 3.60 than one can at SFr. 2."

AN INVENTOR OF BOUNDLESS ENTHUSIASM, DESPITE THE FRANCO-PRUSSIAN WAR OF 1870-71,

Insofar as Nestlé's business methods are concerned, he did not believe in overadvertising, stating that it "cost too much and yielded too small a return." Nestlé simply distributed cans of his infant cereal to pharmacists, promising them a 20 centime commission on cans sold at SFr. 1.25 and a 30 centime commission on those sold at SFr. 1.50. Moreover, he had the unique idea of requesting that physicians "examine the infant cereal, try it, and judge for themselves whether the claims made in the leaflet are justified." Speaking of mothers, he pointed out that "they are delighted to be able to feed their children so easily on 25 to 30 centimes per day."

Nestlé's business had just begun to take off when the Franco-Prussian War broke out. Nestlé's position on this conflict was clear: "I shall not talk about the war," he stated in 1870, "I'm too sick of it. As long as we Europeans have rulers with standing armies, we shall have shameful and savage battles." Despite his being of German origin, Nestlé was to write to his agent in Paris that same year: "France will remain French, but the French people will have to take matters into their own hands. This is a terrible crisis, but even if the army should be defeated, the people shall be victorious. A man must never lose his nerve. Keep calm and things will turn out fine."

The siege of Paris provided Nestlé with another source of outrage: "I have received a letter by balloon from my friend Christen. He is sorry not to have had more powdered baby food available to save the lives of the many starving children. The king of Prussia values gunpowder much more highly than my kind of powder, which keeps children alive."

The war caused sales to stagnate, resulting in financial problems for Nestlé's firm. In his correspondence, Nestlé complained that the German railroads were refusing to allow goods destined for Belgium and Holland to pass through Germany. With his financial situation continuing to worsen, Nestlé remarked in August, 1870: "Everyone insists on being paid, but no

HIS FIRM FLOURISHED. NESTLÉ UNDERSTOOD THE IMPORTANCE OF HIS WORK FOR CHILDREN;

one will pay; bankers refuse to grant credit, and I am no longer able to discount even my best securities. It's a painful situation, and everyone is trying to get by as best he can."

Toward the end of the war, Henri Nestlé wrote to his American agents concerning events in Europe: "Soon we shall be able to send shipments with the same regularity as before.... Peace has come again. World statesmen shake hands, while the common man picks up the pieces." Higher milk, sugar, and grain prices (causing Nestlé's firm to be less profitable) were among the consequences of the Franco-Prussian War. A shortage of tinplate drove up the price of cans 40 percent; moreover, there were increases in transportation costs and customs duties as well. In time, however, conditions returned to normal. Trade began to pick up, and Nestlé became confident once more. And he had good reason: in 1871, the volume of shipments from Nestlé's company—which now had about thirty employees—totaled between eight hundred and a thousand cans per day.

Owing to the particular type of product he manufactured, Nestlé was always sensitive to any signs of approval he might receive from medical authorities. As early as 1868, Dr. Barthez, court physician to France's *prince impérial,* was convinced of the advantages of Nestlé's new product and had introduced it into aristocratic circles in Paris. After analyzing Nestlé's product, a famous chemist of the time agreed to test it on his five-week-old grandson, promising its inventor his backing as a man of science. "Sir," he wrote Nestlé, "you appear to have entirely succeeded in providing a practical solution to a problem that is of the utmost importance to public health and the preservation of human life," adding, "The use of your powdered baby food will undoubtedly reduce the high infant mortality rate."

Nestlé's infant cereal was soon adopted by hospitals in a number of countries. By 1873, it was already marketed in America, Argentina, Australia, Austria, Belgium, England, France, Germany, Holland and the Dutch East Indies, Italy, Mexico, Russia, Scandinavia, Serbia, Spain, and, of course, Switzerland.

Nestlé's world view is apparent in the following statements: "Let us continue along the right path, the path we have always followed, that of obtaining scientific approval for our firm. This is worth much more to us than a full coffer." Or: "I have never regretted spending money to do good, but it goes against my grain to spend even 1 centime on quackery." Or again: "Let us be at once cautious and bold, and we shall succeed."

Nestlé prided himself on being a self-made man. When one of his agents suggested that the famous logo of the company—the Nestlé nest—might be replaced by the cross of the Swiss flag, he reposted: "I regret that I cannot allow you to change my nest for a Swiss cross. My product must be recognizable at first glance. The nest is not merely my trademark, it is also my coat of arms. [Nestlé means "little nest" in Swiss German dialect.] I cannot have a different trademark in every country; anyone can make use of a cross, but no one else may use my coat of arms." These are the convictions of a man who considered his name, his trademark, his invention as his birthright.

AND TOOK PRIDE IN IT, WORKING DILIGENTLY TO ACHIEVE HIS GOAL. BUT THIS WAS NO EASY TASK FOR A MAN OF SIXTY...

Nestlé had enlarged his factory shortly after the end of the Franco-Prussian War, thus enabling him to double the output of his infant cereal from July, 1871 to July, 1873. His privileged clientele were unanimous in their appreciation of his product. Nestlé maintained close contact with his distributors in a variety of countries. A fervent defender of freedom, Nestlé helped to bring the French artist Gustave Courbet to La Tour-de-Peilz, Switzerland, when Courbet was exiled following the fall of the Commune of Paris.

As the fame of Nestlé's small firm at Vevey continued to spread, its owner was faced with problems he had never before encountered. Not only was it necessary for him to continue shipment of his product throughout Switzerland, but he now had to establish distribution networks in Germany, France, England, and Italy as well. The problems related to overseas shipment were becoming increasingly difficult, compelling Nestlé to work out, on a case by case basis, the most economical and rapid means of ensuring that his powdered baby food arrived in perfect condition at its destination, be it New York, Melbourne, Buenos Aires, or elsewhere. Nestlé always tried to utilize "state-of-the-art sailing vessels" to transport his products. His international transactions had brought him in contact with ticklish tariff questions, particularly in Belgium, Holland, and Germany, where all goods containing sugar were subject to exceptionally high import duties.

Railroad station at Vevey, ca. 1865

In 1873, Henri Nestlé was already selling 500,000 cans of his infant cereal per year. The firm had reached its critical mass, and this new situation called

AND HE DECIDED TO SELL HIS BUSINESS IN 1875. A NEW COMPANY, FARINE LACTÉE HENRI NESTLÉ, WAS CREATED AT VEVEY.

for hard thinking on Nestlé's part. In view of the company's constant expansion, it would not be long before it would become nearly impossible for a man of Nestlé's age (he was nearly sixty at the time) to retain control of it. Thus, Nestlé was obliged to begin searching for a buyer. By 1874, Nestlé was looking forward to a well-deserved retirement after a life of hard work and struggle. We must not forget that he had launched a business in his fifties and, in a mere seven years, had transformed it into an enterprise that would still be in existence more than a century later.

Henri Nestlé did not have to look long for a buyer; soon the representative of a group of Geneva businessmen made him an offer of SFr. 1,000,000 for the purchase of the company. However, just as the deal was about to be concluded, the brother of Jules Monnerat—the syndic of Vevey and a former member of the Swiss parliament—received news of it. Jules Monnerat had been planning to acquire Nestlé's firm in association with Pierre-Samuel Roussy—one of Nestlé's suppliers—and Monnerat's nephew, Gustave Marquis, a landowner at Châtelard above Montreux. As soon as his brother told him the news, Monnerat urged Roussy to immediately meet with Nestlé and negotiate the purchase of his firm for SFr. 1,000,000. During their meeting, Nestlé at first hesitated; but Roussy knew how to be persuasive, and to clinch the deal, he offered Mr. and Mrs. Nestlé a splendid coach and team of horses that the people of Vevey would remember for years to come. The contract was signed. Nestlé turned over his company and his clients—as well as the exclusive use of his name—to the new owners, who, on March 8, 1875, changed the firm's name to Farine Lactée Henri Nestlé. There were three men on the new company's board of directors: Jules Monnerat, Pierre-Samuel Roussy, and Gustave Marquis.

Jules Monnerat (1820–1898)

As one might imagine, the sale of Henri Nestlé's firm caused quite a stir around Vevey. The town's newspaper, the *Feuille d'Avis,* reported the sale in the following terms on January 12, 1875: "A sale that is creating a sensation in our locality has just transferred to a group of local financiers, for the considerable sum of one million [Swiss] francs, the business establishment of the chemist, Mr. Nestlé, active in the manufacture of his infant cereal. Over the past two years, sales of this product have grown to such an extent that, in spite of repeated expansion of his premises, Mr. Nestlé has been unable to keep pace with demand. . . ."

According to the contract dated March 8, 1875, the new company, Farine Lactée Henri Nestlé, acquired not only Nestlé's factory, his machinery, and the equipment used in the preparation of his infant cereal, but also his manufacturing process, the patents granted him in various countries, the signature of the firm, his medical correspondence, and virtually everything else connected with the original firm. The deed of partnership, according to which Nestlé transferred his right to use the company name as well as his signature to the new owners, was signed in the presence of two witnesses, in accordance with laws in effect in the canton of Vaud at that time. One of the two witnesses was Daniel Peter, then a small manufacturer, who would later become famous as the inventor of milk chocolate. Peter's name would be associated with Nestlé in 1929, when Peter, Cailler, Kohler merged with the Nestlé and Anglo-Swiss Condensed Milk Company. Making a clean break with the past, Nestlé retained no proprietary interest in the new company; never was he a shareholder. He merely led a quiet life at Montreux and Glion, taking an interest in public affairs. The Nestlés had no children. On July 7, 1890, Nestlé died at Montreux and was laid to rest at Territet, where his grave can still be seen. The Nestlé name, the infant cereal he had invented, as well as the nest that he chose as the logo of his company were destined to survive the various mergers and acquisitions that the future held in store for Farine Lactée Henri Nestlé.

HENRI NESTLÉ DIED IN 1890. THE NEW FIRM GOT OFF TO A GOOD START IN 1875, WITH A SOLID MANAGEMENT STRUCTURE...

During the early years of its existence, Farine Lactée Henri Nestlé limited itself to the manufacture and sale of Nestlé's infant cereal. The new owners concentrated mainly on consolidating their company's position and securing the means necessary for its continued growth. Open to modern ideas, they decided to incorporate the company in 1875. The company's original capitalization was SFr. 1,000,000.

Soon afterward, the new owners divided the tasks of company operation among themselves. The true head of the company, Jules Monnerat, its chairman, was given responsibility for sales. Pierre-Samuel Roussy took charge of production; Gustave Marquis was entrusted with the purchase of milk supplies. Together, the three new owners possessed the talent necessary to organize and expand their firm: be it in the field of finance (Jules Monnerat was already a well-known financier beyond the canton of Vaud),

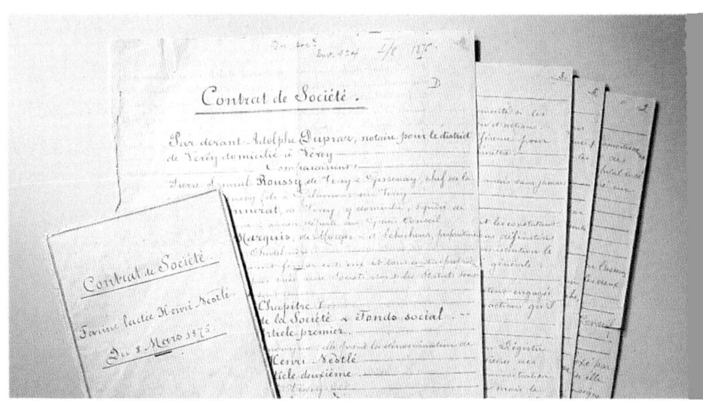
Contrat de Société.

Contrat de Société

Chapitre I
de la Société – Fonds social

Handwritten contract of March 8, 1875, founding a new company, Farine Lactée Henri Nestlé

AND A CLEAR IDEA OF EACH INDIVIDUAL'S TASKS. THE COMPANY REMAINED FAITHFUL TO ITS FOUNDER'S IDEALS. ITS RAPID SUCCESS...

industry (Pierre-Samuel Roussy owned a milling enterprise of considerable size), or trade (Gustave Marquis was intimately acquainted with the economic and cultural life of the canton of Vaud). From the start, these men had a flair for choosing young, bright assistants (many of them relatives or friends), who contributed a great deal to ensuring the company's rapid development and who strengthened both its sales potential and production capacity. Among the men of this new generation was Emile-Louis Roussy, the son of Pierre-Samuel Roussy and nephew by marriage of Jules Monnerat. Following the death of his father in 1880, Emile-Louis became chief executive officer (c.e.o.), and, together with his uncle, Jules Monnerat—chairman until 1899—Emile-Louis remained the guiding spirit of Farine Lactée Henri Nestlé until 1905. For a decade and a half, i.e., from 1905 until 1920, Emile-Louis Roussy was to serve as chairman of the board. In 1883, he had invited his brother-in-law, the banker Gustave Aguet, trained in Italy and also a nephew of Jules Monnerat, to join the firm. Named manager of the company's London branch that same year, Gustave Aguet set up the sales network required to distribute Nestlé products in Great Britain and overseas. (Aguet became chairman of the company in 1920.) In 1885, Emile-Louis Roussy invited Auguste Mayor—also a nephew of Jules Monnerat—to participate in the company. Mayor joined the company's board, in charge of Swiss operations, and remained in that position until 1905. Later he became c.e.o. and vice-chairman of the board.

As a result of having been incorporated, by 1875 the firm had achieved a place in the sun. It possessed a solid financial and administrative structure, geared to meet both present and future needs. However, production was no longer able to keep pace with demand. Delivery dates were not being met, as production capacity was insufficient. (One of the reasons, incidentally, that Nestlé had sold his business.) The new management of the company bought machines, had warehouses built, enlarged workshops, and did everything in its power to keep the market supplied with its high-quality product. Modern manufacturing methods had given rise, however, to new difficulties that required time and patience to resolve. Milk supplies were of prime importance: milk is a delicate substance requiring a great deal of care. As a result, the Nestlé Company very rapidly turned its attention to improving the quality of this precious raw material. It advised farmers on methods of feeding their cattle and insisted that stables and dairies be kept impeccably clean. In short, the company was already engaged in the educational and social

Emile-Louis Roussy (1842–1920)

programs it would carry out throughout both the developed and the developing world.

In terms of business strategy, the new management's approach at the outset was merely to continue to ensure company expansion after the manner of Henri Nestlé, witness a letter dated March 12, 1875: "We want our product to be available not only in bigger cities, but also in small towns and villages. It is obvious that all we need do to achieve this is to increase the scale of our distribution network, while ensuring our agents a sufficient profit margin." A simple idea; however, agents were not always totally competent. There was increasing competition, and customs barriers hampered the free movement of goods.

RESULTED IN STIFF COMPETITION FROM ITS RIVALS. IT RETALIATED AGAINST THE ANGLO-SWISS CONDENSED MILK CO. BY MANUFACTURING CONDENSED MILK. SALES ROSE IN EUROPE...

Fortunately, this initial period of uncertainty and adjustment was short-lived. Production of infant cereal soon rose to more than four thousand cans per day. Of course, the Swiss market was at first the company's largest. On foreign markets, the company had to struggle to maintain its position in the face of rival brands produced locally. Nevertheless, the Nestlé Company continued to do all manufacturing in Switzerland—a policy that was to remain unchanged for many years.

Early in 1878, economic conditions were ripe for the Anglo-Swiss Condensed Milk Company to launch its own brand of infant cereal. This company, with headquarters in central Switzerland and specialized in canned condensed milk, was concerned that Nestlé's product might one day replace its own as a baby food. The directors of Nestlé were quick to realize that the Anglo-Swiss Condensed Milk Company might soon become a dangerous competitor, as it was already requiring its agents to exclusively handle its own infant cereal. Nestlé promptly reacted by deciding to launch production of condensed milk that very same year. From that moment on, the two companies—not knowing that they were one day to merge—waged a violent economic battle against one another.

The Nestlé factory at Vevey: packaging infant cereal

If the Nestlé Company had not already established an excellent reputation for quality, it would never have been able to assert itself on the highly

BUT THE STRUGGLE WITH ANGLO-SWISS INTENSIFIED IN 1878. NESTLÉ EXPANDED...

competitive condensed milk market. As early as 1879, however, the London office wrote to its headquarters at Vevey: "Orders for condensed milk are increasing rapidly" and "if we are not to run out, you must send two wagon-loads per week during one month so that we may replenish our stock." It soon became clear that it was no longer possible to supply all of Nestlé's markets from a single production facility at Vevey. Given the growing volume of orders, the company was forced to face the fact that, while its plant at Vevey could, theoretically, process up to 3,745 gallons of milk per day, its stock of fresh milk would no longer have sufficed at such a level. Thus, in March, 1880, the company decided to acquire a mill at Bercher, in the agricultural center of the canton of Vaud, with a view to transforming it into a condensed milk factory.

Despite its success, the company was to encounter a certain number of obstacles, however. Butter producers complained that Nestlé was responsible for a rise in milk prices. Moreover, some countries decided to raise their customs duties, which put considerable pressure on the large-scale exporter. The firm found means of resolving these problems, however, and Nestlé was able to carry on with production until the end of the century without setting up factories abroad.

As the years went by, competition with the Anglo-Swiss Condensed Milk Company at Cham became increasingly fierce. For example, Anglo-Swiss reduced the price of a case of its condensed milk from SFr. 28.80 to SFr. 26.40. Nestlé retaliated by reducing the price of its own condensed milk. This did not cause the latter particular hardship, for condensed milk was a new product that did not increase overhead to any great extent.

The Nestlé factory at Payerne: vacuum pump room

Since the Swiss market was rapidly becoming too small a setting for their battle, the two competitors moved onto the larger British market. Nestlé had acquired an enviable position on that market, thanks to the activity and influence of its highly respected local agents. With only two factories—both in Switzerland—Nestlé was defending itself quite well against its rival. In Australia, too, Nestlé was holding its own.

Encouraged by these results, the firm increased its production capacity in Switzerland by opening a plant at Payerne in 1890, to supplement those already existing at Vevey and Bercher. However, when fresh milk supplies became difficult to obtain and costs increased due to customs duties on sugar and tinplate, the company realized that, in certain countries, it could no longer hold its own against international and local competition. Tariff barriers remained strong in France and were strengthened in Germany and, particularly, in the United States. Consequently, Nestlé decided to change its policy. Seven years later, the company decided to build its first factory outside Switzerland. As Norway was a country that maintained close ties with Britain and in which economic conditions were favorable, it was decided that the plant would be built in Norway. Thus, in 1898, Nestlé acquired the Norwegian Milk Condensing Company, with its well-equipped facilities at Kap. And, in a daring move some two years later, Nestlé launched its infant cereal on the other side of the Atlantic. The factory Nestlé built at Fulton, New York, and provided with state-of-the-art equipment, began production in 1900.

OPENING TWO NEW FACTORIES IN SWITZERLAND, ACQUIRING A PLANT IN NORWAY IN 1898, BUILDING A MODERN U.S. PRODUCTION FACILITY IN 1900, ESTABLISHING ITSELF IN GREAT BRITAIN IN 1901, IN GERMANY IN 1903, AND IN SPAIN IN 1905. BRANCH OFFICES WERE SET UP THROUGHOUT EUROPE.

The company's overseas investment in the production of baby food had no negative influence on the development of Nestlé's condensed milk division. As milk supplies for the Norwegian factory at Kap were inadequate, Nestlé decided to set up another factory in Great Britain. A small cream-sterilizing facility at Tutbury, purchased in 1901, was converted and enlarged, and it became the supplier of the English-speaking market and merchant shipping fleet. When Germany substantially raised its customs duties on infant cereal in 1903, Nestlé decided to build a new factory at Hegge, Germany, and to form a company with limited liability, Nestlé Kindermehl GmbH, with head offices in Berlin. Meanwhile, Nestlé boosted its manufacturing capacity in Switzerland by opening a fourth factory at Neuenegg in the canton of Bern. Finally, in 1905, when Spain also imposed drastic import duties, Nestlé responded to the challenge by opening a facility at La Penilla, near Santander.

So much for the history of the expansion of the company's production facilities. As for sales, from 1888 onward there was a growing trend to replace its representatives or agents with Nestlé branch offices or sales companies. This new policy was pursued, for example, in London in 1883, and in Berlin and Paris in 1903. The trend was even more pronounced after 1904, when Nestlé added chocolate to its range of food products. Auguste Roussy, one of Nestlé's directors, reached an agreement with the chocolate

THE NESTLÉ COMPANY TURNED ITS ATTENTION TO CHOCOLATE IN 1904 AND ENTERED INTO NEGOTIATIONS LEADING TO ITS MERGER WITH ANGLO-SWISS IN 1905.

manufacturers Daniel Peter of Vevey and Jean-Jacques Kohler of Lausanne, authorizing their firm, the Peter & Kohler Swiss General Chocolate Company, to produce milk chocolate under the Nestlé trademark. This, as we shall see later, was the first in a long series of alliances, such as that of 1929, when Nestlé merged with these chocolate makers.

As for the merger that took place in 1905 between Nestlé, Vevey, and the Anglo-Swiss Condensed Milk Company, Cham, it was brought about through the efforts of two bankers: Wilhelm Caspar Escher, c.e.o. of the Crédit Suisse bank in Zurich (and a member of the board of Anglo-Swiss), and Benjamin Rossier, a native of Vevey and c.e.o. of Banque Suisse et Française in Paris. On January 23, 1905, Rossier wrote to Emile-Louis Roussy to brief him on his interview with Escher: "We agreed on the great advantages to the company and to Anglo-Swiss if the two firms were to merge. . . .The upshot of our conversation was that, subject to examination of Nestlé's balance sheet and its sales figures for the past few years, Mr. Escher would be prepared to accept a merger based on an equal contribution of capital by the two companies."

Aided by the skillful mediation of these men, the Nestlé and Anglo-Swiss Condensed Milk Company was born. (Later, the reference to Anglo-Swiss would be dropped from the company name.) In 1905, however, Anglo-Swiss actually made a larger contribution to the merger than did Nestlé, even though each company had an equal number of plants to pool.

We have already traced the fortunes of Henri Nestlé's company from its inception. Let us now turn our attention to what was happening a mere 150 miles from Vevey, at Cham in central Switzerland, the source of the other tributary flowing into the Nestlé Company as it is known today. Indeed, it is to the first annual report of the Anglo-Swiss Condensed Milk Company, published in 1866, that the story of the modern Nestlé Company may be traced.

The factory at Payerne: engine room

1866: OWING TO THE PAGE BROTHERS, THE ANGLO-SWISS CONDENSED MILK CO. ESTABLISHED ITSELF IN CENTRAL SWITZERLAND...

1905: The Advent of the Anglo-Swiss Condensed Milk Company—An American Venture

☐ Cham—a little town in the canton of Zug—was the site chosen by the Americans, Charles and George Page, for their condensed milk factory. As mentioned earlier, Henri Nestlé was foreign-born. And the 1905 merger was to bring two new "foreigners" into the firm—this time from the United States. That the Page brothers should hail from America is no coincidence, for in 1856, Gail Borden had founded his first factory and thus created the canned milk industry in the United States. The growth potential for this branch of the food industry attracted the interest of the enterprising Charles A. Page, then American consul in Zurich. He was from a family of thirteen and well-acquainted with pioneer life, for he was born on a settlement of hardy and tenacious farmers surrounded by hostile Indian tribes. During the Civil War, Page had been a war correspondent for the *New York Tribune* with the Potomac Army.

Arriving in Switzerland at the age of thirty, Charles Page soon thought of making use of the excellent and abundant Swiss milk supply he found there. He discussed his plans with his elder brother George, who, at that time, was working for the War Department in Washington, D.C. George gathered information on the machinery and equipment required and initially envisaged marketing condensed milk in Switzerland under the Borden Milk trademark, paying a modest fee to this American company for the right to do so. Interest in this project was not as keen as the brothers expected, however, and they soon decided to form their own firm. On April 23, 1866, Charles Page informed his brother George that he was forming a corporation whose initial capital was SFr. 100,000 (five hundred shares with a par value of SFr. 200). In addition to the Page brothers, a circle of business friends of Charles Page subscribed for these shares. Among these were D. H. Wheeler, former American consul in Genoa, who had settled in Zurich, P. E. Lockwood, and L.P. Merriam. The only Swiss citizen in the group was the banker

Anglo-Swiss factory and the town of Cham

J.H. Kerez-Paravicini, elected chairman of the board at the first meeting of the new corporation.

With modern equipment from the U.S.A. Anglo-Swiss: a corporation with American founders.

This meeting took place on August 6, 1866, the date of the founding of the Anglo-Swiss Condensed Milk Company. Why such a complicated name for a company created to sell milk from Switzerland? (And an English one at that!) The explanation is simple: although its founders intended to manufacture their product from milk collected in central Switzerland, they planned to export it to other European countries, especially to England, which, as we have seen, dominated world trade at the time. Thus, the company's founders were, in fact, flattering British national pride with a name that gave an international flavor to a Swiss company created by Americans!

On August 22, 1866, the board—which had appointed George Page chief executive following his arrival in Europe in July—decided to purchase a suitable site for the company. George Page brought the necessary equipment from the U.S. to set up a small condensed milk facility in Switzerland. And after conducting a thorough study of the region, a site was found at Cham, on the shores of Lake Zug. In October, 1866, the board, with considerable foresight, appointed London-based L.P. Merriam sales manager. Merriam was to open an office and warehouse in his name; however, his first and most important task—and this was a sign of the times—was to try and secure the vital patronage of shipping companies located at various European ports. For a time, Merriam was virtually the sole agent of the company's milk products in England and its overseas possessions. The wholesale price, ex factory, of a 1 lb. can was SFr. 1 or its equivalent in foreign currency. Thus, even before commencing production of his high-quality condensed milk, (George Page did not manage to begin production until February, 1867), the company had already clearly defined its sales policy.

Thus, some six months before Henri Nestlé distinguished himself outside the canton of Vaud as the inventor of infant cereal, the well-organized manufacturers of condensed milk at Cham were already turning out their product. We must bear in mind that the founders of the Anglo-Swiss Condensed Milk Company were international businessmen who made use of up-to-date methods and who took all the necessary financial measures to set up a corporation that would soon rank among the many others being formed during that period. They had created a firm that was backed by a close circle of relatives and friends and ensured its success by state-of-the-art production techniques and an intelligent marketing approach; whereas Henri Nestlé had

FOLLOWING INITIAL DISAGREEMENT, THE FIRM'S PRODUCTS ENJOYED SUCCESS IN GREAT BRITAIN.

been an empiric who, buoyed up by a solid belief in the value of his invention, had managed his business and explored new markets all on his own. The Americans and Britons of Anglo-Swiss had merely picked their techniques from the shelf, as it were: they had not invented them by themselves. Moreover, unlike Henri Nestlé, who had many friends in Vevey and who considered Switzerland to be his homeland, the directors of Anglo-Swiss failed to sink real roots in their adopted country. Nevertheless, the two mainstays of the Nestlé Company, serving to reinforce it as it prepared to conquer world markets, were both founded by foreigners who succeeded thanks to their determination and their choice of Swiss employees with their proverbial pride in a job well done. From its inception in 1866, Anglo-Swiss benefited from a Swiss banking system already powerful in Zurich, even though Anglo-Swiss's founders contributed its initial capital from their own funds. Henri Nestlé, on the other hand, was virtually isolated as he was taking his first steps in the world of business.

Well organized, the Page brothers published their first annual report in 1867; whereas Henri Nestlé's successors did not follow suit until 1875. The following year, the annual report of the Anglo-Swiss Condensed Milk Company—already an international concern—showed a net loss of SFr. 1,500.84. But the factory at Cham represented an asset of SFr. 50,681.46, a sum that Henri Nestlé would never have imagined even in his wildest dreams. Initial sales showed that Anglo-Swiss's growth potential was good. Fired with an optimism that would prove to be justified, those attending the annual shareholders' meeting on November 28, 1867, decided to increase the company's share capital from SFr. 100,000 to SFr. 150,000.

George H. Page (1836–1899)

There was trouble brewing, however, among Anglo-Swiss's founders. George Page had asked that his annual salary be raised to SFr. 1,500 and that he receive a 5 percent commission on all sales outside Great Britain. In January, 1868, Page even threatened to resign from his position as chief executive. He also wished to increase the size of his staff so that he might devote more of his time to improving sales. (Page complained that Merriam, Anglo-Swiss's sole agent in London, was not moving his stock quickly enough.) A total of 1,300 cases of condensed milk remained unsold, thus reducing the amount of working capital. This serves as yet another indication of the enormous difference in the approach of this Swiss German company and Henri Nestlé's small firm in French-speaking Switzerland.

THE FRANCO-PRUSSIAN WAR HAD LITTLE EFFECT ON THE COMPANY'S DEVELOPMENT.

In reality, George Page's complaint reflected his frustration over the problems inherent in the operation of any condensed milk facility: to ensure the regularity of its milk supplies, it must purchase them in fixed quantities from a number of dairy farmers, despite the fact that it can only roughly estimate its own requirements. When milk is unexpectedly plentiful—especially in the spring—stocks increase. To deal with this problem, Page suggested halting the production of condensed milk temporarily and manufacturing butter instead. This did not appeal to the board, however; and the second annual shareholders' meeting, which opened in Zurich in July, 1868, sent the board's report back to the auditors with instructions to investigate whether expenditures were not too high. At the same meeting, during election of the company's board of directors, George Page received only a few votes. Now, for the first time, family considerations came into play: Charles Page resigned, and his brother gave up his position as chief executive while remaining a member of the board. This was a moment of serious crisis, the likes of which Henri Nestlé never had to face.

Three months of maneuvering and struggle were necessary to overcome this situation. M. Lippincott was appointed chairman. George Page became c.e.o. once again, while L.P. Merriam left the board and was replaced by Charles Page, who introduced another brother on the board, David. The Page clan had not only survived another battle for power, but had won the war.

The business sailed ahead smoothly. In 1868, the company's share capital was increased to SFr. 300,000; and in spite of its losses for 1867, profits now reached SFr. 30,372.12, more than half of which was returned as dividends to the shareholders. Further company growth occurred in 1870, at which time the Cham facility was valuated at SFr. 153,947 and net profits totaled SFr. 116,051.84. To expand their production facilities, the three Page brothers recommended resorting to a loan. Once again the board was divided, but the Page brothers won the day this time, too. P.E. Lockwood, a member of the board, resigned. Charles Page did so, too; however, this time it was in order to take over as manager of the firm's most important branch—the London office. The result of such intrigue was actually quite salutary, for, as the Page brothers emerged victorious, it helped clarify the situation within the company.

The Franco-Prussian War of 1870–71 created new sources of difficulty. From the outset of the war, payments between England and Switzerland

IN 1872, IT OPENED PLANTS IN GREAT BRITAIN AND GERMANY AND CONTINUED ITS RAPID GROWTH...

were suspended, which put the Cham plant in a difficult position, as most of its sales were on the other side of the English Channel. It appeared, for a time, as though Anglo-Swiss would be unable to pay its suppliers for their milk. Charles Page—who was in London at the time—lost no time in loading his bags with sacks of gold and leaving for Switzerland. Thanks to this astute action, farmers around the village of Cham received their payment—and in English gold sovereigns at that! For the first time, however, demand began to outstrip production.

When peace returned to Europe in 1871, its borders were reopened, which furthered industrial expansion, first in Switzerland, then in Great Britain and Germany (Anglo-Swiss's two biggest markets). Orders poured in so rapidly that an effort had to be made to increase production capacity. In 1872, share capital was increased once again from SFr. 300,000 to SFr. 1,000,000, with two thousand new shares made available at a par value of SFr. 500. The company was now moving ahead at full speed. It enlarged its factory at Cham and purchased two other factories in Switzerland: one at Guin in the canton of Fribourg, the other at Gossau in the canton of Saint Gall. Of the company's total production, 75 percent was sold in England—compared to 15 percent in continental Europe and 10 percent overseas. Thus, six years after being founded, the firm transferred a portion of its production abroad. It set up a factory at Chippenham, England, on the River Avon; and, a few months later in 1872, production started up at Rickenbach, Bavaria, near Lindau. (The equipment for the Bavarian plant came from that at Gossau, which was subsequently closed.) The tinplate works at Cham were also modernized: the expensive charcoal used previously was replaced by gas energy.

Gold sovereign with the effigy of Queen Victoria

Despite the general decline in the world's economy, Anglo-Swiss continued to prosper, which proved that the company's condensed milk was being adopted on a wide scale and was virtually unaffected by economic fluctuations. Another indication of the success of Anglo-Swiss is provided by the following statistics for the period 1866–72: out of a total of twenty-five condensed milk producers active in Europe during that period (six in Switzerland, six in Great Britain, four in Germany, two in France, two in Austria, and one each in Holland, Ireland, Hungary, Norway, and Spain), eleven had already closed down, and eight were in financial trouble. In order to retain a share of the market, six others were forced to sell their products at a lower price than Anglo-Swiss, which continued to perform well. Anglo-Swiss's turnover for 1873 was SFr. 3,531,620—a 40 percent increase over the preceding year.

FRANCE BEING THE ONLY EXCEPTION. OVERSEAS SALES CONTINUED TO PROGRESS, DESPITE CHARLES PAGE'S DEATH IN 1873.

Sales were soaring in Great Britain, but not in Belgium (where import duties presented a certain obstacle), nor in France, where public mistrust of foreign canned goods curbed expansion considerably. French consumers were not averse to all canned food products. Indeed, it was a Frenchman, Nicolas Appert, who, some seventy years earlier, had discovered this method of preventing foods from spoiling—a method more efficient than such centuries-old ones as drying, salting, pickling, preserving in sugar, or utilizing natural cold for storage. Around 1804, the father of the canned food industry (Appert had developed a revolutionary method of heat sterilization) opened a tiny factory at Massy, near Paris. There he sealed food in glass jars or bottles after heating them in copper tanks.

The overseas market was a promising one—or so George Page thought. And insofar as Anglo-Swiss was a flourishing company, the views of its chief executive carried considerable weight. Charles—the true founder of the company—was satisfied with his role as an astute and enterprising salesman in the capital of the mighty British Empire. George's authority as head of the firm was unchallenged, while Charles enjoyed an excellent vantage point from which to direct overseas sales and a certain amount of export business from England. In a letter dated May, 1872, Charles wrote to his brother: "Do you realize that, from January 1, 1873 on, London will require over 500 cases a day?... And that our only hope is to receive milk from Switzerland this summer?..." Obviously, George took this comment to heart and took the necessary measures to ensure adequate supplies. Charles Page died in 1873. And with his death, Anglo-Swiss lost not only its founder, but also a man whose shrewd business sense and tenacious optimism had commanded respect for seven years.

Anglo-Swiss factory at Rickenbach, Germany, 1877

Anglo-Swiss continued its rapid development nonetheless: in 1874, it acquired the English Condensed Milk Company of London. It opened two new production centers in England: one at Middlewich, the other at Ayles-

ANGLO-SWISS AND NESTLÉ CONFRONTED EACH OTHER IN THE FIELD OF BABY FOOD.

bury. Its share capital doubled in 1874. Moreover, there was now new evidence of the soundness of the company: It issued SFr. 1,000,000 worth of bonds at 6 percent interest, which were purchased by the company's shareholders on their first day of issue. Once again we see the distance separating Anglo-Swiss from Henri Nestlé, who was to sell his firm the following year. The depression of 1875 had no effect on George Page. The company's Paris agency was converted into a branch office, after the manner of the London office. The 1876 turnover (SFr. 8,188,217.41) was nearly four times that of 1872. And share capital followed the same performance curve, rising from SFr. 2,000,000 to SFr. 3,000,000 in 1876, and reaching SFr. 4,000,000 in 1878. This fresh capital was used to enlarge factories, improve equipment, finance growth, and streamline production. To avoid the problem of accumulating stocks of condensed milk when the supply of fresh milk outstripped demand, equipment for cheese production was installed at Cham in 1887. Anglo-Swiss now produced a range of five products: cheese, condensed milk, coffee and milk, cocoa and milk, and chocolate and milk. Henri Nestlé's successors in Vevey continued to produce only one highly successful product: his famous infant cereal. Thus, in 1877, Anglo-Swiss decided to challenge Nestlé's leadership in this area by producing its own brand of infant cereal.

The rivalry between the two companies was to go on for the next twenty-eight years, that is, until the two firms merged. In 1876, the prosperity of the Page brothers' firm inevitably attracted a certain amount of criticism. The skill of its management and years of intense effort on the part of its employees had enabled the company to become a top performer. In Switzerland, however, Anglo-Swiss was accused of being partially responsible for the rising cost of butter and milk. (The Nestlé Company was criticized for the same reason at around the same time.) These accusations were unfounded, however, since Anglo-Swiss's purchases of milk amounted to only 1 percent of total Swiss milk production.

Anglo-Swiss offices in Paris, on the Boulevard des Capucines

Let us return to the source of friction between Anglo-Swiss and Nestlé: namely, infant cereal. Anglo-Swiss started out with some difficulty in this area; the factory it had bought at Flamatt in 1877 was destroyed by fire, and production had to be transferred to Cham. The Nestlé Company responded to Anglo-Swiss's encroachment into the infant cereal market by producing its own condensed milk. And indeed, Nestlé condensed milk was soon to outperform Anglo-Swiss's Milkmaid brand on a variety of markets, particularly in Europe.

ANGLO-SWISS ESTABLISHED ITSELF IN THE U.S.A. IN 1882,

The constant struggle between these two firms, active in virtually the same areas, exercised a major influence on their respective destinies. George Page had foreseen this difficulty; and, in 1881, he favored the solution of simply taking over the rival firm (valuated by the board of directors of Anglo-Swiss at SFr. 1,500,000). Unfortunately, however, the Nestlé Company was not for sale.

The share capital of Anglo-Swiss was increased from SFr. 4,000,000 to SFr. 10,000,000 in 1880. Thus strengthened, Anglo-Swiss was well-armed for future expansion. The years 1881 and 1882 were turning points in that firm's history. In December, 1881, the total average daily production of condensed milk reached 1,063 cases (Cham 402 cases, Lindau 182, Middlewich 133, Aylesbury 129, Chippenham 110, and Guin 107), with each case containing forty-eight cans. Since deliveries to the United States that same year amounted to sixteen thousand cases per month, the company's British factories could no longer keep up with demand. It was at that point that George Page had the idea of setting up a factory in the United States (mainly to avoid having to pay that country's customs duties). On May 4, 1882, the annual meeting of shareholders approved his scheme.

During this period, the Borden Company was virtually the only company in the United States manufacturing condensed milk. However, it did not control the market. Thus, in 1882, George Page, still proud of his American origins, immediately decided to purchase a factory at Middletown, New York, from the Orange County Milk Association.

The decision to begin production in the United States soon proved to have serious drawbacks: George Page now had to spend at least half his time across the Atlantic and, consequently, began to neglect his company's European interests to some extent. Nestlé seized the opportunity to challenge Anglo-Swiss's dominant position in the Old World. Moreover, the presence of Anglo-Swiss in the United States caused Borden to take certain countermeasures. Indeed, a veritable "milk fever" took hold of the United States, with a variety of new companies being formed. Borden's brand, Eagle, had

RESULTING IN IMMEDIATE PROBLEMS FOR THE FIRM. ATTEMPTS AT A RAPPROCHEMENT WITH NESTLÉ FAIL.

no trouble holding its own in this highly competitive environment, and it was not long before the same firm marketed several other low-priced brands in an attempt to eliminate competitors. A newcomer to the American market, Anglo-Swiss found itself at a serious disadvantage and soon had to make certain sacrifices in terms of profits in Europe and other parts of the world. Thus, as of 1882, the year of its American venture, Anglo-Swiss began to weaken, and while it was yet to boast that "...a single day's production from the two Swiss plants is sufficient to cover the country's requirements for a year," the company no longer enjoyed the same rapid pace of expansion. From this point on—and despite certain good years—the performance of Anglo-Swiss would be unsteady, and the days when that company dominated markets in Europe and overseas were over. (In 1882, its production was nevertheless 25,500,000 cans, half of which was produced in Great Britain.)

In that same year, manufacturers began to question whether sugar would always be a key ingredient of condensed milk, as chemists had developed patented processes for producing evaporated milk, which did not require sugar. Page turned down both the offer of a production process and a factory designed to produce this new unsweetened product in the United States, as he had no intention of launching a new product that would involve too many risks or was liable to increase his worries. The chief executive of Anglo-Swiss already had more than enough problems on his hands, for the Nestlé Company was becoming an increasingly dangerous competitor. Page defended himself by creating two new brands: Wilhelm Tell and Star Brand. Moreover, he stimulated sales of his own infant cereal in the hope of weakening the performance of his competitor's. He was even ready to draw on the firm's reserves and forgo any profit for an indefinite period in order to cut prices to such an extent that Nestlé would be forced to abandon production. The board of directors, however, refused to agree to this daring proposal.

Anglo-Swiss office at Cham, 1885

In 1883, another attempt was made to bring Anglo-Swiss and the Nestlé Company together. In that year, Paul Wild, chairman of the board of Anglo-Swiss at the time, received a visit, "not," as he wrote, "from Nestlé's strong man [Jules Monnerat], but from his nephew, the wealthy miller Emile-Louis Roussy," whose task was to investigate the possibility of reaching an agreement between the two firms. Roussy valuated Anglo-Swiss at SFr. 18,000,000 and Nestlé at SFr. 10,000,000, i.e., ten times the amount received by Henri Nestlé eight years earlier. In addition, Anglo-Swiss's

Ad for Milkmaid condensed milk, enameled on a metal plate, ca. 1905

GEORGE PAGE DECIDED TO RESIDE IN THE U.S.A.

1889: A YEAR OF SETBACKS FOR ANGLO-SWISS IN AUSTRALIA AND THE U.S.A.

financial strength reflected its industrial strength, with three factories in England, one in Germany, and three in Switzerland; whereas Nestlé possessed only two factories in Switzerland. George Page was opposed to any agreement, as he mistakenly thought that Nestlé's strength was waning fast. Page's unyielding attitude can be explained to a certain extent: he estimated Anglo-Swiss sales at approximately 700,000 cases for 1884. In Africa and Asia (especially in India), Anglo-Swiss's turnover was growing steadily, thanks to the reputation for high quality enjoyed by its Milkmaid brand.

Yet despite the positive social impact of the company—remarkable for that time—and its high level of production, Anglo-Swiss was forced to reduce production in 1886 to avoid building up too high an inventory. Net profits for 1887 were a mere SFr. 307,843—six times less than those of the previous year.

It was at this point that George Page realized his company could enjoy certain advantages from transferring the bulk of its production to the areas of the world that offered the most favorable economic conditions. This policy of decentralized production would become increasingly important from this point on in Anglo-Swiss's history. From a commercial point of view, using agents overseas made it difficult to keep track of local market conditions; it also made it impossible to cooperate effectively with country-based suppliers not connected with the company. It was becoming urgent, then, for Anglo-Swiss to set up its own sales organization. George Page was also increasingly attracted to countries with a large market potential, such as the United States (despite the unfortunate experience of 1882). And so, Anglo-Swiss built a second factory at Dixon, Illinois. The Dixon plant made use of the latest production techniques and was to exceed the one at Cham in terms of output. Despite a risk of orienting the firm too much toward the United States, George Page decided to settle permanently in that country. Of course, Europe, and not the U.S., was the main source of the company's success. Page's decision had a very negative effect: year after year, following his move, U.S. sales showed losses that had to be made up by success in Europe.

By 1889, George Page had borne the responsibility of guiding the business for twenty-three years—a Herculean task. The economic picture continued to look bleak. Exports had fallen to such an extent that British exports to Australia—which were 75 percent of all Australian imports—had dropped to 25 percent. Moreover, Anglo-Swiss varied its pricing in Great Britain far too often, thereby encouraging disgruntled retailers to replace Milkmaid with Nestlé's brand. From 1890 on, tariff barriers were increased in Spain, Germany, Italy, Austria, Holland, Australia, Canada, and France. (Great Britain was the only country that imposed no customs duties whatsoever.) In the United States, the situation was even worse. No sooner had the Dixon factory been completed than five competitors (among them Borden) launched similar products. As it was well-established and had considerable financial resources behind it, Borden was able to adapt its production to changing conditions, whereas smaller manufacturers would be driven into bankruptcy. In spring and summer, when fresh milk was abundant, Borden would step up production of its Champion brand condensed milk to hundreds of thousands of cases, thus flooding the market with its low-priced brand. In winter, Borden put a brake on the sale of Champion condensed milk while encouraging that of Eagle, its higher-priced brand. This successful move by Borden taught George Page that only large-scale production could cushion the negative effects of increased costs for raw materials such as milk (which could not be offset to any extent by raising prices). Page aimed at achieving a weekly output of two thousand cases, giving very little consideration to the problem of finding markets for his product. Producing products at a constant volume in order to stabilize costs ignores the fact that selling prices are always subject to market fluctuations; therefore, logically, any sizeable decrease in sales must be followed by a cutback in production. Page tried to impress upon his agents the need for economy: he told them to avoid all nonessential expenses and to limit the scale of their organizations. In addition, Page raised or lowered prices for his products according to available stocks. This irritated customers, however; and he had to admit, rather vexed: "It seems that Nestlé has a reputation for stable prices, and that it intends to remain faithful to that principle."

THE COMPANY HAD TO STREAMLINE ITS OPERATIONS AND IMPROVE QUALITY CONTROL.

Additional measures needed to be taken to improve Anglo-Swiss's operations. Among these was more stringent control of milk supplies so as to ensure the high quality of the company's milk-based products. Page carried out tests of his stocks and came to the conclusion—which soon became a company rule—that it was essential to check batches of processed milk for a specified period before permitting them to be sold. Page also reorganized the administrative structure of Anglo-Swiss, replacing agents and wholesale dealers with sales offices whenever possible.

A STORM BEGAN TO BREW, WITH SERIOUS PROBLEMS IN THE U.S.A., AND, IN 1891, IT HIT THE BOARD OF DIRECTORS.

In the last decade of the nineteenth century, the major concern of this tireless man was still the American portion of Anglo-Swiss's business. In 1891, sales were still not up to forecasts. Profits had dropped 40 percent. The eight production centers in Switzerland, Germany, Great Britain, and the United States were operating, by and large, at only half their capacity. Indeed, the two American facilities were not even working at 25 percent capacity. The decision to start up operations in the United States was, indisputably, a direct result of utopian ambitions. Since there could be no thought of withdrawing from that market, Anglo-Swiss resolved to boost both production and sales in order to bring costs in line with those of its competitors, in particular the New York Condensed Milk Company (owned by Borden). That company supplied half the requirements of the United States and was far ahead of Anglo-Swiss (the second largest manufacturer of condensed milk in America at the time). To add to the difficulties of the Dixon plant, unsweetened evaporated milk began to gain ground on the American market. In the face of this, Anglo-Swiss, too, was forced to start producing this new product while not really believing in its potential. Though times were difficult, Page refused to consider a mortgage loan. Nor did he believe newspaper advertising to be advisable.

The firm's financial troubles had repercussions in terms of the cohesion of its board of directors. The Page brothers felt that the board should limit itself to scrutinizing the company's annual accounts and suggesting ways in which to distribute company profits. Paul Wild, chairman of the board, thought otherwise. At the company's annual shareholders' meeting in 1891, those present learned just how serious the situation was. The price of one share had fallen on the stock market to SFr. 530. In an alliance with plant managers, the Pages had decided to resign en bloc if those present at the meeting demanded that the chief executive return to Cham and liquidate U.S. plants, replacing them with only an agent in that country. Once again, the crisis was resolved to the advantage of the Page brothers. Wild left the board, and Adolf Gretner—an employee of the company until that time

Staff at the entrance to Anglo-Swiss headquarters at Cham, 1893

and the man George Page wished to see in that position—became chairman.

THE SITUATION IMPROVED FROM 1892 ON. IN 1895, ANGLO-SWISS ESTABLISHED ITSELF IN NORWAY. IN 1899, GEORGE PAGE DIED.

Fortune now began to favor the company once more: profits doubled; condensed milk suddenly came into fashion as a baby food in both the United States and Great Britain. By 1893, however, the United States was in the throes of a deep economic crisis. Borden launched a brand of condensed milk—Magnolia—whose low price Anglo-Swiss was unable to match. In Australia, Nestlé began to overtake its Swiss rival. Page was forced, against his will, to close his agencies on that great continent and handle sales in Oceania from faraway London. Sales were down in China as well as in Japan ever since the Japanese had restricted the right to register trademarks in that country to Japanese citizens. Germany was now virtually the only country in which Anglo-Swiss was not plagued by fierce competition. Despite all these problems, shareholders received a 10 percent dividend in 1893.

Another important decision was reached in 1895: Anglo-Swiss decided to establish itself in Norway by acquiring the Scandinavian Condensed Milk Company, whose Gold Medal brand had been Anglo-Swiss's main competitor in Australia. So, by 1896, with the acquisition of plants at Hamar and Sandesund (formerly owned by Scandinavian Condensed Milk), Anglo-Swiss possessed a total of ten production centers. A bond issue of SFr. 2,500,000 at 3 1/4 percent—oversubscribed by 200 percent—showed that public confidence had been restored in the firm. Profits for 1896 exceeded SFr. 2,500,000, and the following year these leveled off at just over SFr. 3,000,000. To make up for losses from its unfortunate experience in the United States, however, the company was tapping funds from its total worldwide sales.

The year of George Page's death—1899—was a crucial one for Anglo-Swiss, as it marked a change in policy that would result in the abandoning of its U.S. venture. The death of George Page, who had been the chief executive of Anglo-Swiss for thirty-three years, came as a particularly hard blow, insofar as it was he who had shaped company policy all those years. From the start, that bold, resourceful, and hardworking man had served as an extraordinarily competent, technically oriented manager who soon eclipsed his brothers Charles and David by the strength of his personality (even after David had become his closest associate). George Page's job had been relatively simple in 1866, but his responsibilities became very great with the expansion of the firm. Page was in charge of manufacturing facilities for six

AND, FOR A TIME, HIS BROTHER DAVID FOLLOWED IN HIS FOOTSTEPS, FINALLY RESIGNING OVER THE IMMINENT SALE OF THE U.S. SIDE OF THE COMPANY.

products in five countries and a sales network which, though originally limited to Great Britain, eventually spanned the entire globe. All problems would end up on his desk. While raw materials were usually delivered without a hitch and project financing was forthcoming, the production side of the business—installation of new equipment and modernization of existing facilities—called for a highly inventive individual with a true pioneer spirit. George Page devoted a great deal of his time and effort to these problems (sometimes at the expense of sales). Anglo-Swiss had three central sales offices: one in the small Swiss town of Cham, for continental Europe; one in London, for Great Britain and exports overseas; and a third in New York, for the United States. At times, coordination between these offices was far from perfect. Whenever Page was in Europe, the American side of the business suffered from his absence; conversely, when the chief executive was in America, its European side lacked effective leadership. With his keen mind, Page quite clearly saw the disadvantages inherent in this situation; but being a strong-willed man, he found it difficult to change certain of his deeply engrained ideas such as his prejudice against advertising.

Following the death of this key figure of Anglo-Swiss, who had bought and converted a factory at Staverton, England, in 1897, and built another as late as 1898 at Sterling, Illinois, in the United States, George Page's brother-in-law, Aloys Bosshard, joined the board in 1899; and David Page, who had been executive vice-president, now became head of the firm. Like his predecessor, David Page was more technically oriented than business oriented. A man of common sense, David placed a high value on clarity and precision. He, too, had played an important role in considerably improving manufacturing facilities, which helped move the company forward in the wake of George Page's death. Anglo-Swiss continued to expand, purchasing a small factory at Monroe, Wisconsin, in 1899, and another at Walton, New York, in 1900. The feasibility of opening a factory in Russia was also studied, as well as that of opening production centers in Denmark, Spain, and Argentina. The new management, however, had other problems to deal with.

Factory at Staverton, England

(IT WAS SOLD IN 1902.) WHAT BEGAN AS A RAPPROCHEMENT WITH NESTLÉ...

The year of George Page's death, the company's net profits totaled SFr. 3,300,000. The board of directors proposed a dividend of 11 percent; but, those present at the annual shareholders' meeting voted for 12 percent. In addition, Fred H. Page—whose views on bringing Anglo-Swiss and Nestlé together were far afield from those of his father George—was elected to the board without the board's having proposed him for this position. To the mind of David Page, this signaled a new company policy: namely, a renunciation of the American side of the business and an attempt at a rapprochement with Nestlé—a policy diametrically opposed to that of the late chief executive, whose spiritual heir David considered himself. When he was asked by the board to take over the negotiations the company had begun with Borden with a view to finding areas of common interest or even selling its factories in America, David Page relinquished his position as chief executive in 1900 and resigned from the board entirely the next year. A triumverate, consisting of board members Adolf Gretner, Aloys Bosshard, and, in 1902, Fred Page, collectively assumed the function of chief executive, thereby enabling the company to sell off assets to Borden. Borden acquired all buildings and equipment at Dixon, Middletown, Burneside, Monroe, Goshen, Sterling, Walton, New York, Brooklyn, and Chicago for $ 2,000,000. Moreover, Borden kept on all the U.S. employees of Anglo-Swiss. The company emerged from this transaction with greatly increased liquid assets. It was able to settle its remaining bond debt and, in 1903, reduced its capital from SFr. 24,000,000 to SFr. 19,000,000 by offering a cash payment of SFr. 100 for each of its forty-eight thousand shares.

At this point, it was not yet clear whether the company was going to use its liquid assets to increase its production potential. First of all, Anglo-Swiss purchased a little Swiss company, the Erste Schweizerische Alpenmilch-Export-Gesellschaft, together with its small factory at Egnach, near Romanshorn, for SFr. 500,000. Its chief product was Superb brand condensed milk.

Various other projects for industrial expansion were put on the back burner, however, as the company turned its full attention to reaching an agreement with Nestlé. (During this time, Anglo-Swiss continued to enjoy profits exceeding SFr. 3,000,000 per year. And, on the eve of the merger in 1904, it showed a record profit of SFr. 3,691,004.49.)

In 1905, a variety of factors contributed to Anglo-Swiss's rapprochement with Nestlé, which had just reached an agreement with the French Swiss chocolate makers Peter & Kohler to sell their own chocolates as well as the

EVENTUALLY RESULTED IN A MERGER WITH IT IN 1905.

Nestlé brand chocolate that they were authorized to produce. Anglo-Swiss's financial position had been strengthened by the sale of its American interests in 1902. Initially, the management of Anglo-Swiss wanted to exploit that advantage to wage a prolonged price war with Nestlé. The board members of both companies, who, for several years, had been considering the possibility of a merger, were quite alarmed; but thought it wiser to wait until things had quieted down somewhat. Indeed, there was good reason for hope—after all, serious talks had been under way for years.

As George Page had been opposed to any agreement, contacts between the two companies in 1883 made little progress. In 1888, Anglo-Swiss had tried unsuccessfully to sell Nestlé its factory at Guin in the canton of Fribourg. Anglo-Swiss put forward more attractive proposals in 1889, and the question of a merger arose. A letter from Anglo-Swiss provides clear evidence of the way in which that company attempted to influence its future partner: "Only for the time being are Nestlé's factories located in the right countries; they are in the wrong countries in the long run, however. These can only be kept going by investing large sums in advertising, and these sums must be financed by the consumer, who is forced to pay a higher price for every can he buys. This system has worked on the British market alone; it is too late to extend it to other markets. . . ." Moreover, Anglo-Swiss's management wrote to Nestlé: "You will soon have to rely solely on the British market, unless you set up factories in America, the Argentine Republic, or New Zealand, which are all so far away that supervision would be a problem—or at least an inconvenience—unless you prefer traveling to the comforts of home. . . ." Nestlé's management replied to this ironic letter with an explicit proposal: to provide the new company with a capital of SFr. 40,000,000, each group contributing one half of this amount; to take liquid assets into account, a cash dividend of SFr. 2,000,000 would be distributed to Anglo-Swiss shareholders. The failure of this proposal may be traced to George Page's opposition to it.

Following George Page's death in 1899, the question of a merger was once again raised; but stock market conditions were hardly favorable at the time. Nevertheless, the foundations were now laid for a new proposal: Nestlé would be acquired—with its assets and liabilities—by the Anglo-Swiss Condensed Milk Company, whose capital would rise from SFr. 19,500,000 to SFr. 40,000,000. This proposal was rejected by the shareholders of Anglo-Swiss at their annual meeting.

In January, 1905, two bankers—Wilhelm Caspar Escher, from the canton of Zurich, and Benjamin Rossier, from the canton of Vaud—laid the foundations for the merger of the two companies, though the behind-the-scenes struggle continued to rage in the months that followed. Upon learning that Nestlé had acquired an interest in Peter & Kohler, Anglo-Swiss at once sought a merger with Cailler or Suchard. However, this was little more than a final skirmish, for the views of Messieurs Escher and Rossier prevailed.

THOUGH NESTLÉ WAS ABSORBED BY ANGLO-SWISS, IT RETAINED ITS IDENTITY.

The final balance sheets drawn up in preparation for the 1905 merger clearly show the distance separating the attitudes of the directors of the two companies. Anglo-Swiss's balance sheet showed debts only in the area of its routine business (milk purchases, dividends, etc.), the value of its factories being covered by the amount of its share capital. Nestlé's, on the other hand, showed certain liabilities, such as expenses associated with its factories and, especially, SFr. 9,200,000 in bonds. Clearly, Anglo-Swiss was in far better financial condition than Nestlé, and it was to remain keenly aware of this for several years. Indeed, it took some time before the staff at Cham, with their American and Swiss German mentalities, would learn to adapt themselves to the Latin mentality of the people at Vevey. As in the case of a family, whose members treat each other with mutual respect, a conscious effort was made to minimize tensions and smooth out interpersonal conflicts. For more than twenty years, their sense of commitment to a common goal was to triumph over personal idiosyncracies. It was not before 1923 that the senior executives of both branches of the company were to settle down on the shores of Lake Geneva. By then, Nestlé had learned to coexist with its partner so as to maintain harmony in their "marriage." In 1905, Nestlé had chosen—for better or worse—a partner stronger than itself.

In order to expedite the merger, Nestlé was absorbed by the Anglo-Swiss Condensed Milk Company. However, the choice of the new company name—Nestlé and Anglo-Swiss Condensed Milk Company—indicated clearly both the nature of this merger and the spirit in which it had been carried out. Indeed, it was not a question of the stronger of the two companies merely ingesting the other, as it were;

Cans of condensed milk for various countries, from the early twentieth century

THANKS TO THEIR MERGER, THE NESTLÉ AND ANGLO-SWISS CONDENSED MILK CO. CONTROLLED A TOTAL OF 18 PRODUCTION FACILITIES ON SEVERAL CONTINENTS.

rather, as stated in the preamble to the deed of amalgamation, it was more a matter of "turning to mutual advantage the processes and experience gained by the two companies in the manufacture and sale of condensed milk, infant cereal, and other related products." Therefore, it was decided that the two companies would be on an equal footing as regards their rights.

According to the terms of the contract, the Henri Nestlé Company contributed to the newly formed entity all assets without exception (premises, rights and claims in respect of third parties, etc.); while the Anglo-Swiss Condensed Milk Company, though retaining its own assets under the new company name, assumed the direct and indirect liabilities of the Henri Nestlé Company. Strengthened by this pooling of interests, sales policies, and working methods, the new firm that evolved from the merger was soon to show signs of its dynamism and expertise in the food industry. And the issue of fifty thousand new shares of stock at a par value of SFr. 400 was to stimulate the activity of the company.

The purpose and terms of the merger were approved at the annual meeting of the two companies' shareholders in 1890 (on February 3 and April 15). As previously mentioned, each firm contributed nine of its factories to the new company. The industrial assets of Anglo-Swiss included three factories in Switzerland (at Cham, Guin, and Egnach), four in Great Britain (at Chippenham, Aylesbury, Middlewich, and Staverton), and two in Norway (at Sandesund and Hamar). The Henri Nestlé Company contributed four Swiss factories (at Vevey, Bercher, Payerne, and Neuenegg), one in Norway (at Kap), one in the United States (at Fulton, New York), one in England (at Tutbury), one in Germany (at Hegge), and one in Spain (at La Penilla). This list clearly shows to what extent Anglo-Swiss was oriented toward the British and Norwegian markets; whereas Nestlé was active primarily in the United States, Germany, and Spain. Thanks to these eighteen modern production centers, the new corporation, Nestlé and Anglo-Swiss Condensed Milk Company, was to benefit from a network of strategically located production facilities, destined to play a decisive role in the company's future.

Chapter III

1905–1929

In the Wake of the War That Shook the World, Nestlé Merges with Peter, Cailler, and Kohler

23 YEARS OF WAR AND POLITICAL TENSION LED TO THE ECONOMIC CRISIS OF 1929. FROM 1905 ON, THE RUSSIAN EMPIRE WAS IN DECLINE...

In the Years Before and After World War I (1906–1929)

☐ *In 1929, nearly a quarter of a century had elapsed since the balance of European power had irreversibly shifted with the decline of Russia in 1905. This was the eve of the New York Stock Market Crash that would resound the world over, and the Great Depression was about to sweep over the United States.*

To be sure, some farsighted economists had warned that the artificial prosperity Americans were enjoying could lead to disaster. Yet, at the time, few observers predicted that the Stock Market Crash would result in a worldwide economic catastrophe. (This, despite the fact that there was ample cause for worry: the events of the previous twenty-three years should have made it clear to world leaders—indeed, to all mankind—that fortune was a fickle friend and could change overnight.) From the turn of the century, with its imperialist extravagance, to the horrors of World War I and the ultimate victory of the Allies, whose unity was little more than a facade, Europe, for many years, had been on a political roller coaster. Thus, while 1929 marked a turning point in the world economic climate, international politics had already been in turmoil for quite some time.

In 1905, after suffering defeat at the hands of the Japanese, the czarist regime began disintegrating. On January 22 of the same year came the infamous events of Red Sunday, which were followed by unrest in Poland, the Ukraine, Finland, and at Baku. The general strike in the country became so widespread that the czar was forced to convene a meeting of the national parliament, the duma. Four successive dumas were unable to quell the unrest. Moreover, a power struggle between the czar and this parliament contributed greatly to the success, in 1917, of the October Revolution.

Germany took advantage of Russia's weakened position, owing particularly to the fact that Britain was occupied, in 1905, with the question of Irish independence and was thus ill-disposed to playing the role of peacekeeper in Europe. Britain, with its imposing navy and strong ties within the Empire, was still indisputably Europe's greatest power. However, Britain's prosperity had its negative side, insofar as it strained the social fabric of the nation, and liberal politicians were thus forced to devote considerable energy to resolving their country's social problems.

Germany exploited a disagreement with France over Morocco for a calculated show of strength that reached its peak just before the Algeciras Conference of 1905. Germany's strengthened position was made possible by several factors: a rift between Russia and Britain over the Anglo-Japanese Treaty of 1902, the relative weakness of the Franco-Russian alliance, and growing support of the German military for a preemptive strike against France.

WITH GRAVE CONSEQUENCES FOR THE BALKANS. RIVALRY BETWEEN THE BRITISH AND GERMAN NAVY HELPED FORGE CLOSER TIES BETWEEN BRITAIN, FRANCE, AND CZARIST RUSSIA.

Another direct consequence of Russia's vulnerability was instability in the Balkans. In 1908, the Austro-Hungarian Empire, vexed by the Serbian coup d'etat of 1903 (which had displaced Vienna's protégé, Alexander I, by the less friendly Karageorgevich), annexed the turbulent province of Bosnia-Herzegovina, which had been administered by it since the Berlin Conference of 1878. When the czar protested, Germany took the side of Austria. Vienna sent an ultimatum to Belgrade, while Berlin sent one to St. Petersburg. In 1909, the Slavs bitterly admitted defeat, thus setting the scene for the dramatic events that would take place in Sarajevo in 1914. By now, Germany had alienated France as a result of the Moroccan incident and Russia as a result of the Balkan affair. By reinforcing its navy with twelve large battleships, Germany now presented a serious challenge to Britain, which had only nine. A costly naval arms race ensued. In 1907, after expressing approval of France's policy in Morocco, London reached a favorable accord with St. Petersburg, which confirmed Britain's domination over India and Afghanistan, divided Persia into two zones of influence—one Russian, the other British—and resulted in Britain's definitive renunciation of control over Tibet. While the alliance between these three powers was being consolidated, Germany formed the Triple Alliance with Austria-Hungary and Italy. Thus, William II's global strategy forced France back into the ranks of the world's great powers, incited Britain to challenge German expansion, and brought about the unlikely 1908 encounter at Reval on the Baltic, between Edward VII and (the pro-German) Nicolas II.

This set into motion the terrible chain of events that was to lead to World War I. With a feeling of being hemmed in, William II turned his attention to Russia. He took advantage of a meeting with the czar at the Potsdam Conference of 1910 to discuss not only the Baghdad Railway, which the Germans were building with the help of the Turks, but also

TURKEY'S WEAKENED POSITION IN EUROPE STIRRED UP CERTAIN ACQUISITIVE INTERESTS. A MURDER AT SARAJEVO SPARKED WORLD WAR I IN 1914.

Russia's relations with France and Britain. The kaiser then resolved to put pressure on France again; in 1911, he sent a gunboat to Agadir in Morocco. Tension mounted between Paris and Berlin. Britain, fearing the establishment of a German port on the Moroccan coast that could endanger its links with South Africa, intervened in the dispute. Germany withdrew from the conflict, leaving France free to act in Morocco. French Algeria was finally surrounded by friendly nations, with Tunisia to the east and Morocco to the west. Portugal, a distant neighbor of Morocco, proclaimed itself a republic in 1910, deposing Manoel II, who had succeeded Carlos I, assassinated in 1908.

Unrest was rife elsewhere in Europe, too, particularly in the Balkans. By 1913, Turkey had been weakened by a whirlwind of events. Among these were: the 1908 coup d'etat organized by the Young Turks against the Sultan Abdul Hamid, the reestablishment of a parliamentary system, the declaration of Bulgaria's independence by Ferdinand I, the overthrow of the Turkish sultan by his brother Mohammed V, Italy's 1912 declaration of war against Turkey (resulting in the loss of Tripolitania), and the 1912 Treaty of Lausanne between Rome and Constantinople. Not long afterward, in 1913, Serbs, Greeks, and Bulgarians seized Macedonia, threatening the Turkish capital. Ultimately, the fierce nationalist, Enver Pasha, was unable to avoid renouncing most of Turkey's territory in Europe, except for a small portion of Thrace.

This first Balkan war was followed by another, this time between the Bulgarians and their former allies: the Serbs, Montenegrins, Greeks, and Romanians. Ferdinand I of Bulgaria had to find some way to make peace. The two Balkan wars resulted in a larger Serbia, which, in turn, brought about a rapprochement between Austria and Turkey and Austria and Bulgaria in the spring of 1914.

By the summer of 1914, events had begun to run out of control. In the midst of an accelerating arms race, much of Europe braced for war: Sweden, Holland, and Belgium built up their defense forces, and France announced a three-year period of military service. Britain, however, was still plagued by the Irish question, Austria by its national minorities, Russia by fear of a revolution, and Italy by widespread strikes. Only Germany was without major domestic preoccupations, when, on August 1, 1914, World War I broke out, which was to drain Europe of its vital forces for many years to come.

Despite this political turmoil, however, since the turn of the century Europe had been experiencing unprecedented economic prosperity. It is true that the Continent was no longer what it had been in 1895, at the peak of its period of colonial expansion. Europe was beginning to feel the effects of a poor demographic situation as compared with younger, more vigorous countries. A declining birthrate was barely offset by improved nutrition and medical advances, resulting in increased life expectancy. Indeed, these advances had been especially remarkable during the previous three decades and included the identification of several deadly bacilli, including typhoid, in 1830 (by Eberth), cholera, in 1883 (by Koch), bubonic plague, in 1894 (by Yersin and Kitasato), and identification of the four blood groups (by Landsteiner) in 1900. Biologists and chemists were now coming to the aid of physicians in the fight against disease. In 1885, Pasteur's discovery of a vaccine for rabies paved the way for the development of vaccines for other contagious diseases. In addition, research in the fields of asepsis, antisepsis, and anaesthesia radically transformed the art of surgery.

IN AN ERA OF EUROPEAN PROSPERITY, TECHNOLOGICAL ADVANCES PROVED A PARTICULAR BOON. LOWER BIRTHRATES AND ACCELERATING EMIGRATION STRAINED THE SOCIAL FABRIC OF EUROPE, BUT EUROPE'S ECONOMIC POWER CONTINUED TO GROW, THANKS TO ITS COAL, PETROLEUM, AND STEEL...

These advances notwithstanding, lower birthrates in the industrialized countries of Europe had resulted in a smaller work force. Emigration, too, had a drastic effect on the vitality of the Old World: between 1906 and 1914, more than 8,000,000 Europeans settled in the United States; from 1901 to 1914, 2,700,000 left for Canada; and in 1911 alone, 100,000 Spaniards and Portuguese emigrated to Brazil, and 120,000 Spaniards and as many Italians sailed to Argentina. Moreover, countless numbers of Europeans sought a better life in Australia and South Africa. This influx of manpower, knowledge, and skills gave an enormous boost to industry in all the developing European countries and soon gave rise to fierce competition between them.

During this period, coal was as yet the main source of energy. Worldwide production increased from 240,000,000 tons in 1870 to 1,215,000,000 tons in 1913. Half the available coal was used in steam engines, whose efficiency was greatly increased by Parson's invention of the turbine in 1884. A quarter of the coal produced was used by locomotives and the rest for home heating in countries enjoying temperate climates.

Two other sources of energy were gaining importance: electricity and oil, which, along with steel, was to bring about the extraordinary devel-

ITS NONFERROUS METALS...

opment of the automotive industry. Gramme's invention of the dynamo in 1869 was followed by improvements both in the harnessing of water power and in the means of transporting electricity in 1877. Edison invented the electric lamp in 1879; electric heating and motors began to be used from 1900 on, and electric power was being used on an increasingly wide scale in the metallurgical and chemical industries. The gasoline-powered internal combustion engine was introduced by Benz in 1886 and was soon to be perfected by Daimler and Forrest. It was several years, however, before large-scale production of motor vehicles was to get underway in Detroit in 1904. A decade later, Ford was producing 1,000 cars per day, giving the United States a commanding lead in the automotive industry. The diesel engine (invented in Germany in 1895) was used in naval vessels from 1904 on, and oil pipelines and tankers began to multiply.

Coal and petroleum were also the basis for a burgeoning chemical industry, particularly in Germany and the United States. Chemists were busy producing everything from perfumes and dyes to fertilizers and dynamite (patented in 1867 by the Swede Alfred Nobel). The first plastic—celluloid—was perfected in the U.S. in 1870; in 1888, George Eastman used this substance to produce photographic film. The first artificial fiber—rayon— made from nitrocellulose (discovered by the Swiss Schönbein) was created in 1884.

The steel age had begun shortly after 1860—in Britain, with Sir Henry Bessemer's discovery of a process for removing carbon from molten metal and Sydney Thomas' treatment of phosphorous minerals; in Germany, with inventions by Siemens; and in France, with Pierre Martin's large-scale recycling of scrap iron. The price of steel fell steadily as production increased. By 1894, its production in Germany, including the Lorraine and Ruhr regions, exceeded that of Great Britain. The production of nonferrous metals increased as well: copper was used for electric wiring, zinc for galvanization, and tin for tinplating. Europe was becoming increasingly dependent on the Americas, Africa, and Asia to meet its growing demand for these substances. At the same time, France was still producing enough bauxite for the European aluminum industry. And thanks to a production method based on electrolysis (introduced in 1886 in both France and the U.S.), the aluminum industry was growing at an increasingly rapid pace in America,

Germany, France, Britain, Canada, Austria, Norway, Italy, and Switzerland.

By 1914, the world's major railway systems were already in place. Compressed air brakes had been invented by George Westinghouse in 1869. The construction of major tunnels—the Mont Cenis between France and Italy (1871), the St. Gotthard (1882), the Simplon (1906), and the Lötschberg (1913) in Switzerland and the Arlberg in Austria (1884)—enabled railway networks to go beyond the Alps. In the United States, four transcontinental railway lines came into being after the first Atlantic-Pacific track was laid in 1869. Canada followed suit in 1886. In Latin America, the first trans-Andean line, between Buenos Aires and Valparaiso, was inaugurated in 1910. From 1904 on, the Trans-Siberian Railway reduced the traveling time from Moscow to Vladivostok from forty days to fifteen.

ITS RAILWAY NETWORKS, THANKS TO DEVELOPMENTS IN AIR TRAVEL...

Lower rail fares brought down the cost of transporting merchandise. In cities, the first streetcars were put into service at the turn of the century. The development of rail networks resulted in a decrease in the importance of water routes. The bicycle, invented at the end of the previous century, still enjoyed its nickname, "the little queen," despite the fact that, by 1914, 2,000,000 motor vehicles now traveled along the many routes crisscrossing the countryside on an ever-expanding network of roads. Ocean-going vessels were, for the most part, powered by steam; from 1910 on, it was only a six-and-a-half-day voyage between Europe and the United States. Cargo vessels, equipped with refrigeration for the first time, made it possible to transport perishable items. Generally speaking, the greater speed at which ships could now travel coupled with an increase in their cargo capacity (made possible by the use of steel in their construction) resulted in a decrease in freight costs by a factor of six over a period of fifty years. In addition, the canals of Suez (1868), Corinth (1893), Kiel (1895), and Panama (1914) shortened the duration of sea voyages considerably.

With the new century also came the birth of aviation. In 1884, J. C. Renard launched the first dirigibles, followed by the famous ones of Graf Zeppelin. The airplane, which first took to the air in 1897, powered by a steam engine invented by Clément Ader, was soon to benefit from improvements made to the internal combustion engine. In the U.S. the Wright brothers flew more than 800 feet in 1903; Blériot crossed the

AND TELECOMMUNICATIONS. IN 1914, WAR CHANGED THE FACE OF EUROPE.

English Channel in 1909, Chavez the Alps in 1910, and Roland Garros the Mediterranean in 1913.

Postal service had improved since the creation of the Universal Postal Union in 1875, which resulted in a greater uniformity in postal rates. The telegraph, used for railway systems since its inception in the mid-nineteenth century, was soon made available to newspapers, as well as to the general public. Operated by government agencies, it became a powerful tool for unifying world markets. The use of underwater cable—introduced in 1851 by a British company to link England and France—was expanding rapidly. Before long, it was to reach Moscow and the Mediterranean, by 1865 Calcutta, by 1866 the United States, and by 1875 Austria. The telephone, invented by Graham Bell in 1876, was already in general use in the U.S., and by 1913, one out of every sixty British citizens had such a device. Radio made its début around 1886, thanks to the efforts of Maxwell, Hertz, and Branly. Marconi established a radio link between France and Britain in 1899 and between Newfoundland and Cornwall in 1901. The phonograph had been invented by Thomas Edison in 1878, the movie camera by Etienne Jules Marey in 1888, and a primitive form of the modern tape recorder by Waldemar Poulsen in 1898.

This veritable explosion of technological advances reinforced the sense of well-being that characterized Europe's Belle Epoque, *whose center was, without a doubt, Paris. Ironically, it was also in that city that the infamous Dreyfus Affair had just sparked violent emotions and bitter political controversy.*

This, then, was the political and economic scene on the eve of "the war to end all wars"—a war that would witness the first foray on the part of the United States onto European soil and would bring about the demise of czarist Russia, the dismantling of the Austro-Hungarian Empire, and the end of the Ottoman Empire.

World War I also transformed the way of life of 452,000,000 Europeans, nearly half of whom lived in rural areas. Social conditions had already changed radically in the industrialized countries during the previous fifty years. Workers were attracted to towns, with their concentration of factories and ever-increasing wages. (Although new production methods—in particular, the assembly line—made work far less satisfying.) Alongside the upper middle class, which was concerned more with business now than public affairs, a new type of white-collar worker came into existence, created by the growth of minor commercial fields, the burgeoning of administrations and the abundance of subordinate positions thus created. The movement for the emancipation of women was underway throughout the world, though it was strongest in the Scandinavian and English-speaking countries. Only rural areas remained relatively unaffected by these developments.

FOLLOWING AN UNPRECEDENTED DIPLOMATIC CRISIS...

By 1914, the trade union movement, essentially pacifist in nature, already had more than 16,000,000 members worldwide, yet it did not constitute a sufficiently influential international force to prevent the outbreak of hostilities. Indeed, in the economic sphere, world competition had become much fiercer and markets more difficult to secure. On domestic markets, too, supply was beginning to exceed demand.

Despite increasing tension, the world was caught unawares by the events that directly sparked the war. In fact, as seen earlier, the diplomatic crisis that occurred in July, 1914, was merely the culmination of a decade of international turmoil. On July 23, 1914, a month after Austria-Hungary's Archduke Franz Ferdinand was assassinated by two Serbs at Sarajevo, the Viennese government, with Germany's backing, issued an unreasonable ultimatum to Serbia, demanding, among other things, that Austrian officials be allowed to participate in an investigation into the murder. On July 25, Belgrade refused to comply with the ultimatum. Austria-Hungary mobilized its army; Serbia followed suit, and diplomatic relations were broken off. Vienna's declaration of war came on the 28th. Russia, unwilling to risk Serbia's destruction, mobilized its army on July 31. That same day, the German government sent Russia an ultimatum and demanded a clarification from France as to its position with respect to the crisis. By August 1, France, Germany, and Russia were preparing for war. On August 2, Berlin demanded free passage through Belgium for German troops; the next day it violated Belgium's neutrality and declared war on France. On August 4, Great Britain entered the fray by declaring war on Germany. Previously formed alliances were respected, except in the case of Italy, which did not enter the war until 1915—and when it did so, it was on the side of the Allies. Owing to their various alliances, the belligerents consisted of Germany and Austria-Hungary on the one side, and France, Russia, Britain, Japan, Belgium, and Serbia on the other. These countries quickly

A CRUEL EUROPEAN "CIVIL WAR" BROKE OUT IN THE EAST, THE SOUTHEAST, AND THE WEST.

prepared for war, entrusting their governments with emergency powers, taking special economic measures, and organizing the rationing of food.

The war began on three European fronts: from the North Sea to neutral Switzerland, German troops confronted the French and British, as well as Belgium's small army; from the Baltic to still neutral Romania, Russia fought the Germans and the bulk of the Austro-Hungarian Army; in the Balkans and on the Danube, the Serbs faced the latter as well.

What ensued amounted to a kind of huge European civil war, for, while Japan joined forces with the Allies in 1914, it never actually sent troops to Europe. Despite the prediction of some optimists, the war was not over in four months (though the intensity of the fighting was such that a certain number of governments found themselves short of munitions after only a few weeks). Moreover, food shortages quickly became acute, and the warring nations found it necessary to increase their production, find substitutes for unavailable products, and ration certain foods. As the war dragged on, it drained much of the manpower needed to ensure economic stability. Moreover, during four long years, industrial and economic questions became of secondary importance. In the warring countries, as well as those under occupation, resources had to be utilized as efficiently as possible. As it turned out, Germany and Britain were, at least initially, to suffer the most serious effects of a wartime economy.

In 1914, German generals anticipated a quick victory on the Western Front. For their part, the Allies' strategy was based on a strong Russian offensive and stiff resistance on the part of the French. The Austrians expected to crush Serbia with ease. But all of these strategies backfired. Hindenburg defeated the Russians at Tannenberg, while the Austrians gave way to the might of their foes. Joffre's victory on the Marne allowed the French to regroup their forces, and Serbia stood firm. By the end of 1914, the battlefronts were firmly established. Turkey had entered the war on Germany's side, while the United States remained neutral. Following the British victory at the Falkland Islands, however, the Allies controlled the seas for the duration of the war, despite losses inflicted by German submarines (modern versions of the first such vessels developed by the Frenchman Laubeuf in 1899).

In the end, finding a solution to the acute lack of munitions became the key to gaining the upper hand in the conflict. In 1915, the fighting shifted to the trenches, which required vast quantities of mortars, machine guns, and grenades. Beginning that same year, economic warfare also raged, first with a blockade initiated by the Allies, then with a counterblockade by German submarines. The Allies' diversionary tactics in the Dardanelles and in France proved ineffective. Italy entered the war on the side of the Allies, while Bulgaria joined the Austro-German bloc. Several French and British divisions landed at Salonika but failed to win a decisive victory there. In 1916, both the Western Front and the Eastern Front were locked in a stalemate, despite huge French losses at Verdun. German forces were by now suffering the effects of the blockade, and the German arms industry was struggling to keep pace with its allies' needs. At sea, the Battle of Jutland reaffirmed the supremacy of the British Navy; while on land, Allied forces were unable to win a decisive victory on the Somme.

THE BATTLEFIELD FROM 1915 TO 1918: A MACABRE THEATER OF MECHANIZED DESTRUCTION. AMERICA'S ENTRY INTO THE WAR MARKED THE BEGINNING OF THE END FOR GERMANY.

The German Army was beginning to suffer from an acute lack of manpower. The appointment of Hindenburg, seconded by Ludendorff, to the German high command did little to remedy the situation. Still, by the end of 1916, German forces occupied most of Romania, a land rich in wheat and oil. In the face of heavy human losses and economic hardship, the Russian people soon became disillusioned with the war. President Wilson issued a U.S. offer of mediation, but to no avail.

Two key events brought about radical changes in the situation in 1917: the United States declared war against Germany in April (and in December, against Austria) and the October Revolution erupted in Russia. Immediately following Washington's declaration of war, ten Latin American countries followed suit. Panama, Cuba, Brazil, Guatemala, Nicaragua, Costa Rica, and Honduras officially declared war on Germany; while Peru, Uruguay, and Bolivia recalled their ambassadors. The psychological boost of the New World's entry into the war, as well as its economic and financial support to the European Allies could not have been more timely, for the Germans were beginning to profit from social unrest in Russia, where the czar had abdicated on March 15. And, despite Greece's entry into the war, the Balkan and the Italian fronts were suffering. In France, the Battle of Aisne was a fiasco. The offensive in Flanders, however, introduced much-needed American supplies. (The Russians, on the other hand, lost the whole of Galicia and Riga.)

SOCIAL UPHEAVAL PLAGUED THE BELLIGERENTS, WHILE GERMANY MADE PEACE WITH SOVIET RUSSIA. GERMANY, DEFEATED, WAS FORCED TO SIGN AN ARMISTICE IN 1918.

Social unrest was spreading throughout Europe. French soldiers began to desert; strikes broke out in the British metallurgical industry and in Italy. The German Socialists demanded "peace without annexation." Charles I, emperor of Austria since 1916, sought peace.

Russia's weakened position had left an opening for the Austro-Hungarians to rout the Italians at Caporetto. Just when all fronts seemed once again locked in a stalemate, revolution broke out in Russia. On November 6, 1917, Lenin, who had arrived a few months earlier from Switzerland in a sealed railway car that the Germans had allowed to pass through their territory, led troops in Petrograd against the new head of state, Kerenski. The Bolsheviks seized power, and on November 21, Lenin began negotiations leading to an armistice. In March, 1918, the treaty of Brest-Litovsk was signed by Russia and the Central Powers.

In early 1918, then, all indicators seemed to be pointing toward a German-Austro-Hungarian victory, but the arrival in July of thousands of American troops dealt the Germans a decisive blow. After suffering heavy losses in costly offensives at Saint-Quentin and Chemin des Dames, German generals were unable to prevent Allied forces, bolstered by reinforcements in the form of U.S. arms and troops, from breaking through German lines in August. Not long thereafter, French and Serbian troops, led by Franchet d'Esperey, defeated the Bulgarians at Salonika, and the British General Allenby and his Palestine Expeditionary Force crushed the Turkish Army and arrived at Damascus. In October, Turkey requested an armistice. On October 4, the new German chancellor, Prince Max of Baden, under pressure from military leaders desirous of avoiding total military defeat, asked President Wilson for an armistice. Wilson responded by demanding that all German leaders, both military and civilian, be removed from power. At the same time, the Italian General Diaz led a major offensive against Austro-Hungarian troops and occupied Vittorio Veneto. Czechoslovakia declared its independence and Slovenia seceded from Austria. Charles I signed the armistice of Villa Giusti with Italy and left Vienna on November 11, the final day of the war. William II had already abdicated at Spa two days earlier and fled to Holland. Germany and Austria were both declared republics.

The terrible war that had taken 9,000,000 military and civilian lives was over. Europe, weakened not only by its war losses but also by a drop in the birthrate, exacerbated by the war, had lost much of its prestige, while that of the United States and Japan was on the rise. The recently all-powerful Russian, German, and Austro-Hungarian empires, had been reduced to ruins.

SWITZERLAND WAS PARALYZED, DURING THIS TIME, BY A GENERAL STRIKE.

For Switzerland, November 11, 1918, the first day of peace, was a day of joy tinged with disquiet. Its army could finally be demobilized; but there were social problems to be addressed. During four long years of war, this neutral country (which had taken in 30,000 refugees and 85,000 civilian and military internees) had experienced sporadic but serious internal tension. Because of their linguistic links, the German- and French-speaking Swiss were highly susceptible to political propaganda penetrating the borders from both east and west. The French-speaking Swiss were outspoken in their disapproval of the invasion of Belgium, while the German-speaking Swiss could hardly forget that, since 1870, Germany had been for them the paradigm of a hard-working and orderly society. Tension mounted between these two components of the Swiss population. In February, 1914, a group calling itself the New Swiss Society was created with the objective of fighting what it called "the mental derangement of the country." Yet, in the autumn of 1918, Switzerland seemed less unified than before the war. Things should have improved after November 11; instead, a general strike was called—the first in Swiss history—and, to make matters worse, that same autumn an epidemic of influenza killed thousands of soldiers and civilians.

The strike was a product of the fatigue and frustration brought about by four long years of war. It was true that Switzerland's army of citizen-soldiers had fulfilled their mandate of safeguarding the country's neutrality and of allowing humanitarian organizations—in particular the International Committee of the Red Cross—to succor the populations of the warring countries. But most Swiss soldiers had no other source of income but their army pay, and many families had been financially strapped since 1915. Between 1914 and 1918, food and coal prices had doubled. And an increasingly active black market widened the gap between rich and poor. Some political extremists who had been in the entourage of Lenin while he was living in Switzerland thought conditions ripe for the wave of revolution from Russia and Central Europe to engulf the Swiss Confederation as well. When the general strike was called by a committee of trade union and socialist leaders, 139,000

1918: THE OLD WORLD BANDAGED ITS WOUNDS, WHILE CERTAIN COUNTRIES TOOK ADVANTAGE OF THIS SITUATION TO...

workers responded, including the railway employees. The federal government had to act quickly to defuse the situation.

That date, November 11, 1918, marked a profound change of political orientation for Switzerland, transforming it from a prewar, liberal society into the socially oriented one it is today. Though the country had been able to maintain its system of semidirect democracy as set forth in its constitution of 1848 (revised in 1874), and a basic respect for individual rights remained unchallenged, government intervention during the war had left its mark: in 1919, the eight-hour workday was introduced throughout Switzerland, and from this time on, it became more and more the rule in that country for working conditions, vacations, pension plans, and the like to be negotiated collectively between trade unions and employers. And this holds true today as well.

With the end of the war came hopes that agricultural production (which had dropped by one-third during the years of the war), industry, and savings would recover quickly. Scientific progress had not stood still during those years, especially in areas of research with potential military applications. But the working and middle classes had suffered the most from the disastrous effects of inflation and the high cost of living.

The next ten years were years of hope in Switzerland, of disillusionment elsewhere, and of sweeping social changes virtually everywhere. By 1929, economic, monetary, and financial disorder had brought the industrialized world once again to the brink of armed conflict. Indeed, despite the high hopes that accompanied the war's end in 1918, the world entered a period fraught with difficulties at least in part engendered by the war itself and by the decisions reached at Versailles.

World War I had brought about radical changes in the balance of world power. Great Britain now had to accustom itself to the idea of ruling the waves alongside the United States. Moreover, its two largest former dominions, Canada and Australia, now both independent, began moving into the American sphere of influence. The political and economic importance of Latin America was far greater than before the war. In Asia, Japan had become a force to be reckoned with. Europe, which had been deeply shaken by the war, now had to accept the existence of all these new forces in the world.

On the European continent, the Austro-Hungarian Empire had been splintered into many small states; France was weakened; Germany ruined; and Russia torn apart by revolution. While most European countries had maintained control of their colonies, the Continent itself had become such an active arena for political and social movements that its moral fabric was now weakening and signs of decline becoming increasingly apparent.

FREE THEMSELVES OF THE EUROPEAN YOKE.

THERE WAS A NEW SPIRIT IN EUROPE. ATTITUDES CHANGED...

In the early postwar years, thousands of soldiers had to be reabsorbed into a civilian population unsatisfied with this precarious peace. Because of their wartime experience and because the world was now such a different place, those ex-soldiers viewed everything with new eyes. Prewar liberalism, with its emphasis on the rights of the individual had now lost ground to socialism, with its emphasis on society's collective needs. Trade unions, formed to defend workers' social and professional interests, began growing in size and stature, while highly organized and powerful socialist parties began to make their influence felt.

Despite its might, the socialist movement was divided into two tendencies: revolutionary and reformist. And it was this internal conflict which was partially responsible for the failure of the Second International in 1914. Faced with the terrible choice of defending their countries from outside aggression or representing a proletariat that ignored all national borders, party leaders thought first and foremost of their own particular countries. However, the socialist movement survived the war. Indeed, it seemed to draw renewed energy from the war and to rekindle its revolutionary fervor, which culminated in the Bolshevik Revolution of 1917.

Another factor must be mentioned: the war had trained millions of men to obey orders and to consider world events through the prism of government censorship. The notion of individual freedom was further eroded by the strong emphasis placed on national interests, which involved the shaping of attitudes, the artificial stimulation of public enthusiasm, collectivization of the means of production, and the rationing of goods. In addition, there were important changes in the distribution of wealth. The rural population, while suffering heavy losses of manpower, enjoyed a certain degree of consolation in that there was now a greater availability of food. Factory workers, on the other hand, bore the brunt of the disastrous effects of a surge in the cost of living with no corresponding increase in salaries. And when, after the armistice, millions of demobilized soldiers reentered the work force, social unrest

MONETARY SYSTEMS EVOLVED; THE PUBLIC DEBT GREW. THE UNITED STATES BECAME THE WORLD'S CREDITOR.

intensified. From 1919 on, liberal democracy was under attack on all sides: on the Right, the fascists argued—as did Oswald Spengler—that the masses were ready to place their destiny in the hands of a strong leader capable of imposing his will in the midst of a profusion of individual interests, while on the Left, the proletarian movement, with the Russian Revolution as its model, favored a dictatorship of the proletariat.

World War I had totally transformed the world's monetary system. Before the war, economies had functioned, both domestically and internationally, through the exchange of goods and services whose value was expressed in terms of the gold standard. This system was completely torn asunder by the war. Moreover, during the course of fifty-one months of war, a decrease in production and transportation problems disrupted international trade patterns. Because Russian wheat could no longer be shipped through the Dardanelles, it was replaced on world markets by American wheat. Germany's chemical industry had succeeded in producing a variety of man-made materials. The U.S. had enlarged its merchant fleet to make up for the shortage of European cargo vessels. Thus, by the end of the war, a certain number of countries that had been too preoccupied with the war effort to devote much attention to international trade, suddenly discovered that they had been taken overtaken by other countries that refused to relinquish the new position they had achieved on world markets. This new world order—created in large part by the war and marked by both a decline in Europe's sphere of influence and a concomitant rise in that of the American and Soviet superpowers—would continue to exist throughout the twentieth century.

In purely economic terms, the war had cost more than $180,000,000,000. The public debt was enormous, because most of the warring nations had not been able to collect sufficient revenues through taxation and thus had been forced to borrow. In addition, there was widespread destruction of property and the repair or replacement of equipment and machinery to be reckoned with. The expenses involved amounted to a third of the national wealth of France and Britain and a fourth of that of Germany and Italy. Inflation was rampant throughout the Continent, wreaking further havoc with national economies. In Britain, wholesale prices were about 11 percent higher in March, 1919, than before the war. The convertibility of currencies was gradually done away with in continental Europe.

WHILE ECONOMIC CRISES ERUPTED.

Suddenly, Europe, which had once been the world's creditor, was now a debtor continent. Moreover, its principal creditor, the United States, where the dollar had retained its value in relation to gold, had begun retreating into political and economic isolationism. Revolutionary Russia was no longer an actor in the European decision-making process. And the strong economic cohesion between the Allies during wartime had given way to financial rivalry in a continent fragmented by the creation of many small countries, following the breakup of the Austro-Hungarian Empire.

Prices rose more sharply after the war than during it, reaching their peak by 1920, when the needs of most buyers had been met and personal savings had been used up. Some governments, including that of Britain and the U.S., were able to control spiraling inflation by drastically cutting back on expenditures, with several key banks raising their discount rates.

By the end of 1920, a slump in U.S. sales—due to the return to the marketplace of European agricultural products and, in the industrial sector, to a certain degree of market saturation—brought about a short-lived economic crisis. In that same year, the Republican party returned to power, challenging President Wilson's support for the League of Nations and, as an indirect result of their isolationist policy, halting both military and civilian government spending. Farmers, who had been forced to borrow continually since 1916 to increase their agricultural output, were hard hit by a drop in prices for their crops and continued to be plagued by this situation as late as 1934. In industry, repeated waves of layoffs resulted in high unemployment. To counteract the economic depression, the government raised customs duties, lowered taxes and restricted immigration. Despite such measures, however, in 1921, steel production dropped by some 50 percent.

The effects of this crisis in the U.S. were soon felt in Japan, Britain, and Western Europe. In France, the gross national product dropped dramatically. Italy, too, was suffering its own economic and social ills. Because of a lack of mineral resources and adequate soil for farming, that country was forced to import from abroad 80 percent of the raw materials needed for its domestic industry. In 1921, widespread unemployment, inflation, strikes, and the takeover of factories by angry workers, as well as unrest in rural areas, helped bring Benito Mussolini and

FASCISM ENGULFED ITALY IN 1922, AND GERMANY STRUGGLED WITH A MYRIAD OF PROBLEMS FOLLOWING THE TREATY OF VERSAILLES. AUSTRIA-HUNGARY WAS DISMANTLED.

the Fascists into the Italian parliament. Mussolini, a former socialist, possessed considerable charisma and was a gifted public speaker. He was a strong believer in the use of force to achieve political ends and was also highly cunning, playing deftly on national sentiments of frustration and disappointment over Italy's so-called lost peace, i.e., its dashed hopes of expansion south toward Africa and east toward the Adriatic coast. Aided by a group of cohorts from World War I, Mussolini used the threat of a Russian-style communist revolution to intimidate his countrymen into backing a totalitarian regime (he and his entourage were the first to use this term), which he promised would transform Italy into a great world power. Mussolini took advantage of Italy's weak parliamentary government to organize a March on Rome with the infamous Blackshirts. On October 28, 1922, Mussolini came to power in Italy, thus commencing more than twenty years of dictatorship there.

Meanwhile Germany was experiencing a monetary crisis unparalleled in that country's history: by July, 1922, the mark had lost 99 percent of its value. The country's economic crisis during those early postwar years would have important repercussions worldwide—as would the political events that accompanied that crisis.

After signing the Armistice of 1918, the Social Democratic Weimar Republic initiated peace negotiations with Russia (which had lost Finland in 1917), with the newly independent Baltic states of Latvia, Estonia, and Lithuania being absent from these. The Treaty of Versailles, signed on June 28, 1919, sealed Germany's fate: Alsace-Lorraine was returned to France; Poland was given access to the sea via a corridor to the free city of Danzig (Gdansk), under control of the League of Nations (founded the year before). Germany's former colonies were divided among France, Britain, Belgium, New Zealand, Australia, and Japan; its army was reduced to 100,000 men, and a Reparations Commission was set up to administer the settlement of payments, which had been initially established at 269,000,000,000 gold marks. Reaching these decisions had necessitated a great deal of hard bargaining between the Allies, especially when it came to the question of France and Belgium's occupation of the left bank of the Rhine, France's administering the Saar, and Italy's claim to Fiume.

The future of the six states that had been created or redefined following the dismantling of Austria-Hungary was determined by the Treaty of

Saint-Germain, in September, 1919, and that of Trianon, in June, 1920. The population of Austria was reduced to 6,000,000; Hungary lost more than half its territory; Czechoslovakia was formed by joining Bohemia, Slovakia, and Carpathian Ruthenia; Yugoslavia was constituted by bringing together the Serbs, the Croatians, and the Slovenians; Romania gained territory taken from Hungary and Bulgaria; Poland was declared independent. It was forbidden for Austria to reenter into an alliance with Germany without the prior agreement of the League of Nations. In November, 1919, the Treaty of Neuilly awarded parts of Bulgaria to Greece, Romania, and Yugoslavia. In August, 1920, Turkey signed the Treaty of Sèvres with the Allies. However, Ataturk's newly founded republic refused to acknowledge this treaty and soon embarked on a war with Greece which dragged on until the Treaty of Lausanne in 1923.

THE INTERWAR PERIOD BEGAN, WITH ITS TRAIN OF MILITARY AND SOCIAL CONFLICTS, MONETARY CRISES, AND THE RISE OF NATIONALIST EXTREMISM.

Never before had a peace treaty been so difficult to draw up. And many of the belligerents remained dissatisfied once it had. Even the creation of the League of Nations in Geneva in 1918, in which the European Allies had placed so much hope, was dealt a severe blow by the U.S. Congress's refusal in 1919 to authorize the U.S. to join it. Woodrow Wilson, the Democratic president who had first initiated the idea of a global organization for common security and whose views, as expressed in the famous Fourteen Points program of 1917, were challenged in 1918 by a Republican Congress with isolationist tendencies. Obviously, the failure of the U.S. to join the organization seriously undermined its effectiveness. Thus, the interwar period, marred at the outset by diplomatic quarrels, economic crises, social unrest, political change, and unsolved problems, did not have auspicious beginnings. In fact, World War I gave rise to a series of minor conflicts, indicative, nonetheless, of a certain tension in the world. Among these were: the war between Turkey and Greece; the struggle in Germany between the anti-communist Freikorps *and the pro-Soviet Spartacists; a Russian threat to Poland; an attempted communist putsch by Bela Kun in Hungary; and the occupation of Syria by France. Ireland—with the exception of Ulster, which remained British—won its independence in 1921, after a long struggle and the threat of revolution. The defeated countries of Central and Eastern Europe languished in poverty. The European Allies snubbed Soviet Russia, where anti-Communist forces led by General Wrangel*

MEANWHILE, THE U.S. ENJOYED SOCIAL AND ECONOMIC STABILITY, THOUGH THE QUESTION OF GERMAN WAR REPARATIONS REMAINED UNRESOLVED.

and Admiral Kolchak were defeated. All this time, the United States remained strongly isolationist.

This chaotic situation, resulting from misunderstanding, bitterness, and arrogance on the part of the victors and resentment on the part of the vanquished, lasted until 1923. At that time, the liquidation of stocks gave the U.S. economy a much-needed boost, with social stability contributing to its recovery. The Ford Company announced a policy—soon to be adopted by other firms—of higher wages, even in the case of a drop in the cost of living. Easy credit served to stimulate sales, as did increased publicity. Moreover, chain stores, with their wide range of attractive products, whet the nation's appetite for consumer goods yet further. Most important, economic recovery in the U.S. had a strong impact on Europe's economic situation.

Germany's defeat notwithstanding, it continued to play an important role in shaping events in Europe. In 1922, it signed the Treaty of Rapallo with the Soviet Union, a nation that also found itself in quarantine, as it were. In 1923, an attempted coup by the former German general, Ludendorff, and a certain Adolf Hitler foreshadowed the dire events in store for this economically ruined country. In 1921, interest on Germany's war debts, pensions paid to war victims, and its reparations payments amounted to more than twice the level of government revenues. Beginning with the Franco-Belgian occupation of the Ruhr in 1923, Germany's expenditures increased tenfold. To remedy the situation, the Reichsbank stepped up the issuance of banknotes, and the resulting flood of currency in circulation created a situation in which consumers preferred to immediately acquire goods with their money rather than putting it away as savings. Germany owed its salvation—at least temporarily—to the Reparations Commission, established to study that nation's financial predicament. It included two Americans, Charles G. Dawes and Owen Young, whose main task was to examine the question of Germany's reparations payments. The total amount of payments had been assessed at 132,000,000,000 gold marks, part of which could be paid in kind, in the form of naval vessels, machines, building materials, and livestock for war-ravaged areas of France and Belgium. Other forms of reparations included the supply of 25,000,000 tons of coal per year; the transfer of ownership of German property and investments abroad; and the maintaining of Allied occupation armies on German soil. The outstanding debt was to be paid off within a period of forty years. In January, 1923, however, the Reparations Commission judged that Germany, which had just requested a moratorium on payments, was "willfully in default." French and Belgian troops moved in to occupy the mineral-rich Ruhr, which produced widespread, albeit passive, resistance on the part of the local population. (The region provided three-quarters of Germany's steel and coal.) Inflation reached such heights that in November, 1923, the German government, headed by Gustav Stresemann, was forced to take drastic monetary measures: it issued a new unit of currency called the Rentenmark, *each worth 1,000,000,000 original marks.*

IN 1925, GERMANY, ENGLAND, BELGIUM, ITALY, FRANCE, POLAND, AND CZECHOSLOVAKIA SIGNED NONAGGRESSION PACTS IN LOCARNO.

The 1924 announcement of the Dawes Plan restored German confidence to a certain degree, despite raging inflation that had annihilated savings, undermined the value of government loans, bonds, and mortgages, and brought misery to people living on fixed incomes or pensions. The plan called for initial annual payments of $250,000,000 up to a sum of $625,000,000, after which regular payments would be made. Germany accepted the plan, which was clearly in its interest (as was the Young Plan, put forward and accepted in 1930, which reestablished Germany's outstanding debt at $9,000,000 instead of the $33,000,000 figure reached a decade earlier).

By early 1929, the German economy had recovered to such an extent that the volume of its exports equaled that of 1913. By offering 2 percent higher interest rates on foreign investments than those offered by other industrialized countries, the Weimar Republic was able to attract much foreign capital. In 1925, the election of Marshal von Hindenburg as president served to further strengthen confidence in the economy. In that same year, Stresemann put his signature to the Locarno Pact, along with Briand for France, Chamberlain for Britain, Vandervelde for Belgium, Mussolini for Italy, Skrzynski for Poland, and Beneš for Czechoslovakia. And the situation might have continued improving, were it not for the economic storm that was brewing in the United States.

1929 was a fateful year in modern economic history, and while we shall discuss the New York Stock Market Crash per se later on, it might be useful here to trace the events leading up to those dark days in October, 1929. As we have seen, the period preceding the Stock Market Crash—seven years in the U.S. and five in Europe—was marked by a

ECONOMIC RECOVERY GAVE RISE TO A KIND OF EUPHORIA; AND INFLATION FELL, AT LEAST TEMPORARILY. BUT THIS ILLUSION OF WELL-BEING WAS SHORT-LIVED...

peculiar sort of economic recovery. Abundant credit had enabled industries to increase their production while not necessarily considering the marketability of their products. In the U.S., widespread stock market speculation created a false sense of prosperity, with sums being invested exclusively with a view to making huge profits. Ironically, this situation contributed to Germany's rapid recovery. As the economist André Philip suggested in this connection: "...in the end it was the United States that paid a large part of Germany's war reparations."

During this period, the production of coal slowed, while that of petroleum products (three-quarters of which were produced in the U.S.) increased dramatically. Steel production, too, was on the rise. New means of transportation, such as the automobile and the airplane, contributed to the expansion of the aluminum and rubber industry. In 1929, 84 percent of all vehicles were made in the U.S.A., and civil aviation was a booming industry as well, particularly after Lindbergh's spectacular crossing of the Atlantic in May, 1927. During that same year, talking movies made their appearance in America. Electrically powered devices such as refrigerators, telephone exchanges, and household appliances began to be produced on a wide scale, and radio technology was making great strides. In the U.S., large industries, using methods of mass production, were fast becoming economic giants. At the same time, European industrialists began providing machinery and equipment to their colonies and to developing countries. Increasingly sophisticated forms of advertising—especially in the U.S.—fostered increased demand on the part of consumers.

The high rate of inflation that had raged in some European countries and which caused a flight of capital abroad, began to subside; and by 1923, the situation had improved in France, Germany, and Central Europe. At the same time, British and American investment was contributing to the development of Latin America and the British dominions. Following the 1922 establishment of the gold exchange standard at the World Economic Congress in Genoa, the central bank reserves of many developing countries often consisted of sterling credit notes convertible into other currencies.

In the United States, an agricultural crisis had been brewing since 1920. During World War I, American farmers had invested heavily in methods of increasing their production, and the resulting indebtedness led to financial disaster when prices began falling after the war. Each time the situation began improving, farmers increased production in the hope of paying off their debts. From 1928 on, agricultural stockpiles were growing and food prices dropping, while the prices of industrial goods remained high. Farmers' buying power decreased and they were forced to mortgage more and more of their land.

In retrospect, it is easy to say that the worldwide economic recovery that led to the New York Stock Market Crash was, in fact, artificial; but at the time, and despite the worsening plight of American farmers, few observers predicted a financial catastrophe. In the area of international politics, the Kellogg-Briand Pact, signed in 1928 by fifty-four governments, with a view to proscribing war, helped foster an illusion of tranquility. By the end of 1929, the collapse of the American stock market had replaced the general euphoria with deep disenchantment. And the consequences of the economic disaster soon to come would be felt—like a major earthquake—in many countries around the world. The suddenness with which it hit revealed the extent to which American prosperity had been illusory; moreover, it caused a series of shock waves to reverberate throughout an economically and politically fragile Europe, unprepared for such instability.

In 1929, after the armed peace that, in 1914, marked the end of Europe's Belle Epoque, *after the horrors of World War I, and the economic, social, and political upheaval of the postwar period, a world hoping blindly for peace and prosperity was still unaware that the worst was yet to come: that World War II, already in the making, would result in far greater loss of life, far greater physical destruction, and more profound and sweeping changes in the minds and hearts of men and women throughout the world than any previous conflict in the history of mankind.*

AND TEN YEARS AFTER THE NEW YORK STOCK MARKET CRASH, A SECOND WORLD WAR BROKE OUT, FAR MORE TERRIBLE THAN THE FIRST.

NESTLÉ
NESTLÉ'S
GENUINE MILK
CHOCOLATE
NESTLÉ
NESTLÉ'
GENUINE MILK
CIOCCOLATO
NESTLÉ'S GENUINE MILK CHOCOLA

Chapter III – Nestlé

1905–1929 Nestlé Becomes a Full-Fledged Chocolate Manufacturer

1905: AN EXCELLENT START FOR NESTLÉ AND ANGLO-SWISS CONDENSED MILK CO.,

☐ 1929 was the year of Nestlé's second merger—this time with the chocolate makers Peter, Cailler, and Kohler. They had earlier pooled their resources to found Chocolats Suisses S.A., which also produced a Nestlé brand chocolate (marketed by Nestlé and Anglo-Swiss Condensed Milk Company). This merger took place just a few months before the U.S. Stock Market Crash.

The firm that evolved from the 1905 merger of Nestlé and Anglo-Swiss had indeed gotten off to an excellent start. A sign of the complete equality that had prevailed upon the merger of the companies: the new firm now possessed two headquarters—just as it does today—one at Cham; the other at Vevey. With Emile-Louis Roussy as chairman, the first board of directors consisted of ten members, five of whom were nominated by the branch of the company in eastern Switzerland and five by the branch in western Switzerland. The company's authorized capital of SFr. 40,000,000 provides us with a good idea of its economic strength.

The senior executives of the organization exemplified, in 1905, the hazards involved in a union between two firms that had been rivals in both manufacturing and marketing for so long. Ever since the merger, questions of personality and prestige had played a role in management decisions, and it was to take nearly two decades of gradual efforts (until the 1921–22 crisis at Nestlé discussed later) to make the merger complete and create a company with genuinely centralized control.

Gustave Aguet needed to muster all his diplomatic skills in this process of unification, insofar as he was not only closely related to both Emile-Louis Roussy, chairman of the board, and Auguste Mayor, one of the firms's executive vice-presidents, but was also a friend of the Page family, especially of young Fred H. Page, the company's other executive vice-president.

Gustave Aguet (1852–1927)

So as not to break with tradition, from 1905 on, the senior executives of the former management (at Cham, Vevey, and in London) all retained their positions. Therefore, complete centralization of resources, with all services in one place within one management structure, did not take place. The team at Cham handled accounts, legal affairs, insurance, taxes, and transportation, together with technical problems, construction work, and milk sales in Germany and Austria. Vevey was in charge of the distribution of Nestlé infant cereal as well as sales of all the company's other products in continental Europe— with the exception of Germany and Austria—as well as running the four factories located in western Switzerland. The two sales departments in London were combined, creating what was virtually a third head office. It mainly handled sales to Great Britain, Asia, Australia, Latin America, and Africa. In 1905, the new company was managed by four men: the headquarters at Cham was controlled by two executive vice-presidents, both having been in the same position at Anglo-Swiss: Aloys Bosshard and Fred Page. The position of executive vice-president at Vevey was held by Auguste Mayor, assisted by Auguste Roussy, son of the chairman of the board. The fourth executive vice-president, Gustave Aguet, resided in London and was soon to be assisted by his future son-in-law, Alfred Liotard-Vogt. Thus, before and during World War I, the new company was clearly far from possessing the most satisfying and efficient management structure. In spite of, or rather, because of events over which the firm's directors had no control, it continued to expand: before the war it profited from the dynamism of the world economy; during the war, it profited from the fact that the belligerents required large amounts of its milk products.

WHICH HAD A HIGHLY DECENTRALIZED ORGANIZATIONAL STRUCTURE. PRODUCTION IN AUSTRALIA STARTED IN 1907;

While the year 1905 mainly involved adjustments and reorganization, as of 1906, shareholders were gratified to see the rapid increase in sales of the company, with a net profit of more than SFr. 7,500,000 that year. In the following years, as the trend toward protectionism began to create a serious obstacle to the export of Swiss products, the consistently high sales figures enjoyed by the company were viewed with particular satisfaction. Given the increasingly protectionist environment, it soon became less expensive to produce goods outside of Switzerland, as raw materials were cheaper abroad, and wages and transport costs lower there. As a result, the Swiss factory at Egnach, near Romanshorn, was closed down in 1906.

The company started manufacturing in Australia—the second largest export market for its products—in 1907. For this purpose, the firm purchased a large Australian condensed milk company, the Cressbrook Dairy Company of Brisbane, which owned a rather rudimentary condensed milk plant at Toogoolawah, Queensland, and a small plant at Wilson Park in the same state. The seventeen farms supplying those two production centers produced approximately 370,000 gallons of fresh milk in 1906, whereas the factory at Bercher, Switzerland, was handling

"Vevey with the Dent du Midi," a 1903 postcard

cloven times that quantity. Thus, the company decided to investigate the possibility of strengthening its presence in Australia. As it had not forgotten its unfortunate experience in America, the board was wise to make it clear, however, in its report to shareholders, that the purpose of manufacturing in what was then a developing country was not to try and capture a new market. That report stated: "in Australia, we must safeguard our position: our products enjoy undisputed supremacy there."

With the acquisition of Cressbrook in the Land Down Under, Nestlé acted very briefly against its policy of never acquiring farms or cattle. For a time, the company owned four farms and 1,443 head of cattle. Nestlé and Anglo-Swiss had been selling two hundred thousand cases of imported condensed milk per year in Australia, which was more than the output of the two Australian factories combined. Thus, in 1910, it decided to build an industrial complex at Dennington, Victoria. The region had everything needed to run an efficient plant: a good milk supply, plenty of water, and an adequate source of labor from nearby Melbourne, the capital of Victoria. By 1912, production at Dennington was so high that it was now possible to sell the Wilson Park factory. In the meantime, the enlarged Toogoolawah factory had been supplied with equipment and machinery from Switzerland. (The purchase and production of all Nestlé and Anglo-Swiss technical equipment was centralized at Cham.) At the same time, steps were being taken to increase the output of Australian farms, to clear more land, to improve farmers' livestock, etc. The opening of an office in Sydney added the final touch to the Australian venture, which was Nestlé's first attempt to manufacture its products in a country possessing only a rudimentary industrial infrastructure. This trend toward industrial expansion, which began in 1907, was to continue to develop over the years.

Factory at Dennington, Australia

In addition to high customs duties, another obstacle hindering the exports of any given firm is, of course, competition, which may take many different forms. For example, the advent of condensed skimmed milk—an inherently cheaper product—forced Nestlé and Anglo-Swiss to alter its basic policy of giving preference to condensed whole milk. Competition thus obliged the firm to fight for a position of prominence in this unfamiliar area. Holland, where the firms of Van den Bergh, Aurora, and Hollandia had already been established, was one of the most suitable countries in which to start manufacturing this type of milk. Another was Denmark. Both of these countries had long held a privileged position in the manufacture of butter and condensed milk. It did not take long for Nestlé to acquire a substantial interest in the Galak Condensed Milk Company of Rotterdam, which had at its disposal abundant milk supplies from surrounding districts. On behalf of that company, Nestlé set up a skimmed milk factory, geared exclusively to overseas markets; it began production in 1912. Nestlé and Anglo-Swiss was merely protecting itself against a potentially dangerous situation, especially in the Far East, where the consumption of skimmed milk—served with tea—had risen appreciably within a very short period of time.

IT GREW IN HOLLAND AND DENMARK; AND SALES INCREASED IN GREAT BRITAIN AND ASIA.

In 1912, a variety of factors led the company to set up a factory at Ashbourne, England. Among these were demand in urban areas for ever-increasing supplies of fresh milk, the prospect of preferential tariffs for British goods on Dominion markets, the possibility of import duties being levied on imported condensed milk, comparatively low cost price, as well as excellent transportation facilities overseas. The Ashbourne factory had an annual output of two hundred thousand cases. The rise in Nestlé's sales the previous year had encouraged the company to acquire "a substantial interest in an English firm, Messrs. Fussell & Co., Ltd. of London, which possessed a plant producing evaporated milk and sterilized cream at Salisbury, England, and another at Holmestrand, Norway." From 1910 on, production grew in practically all countries—even in Switzerland. In 1912, the board announced that it was purchasing a small factory at Yverdon, Switzerland, which had been manufacturing products for Nestlé since the previous year. This increase in manufacturing capacity was accompanied by an increase in sales. In 1910, sales were 22 percent higher than in 1908. Thanks to an intensive publicity campaign, dairy products began to be appreciated not only in all classes of society, but also in regions where milk was too scarce to be a regular part of the staple diet.

Simultaneously, the firm was improving its sales organization by progressively replacing its network of agents with branch offices. From the very start, the main Singapore warehouse played an important role in grouping orders and splitting up consignments for the Far East. Warehouses were opened in Hong Kong, Calcutta, Madras, Bombay, Colombo, and, in 1913, in

THE FOUNDING OF LOCALLY BASED COMPANIES CHARACTERIZED THE PERIOD PRIOR TO WORLD WAR I, WHICH SOON RESULTED IN ADMINISTRATIVE DIFFICULTIES...

Japan. Thanks to this method of operation, supervised from the central office in London, sales curves for condensed, evaporated, and sterilized milk rose rapidly. The success of this venture had an influence—on a more modest scale perhaps—on the introduction of warehouses in other parts of the world, notably in Buenos Aires and Constantinople.

In addition to expanding sales and purchasing existing companies, Nestlé acquired an interest in companies that had been formed as a result of its initiative and had set up factories to manufacture Nestlé products. Nestlé placed increasing emphasis on creating country-based firms responsible for setting up their own production centers abroad. In Italy and later in Germany, companies were formed such as Società Henri Nestlé, Milan, in December, 1913, to which Nestlé and Anglo-Swiss granted certain rights.

By the beginning of World War I, Nestlé had at its disposal unparalleled expertise in the milk industry; it was also in a position to market its chocolates internationally, thanks to a 1904 agreement with the Société Générale Suisse de Chocolats, which Peter and Kohler had founded. The expertise acquired by the Nestlé Company and by Anglo-Swiss over more than fifty years of activity later proved quite useful when, during the war, the new firm resulting from their merger had to adapt to conditions totally different from those it had encountered previously.

At the outset of the war, Nestlé's activities were initially disrupted by Europe's mobilization, since most of its factories were located on the Continent. Obviously, production centers in such countries as Germany, Austria, and Great Britain were more seriously affected by protective economic measures than those in neutral countries such as Spain, Norway, and Switzerland. These difficulties were administrative rather than commercial in nature, however. And, as there were technical means of overcoming them, production continued everywhere in the early months of the war.

Factory at Hiroto, Japan

As with all firms obtaining their raw materials from a variety of countries and shipping their products long distances by sea, Nestlé and Anglo-Swiss Condensed Milk Company was immediately confronted with serious transport problems, owing to the restrictions placed on shipping by the belligerents. Freight and insurance fees soon rose to extremely high levels, and at times it was simply impossible to ship goods at all. In addition, reserves of a certain number of raw materials had to be maintained in order to ensure the long-term requirements of factories, which tied up large amounts of capital.

AS WELL AS TRANSPORTATION PROBLEMS, BOTH OF WHICH WORSENED AS THE WAR SPREAD. THE COMPANY'S FIFTIETH ANNIVERSARY, IN 1916, PASSED IN SILENCE;

Due to the sheer volume in certain areas of production and also to the very nature of its products (i.e., basic foodstuffs) it was possible for Nestlé to continue its activity in nearly all countries. As of the first year of the war, the company promised financial compensation for all members of its staff who had been called up for military service in all the countries in which it was present.

The difficulties generated by the war grew more acute in 1915. Since the hostilities created a tremendous demand for dairy products, the problem was not so much one of expanding into new markets as it was of how to meet the growing demand of Nestlé's existing customers. The Allied blockade and German submarine warfare directed against ocean-going vessels were to remain major concerns of the company until the end of the war.

Faced with increasing demand—largely in the form of government contracts—Nestlé strengthened its policy of decentralization by setting up new country-based firms to handle manufacturing and sales: in Norway, the A/S De Norske Melkefabriker operated the factories at Hamar, Kap, and, from 1916 on, Levanger; in Austria, Nestlé's Kindermehl Gesellschaft took over the Grimmenstein factory.

In 1916, the fiftieth anniversary of the company's establishment passed in silence, for the anxiety the war caused was far too great to permit celebration. A shortage of fresh milk was beginning to be felt, especially in Switzerland. For long periods at a time, the factories had to forgo the processing of virtually all milk received so as to meet the needs of urban centers. The Guin and Yverdon factories were closed down. However, the company managed to find other sources of supply. In Norway, for example, it purchased Egron, with headquarters at Christiania, which had factories at Kloeften, Norway, as well as Vernamo, Sweden. Egron held the patent for a manufacturing process for powdered milk. (Later—after improvements to it—this process was to be of enormous benefit to the majority of the factories that manufactured Nestlé products throughout the world.) In addition, the firm's business interests in South Africa were transferred to the Nestlé

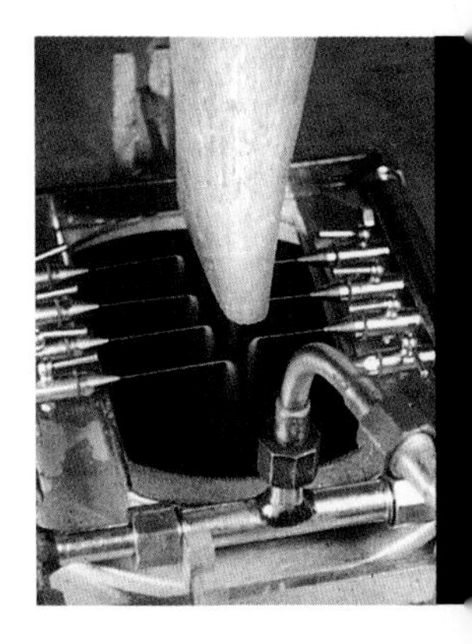

Part of the old equipment used to manufacture powdered milk

A COMPANY WAS SET UP IN FRANCE THAT SAME YEAR.

and Anglo-Swiss Condensed Milk Company (Africa), Ltd., with headquarters in Cape Town.

At that time, there were already about a dozen companies either selling or manufacturing Nestlé products, located mainly in Europe, the U.S., and Australia. Before long, similar firms were set up for other major markets. Working along the same lines, Nestlé helped to create a corporation in France, authorized to manufacture and market Nestlé products in that country—as well as in the French colonies—which began production at Cherbourg in 1916. The same year, the capital of Nestlé and Anglo-Swiss increased from SFr. 40,000,000 to SFr. 60,000,000.

Tight restrictions were placed on the company's use of its own production facilities in 1917. Moreover, during this same period the company felt the effects of the general rise in manufacturing and operating costs and of a low liquidity ratio. There was a reduction in the number of head of cattle, and poor fodder caused a decline in milk production. Once again, Nestlé was forced to cut back on production so that a large part of its milk supplies could be diverted to the civilian population. The company made considerable sacrifices in the public interest in agreement with governments that were not yet capable of finding a rational means of ensuring the supply of fresh or canned milk. In Switzerland, Nestlé again decided to forgo a part of its supplies of fresh milk to permit the production of butter and to provide milk for the urban population, thereby resulting in a sharp drop in the export of Swiss condensed milk.

Times were no longer as they had been in the early days when Anglo-Swiss and Henri Nestlé had obtained enough milk in Switzerland alone to meet all their requirements. By 1917, the volume of Swiss milk available to Nestlé to produce condensed milk was barely 6 percent of that needed for the manufacture of its products the world over. There were three avenues open to Nestlé, permitting it to offset a drop in Swiss exports while meeting a growing international demand: 1) to purchase condensed milk from existing facilities (or acquire such factories and improve their output—the quickest solution); 2) to build its own factories utilizing new or traditional milk-supply networks (a sensible but slow solution); 3) to increase the production of factories already owned by the company by improving equipment and collection techniques. Owing to the urgency of the situation, Nestlé was forced to adopt the first of these three courses of action.

Fresh milk arriving at the condensed milk factory in Payerne, Switzerland

ACQUISITION OF FACTORIES IN THE U.S. AND IN AUSTRALIA POSED FINANCING PROBLEMS.

Nestlé had begun purchasing condensed milk in America as early as 1915 and had increased these purchases until 1917. Some forty suppliers were now providing Nestlé with products manufactured according to its specifications, which it resold to the civilian population and to the armed forces during the war. Several of the American factories specializing in the manufacture of condensed milk for Nestlé increased their production level fivefold within a very short time. However, their financial resources were soon exhausted, and Nestlé was obliged to come to their aid. These transactions were carried out by Nestlé's Food Company, New York, established in 1905 (with a capital of $250,000) to manufacture infant cereal at Fulton, New York, and to market it in the U.S. In 1917, Nestlé purchased such a great amount of products from American manufacturers that its board of directors decided to send a delegation to the U.S. to negotiate the acquisition of several factories there.

That delegation set its sights on the John Wildi Evaporated Milk Company, Columbus, Ohio—founded by a Swiss—and the Hires Condensed Milk Company, Philadelphia. By purchasing shares in these companies and their subsidiaries, Nestlé ensured itself the output of twenty-seven condensed milk factories. In the United States alone, Nestlé's production capacity was now five times greater than that of its Swiss factories before the war. And, in 1918, the company's worldwide production capacity was twice that of 1914. To provide the liquid assets and credit needed to finance development in the U.S., Nestlé's Food Company, New York, increased its capital to $15,000,000.

Building on William Street in New York City, housing Nestlé's Food Company, Inc.

A similar policy was adopted in Australia during the final months of the war. In autumn of 1918, the company took the risk of purchasing considerable quantities of condensed milk from local companies such as Bacchus March Concentrated Milk Company, Australian Milk Products, Ltd., and Standard Dairy, Ltd., with eleven factories ensuring delivery. In 1920, Nestlé continued in this rather risky direction, acquiring a controlling interest in these companies.

During this time of economic instability in the world, such acquisitions obviously required proper financing. Nestlé had raised loans, of course, as early as 1912. The company adhered to an unchanging principle: to purchase its suppliers' total output of fresh milk. Under normal circumstances, this output was approximately equivalent to the quantity that was used in the production process. In 1912, however, Nestlé suddenly found itself with unexpectedly large quantities of fresh milk on hand. Since it was bound by contracts with milk suppliers, it had no other choice but to expand production in order to absorb the surplus. This resulted in an accumulation of unsold stocks, which tied up a considerable amount of capital. The only viable solution was to raise a SFr. 12,000,000 loan. This was the first in a total of five loans raised by the Nestlé Company from 1912 until 1917: SFr. 2,000,000 in 1913, SFr. 10,000,000 in 1915, SFr. 10,000,000 in early 1917, and SFr. 20,000,000 in the autumn of that same year.

IN 1918, THE COMPANY REMAINED CONFIDENT, DESPITE A REEVALUATION OF WARTIME PRIORITIES.

Toward the end of the war, the scheme for acquiring twenty-seven factories in America, the plan to take over a chocolate firm in Australia, and the purchase of large quantities of condensed milk forced the company once again to raise bank loans amounting to SFr. 30,000,000. In 1919, the board of directors was still using price increases and the need to finance production and build up inventory to justify increasing its holdings from SFr. 17,725,625 in 1917 to SFr. 100,562,573. In 1916, the board had offered the same justification for increasing capitalization from SFr. 40,000,000 to SFr. 60,000,000, by issuing fifty thousand new shares, each worth SFr. 400.

In its annual report for 1918—the year of the Armistice—the board of directors still expressed the hope that a large number of consumers who had grown used to condensed milk because of the shortage of fresh milk would remain customers of Nestlé now that the war was over. Like all wars, World War I had left in its wake great suffering, tragedies, and hardship. More than any previous war, however, it had resulted in a tremendous leap forward in the area of science and technology. And this helped shape new consumer patterns. But once armies were demobilized and government food-supply centers gradually closed down, there was no compensatory increase in civilian orders for the canned milk products that had been essential to millions of people for four years. The end of hostilities put a sudden end to government contracts and marked the return to a peacetime economy. For Nestlé, this meant the need for rapid readjustments with top priority given to feeding the war-ravaged civilian population.

Delivery carts in Sydney, Australia, 1920

STEPS WERE TAKEN TO REORGANIZE SALES. IN 1920, MANUFACTURING BEGAN IN LATIN AMERICA...

For the first few months after the Armistice, sales levels were easily maintained, even though the company's production capacity had increased tremendously since 1914. In the confusion of the immediate postwar period, fluctuations in exchange rates and the rising cost of raw materials foreshadowed the difficulties that were soon to plague the Nestlé and Anglo-Swiss Condensed Milk Company.

In 1919, management's optimism coupled with cash-flow problems for the company's chocolate suppliers, Peter & Kohler (which had merged with Cailler in 1911), led Nestlé to consider manufacturing chocolate itself. Nestlé took control of the Peter, Cailler, Kohler Company in Australia, with the idea of constructing new chocolate production centers in that country. In addition, Nestlé obtained exclusive rights to market that chocolate maker's products in all the countries of the world, with the exception of Switzerland, Germany, Austria, the U.S., and Canada.

As late as 1919, it looked as though the civilian consumers who had grown used to condensed milk during the war were likely not only to retain their taste for it, but to continue to purchase it in large quantities as well. However, this was not to be the case.

During the Paris Peace Conference, Nestlé was restructuring. The department responsible for all European sales other than those for Great Britain was transferred to Paris, while the London office retained responsibility for sales in Britain and exports overseas. The company felt that it was necessary "to open up in Europe new sales centers controlled by a single management structure." To varying degrees, the company controlled a total of forty-two factories in the U.S., which created false hopes of serving as suppliers for the Pacific Islands, the Philippines, and particularly Japan. In this general climate of euphoria, Nestlé and Anglo-Swiss doubled its share capital, which now reached SFr. 160,000,000, by issuing two hundred thousand shares of stock at SFr. 400 per share. As its liquid assets were still inadequate in 1919, the company was obliged to seek a loan of SFr. 100,000,000 from certain large commercial banks. In 1920, a bond issue of SFr. 25,000,000 brought the total value of its bonds to SFr. 85,000,000.

The year 1920 was a memorable one in Nestlé's history. The company, which already had manufacturing facilities in one developing country—Australia—decided to start production in South America. The region selected for the construction of a production center was Araras, in Brazil, the biggest country in South America. It was the first in a series of links that Nestlé

Factory at Araras, Brazil

A sign of Nestlé's desire to produce its products locally in the world's developing countries. Management was optimistic in 1920...

would forge over the years, manufacturing its products in Latin America, and it was a vital one, insofar as it not only opened the way to production in the South American subcontinent, but also bore witness, once again, to the entrepreneurial spirit that Nestlé always demonstrated when it was required. Of course, this part of the world was far from being unknown territory to Nestlé and Anglo-Swiss: indeed, Anglo-Swiss had advertised in local Cuban newspapers, for instance, as early as 1880. Nevertheless, there is a vast difference between selling products imported from Europe or elsewhere and setting up production facilities in a region devoid of an industrial infrastructure. The 1920 decision was all the more significant insofar as the company, originating in the small, landlocked, neutral country of Switzerland, did not have the luxury of resorting to the methods that the world's great powers are sometimes tempted to use to promote their industries. Then, as now, Nestlé had to learn to adapt itself to prevailing conditions and always to operate within the limits of its own resources.

What, exactly, were the preconditions for setting up a factory in Brazil in 1920? First of all, Nestlé had to adopt a policy diametrically opposed to that of its main rivals, who enjoyed large domestic markets and saw no reason to create production centers in countries whose markets they could supply from abroad. Next, it meant finding a milk-producing area and building a factory in a region where it was impossible to obtain the necessary equipment and where the local inhabitants had no experience either in efficient dairy farming or in factory work. Livestock had to be improved, and transport organized. Capital was needed, foreign experts brought in, and equipment imported. Farmers had to be advised and local workers trained for industry. Owing to its experience in Australia, however, Nestlé undertook this task in Brazil with determination—and was successful there.

Management's faith in the future of the firm was even more apparent in its purchase of eleven plants in Australia in 1920. In addition, the company acquired, directly or indirectly, eleven others in the U.S. (primarily in California and Wisconsin). During this period, the company possessed a total of eighty factories and more than three hundred distribution depots, sales offices, and agencies around the world.

Rapid expansion soon had unanticipated effects on the firm's stability. Signs of fatigue began to appear in 1921. The board of directors realized what was happening by November and feared that losses for the 1921 business year would be considerable. Moreover, stock market activity made matters worse in that it reacted sharply to rumors that Nestlé's dividend, which had reached SFr. 65 the previous year, might be canceled for the current year. Nestlé was in the throes of a crisis, the company's first, and by far the most serious it had experienced, with a chain of alarming figures following month after month. Let us take a closer look at this dark moment in Nestlé's history.

BUT WAS UNABLE TO SUSTAIN THIS OPTIMISM IN 1921. INVENTORY ACCUMULATED, AND FEAR OVERTOOK THE STOCK MARKET.

November 20, 1921: owing to panic selling of Nestlé stock, its share price fell to below par. Nestlé shares, which had a par value of SFr. 400, plummeted from SFr. 1,020 in January, 1920, to SFr. 550 in July, 1921. By December, 1921, its share price had dropped to SFr. 225, sinking yet further, to SFr. 145, by the beginning of 1922. Shares of Peter, Cailler, Kohler stock—Nestlé's regular chocolate supplier—with a par value of SFr. 200, fell to SFr. 135. Stunned by the initial shock wave, bankers joined the press in blaming the company for not having foreseen the crisis. Of course, they neglected the fact that the firm was—as the future would show—in far better shape than was indicated by the market value of its shares. In December, 1921, ten thousand Nestlé and Anglo-Swiss shares were offered on the Swiss stock exchange: "a market," in the words of the *Gazette de Lausanne,* "dominated by the performance of these shares, and which has collapsed under an avalanche of orders to sell to a point that would have seemed impossible less than a month ago."

Given the nervousness of the market and the resulting panic selling, the company's board of directors was forced to issue a statement on December 1, 1921, to the effect that the firm's difficulties were due to the fact that it had built up a large inventory of products when raw material prices were high and now had to sell them "when prices were falling." This caused considerable losses, even though current sales were being maintained at a higher level than before the war. Not at all reassured by this statement, from this point on, until the annual shareholders' meeting of May 29, 1922, the press continued to discuss the question of whether the company's losses exceeded its total assets and whether

Warehousing Nestlé products in Christiana (modern Oslo), Norway

LOSSES REACHED SFR. 100,000,000. SALES DECLINED OWING TO FLUCTUATING EXCHANGE RATES...

the value of its reserves of raw materials and products awaiting delivery was not greater than its share capital.

Business people today tend to have a very different view from those of 1921. All the same, the speed with which the company was to recover after 1923 shows that, whatever errors of judgment the company's management may have made following the end of hostilities, and the cessation of orders for its products due to the war, such errors do not provide an adequate explanation for the sharp drop in the company's share prices. This drop was due—at least in part—to a kind of collective anxiety vis-à-vis the inherent fragility of the stock market. At that time—and even today—once such anxiety begins, it may lead to a drop in the price of a particular stock totally incommensurate with the health of the company that issued it.

Here is a passage from the annual report for the year 1921, published in the spring of 1922: "For the first time since the establishment of the company, the balance sheet shows a substantial deficit. Its board of directors wishes to express to shareholders its deep regret at having to announce such disappointing results after so many years of prosperity." Losses totaled nearly SFr. 100,000,000 and were chiefly caused by unfavorable exchange rates, falling prices, and the world economic crisis.

In addition, the report stated: "The serious crisis in foreign exchange rates, which seemed likely to ease somewhat early in 1921, owing to an improvement in the strength of certain currencies and the stabilization of others, unfortunately continued to have disastrous effects throughout the entire fiscal year. It has had particularly harmful effects on our company, as its activities are global in nature and our products are sold in nearly all the world's currencies. These effects have made themselves felt not only in losses suffered when transferring foreign funds to this country, but also in terms of the need to raise the prices of our goods in order to offset these unfavorable conditions, which serves to effectively close certain markets to us."

The company's sales figures for the Middle East had dropped greatly, owing to the depreciation of the leu, the drachma, and the Turkish pound. Fluctuations in the value of the French franc and the Italian lira also forced Nestlé to constantly readjust the prices of its products. However, "the most disturbing effect of exchange-rate fluctuations on our results for the fiscal year was the variation in rates between December 31, 1920, and December 31, 1921. On the eve of 1922, the two currencies in which the company conducts the major part of its business, the pound sterling and the dollar, had fallen markedly from their levels of the previous year." The same held true of the peseta, the Norwegian crown, and the Dutch florin. The total sum of these differences reduced the value of the firm's foreign sources of revenue by SFr.30,900,000.

AND TO THE WORLDWIDE ECONOMIC CRISIS. FINANCIAL MEASURES WERE INADEQUATE.

The prices of raw materials had risen to very high levels by mid-1921. Sugar and tinplate had shot up 400 percent and coal by more than 500 percent as compared to their prewar prices. By the second half of 1921, however, raw material prices had dropped to such a low level that they were almost back to their 1914 levels. (According to the annual report, this drop amounted to SFr. 30,000,000.)

Moreover, the world economic crisis that first became perceptible toward the end of 1920 was producing a steady drop in consumer purchasing power. Production had to be cut back; this meant heavy operating losses at the very moment when milk production was reaching very high levels, not only in Switzerland and England, but in Norway and Australia as well. Several factories in Switzerland, Norway, Australia, and the U.S. had to be shut down. As the annual report to shareholders concluded, "two-thirds of the deficit is the result of either inventory losses or due to unfavorable foreign exchange rates."

Thus, the company's future was far from sunny at the close of 1921. Since its own funds were insufficient, it was essential for the firm to seek financing elsewhere in order to meet its growing needs. This was no easy task, for the company had virtually exhausted all its available sources of credit. Moreover, this was no time to try and raise money on the capital market in Switzerland, as the Confederation, the cantons, and the communes had strained that market. At the extraordinary shareholders' meeting on April 28, 1921, it had already been agreed to issue two million shares of cumulative preferred stock in Great Britain; these were to be registered shares with a par value of £ 1 and a fixed annual dividend of 8 percent. As a result, the firm's share capital grew by SFr. 45,000,000 and now totaled SFr. 160,000,000. This sum, however, was

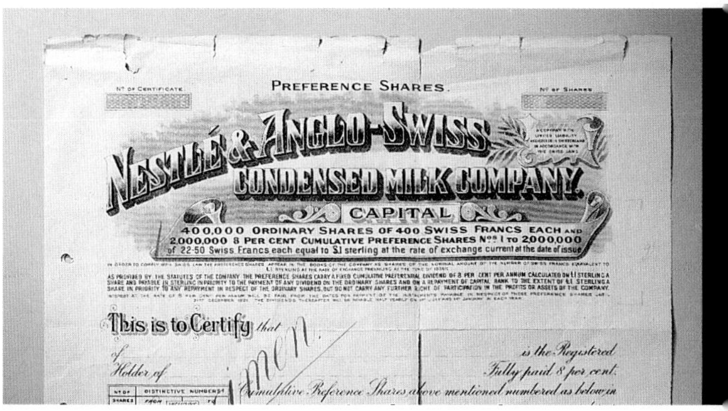
PREFERENCE SHARES.
NESTLÉ & ANGLO-SWISS CONDENSED MILK COMPANY.
CAPITAL
400,000 ORDINARY SHARES OF 400 SWISS FRANCS EACH AND 2,000,000 8 PER CENT CUMULATIVE PREFERENCE SHARES Nos. 1 TO 2,000,000 of 22·50 Swiss Francs each equal to £1 sterling at the rate of exchange current at the date of issue
This is to Certify that
of
is the Registered Holder of
Fully paid, 8 per cent. Cumulative Preference Shares above mentioned numbered as below in

Preference share issued in 1921 by Nestlé and Anglo-Swiss Condensed Milk Company

EMERGENCY MEASURES HAD TO BE INTRODUCED AT ALL LEVELS OF THE COMPANY: MANAGERIAL STAFF WAS REDUCED...

insufficient to meet the company's financial obligations, which included payment of the eleven Australian factories purchased at the end of 1920. For this reason, in the summer of 1921, the board decided to issue in Australia, where a locally based company had been set up, bonds totaling £ 820,000 (SFr. 20,500,000) at 7.5 percent interest, with maturity dates of three, six, nine, or twelve years. During this same period, the company's management was seriously concerned about another market: the American one. Indeed, it had been necessary to sell five of the fifty-three American condensed milk factories and their affiliates controlled by Nestlé's Food Company, Inc. Moreover, twenty had to be shut down; twenty continued to manufacture their products in December, 1921, and eight were distributing fresh milk in order to maintain their milk supply networks.

Undoubtedly, the company was on a dangerous course, but its heading simply had to be maintained. Emergency measures were necessary. The first was to abolish its outdated status as a family or pseudo-family concern. No longer would the majority of its top executives be close relatives, and it was now time to effect a truly harmonious blending of the former directors of Anglo-Swiss and Nestlé into a new managerial entity. Thus, Nestlé's new policy was to select its executive staff henceforth on the basis of proven ability and years of experience in the business world. In addition, these had to be men in the prime of their lives. The first step, then, was to reorganize the company's management structure. A committee consisting of a chairman, two vice-chairmen, and an executive vice-president was set up; it met in Paris every two weeks.

As the previous four-person management team was highly decentralized, its reaction time was far too slow, for its members lived in three countries: Great Britain, Switzerland, and France. (Gustave Aguet was living in London; as mentioned, he had become chairman of the company when his brother-in-law Emile-Louis Roussy died in June, 1920. The second executive vice-president, Alfred Liotard-Vogt, Aguet's son-in-law, was living in Paris. Fred Page, who often traveled to America, resided at Cham. Auguste Roussy, Emile-Louis's son and Gustave Aguet's nephew, was living at Vevey.) The result of this partial restructuring of the company's management in 1921 was, in effect, to separate the chairmanship of Nestlé and Anglo-Swiss Condensed Milk Company from the management of the London market. This administrative shake-up was the prelude to a thorough restructuring of the company's operations. Of course, it could not simply sever its links to the past overnight, no more than it could renounce commitments, which, in many cases, had been entered into several years previously. However, stock market upheavals and the drop in Nestlé share prices made it essential that the company cut down on a certain number of its staff, reduce expenditures, and put its house in order from a financial point of view. In a word, like it or not, Nestlé was forced to do everything in its power to prevent the drop in the price of its stock from getting any worse. But time was of the essence.

ALONG WITH INVENTORY; PRODUCTION WAS STREAMLINED; AND, IN 1922, THE FIRM SOUGHT THE EXPERTISE OF LOUIS DAPPLES,

As the urgent questions confronting the company at the beginning of 1922 were interrelated, they raised a variety of complex and delicate problems: inventory had to be further reduced, and the prospect of considerable losses accepted, with an ever-widening differential between cost and sales prices due to the drop in the latter. Statistics for this period show total sales in 1922 to be 20 percent lower than in 1921 (although these were nonetheless some 40 percent higher than before the war).

The company faced another serious problem: namely, production. Production capacity was four times greater than in 1914, and it was becoming increasingly important to bring it back in line with current sales. In spite of substantial operating losses (the result of using raw materials purchased at high prices), another group of factories had to be closed down in the U.S., Great Britain, Australia, Norway, and Switzerland. At the same time, Nestlé had to sell off—at a loss—a considerable quantity of the Peter, Cailler, Kohler (P.C.K.) chocolate it marketed.

Initial remedial measures failed to provide a definitive solution to the problem of how to get the firm back on a solid footing. Nestlé's financial difficulties began to assume enormous proportions, and in the beginning of May, 1922, the board of directors felt obliged to call on the well-known financial wizard Louis Edmond Christian Dapples to help undertake the critical task of thoroughly reorganizing Nestlé and Anglo-Swiss, while striving, at the same time, to renew bankers', shareholders', and employees' confidence in the company. Dapples's expertise and the keen mind of this financial specialist, coupled with his vast business experience and strong character, literally worked a miracle at Nestlé and Anglo-Swiss. The Dapples family hailed originally from the canton of Vaud, though Louis was born in Genoa in 1867, where his father was a banker. Dapples pursued classical studies in Zurich, and when his father thwarted his original dream of becoming a surgeon, he entered the London branch of Crédit Lyonnais, a French bank, in 1888, soon rising to the level of deputy manager. Fifteen years later, he helped direct

A SEASONED FINANCIER, WHO HAD REACHED THE AGE OF RETIREMENT. LOUIS DAPPLES FIRST MOVED TO REGROUP ALL OF THE FIRM'S SENIOR EXECUTIVES IN LONDON,

the Banca Commerciale Italiana, in Milan, and was later appointed head of the Banque Française et Italienne pour l'Amérique du Sud, spending several years in Brazil and Argentina as a result.

Louis Dapples had acquired considerable experience as a leader of men, particularly in São Paulo, Rio de Janeiro, and Buenos Aires, and was thoroughly familiar with the most efficient methods of work in countries at the dawn of their economic expansion. A man of this caliber, with vast international experience, had little interest in settling down to a life of leisure after retiring and returning to his native Europe. This polyglot (Dapples spoke French, Italian, German, English, Spanish, and Portuguese) was neither a businessman nor an industrialist. However, his organizational talents, his qualities as a born leader, and his keen judgment resulted in his skills being solicited long after he had retired and moved to Italy. (The French government and the Industrial Bank of China, for example, entrusted him with a variety of missions.) Indeed, Dapples knew the rules of business in the four corners of the world.

British banking circles recommended that Nestlé and Anglo-Swiss Condensed Milk Company contact him while Dapples was living in Florence. He immediately agreed to bring order to the company's chaos and set to work at once. Dapples proposed close budgetary scrutiny at all levels of the firm and reorganized its administrative structure. He directed this entire operation with an iron hand, sparing no one—not even himself.

Dapples was elected to the board of directors at the annual shareholders' meeting of May 29, 1922, where it was decided to increase the number of board members from seven to fifteen and the number of executive vice-presidents from four to five. (One of these was Dapples.) Following discussions with Gustave Aguet, the company chairman, the reins of the company were transferred to Dapples. The idea of bringing together, under one roof in London, all of the company's senior executives, thereby strengthening their authority, meant that Fred Page had to leave Cham, and Auguste Roussy Vevey. For a time, Alfred Liotard-Vogt remained in Paris, but soon the continental sales organization there was transformed into a mere distributor, with control being exercised from Vevey.

Louis Dapples (1867–1937)

Alfred Liotard-Vogt played an important role in stimulating company sales. Liotard-Vogt reorganized the company's system of distribution so that it would be flexible enough to meet varying market conditions. The sales networks, created before the war and expanded immediately thereafter, were

AND IMPROVED COMPANY PERFORMANCE, PARTICULARLY IN THE U.S.

capable of keeping tabs on a given product from the moment it left the factory until it reached the consumer. Moreover, it was Alfred Liotard-Vogt who set down a guiding principle that would remain applicable until today: namely, to establish the company's own extensive sales network rather than relying on independent agents working on a commission basis. Furthermore, he was among the first to carry out a rather primitive form of what is now known as market research. Alfred Liotard-Vogt's powerful personality enabled him to continue his career at the Revenue Court in Paris after leaving Nestlé. Despite certain differences of opinion between the company chairman, Louis Dapples, and Alfred Liotard-Vogt, some ten years after his father had left the company Pierre Liotard-Vogt joined the firm. Nearly fifty years later, he was to become both chairman and chief executive of Nestlé.

In 1922, Nestlé's key problem was cash flow. By September 1, 30 percent of its bank loans, which amounted to SFr. 293,000,000 at the end of 1921, had been repaid. On December 16, 1922, the level of the company's common stock was reduced from SFr. 160,000,000 to SFr. 80,000,000 by lowering the par value of each share from SFr. 400 to SFr. 200. These measures, though successful, were not yet sufficient; the various causes of the company's deficit had to be found and a return to profitable operations ensured.

The company's thorniest problem was in the U.S. Owing to its high production levels during the war years, Nestlé's Food Company found itself with a large inventory of manufactured products on its hands—which had to be sold off rapidly at the time of the Armistice. Following the sudden drop in production, the company's reserves of raw materials (accumulated during 1920 and 1921) had now been reduced. However, in 1922, it was still burdened with debt. A solution existed, of course: namely, to sell a certain number of the company's forty-eight factories—twelve of which were closed down. However, it was out of the question to relinquish the company's extensive milk-supply networks, which were, in fact, the truly valuable part of its production centers. Instead, output was adapted to the specific conditions of the U.S. market. As it had been noted that Americans consumed large quantities of ice cream, fresh cream, powdered milk, and particularly evaporated milk, all factories on the Pacific Coast (well-situated to serve the Far East) were kept in operation. And, since it was easy to transport fresh milk over long distances in the U.S., Nestlé's Food Company took a serious

THANKS TO DAPPLES, THE COMPANY WAS ABLE TO REIMBURSE ITS BANK LOANS. BY 1925, THE STORM HAD PASSED, FOLLOWING THE RESHAPING OF THE MANAGERIAL STRUCTURE AT VEVEY;

interest in ensuring its distribution, with any surpluses being used to produce evaporated milk.

Bank loans were reduced along with inventory in various countries, so that, by the end of 1922, there were a certain number of signs of a true recovery. (It should be mentioned that, in Spain, the Sociedad Nestlé, founded in 1920, was financially sound as it had no problem of surplus inventory to deal with.) At the same time, Nestlé had reached a temporary compromise with P.C.K. after four years of disagreement over the responsibility for heavy losses incurred because of the large surplus of high-priced chocolate that remained unsold following the end of the hostilities.

From 1922 on, the basic guidelines for company policy were laid down: rebuild the reserves needed both to repay bank advances in their entirety and to clear certain liabilities on the balance sheet; streamline the company's sales organization; cut manufacturing costs for products that yielded little or no profit despite a large volume of sales. The firm decided to pay off its debts once it had regained a certain freedom of action and independence. By December 31, 1923, these had dropped to SFr. 54,477,000 from SFr. 293,000,000 in 1921, which resulted in a considerable reduction in interest charges.

By 1925, Nestlé and the various companies selling or manufacturing its products had repaid all of their outstanding debts with commercial banks. The company's balance sheet showed SFr. 100,500,000 in bonds. It had also resumed paying a modest dividend on common stock. Thus, in less than four years, Nestlé's major financial problems had been resolved in spite of the unsettling economic conditions in the world at the time.

1925 was also the year of the second stage of administrative reforms. Nestlé now totally accepted the concept of the professional manager, of which it had been slightly wary until this time. The executive vice-presidents relinquished their posts, while remaining members of the board. Among those called upon to participate in the new management structure were Gustave Huguenin and Edouard Muller, who was to become chairman of the company later on. Those responsible for the 1905 merger—Wilhelm Caspar Escher and Benjamin Rossier—were now on the board, as was Auguste Mayor; while Louis Dapples served as the chief executive. Owing to the powerful influence of Dapples, described as having "an iron hand and a steel fist," all of the company's directors were now under one roof at Vevey.

The American and Australian markets were still sources of concern. In the U.S., the measures taken to put Nestlé's Food Company on sounder footing had proved inadequate, for the factories there that had been closed down since 1921 involved considerable expenses. In addition, competition was fierce, particularly in the field of evaporated milk. Contrary to its policy three years earlier, the firm did not hesitate to adopt new reforms in order to minimize maintenance charges and realize considerable tax savings in 1925. Nestlé significantly reduced the scale of its activities in the U.S., selling off a number of its factories there and concentrating production in those that were well-situated from the standpoint of both milk-supply networks as well as transportation.

THE SCALE OF THE U.S. SIDE OF THE COMPANY WAS REDUCED, AND IT DECIDED TO ADOPT A CAUTIOUS POLICY OF ADAPTING ITSELF TO EUROPE'S ECONOMIC ENVIRONMENT.

Similar decisions were made concerning the company's plants in Oceania: three factories and all of the farms belonging to Nestlé and Anglo-Swiss Condensed Milk Company (Australasia), Ltd. were sold; new agreements about production for export were made with the dairy farmers' cooperative New Zealand Co-operative Dairy Company; and a chocolate factory was built at Auckland. However, despite these measures, the company was not yet completely out of danger.

In other parts of the world, especially in Europe, steps were taken to better adapt each of the various locally based companies to the specific conditions of its particular economic environment. In France, where there was an expected rise in customs rates, Société Nestlé (France) decided to manufacture its products domestically. A production center was set up at Lisieux, Calvados, in 1925, and another built at Boue, Aisne, in 1927. The Belgian market was now separated from the French market, with Société Nestlé (Belgique) about to start production of its own products and to operate a chocolate factory in cooperation with P.C.K. in Antwerp. In Italy, Società Nestlé, founded in 1923, built a factory at Abbiategrasso. In Germany, Linda-Gesellschaft acquired a factory at Kappeln in Schleswig from Milchwerke Angeln GmbH, equipping it for the production of evaporated milk and packaged cheese. In 1927, Nestlé (South Africa), Ltd. was on the point of acquiring two factories from a local

Packaging confectionery items in Auckland, New Zealand

IN 1929, NESTLÉ PREPARED TO FACE THE GREAT DEPRESSION, WHICH IT SURVIVED.

South African company and, from 1930 on, was able to dispense entirely with imports, thanks to its factories at Donnybrook, Estcourt, and Franklin.

Nestlé's policy of adapting its operations to prevailing economic conditions (in particular, to the problem of tariff barriers) was both wise and well-thought-out. Unfortunately, however, it could not be implemented in all cases—for example, in Great Britain. From 1924 on, production levels at the Aylesbury and Salisbury factories were lowered, and, at times, production was even halted. Arriving from the farmers, the incoming fresh milk was sold in London through a department that specialized in its distribution. Fortunately, the five other factories in Great Britain were in a position to meet a large part of the demand, and the British company chose to follow the distribution policy adopted by the other companies of the group.

In Switzerland, the economic slump, higher production costs than those of other countries, and the customs duties to be paid to importing countries, forced Swiss manufacturers to adapt their factories' production levels to these new conditions. In 1917, Nestlé and Anglo-Swiss Condensed Milk Company was obliged to close its factory at Guin, as well as those at Neuenegg and Bercher in 1921. (The last two were eventually taken over by another company.)

On the eve of 1929, the many locally based Nestlé companies throughout the world had achieved varying degrees of importance, yet each of them played an essential part in ensuring the success of the company as a whole. The process of consolidation, expansion, and streamlining had enabled Nestlé to widen its range of activities; a management team of bright young men began to introduce new items with considerable consumer appeal to the company's traditional range of products: condensed milk, infant cereal, powdered milk, and chocolate, thus making it possible to spread overhead over a wider base. For years, this policy of expansion was pursued by acquiring an interest in food-manufacturing firms or through the creation and development of completely new products in the research laboratories of associated companies. Thus, in 1927, Nestlé entered into an agreement with T. & E. Plum, Ltd., Copenhagen, for the sale of butter in Denmark. In that same year, a proposal from Gerber & Co., AG of Thun, Switzerland, the originators of packaged cheese, resulted in Nestlé and Anglo-Swiss Condensed Milk Company reaching an agreement with Gerber, according to which Nestlé was granted the right to sell the former's products in all countries except Switzerland and, for a certain period, the U.S. (In France

Nestlé has been producing packaged cheese at a factory in Pontarlier under the brand name Gerber since 1928.)

By the end of 1928, the manufacture of chocolate was the company's second most important activity after milk products. It is for this reason that, on March 27, 1927, shortly after the death of Gustave Aguet, Louis Dapples, who had become chairman of the board, quickly decided to see whether Nestlé could reach a new agreement with the management of Peter, Cailler, Kohler Chocolats Suisses S.A., which would be of benefit to both parties. Judiciously ignoring certain areas of disagreement between the two companies in the past, discussed further on, the two firms began negotiations. In the course of their talks, Alexandre Cailler and Jean-Jacques Kohler, the executive vice-presidents of P.C.K., informed Nestlé that they would give their approval to a complete merger as long as certain conditions were met.

IN 1928, NESTLÉ WAS CONTACTED BY CHOCOLATE MAKERS IN VEVEY WHO WISHED TO STRENGTHEN THEIR POSITION ON WORLD MARKETS.

Apart from the fact that a merger would simplify the operation of the two companies, there were clear advantages in this from the point of view of the chocolate makers. Nestlé was a sound firm that had stood the test of time and possessed the financial resources necessary to market chocolates on an international scale. Nestlé had also reached its critical mass, thus enabling it to finance the setting up of new factories around the world, required in order to tailor new chocolate products to the varying tastes of local consumers, as well as to ward off competition.

For several years, the Swiss chocolate industry had had to face a triple-headed threat: 1) the rapid expansion of chain stores, which had started to manufacture their own chocolate products; 2) a growing spirit of nationalism, and 3) tariff barriers that had already led some companies to set up country-based chocolate factories (much to the dismay of Swiss chocolate exporters). The merger that Messrs. Cailler and Kohler were proposing was indeed a tempting one for Nestlé.

Nestlé and Anglo-Swiss Condensed Milk Company (Australasia), Ltd., which had opened a chocolate factory in Australia, acquired an interest in Société anonyme belge des Chocolats Peter, Cailler, Kohler, with headquarters in Antwerp. In 1924, Nestlé also acquired an interest in an Italian firm, Industria Riunita Cioccolata at Intra.

In 1927, in cooperation with P.C.K., Nestlé opened a factory in Turkey; it also set up a production center run by a small independent company, Sociedad Española de Chocolates S.A., at La Penilla, Spain, where Nestlé already possessed a condensed milk factory. Local manufacture in New

THE IDEA OF A MERGER WAS ACCEPTED IN 1928; IT TOOK PLACE THE FOLLOWING YEAR.

Zealand had been entrusted to New Zealand Milk Products, Ltd. Naturally, all of these firms were granted the right to use the Peter, Cailler, and Kohler trademarks. Nestlé had set up its Saavedra factory in Argentina in 1927; and in the midst of negotiating its merger with P.C.K., it created Deutsche Aktiengesellschaft für Nestlé Erzeugnisse in cooperation with P.C.K. From that time on, this new German company was responsible for the manufacturing and sales divisions of Linda-Gesellschaft GmbH and Otto Quantz Schokoladenwerke AG, which marketed products bearing the Nestlé and P.C.K. trademarks in Germany. In 1928, Nestlé again forayed into the German chocolate market by acquiring an interest in Sarotti AG, a large Berlin chocolate maker. In addition, Nestlé began to market its products in Peru and Portugal in 1927.

Despite the risks involved, expansion was justified. In 1928, the board of directors unanimously accepted the terms for a merger with Peter, Cailler, Kohler Chocolats Suisses S.A. But just when it appeared that the proposed merger would go through, a snag occurred: an American company, Lamont, Corliss & Company, in which P.C.K. had acquired a 37 percent interest, objected to so great an amount of its capital falling into the hands of Nestlé. Because of the important role that Lamont, Corliss played in the distribution of P.C.K. chocolates in the U.S., it was impossible to ignore its objection. Several months were necessary before an agreement could be reached enabling Nestlé to acquire this interest, which meant that the merger between it and P.C.K. did not actually take effect until January 1, 1929. The merger was a logical step in a series of rapprochements that had moved Nestlé increasingly close to the firms of Peter and Kohler ever since 1904, and to that of Cailler ever since 1911. We shall now trace the history of these three Swiss chocolate makers.

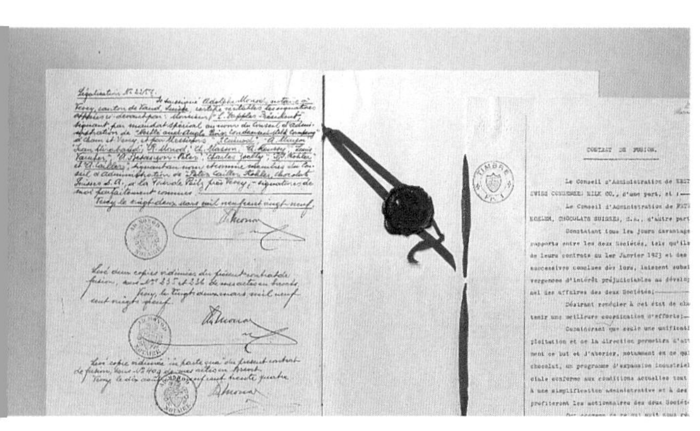
CONTRAT DE FUSION.

Contract for the merger of Nestlé and Anglo-Swiss Condensed Milk Company with Peter, Cailler, Kohler

The Story of Peter, Cailler, and Kohler, Chocolate Makers in Western Switzerland

F.L. CAILLER FOUNDED HIS FIRM AT VEVEY IN 1819.

☐ Nestlé's decision to manufacture chocolate was not a spur-of-the-moment one; force of circumstance drew it and the chocolate makers P.C.K. together. We have already mentioned that Daniel Peter, the inventor of milk chocolate, was a friend of Henri Nestlé. Now we shall discuss the reasons why Vevey was an important center of the Swiss chocolate industry in 1929 and had been one for nearly a century.

In 1819, at only twenty-three years of age, François-Louis Cailler, scion of an old, established family of Vevey, founded a small business for the manufacture and sale of cocoa and chocolate near the town of Vevey (at En Copet in the neighboring commune of Corsier, to be precise). Of course, handmade chocolate was not unknown in Switzerland, as it had been imported from France and Italy; but Cailler, who had observed the hand-crushing of cocoa and sugar in northern Italy, was the first in Switzerland to envisage production on a relatively large scale of a superior chocolate at a reasonable price by harnessing the power of machines. At En Copet, Cailler installed a crushing machine that he had invented, consisting of two stone cylinders turning at the same speed.

As Cailler was something of an industrial pioneer in the field, he did not have to worry about competition at the outset. However, he did have to worry about supplies. Sugar and cocoa were expensive commodities that entered Switzerland in small quantities after having traveled long distances and gone through the hands of numerous middlemen. Transport was slow and difficult, for raw materials had to pass through several countries and were liable to be held up at times, because of political troubles in the aftermath of the Napoleonic wars, or merely due to the weather. In 1821, Cailler—who was manufacturer, inventor, designer of his packaging's graphic artwork, marketing agent, and traveling salesman—was deeply involved in making constant improvements to his machines, which, while rudimentary, were nonetheless the prototypes for today's conching machines and blenders. Cailler's clients received their chocolate in the form of small individual blocks—another of Cailler's ideas—improving on the method of the Italians, who produced their handmade chocolate in long rolls, which were cut into slices of varying length for the customer. Cailler soon introduced his own specialty products, by adding vanilla or cinnamon to the

François-Louis Cailler (1796–1852)

HIS SUCCESSORS FOLLOWED IN HIS FOOTSTEPS, AND THE CAILLER COMPANY BEGAN PRODUCTION AT BROC IN 1898.

cocoa and sugar mixture during manufacture. His so-called *pur caraque* and *commun sucré* varieties were sold beyond the borders of Switzerland. And the famous French statesman Talleyrand was among Cailler's early customers.

François-Louis Cailler died in 1852, on the eve of his fifty-sixth birthday, leaving a widow and two young sons, Alexandre and Auguste, to carry on in his footsteps. Cailler's widow assumed responsibility for directing the family business until her sons were old enough to take hold of its reins. In 1853, she moved the business across the Veveyse River to an area of Vevey known as En Clergère, which was situated near a source of water power abundant by the standards of those days. The new railroad line also passed nearby. By the end of 1865, just as the business was taking off, Alexandre suddenly died. Until Alexandre Cailler, Jr., born in February, 1866, was ready to take his father's place as director of the company founded by his grandfather, it was operated by his mother, his childless Uncle Auguste, and by his stepfather, L. Gétaz-Cailler. For a time, the business experienced serious difficulties, not so much because of the inexperience of its directors as because chocolate sales were yielding smaller and smaller profit margins.

In 1888, after having trained at Turin, Italy, and in Germany, Alexandre Cailler, Jr. became director of his family's small factory, employing eight workers and operating two machines. Initially, Cailler worked on his own; later he brought his brother-in-law Jules Bellet into the firm, who was in charge of technical questions and manufacturing. In 1895, the two of them set up a joint-stock company with a capital of SFr. 100,000 to manufacture the milk chocolate that Alexandre's uncle, Daniel Peter, had invented in 1875. While concerned with maintaining the extremely high quality of his products, Alexandre Cailler, Jr. decided to transform the family business into a major industry in 1898, building a factory at Broc in the Gruyère region of the canton of Fribourg, which had an excellent supply of labor and milk, as well as water power that could be harnessed as a source of electricity.

On October 8, 1898, the company's factory at Vevey was vacated, and production began at Broc. In 1900, the firm was transformed into a corporation with a capitalization of SFr. 1,000,000 (two thousand shares at SFr. 500 per share). The company's capital was doubled in 1902, by issuing a bonus of one new share for each original one. Just seven years after it opened, in 1905, the factory at Broc, which had been built with the intention of doubling the production level of the original factory at Vevey, was now employing a

The second Cailler factory in Vevey, 1889

SINCE 1830, THE KOHLER COMPANY HAD BEEN PRODUCING CHOCOLATE IN LAUSANNE, BEFORE TRANSFERRING ITS PLANT TO ECHANDENS.

total of 1,373 workers as compared with the 120 workers employed the year the factory was opened at Broc in the Gruyère.

The business was beginning to feel the pressure of competition, however. Since the founding of Cailler's firm in 1819, a number of other companies had followed its lead: Suchard in 1826; Kohler in 1830; Sprüngli in 1845; Klaus in 1856; Peter at Vevey in 1867; Tobler, in 1869; and Lindt in 1879. As a result, by the turn of the century, the chocolate industry had become an important sector of the Swiss economy. Of all these companies, however, only those of Amédée Kohler and Daniel Peter are of interest to us, for, along with Cailler, they were to form the group of chocolate manufacturers that would merge with Nestlé in 1929.

Gottlieb Kohler (who changed his Christian name to Amédée on his arrival in French-speaking Switzerland) was born in 1761, in Büren, near Bienne, in the canton of Bern. In 1793, he left Bienne for Lausanne in the canton of Vaud to open a shop dealing in colonial food products. While his business soon began to thrive, Kohler had no intention of remaining merely a small shopkeeper. By banding together with his sons Charles-Amédée and Frédéric, he expanded his business under the name Amédée Kohler & Sons in 1818. Amédée's two sons had the same entrepreneurial spirit as their father, and, in 1830, when Charles-Amédée decided to devote himself exclusively to the manufacture of chocolate, both his father and brother backed him. Charles-Amédée started off in business quite modestly, although this was far less of a problem for him than it had been for F.L. Cailler, as the Kohlers were a very wealthy family, with considerable experience in the sale of colonial food products. The Kohlers bought a mill in Lausanne at 11 Rue du Petit-St-Jean, converting it into a factory. In 1833, thirteen years after Amédée Kohler died, his son Charles-Amédée acquired a sawmill at Sauvabelin, above Lausanne, converting it into a factory as well. (Its offices and warehouse were to remain on Rue du Petit-St-Jean.) When Charles-Amédée Kohler died in 1874, his son Charles-Amédée, Jr., inherited the company's new ultramodern facilities. In 1884, following Charles-Amédée, Jr.'s death, his two sons Amédée-Louis and Jean-Jacques, in turn, inherited the company. Upon taking control of it, they changed the company's name to Les fils de Charles-Amédée Kohler, and the Sauvabelin chocolate plant was improved still further to facilitate production of the chocolates that had given it an excellent reputation.

Charles-Amédée Kohler (1790–1874)

DANIEL PETER, F.L. CAILLER'S SON-IN-LAW, WHO BEGAN HIS CAREER AS A CANDLE MANUFACTURER, EVENTUALLY ENTERED THE FIELD OF CHOCOLATE MAKING, LATER INVENTING MILK CHOCOLATE AT VEVEY.

In 1897, the founder's great grandsons moved from Sauvabelin to Echandens, near Morges, in the canton of Vaud; they had built a factory there and equipped it with the latest technical innovations. In 1898 (the same year Alexandre Cailler started production at Broc), the Kohlers' concern, with help from financiers in Geneva, became a corporation, Fabrique de Chocolat Amédée Kohler & Fils, with a capital of SFr. 3,000,000. When the family business was still in its infancy, the Kohlers, like the Caillers, considered each export contract as an exceptional event; things changed, however, with the advent of milk chocolate. New horizons opened up for the chocolate industry—not only in Switzerland, but all over the world.

As mentioned earlier, it was Daniel Peter who invented milk chocolate, thanks to painstaking repetition of a series of meticulous experiments that finally helped him to realize his original idea. Curiously enough, it was in the premises of his firm in the Rue des Bosquets in the En Rouvenaz area of Vevey (not far from F.L. Cailler's factory and virtually next door to Henri Nestlé's) that Peter made his historic discovery. Born in 1836, at Moudon in the canton of Vaud, where his father was a butcher, Peter had gone to Vevey to learn to become a businessman. Peter was in charge of the Frères Peter candle company when he made his discovery. Together, Daniel Peter and his brother Julien had operated their factory until the introduction of oil lamps ruined all chances of future success. Headstrong and persistent, Daniel Peter did not let this setback discourage him. On the contrary, following the example of his father-in-law Mr. Cailler (Peter had married the latter's daughter, Fanny, in 1863), he decided to go into the chocolate business himself. This was a field that particularly attracted Peter. As he explained: "Industrial products intended as food are, without a doubt, among those offering manufacturers the best prospects for success. They are consumed every day, and, unlike other items, there is a constant demand for them that is not subject to the whims of fashion. Some specialty foods, it is true, were a great success for a time and then, rightly or wrongly, were superseded by others." And Peter added, "In my opinion, this will not happen to chocolate. Since the Spaniards brought it to Europe at the beginning of the seventeenth century, it has come into more and more widespread use. Like coffee, it is a now a regular part of people's diet, but its nutritional value is higher."

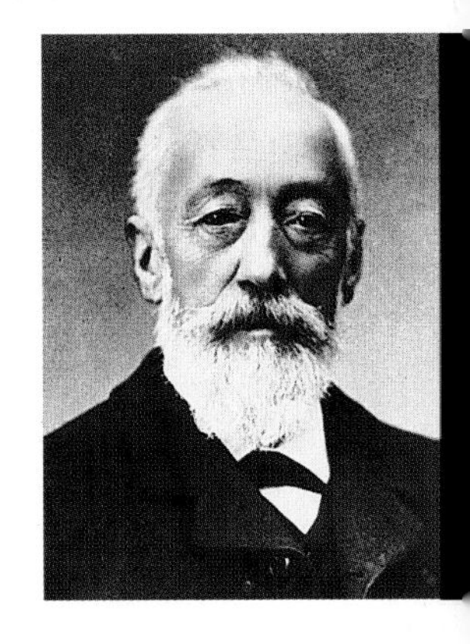

Daniel Peter (1836–1919)

Peter left his native Switzerland for a time to seek employment as an ordinary factory worker in a chocolate factory in Lyons, France. In 1867, he returned to Switzerland and founded a new company with his brother Julien.

PETER EXPORTED TO GREAT BRITAIN, AND LATER TO THE ENTIRE WORLD...

Daniel Peter intended to continue operation of the candle factory he and his brother already owned and, at the same time, to diversify, establishing a chocolate firm under the name Peter Cailler & Companie. Peter was thirty-one years of age. The presence nearby of his friend Henri Nestlé, who was producing his milk-based infant cereal, gave Peter the idea of producing a milk-based form of chocolate. Initially, he had only one employee to help him in this task, along with his wife, who helped him package his products. Peter's plant functioned continuously, twenty-four hours a day. During the day, he produced plain chocolate in order to make ends meet; at night, he searched endlessly for a way to combine milk and cocoa powder. Peter contacted Anglo-Swiss during this period, with a view to obtaining the condensed milk he needed for his research. Peter visited the Anglo-Swiss factory at Guin and placed an order for "condensed milk, to be used," as he stated, "in the manufacture of a new product, for which I am sure there will soon exist great demand." And he concluded: "Considering your high production levels, I trust that I shall find it as much to my advantage to order the milk I need from you as to produce that milk myself."

After years of trial and error, Peter finally began to make rapid progress with his milk chocolate. First produced in 1875, it won a silver medal at the International Exhibition in Paris as early as 1878 and was awarded a gold medal at the International Exhibition in Zurich in 1883. Peter was particularly pleased with these awards, as he had had to manufacture and market his discovery on extremely limited resources.

Wrapping for Gala Peter, the first milk chocolate

As in the case of Anglo-Swiss and Nestlé, Peter received his first export orders from England. This was understandable insofar as Great Britain was the undisputed superpower of the period, and many tourists from that country spent their leisure time in "exotic" Switzerland, made famous through the works of the English Romantics several decades earlier. One of these tourists, a pharmacist from a small English town, ordered more than 100 pounds of Peter's new milk chocolate over a period of two years. At the time, Peter wrote: "If a town of eight thousand inhabitants can consume more than 100 pounds per year, then the six million inhabitants of London could easily consume more than 40 tons." And he went on to explain: "This is what led me to pay several visits to that country, in which I ensured myself a market. . . ." Nor did Peter neglect the German, Austrian, and Italian markets. Thus, the inventor of milk chocolate was fortunate enough to see the fruits of his labor travel around the world. Of course, this softened, to a certain extent, the hardships Peter had had to endure when starting out. However, it did little to help him resolve his persistent financial problems.

BEFORE BUILDING A FACTORY AT ORBE IN 1901.

Peter tried initially to interest the directors of Nestlé—Jules Monnerat, Emile-Louis Roussy, and Auguste Mayor—in his business, but his discussions with them proved fruitless. Soon thereafter, a banker from Vevey, Gabriel Montet, found financial backing for Peter's firm. In 1896, with the aid of two prominent men of the area, Albert Cuénod and L. Rapin, Peter founded Société des Chocolats au Lait Peter, a corporation with a capitalization of SFr. 450,000 (one thousand eight hundred shares at SFr. 250 per share). In a report dated that same year, Peter wrote proudly: "I think I can say with a pretty high degree of certainty that the majority—if not all—of the chocolate makers in Switzerland have tried to copy me. This is proof of how highly they value my invention. But, after unsuccessful trials, all have had to give up; and except for the milk chocolate paste produced by Anglo-Swiss Condensed Milk Company at Cham—a sort of jamlike substance that does not keep very well—I know of no rival product at present that meets the same needs." Peter claimed that his success had been achieved without advertising; it was a success achieved "solely as a result of the merits the consumer has discovered in the product." Peter conveniently neglected to mention that his nephew Cailler also manufactured milk chocolate during this period—which caused a certain amount of dissension between their families. Nevertheless, the value of Peter's new discovery was so obvious that orders for it literally came pouring in from abroad. Sales in Switzerland reached a relatively high level. And during the first half of 1895, Peter's company sold a total of around 10 tons of chocolate, which was more than what he had sold during the entire previous year.

The authorized capital was increased from SFr. 650,000 in 1899 to SFr. 1,000,000 in 1900 and again increased in 1903 to SFr. 1,500,000. Peter's firm was expanding by leaps and bounds. In 1901, he opened a remarkably well-designed factory at Orbe, an important region for milk production in the canton of Vaud, in order to supplement the output of his factory at Vevey.

PETER AND KOHLER JOINED FORCES IN 1904...

At the beginning of the century, the three chocolate manufacturers Cailler, Kohler, and Peter were each known for a particular product. While they all manufactured ordinary chocolate, Cailler had launched a *fondant* variety; Kohler specialized in candies; and Peter, in his invention—milk chocolate. As Peter's recipe soon became widely known, this "leak" actually helped serve the cause of the chocolate industry as a whole, both in Switzerland and beyond its borders. Initially, Swiss chocolate manufacturers had a monopoly on the production of milk chocolate, and they were thus able to start production outside of Switzerland. Their first target was Great Britain, then France, Germany, Belgium, and Russia. This expansion in trade soon transformed Swiss chocolate making from a domestic industry into a full-fledged export industry. Development of this kind was unthinkable without financial support, however. And no matter how healthy they were, these firms lacked the necessary capital to continue expanding their operations indefinitely. Whether they liked it or not, they were obliged to try and reach an understanding among themselves if they wished to exploit their full potential in those countries enjoying an economic boom at the time: Great Britain, the U.S., Japan, Germany, France, and Russia.

In January, 1904, Jean-Jacques Kohler, who now headed the firm founded by his great grandfather, asked a mutual friend to sound out Daniel Peter about a possible merger or any form of cooperation between the two companies. Kohler felt that an agreement with Peter would bring his company a share of the milk chocolate market the latter had succeeded in generating, especially in Great Britain and the U.S. For Peter, the idea of eliminating a competitor on those markets and the possibility of profiting from sales of plain chocolate as well as assortments of quality candy, which comprised the bulk of Kohler's production in both Switzerland and France, argued strongly in favor of reaching an agreement with Kohler.

Sales of the two firms were far from being on the same scale: in 1903, Peter's totaled SFr. 6,000,000, 50 percent generated in Great Britain and 5 percent in Switzerland. Kohler had a total sales figure of SFr. 2,800,000, 16 percent in Great Britain, 18 percent in France—where the company owned a factory in Paris—and almost 50 percent in Switzerland. However, as far as Peter's firm was concerned, the personality of a competent man the likes of Jean-Jacques Kohler offered it an appreciable guarantee that the potential company would be a profitable venture. Taking Jean-Jacques Kohler's views into account, Peter agreed to include the Suchard Company in the merger, should it take place. (Negotiations did not break off when the latter refused to participate.) On January 11, 1904, Peter acquired the net assets of the Kohler firm, paying SFr. 600,000 in shares of stock and SFr. 1,500,000 in cash. The authorized capital of the new company, Société Générale Suisse de Chocolats, was increased to SFr. 2,500,000. The firm's new name made it clear that those responsible for the merger wished to leave the door open to the possibility of other firms joining the new company. They decided, however, to retain the words *Peter et Kohler réunis* on product packaging. Managerial integration of the two companies was not achieved until June 1, 1904. The factory at Echandens continued operation until 1907, when it was transformed into a printing plant (at which time its chocolate production was transferred to Orbe and the manufacture of assortments of quality candy to Vevey). Except for those in France, all agencies around the world passed into the hands of the various sales representatives of Peter.

TO FORM SOCIÉTÉ GÉNÉRALE SUISSE DE CHOCOLATS, WHICH SOUGHT A RAPPROCHEMENT WITH NESTLÉ THAT SAME YEAR. THE FIRST NESTLÉ BRAND CHOCOLATE WAS MANUFACTURED BY PETER & KOHLER.

Owing to his age, the inventor of milk chocolate could no longer take an active part in operating his business; thus, Jean-Jacques Kohler assumed control of the firm, introducing significant reforms and improvements—especially technical ones. Shortly after the Peter-Kohler merger, Auguste Roussy (a member of the board of Société Anonyme Henri Nestlé) paid a visit to Kohler to inform him that Nestlé, too, had decided to produce chocolate. Kohler's visitor added that, since he had always been on friendly terms with Mr. Kohler, he wished to make him aware of the project. On learning of it, Kohler replied: "If Nestlé needed to cooperate with a chocolate maker, it should be with Peter & Kohler." For Jean-Jacques Kohler, such an arrangement, which would bring Nestlé into the club of chocolate producers, was wholly in keeping with the spirit of his company's merger with Peter; indeed, the terms of that merger did not preclude other similar agreements. In July, 1904, the board of directors of the two companies were informed of talks between Daniel Peter and Jean-Jacques Kohler, on the one hand, and Auguste Roussy and Auguste Mayor on the other.

These resulted in an agreement according to which Nestlé committed itself to raising the authorized capital of Peter & Kohler by SFr. 1,000,000, by subscribing to ten thousand of its shares at SFr. 100 per share. Peter & Kohler was entrusted with manufacturing the first in what was to be a long series of Nestlé brand milk chocolates and was authorized, in certain circumstances, to use Nestlé's factories abroad. Moreover, Nestlé agreed to supply Peter & Kohler with any surplus milk it might have at its disposal. As a

Cailler merged with Peter & Kohler in 1911; and, thus, it was the firm of Peter, Cailler, Kohler that finally merged with Nestlé in 1929.

result of this 1904 agreement, Nestlé assumed responsibility for foreign sales—an area in which it excelled—and abandoned its project of manufacturing or marketing chocolates (other than those specified in the contract with Peter & Kohler). In return, Peter & Kohler undertook to refrain from manufacturing or marketing products similar to those produced by Nestlé. The position of both parties to the agreement was clear, and the contract—valid for ninety-nine years—ensured that, from that moment on, Peter, Kohler, and Nestlé brands of chocolate were to be manufactured by true specialists in chocolate making and marketed by Nestlé and Anglo-Swiss, which had a proven track record in sales.

By 1929, this agreement had been in force for a quarter century. However, the situation of the two parties to the agreement changed somewhat after 1911, when Cailler joined forces with Peter & Kohler. Société Anonyme des Chocolats au Lait F.-L. Cailler merged with Société Générale Suisse de Chocolats in that year, thus forming Société Peter, Cailler, Kohler, Chocolats Suisses S.A. This merger marked the end of negotiations between the two firms, which had engaged in fierce competition up to that time.

Why had Alexandre Cailler—grandson of François-Louis Cailler, the firm's founder—first suggested this merger? Peter & Kohler chocolates had secured a leading position on British and foreign markets, thanks to the vast sales network that Nestlé had placed at its disposal. This network also contributed to Peter, Kohler, and Nestlé brand chocolates' popularity in France, Germany, and the U.S., where negotiations with the U.S. firm Lamont, Corliss & Company (which marketed Peter & Kohler products in the U.S. and Canada, in addition to manufacturing and marketing their own products) had resulted in a merger with the American side of Peter & Kohler in 1909. Cailler had quadrupled its total sales between 1900 and 1910; it was represented by agents in Great Britain, the U.S., and Germany, as well as such distant export markets as Africa and Australia. But apart from Switzerland, Cailler's sales did not reach the level of Peter & Kohler's. This situation led Alexandre Cailler to seek, via intermediaries, an agreement with Jean-Jacques Kohler in June, 1911. Cailler preferred to contact Kohler rather than his uncle, Daniel Peter, due to the fact that Kohler did not always see eye to eye with the inventor of milk chocolate.

In the 1911 merger between the chocolate makers Cailler and Peter & Kohler, both firms were treated on an equal basis. Owing to space constraints at Vevey, it was impossible to fully integrate the managerial staff of the two concerns until 1917. We shall merely mention here that the agreement, signed on September 21, 1911, stated that Nestlé was to acquire a 39 percent interest in P.C.K., which now not only possessed the Swiss factories at Orbe, Echandens, and Broc, but, more importantly, was henceforth able to take advantage of the active involvement and expertise in the field of chocolate making of the chief executives of the firms that had merged. As the 1904 agreement with Nestlé applied to P.C.K. as well, during World War I, the latter profited greatly from Nestlé's assistance. The company had so great a quantity of chocolate on hand at the Armistice that large quantities of it, manufactured by P.C.K. (whose products, as the reader will remember, Nestlé marketed in several countries), had to be sold at a loss.

IT TOOK SOME TIME BEFORE A HARMONIOUS RELATIONSHIP COULD BE ACHIEVED BETWEEN NESTLÉ AND P.C.K.

By 1929, there was a considerable degree of overlap in the activities of the two companies, and, thus, a certain rapprochement seemed natural. Indeed, the directors of the two companies had too many points in common to remain insensitive to such an idea, inasmuch as they were active in the same field, knew each other well, and had worked together for many years. Moreover, Lamont, Corliss & Company's opposition to the merger proved to be only temporary. It should perhaps be mentioned here that the premises of the chocolate factory at Fulton, New York, which Lamont, Corliss had acquired in 1917, reverted entirely to Nestlé in 1951 and, subsequently, became the biggest chocolate production facility of the entire group.

The shareholders of P.C.K. approved the terms of the merger on March 25, 1929, and the shareholders of Nestlé and Anglo-Swiss Condensed Milk Company did so two days later. Nothing in the company name, which remained the same, indicated that Nestlé had become a full-fledged member of the select circle of Swiss chocolate makers. In 1904, it had made a cautious foray into this field and had soon proved its ability to market chocolates on an international scale. Nevertheless, all of the chocolate making experts were employed by P.C.K.

Factory at Orbe, Switzerland

For a time, these specialists felt somewhat ill at ease in the new company. While condensed or powdered milk, be it sweetened or unsweetened,

A.CAILLER AND J.J. KOHLER JOINED THE BOARD OF DIRECTORS OF NESTLÉ AND ANGLO-SWISS CONDENSED MILK CO.

has the same taste everywhere, this does not hold true in the case of bars of chocolate. The specialists at P.C.K. had mastered the art of manufacturing high-quality chocolates; while Nestlé's sales network had mastered the art of of marketing those chocolates with great success. Of course, perfect harmony between production and marketing had not been necessary during the twenty-five years the two companies had merely cooperated with one another. The situation changed considerably, however, once the two firms merged. Now everyone was working for the same company, and the relationships between staff working in different divisions of the same company had to be quite close. However, a lack of harmony between these two divisions was less surprising in 1929 than it had been in 1905, in the wake of Nestlé's merger with Anglo-Swiss. Following the first merger, the company's managerial staff were geographically separated from one another, with a certain number of them at Cham, where the technical division was located; at Vevey, where the financial division was located; and in London, where the sales division was located. In the case of Nestlé's first merger with another company, however, both firms produced the same products; while that with P.C.K. brought Nestlé into a new field with which the company did not yet feel entirely familiar. Moreover, contrary to what had occurred twenty-five years earlier, Nestlé was now joining forces with a business smaller than itself, which influenced the way in which the staff of the two companies behaved toward one another as well. It soon became clear that new products required new habits and a somewhat new way of thinking. Finally, the staff of P.C.K. had been working for a company that had remained a highly family-oriented concern; whereas in the case of Nestlé and Anglo-Swiss, although the majority of its employees were Swiss citizens, they were used to a more international organizational structure and the way in which they worked was more international in nature.

In addition to Alexandre Cailler and Jean-Jacques Kohler, in keeping with the spirit of the 1929 merger, two former members of the board of P.C.K. were soon elected to the board of Nestlé and Anglo-Swiss: Jean Cuénod, whose father had founded Société des Chocolats au Lait Peter with Daniel Peter in 1896, and R. Monod of Geneva. Unfortunately, Jean-Jacques Kohler did not enjoy the fruits his efforts, for he died in 1930. This was indeed a period of transition, for among the members of the board who had originally been with Anglo-Swiss, Wilhelm Caspar Escher, who had worked to bring about the 1905 Anglo-Swiss merger, died a few months before the

Poster advertising Cailler chocolate, ca. 1920

A. CAILLER AND J.J. KOHLER JOINED THE BOARD OF DIRECTORS OF NESTLÉ AND ANGLO-SWISS CONDENSED MILK CO. NESTLÉ NOW POSSESSED 13 CHOCOLATE FACTORIES THROUGHOUT THE WORLD, IN ADDITION TO SAROTTI IN GERMANY.

merger with P.C.K. And Fred H. Page, another former Anglo-Swiss board member, died just a month after the 1929 merger. Of all those who had been among the actors in Nestlé's first merger, only Benjamin Rossier and Auguste Roussy remained in the upper echelons of the company's management; twenty-five years earlier, both had originally come from Nestlé to board of Nestlé and Anglo-Swiss Condensed Milk Company.

The contract for the acquisition of P.C.K. was drawn up on January 23, 1928, but it did not take effect for more than a year due to negotiations over the Lamont, Corliss issue. The contract stipulated that the net assets of P.C.K., which it had contributed to the merger, would be paid to Nestlé and Anglo-Swiss in the form of eighty-seven thousand shares of common stock, each share having a par value of SFr. 200, with dividend rights as of January 1, 1929. Once the net assets of P.C.K. had been "duly valuated by both parties," it was decided that one share of Nestlé and Anglo-Swiss Condensed Milk Company stock would be equivalent to four shares of P.C.K. stock. The authorized capital of the new company was increased from SFr. 125,000,000 to SFr. 145,000,000 (i.e., SFr. 100,000,000 in the form of five hundred thousand bearer shares of common stock having a par value of SFr. 200 per share, and SFr. 45,000,000 in the form of two million senior shares of stock).

Nestlé had now become a true giant in the food industry, with three factories in Switzerland (at Broc, Orbe, and Echandens) as well as six chocolate manufacturing plants (in Turkey, France, Belgium, Italy, Great Britain, and Germany). The newly merged companies now possessed a total of thirteen production centers: the nine just mentioned, plus plants in New Zealand, Spain, Argentina, and Australia, as well as the Sarotti Company in Berlin, which had begun manufacturing products bearing the Nestlé, Peter, Cailler, and Kohler trademarks. The Nestlé Company's chairman, Dapples, whose sole responsibility it was to negotiate with P.C.K., stated in the company's 1929 annual report that he was, "pleased to be able to report that our amalgamation with Peter, Cailler, Kohler, Chocolats Suisses S.A. has been carried out in a most harmonious and accommodating manner, causing no inconvenience to our production and sales departments. This centralization has already had a positive impact on 1929 sales figures. However, we must wait for future years before our own balance sheets begin to reflect the many advantages that we hope to reap from this decision of the stockholders of both companies." By the end of 1929, and despite the New York Stock

Market Crash of October, Nestlé's profits had risen from SFr. 23,614,314.82 to SFr. 30,272,320.87. In Dapples's view, the total profits that the newly merged companies had earned that fiscal year "reflect the normal expansion of our business." Dapples was rather reserved in his optimism, especially in view of the enormous difficulties Nestlé and Anglo-Swiss had experienced toward the end of 1921.

Chapter IV

1929–1938
Nestlé Invents Nescafé on the Eve of World War II

1929–1939: THE WORLD MOVED FROM ECONOMIC CRISIS TO POLITICAL DISSENSION...

From the New York Stock Market Crash (1929) to the Eve of World War II

☐ *Nescafé first appeared on the market in April, 1938. In the preceding chapter we discussed world events up to the beginning of 1929. Now we shall turn to the decade preceding World War II.*

The New York Stock Market Crash of October, 1929, reverberated around the world for more than four years. When the world began reemerging from the ensuing depression in 1933, it found itself plagued by social, political, and economic problems due in large part to the rise of European dictatorships. From 1929 on, more than ten years of unrest, tension, and insecurity culminated in a war that, while certainly foreseeable, proved infinitely more atrocious than even the most pessimistic observers had predicted.

During that decade, events followed one another in rapid succession. For our purpose, it will suffice to mention them briefly.

The Depression hit the United States in 1929; by 1930, the crisis had spread to Europe and the rest of the world. The French withdrew from the Ruhr; the National Socialist and Communist parties won elections in Germany; Japan and the U.S. signed an agreement on naval strength; and authoritarian regimes came to power in Egypt, Poland, Brazil, and Japan. In 1931, in the throes of economic depression, Great Britain devalued its currency and several other countries followed suit. President Hoover declared a world moratorium on war debts and reparations, while Germany and Austria sought to establish a customs union; Japan seized Manchuria; Spain declared itself a republic; and Canada was granted total political autonomy. In 1932, Franklin Delano Roosevelt, a Democrat, was elected president of the United States. In Europe, the Geneva Disarmament Conference was faltering; at the same time, the Lausanne Conference virtually put an end to Germany's payment of war reparations. In Berlin, the short-lived von Papen government was replaced by that of General von Schleicher. Albert Lebrun became president of the French Republic, following the assassination of Paul Doumer, and Salazar became head of state in Portugal. The U.S.S.R. signed non-aggression pacts with Finland, Poland, Latvia, Estonia, and France. In Canada, the Imperial Conference implemented a system of preferential tariffs for British products, and Great Britain allowed the duty-free

REGIONAL CONFLICT, ASSASSINATIONS, UPHEAVAL IN EUROPE...

import, under certain conditions, of products originating from the British Commonwealth. In Latin America, the Gran Chaco War broke out between Bolivia and Paraguay; in Asia, Japan created the state of Manchukuo.

In 1933, the recession abated. Roosevelt announced his program of economic and social reform known as the New Deal. On January 30 of that year, Hitler came to power; Germany withdrew from the second Disarmament Conference and from the League of Nations. In Vienna, Chancellor Dollfuss, relying on the support of the "Heimwehr", outlawed the Austrian National Socialist party. Germany, Great Britain, France, and Italy entered into a short-lived alliance. In 1934, the world economic situation improved. Poland and Germany signed a nonaggression pact. Hitler had the heads of the German police (Sturmabteilung) *executed and gave greater power to the SS* (Schutzstaffel) *shortly before assuming the position of head of state left vacant after the death of President Hindenburg. In Vienna, Chancellor Schuschnigg succeeded Chancellor Dollfuss, assassinated after two years in power by the National Socialists. Alexander I of Yugoslavia and the French minister Barthou were assassinated in Marseilles in a plot carried out by one of the king's subjects. In Belgium, Leopold III assumed the throne. In China, proclaimed a republic in 1911, Chiang Kai-shek, in power since 1928, defeated the communist armies of the south; those forces eventually regrouped under Mao Zedong and set out on the 4,000-mile Long March to the northern province of Yenan. In 1935, the Saar region voted overwhelmingly to return to German control. An accord between Germany and England authorized the former to maintain a fleet equivalent to one-third the size of the British Navy. Italy attacked Albania. General Pilsudski, since 1926 the "uncrowned king" of Poland, died in Warsaw. In Czechoslovakia, the German National Socialist party, centered in Sudeten, gained power. In Moscow, the Komintern declared itself in favor of a union of "bourgeois republics" against fascism; while, at the same time, Stalin's great purge was thinning out the ranks of old guard Leninists. The monarchy was reinstated in Greece with Georges II. The Gran Chaco War between Paraguay and Bolivia resulted in most of their disputed territory being awarded to the former. The Japanese invaded northern China.*

MILITARY INTERVENTION, THE SPANISH CIVIL WAR, THE SHORT-LIVED MUNICH AGREEMENT...

1936 was also marred by dire events. The occupation of the demilitarized Rhineland met with little foreign protest; meanwhile, the Austrian National Socialist party, now legalized, was gaining power. Great Britain had three kings in the space of one year: George V died; his successor, Edward VIII, abdicated; and Edward VIII was followed by George VI. Japan withdrew from the Naval Disarmament Conference in London. Egypt, ruled by King Faruk, was moving towards greater independence. Leon Blum formed a Popular Front government in France. The king of Italy declared himself emperor of Albania. General Franco's troops rose up in Spanish Morocco, triggering three years of Spanish civil war. General Metaxas installed himself as dictator in Greece. The Treaty of Montreux restored Turkey's rights to the Dardanelles. Roosevelt was reelected president of the United States.

In 1937, the situation deteriorated yet further. The Swiss, C.J. Burckhardt, arrived in Danzig as the new commissioner of the League of Nations. Civil war was raging in Spain; leftist democrats and communists from all countries joined together in the International Brigade, while the Reich and Italy sent troops to bolster Franco against the republicans. Mussolini and Hitler met in Berlin. Thomas Masaryk, who preceded Eduard Beneš as president of the Czechoslovak Republic, died in Prague. In the Indies, massive strikes were causing widespread unrest. Australia appointed its first diplomatic representative. Italy withdrew from the League of Nations. Stalin purged the Red Army; its leader, Commander Tukhachevski, was executed. War broke out between China and Japan; Beijing, Shanghai, and Nanjing fell to Japanese domination; and after signing a nonaggression pact with the Soviet Union, Chiang Kai-shek withdrew, along with the Chinese government to Chungjing. Under Prince Konoye, Japan intensified its policy of economic self-sufficiency and independence.

In 1938, all eyes were on Germany. As recently as 1936, the Olympic Games had been held in Berlin. Following their meeting in Rome, Hitler and Mussolini strengthened their alliance. Hitler reorganized the German Army, demanded the return of the Sudetenland to the Reich, and precipitated the union of Germany and Austria, which was overwhelmingly approved in Austria by popular vote; Prime Minister Chamberlain sponsored the Munich agreement between Great Britain, France, Italy, and Germany, separating the Sudetenland from Czecho-

slovakia, which, despite Soviet backing, offered no opposition. President Beneš fled to the United States. In Germany, pogroms against Jews became increasingly frequent. Horthy, regent of Hungary, met with Hitler, an ominous sign of the extent of Germany's penetration into the Balkans.

1939: tension, on the eve of combat, persisted until September. The German Reich divided Czechoslovakia into a protectorate of Bohemia and Moravia and declared Slovakia an independent state. Italy occupied Albania. Franco won the Spanish Civil War. Germany claimed the Memel region as well as the corridor surrounding Danzig, signed the Axis agreement with Italy, and then, in August, forestalled negotiations between the Allies and the Kremlin by signing a nonaggression pact with the U.S.S.R.; while Poland, and Great Britain concluded a mutual assistance treaty.

By the fall of 1939, the stage was set for tragedy. The curtain opened on the first act of the drama: the German invasion of Poland, foreshadowing in its suddenness and devastation later attacks that would set the world ablaze.

Such was the political landscape of the period. In the economic and social areas, the ten years following the Depression were fraught with so many problems and such great international tension that the decade might well be viewed as one of the worst in history. Everything seemed to conspire to demoralize a world already disillusioned after Wall Street's Black Thursday stock market crash.

The financial debacle began on October 24, 1929. On the 29th, more than 16,000,000 shares changed hands in New York. Although most speculators were unaware of it, two dangers were threatening market stability: first, the discrepancy between production, which had increased 25 percent since 1919, and available markets; second, the disparity between production and share prices. Indeed, since 1924, speculation had increased dramatically. New and increasingly sophisticated advances in communication, such as telephone, telex, and radio, now enabled Americans to follow the market more closely than ever before. Everyone scrambled to buy shares whose value skyrocketed. Rich and poor alike viewed the stock market as a foolproof way to make money, especially when shareholders could easily obtain bank loans to buy more stock (provided loans were guaranteed by securities and dividends or

AND WORLD WAR II. THE EFFECTS OF THE NEW YORK STOCK MARKET CRASH OF 1929...

THREW
THE U.S. ECONOMY
INTO DISARRAY.
ROOSEVELT'S NEW
DEAL, PRESENTED
IN 1933,
MET WITH SUCCESS.

increases in share prices exceeded the level of credit). Of course, it didn't take very much to upset this artificial balance. And when that day came, a crisis of confidence hit Wall Street which reverberated far beyond the U.S., shaking the entire world economy and its monetary systems. So great was the cataclysm that neither industry nor agriculture was spared; widespread unemployment resulted almost immediately. Even the most solid financial institutions were devastated by the storm. By mid-November, speculators had already lost $30,000,000,000.

After the Stock Market Crash, President Hoover, driven by the classic Republican conviction that all direct goverment action on the economy was contrary to that spirit of free enterprise upon which the American economic system was founded, refused to allow the Treasury to intervene. Market jitters soon escalated into a full-scale economic crisis. Between 1929 and 1932, the U.S. gross national product fell from $81,000,000,000 to $49,000,000,000; salaries fell by 40 percent, dividends by more than half. The situation of indebted farmers worsened; industries cut back on production and were forced to lay off workers. Unemployment spread to every economic sector and social milieu. And by the end of 1930, 5,000,000 persons—10 percent of the working population—found themselves out of a job. The crisis soon affected the worldwide economic situation.

In 1931, in a move designed to rescue both the European countries most affected by the crisis as well as American investments abroad, President Hoover declared his famous one-year moratorium on war debts and reparations. This had the effect of stopping the payment of reparations by Germany, but did not encourage the return of floating capital to the U.S. By October, 1931, unemployment exceeded 7,500,000. Thus, it came as no surprise when, in 1932, the presidential election was won by the Democrat Franklin Delano Roosevelt, who promised Americans a New Deal.

In March, 1933, when Roosevelt took office, one worker in four was unemployed. Farmers were desperate. But Roosevelt had the gift of restoring the nation's confidence in itself. Government control at the administrative level over banks, currency rates, and production gradually served to rebuild the economy. A gold embargo, declared on March 6, 1933, substantially reduced farmers' debts. The stock market was reorganized, with strict regulations governing the issuing of shares, *as well as on the amount of credit brokers could extend to their clients. Roosevelt also took direct economic measures; for example, he reduced civil servants' salaries and government officials' pensions and virtually put an end to prohibition, which drained huge sums of money from the national treasury into the pockets of a few black marketeers. By implementing his New Deal, Roosevelt was able to allocate nearly $3,000,000,000 for public works. The Tennessee Valley project, for example, with its twenty-seven dams built in seven states, illustrates Roosevelt's ability to combine the need to provide jobs for the unemployed with another important need, that of controlling the flow of a river. At the same time, the project promoted cooperation between the federal government, state government, and local farmers. In order to stimulate agriculture, Roosevelt created agricultural credit funds, controlled by the federal government, which provided farmers with fixed-interest loans. In 1933, the passage of the National Industrial Recovery Act instituted a shorter work week, a minimum wage, and a means by which companies in a given industry could agree on prices, salaries, and regulations, with a view to limiting excessive competition. In the area of social welfare, Roosevelt introduced, in 1935, a law authorizing the federal government to help individual states meet the needs of sick, elderly, and handicapped citizens and to create both a national social security and an unemployment insurance fund.*

ECONOMIC SHOCK WAVES FROM NEW YORK REVERBERATED THROUGHOUT THE WORLD.

All these decisions, taken in rapid succession, were completely new for a highly liberalist country such as the United States. And not surprisingly, they caused a certain amount of opposition. Nevertheless, in 1936, Roosevelt was reelected. From 1937 on, strengthened by the support of an overwhelming political majority, the president set out to improve and consolidate his system of reform (created not through violent revolution, but through democratic means). In 1938, economic recovery was beginning to be felt. However, it was not until the outbreak of the war in 1939 that the United States was to achieve a level of production greatly exceeding that of 1929.

The storm originating in New York in 1929 first hit the London Stock Exchange, then those of continental Europe, and finally of the other industrialized nations. The effects on the European economy were somewhat delayed, though as early as 1930, American and French investments were withdrawn from Germany and Austria. The Americans

ENGLAND DEVALUED THE POUND IN 1931.

withdrew their capital as a direct result of the Stock Market Crash; while the French withdrew theirs owing to their fear of an Austro-German alliance—and this, even before Hitler's rise to power. British banks attempted to bolster their Austrian and German counterparts, but in vain. In the spring of 1931, one of Europe's largest banks, the Boden-Credit-Anstalt of Vienna, faltering since 1923, now suspended all payments. In extremis, and despite the heavy losses involved, the Austrian government converted it into a state-owned bank. In Germany, the sudden loss of American capital combined with fears surrounding the mounting success of the National Socialist party resulted in a draining of the foreign currency reserves of the Reichsbank, in July, 1931; during that same month the important Darmstädter Bank was also forced to suspend payments. The German government closed all banks for two days. This had a devastating effect on Great Britain: within a few days, the capital invested by British banks in Germany was frozen, and the gold reserves of the Bank of England plunged by £32,000,000.

Thus, the storm from America, fed by upheavals in Austria and Germany, passed through London on its way back to New York, but not before striking Italy, Latin America, Asia, Africa, and the Far East. Even the Soviet Union, isolated by Stalinist Communism, felt the impact of that storm on imports and exports.

Beginning in 1931, each country attempted to resist economic crisis as best it could. Germany, Italy, and Japan opted for the most radical measures. Other countries sought to find remedies more in keeping with their political traditions. Before we turn our attention to each country's particular economic situation—beginning with the democracies and then dealing with the totalitarian regimes—we should point out that nearly every country saw its salvation in stronger government intervention, designed to bolster the currency, stimulate industry, and prevent prices from plummeting. Economic liberalism found very few disciples during this troubled period.

England opted for devaluation; on September 21, 1931, it abandoned the gold standard. With the exception of Canada and British Honduras, the British Empire followed London's example. In rapid succession, Portugal, Denmark, Norway, Sweden, Finland, the Baltics, Ireland, Greece, Iran, Iraq, and Egypt devalued their currencies. This was the basis of the Sterling Area. The Bank of England's raising of the discount

FRANCE FARED SOMEWHAT BETTER ECONOMICALLY...

rate to 6 percent led, in the years that followed, to a flight of capital from the U.S., owing to the implementation of the New Deal, from France, owing to the Popular Front, from Germany, owing to Hitler's rise in popularity, and from Spain, owing to the civil war brewing there. This capital allowed a resurgence of British industry that continued until 1939. From 1932 on, protectionist Britain profited from tariff agreements signed in Ottawa between it and the Commonwealth countries. Preferential treatment enabled products—especially foodstuffs—arriving in England from those countries to benefit from considerably reduced customs duties. Similarly, the other nations of the British Empire, themselves protected by a solid tariff barrier, granted preferential tariffs on industrial products from Great Britain. Such preferential treatment was soon extended, by means of a series of bilateral accords, to the Scandinavian countries as well. Thus protected by the establishment of quotas on imports and exports, as well as by subsidies, agricultural and industrial production improved. For the first time ever in England, the government intervened to bring about the reorganization of the coal industry and the consolidation of the steel industry. Between 1932 and 1937, the unemployment rate decreased by 50 percent, leaving fewer than 1,000,000 persons unemployed just prior to World War II.

In France, the impact of 1929 was felt somewhat later. The very name, Raymond Poincaré, French president from 1926 to 1929, inspired such confidence that France was able to bolster and stabilize the franc in 1928. Furthermore, Paris had not been the site of as much speculation as New York and a certain number of other capitals. Finally, the caution of credit institutions and the scepticism with which sensible capitalists viewed the overvalued currencies of the English-speaking world allowed France to weather the Depression better than some other countries—at least until the devaluation of the pound sterling in 1931. Still, France's deflationary policy meant that from 1931 to 1936, its products had difficulty competing with foreign goods, whose prices had been much more drastically cut. The Laval government's statutory orders sought to bring prices down in order to stimulate exports. But the halting of German reparations and the decline of tourism took their toll on France's balance of payments. Restrictions on imports, combined with a general drop in both foreign and domestic prices, resulted in decreased revenues from direct taxation and customs duties.

BUT NOT IN THE SOCIAL SPHERE. JAPAN, TOO, WAS AFFECTED.

In addition to the budget deficit, there were the effects of political changes. In 1932, the Cartel of the Left came to power, causing a flight of capital from France. The policy of lowering prices brought about layoffs, which increased unemployment and resulted in the formation of political groups on both the extreme Right and Left that took to the streets in violent confrontations like the one that took place on February 6, 1936, in Paris. When, in 1936, Leon Blum took over the leadership of the Popular Front government, 1,000,000 striking workers were engaged in factory sit-ins. Blum, a Socialist, raised salaries, instituted annual paid vacations for workers, and reduced the work week from forty-eight to forty hours. This latter measure unfortunately resulted in higher cost prices for industry and an increase in the cost of living. Blum moved to nationalize a certain number of arms factories and the National Wheat Board; he tightened the government's control over the Bank of France and the railroads. In 1936, he devalued the franc by 25 percent. A second devaluation, decided by the minister Chautemps, took place in 1937. Following the demise of the Popular Front government, Daladier, the new president, once again devalued the franc. Capital began to flow in again, and this trend continued until the outbreak of the war. When, as early as 1929, the effects of the stock market disaster in the U.S. reached Japan, that country's economy was largely centered on exporting manufactured goods—in particular, textiles, bicycles, and watches—and thus was dependent on a steady supply of raw materials from abroad. As capital became scarce, Japan's financial problems worsened. Its precarious economic situation led it to undertake a military buildup in order to ensure continued expansion. Heavy industry was becoming increasingly geared toward producing arms, and a series of military conquests ensued: first in Manchuria, then in China, and finally, at the height of World War II, throughout all of Asia. This new shift in economic priorities took a heavy toll on the production of consumer goods. The Japanese government intervened vigorously by arranging mandatory industrial mergers and creating cooperative associations that granted credit and determined prices. In the territories occupied by Japan, local industry was subjected to strict military control.

Italy and Germany, both ruled by dictators, adopted a somewhat different approach to the economic crisis. There, the capitalist system was not placed under military control, but became, over time, the instrument of a political clique.

ITALY AND GERMANY TOOK REFUGE IN AUTHORITARIANISM. HITLER PROMISED A ROSY FUTURE...

Fascism had been gaining influence in Italy since 1922. In 1927, Mussolini, firmly in power, proclaimed the Charter of Labor, that outlined the status of trade unions (whose leaders reported directly to the Fascist party, the country's de facto government). When, in 1931, the economic crisis hit, Italy was a monolith with government power firmly concentrated at the top. Mussolini resolved to come to the aid of the banks, struggling to support industry, which were required to hold corporate securities in their portfolios. The Italian government took possession of those securities, placing them in a newly created government body, the Industrial Reconstruction Institute. The I.R.I. thereby acquired a substantial interest in banks and a number of major industries. And thus, the economic crisis may be seen as a contributing factor in the movement in Italy toward increasingly pervasive state control.

It was in Germany that the world economic crisis had the strongest impact, however. When, in 1930, the effects of the Depression reached that country, the Reich first attempted to maintain the gold standard, cut spending, and raise taxes, while reducing reparations payments to the Allies. Chancellors Bruning and, after him, von Papen pursued this policy, but by 1932, public discontent had given rise to greater representation of extremist parties in the Reichstag. Clearly, the causes of the economic crisis in Germany were largely external: the pulling out of foreign capital caused panic in the banks, and the drop in world prices for agricultural products had plunged the powerful landowners of eastern Germany into debt—a situation which President Hindenburg sought to remedy. But the domestic political situation was no less a determining factor. The number of Communist and National Socialist members of the Reichstag was distressing to foreign investors. Furthermore, the fear of returning to the hard times of 1921–23 caused the German people to turn to a nationalism that smacked of xenophobia. From 1930 to 1933, the country floated between democratic and authoritarian government. But the unstable political situation, combined with an unemployment figure of more than 6,000,000, worked in favor of the nationalists.

Indeed, Hitler promised the German people a welfare state in which they slowly but surely began to believe. Playing on the general resentment toward foreign capitalists, Hitler managed to win over small inves-

AND CAME TO POWER IN 1933.

tors. By speaking out against the Treaty of Versailles, he assuaged the nationalists and former professional soldiers whom the Reichswehr, limited to 100,000 men, had to turn away. By attacking large stores, owned by Jews, he won the support of small shop owners. By criticizing industrial conglomerates, he also won the support of small manufacturers who were opposed to the Konzern, *i.e., permanent organizations that grouped together the small industries in a given field, deciding on everything from the purchase of raw materials to the sale of finished products. Hitler's growing group of supporters included non-Communists, dissatisfied government workers, and even a handful of poor intellectuals. When he attacked the Communists, right wing groups approved, even though they did not necessarily agree with all the ideas embodied in his slogan "service, not self." Finally, when Hitler called for strong central government, nationalization of the banks, the return of national prosperity through the elimination of unemployment, and the establishment of a political system which would exclude Communists and prohibit all disputes between political parties, the German people rallied around him, despite his racist policies that were eventually to lead to the extermination of millions of European Jews.*

In 1933, to the surprise of many observers, Hitler became chancellor. He soon brought his iron hand to bear on everything from the life of the labor unions to the wheels and pinions of the state. By the time Marshal Hindenburg—who had helped bring him to power—died in 1934, Hitler had already eliminated the Communists through the Reichstag Fire affair, had put an end to the Weimar Republic by proclaiming absolute political power, had established the first concentration camps, had placed Goering in charge of Prussia (whose parliament was dissolved), had instituted a one-party system, had obtained 92 percent of the popular vote, and had withdrawn Germany from the League of Nations. By 1935, Hitler's social organization, with its motto "force through joy," was already in place. In the economic sphere, the National Socialists placed capitalism at the service of the state. By 1938, Hitler had eliminated unemployment; he accomplished this by building highways and airports, by employing 1,000,000 Germans within the party, by hiring vast numbers of persons to work in the arms industry, by establishing a large industrial complex for the manufacture of synthetic goods, and by freezing foreign assets, thereby forcing foreign buyers to pay for at least part of the goods bought from Germany in foreign currency.

Before long, the countries along the Danube became economically dependent on the Third Reich, which explains the ease with which Berlin, which already dominated the non-Slavic region of what had been Czechoslovakia, was able to negotiate a number of wartime alliances: with Bulgaria, Hungary, and Romania (Yugoslavia remained independent). Just before the war, Hitler had his sycophants in a number of countries. He made use of them both to infiltrate movements opposed to his expansion and to further his diplomatic agenda, which sought to "reunite" ethnic Germans dispersed throughout Europe. At the same time, Hitler cultivated friendships with the leaders of Italy and Spain, after Italy's war with Ethiopia had alienated it from Western democracies and the Spanish Civil War had divided Europe into two opposed camps, thus destroying the accomplishments of the 1935 Stresa Conference involving France, Italy, and Britain. As those present at that conference had sought to protect Austria, the breakup of the Stresa alliance in 1938 provided Hitler with a perfect opportunity to enter Vienna in great pomp and to annex Austria.

Clearly, the political and social atmosphere in Europe could hardly have been more troubled when, from Vevey, Nescafé began its international career.

NESCAFE

CHAPTER IV – NESTLÉ

1929–1938

Nestlé and Anglo-Swiss and the Invention of Nescafé

ALONG WITH NEW ACTIVITIES IN THE FIELD OF CHOCOLATE MAKING, NESTLÉ STARTED PRODUCTION IN ARGENTINA AND CUBA IN 1930 AND FORGED SOLID LINKS WITH ITS WORLD MARKETS,

☐ Though the situation would change somewhat later, in 1929 the Depression had practically no effect on Nestlé and Anglo-Swiss Condensed Milk Company, nor on the success of Nestlé's Food Company, Inc., New York—located in the eye of the hurricane, as it were. Mastering its own crisis so well in 1921 had prepared Nestlé particularly well to survive the economic shock of the following years. In the meantime, the merger with P.C.K. affected the structure of other companies, such as Società Nestlé in Milan, Italy, which had merged with Società Italiana Peter, Cailler, Kohler at Intra.

The Nestlé and Anglo-Swiss Condensed Milk Company, which had increased its capital to SFr. 97,500,000, continued expanding its other activities. It strengthened its milk-processing division by acquiring a substantial interest in Hollandia Anglo-Dutch Milk and Food Company, Vlaardingen, Holland.

Two new locally based companies were created in 1930: Nestlé (Argentina) S.A.P.A. and Compañia Nestlé de Cuba—showing clearly the importance of Latin America to the Swiss firm. Nestlé was one of the first companies to show confidence in the future of that part of the world, at a time when starting industrial production there was often considered a foolhardy step for a European-based company. The milk processing factory at Bayamo, Cuba, was created from scratch in a region that had no previous experience with such industrial and agricultural facilities. In the U.S., the company acquired a production center at Ripon, California, while in the French town of Gap, it converted a small dairy into a condensed milk factory.

The managers of the factory at Bayamo, Cuba

From 1922 on, considerable stress had been placed on improving communications among the various locally based companies when the project for reorganizing the company was put forward. In June, 1929, Louis Dapples set out on a voyage that lasted nearly a year and took him to the U.S., Australia, the Middle and Far East. It was a voyage that reinforced links between the firm's widely scattered locally based companies and the man at the helm, who had carried out the company's comprehensive recovery program by dint of his personal authority. Another foreseeable outcome of the voyage was to enable Dapples to devote himself entirely to his duties as chairman of the board and leave the task of running the company to its executive vice-presidents: Edouard Muller, Gustave Huguenin, Maurice Paternot, and Frank Britain, who had already assumed their functions prior to the merger with P.C.K. Edouard Muller acted as executive chairman during Dapples's absence and became a member of the board in 1930, with the title of chief executive officer. As Dapples was a financial expert, a particularly valuable result of his voyage was the advice and counsel he could give those in charge of distant markets at the outset of the disaster on Wall Street.

IN PARTICULAR, WITH THOSE IN THE U.S. AND SOUTHERN AFRICA.

The company had not limited its restructuring to the technical, commercial, or administrative levels; other important measures sought to develop a comprehensive corporate philosophy and, especially, to formulate specific policies with regard to its raw materials suppliers. Nestlé avoided being too adversely affected by the Depression by closely monitoring the rise and fall of raw materials prices and purchasing them at the most advantageous moment. By 1930, the company experienced no further cash-flow problems; its factories maintained their output levels, and chocolate sales increased. The managerial structure was by now well-tuned and managers' responsibilities well-defined.

In the U. S., the milk sales of Nestlé's Food Company, which had only recently changed its name to Nestlé's Milk Products Company, Inc., New York, remained steady in spite of the Depression; whereas chocolates, being a less essential item, encountered some resistance. Broadly speaking, however, the adaptation of production levels to market demand was so successful that Nestlé was able to repay a certain number of loans and outstanding debts. The company in South Africa published excellent sales figures and was planning to build a new factory at Pietermaritzburg; while the chocolate manufacturing factory at Auckland, New Zealand, was able to defend itself quite well against severe competition. In 1931 and 1932, when the worldwide economic slump was at its high point, the Nestlé organization was able to prove conclusively how strong it really was. Naturally, profits were down for 1931, but the company's financial position was healthy, owing to a sound policy of amortization. As the company's policy of decentralization had been in effect for many years, it was possible for it to overcome what for another company would have been prohibitive tariff barriers.

Great Britain's decision, in 1931, to come off the gold standard had inevitable repercussions on Nestlé's financial dealings. In addition to the compli-

NESTLÉ CONSOLIDATED IN THE FACE OF CURRENCY DEVALUATIONS AND FIERCE COMPETITION WORLDWIDE.

cations caused by devaluation in the countries that had followed Britain's example, there was the difficult problem of supplying those markets that depended on provisions from countries remaining more or less true to the gold standard. There were two major obstacles preventing countries that had remained on the gold standard from successfully exporting their products: strict exchange control in the importing countries and competition from lower-priced products originating from countries where the currency had been devalued. Production levels, particularly in Norway and Holland, were gradually readapted to the realities of the market. The transfer of money was a major problem. Once Nestlé products had been sold (with the help of increasingly expensive publicity), it was necessary to transfer funds to Switzerland; this was no easy task at a time when drastic controls had been imposed on currency leaving many countries.

As the economic crisis deepened, Nestlé pushed ahead even more energetically with its policy of consolidation; by 1933, the company's bonded debt had been reduced from SFr. 116,841,500 (in 1929) to SFr. 5,000,000. And by 1935, it had been eliminated entirely. In 1934, the company's share capital was reduced to SFr. 116,000,000 through the conversion of senior shares at an equitable conversion price.

Overcoming current difficulties was insufficient; plans had to be made for the future as well. However, considerable caution had to be exercised in this. Annual reports from this turbulent period expressed the hope that monetary stability and normal price increases for raw materials and manufactured goods would return. But all of them emphasized that prosperity was not around the corner. They pointed out that consumers had become poorer and thus preferred cheaper goods to brand-name articles, as the unfortunate experience with evaporated milk had shown in the U.S. As profit margins on products such as evaporated milk were extremely low, large firms specializing in their manufacture concentrated on high sales volume—prepared, if necessary, to lower prices to a ridiculous level. Such cut-throat competition continued until 1933, when the Roosevelt administration established price floors and introduced the control of sales terms. Moreover, from 1932 on, it became easier for Great Britain to export to countries that were signatories to the Ottawa Agreement.

One nation after another resorted to devaluation; those that had devalued first had no difficulty in selling their exports. But once more radical devaluation took place elsewhere, the volume of the former's exports dropped, and a period of fierce competition ensued. The Australian market is a typical case in point. When the international crisis began, the devaluation of the Australian pound stimulated exports of Australian condensed milk. But by 1933, after other countries had devalued their currency, Australia, whose economy had become sounder in the interim, was no longer an important exporter of this product. From this point on, a large part of Australian condensed milk production was absorbed by the domestic market.

From 1934 on, sales were on the rise once again, and locally based companies were set up in the four corners of the earth.

Of course, markets that had felt the effects of the slump earliest were also the earliest to show signs of recovery, as demonstrated by the increase in Lamont, Corliss's chocolate sales from 1934 on. Thus, the U.S., where Nestlé had fourteen factories in operation in 1934, recovered from the Depression in advance of Europe. Despite its monetary difficulties, sales of milk, chocolate, and cheese in Spain had raised high hopes there; but the political situation prevented economic activity from getting under way again. From 1936 on, all industrial and commercial activity was paralyzed by the Spanish Civil War. With the return of a certain degree of stability in Germany, sales of milk, chocolate, and cheese had increased, but the difficulties of transferring funds to Switzerland were still not resolved. In addition to the problems inherent in the economic situation, Società Nestlé in Italy had to cancel all of its commercial and financial agreements with a canned food company in Naples and move its sales directors back to Milan.

Competitors had to be watched constantly in times as unsettled as these. To avoid the risk of being squeezed out of a market, it was essential that production be started before established competitors could control the market. Thus, factories were built that might never have seen the day had the company's management at Vevey limited itself to thinking only in terms of the present. Several newcomers were added to the list of producers of Nestlé products: in Denmark, Nestlé Nordisk A/S, Copenhagen, and a chocolate factory in 1933; in Czechoslovakia, Nestlé Akciova Spolecnost Provyrobu a Prodej Potravin in Prague in 1935, and a small factory producing Nescao, infant cereal, and evaporated milk at Krumlov in Moravia in 1936. In other countries, local production was stepped up in other ways: for example, in South Africa, through the addition of a new dairy products unit; in Argentina, through a powdered milk plant that started production in 1933; in Brazil, through a second milk-processing factory; and in Belgium, through the construction of the milk-processing factory at Hamoir in 1932. Nestlé acquired an interest in a locally based company in Chile, Sociedad Comercial

SOME FACTORIES HAD TO BE CLOSED DOWN, HOWEVER.

Industrial Lechera Miraflores, which merged with Sociedad Nacional Lechera de Graneros in 1935. The new firm retained its own identity, while Nestlé provided various forms of technical expertise, including the building of a factory at Retiro. In the U.S., three new condensed milk plants were set up at Greenville, Ohio, Weynwega, Wisconsin, and Tuscaloosa, Alabama, to improve the competitive position of Nestlé's Milk Products Company in the heartland of America. The first condensed milk plant in Mexico started production at Ocotlán in 1935. Still other approaches were adopted to increase Nestlé's presence abroad. For example, in Japan, the manufacture of Nestlé products was entrusted to an all-Japanese company in 1933. And an agreement was signed in Portugal with the Sociedade de Produtos Lacteos, authorizing it to utilize Nestlé's manufacturing processes as well as to market products bearing the Nestlé trademark.

More locally based companies were formed in 1935 to replace the existing organizations. Nestlé's Milk Products, Ltd. was founded in London. At Gibraltar, a British company, Nestlé and Anglo-Swiss Milk Products, Ltd., was formed to coordinate the work of sales organizations in countries supplied through the import of Nestlé products.

Of course, there was a negative side to such growth; we shall discuss it here in detail in order to help the reader better understand the secret of how Nestlé was able to expand throughout the world in spite of the Depression. The company closed down its factory at Lindau, Germany, and disbanded Nestlé's Milk Products Company in California as well as A/B Nestlé in Stockholm, Sweden. The Depression had finally left its mark on Nestlé's manufacturing network in Switzerland. Exports from Switzerland encountered even greater obstacles than they had prior to the 1929 slump and could no longer hold their own against foreign competitors. (The Swiss franc was not devalued until 1936.) As strict as they were, the guidelines Nestlé issued prior to the Depression in an attempt to streamline its production had not succeeded in ensuring that production at the company's five Swiss factories continued a normal levels. Once again, the company had painful decisions to make in order to concentrate its

The Ocotlán plant, the first condensed milk factory in Mexico

production in a reduced number of factories. The two oldest production centers—at Cham and at Vevey—had to be closed down in 1932 and 1934 respectively. Also in 1934, the company was forced to close its factory at Payerne. Nestlé was aware that such drastic measures had social consequences, and it decided to financially compensate members of its staff who had been laid off through the force of circumstance. Production of processed milk was centralized at Orbe, and chocolate production divided up between Orbe and Broc.

AMONG THESE: CHAM (1932) AND VEVEY (1934). NESTLÉ VARIED ITS RANGE OF MILK-BASED PRODUCTS...

Throughout this period, Nestlé was also endeavoring to diversify its range of products, which were essentially milk-based items. As we saw earlier, it was impossible to regulate fresh milk supplies, which arrived at the processing plants at a rapid pace. Most plants had signed contracts with the dairy farmers according to which they agreed to purchase their entire milk supply. Any surplus had to be used in the manufacture of other dairy products such as cheese.

The reader will recall that, at the end of the nineteenth century, in addition to its condensed milk and infant cereal, a new product, evaporated milk, was added to Nestlé's range of products, followed, in 1921, by powdered milk. Another type of powdered milk was the special milk formula that Nestlé sold under the brand name Lactogen, indicating that the product was very similar to mother's milk in terms of its composition. Nestlé factories also produed malted milk and Elédon, a powdered form of buttermilk for babies suffering from digestive disorders. In 1929, a beverage containing wheat flour was marketed under the brand name Milo. In 1930, Nestlé developed the low-fat, protein-rich milk Nestogen, enriched with malto-dextrin and sucrose. Pelargon, a type of whole milk combined with lactic acid to improve digestibility, was added to Nestlé's range of special milk products for children in 1934; while instant Nescao was soon to complete its line of chocolate-based products. In 1936, in cooperation with the Swiss pharmaceutical company Hoffmann-La Roche of Basel, the company began producing Nestrovit, a vitamin-enriched product based on condensed milk (also available in cocoa-butter-based bars). Nestrovit was the precursor of such products enriched with vitamin B or D as Nesviton and Nestamine. All of Nestlé's dietetic products were developed by its various scientific departments in close cooperation with pediatricians. And none of them was ever put on the market before it had undergone a stringent series of clinical tests and had been approved by medical authorities. Considerable caution was

1938 ad for Nestrovit

AND DEVELOPED TOTALLY NEW ONES.

exercised in the advertising of such products, for the question of choice and dosage was, and still is, to be determined by the physician alone.

Since its inception, apart from its dark chocolate and, in France, its specially prepared vegetable baby food, Nestlé had never departed from its tradition of manufacturing only products containing milk in one form or another. It was to deviate from this policy, however, in 1938, a year before World War II, when the company created Nescafé instant coffee.

There are three ways for a company to grow: by expanding on its own, by acquiring other firms, or by combining these two methods. Thus far, we have discussed the series of mergers in which the Nestlé Company participated. Before the year 1938, only Nestlé's merger with P.C.K. in 1929 had resulted in its manufacturing an additional specialty—chocolate—on a large scale. In this chapter, we shall focus our attention on a new Nestlé product, produced from raw materials far different from those it had utilized until that time. In fact, Nescafé was a product that was so totally new it was unequaled by any other coffee-based product in the world.

When Nestlé's research laboratories succeeded in developing the world's first instant coffee, it was with the conviction that this new product had a great future in store for it. As early as half a century ago, life was becoming increasingly fast paced, and it was becoming quite apparent that consumers preferred food products that were quick and easy to prepare. It was with this change in mentality in mind that the company's management—Louis Dapples and Edouard Muller in particular—decided to ask its research team to study the feasibility of producing such a product. The story of the discovery and marketing of instant coffee is quite an interesting one. In 1930, Louis Dapples, who was well-known in Brazil, where he had lived for several years before becoming company chairman, was approached by a gentleman from São Paulo and by a representative of the Brazilian Coffee Institute, who asked Nestlé if it could manufacture coffee in the form of cubes. It was thought that coffee cubes would have the twofold advantage of maintaining the flavor intact and, at the same time, being soluble in hot water. During the 1930s, Brazil was accumulating such huge coffee surpluses that it had to destroy part of its coffee harvest to prevent prices—already considered too low—from plummeting yet further. It was felt that coffee consumption would increase if a new product could be developed that was easy to use and if that product was promoted by Nestlé's expert sales organization. At the time, there already existed on the market various forms of crystalized or

1952 ad for Nescafé and Nescoré

IN 1937, NESCAFÉ WAS INVENTED AT VEVEY AND FIRST MARKETED IN SWITZERLAND IN 1938.

liquid coffee. However, none of these were really successful items. Apart from the fact that they were not readily soluble, they were wanting in terms of taste and aroma. Thus, sales of these products had been insignificant, and the problem of reducing the overabundance of coffee beans remained unsolved.

Louis Dapples, therefore, instructed the Nestlé research laboratory in Switzerland to search for a solution. After years of painstaking research, the desired result was at long last achieved in the spring of 1937, through the efforts of a group of researchers headed by Max Morgenthaler. First, the delicate problem of preserving the coffee's aroma was resolved by the addition of carbohydrates. Next, researchers helped overcome the problems arising when the process was implemented on an industrial scale. When the totally new product was finally marketed, it was not in the form of cubes but in the form of a water-soluble powder, which meant that the consumer could vary the concentration of the product as desired. Thus was born Nestlé's innovative product: Nescafé, the next important development at Vevey, following Henri Nestlé's infant cereal and Daniel Peter's milk chocolate.

Originally, Nescafé was to be manufactured in Brazil. Nestlé had to relinquish that idea, however, as there did not seem to be any chance that the Brazilians would modify their regulations governing the utilization of coffee. Moreover, customs regulations and clearing procedures were making exports increasingly difficult in that country. Therefore, it was decided that the new product would be manufactured by locally based companies in the countries in which it was to be consumed, and that production would begin immediately in Switzerland. The first Nescafé production unit was installed at the Orbe factory, and the new product was introduced in Switzerland on April 1, 1938. Initially, it was not widely advertised, owing to low production capacity and to the need to eliminate any bugs in the system. In 1939, in spite of the complications caused by the approach of World War II, Nestlé succeeded in starting up production of Nescafé in France, Great Britain, and the U.S.

The Nestlé laboratory, Vevey, in which Nescafé was invented

Meanwhile, important events were taking place at Vevey. The policy of decentralization had gradually modified the company's structure. By 1936, the industrial and commercial activity of Nestlé and Anglo-Swiss Condensed Milk Co. was very limited in comparison with the considerable interests it had acquired in companies manufacturing or selling its products. There were more than twenty such companies around the world at this time: in Argentina, Australia, Austria, Belgium, Brazil, Chile, Cuba, Czechoslovakia, Denmark, France, Germany, Great Britain, Holland, Italy, Japan, Mexico, Norway, Portugal, South Africa, Spain, Yugoslavia, and the U.S. Apart from the Swiss market—which the company supplied itself—the Nestlé and Anglo-Swiss Condensed Milk Company now possessed only a handful of manufacturing and marketing firms scattered abroad. All the requirements for transforming Nestlé and Anglo-Swiss into a holding company were now met.

LOOKING AHEAD TOWARD THE FUTURE, NESTLÉ RESTRUCTURED, CREATING TWO HOLDING COMPANIES: NESTLÉ AND ANGLO-SWISS HOLDING CO., LTD., IN 1936 AS WELL AS UNILAC, INC.

Nestlé and Anglo-Swiss only needed to create a company responsible for production and marketing in Switzerland. Nevertheless, owing to the firm's size and the precariousness of the international situation, this was not a sufficient guarantee that Nestlé would continue to expand. The highest echelons of Nestlé were of the opinion that another company—this one domiciled outside of Switzerland—would be better equipped to handle the task of creating and launching new products targeted especially at U.S. and overseas markets. This holding company would assume responsibility for Nestlé's interests in the Western Hemisphere.

A number of decisions bearing on these plans were approved by the shareholders at the extraordinary shareholders' meeting held on November 27, 1936. Three important moves were made during that meeting: a Swiss company, Nestlé and Anglo-Swiss Condensed Milk Company, Ltd.—which later was to became today's Société des Produits Nestlé S.A.—was established; the parent company was transformed into a holding company, Nestlé and Anglo-Swiss Holding Company, Ltd.; and a second holding company, Unilac, Inc., was created by a number of Nestlé's overseas associates. Unilac's headquarters were in the Republic of Panama, where Nestlé and Anglo-Swiss had been present for many years. It remained in existence until 1985.

The operating company for the Swiss market—with a capital of SFr. 5,000,000—had its headquarters at Vevey; it assumed responsibility not only for the manufacturing and marketing activities carried out previously by the parent company, but also acquired all of the latter's trademarks throughout the world, since these could not be the property of a holding company

SHARE CAPITAL WAS REDUCED FROM SFR. 116,000,000 TO SFR. 58,000,000 IN 1937, THE YEAR OF LOUIS DAPPLES'S DEATH.

at the time. As for the staff, it became subordinate to the new company's management, with the exception of certain senior managers who remained under the control of the holding company, with headquarters in Cham and Vevey. This was an important step, although at first, it appeared merely to have given formal recognition to a situation that had existed de facto in any case. Having transformed itself into a holding company with a capital of SFr. 116,000,000, Nestlé was now in a position to make its next important move. In 1936, Unilac's capital totaled $7,500,000 and consisted of both common stock and founders' shares, both of which ensured those possessing them the right to participate in company profits. The founding companies held the founders' shares; while common stock, representing Nestlé's investment in the new company, was distributed free of charge to Nestlé shareholders. Unilac shares were distributed in such a way that the holder of each share of Nestlé stock (whose par value was SFr. 200 as of December 31, 1936) received a $12 share of Unilac stock bearing the same serial number and attached to the corresponding Nestlé certificate.

These structural changes facilitated operation of the firm. The company's cash-flow situation was excellent, though owing to international tensions, it became increasingly difficult and hazardous to utilize such funds. Therefore, in 1937, the board of directors decided that it was advisable to reimburse shareholders, which would reduce share capital without hampering company expansion. The shareholders agreed to reduce the capital from SFr. 116,000,000 to SFr. 58,000,000 by halving the par value of each SFr. 200 share and ensuring an immediate cash payment of SFr. 100 per certificate. In addition, each share would be accompanied by an amortization certificate, thus enabling shareholders to participate in distributions up to a maximum of SFr. 12.50 per year. This was to expire, however, as soon as distributions totaled SFr. 200, i.e., the equivalent, per shareholder, of the company's 1922 reduction in capital.

Maurice Paternot (1891–1973)

This move would certainly have met with the approval of Louis Dapples, who had died suddenly a few months earlier, since it was totally in keeping with his way of thinking. That great financier and businessman died, where he was born, at Genoa on July 31, 1937, at the age of seventy, after returning from a trip to the U.S. Widespread repercussions were felt as a result of the loss of a man who had restored the company's financial health with consummate skill, who had masterfully negotiated the merger with P.C.K., and who was the first to launch the idea for the product that was eventually to become Nescafé. The untiring Dapples had assumed enormous responsibility. For fifteen years, he had worked to form a top-level team of associates with proven track records. Among these were Edouard Muller, marketing specialist; Maurice Paternot, production and financial expert; Gustave Huguenin, head of the technical department; and André Perrochet, legal expert. Such men had assisted Dapples in his work of reorganizing the company—infusing it with new life and a new spirit—with remarkable competence.

EDOUARD MULLER WAS ELECTED CHAIRMAN. THE COMPANY COMPLETED ITS REORGANIZATION IN 1938, IN THE MIDST OF INTERNATIONAL TENSIONS.

The board of directors elected Edouard Muller, the former chief executive, to the position of company chairman; Carl J. Abegg, an important businessman from Zurich, became vice-chairman; and Maurice Paternot took over the duties of chief executive upon Muller's election as chairman. The destiny of Nestlé was now firmly in the hands of a group of vigorous young men who had matured with the organization and knew all of its intricacies. The sole representative of the prewar generation remaining on the board was Auguste Roussy. The Great Reaper had indeed decimated the old brigade of Cham and Vevey as well as the the directors of the chocolate industry: men like Wilhelm Caspar Escher (vice-chairman) in 1929, Fred Page in 1930, Jean-Jacques Kohler in 1921, Auguste Mayor (vice-chairman) in 1933, and Alexandre Cailler (vice-chairman) in 1936. Alfred Liotard-Vogt had withdrawn from the board as early as 1922; and Benjamin Rossier, the banker whose discussions with Escher had led to the merger of 1905, had had to vacate his seat on the board due to poor health.

In 1938, Nestlé had behind it the strength of more than one hundred factories around the world: in Panama, Japan, Mexico, the U.S., Western Europe, and Great Britain. The Barra Mansa plant increased its production capacity in Brazil; the Sancti Spiritus plant its capacity in Cuba; the Los Angeles (Chile) factory (built to support the efforts of the factory at Graneros) its capacity in Chile. Two more condensed milk plants were acquired in Denmark. Even in Spain, where the Spanish Civil War was coming to an end, there were plans for opening two new production centers in 1939. And projects for the construction of factories in Jamaica, Colombia, Venezuela, and Peru were about to be realized.

Edouard Muller (1885–1948)

However, world events were already casting long shadows over such plans. As they traveled quite extensively, it was not hard for Nestlé's directors to perceive that the international situation was growing steadily worse, which foreboded considerable problems for an international concern marketing its products in the four corners of the earth, wherever economic freedom prevailed. Fortunately, it was easy to take precautionary measures, since Nestlé and Anglo-Swiss Holding Company and Unilac, Inc., though distinct companies, were like communicating vessels. At the moment of the Sudeten Crisis in 1938, the company already possessed adequate manufacturing facilities to cater for more than the usual demand, and there were contingency plans ready to be put into effect in case of difficulties with any important markets.

In the midst of the political tensions that peaked the year Nescafé was launched, the Nestlé Day Nursery, founded by Louis Dapples, was inaugurated at Vevey. Three years earlier, Nestlé had contributed to the building of a hospital bearing its name in Lausanne. Nestlé's activities have always been aimed at helping to improve public health; in this connection, the firm has always heeded the advice of physicians and scientists. And thus, it was only natural that the company should engage in humanitarian activities of this kind.

A year prior to the outbreak of World War II, the management of Nestlé and Anglo-Swiss completed its reorganization of the company, improving communications among the various markets, strengthening the legal status of firms producing or marketing Nestlé's products throughout the world, establishing a purchasing policy for raw materials and a more efficient system of monitoring inventory to avoid a recurrence of the problems encountered during World War I. Despite the difficulties Nestlé initially encountered in its attempt to integrate chocolate manufacturers into the company following the 1929 merger with P.C.K., a certain esprit de corps had developed during years of working together. Although it was not yet as large as it was to become by the end of the twentieth century, Nestlé had already attained its critical mass. By the eve of World War II, it was capable not only of achieving commercial success, but also of fulfilling an important role in the service of the international community.

The Nestlé Day Nursery, Vevey, Switzerland, opened in 1938

Chapter V

1939–1947

A Devastated Europe Struggles to Recover from World War II

Nestlé and Maggi Form a Sweet and Sour Union

IN 1939 THE MOST DEVASTATING WAR IN HISTORY BEGAN IN POLAND AND SPREAD TO WESTERN EUROPE IN 1940...

World War II and Its Troubling Aftermath (1939–1947)

☐ *The year was 1947. The most devastating war of all times had ended two years earlier. What follows is a brief discussion of that war, as someone experiencing it firsthand might have perceived it.*

On September 1, 1939, without warning, German troops crossed the Polish border. Two days later, France and Great Britain—followed by all the Commonwealth countries—declared war on Germany. The rest of the world watched helplessly while Poland was crushed, with Russia moving in to help carve up the spoils. With the most important military operations concentrated on the Baltic coast, the German and French armies watched each other closely without engaging in any significant battles. Even while Finland, which had tenaciously fended off the Red Army for a time, was forced to sign the Peace of Moscow in 1940, the so-called phoney war was still going on along the fortified Franco-German border. The British and French remained vigilant, dominating the seas despite the appearance of a powerful fleet of German submarines.

On April 9, 1940, Germany went on the offensive again, invading Denmark, and occupying Norwegian ports and territory in order to prevent the Allies from cutting off the Reich's crucial iron supply route at Narvik. On May 10, the Wehrmacht *began a westward offensive, not only against France, with whom Germany was officially at war, but also against Belgium, the Netherlands, and Luxembourg, which were neutral countries. On May 14, Holland surrendered, with Belgium doing likewise shortly thereafter.*

On May 28, British and French troops from the Northern Army began the evacuation of Dunkirk. The first part of the campaign was having political effects. The queen of the Netherlands fled to England, the king of Belgium, Leopold III, was taken prisoner, and the French president, Reynaud, appointed Marshal Pétain vice-president of the Council of Ministers and replaced General Gamelin by General Weygand as commander in chief of the French Army. On June 5, the Germans pushed toward the Seine. On the 10th, the republican government withdrew from Paris. On that same day, Mussolini declared war on France and on Britain. On the 14th, General Guderian and his German tanks pushed through Weygand's lines to the Marne. Paris and Verdun fell on that

TO THE BALKANS IN 1941...

same day, and Besançon, Belfort, and Epinal two days later. On the 18th, Rommel reached Cherbourg. Half a million men were surrounded in Alsace-Lorraine and subjected to heavy German attacks. Meanwhile, Lyon was taken and the Rhone valley opened to advancing German troops. One hundred forty German divisions were moving through France, met at every turn by throngs of French and Belgian refugees. Total chaos reigned. The French government, meeting at Bordeaux, rejected a proposal from Churchill to unite with Britain, but also balked at demanding an armistice. Marshal Pétain's government soon took over. On June 17, the old soldier broadcast a request for an armistice, and on the 22nd, an agreement was signed in the very same clearing in the Compiègne forest where imperial Germany had capitulated in 1918. France was occupied as far as the Loire, but was able to keep its colonies and navy. On June 24, an armistice was signed between France and Italy.

The blitzkrieg was over in France on June 25, when Pétain's government began pursuing a policy of rapprochement with Germany. But the war dragged on, just as General de Gaulle had predicted, and on June 18, he issued his call from London for resistance. Britain, still commanding the world's most powerful navy, as well as a strong fleet of fighter planes, had been building up its army since the Battle of Dunkirk; under the strong leadership of Churchill, the British government refused any compromise with Germany. Not long afterward, it won the Battle of Britain. At the same time, the Russians, in accordance with an agreement signed with Germany, in 1939, were taking over the Baltic states and annexing Romanian Bessarabia.

In 1940, President Roosevelt promised to supply Britain with fifty destroyers in exchange for permission to establish military bases in Newfoundland, Bermuda, the Bahamas, Jamaica, Trinidad, and Guyana. Germany's response to this was to sign a tripartite pact with Italy and Japan. Angered by Britain's defiance, Hitler tried to reach an agreement with Spain to block Gibraltar. At the same time, Mussolini, frustrated in his desire to annex parts of France—among them, Nice and Savoy—ordered his troops stationed in Albania to attack Greece. Italian troops also took Sidi Barrani and Salūm, in British-held Cyrenaica.

In 1941, the Italian Army was forced to evacuate Eritrea, while suffering serious setbacks in Greece. Hitler came to Mussolini's aid. In the Bal-

TO NORTH AFRICA, THE U.S.S.R, AND, FINALLY, TO JAPAN AND THE U.S.

kans, where Albania was now controlled by Italy, every country except Greece had joined the tripartite pact by the end of March. Yugoslavia, the last country to join the Axis alliance, changed governments—and foreign policies—immediately after signing the agreement. On April 6, at dawn, Hitler ordered the bombardment of Belgrade and German troops descended on Yugoslavia and Greece. That campaign ended in May with the occupation of Crete. The opening of this new front in the Mediterranean pushed the Reich into Africa, where Rommel's Afrika Korps *began operations in Libya with the ultimate goal of taking Egypt. Meanwhile, Allied naval forces managed to sink the* Bismarck, *Germany's most powerful battleship. On June 22, 1941, Hitler suddenly turned on the Red Army, ostensibly to prevent an attack from the east, but probably also with a view to snatching up the Ukraine's grain reserves. Three million German soldiers, seconded by Finnish divisions to the north and Hungarian and Romanian troops to the south, invaded the U.S.S.R. But Stalin's scorched earth policy, coupled with the onset of winter, finally stopped the German troops on December 6, before they could reach Moscow.*

It was during the month of December, 1941, that the war became a truly global affair. Japan, in search of natural resources and new markets and deprived by American economic measures of essential imported goods—oil in particular—staged an attack on the American Navy. On December 7, Japanese bombers suddenly descended upon American ships anchored in Pearl Harbor. The next day, Hitler, too, declared war on the U.S., fully aware of the mid-ocean summit, in August, 1941, between Roosevelt and Churchill, in which the two leaders had reaffirmed their common goals in the Atlantic Charter and in which Roosevelt had underscored his resolve to protect Allied convoys. This was immediately followed by more diplomatic flurries and a new round of land, air, and sea battles. Japan, which soon occupied Thailand and Indochina and already controlled parts of China and all of Korea, Manchuria, and Formosa, now embarked on a successful campaign to take the Philippines, Malaysia, Indonesia, Burma, northern New Guinea, the Marianas, and the Bismarck Islands. In 1942, Germany stepped up its submarine operations. Britain liberated Ethiopia and restored the emperor to the throne, then it moved to occupy Iraq, Libya, Syria, and Iran. In Africa, Rommel counterattacked in January and recaptured

Cyrenaica. In the U.S.S.R., the Wehrmacht, *having spent a rigorous winter blocked outside Moscow and Leningrad, launched attacks, in May, on Crimea, the Caucasus, and on the Don. But thanks to a decision by Churchill and Roosevelt (who had met in Washington early in the year) to give priority to operations in Russia, the Red Army was receiving substantial assistance in the form of arms. Germany responded by intensifying its submarine attacks against Allied convoys en route to the Russian port of Murmansk. In Africa, Rommel reached the Egyptian border. At that moment, in July, 1942, the signatories to the tripartite pact, Japan in Asia and the Axis countries in Europe, were at the height of their power.*

DESPITE INTENSE SUBMARINE WARFARE, THE AXIS ARMIES BEGAN TO RETREAT. ITALY SURRENDERED IN 1943.

But the moment was short-lived. Already, Japan had suffered its first naval defeat in centuries, losing the Battle of Midway to American forces in the Pacific. At the same time, the Axis powers were suffering from stepped-up Allied air raids, both at home and in occupied territories, resulting in heavy damage to their industrial centers.

The Battle of Guadalcanal began in August, 1942; by November, Japan had lost it. After the autumn of 1942, Japanese forces advanced no further on land or sea. In Africa, following Montgomery's victory at El Almein on October 23–28, Rommel began to retreat. On November 8, American troops suddenly landed in North Africa. Germany responded by occupying the whole of France. Early in 1943, Russian troops stopped the Germans and later defeated them at Stalingrad. In the middle of that year, German submarines lost the Battle of the Atlantic to Allied convoys.

The morale of the Axis dictators was low, and their prestige tarnished. In July, 1943, in Italy, the Fascist Grand Council overthrew Mussolini, just as the Allies, having driven their adversaries out of Africa in the Battle of Tunis, were landing in Sicily. The Badoglio government, which had succeeded Mussolini's, began secret negotiations with the British and Americans. In September, while the Germans were disarming the Italians from Greece to France, an armistice was signed between Italy and the Allies, and Eisenhower's troops landed at Salerno. Mussolini, who had been imprisoned by his compatriots, was liberated by a parachute commando sent by Hitler and proceeded to proclaim the short-lived "Social Republic" in northern Italy.

Meanwhile, the Germans, who had lost ground on the eastern front, were forced to pull back from the Caucasus, Orel, Kharkov, Kiev, and the

THE ALLIES MET IN TEHRAN.
IN 1944, GERMAN TROOPS WERE ON THE DEFENSIVE;

area east of the Dnieper. It was becoming clear that Germany, whose heavily damaged industry was faltering and whose armies were shrinking in size, was sure to lose the war if it did not direct its efforts toward producing new weaponry—namely, rockets, and, especially, the atomic bomb—which was as yet little known except to a handful of military experts.

In November, 1943, Churchill, Stalin, and Roosevelt met at Tehran and discussed the establishment of what was to become, after the war, the United Nations. Also at that meeting, Stalin made a vague promise to attack Japan, and the two Western powers agreed to open a second front in Normandy in 1944. It was decided that part of eastern Prussia would go to the U.S.S.R. and that Poland would receive some German territory in exchange for land it would lose to Russia. In Yugoslavia, the Allies would give their support to the communist leader, Tito, and not to the royalist Mihailovitch.

At the same time that Britain was losing influence in Central Europe, the Soviet Union was spawning a group of small governments and committees in exile whose communist leaders were preparing to take over in Poland, Hungary, Bulgaria, and East Germany.

The retreat of German troops in Russia and in Africa, the fall of Italy, the increasingly devastating air raids, and the reign of terror established wherever the National Socialists were in power all acted to revive and reinforce resistance movements in the occupied countries. By 1944, German leaders had to contend with resistance from every quarter, even within Germany itself. In Russia, partisans hampered the retreat of German troops. Furthermore, even while retreating troops approached the borders of countries friendly to the Reich, the loyalty of those countries was becoming questionable. Hitler was compelled to intervene militarily in Budapest in order to prevent Hungary from defecting. And in France, northern Italy, Belgium, the Netherlands, and Luxembourg, local resistance to German occupation now constituted a veritable secondary war parallel to the one dragging on in the trenches. Indeed, resistance persevered despite brutal reprisals, such as Lidice in Czechoslovakia and Oradour in France, which had already become engraved in the minds of men as unforgettable historical tragedies. In Warsaw, the popular uprising of October, 1944, was crushed by the SS. And, to add to the confusion, rival resistance groups clashed openly in

Yugoslavia and in Greece. Tito finally defeated Mihailovitch, and Greece was paralyzed by civil war until 1950.

In 1944, the Soviet high command, with its powerful artillery forces and highly organized troops, began a series of offensives. Russian troops reconquered the Ukraine and Crimea and reached western Prussia, Poland, and Romania, indirectly causing their adversaries to evacuate Greece. At the same time, Rome was liberated by the Allies in June, 1944, following fierce battles in February at Anzio and Monte Cassino.

Thus, by June, 1944, the Allies were ready for the kill. At dawn on June 6, after intensive air and sea bombardment, Allied troops landed in Normandy under the command of General Eisenhower, chief commander of Allied forces in Europe. By July 25, the Germans could no longer check the advance of Allied troops, backed up by members of the French resistance movement; a second landing in southern France, on August 15, quickened the retreat of the German Army. On August 25, General Leclerc's tanks rolled into Paris and the next day de Gaulle arrived. Allied divisions advanced to Brussels and Antwerp, and when German troops tried to resist in the Ardennes, it was too late. The new arms that were supposedly going to save the day for the Germans arrived too late. And the June bombardment of London by Hitler's V2 rockets was abortive. In July, 1944, an attempt by Hitler's German opponents to assassinate him failed as well. The war dragged on, and the massacres that followed Count von Stauffenberg's unsuccessful attempt to assassinate Hitler cost the lives of many foresightful civilians and military officials such as Rommel. Meanwhile, in German concentration camps, the brutal extermination of innocent Jews and gypsies continued relentlessly.

JAPAN, TOO, WAS WEAKENING. IN 1945, THE ALLIES WERE VICTORIOUS IN EUROPE...

In Asia, Japan's land, sea, and air forces had already lost Guam, the air battle of Formosa, and the largest naval battle in history, near the island of Leyte in the Philippines. In October, 1944, only the kamikazes, or suicide aircraft, still posed a real threat to Allied warships. The Philippines were now within reach of Anglo-American forces. By the end of 1944, in Asia and in Europe, the Allies were preparing to strike the final blow.

1945 was a year of stark contrasts: total devastation for the vanquished, exuberant joy for the victors. Never before, it seemed, had the planet been so totally shaken in so short a time by the destruction of cities and widespread suffering. When peace finally came—a moment of

AND THEN IN ASIA.

rejoicing for some and despairing for others—the awful, final toll of the nightmare became painfully clear: 30,000,000 civilians and 10,000,000 soldiers dead; 15,000,000 others killed in concentration camps; and $1,000,000,000,000 in direct and twice as much in indirect costs.

1945 saw the collapse of Germany and Japan, followed shortly by that of their allies and the end of their occupation of neighboring countries. Finland, Bulgaria, Hungary, and Romania had already surrendered, and Croatia, Slovakia, Mussolini's "Social Republic," and Manchukuo disappeared from the map. Albania, Belgium, Denmark, France, Greece, the Netherlands, Luxembourg, Norway, Poland, and Czechoslovakia regained their independence as the last Japanese troops pulled out of Burma, Borneo, China, Korea, Indochina, Indonesia, Malaysia, the Philippines, and Thailand. Austria remained occupied by the Big Four. Estonia, Lithuania, and Latvia had already lost their autonomy at the beginning of the war.

Also in 1945, the month of April was marked by the deaths of three of the war's main protagonists. The euphoria of victory was shattered for Americans by the death of President Roosevelt, on April 12; his successor, Harry Truman, was faced with the enormous task of post-war recovery. Eighteen days later, on the 30th, Hitler and Goebbels committed suicide in their Berlin bunker. Mussolini had been executed near Milan two days earlier. On April 22, the victorious armies—the Soviets returning from Poland and Bohemia and the Western Allies emerging from France and Belgium—shook hands on the Elbe. On May 1, the Germans in Italy surrendered, followed by the unconditional surrender of the remaining fragments of the German Army.

In August, American air and naval forces, having made their way across the Pacific from island to island, reached Japan. The fatal decision was made: on August 6, the atomic bomb was dropped on Hiroshima; on the 9th, Nagasaki was also bombed. The atomic age had descended upon humanity.

The Germans had officially surrendered on May 7; on August 14, it was Japan's turn. Everyone laid down his arms. Now it was up to political leaders and diplomats to pick up the pieces. They had already accomplished a great deal: in February, an ailing Roosevelt, uneasy Churchill, and shrewd Stalin had met in Yalta. The result was the division of the world into zones of influence and of Germany into zones of occupation. In addition, trials were to be held for war criminals, reparations imposed on the former Reich, and free elections held in Eastern Europe. Five months later, in August, on the eve of the bombing of Hiroshima, Stalin, Truman, and Churchill—succeeded by Attlee—met in Potsdam. There they finalized their policy toward Germany, gave Silesia to Poland, and made the Saar a French protectorate. Königsberg was to become Kaliningrad and Berlin a divided city within a divided country. Between the summit meetings of Yalta and Potsdam, the United Nations was born in San Francisco on June 26.

THE VANQUISHED WERE SUBJECTED TO OCCUPATION.

The war was finally over; now came the task of reconstruction. After the two armistices of 1945, people's thoughts first turned to demobilization, but this was not accomplished everywhere as quickly as in the U.S. The vanquished countries were now under occupation; the victors, in Europe and Asia, were exhausted. All of them, with the exception of Britain, were faced with severe shortages of food. The warring nations whose territories had escaped military operations were in the strongest position. But in every country, the main objective was to rebuild—to emerge from the shadow of murderous destruction into the daylight, however dim it might seem at first. The victors of the war declared their solidarity with one another, while the conquered nations were dismembered. And with the disappearance of the Axis powers, the world looked forward to a new era of unity. In fact, unbeknownst to them, the world would remain divided, initially into halves, i.e., between East and West, and ultimately into thirds, with the emergence of the Third World.

When the fighting ended, every country in the world was living under a wartime economy; no one escaped the hardships of rationing nor government control over industry and commerce, and the needs of each individual were subordinate to those of the military.

Some countries remained powerful despite heavy war losses, rich in spite of the high cost of war, and peaceful despite the burdens of victory. Their military strength remained unimpaired, and the conversion to a peacetime economy was a clear, if not easily attainable, challenge. The United States was one of those countries. The war had elevated it to a dominant position both in terms of world industry and finance. Its gross national product went from $81,600,000,000 in 1940 to $181,200,000 000 in 1945. At the moment of the two armistices, in

THE VICTORS WERE SOON DIVIDED. DEVELOPING COUNTRIES BEGAN CLAIMING INDEPENDENCE.

1945, the U.S. controlled the Pacific zone and Middle Eastern oil pipelines and maintained air and naval bases on five continents. U.S. production had doubled in five years. At the same time, the other most important victor in the war, the Soviet Union, though ravaged by war, was stretching its powerful arms toward its neighbors as well as its European adversaries. The Soviet political system began imposing itself on the Balkans and the eastern part of Germany, then on Poland and Czechoslovakia.

The postwar world was soon split into two. What Churchill, speaking in Fulton and then in Zurich in 1946, called the "Iron Curtain," had fallen in 1945 across the center of Europe; while in China, civil war led to a communist victory in 1949. Two ideologies soon confronted each other openly. On the one hand, the "capitalists" sought to reconcile free enterprise and a market economy with increasing government control; on the other, the "socialists" espoused a Marxist-Leninist single-party system. This dichotomy was exacerbated by the effects, in Europe as well as in Asia, of growing opposition between the two superpowers, one of which, while striving to exclude the other from its sphere of influence, was also driven by an evangelistic desire to spread the "good news" of the revolution. For the Soviet Union, in 1945, there was no peace possible, nor was it possibile to achieve a communist society as long as "war-mongering imperialism" existed in the world. It was therefore necessary to destroy capitalism—considered to be at the root of imperialism—by revolutionary means. The U.S.S.R. thus established itself as a revolutionary power whose goal was to conquer not only the United States but the entire non-communist world.

These two superpowers—still officially allies, but, in fact, already ideological enemies—each had loyal followers. Great Britain, bled white by the war, but justifiably proud of its heroic record during it, and France, defeated in Europe, but reborn five years later, were heavily indebted to the United States.

The European colonies had seen the Japanese, during their conquests of 1941–42, destroy the myth of white supremacy. As soon as the Japanese withdrew, colonies in Asia began proclaiming their independence. The colonial powers had neither the manpower nor the funds to put up much opposition, plagued, as they were, by postwar restrictions and shortages (of food in particular). From 1946 on, and increasingly during the next twenty years, many young countries proclaimed their independence, first in Asia, and later in Africa. Most of them had to suffer hard times in order to fulfill their dream of economic as well as political autonomy.

In 1947, the countries hardest hit by the war were still suffering from extreme hardship: Germany, Poland, the Balkans, and Japan had experienced the worst aftereffects; Italy was hard hit; and France and the Netherlands were struggling to avoid the worst. The vanquished were faced with a totally uncertain future, excessively devalued currencies, thousands of homeless refugees, and a military occupation that was projected to last for at least twenty years.

Peacetime conditions did return—albeit slowly—in Europe, where at least people had the luxury once again to worry about the future instead of living from hand to mouth.

On the other side of the Atlantic, 1945 marked the beginning of an economic boom that astonished economic pessimists. Stalin had miscalculated when he assumed that a postwar economic depression would render the U.S. incapable of coming to the assistance of non-communist countries, but he did not give up hope.

THE U.S. ENJOYED RENEWED PROSPERITY. EUROPE NURSED ITS WOUNDS...

American isolationism was a thing of the past. The country's newfound prosperity, in fact, pushed it to extend a helping hand to Western Europe in the form of the Marshall Plan. The transition from a wartime to a peacetime economy was a smooth one, except for some strikes in 1946. When the government deregulated industry and began encouraging civilian production once again, consumer demand, unsatisfied during the war, was able to absorb nearly everything the country could produce. Virtually all competition—British in Latin America, German in Europe, and Japanese in the Far East—had disappeared. And because of industrial standardization and rationalization, prices of American goods were lower than those of other countries. The dollar thus remained stable.

While the American postwar economy was booming, Europe was recovering slowly and painfully. In 1946, production was lower than in 1937. Consumer demand, no longer subject to wartime restrictions, and stimulated by reconstruction, greatly exceeded supply. Prices went up sharply. At the end of 1947, for example, they had nearly doubled their 1937 level in Great Britain, tripled it in Belgium, increased twelve-fold

AND THE COLD WAR BEGAN.

in France, and fifty-fold in Italy. In Germany, the economy was in a shambles: on the black market, a pound of coffee cost 500 marks and a single egg cost 12 marks.

Moreover, in Europe, the much awaited peace of 1945 had quickly evolved into a cold war, with its alternating periods of hope and apprehension.

In Greece, armed struggle between communists, supported by Stalin, and royalists, backed by the British and Americans, incited President Truman to make one of America's most important postwar policy decisions. On March 12, 1947, assuming responsibility for seconding a militarily and financially weak Britain in its support of the Greek and Turkish governments, Truman announced his plan to aid free countries in their struggle against poverty and hardship. Soon afterward, Truman's secretary of state, George Marshall, announced his plan for aid to European countries. The plan was well received by all the countries of Western Europe; the Eastern bloc refused (after a brief period of hesitation on the part of Czechoslovakia). We will examine more closely, in the next chapter, the way in which the Marshall Plan helped the economy of Western Europe; for the moment, in order to form a general idea of the rate of European recovery, we shall simply mention the decreasing annual amounts granted to Western Europe under this plan: $4,785,000,000 during the first year; $3,380,000,000 the second year; $2,720,000,000 the third year; and $2,000,000,000 the fourth year.

In 1947, the countries of Western Europe slowly began their economic recovery. They had already come a long way since 1945. In that year, slow production on the Continent was exacerbated by a general economic crisis, both in the commercial and financial spheres, of which Great Britain was one of the chief victims. Production woes in France were considerable, despite the fact that the country had regained four-fifths of its industrial potential immediately after the war. There was a shortage of coal, factory equipment was in disrepair, and the transportation system was far from satisfactory. For lack of manpower, fertilizers, and equipment, the agricultural sector produced less in 1945 than in 1944. In addition, France had lost half its merchant fleet.

In 1947, Europe's privileged position on world commercial markets was a thing of the past. The Old World's former industrial powers had lost many of their markets during the war—countries overseas had built their own factories, and the Americans had moved into all markets. To remedy this problem, France opted to borrow and Britain to impose austerity measures. Neither solution proved effective: France went into debt and Britain had trouble exporting its three main products—coal, textiles, and machinery. As for Germany, even though it had become, since the end of the war, a kind of barometer for relations between the superpowers, it was totally stripped of its former might. Its economy was in ruins (all the more so as the Reich was divided into four separate zones). Indeed, owing to widespread destruction, the absence of skilled labor (especially in the mines), the task of repairing factories, a lack of both domestic and foreign raw materials, the need for spare parts, and an influx of refugees, the Ruhr was still suffering from near-famine conditions as late as 1947. This industrial heartland of Germany, now under British occupation, was totally cut off from the agricultural areas of eastern Germany—now controlled by the Soviets—as well as from its southern regions, which were occupied by the French and Americans. The Western Allies, who were opposed to Soviet interference in the affairs of the Ruhr, looked on as the Russians tightened an iron grip on their occupied zone. Finally, in 1947, London and Washington decided to link their zones into one economic entity so that the Ruhr could profit from agricultural supplies from Bavaria. In addition, London, Paris, and Washington began planning a reform of the German mark for the following year, to be followed by the establishment of the Federal Republic in 1949.

We shall return later to these events, for they had not yet occurred when Nestlé and the Anglo-Swiss Condensed Milk Company, spurred on by the success of their milk-based products, chocolate and Nescafé, began extending their range of products with the addition of those of the Maggi Company.

BUY MAGGI'S
PRODUCTS
„Cross-Star"
(Cross-Star)

Chapter V – Nestlé

1939–1947

Nestlé During World War II and in Its Aftermath

FROM 1939 ON, THE COMPANY SPLIT INTO TWO ORGANIZATIONS: ONE IN EUROPE AND ONE IN THE U.S. CHAIRMAN MULLER REMAINED IN THE U.S.

☐ The death knell of the Old World sounded in 1939. Nestlé braced itself for the storm and the perils that could confront a multinational company with headquarters in Europe and a staff appointed solely on merit. The firm had just experienced the severe turbulence caused by the high- and low-pressure areas, as it were, of the global economic climate. Soon it was to be faced with the fury of national, racial, and ideological prejudices, as well as religious hatred, all of which set nation against nation and continent against continent. The flexibility of the company's organization and its moral—even more than its financial—strength, coupled with its loyal staff, saved the Nestlé Company from destruction in a world torn apart as never before.

It had been decided that, when war became imminent, the headquarters at Vevey would be split in two and part of the senior executives would move to the U.S., as it was easier to supervise some of the distant markets from North America than from Switzerland. As we have seen, one of the company's main strong points lay in the numerous contacts between its various units in different parts of the world. It was necessary to divide up jobs that needed to be done while waiting for the political situation to improve. An administrative headquarters with all necessary services was set up at the Unilac offices in Stamford, Connecticut, fifty minutes by train from New York; and it was placed under the control of Edouard Muller, the chairman, and Gustave Huguenin, the chief executive. In Switzerland, Carl J. Abegg chaired board meetings throughout the war, while the business itself was run by Maurice Paternot, the chief executive, assisted by André Perrochet, the general manager, who was elected to the board in 1942. Thus, for nearly six years, the war turned Nestlé, for all practical purposes, into a company under dual control: in late summer of 1939, its chief executives were residing in one of two neutral countries: Switzerland or the United States.

André Perrochet (1891–1976)

The war, which spread as far as the Swiss border, hampered the activity of associated firms in Europe. Italy was still neutral, but France and Germany were locked in battle. And in that tragic autumn of 1939, it was impossible to foresee whether Switzerland was destined to become completely isolated or invaded by foreign troops. In order to safeguard assets, a task entrusted to it by the company's shareholders, the board issued guidelines to conserve assets and ensure a constant yield on them. The board decided that Edouard Muller, the chairman, should devote himself particularly to running the company's overseas business from the U.S., where he was living at the time. Carl J. Abegg, the vice-chairman, and Maurice Paternot, the chief executive, were to deal with European markets. Control of the firm's operations in North, Central, and South America was transferred to Unilac. Dividing up the business interests of the two groups—with each falling within the sphere of influence of one or the other of the two jointly owned holding companies—greatly simplified management's task under such exceptional circumstances. And as long as these prevailed, Stamford and Vevey continued to cooperate closely.

THE EFFECTS OF THE WAR ECONOMY WERE FELT IN EUROPE; AS WAS MOBILIZATION...

The repercussions of a war economy were felt throughout the world. Even the imports and exports of countries that remained outside the conflict were subject to control, their trade with certain countries was reduced, and their transport risks increased. Given the extraordinary budgets resulting from the war, governments began to become concerned over how, ultimately, they would pay for essential but nonproductive expenditures. Taxes were soon increased. Existing ones rose sharply, and new so-called war taxes were also introduced. One country after another restricted industrial and commercial profits by making them subject to special taxes. Some countries instituted a series of special national taxes, which often took the form of a wealth levy. As for exchange controls, which had been common enough even before the war, these became so widespread that countries like Switzerland, with convertible currency, became the exception rather than the rule. Most countries supplemented financial measures of this sort by a whole series of regulations, such as production quotas, price controls, import and export licensing, and limitations on the import of staple goods. Movement of such goods was hindered not only by a shortage of transport, but also by higher freight and insurance charges, not to mention trends toward total self-sufficiency that limited industry to the use of certain raw materials only.

Mobile canteen run by the Welfare Department of western Switzerland, 1940–1945

In Switzerland, as elsewhere in Europe, mobilization brought about a considerable manpower shortage. Nestlé's net profits for 1939 (consisting mainly of sales before the outbreak of the war) were approximately SFr. 6,000,000, SFr. 14,000,000 less than the 1938 figure. While the 1939 report to shareholders still included some information about operations in

AND DIFFICULTIES WITH COMMUNICATION AND SUPPLIES. SALES OF NESCAFÉ WERE ALSO AFFECTED. AND THE WAR AFFECTED THE TRANSFER TO SWITZERLAND OF COMPANY FUNDS.

Italy (e.g., an increase in the production capacity of the Abbiategrasso factory of Società Nestlé at Intra), the 1940 report confined itself to comments on Swiss market developments. The lack of communication—which was sometimes total—and wartime security regulations to which associated companies abroad were subject made it impossible to publish any reports on business in Europe (apart from Switzerland) until 1945. As the German Army advanced across Europe in 1940, some factories were impeded in their export efforts, while others were handicapped by occupation or martial law. With the advent of food rationing—to say nothing of food shortages—the problem of obtaining adequate supplies of raw materials soon became much more acute than that of marketing. Being unable to solve the problem of the scarcity of fresh milk, Nestlé's factory managers did their best to work out production programs consistent both with the limited availability of essential raw materials and with increasingly drastic wartime controls. The company's marketing specialists in Europe were busier cooperating in government rationing schemes than expanding sales.

As for Nescafé, launched in 1938, it had not benefited from the normal market conditions its immense potential deserved. As it was a new invention, the food regulations of many countries had to be changed to encompass its somewhat unusual product description. And legal battles were to be fought in Switzerland after the war over this revolutionary product. At the beginning of the war, Nestlé's Swiss-based company could justifiably claim to be the first to manufacture and sell canned instant coffee. The tremendous success of this product, which had been on the market for only a few months, was a just reward for all those who had worked painstakingly on its research and development. But, from 1930 on, restrictions on the importation of raw coffee beans served to limit production in Switzerland. In other European countries, the war economy was itself a considerable obstacle, though there the shortage of coffee beans was further complicated by the problem of delays in plant construction, as the war was holding up the installation of necessary machinery.

Employees at the Nestlé factory at Intra, Italy

Thus, of the twelve main European markets that were the responsibility of the general management at Vevey, it was the market supplied by Société des Produits Nestlé S.A. in Switzerland that was the least handicapped in the production of Nescafé. Nevertheless, as we shall see, it was in the U. S. that this new product was to make its most spectacular breakthrough and begin to acquire worldwide renown.

However, on the other side of the ocean, Unilac, Inc. was expanding, and additional plants were opened in Latin America.

During this period, it became increasingly difficult to transfer to Switzerland the modest earnings still being made abroad, due to the generalized use of clearing procedures; and, by the end of the war, transfers of this kind had become virtually impossible. Here it might be fitting to digress for a moment and praise the thousands of men and women of Nestlé all over the world who, throughout the war and sometimes at great personal risk, strove to safeguard company property, to come to the aid of the civilian population in countries at war or under occupation, to help the victims of oppression, and to distribute food to those who needed it most.

On the other side of the Atlantic, Unilac, Inc. was highly active, as most of its markets lay outside the various theaters of military operation. But Great Britain—which was also supplied by the management at Stamford—was suffering heavy enemy bombing. Shipping was being disrupted by submarine warfare, and restrictions were in force in most countries (not on the same scale as in Europe, where markets were supplied by the management in Switzerland, but disagreeable nonetheless). As hostilities spread, civilian operations diminished and government purchases increased.

From 1940 onward, the nations of Latin America received practically no further exports from Europe. But their need for canned milk was as great as ever. Immediately, Nestlé's chairman, Edouard Muller, and his team set to work increasing production capacity in those countries that manufactured Nestlé products, either by expanding existing factories or by constructing new ones. At the same time, the company's policy of setting up production centers in other countries was vigorously pursued. In due course, factories were established in Venezuela, Colombia, and Peru to supplement the output of those already established in Argentina, Brazil, Chile, Cuba, Jamaica, Mexico, and Panama. In this way, management was perpetuating the policy—or what might even be termed a tradition—that Nestlé had courageously pioneered more than thirty years earlier in Australia.

From Mexico to Argentina, various new products, such as chocolate, Milo, dietetic foods, and, finally, Nescafé were added progressively to

SALES OF NESCAFÉ IN THE U.S. SKYROCKETED IN 1941,

Nestlé's line of canned milk products that, as mentioned earlier, it first began to manufacture in Brazil. By the end of the war, thirteen manufacturing centers were in operation; and, by 1946, the number had grown to sixteen. Setting up and operating manufacturing centers in Latin America at that time required both great entrepreneurial spirit and patient effort. Agronomists, veterinary experts, and milk inspectors were needed to instruct the peasants in the advantages to be derived from planned cattle feeding, better land utilization, regular quality control, selective breeding, and proper farm hygiene. (The situation is no different today.) These experts that the management at Stamford sent out to Latin America had to cover vast distances in search of suitable areas for the gradual development of milk production. In spite of the careful precautions taken, unforeseen circumstances were always liable to arise and completely upset initial plans. In 1940, for example, it was decided to build a factory at Chiclayo, Peru. Between the start of construction and the start of production, war was to alter the economic situation: the peasants gave up cattle rearing in favor of growing sugar cane and rice, which they thought would be more profitable. As a result, the factory was soon short of milk, and a precondensing factory had to be set up in a dairy farming area at Cajamarca, some 180 miles away on the high plateau of the Andes. The mountain road from Chiclayo, at sea level, to Cajamarca crosses a pass nearly 10,000 feet high. So that even today, tank trucks with two reservoirs make a daily round trip, carrying fuel oil up to Cajamarca in one and bringing milk down to Chiclayo in the other. Another example of the resourcefulness of Nestlé's representatives is the history of the factory at Nata, Panama. Owing to an unexpected shortage of milk, it looked at one time as if the plant might have to be shut down. But Nestlé's experts conceived the idea of growing tomatoes there instead. The local farmers agreed with the suggestion; and, ever since, the factory in Panama has been producing both tomato juice and various other kinds of canned tomato products.

Tomato harvest at Nata, Panama, 1972

From that time on, the Latin American countries derived many benefits from Nestlé's policy of developing the dairy industry; they have not changed even today: since domestic production replaced imports, the drain on foreign currency reserves lessened; agricultural output developed more rationally; local labor was employed (more than 95 percent in the case of Nestlé) in the factories themselves and in such related sectors of the economy as milk, sugar, cocoa, and coffee production, as well as that of packaging. This

THE YEAR AMERICA ENTERED THE WAR.

improved standards of living, encouraged local trade, and increased revenue from taxes.

Yet all this activity in Latin America did not distract the attention of the management in the U.S. from other important questions: Nescafé, being a major one in its own right.

We have already mentioned that Nescafé was manufactured in the U.S. in 1939, one year after it was first launched on the Swiss market, when the U.S. was still a neutral country. Nestlé chose to start up production of Nescafé at its factory at Sunbury, Ohio. It was introduced gradually onto the market, as no one knew what the public's reaction would be to such a product. (After all, the company had had little experience with a product so far afield from the milk industry.) Before the first sales campaign began in July, 1940, Nestlé forecasted sales of 100,000 cases per year. By the end of the year, 6,000 cases per month were being sold in fifty-three of the ninety-three American cities with a population of more than 100,000. And annual production levels of Nescafé in the U.S. were to reach 1,000,000 cases three years later.

The Japanese attack on Pearl Harbor in December, 1941, put an end to American neutrality and roused the American government to action. Drastic economic measures were introduced, and the government focused its attention on the war economy: for the next four years, the needs of the armed forces took precedence over all others. Government agencies bought food products in bulk, and Nescafé was high on their lists. Along with evaporated milk, powdered milk, and special dietetic foods, Nescafé now began to reach all parts of the world. It was not the only instant coffee to do so, however. Wartime measures had considerably reduced the protection that patents afforded, and rival American firms began to exploit the Swiss invention on an international scale. Soon instant coffee was being marketed under various brand names, and Nestlé was powerless to prevent such activity. Instant coffee became a widely known beverage as a result of its use by the army, through its distribution to the civilian populations of liberated Europe and the impoverished

The flag Nestlé received from the U.S. Army and Navy in 1943 in recognition of the services rendered by Nescafé

BY 1944, NESTLÉ WAS ALSO A GLOBAL COFFEE MANUFACTURER. EVEN BEFORE THE WAR WAS OVER, MANAGEMENT HAD TO PLAN...

Mediterranean countries, and later to the countries of Asia freed from the Japanese yoke. (Nestea instant tea—another Swiss prewar invention—was created in the hope of following in the tradition of Nescafé, though it was far less successful.) Nescafé soon reached the countries of South America, where the idea of a water-soluble coffee in powdered form had first originated. And later, Nescafé was even to reach countries in which it was not officially allowed to be marketed for economic or political reasons: the Soviet Union, the countries of Eastern Europe, and, eventually, China.

In 1944, Nestlé's chairman, Edouard Muller, and his associates found themselves at the head of a global coffee concern. However, much of the technical know-how related to the production of Nescafé had all but passed into the public domain. And the company immediately gave considerable thought to its future position in Europe and elsewhere in the face of the fierce challenge from its American competitors. As early as this period, Nestlé already planned to extend the local manufacture of Nescafé—which had been produced for several years in Switzerland, Great Britain, France, Germany, South Africa, Argentina, and Mexico—to coffee-producing countries such as Peru, Brazil, Cuba, and Colombia as well as to Asia, Europe, Oceania, and Latin America.

Toward the close of the war, the general management at Stamford was able to review the achievements of nearly six years of operation. The Nestlé organization had maintained its performance in all countries overseas. In North America, government orders had been given such a high degree of priority that, for one year, the sale of Nescafé to the civilian population had been forbidden, and the entire output of the firm's factories (the original one at Sunbury and a new ultramodern one at Granite City, Illinois) had been earmarked for delivery to government agencies. With its unpleasant experience of 1918 in mind, Nestlé's management took the necessary steps to prepare for a rapid return to peacetime operations in America as the Allied victory approached. The Latin American markets had been—and still were—a source of satisfaction, though inflation was a constant danger. The strength of the markets of the British Commonwealth continued to meet the company's forecasts. It was essential, however, to look to the future and not just sit back in joyful anticipation of world peace. After Pearl Harbor, for example, it was no longer possible to supply all the areas in the Far East now occupied by Japanese forces. In Japan itself, manufacture and distribution networks had been under government control for three long years. Fortunately, certain other problems had fewer unknowns associated with them. Goods being shipped to distant countries that had been on the high seas when war broke out with Japan had been partially recovered. The last and most important reason for the management at Stamford to face the future with confidence was that none of Nestlé's factories in Asia had been destroyed.

The same confidence was shared by Nestlé's management at Vevey in spite of the increasingly furious battles in Europe and the gigantic Allied bombing, behind the lines, of the retreating Axis armies. But confidence may not be equated with blind optimism, and there was no avoiding the fact that difficulties of all sorts existed in the various European countries where Nestlé was active. However, the cash flows of the companies operating on the Continent were sufficient; and hence the situation bore no resemblance to that which had existed at the end of World War I.

THE RETURN TO A PEACETIME ECONOMY AND REPLENISH COMPANY FUNDS. 1945 BROUGHT ANXIETY, SOON FOLLOWED BY RENEWED HOPE. THE COMPANY REUNIFIED ITS MANAGEMENT...

The war was nearly over, and it was necessary to consider the use to which these liquid funds were to be put in the context of a peacetime economy. Management felt, quite rightly, that the transition period would call for heavy investment in production facilities and in new levels of raw materials and finished products. Additional funds were set aside to repair the damaged Tempelhof factory in Berlin and both the Lisieux factory in France and Nestlé's London offices at St George's House, which had been bombed. The company could look calmly forward to the end of the war. But a certain watchfulness was still essential, as all signs pointed to a period of chaos during the last few months of the war.

For Nestlé, the spring of 1945 was a time of anxiety. Early summer was a period full of unknown factors; and this was followed by six months of greater certainty. Peace had returned with its many blessings—and its many problems. It was also a year for reestablishing lost contacts. The staff of companies utilizing Nestlé processes in Germany, France, Italy, the Iberian Peninsula, and Scandinavia reforged their links with Switzerland. The European and American side of the company was now able to discuss plans and calculate losses or gains, with no fear of censorship. Several countries no longer had the same legal status; factories had been destroyed or temporarily put out of operation, but a great number of employees were still at their posts in spite of all the fighting, bombing, illness, injury, and prison camps.

In 1945, Nestlé's two management structures—one in the Old World and one in the New—could report that the war had not succeeded in arousing animosity between members of the staff. While their countries might have

REPAIRED DAMAGED FACTORIES, AND BEGAN TO EXPAND ONCE AGAIN, IN SPITE OF CERTAIN LOCAL PROBLEMS.

been at war, they had performed their duty to the nation without forgetting the ties of friendship and loyalty that bound them together as members of a single team working toward a common goal. Within the Nestlé Company, there were no signs of the rift that had divided Europe. While countless families had been decimated, nations torn asunder, and opinions diametrically opposed, the esprit de corps of Nestlé's staff had remained intact.

There is, of course, no denying the fact that the political orientation of each of the warring countries had influenced the behavior of Nestlé's international staff to a certain extent. But once the war was over, duty to the firm and a sense of the importance of their task in providing assistance to the world community took precedence over all other considerations. Exemplary national loyalty during hostilites did not stand in the way of renewing international friendships. In the belligerent countries, local management had looked toward tiny neutral Switzerland or toward the mighty U.S. in the hope (which turned out to be well-founded) that management would be able to maintain the firm's unity and build for the future. Their fellow employees in neutral countries saw the company's centralized management in Switzerland as the key to guaranteed stability and survival. As for the staff from Vevey, exiled, as it were, in America, they never forgot their brothers in Europe and elsewhere, isolated by the war or living in constant danger.

Reports received in 1945 showed that destruction in Europe had not affected the company's vital network of production facilities. However, there was no time to lose. Premises had to be rebuilt; the company needed to redefine its place in the peacetime economy, locate missing personnel, replace those who had disappeared, start up production and marketing once again, as well as provide financing for some of its worst-hit subsidiaries.

It was essential that positions gained in the Western Hemisphere should at least be maintained. There was an urgent need to reassemble, under one roof, the two central management structures which, for six years, had been forced to work in virtual isolation, influenced by different ways of thinking and operating.

Thus, it was a war-shaken but determined company that was to set out on the peaceful task of concentrating its efforts at a time when the West was increasingly open to its products and the East increasingly closed to them.

At the end of World War II, the tension between the Western world and the U.S.S.R., the emancipation of certain countries in the Southern

SOON IT WAS POSSIBLE TO SUPPLY MARKETS AND TO ENSURE EMPLOYEE TRAINING ONCE MORE.

Hemisphere, and the attitude of various nonaligned nations had not yet assumed major proportions. Nestlé was, of course, concerned with the dangers confronting its factories in Poland and Czechoslovakia, from which no news had been received for some time. (These were soon to become nationalized.) There was also anxiety over the Soviet authorities' dismantling of the Tempelhof factory in Berlin. But obviously, the most pressing problem was to get business going again in Europe.

European production facilities were struggling with obstacles ranging from a lack of fuel to a shortage of raw materials. There were no tires for the trucks used to collect milk; oil-fired boilers, which had been heated with wood during the war, were in a poor state; and, on top of this, there were the repercussions of local manifestations of nationalism. In order to get production going again, the various modifications and improvements that had been planned during the war had to be implemented immediately. Without halting manufacture, plants were enlarged or relocated, improved equipment was installed, and sources of power were adapted to meet new needs. Some factories were now geared simultaneously to turning out products in powdered form based on milk, coffee, or cocoa. For this purpose, spray-drying towers and bean roasting and coffee extraction equipment had to be added to the traditional equipment required for the production of canned milk products. Plants producing a single item were automated in order to overcome the problem of manpower shortages in the countryside, where the majority of Nestlé's factories had been built before the war.

Carrying out this complex project was particularly difficult, since specialized equipment manufacturers in postwar Europe were not yet in a position to supply the necessary machinery. As a result, Nestlé's engineers had to spend a good part of their time working with these manufacturers to modernize plants and simplify production processes.

The first major problem to be solved, with a view to resupplying the company's markets, was that of transport. To address the problem of severe undernourishment, there was an urgent need for baby food, with inadequate local production being supplemented, wherever possible, by imports. Rapid implementation of such programs was nevertheless held up by financial and bureaucratic obstacles resulting from the numerous wartime controls that remained in effect even after the fighting had ceased. At the same time, the functions of sales staff had to be quickly adapted to the new economic situation.

NESTLÉ BEGAN TO REORGANIZE AND TO CENTRALIZE ITS MANAGEMENT IN VEVEY IN 1947.

Of course, strict rationing was to remain in effect for several years in a number of countries, but it was generally known that the situation was bound to ease up in the end and that the work of the sales staff would not always be limited to distributing rations. A time would come when sales would have to be vigorously promoted and when products would no longer be sold virtually for cash, relying on only the most rudimentary forms of advertising. There could be no better way of revitalizing Nestlé's sales organization than by sending the staff back to school, as it were, to learn new sales techniques. Special training courses were organized for senior sales personnel; and schools for training future sales staff were set up first in France and Switzerland, and later in Germany, Britain, Spain, Italy, and Denmark. Eventually, the idea was to spread beyond Europe to Mexico, Australia, Brazil, and South Africa.

Thanks to this training, future salesmen who would one day be called upon to deal with retailers—key elements in the distribution system both in big cities and in the countryside, in the most densely populated as well as the most sparsely populated areas—would be fully briefed on Nestlé's range of products and the particular distribution techniques to be utilized with each. In addition, they were taught advertising, to overcome administrative complexities related to sales, and the importance of analyzing market conditions.

Nestlé accompanied such reforms with a general reorganization of the company; scientific research was intensified, and funds were replenished. To offset losses resulting from state ownership in certain countries, Nestlé also needed to take a new series of initiatives.

Chairman Edouard Muller, returning from the U.S., arrives at Cherbourg, France, in 1947

The first step in the process of reorganization of the company involved the centralization in Switzerland of the general management. The staff at Stamford returned to Vevey, thus restoring cohesion between the American and the European side of the company. During the war, the number of executives and staff working at the administrative center at Vevey had never exceeded 155, but two years after the Armistice, this number had already risen to 490. Steady progress was made toward the ad hoc establishment of a team of managerial staff, which, forty-five years later, was to total nearly 1,600 persons. Without the introduction of new talent into the executive ranks, there could be no true reorganization of the company's administrative structure, for mobilization and war had disrupted the regular selection and promotion process. A number of active and experienced Swiss and foreign men, in the prime of their lives, were appointed to new posts. All these had proven track records, holding positions of responsibility in various markets; they knew the languages, customs, and methods of work of the areas whose economic development they were to monitor from Vevey.

ONCE AGAIN, THE COMPANY PLACED EMPHASIS ON RESEARCH WHILE, AT THE SAME TIME, KEEPING ITS FINANCIAL SITUATION UNDER CONTROL.

In 1947, Edouard Muller returned to Europe. Muller had at his disposal a thoroughly reliable team, thanks to which the company could resume its expansion and take an even more active part than before in the trend toward industrial mergers, made necessary as a result of the rapid development of technology and the high cost of research and advertising (the ultimate weapons of modern business).

Food research specialists turned their attention toward both fundamental research and technological advances. The firm's technical, scientific, and consulting centers in Switzerland already provided great assistance, in the immediate postwar years, to companies manufacturing Nestlé products throughout the world (and particularly in Europe). Such services needed to be further developed in view of three decisive factors that would certainly have an influence on the development of the food industry: increased world population (resulting in increased food consumption) was the first factor, making it essential to devise more rational production methods; the second factor was the rising standard of living of the lower classes of the industrialized countries, calling for new types of food products suited to the needs of modern consumers; and the third factor was the changing social and economic conditions in the countries producing such commodities as cocoa, coffee, sugar, and spices. Therefore, management decided to boost R & D capacity by creating new laboratories and pilot plants at La Tour-de-Peilz, near Vevey.

In that same year, 1945, it was more important than ever, from a financial point of view, that the group should be able to start without delay on a flexible and rapid program of equipment modernization and sales expansion. Thanks to its healthy cash-flow situation—the result of sound financial policies—the company was able to embark on policies designed to increase its

THE MERGER WITH MAGGI TOOK PLACE IN 1947,

economic and commercial strength. Among the products that had to be remarketed as soon as possible, the most important were Nestlé baby foods and Nescafé. The latter had not enjoyed such favorable conditions in Europe as in the U.S., where there had been no significant problems with supplies of raw materials. The war had caused Nescafé—the only product of its kind when first introduced—to lose a surprise factor and had deprived Nestlé of the head start that a pioneering firm generally has on its competitors, particularly when—as in the case of the Nestlé Company—its reputation has been established. Nescafé would certainly have secured a dominant position in the U.S. in peacetime, but patent protection was much weaker during the war, which enabled competitors to gain a firm hold on the market. A shortage of raw coffee beans in Europe, during and after the war, had limited the success of Nescafé; and, after 1946, Nestlé's competitors were set to launch their own brands of instant coffee. The moment rationing ceased, a price war broke out, resulting in the inevitable problems that arise whenever a completely new product is launched simultaneously under several brand names.

In 1947, while still maintaining its previous activities, the Nestlé Company was to become involved in a range of food products no longer based exclusively on milk, cocoa, and coffee; namely, those produced by the Maggi Company. Nestlé wished to combine its eighty years of expertise as a food manufacturer—the work of several generations of dedicated men and women—with the ability of specialists in a related sector of the food industry. The company felt it could put the whole of its administrative structure, its sales organization, and its manufacturing centers to work extending its range of products. In so doing, Nestlé would be better able to increase its sales on those markets where its traditional line of products had not yet made sufficient headway. At the same time, it could step up the distribution of new products in areas where these were virtually unknown but where the company itself was a top performer.

Maggi test kitchen at the laboratory in La Tour-de-Peilz, 1950

The Nestlé Company thus embarked on a period of horizontal expansion, convinced that a steady improvement in the geographical distribution of its activities would be accompanied by the proper diversification of its production. The Nestlé laboratories had already marketed such products as Nescafé, Nescoré, and Nestea; and these were to be followed in the 1950s by various instant beverages such as Nesquik (or Quik). By taking an interest in other brands of food products, the company's management thought that it would be able to combine its experience on international markets with its new partner's expertise in a related branch of the food industry. And this was to be the case with Maggi.

THANKS TO THE NEGOTIATING SKILL OF C.J. ABEGG, VICE-CHAIRMAN OF NESTLÉ AND CHAIRMAN OF MAGGI.

There had, however, to be some point of contact between two firms before they could be brought closer to one another. Such a point of contact was provided by Carl J. Abegg, at the time, vice-chairman of Nestlé and Anglo-Swiss Holding Company, Ltd. The reader will recall that during Edouard Muller's period in the U.S. during the war, Abegg had chaired board meetings and shared in the work of the management team that had remained in Switzerland but whose regular duties had been considerably modified, owing to the difficulty and infrequency of contacts with other markets. Although communications between Vevey and Stamford had been just adequate enough to ensure a minimum of coordination between Nestlé's activities on both sides of the Atlantic, plans had nevertheless been made for the company's activities once the war had come to an end. Carl J. Abegg had played a leading role in this connection. His integrity, tact, and excellent reputation had all helped to maintain a degree of unity between the various components of the company. Even before he rose to become a leading businessman, Abegg had had close contacts with the two companies thanks to family connections. Although they had remained out of the limelight, his grandfather from Zurich and his father had both been industrialists who played an important role in Swiss business affairs. In George Page's time, the Abegg family had invested in Anglo-Swiss Condensed Milk Company. The Abeggs also had a substantial interest in the Maggi Company. Thus, a link was established between the two companies; and, eventually, this was to lead to Maggi's joining forces with Nestlé in 1947, thereby increasing Nestlé's turnover (which was unpublished at the time) from SFr. 833,000,000 in 1946 to SFr. 1,340,000,000 a year later.

Swiss ad for Nestea, 1950

THE MAGGI COMPANY EVOLVED INTO A LEADING MANUFACTURER OF SOUPS AND BOUILLON INVENTED BY JULIUS MAGGI, A FORMER MILLER...

Maggi's Rise to Industrial Prominence

☐ Owing to the structure of the Swiss economy—particularly the small domestic market—Swiss industrialists with vision and energy have always tended to look beyond the frontiers of their country with a view to exporting products made in Switzerland or to setting up factories abroad. This had happened in the case of Maggi as well as Nestlé. We shall relate how the Maggi Company, producing soups, bouillon concentrate, and seasonings secured an important position for itself first in northeastern Switzerland, later in other regions of that country, and eventually throughout all of Europe.

Maggi brand products were the result of the inventiveness of a single individual, who worked diligently in his own firm for more than thirty years, and who, inevitably, left his mark on it. In 1947, this individual had been dead for thirty-five years; but his successors continued in his footsteps with great success, at least until the end of World War II. The name of this inventive individual: Julius Michael Johannes Maggi, born in Frauenfeld in the canton of Thurgau in 1846. His father, of Italian origin, had become a naturalized Swiss citizen in that canton in 1839 and had established himself there as a miller. In 1861, when Julius—who had both the lively temperament of his father and the reflective nature of his mother's Swiss forebears—was only fifteen years old, his father Michael bought a mill at Im Hammer in Kempttal. In 1869, after qualifying as a miller himself, Julius took over his father's mill at the age of twenty-three. Previously, he had trained for two years in Hungary in an ultramodern mill belonging to a Swiss. (During this time, his father was busy operating his mill at Frauenfeld.) More active than studious, Julius Maggi was a capable and imaginative businessman by now. In 1872, he chose his first associate; and in 1874, Julius's adopted brother Eugen enlarged the joint-stock company of J. Maggi et Companie by contributing his mill in Zurich to the family business. Julius was far too aware of economic trends, however, to continue indefinitely with milling at a time when the industry was headed toward a difficult future. During his travels, Julius Maggi became keenly aware of the remarkable changes that were taking place in the European economy. During that era, many people began to consider the changes that the industrial age was bringing to the structure of their society. There were now many opportunities for women to work in factories that had sprung up virtually everywhere. Consequently, women no longer had the time they needed to prepare meals, which resulted in rapid

Julius Maggi (1846–1912)

modifications in the family diet. The problem became so acute that it had to be addressed by public authorities. Julius Maggi, a man with a large circle of friends, was introduced to the Swiss Public Welfare Society through one of its advisors, Dr. Fridolin Schuler. Schuler was both a physician and factory inspector and frequently had the opportunity to study the habits and living conditions of factory workers. Schuler had even taken a leading part in persuading the *Landsgemeinde* of Glarus to pass a Factory Act which, as mentioned earlier, foreshadowed a similar Swiss federal law in 1877.

WHO BECAME AN EXPERT ON LEGUMINOUS PLANTS. MAGGI STARTED MANUFACTURING HIS PRODUCT IN 1885.

At the annual meeting of the Swiss Public Welfare Society, held at Glarus in 1882, Schuler chose as the topic for discussion "The Diet of the Working Population and Its Deficiencies." In his thorough treatment of the problem, Schuler recommended that leguminous plants figure more prominently in people's diet because of their high nutritional value. The society commissioned Dr. Schuler to make a comprehensive study of the question. He needed the assistance of someone possessing the necessary practical and theoretical knowledge to produce and make available to the public easily digestible and quickly prepared leguminous plants. Julius Maggi was the perfect choice. Maggi set to work at once; not content with merely improving the methods of grinding peas and beans into flour, he immediately enlisted the help of chemists and physiologists, and after two years of work and tests, Maggi's powdered pea and bean soups were ready to be marketed. These were demonstrated by Schuler to the Swiss Public Welfare Society, and on November 19, 1884, an agreement was signed between the latter and the firm of Maggi & Companie, whereby the Swiss Public Welfare Society agreed to sponsor the new product and publicize it. In return, Maggi undertook to sell his product at a predetermined price "that could not be altered except by mutual consent."

Im Hammer mill, the former Maggi mill at Kempttal, ca. 1870

Maggi had done all his research at the Kempttal mill, and it was there that the large-scale manufacture of powdered pea and bean soup began in January, 1885. Maggi was rather more optimistic than his two associates, for, by 1886, they had left him. Maggi lost no time in forming a limited partnership with Emil Welti, who unhesitatingly contributed SFr. 200,000 to the

AFTER MANUFACTURING A RANGE OF SOUPS, MAGGI'S AROME WAS LAUNCHED IN 1889. THE FIRM, WHICH HAD BEEN REORGANIZED IN 1890, BENEFITED...

business. The object of the partnership was to "manufacture and sell common food products, specialty foods, and medicinal products."

The new firm attracted other partners: August Rübel brought to it SFr. 100,000 and Georg Stoll, SFr. 50,000. Both men were given the option to double their share in the business within a period of two years. These additional funds brought the capital of the partnership up to SFr. 700,000. In spite of this fresh capital, however, financial results were by no means outstanding. At the end of 1888, the firm's sales figure was barely half of that originally envisaged. This did not stop the incorrigible optimist Julius Maggi from setting up warehouses in Paris, Berlin, Singen (Germany), Vienna, Bregenz (Austria), and London within the first three years, nor from entering into an association with a firm in the U.S.

Pursuing his research, Maggi spent large sums of money on increasing his range of soups from the three (two types of pea soup and one type of bean soup) that had been introduced in 1886 to a wide variety by 1889. At the same time, he was perfecting his famous seasoning, a flavor-enhancing agent with a taste resembling that of meat extract and used to season Maggi bouillon concentrate and powdered soups, still sold today under the brand name Arome. Meanwhile, George Stoll was concerned over the financial situation of the partnership. In April, 1889, Stoll wrote: "Whereas Cham [Anglo-Swiss], Nestlé, [and] Liebig are concentrating their efforts on a small number of high-quality products and are very successful as a result, in Kempttal we are engaged in a myriad of experiments and are constantly turning out new products." To which Maggi replied: "...personally, I should like nothing better than to earn adequate profit from a small number of specialty products, in which case our business would indeed resemble that of Anglo-Swiss, Nestlé, or Liebig." But, as he pointed out, that was scarcely possible in the case of powdered soups, and Maggi ended by asserting that research was sufficiently far advanced for the partners to consider forming a corporation.

1900 Maggi poster advertising leguminous plants

A year later, in the spring of 1890, Fabrique de Produits Maggi S.A. was founded, to which the partners of Société en commandite Jules Maggi sold their firm for SFr. 1,907,750.45, i.e., "the value of assets shown in the balance sheet for June 30, 1889." Following years of development and preparatory work, the management of the new company expected it to expand rapidly, but it was to remain disappointed for a time. Not until the end of the last decade of the nineteenth century—especially after sales offices in Vienna and London were temporarily closed in an attempt to streamline the sales organization—did business begin to improve, owing primarily to the high quality of Maggi products. Once he had passed this critical period, Maggi was to reinforce his sales networks in Germany, Austria, France, Great Britain, and Italy little by little until the beginning of this century. And supplied by his plant in Kempttal, they were to become highly successful. This expansion soon made it necessary to consider establishing production centers in the countries surrounding Switzerland. The Singen factory opened in Germany in 1897, the Paris factory in 1898, the Bregenz factory in Austria, in 1907, and the factory at Sesto San Giovanni, Italy, in 1908. In 1908, Julius Maggi replaced his capsules of bouillon concentrate—first marketed in 1892 and sold in granulated form as of 1906—with the famous bouillon cube that was to ensure his fame. Maggi remained the company's sole chief executive for ten years. Georg Stoll's son Hermann, a member of the board of directors since 1890, backed Maggi up as executive vice-president from 1899 on. Hermann Stoll devoted his entire life to the firm Maggi had founded: in 1924, he became chief executive and, from 1939 until his death in 1947, was chairman of the board of Alimentana S.A., Maggi's holding company. Furthermore, thanks to his father, Hermann Stoll was familiar, from his childhood on, with the development of the big Zurich commercial bank, Crédit Suisse, of which he became an executive in 1929.

FROM THE INVENTION OF THE MAGGI BOUILLON CUBE IN 1908. IN 1901, JULES MAGGI MOVED TO PARIS AND FOUNDED A COMPANY TO DISTRIBUTE FRESH MILK.

In 1901, Julius Maggi—who had changed his name to Jules Maggi—moved to Paris in order to personally supervise bouillon concentrate and soup sales, which were flagging at the time. In 1903, Maggi became involved in another new activity: the distribution of fresh milk, founding La Laitière Maggi, a division of one of his companies in France, which became Société Laitière Maggi in 1912. His basic goal was to sell fresh milk of such high quality that it would reinforce the reputation of all products bearing the Maggi name. The dynamic Jules Maggi, who was, at the same time, an inventor, food specialist, and merchant, was keenly aware of the important role of advertising in an international company such as his. Jules Maggi was particularly generous: in 1892, he built housing for his workers; in 1895, he set up a health-insurance program for the firm; in 1902, the Maggi Company implemented a continuous workday—like the British—with a short break at midday; and, as early as 1906, Maggi employees already enjoyed Saturday afternoons off. Jules Maggi was a man of character, who was what we would today call a workaholic, who demanded the same degree of dedica-

MAGGI DIED IN 1912. HIS COMPANY CONTINUED TO BE A TOP PERFORMER,

tion from all those who worked for him. He also liked to keep physically fit and enjoyed engaging in a number of sports.

While he was working in Paris in 1912, Jules Maggi suffered a cerebral hemorrhage and died in Switzerland a few months later. The death of this dynamic, multifaceted individual dealt a serious blow to the company. Maggi had steadfastly sought both to incease sales and to improve the agricultural techniques utilized on the large farm the company had acquired near the Kempttal factory in 1893, in order to grow the vegetables it needed to manufacture its soups. However, as early as 1903, Maggi's advisors had reorganized the firm's management structure. As Alexander Rübel, son of the first chairman, August Rübel (who died in 1892), was to later relate: "[this reorganization was carried out] independently of Jules Maggi, so that when he had to leave the firm, which was one day inevitable, business would be able to continue with no qualms or anxiety for the shareholders."

Maggi's associates and the members of the board of directors had, for some time, been familiar with the operation of the firm. As mentioned previously, Hermann Stoll was the son of Georg Stoll, one of the silent partners in Maggi's first limited partnership; Ernst Schmid and Felix Suter had been senior managers of the company ever since Fabrique de Produits Maggi S.A. was founded in 1890 in Kempttal. The chairman of the board was Hans Konrad Bodmer, who had also been a member of the company's board from the very start. Apart from Ernst Schmid, who was German but had resided in Switzerland for many years, all these men were Swiss. When Jules Maggi became chief executive officer, a second generation of Maggi executives took over the company's top management positions. Among these were Messieurs Stoll, Schmid, and Suter. Following Jules Maggi's death, Schmid and Suter continued as executive vice-presidents of the German and French companies, while Hermann Stoll retained his position as executive vice-president of the Kempttal factory and the Austrian and Italian companies.

Despite the death of the man who had invented its products and single-handedly steered it safely through the turbulent waters of its earliest years, the Maggi Company, which had increased its share capital twelve times between 1891 and 1913—from SFr. 850,000 following its reorganization to SFr. 21,000,000—continued to expand, seeking all the while, through its registered shares (sale of which was restricted to Swiss citizens or foreigners residing in Switzerland), to prove, at all times, that it was truly a Swiss company.

"The Good Cook," poster for Maggi Arome, 1887

AND EMERGED FROM THE WAR VIRTUALLY UNSCATHED. THE FIRM REORGANIZED ONCE AGAIN IN 1924.

Such arrangements were necessary, for certain competitors who had become uneasy because of the market presence of their new rival, Société Laitière Maggi, organized a campaign against the company, "which was accused of being a front for foreign interests and of engaging in espionage against France under the pretense of regular commercial activity." The Maggi Company had sued its competitors in an attempt to combat the dangerous rumors that began to spread concerning the firm. At the end of July, 1914, just as the case was about to be judged, the first signs of war were now clearly perceptible, and "shortly afterward, during the nights before the mobilization, the rabble of Paris, incited by agents of the competition, destroyed the sales offices of Société Laitière Maggi, thus paralyzing that firm for almost the entire duration of the war." Thus, in 1914, Ernst Schmid (himself not a Swiss citizen) withdrew from the company's board of directors, as did R. Cambefort, who had been a member of the board representing French shareholders since 1897. From that date on, Hermann Stoll became the sole general manager. In 1916, following the death of Chairman Bodmer, Carl J. Abegg, whose father had provided Jules Maggi with financial support in 1890, was appointed chairman of the board. The Maggi Company remained basically a family firm, a fact that must be borne in mind in order to appreciate the ramifications of its 1947 merger with the Nestlé Company, itself a Swiss company, but one that had already rid itself of the yoke of family ties.

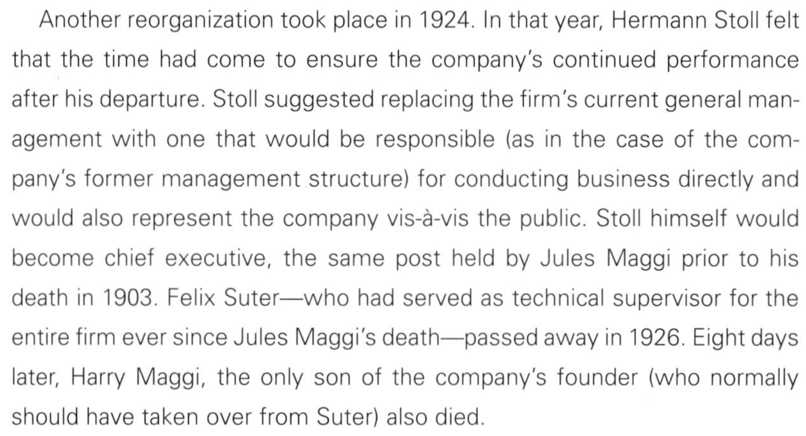

Another reorganization took place in 1924. In that year, Hermann Stoll felt that the time had come to ensure the company's continued performance after his departure. Stoll suggested replacing the firm's current general management with one that would be responsible (as in the case of the company's former management structure) for conducting business directly and would also represent the company vis-à-vis the public. Stoll himself would become chief executive, the same post held by Jules Maggi prior to his death in 1903. Felix Suter—who had served as technical supervisor for the entire firm ever since Jules Maggi's death—passed away in 1926. Eight days later, Harry Maggi, the only son of the company's founder (who normally should have taken over from Suter) also died.

Carl. J. Abegg (1891–1973)

By 1924, the company had come a long way from the difficult period of its first three years of existence, when no dividends were paid. As August Rübel stated: "When our sales figure reaches SFr. 1,000,000, the worst of our problems will be behind us." The advantage of the company's difficult beginnings was that its work force was obliged, from the start, to work very hard; and this was to became a Maggi tradition. Nevertheless, owing to inflation, in the spring of 1924, Société Générale Maggi, which had possessed a considerable amount of funds at the beginning of the war, was forced to "reach deep into its pockets in order to pay a 6 percent dividend." The company's dividend was increased to 8 percent in 1925; and, from 1926 on, it returned to its prewar level of 10 percent.

IN 1930, IT WAS FLOURISHING, DESPITE A DEGREE OF ECONOMIC UNCERTAINTY, ESPECIALLY IN GERMANY.

In 1930, the Maggi Company celebrated, with little fanfare, its fortieth anniversary as a corporation. We shall now view that period from the perspective of people sixty years ago in order to better understand the problems and successes of Maggi's managers at the time. In 1912, the year of Jules Maggi's death, the company had become the holding company, Société Générale Maggi. Only the Swiss operating company retained the name Fabrique de Produits Maggi S.A. In 1930, the latter was doing well and had not suffered the effects of the New York Stock Market Crash of 1929. Although the Depression was growing worse, the company's performance, thanks to intensive streamlining, was "generally satisfactory" and its profits hardly less than those of the previous year (i.e, SFr. 6,600,000, with its dividend remaining at 10 percent). Sales rose in Switzerland, but since the managers were cautious, they added, "the proportion of our per-capita sales is already so high that no sudden increase is forecast." Exports from the Kempttal factory, which had grown every year since the end of World War I, were still quite high, although there was a drop in the level of trade with Holland, Spain, and England. And that factory was further expanded at this point.

Vegetable peeling department in a Maggi factory, around the turn of the century

Germany's economic situation was a source of worry; however, the performance of the German Maggi Company was satisfactory, despite the fact that sales had dropped from their 1929 level. Market penetration was difficult, and this situation was exacerbated by the political situation within Germany and without as well as by the Reich's decision to implement a "campaign of price reductions." The firm's management discovered that lower prices for raw materials could only be passed on partially to customers, "since the

IN FRANCE, SOCIÉTÉ LAITIÈRE MAGGI ESTABLISHED ITSELF AS A LEADER. DIFFICULTIES CAUSED BY THE WAR BEGAN TO BE FELT IN 1940, FIRST IN FRANCE...

government, in its eagerness to help farmers, has raised customs duties on several products of importance to Maggi." On grain selling for 18 marks on world markets, German customs imposed a 25-mark import duty, whereas it had been a mere 7.50 marks a few years earlier. However, this situation had not prevented the German Maggi Company from expanding its Berlin facilities the previous year.

Maggi had two companies in France: one producing and marketing bouillon, soups, and flavoring for continental France, the French colonies, and Luxembourg; the other involved in the distribution of fresh milk. Although company performance was not what it had been the year before, it was considered satisfactory, nonetheless.

In 1930, Société Laitière Maggi, Paris, had seventy-six collection points for fresh milk and one thousand two hundred shops or stores selling cheese, butter, cream, and eggs—in addition to fresh milk. To get a better idea of how large the firm had become: in 1929, it sold 95,500,000 liters of fresh milk! In Austria, the economy was plagued by bank failures, unemployment, rising interest rates, and very high taxes (nine times higher than the net profits of the local Maggi company). Thus, the Austrian Maggi Company showed a slight loss, as did the Italian Maggi Company, in spite of a marked increase in the sale of bouillon cubes. Profits in Belgium—where a sales company had been founded in 1928—were modest. The Belgian firm acquired land for a new warehouse, but local production did not start until 1933. In Poland, there was a certain optimism over company performance there; thus, it was decided that a plant should be equipped for production in Poland, which began in 1932. The Czech Maggi Company, based in Prague, was operating at a loss (though less serious than that of 1929), which provided the justification for raising prices in that country.

Overseas, Maggi, whose products had been available in the U.S. for two decades, was preparing to found the U.S. Maggi Company, which was to begin its activity in February, 1931. Analyses carried out in 1920, 1926, and 1929 to determine the feasibility of entering the highly lucrative American market encouraged the management of Maggi to take the step of crossing the Atlantic. However, production at the factory in New Milford, Connecticut, did not start until eleven years later.

In 1940, there was no special celebration of the firm's fiftieth anniversary; indeed, it was no time for celebration. In Germany, which was winning the war at that time, the company enjoyed a strong market position. The same

Old Maggi poster advertising bouillon cubes

held true for occupied France, devastated Poland, Czechoslovakia, which had been annexed by the Third Reich, and Italy, which had entered the war on the side of Germany. Following its experience in World War I, in 1940, the Maggi Company—whose expansion in Europe had been extraordinary—paid particular attention to remaining a Swiss company, with a Swiss general management, Swiss capital, and Swiss shareholders, even though its staff abroad was highly international.

As the reader will recall, in Jules Maggi's time, the Maggi Company had first expanded by setting up sales companies and, later, production centers located just beyond the Swiss border at Singen in Germany; Bregenz in Austria; Milan; and even Paris. Starting in 1925, a second period of expansion had led the firm to open factories in Czechoslovakia, the Netherlands, Poland, Belgium, and finally, as we have said, in the U.S. in 1940.

In that same year, there was a certain amount of anxiety at company headquarters. Though the factories of most locally based Maggi companies, their administrative buildings, and wealth were not in jeopardy in the case of France, dairies situated along railroad lines had been damaged, as well as factories producing cheese and cold cuts, and storehouses for canned milk). Although Chairman Stoll was able to tell the shareholders that, all in all, the company's financial situation was relatively satisfactory, he also asked them—a sign of the times—to keep that information secret. He even had to request that shareholders not take notes, for, as he stated, "a good many of Maggi's companies, except for [those in] Switzerland and the U.S., are located in countries at war with one another." Indeed, the war had an adverse effect on company profits, which now totaled SFr. 2,838,360.62— a drop of SFr. 1,146,184.44 from the previous year. In order to understand the way in which a Swiss company operated in Europe during the war, it is worthwhile to relate certain remarks made at the virtually private annual shareholders' meeting at which the company's performance for 1940 was discussed. Two factors made the Maggi Company a special kind of firm: first, it belonged to the food industry, which made it remarkably resistant to an economy in the throes of crisis, and, second, its profits on the products it manufactured and marketed were small, which meant that when the economy was strong, the firm could not recoup its losses after long periods of financial difficulty. Furthermore, the food industry was particularly vulnerable to wartime economic measures. Business was hampered by difficulties that varied from country to country, with supplies of raw materials and energy in the form of coal being the most problematic. "Moreover," as Stoll pointed out, "they [the Maggi companies abroad] are totally subjugated to an increasing tax burden."

AND LATER WITH RESPECT TO THE INTERNATIONAL TRANSFER OF FUNDS. THERE WERE INCREASING CAUSES FOR ANXIETY IN SEVERAL AREAS.

A holding company is always hit the hardest by problems involved in the transferring of funds. These "have continued growing in the field of international payments, making it increasingly hard for us to get funds into [Switzerland]." Yet, in spite of unfavorable conditions and high manufacturing costs, demand for Maggi products "remained strong," which explains the level of the firm's profits for 1940. In those troubled times, people were quite worried about the future. There were obvious disparities among the operating companies. In Switzerland, due to the introduction of Maggi's new *sauce claire* (thin sauce), sales had gone up, whereas exports from the factory in Kempttal had dropped sharply "due to problems in delivery and steps taken to protect the factory's inventory. Sales in Switzerland have not enabled us to recoup our losses on sales abroad." Business with Spain was at a standstill. Fortunately, the company had given up on the idea of opening a plant there, although it had been considering it for some time. Exports to England of bouillon and soups had been stopped. In Germany, which had adapted itself to a war economy, production and sales had been able to continue in keeping with the general guidelines for rationing issued at the outset of the war. The situation was the same in Austria, where the Maggi Company still considered its local companies as Austrian, despite the *Anschluss* of 1938.

Although work stopped briefly as France was invaded by German troops in May and June, the French Maggi Company continued to do business almost normally, though the authorities announced severe restrictions on deliveries to customers in occupied France. The companies distributing fresh milk had greater worries, for it was easy for the activity of milk-producing districts to be disrupted by troop movements through the countryside or along railroad lines.

Maggi's market share improved in Italy. In Belgium, however, the local company had only a very limited supply of finished products available; and, throughout 1940, it had a very hard time obtaining new supplies from France or Switzerland. As for the Dutch Maggi Company, it had to resort to taking from its inventory in order to keep the Dutch market supplied with Maggi Arome, for it was impossible to obtain this product from Switzerland, and the Dutch management had delayed establishing quotas for its customers.

THE DEATH OF MAGGI'S TOP EXECUTIVES, IN 1947, CAST AN ADDITIONAL SHADOW OVER THE FIRM'S FUTURE...

The Polish Maggi Company, "which depended on other Maggi companies for its supplies," finally managed to adapt to the new conditions, but not without difficulty. Because of a food shortage in Czechoslovakia, "sales figures went up," but deliveries to customers were also subject to strict quotas. It was still possible to import Maggi products from Switzerland to the U.S. Planning ahead, the managers of the Swiss holding company provided the U.S. Maggi Company with funds to build a factory in America.

World War II, which had resulted in great slaughter, destruction, and socio-economic upheaval, was finally over by 1946. Although the Maggi Company was far from bankrupt, it was nowhere near as prosperous as it had been before the war.

At the annual shareholders' meeting held on June 25, 1947, as he discussed company performance for 1946 and early 1947, Chairman A.L. Tobler, Hermann Stoll's successor (Stoll had died three months earlier, a month before Vice-Chairman Bodmer) had no way of knowing that he was presiding over the final ordinary shareholders' meeting of Alimentana S.A., Maggi's holding company. As the reader will recall, the merger with Nestlé was to take place after the extraordinary shareholders' meetings of both companies held on December 5, 1947. In the summer of 1947, Tobler could only repeat what had been disclosed twelve months earlier in the annual report on company performance for 1945 trading: "Events have unfortunately shown fears about the profitability of our business to be entirely justified." Indeed, in 1946, Chairman Stoll had painted a gloomy picture of the extraordinary damage "that the war and its consequences have done to our most important companies." Among those consequences were a generally very bad economic situation, extreme difficulty obtaining raw materials, nationalization (which had already affected the factory in Poland), and price controls. Losses were heavy even on the Swiss market. Moreover, overhead expenses, including salaries and considerably higher taxes, were also sources of concern.

Maggi factory at New Milford, Connecticut, 1950

According to the chairman, Maggi's German business was in difficult straits in 1945: "even though the production facilities of the factory at Singen were not damaged," it was only able to work "at reduced capacity since the end of the war," for the limits of the Allied zones of occupation in Germany had cut the company off from its sources of raw materials and from its customers (to the advantage of the firm's competitors). The same applied to Austria. Although the Czech Maggi Company was losing money, there was no talk as yet of nationalizing factories. (However, in 1948, Maggi's factory in Czechoslovakia was to become nationalized.) The French Maggi Company was showing a loss because of the poor quality of its raw materials. The dairy business was doing badly in France, and rumors of nationalization created a degree of uncertainty, which hampered reconstruction. Fluctuations in exchange rates resulted in substantial losses for the company. While the Belgian Maggi Company was doing relatively well, the Dutch company had been forced to stop working in the year of the Armistice, and losses had been heavy. In spite of the circumstances, the Maggi Company in Italy had managed to continue doing business as usual there. In the U.S., the company suffered losses which, while bearable, signaled that its "future [was] uncertain, for we no longer deliver to the government, and civilian business is not profitable."

WHICH, SINCE 1945, HAD NOT BEEN VERY HEARTENING. IN 1947, SALES WERE DOWN IN GERMANY, AND IN SWITZERLAND AS WELL...

At the shareholders' meeting on June 25, 1947, Chairman Tobler was no more optimistic than his predecessor. Discussing the collapse of the German economy, he said: "We cannot yet foresee the day when the balance sheet of our German firm will once again be in the black." (The reader will recall that Germany and Switzerland together comprised Maggi's biggest markets in Europe.) In France, Tobler went on to say: "the situation is still gloomy and alarming, especially insofar as our financial interest in the dairy industry is concerned." The situation in Switzerland had improved somewhat, but the Swiss company was still not profitable. Although Maggi companies in other countries were all doing relatively well, Tobler pointed out that "even when they do make a profit, it is generally insufficient to offset their liabilities, and, in view of the volume of our business, it fails to offset our losses at present." Tobler hinted at the firm's precarious financial position even more clearly when he stated: "even what I am telling you now—which I must ask you to keep secret—does not enable me to paint a more favorable picture of the future." No one knew when the political and economic situation of postwar Europe would become stable. Moreover, along with the relatively small profit margins prevailing in the food industry, increasing expenses in the form of overhead—in particular, salaries—were

EVEN THOUGH, ELSEWHERE IN EUROPE, BUSINESS ON SMALLER MARKETS APPEARED TO BE MORE PROMISING.

creating a financial burden that the company could not pass on to consumers due to price controls.

Business was beginning to pick up somewhat. Yet, despite the hard work of its salesmen, the Swiss firm in Kemptal was still showing a loss, and exports remained at only a modest level. The factory at Singen, Germany, had been operating from hand to mouth, as it were, ever since the end of the war. Although its output was substantial, it was obliged to adapt itself to the situation in postwar Germany, which meant that it had to "participate in supplying the population with pasta and a certain number of other food products." In short, "nothing was stable," and business was down, "owing to problems with raw materials suppliers as well as customer relations." As late as June 25, 1947, all of the company's accounts were not yet settled for the previous year. Competition was becoming increasingly fierce, and it was impossible to transfer any existing funds from Germany to Switzerland. This was a great disadvantage for Alimentana S.A., the majority of whose profits—as we have mentioned—were generated in countries beyond the Rhine. In Austria, the heavy losses the firm suffered in 1945 were followed, in 1946, by a small degree of profitability. However, up to that time, no funds from licensing fees—of considerable importance to Alimentana—had been transferred to Switzerland. Although, according to company records, there was no mention of impending nationalization in Czechoslovakia, fear of this was a constant factor. A sharp jump in production took place in France in 1946, despite that country's difficulties. (Profits in France that year offset losses for 1944 and 1945.) It was still impossible, however, to transfer licensing fees to Alimentana S.A. in Switzerland. The dairy industry in France was affected by the repercussions of France's serious economic situation. Profit margins were insufficient. "We must continue to remain steadfast for the time being..." was the only advice that Chairman Tobler could honestly give in the circumstances. Sales were up in Belgium as well as in Holland, where a new factory for Arome had begun production in the second half of the year. Sales were improving in Italy, too; but, again, the problem of transferring licensing

Maggi factory at Kemptal, Switzerland, 1950

fees was becoming acute there. In the U.S., the company's management felt that "developments were far from satisfactory," in spite of a large amount of investment for the distribution of locally produced Maggi products.

THE FUTURE LOOKED QUITE GLOOMY IN 1947, AND MAGGI DECIDED ON ITS MERGER WITH NESTLÉ.

Indeed, 1947 looked as if it was going to be a rather disappointing year. Maggi's board of directors were continually trying to underscore the essentially Swiss character of the firm. In February, the board of directors voted not to accept the transfer of shares of stock to foreigners, even those domiciled in Switzerland (unless the shares in question had been previously owned by foreigners); to banks, fiduciaries, or other institutions of that kind; or to individuals working for such institutions. (According to the statutes of the company, the board was not required to reveal the grounds for its refusal.) The board committee had decided on October 4, 1946, to have a manager of the Swiss Maggi Company look into the possibility of local manufacture in Spain, but the idea was subsequently scrapped.

It took the Maggi Company only a few months to reach a decision concerning its merger with Nestlé. The secret was well kept. Carl J. Abegg—virtually the sole survivor among the former team of managers—was the first to consider seriously the possibility of an agreement with Nestlé. Contacts were made in private. And there was no mention of these at Maggi's ordinary annual meeting of shareholders held on June 25, 1947. However, as the end of summer approached, the negotiations between the two firms—still highly secret—began to bear fruit.

Early in September, Nestlé's chairman, Edouard Muller, pointed out that great strides had already been made in these negotiations. He was sure enough of the outcome to write in a letter to be circulated within the company: "Once we take over this concern, it will surely be easy to develop it on the Latin American markets, in Spain, and in Portugal. [Though development will be] a bit more difficult in the English-speaking countries, I believe that in England, the U.S., and Australia these products have very great potential, provided that we are willing to work tirelessly, and, perhaps, in certain cases, to change certain

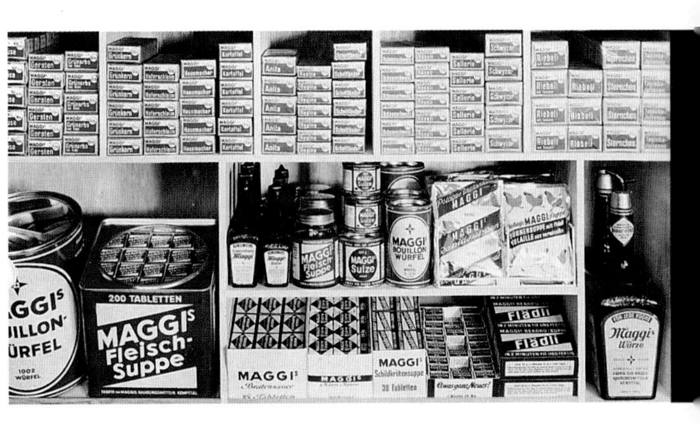

Maggi's suggestion for a store display of its products, 1948

THEIR MERGER AGREEMENT WAS DRAWN UP AND SIGNED IN DECEMBER, 1947. SHARES WERE SWAPPED, AND NESTLÉ ALIMENTANA S.A. WAS BORN.

ingredients to tailor our products to their tastes." In addition to studying the particularly complex case of Maggi's market in Germany (a completely chaotic country at the time, where a good many of the company's employees were coming back, at a trickle, from prison camps), Nestlé was carefully examining the situation of Société Laitière Maggi, which was performing well. It was Nestlé's policy in France not to distribute fresh milk—since political factors played such an important role in that field there—preferring to remain active solely in the canned milk industry. Société Laitière Maggi owned some eight hundred shops in Paris, which also did not fit easily into an industrial organization such as Nestlé's, whose policy it was not to possess its own stores.

After a few months of talks, however, agreements were drawn up. And these were approved at extraordinary shareholders' meetings held by both companies on December 5, 1947. The merger did not result in any important modifications. The two sales organizations remained, for the most part, independent of one another, with Maggi and Nestlé free to cooperate, to a greater or lesser extent, whenever the opportunity should present itself in a particular area of endeavor.

At the time of the 1947 merger, Maggi possessed a total of eleven factories, with those at Kralupy nad Vlatvou, Czechoslovakia, and Poznan, Poland, ultimately becoming nationalized in 1948. (The company received financial compensation for this.)

Nestlé was entering what for it was uncharted waters. Its association with the chocolate manufacturers P.C.K. had shown that quality control for chocolate was a much more ticklish business than quality control for canned milk. In the case of Maggi, a company producing mainly low-priced products for a wide range of consumers, quality would play an even more important role, since glutamate-based soups and bouillon were to appear on the market shortly after the merger, and these would compete directly with Maggi's traditional Arome-based articles. The postwar economic boom and the resulting improvement in consumer purchasing power were to encourage the introduction of new products targeting an even wider segment of the population. Originally aimed at lower-class consumers, Maggi products were eventually to gain the respect of all classes of society.

The financial aspect of the merger involved the exchange of thirty Nestlé shares for one Alimentana S.A., share. From the standpoint of human resources, Maggi's employees were placed either directly or indirectly under

Nestlé's control. Nestlé's senior executives became members of the boards of the extant Maggi companies. Thanks to what Nestlé had learned during its merger with P.C.K., changes took place slowly and disturbances were minimal, in spite of the risks inherent in the pooling of interests of different-sized companies.

THE NEW COMPANY DECIDED TO DROP "ANGLO-SWISS CONDENSED MILK CO." FROM ITS NAME, BUT RETAIN THE SURNAME OF HENRI NESTLÉ.

Its association with Nestlé ensured Maggi that its products would be distributed on a global level and that its financial basis would be strengthened. At the same time, the Maggi Company represented a source of new products for Nestlé. The range of Nestlé's special food products—consisting, prior to the merger with Maggi, of chocolate, milk products, and instant coffee—increased to include soups and bouillon—and soon a wide range of other food products. Nestlé did not have to start from scratch, but could take advantage of the technical know-how of an old and established firm. Nestlé's management had no worries over either the immediate or the distant future. It had fine-tuned its organization and was in a position to distribute a range of traditional items (such as the food products of Maggi) throughout the world. As Chairman Muller was to point out during the shareholders' meeting of December 5, basic food products have the advantage "of appealing to every household and of being distributed via networks and middlemen much like ours are."

Indeed, there are still certain markets, especially overseas, where such items, though existing in other forms, have a good chance of performing well. We are all the more optimistic, insofar as Maggi products are of superior quality, which makes them No. 1 in their field."

A few details concerning this merger to conclude this chapter: Alimentana S.A. became Maggi Unternehmung AG, and what was previously known as Nestlé and Anglo-Swiss Condensed Milk Company retained the name Nestlé in its change of name to Nestlé Alimentana S.A. Management was convinced that the new name of Nestlé's holding company would provide a better description of the firm's activities in the food industry and in the field of dietetic foods. According to Chairman Muller, Maggi's factories, located chiefly in Europe, represented "a precious tool that the combined efforts of both organizations will take full advantage of in an international political climate somewhat calmer, I hope, than today's."

Chapter VI

1947–1962

As East-West Relations Thaw, a Fascination with the Great North Brings Together Nestlé and Findus

IN THE MIDST OF WORLDWIDE ECONOMIC CONFUSION...

The Cold War and Beyond: the World Situation in 1962

☐ *1962 was another crucial year in modern history. The forceful resistance of President Kennedy to Soviet designs on Cuba and Latin America marked both the end of the cold war, which had begun with the division of Berlin, and the beginning of improved relations between the superpowers. This, in turn, led to a period of relative stability and prosperity in democratic, industrialized countries that continued until the oil crisis of 1973. In order to understand how events unfolded during this time, we must reflect for a moment on the differences between the postwar recovery period in 1918 and in 1945. After World War I, the horrors of war had given way to concerns about rebuilding democracy. The victorious nations had succeeded in isolating the Soviet Union and preventing communist expansion. Reconstructing war-torn areas had been accomplished relatively quickly. The desire to forget the nightmare begun in 1914 had engendered an optimism and joie de vivre that were especially apparent in the United States until 1929.*

On the other hand, efforts on the part of statesmen to bring about political stability had met with failure. Insecurity and instability became chronic after the outbreak of the Depression of 1929–30. Several countries in Eastern, Southern, and Central Europe, lacking a strong democratic tradition to draw upon, and gripped by poverty and despair, turned to fascism. Almost every government adopted autarkical and protectionist policies which themselves stimulated nationalist fervor. The world was thus a highly unstable place, in which the most basic equilibrium essential to international peace was utterly lacking, when the war finally broke out in 1939.

In 1945, the world economy was in complete disarray. While some countries were becoming poorer, others were becoming increasingly prosperous, a situation that resulted in even greater inequality than had existed in 1919. Countries like Britain and France had suffered economic slowdowns during the war; others, such as the Soviet Union, were thwarted in their hopes to expand. As for Germany and Japan, whose armies had been totally dismantled, their national product was barely half of what it had been in 1939.

In the entire industrialized world, the United States proved to be the only beneficiary of both world wars. That country's forced entry into the

EAST-WEST RIVALRY CAME TO A HEAD IN EUROPE ESPECIALLY IN GERMANY.

war, in 1941, allowed it to stave off the threat of depression; the U.S. gross national product had doubled since 1930 and, by 1945, it amounted to two-thirds of the combined national product of all the countries in the world. Its strong economic position, combined with its exclusive possession of the atomic bomb, turned the U.S. into the world's leading power. When, in 1949, the Soviet Union achieved a nuclear capability, the military domination of the U.S., if not its economic supremacy, was seriously challenged.

Bolstered by their nuclear exploit, in 1948 the Soviets attempted a double maneuver meant both to prevent an extension of the Marshall Plan in Europe and to enhance Soviet influence there. They first staged the Prague coup in February, in which President Beneš was forcibly replaced by the communist leader Clement Gotwald; similar operations took place soon afterward in Poland and Hungary. In June, 1948, came the blockade of Berlin, resulting in a state of alert in Germany.

Since the end of the war, the remnants of the Third Reich had become the testing ground for strained relations between the superpowers. It is true that the quarrel between Moscow and Washington in the United Nations over nuclear arms control reflected the ongoing rivalry between East and West. But on German territory, where the superpowers were supposedly operating side by side, they were, in fact, on the verge of daily conflict. The slightest local incident might have dire consequences. The Soviet Union was trying to gain time to secure its strategic position in Eastern Europe and to perfect its arsenal of nuclear weapons. At the same time, the Western countries were trying to prevent Germany from becoming a conduit by which communism would reach the Rhine.

The world political situation was thus galvanized by Germany and its reconstruction. The U.S.S.R. kept a firm grip on its buffer zone beyond the Elbe. But Berlin, divided into four sectors, was a thorn in the Soviets' side. In Germany's internal affairs and between the two halves of the former Reich, economic struggle began where military conflict left off. In June, 1948, the Western Allies decided that it would be impossible to create a West Germany without currency reform. The Russian response was swift and fierce: within days, Berlin—an island in a sea of communism—was split into two parts: one Soviet, the other Western. The Soviets and the East Germans cut off all land routes into the city. This economic blockade was life-threatening to the American, British, and French

THE MARSHALL PLAN CAME TO EUROPE'S ASSISTANCE, AND EUROPE BEGAN ITS RECOVERY.

sectors, and the Allies immediately began a massive airlift, which in one year and 270,000 flights brought 2,500,000 tons of food to the city's 3,000,000 inhabitants. By their swift response, the United States, Britain, and France demonstrated their firm opposition to any change in the agreement reached at the Yalta Conference of February, 1945. In areas where the Western powers had a military presence, they put a stop to the extension of Soviet influence.

Also in June of 1948, Tito, the communist president of the People's Republic of Yugoslavia, was expelled from the Cominform, an international organization of communist parties founded in 1947; this constituted early signs of fatigue in the strength of the Eastern bloc.

Thus, the double warning shots of Berlin in 1948–49—first from the Soviet side, then from the West—divided the industrialized world even more clearly into two camps—one Marxist, one democratic. The communist countries were increasingly fearful of a capitalist victory on the economic front comparable to the military victory they had achieved together. Indeed, the democratic countries were profiting from the Marshall Plan, which, between 1947 and 1950, raised the gross national product of the beneficiary countries by 25 percent, thus contributing greatly to Europe's economic recovery. Aid from the Marshall Plan totaled $13,000,000,000 over four years; from January, 1948, to October, 1949, more than $7,000,000,000 were distributed. Half of this aid was used for importing goods and raw materials for industry into Western Europe. In addition, food donations sent from the United States further facilitated European economic reconstruction.

Important though it was, American aid would have been in vain if Europe had not worked hard to pull itself out of its postwar slump. It was clear that the industrial era begun in the U.S. with the advent of automation and atomic power, forced Europe to increase and improve the production of traditional sources of energy such as coal and electricity. European production began improving, aided by better food supplies and higher salaries. Prices, which had gone up 20 percent between 1946 and 1947, rose only 5 percent in 1948, when they also began stabilizing worldwide.

To combat inflation, the governments of Belgium, the Netherlands, Denmark, Norway, and Germany took measures to cut monetary circulation and restrict credit. Little by little, commercial activity also began to stabilize. Rationing, which remained in effect in Britain and the Netherlands, and increased agricultural production reduced the need for increased food imports; likewise, they made it unnecessary for these countries to seek new sources of raw materials.

THE NORTH ATLANTIC TREATY ORGANIZATION WAS CREATED IN 1949.

By the end of 1948, Western Europe ranked second in world industrial output and third in agricultural production. But the international turmoil that lay ahead would have a significant, if only indirect, effect on Europe's continued development.

This time, trouble was not brewing on European soil (though the Berlin blockade continued until 1949), but rather, in Asia, Africa, and Latin America, where the architects of communism had chosen to challenge the West.

In short, 1949–50 marked the turning point between the end of the postwar era, during which Western democracies had sought to consolidate their power, and the beginning of a new phase in modern history in which the struggle between pro-American and pro-Soviet forces dominated the evolution of political and economic affairs throughout the world. This transition was marked by two important events: the creation of the North Atlantic Treaty Organization (NATO) and the Korean War, which had the effect of extending to Asia the futile political standoff begun in Berlin.

NATO—first and foremost a military alliance—brought together the majority of Western nations. Its inception was not without difficulties, however. To be sure, the Allies' second wartime association, from 1939 to 1945, had united them in their opposition to Germany. Europeans understood that only a united front could prevent new hostilities from flaring up. The double threat of a new military buildup in Germany and of an advance of the Red Army toward the Rhine spurred European countries to formalize their solidarity. In March, 1948, five countries—Britain, Belgium, France, the Netherlands, and Luxembourg—met in Brussels to form the Western European Union (WEU), designed to ensure mutual assistance in case of attack. When, several months later in Berlin, the cold war between East and West began heating up, the WEU member nations looked to the United States for support, and Washington agreed that a military alliance was essential to guarantee Western security. Thus, the fear of the advance of Stalinism brought about what neither Hitler's prewar threats nor the horrors of

THE KOREAN WAR BROKE OUT IN 1950...

war itself had managed to achieve: a peacetime defensive military alliance between Western democracies. On August 4, 1949, the North Atlantic Treaty for mutual military assistance was signed in Washington by Belgium, Britain, Canada, Denmark, France, Iceland, Luxembourg, the Netherlands, Norway, Portugal, and the United States, thus proclaiming the solidarity of the two Atlantic coasts.

Suddenly, the split between East and West, already visible in Berlin and elsewhere in Europe, widened into a veritable chasm within the United Nations. A strong, unified Western bloc now confronted the communist regimes established in Eastern Europe by the Soviet Union. Two years later, the Warsaw Pact consolidated Soviet influence in Eastern Europe and further widened the gap between East and West.

The Korean War, which broke out in June, 1950, had the effect of heightening tension to such a level that people feared the worst. In fact, it seems that the communist leaders assumed that Western countries would not come to the military assistance of a small Asian country threatened by communism. Korea may seem, at first, to have been an unlikely choice for a standoff. But, while Europe was protected by NATO, South Korea was quite vulnerable, wedged in between communist North Korea and the sea. More important, Korea's giant neighbor, mainland China, had, come under the control of Mao Zedong in 1949. Only Hong Kong and Macao remained independent; Taiwan, powerless, had only the remnants of Chiang Kai-shek's nationalist army for its defense, and Japan, which had formerly occupied Korea and was not trusted by Seoul, provided little in the way of reassurance.

Given all this, the Soviet Union shrewdly wagered that South Korea's friends would not risk igniting the entire planet by coming to its defense with the atomic bomb. The communist leaders concluded that Korea had no one to turn to in case of attack, especially as the country lay outside the "defensive perimeter" referred to by certain American leaders, which included only Japan and the Philippines.

In June, 1950, the North Korean Army invaded the South. Within days the war became an international crisis. The United States responded swiftly and forcefully; President Truman ordered arms shipments to South Korea and mobilized the 7th Fleet. Popular support for a military response was overwhelming. This resolve was soon reiterated on the floor of the United Nations, where the Soviets had resigned from the Security

Council in protest over the presence of a representative from Taiwan. Truman's envoy obtained a majority vote in the Assembly, thereby authorizing American forces to be sent to Korea on behalf of the United Nations. General MacArthur, who had helped ensure Japan's defeat in World War II, took command of these forces. A difficult, two-year war ensued, during which both sides—North Korea, assisted by volunteers from China, and the United Nations forces, of which a majority were American—engaged each other, alternately scoring victories or suffering defeat. Within the U.N. forces, a split soon became evident between Truman, who saw the war as a campaign carried out in the name of world solidarity against the North Korean aggressor on its own soil, and MacArthur, whose goal was to eliminate Chinese influence in Asia by whatever means necessary—including the atomic bomb. In the end, MacArthur was dismissed.

REAFFIRMING WESTERN SOLIDARITY. EUROPE WAS DIVIDED.

The Korean War came as a psychological shock to the West. Western Allies closed ranks, and the communists did the same. International tension rose to a dangerous level in 1956 and remained there until 1962.

In 1950, the United States began seeking closer ties with Great Britain. The Labour prime minister, Attlee, and, from 1951 on, Winston Churchill, welcomed this American initiative. Washington then concentrated on expanding the North Atlantic Treaty Organization. In 1951, Greece and Turkey became members of NATO; Italy and Germany joined in 1955. At the same time, European unity was the principal theme of talks between France's Robert Schuman, Germany's Konrad Adenauer, and Italy's Alcide de Gasperi. The Schuman Plan for the production of coal and steel was ratified by the parliaments of Belgium, France, Germany, Italy, Luxembourg, and the Netherlands in 1951, and went into effect in 1952.

European security was still the West's chief diplomatic concern. Government leaders knew that the mere presence of powerful military forces stationed on either side of the Iron Curtain was no guarantee of security. But before any meaningful discussions could take place on this issue, the problem of Germany's status had to be resolved. Indeed, Germany remained a source of anxiety in Europe, especially in light of the extraordinary economic recovery West Germany had made since 1949. (This was in stark contrast to the painfully slow development of East Germany.) The Federal Republic of Germany, backed by the U.S.

THE THIRD WORLD MOBILIZED ITS FORCES. EISENHOWER ENDED THE KOREAN WAR IN 1952.

and declaring itself the sole official voice of the German nation, considered the border between East Germany and Poland to be merely a temporary one. On the other hand, the East German government, supported by the communist bloc, held that the Oder-Neisse line was to be the definitive border between the two countries. Diplomatic efforts at the many preliminary conferences that were held regularly in Paris, until 1951, were fruitless; there could be no real progress in extinguishing such smoldering European issues as long as the two superpowers refused all compromise. (And they resembled cats and dogs in their suspicion of one another.)

The cold war was also heating up in Asia and in Africa. During the postwar period, the countries of those continents could be placed in one of two distinct categories depending on the pace of their industrial development. On the one hand, there were the industrialized nations and, on the other, the so-called developing nations. The disruptions of the war and of the continuing struggle between the superpowers served to arouse considerable nationalist fervor.

When the Korean War broke out, the world was actually divided into three blocs: East, West, and the "Third World," a rather amorphous group in which leaders such as Nehru of India, Nasser of Egypt, N'Kruma of Ghana, Tito of Yugoslavia, and Sukarno of Indonesia would soon distinguish themselves. Unlike its European allies, the United States would only lend assistance to these developing countries if it judged a threat of communism to be imminent there. Instead, the U.S. encouraged the formation of military alliances in Southeast Asia and the Middle East with the objective of forming—from Northern Europe to the Sea of Japan—a kind of chain designed to hem in the communist bloc along its southern and western frontiers. In 1951, the U.S. signed a peace treaty with Japan, which was still largely demilitarized; from then on, Japan, too, joined the economic ranks of the Western nations.

It was not long, though, before Washington began feeling the economic and military costs of waging war in Korea. In 1952, the Republican Dwight D. Eisenhower, former commander in chief of Allied forces and of NATO troops, was elected president on the strength of his promise to end the war. In 1953, the armistice of Panmunjon was signed. Eisenhower, and his newly appointed secretary of state, John Foster Dulles, proceeded to commit the United States to a policy of defending any country threatened by communism. From that moment on, the U.S. seized every possible opportunity to secure the backing of the United Nations in its self-appointed role as policeman of the world.

GERMANY, KOREA, AND VIETNAM REMAINED DIVIDED.

In 1954, the world's major powers undertook to resolve geopolitical imbroglios in Germany, Korea, and Indochina. The Berlin Conference, convened in February of that year, brought about neither a change in Germany's status nor improved security arrangements in Europe. The only positive result of the conference was an agreement in principle to begin talks in Geneva on the Korean question. But in April, when the talks got under way, it became clear that no solution would be found; like Germany, Korea was to remain divided: one part communist and the other pro-Western. As for the quagmire in Indochina, where for seven years France had intervened in a civil war between communist and pro-Western forces in Vietnam, it was also the subject of lengthy discussions. In July, a solution was reached: Vietnam, too, would be divided into two parts, a communist North, with Hanoi as its capital, and a pro-Western South, whose capital was Saigon. Twenty years later, the country was reunified, with the victory of the North over the South. Cambodia and Laos—declared neutral at the conference—nonetheless remained within North Vietnam's sphere of influence until 1989. The Geneva Conference also marked the first appearance of communist China on the international diplomatic scene, with the presence of the Chinese prime minister and minister of foreign affairs, Zhou Enlai.

The governments of independent developing countries as well as colonized countries read the Geneva Conference as a clear signal that the superpowers were seeking above all to quell conflict through diplomatic channels. Some of them decided the time was ripe to free themselves of European influence. One expression of that spirit of independence was the Algerian revolt, which broke out in November, 1954.

1954 was also the year that Pierre Mendès-France, the French prime minister, and Konrad Adenauer, chancellor of West Germany, tried unsuccessfully to reach an agreement in Brussels on a treaty leading to the establishment of a European defense community. For the next thirty years, those two countries, as well as the Benelux countries and Italy, worked instead to build an economic alliance within the framework of the Common Market. In 1973, Britain, Ireland, and Denmark joined the Common Market; Greece followed in 1981; and Spain and Portugal in

THE ATOM BOMB BECAME THE GREAT EQUALIZER. 1956 WITNESSED A WAR IN EGYPT...

1986. Within the decade after World War II, a certain number of outstanding issues had already been resolved: in 1954, an agreement with Yugoslavia returned Trieste to Italy; the Saar was restored to Germany in 1955; also in 1955, Austria declared its neutrality, thereby freeing itself of military occupation. This was the first case of Soviet troops withdrawing from previously occupied territory.

The agreements reached at the Geneva Conference demonstrated that the superpowers could negotiate on some important issues, despite the fact that their relations were still fraught with tension. One fact was indisputable: those countries in possession of the atomic bomb had shown that they would abstain from using it unless their own security was threatened. Indeed, the cold war was coming to an end; barely three years after Stalin's death in 1953, the Soviet Union declared itself in favor of reducing world tension.

At the 20th Congress of the Soviet Communist Party in early 1956, Nikita Khrushchev proclaimed a policy of peaceful coexistence, whereby the communist countries were prepared to maintain relations with any country in the world, regardless of political affiliation. In the same address, he reaffirmed the Soviet Union's support of "wars of liberation." Khrushchev's remarks had a favorable effect on relations between the American and Soviet governments, while, at the same time, publicly exacerbating the ideological rift between the Soviets and the Chinese communists, who remained faithful to the Stalinist doctrine of relentless struggle against capitalism. Thus, the communist bloc was split asunder by disagreements over political dogma.

The tacit understanding that was growing between the U.S. and the Soviet Union, and its corollary of Sino-Russian opposition, had the effect of further arousing the desire for political self-determination on the part of some developing countries. In the Third World, President Nasser was the first to take a step in this direction by nationalizing the Suez Canal in 1956. When the Israeli Army responded and French and British paratroopers attacked, Nasser benefited by the fact that the Soviet Union was turning its rockets toward London and Paris. At the same time, the United States spoke out against France and Britain. The United Nations sanctioned the Anglo-French action, and the canal remained under Egyptian control. Nasser's success inspired Iraq to leave the Western fold in 1958; and, in 1959, the revolution in Cuba was also successful. The political situation changed radically in both those countries: in Iraq, the pro-Western King Faisal was assassinated, and in Cuba the American-backed dictator Batista was overthrown. The West refrained from bringing pressure to bear on Iraq. The arrival in Lebanon of American troops and the dropping of British paratroopers in Jordan were seen as security measures, albeit spectacular ones. Cuba, on the other hand, now governed by Fidel Castro, became a thorn in Washington's side, while winning the warm support of Moscow. From this point on, the rest of Latin America could not help but be affected by the Cuban revolution.

AND A REVOLUTION IN BUDAPEST. MORE THAN SIXTY FORMER COLONIES GAINED THEIR INDEPENDENCE.

The communist governments in Eastern Europe welcomed the idea of peaceful coexistence and reconsidered their policies accordingly. Hungary was the most sensitive to this change in policy. In October, 1956, at the very same time that the Franco-British and Israeli attacks were being launched against Egypt, a bloody uprising took place in Budapest. The uprising was brutally crushed by the Soviets and their supporters. One such Soviet protégé, János Kádár, nonetheless became for thirty years the architect of a brand of communism quite distinct from that of the other members of the Warsaw Pact. But something had changed among communist governments as well as among extreme leftist parties: allegiance was divided between the Soviet Union—with its Marxist ideology spiced with remnants of a Great Russian sentiment—and China, the self-appointed champion of the Third World, whose population was rapidly approaching 1,000,000,000—90 percent of whom were peasants.

In Western Europe, France, which had been sharply admonished over Vietnam at the 1954 Geneva Conference, had learned its lesson, not only from such military defeats as that of Dien Bien Phu, but also by its gradual eviction from Indochina both by communist pressure and by American diplomatic support for the anti-French South Vietnamese president, Diem. In Africa as well—except in Algeria, where civil war was still raging—France began following the example of Great Britain, which, from 1945 on, had begun replacing its military personnel in Asia and Africa with civilian envoys. Several former colonies had already joined the Commonwealth, which had hitherto been the exclusive domain of whites. Within a few years, this new policy of Great Britain and of France resulted in the independence of more than sixty countries, which, in turn, served to greatly disrupt the delicate balance of political

IN 1958, DE GAULLE WAS RECALLED TO POWER, AND QUICKLY ENDED THE WAR IN ALGERIA. DISSENSION BETWEEN THE U.S.S.R. AND THE U.S. OVER SOVIET MISSILES IN CUBA ESCALATED INTO A FULL-BLOWN CRISIS IN 1962.

forces within the United Nations. Henceforth, the African and Asian countries would hold a majority of the seats in the Manhattan headquarters of the U.N.

On the domestic front in 1958, the French people, weary of waging near-continual warfare in one part of the world or another ever since World War II, dissatisfied with more than twenty different governments since 1946, and eager to find a solution to their war in Algeria as well as other colonial problems, recalled to power General de Gaulle, who had stepped down in 1946. De Gaulle lost no time in ending the war in North Africa, initiating a rapprochement with Chancellor Adenauer, and fully assuming his role as a European with a firm belief in his country as a world power.

To sum up, several salient features marked the world situation in 1962: the presence of three major poles of attraction—Washington, Moscow, and Peking; the splintering of political blocs by certain countries determined to break away from the influence of the superpowers; the strengthening of economic ties between the industrialized countries, which, since the late 1950s, had seen a decline in their populations and a corresponding drop in domestic consumption (and especially investment); and the difficulties of developing countries to direct their efforts toward improving their economic situation. (Among such countries, the gap was widening between those which had managed to acquire the technological skills required for economic expansion and those which had not.)

In 1962, two major historical events occurred. The first of these was the end of the war in Algeria. The French departments of North Africa gained their independence, whereupon the majority of French nationals and most French military units returned home. The second was the Cuban missile crisis between the United States and the Soviet Union.

Fidel Castro, in power since 1957, had been drawing closer to the Soviet Union; finally, he agreed to allow the Soviets to establish missile bases on Cuban territory. John F. Kennedy, president of the United States since 1961, interpreted the move as a direct threat to American security. As soon as it had been proven beyond a doubt that Soviet technicians were working in Cuba, the U.S. government responded swiftly: in October, 1962, it announced a military blockade of the island and declared that the presence of nuclear missiles in Cuba would be considered an act of war on the part of the U.S.S.R. For one anxious week, the whole world watched and waited, fearing an incident involving Russian ships delivering arms. Finally, realizing that the threat of nuclear war was very real, Nikita Khrushchev backed down, and the two countries agreed on a timetable for dismantling the bases. This agreement, symbolized the following year by the establishment of a hot line between Moscow and Washington, seemed to mark the end of a long postwar period dominated by both covert and overt hostilities between the two superpowers. Indeed, now that they had resolved the Cuban crisis without even consulting their allies, the U.S. and the U.S.S.R. went a step further: they adopted the common goal of maintaining peace.

THE SOVIET-AMERICAN AGREEMENT REACHED AFTER THE CUBAN CRISIS HAD A FAR-REACHING EFFECT ON THE WHOLE OF LATIN AMERICA.

This agreement between the superpowers had two important consequences for the Third World. First, it weakened the role of the United Nations, where the dispute between East and West had granted a certain degree of power to the nonaligned countries. Second, it indirectly forced African and Asian countries to give top priority to their own national interests rather than to the question of U.S. and Soviet rivalry.

In Latin America, ever since the signing of the Bogota agreement in 1948, the political situation had been influenced by the Organization of American States (OAS), whose membership included every country on the American continent, from Alaska to Patagonia, with the exception of Canada. North America's influence in the organization had been of paramount importance since World War I. Were it not for the relaxing of relations between the U.S. and the U.S.S.R., Castro might have been able to play on anti-American sentiment in some Latin American countries to bring some converts into the communist fold. Indeed, all nineteen Latin American countries had been watching the situation in Cuba closely since 1959. Cuba's problems resembled their own: rampant inflation, a tremendous gap between rich and poor, and growing aspirations on the part of the masses for better living conditions. The appearance in the Caribbean of a government based on Marxist-Leninist principles aroused divided sentiments on the Latin American continent and eventually gave rise to political unrest.

In 1962, sensing the urgency of the situation in Latin America, the Kennedy administration launched the Alliance for Progress. This ten-year plan was designed to accelerate economic and social development in Latin America by carrying out certain reforms and gradually *distributing $20,000,000,000. Washington was convinced that the process of democratization would facilitate the struggle to overcome poverty—Castro's principal ally. In some countries, more liberal U.S.-backed governments began replacing dictators such as Rafael Trujillo of the Dominican Republic, a trend reminiscent of the reform movement in Argentina, sparked off by the fall of Juan Peron in 1955.*

Chapter VI – Nestlé

1947–1962 Nestlé Enters the Frozen Food Industry After Its Merger with Maggi

CHAIRMAN EDOUARD MULLER DIED IN 1948. HIS SUCCESSOR WAS C.J. ABEGG, WITH MAURICE PATERNOT AND ANDRÉ PERROCHET ACTING AS EXECUTIVE VICE-PRESIDENTS UNTIL 1952. AFTER 1952, ENRICO BIGNAMI AND JEAN-CONSTANT CORTHÉSY WERE TO TAKE CHARGE.

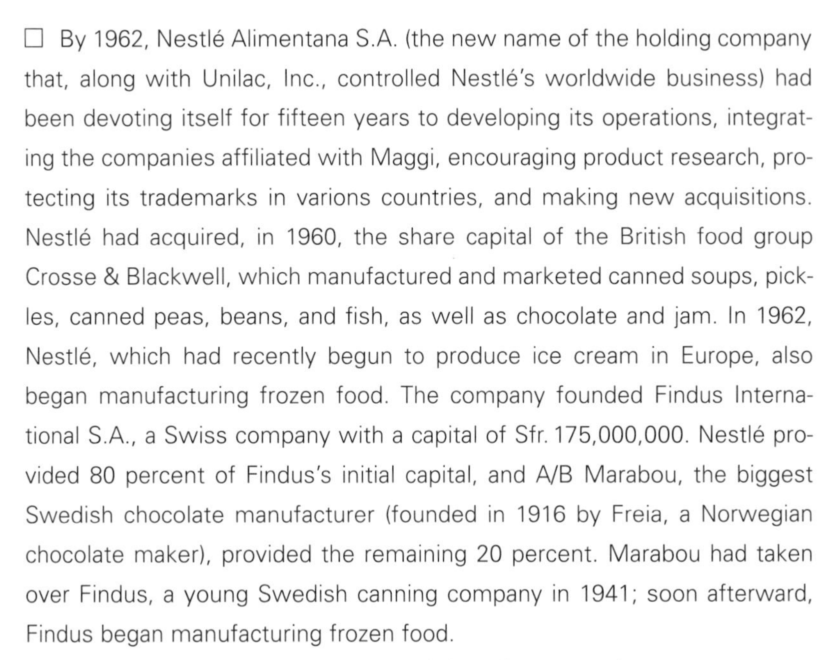

☐ By 1962, Nestlé Alimentana S.A. (the new name of the holding company that, along with Unilac, Inc., controlled Nestlé's worldwide business) had been devoting itself for fifteen years to developing its operations, integrating the companies affiliated with Maggi, encouraging product research, protecting its trademarks in varions countries, and making new acquisitions. Nestlé had acquired, in 1960, the share capital of the British food group Crosse & Blackwell, which manufactured and marketed canned soups, pickles, canned peas, beans, and fish, as well as chocolate and jam. In 1962, Nestlé, which had recently begun to produce ice cream in Europe, also began manufacturing frozen food. The company founded Findus International S.A., a Swiss company with a capital of Sfr. 175,000,000. Nestlé provided 80 percent of Findus's initial capital, and A/B Marabou, the biggest Swedish chocolate manufacturer (founded in 1916 by Freia, a Norwegian chocolate maker), provided the remaining 20 percent. Marabou had taken over Findus, a young Swedish canning company in 1941; soon afterward, Findus began manufacturing frozen food.

Edouard Muller, Nestlé's chairman, did not live to see these many accomplishments. In 1948, while on a visit to the U.S., Muller died suddenly. A supremely competent businessman, who was intensely human—jovial, approachable, and bursting with energy—Nestlé Alimentana's first chairman had the gift of infecting his colleagues with his own enthusiasm. Having loked after the company's interests during the most devastating war in history, Muller died just as the sound policies he had formulated were about to put a united and financially strong company on the road to a new exciting future.

Enrico Bignami

Carl J. Abegg took Muller's place as chairman of the board of directors. From that moment on, Nestlé was placed under the direct control of two executive vice-presidents: until 1952, the Frenchman Maurice Paternot and the Swiss André Perrochet and, after that date, the Italian Enrico Bignami and Jean-Constant Corthésy (a Swiss from the canton of Vaud). In spite of the sudden disappearance of Chairman Muller, who had conducted negotiations for acquiring the Alimentana holding company with a firm hand, the changing of the guard took place without a mishap, proving that Nestlé had a large reserve of executives and employees capable of ensuring the company's development. These were responsible for the firm's rapid rise to the position of one of the foremost multinational food companies.

THEY CONCENTRATED ON POOLING THE RESOURCES OF NESTLÉ'S AND MAGGI'S EUROPEAN OPERATIONS, ESPECIALLY IN GERMANY...

Individuals are of capital importance to all firms; so much so that one sometimes hears that the success of a company depends primarily on its chief executive, on top-quality products, and on the staff that the chief executive or his assistants have trained. A chief executive can delegate a great number of jobs; however, after a merger, for example, he cannot leave the task of integrating new people solely to personnel experts. There are certain burdensome responsibilities that no boss can delegate. Owing to its importance, Nestlé's 1947 merger with Maggi had to be handled with a mixture of tact and decisiveness. Maggi was not fully integrated overnight, for Nestlé's employees were entering a new field of production and still depended to a great extent on the know-how of Maggi's own experts. At times, the learning process was harsh and difficult, not only for the new arrivals in the Nestlé group, but also for Nestlé employees themselves. The experience was a good one, however, and it soon bore fruit.

Maggi had established itself primarily in continental Europe. The nationalization of its Czech and Polish factories and, above all, the erratic trend business in Germany that followed, had been bitter pills for the firm to swallow. Aware that Maggi's share of the food products market was in jeopardy in Germany, Nestlé's general management made an effort to regain what had been lost. Naturally, Nestlé was confident that it could hold its own against a growing number of competitors (particularly, big American companies now turning their attention to the Old World) and successfully overcome the various market pressures there. But it was very hard going, especially in West Germany. Since material damage to Maggi's facilities at Singen was insignificant compared to that inflicted on its administrative center in Berlin, efforts were concentrated on reviving Maggi's Singen operations first, and only later its operations in Frankfort on the Main. Before 1945, Maggi products had been top performers in their field in Germany, particularly in the eastern part of the Third Reich, which had now become a part of East Germany. Maggi's operations in the Federal Republic of Germany had to be reorganized and streamlined in order to give its employees new confidence and—even more important—to enable them to gain or regain a significant share of the market.

Jean-Constant Corthésy (1907–1976)

This was a long and arduous task, and the men sent by the company headquarters to manage Maggi often disagreed with their superiors, who continued to feel—with reason, perhaps—that the major emphasis should be placed on milk products, chocolate, and, above all, Nescafé instant

WHERE, LITTLE BY LITTLE, MAGGI WAS MAKING INCREASING PROGRESS. IN FRANCE, IT WAS MORE COMPLETELY INTEGRATED WITH NESTLÉ . . .

coffee. One of the characteristics of this relatively long postwar period was the great contribution made by the men from Nestlé working in the German Maggi Company to harmonize the activities of the various Nestlé concerns in West Germany, even though, initially, Nestlé, Maggi, and Sarotti—the German chocolate manufacturer in which Nestlé had been acquiring a growing interest since 1929—were completely independent of one another.

By the end of the 1950s, Maggi was once again a highly motivated company that had recovered its dominant prewar position on the West German market. This proved that, with hard work, qualified executives, and a strong sense of team spirit, a company could pass through periods of hardship and yet emerge unscathed. Shortly after the war, the Maggi Company was plagued by several problems. It was poorly organized and its activity was hampered by the slow return of employees from prisoner of war camps. Moreover, Maggi's senior management preferred working in the traditional way, producing low-priced products targeted at the lower classes; whereas new ingredients, a change in eating habits, and new consumer requirements incited the more progressive members of management to develop new products of higher quality that would appeal to middle-class consumers as well. It was these progressive managers who won the day, and the company soon began developing new products, while continuing to manufacture and market those that had made it so successful with the working class. Thus, from the late 1950s on, the German Maggi Company was once again a dynamic firm, marketing products adapted to contemporary tastes.

By 1962, in the Federal Republic of Germany, Maggi was selling, in addition to soups: its traditional bouillon and Arome, glutamate-based bouillon, seasoning in cube and powdered form, dehydrated and canned stew, ravioli and other ready-to-eat dishes, canned soups, as well as a wide range of sauces that enabled housewives to vary their menus. In the years that followed, Maggi put new products on the market: liquid and powdered condiments, new ready-to-eat dishes, and four kinds of potato-based dishes. Soon Maggi sauces were to become the best-selling items among the company's many products.

In France, Maggi was more completely integrated with Nestlé, owing to the authority exercised by the head of Société des Produits Alimentaires et Diététiques (SOPAD), Pierre Liotard-Vogt, the future chief executive officer and chairman of Nestlé Alimentana S.A. Apart from the Alsace region, in France sales of Maggi soups were relatively limited. In addition, they were

Bottles of Maggi Arome being automatically filled in a German factory, 1935

AND MAGGI'S DAIRY ACTIVITIES WERE TAILORED TO SUIT NESTLÉ'S REQUIREMENTS.

targeted at working-class customers and often could not even be found in the best stores. Maggi needed to develop a range of high-quality glutamate-based products making use of new ingredients. The case of Maggi soups in France was not exceptional: the same changes in customer tastes had taken place elsewhere. (Meat and vegetable bouillon were not as seriously affected by such changes, however.) Over the years, the French Maggi Company worked on improving the quality of its bouillon so that it would appeal to more discerning customers. From this point on, Maggi's were the best-selling bouillons on the French market. In 1962, Société Industrielle de Spécialités Alimentaires (SISA)—which Jules Maggi had established in Paris at the turn of the century—was still responsible for the manufacture of Maggi products. And this was the case until 1968, i.e., until SOPAD, the company that produces and markets Nestlé's products today, absorbed SISA.

Soon after the 1947 merger, however, the administrative and sales departments of SISA were incorporated into Nestlé: former SISA employees now found themselves holding the same position at Nestlé, and vice versa. Soon it was virtually impossible to distinguish between those who had come from Maggi and those who had always worked for Nestlé. This integration was very successful, especially since SISA employees had, in the words of Pierre Liotard-Vogt himself, "perhaps found at Nestlé the dynamism their own firm lacked; Maggi's business was doing extremely well; and, all things considered, Nestlé's move had been beneficial to everyone." As far as new products were concerned, in 1962, the success of Maggi's fish-soup mix, sold in small bags, had greatly enhanced the company's reputation for quality. That same year, the Nestlé group marketed its first mashed-potato flakes in France under the Mousline trademark.

Maggi soup being distributed to Swiss girl scouts, 1935

The reader will recall that the French market was of special importance to Maggi because of Société Laitière Maggi, whose sales figure for 1938 was more than five times higher than nondairy food products. In addition, when the question of a possible merger with Maggi was being discussed, Nestlé had clearly indicated that it did not wish to become involved in the distribution of fresh milk. Therefore, in 1947, Nestlé ceased to distribute fresh milk and sold its milk distribution network to a French company with which Maggi had an excellent relationship. Negotiations went on for over a year; and, in the end, Nestlé retained a few factories and shops. All things considered, this sale enabled the company to unburden itself of an unnecessary part of its dairy activity, while keeping its milk distribution networks and related factories, thereby helping Nestlé to expand its own canned milk operations. As for its more than 1,400 shops, over five hundred had already been closed; and more than eight hundred others, still in operation, were not doing particularly well. Nearly three-fourths of the shops were sold, and SOPAD kept the 224 best-located ones, which evolved into the Cercle Bleu group in 1948. The aim of this operation was to put at the company's disposal a distribution chain for quality food products that other big food companies might also wish to utilize. The same approach was used a short time later in the case of Laiterie Amiot's 146 shops, which belonged to Maggi but were completely independent. It was not until around 1962 that all of these shops were sold off, thus putting an end to this single exception to Nestlé's rule of not selling directly to customers.

NESTLÉ ALIMENTANA S.A. CONTINUED TO PROSPER THROUGHOUT THE WORLD. . .

By 1962, the Maggi and Nestlé companies in Switzerland had long since resolved the problems involved in pooling their staff. Although the competition had managed to stir up public opinion to a certain extent at the time of the 1947 merger, these tensions soon disappeared.

We have dwelt at some length on the subject of how the Maggi Company was absorbed by Nestlé in order to provide the reader with an example of the mechanism of a typical Nestlé merger. And in our discussion of the subsequent mergers that were to contribute to making the company what it has become today, we shall leave this aspect aside. It is necessary, however, to draw the reader's attention to certain complex and little-known aspects of a merger—which cannot be avoided even when both companies are based in the same country. Perhaps this will also help demonstrate how much more cautiously Nestlé had learned to operate in such critical situations. While existing structures must be modified after a merger, moral, social, and psychological considerations must also be taken into account. Success, and success alone, is what counts in human relations, and know-how is not something one can learn from books; it must grow out of practical, day-to-day experience.

One of the shops in Paris belonging to Société Laitière Maggi

In view of its activities throughout the world, by 1962, Nestlé was becoming an increasingly global company, with a total turnover of nearly

IN EVERY FIELD OF ACTIVITY (DESPITE THE NATIONALIZATION OF ITS CUBAN FACTORIES IN 1960).

SFr. 5,000,000,000 (SFr. 4,934,000,000 to be precise), which was more than 33 percent greater than that of 1959. The company was careful to protect its trademarks in several countries. As a result, wherever possible, Nestlé tried to gain full control of the firms bearing its name and utilizing its manufacturing processes. In 1949, Unilac, Inc. had taken over Lamont, Corliss & Company for precisely that reason. When Peter, Cailler, and Kohler merged in 1911, those three companies granted Lamont, Corliss the exclusive right to manufacture and market the chocolates of the new company that evolved from their merger both in the U.S. and Canada. The 23,000 shares (37 percent of Lamont, Corliss's capital) owned by Société Suisse de Chocolats had passed into Nestlé's hands when it merged with P.C.K. in 1929. Over the years, Lamont, Corliss had developed into one of the biggest chocolate manufacturers in the U.S. When Thomas V. Lamont, founder of Lamont, Corliss, died in 1948, Nestlé began negotiations with his heirs. The following year, Unilac acquired all of the American company's capital, thereby ensuring itself control over the manufacture and marketing of Nestlé brand chocolates in the U.S. and Canada.

Despite the fact that the company was busy continually extending its range of products and ensuring the protection of its trademarks, Nestlé could not afford to reduce the production levels of its traditional range of products whatsoever. From 1951 to 1966, Nestlé established more than forty new production centers in all parts of the world to manufacture condensed and powdered milk, Nescafé, Nesquik, baby food, enriched foods, chocolate, as well as other food products. Such expansion was not without risks, of course, particularly in the case of the Third World. For example, Nestlé companies in Cuba, employing a total of 1,200 Cubans, were nationalized in 1960, which put an end to Nestlé's manufacturing and sales there. (This, despite Nestlé's long tradition on the island, starting with the opening of the Bayamo factory in 1930 and continuing, subsequently, with the creation of three additional production facilities.)

Carrier tricycle delivering Nestlé, Peter, Cailler, and Kohler chocolates in Amsterdam, ca. 1930

In addition to building new facilities from scratch, Nestlé also incorporated a number of existing, hitherto independent, manufacturing centers into its production network. One characteristic of the firm that has remained the same throughout its existence is its basically horizontal organization. As mentioned before, Nestlé neither produces its own raw materials nor distributes its products directly to consumers. And it was a major event when it decided to manufacture certain packaging materials for its products. (For example, it is Nestlé that produces the billions of tin cans it uses every year.)

IN 1956, NESTLÉ TOOK STEPS TO ENSURE THAT IT WOULD REMAIN A SWISS COMPANY. ONCE AGAIN, EMPHASIS WAS PLACED ON RESEARCH AND DEVELOPMENT.

By expanding its activities, Nestlé became increasingly international in character, and the soundness of its organizational structure enabled it to rise to the level of one of the world's leading firms. The experience of World War II convinced Nestlé's management that the great majority of shareholders welcomed the firm's expansion throughout the world. In order to protect these characteristics, the management proposed that the issuing of registered shares—whose registration would be subject to authorization by the board of directors—be limited to Swiss citizens. This ensured a certain amount of stability and balance in the way the company's shares were distributed both inside and outside Switzerland. In April, 1959, the board of directors proposed tripling the share capital by issuing 1,304,000 registered shares with a par value of SFr. 100—to which the shareholders agreed in May. These new shares were offered at the rate of two new registered shares for each old bearer share. As a result, Nestlé's capitalization rose from SFr. 65,200,000 to SFr. 195,600,000. At the same time, Unilac, Inc. issued 1,304,000 shares with a par value of $12, thus increasing its capital from $7,824,000 to $23,472,000. (The reader will recall that Unilac shares, at that time, still formed a part of Nestlé stock certificates.)

Nestlé continued to place particular emphasis on research. The new research laboratories that the company had begun building in Vevey in 1947, were inaugurated in 1950. In order to provide the reader with a better understanding of the important task of Nestlé's quality-control and research specialists—both in Switzerland and abroad—we shall spend a few moments observing their work in detail.

A company wishing to maintain the highest standards of quality is obliged to keep a close check, at all times, on its raw materials, manufacturing processes, and finished products. But constant control is particularly important in the food industry, and it is absolutely essential in the case of the Nestlé Company, which utilizes a raw material as perishable as fresh milk.

In order to keep milk properly, its constituent parts must be put into a state of "suspended animation" during particular periods and under particular conditions. Fresh milk is produced within the cow's body—a kind of highly efficient living laboratory—and its quality depends on that of the fodder used to feed it, the level of hygiene in the cowshed, etc. Fresh milk must possess particular chemical and bacteriological qualities making it fit to be canned. During the canning process, strict controls must be maintained, for a foodstuff intended primarily for babies must be of uniform quality. Nestlé applies extremely strict quality-control procedures to every stage of the production process—from the collection of fresh milk to the sale of finished products. Nestlé applies the same strict quality-control procedures to all the products carrying its trademark. These involve on-site inspection by factory chemists, checks at the regional level, as well as analyses carried out by the central laboratories at Vevey. This is the only way to ensure the uniform quality of the great variety of foods produced by the group's factories throughout the world.

Today, as in the past, the vitality and creativity of the Nestlé Company has always been reflected in the work of its research scientists. Creative brains wage battles not only to discover new products, but also to solve the problems inherent in applying laboratory results to an industrial environment. New manufacturing processes and production techniques adapted to ever-changing customer tastes are constantly needed to ensure efficient production. Within a period of eleven years, the number of staff working in Nestlé's research laboratories tripled, thus underscoring the importance Nestlé attached to research as early as 1962. Having outgrown its laboratories opened in Vevey in 1950, Nestlé enlarged them in 1963, by remodeling several floors of an adjacent building. Finally, in 1986, Nestlé transferred its research laboratories to a new state-of-the-art complex located in the small town of Vers-chez-les-Blanc, just above Lausanne.

The Nestlé laboratories opened in Vevey in 1950

In the field of chocolate making, attention was devoted to ensuring more efficient mass production while maintaining the unique qualities of the various Nestlé brands. Thanks to the efforts of its research scientists, Nestlé was able to market a great many new food products, to improve automation, and to perfect its freeze-drying techniques. Since 1959, Nestlé engineers and research technicians have been able to tap the potential not only of the company's pilot plant at Vevey, but also of its new industrial laboratories at Orbe and Marysville, Ohio, to test new types of equipment and to study the feasibility of manufacturing newly developed products on an industrial scale.

THE BRITISH COMPANY CROSSE & BLACKWELL WAS ACQUIRED IN 1960.

Nestlé's Acquisition of Crosse & Blackwell (1960) and Locatelli (1961)

☐ In 1962, the Nestlé Company derived its strength from its own internal dynamism and from its various acquisitions. In the two preceding years, the company had acquired Crosse & Blackwell in Great Britain, La Gragnanese S.p.A. and Locatelli S.p.A. in Italy, as well as Cain's Coffee in the U.S. It had also acquired an interest in ice cream and frozen food companies in order to ensure its horizontal expansion.

By acquiring the share capital of the Crosse & Blackwell group in 1960, Nestlé gained control of that company's affiliates in Britain, Australia, South Africa, the U.S., and elsewhere, manufacturing canned soups, pickles, canned peas, beans, and fish, as well as chocolate and jam. This acquisition increased Nestlé's output capacity considerably by providing it with eleven additional factories, among which was the largest fish-canning factory in the United Kingdom, located at Peterhead in northern Scotland. (This was the first time that Nestlé had ventured into the seafood market.)

The origins of Crosse & Blackwell may be traced back to a firm established in London in 1706 for the sale of colonial produce. The business was operated for more than a century under the Jackson brand, and later under that of West & Wyatt, before eventually turning to the manufacture of food products. In 1830, two friends, Edmund Crosse and Thomas Blackwell—who had entered the firm eleven years earlier as apprentices—bought the company for the sum of £600 and gave it their names. In 1864, Crosse & Blackwell took over a small firm, Gamble & Company, whose founders had set out in 1811 to produce canned fruit, vegetables, and meat for the galleys of ocean-going vessels. After World War I, Crosse & Blackwell, which had been incorporated in 1892, with an initial share capital of £500,000, joined forces with two old established firms: E. Lazenby & Son, Ltd. and James Keiler & Son, Ltd. Elizabeth Lazenby, the wife of a London grocer, had started the first company in her kitchen, producing a sauce that enjoyed an excellent reputation as a seasoning for meat dishes. Manufacture on a commercial scale began in 1776, and the firm remained a family business until it was taken over by Crosse & Blackwell in 1919. As for the firm of James Keiler & Son, it was was well-known as the originator of Dundee Marmalade, made from bitter oranges, and famous in English-speaking countries.

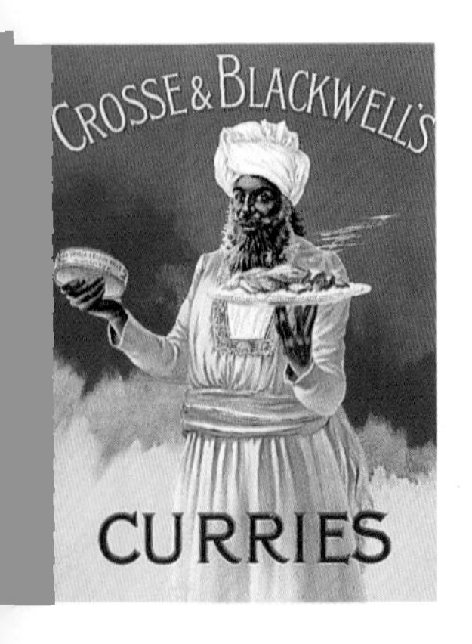

Crosse & Blackwell poster advertising exotic spices, ca. 1900

THIS ACQUISITION MET WITH THE FULL APPROVAL OF BOTH PARTIES.

Nestlé decided to acquire Crosse & Blackwell in 1960, above all, because, like Maggi, its products were targeted at the same clientele as Nestlé's. Maggi was a Swiss company, and Crosse & Blackwell a purely British one, mainly producing products for customers of the English-speaking world. As mentioned, Crosse & Blackwell's markets were primarily located in the sterling area, and this was of considerable importance to Nestlé. Nestlé's management realized at the time that this acquisition would help simplify and synchronize its sales networks. What is more, the products of the newly acquired company would benefit from Nestlé's R & D facilities. The new firm did not seem to require a great deal of new technical assistance to ensure its expansion. And the staff of Crosse & Blackwell did not have the same reservations as did a certain number of Maggi's senior executives in 1947 concerning the merger of their company with Nestlé. Crosse & Blackwell's employees realized that Nestlé could give their firm a needed boost. As for Nestlé, it felt that the acquisition of a typically English firm would serve to reinforce its presence in the English-speaking world.

There were other differences between Nestlé's 1960 take-over of Crosse & Blackwell and its 1947 merger with Maggi. In 1947, Carl Abegg was on the board of directors of both companies. Abegg was not a specialist in the food industry, but rather a general businessman who, at Alimentana, had seen the company's managers disappear at a time when the German Maggi Company was proving extremely difficult to rebuild. Owing to the difference in size between the Nestlé Company and Crosse & Blackwell, the acquisition of the latter posed no major problems, as Nestlé had the financial resources it needed to carry it out without a hitch.

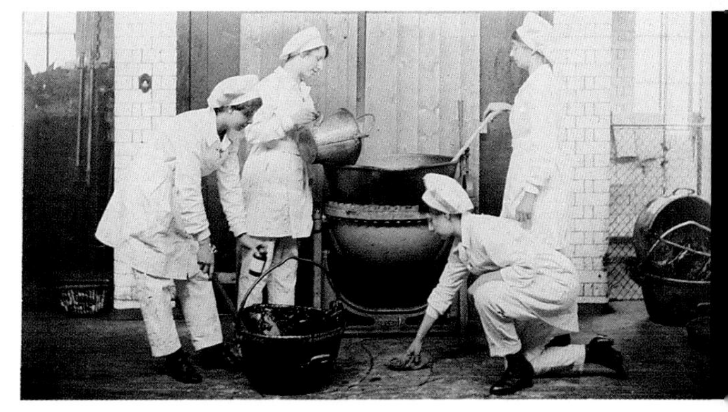

Preparing Crosse & Blackwell jam in London, 1914

Nestlé's acquisition of Crosse & Blackwell did not simply fall from the sky. Indeed, men played a decisive role in the operation. The chairman of the British company had revealed to Reginald Worth, general manager of Nestlé Alimentana S.A. and former head of its English market, his desire to secure the backing of a powerful group. However, the possibilities in this area did not look very promising at the time. Therefore, Enrico Bignami traveled to England to inform Crosse &

THE ACQUISITION OF LOCATELLI S.P.A., IN ITALY, FOLLOWED IN 1961. NESTLÉ WENT FROM THE MANUFACTURE OF ICE CREAM TO THAT OF FROZEN FOODS, THANKS TO THE ACQUISITION OF THE SWEDISH COMPANY FINDUS.

Blackwell's management that he intended to buy their firm. And an agreement was reached soon afterward. Nestlé acquired six production facilities in Great Britain (including Crosse & Blackwell's fish-canning factory in Scotland), one in the U.S., one in South Africa, and three in Australia. Crosse & Blackwell had employed 4,700 workers in production and 1,900 other employees and salesmen; their absorption into the Nestlé group brought the total number of its employees up to 69,000 in 1960.

In 1961, Nestlé acquired a considerable interest in Locatelli S.p.A., Milan. Locatelli, founded in 1935, was one of the main manufacturers and marketers of cheese in Italy. Over the years, thanks to the energy of its chief executive officer, Ettore Locatelli, the company had expanded its activities to include cold cuts and canned tomatoes. Locatelli possessed ten factories in Italy. In 1961, Nestlé also took over La Gragnanese S.p.A., with headquarters at Piacenza, and a tomato processing factory at Gragnano. From then on, that factory alone was to ensure the steady supply of tomato-based products to Maggi and Crosse & Blackwell production centers.

Nestlé's acquisition of Cain's Coffee in the U.S. in 1960 was a first, hesitant step in the marketing of coffee beans and ground coffee; whereas twenty years later, the company was to show much greater resolve.

By 1962, Nestlé had entered the field of ice cream production in Europe as a result of agreements signed by associated companies: with Heudebert, Gervais, France-Glaces in France; Jopa in Germany and Austria; and Derivados Lacteos in Spain. Although ice cream comprised only a relatively small part of Nestlé's huge manufacturing operations, its handling and sale required an uninterrupted series of refrigeration systems at every stage of the distribution network. Given Nestlé's experience in this area, the next logical step for it was to enter a new, much larger field, namely, that of frozen foods.

Mirabelle, Crosse & Blackwell's first motor-driven tugboat, London, 1913

The expertise acquired in the production of ice cream was indeed to prove quite valuable when Findus International S.A. was established in 1962. This was Nestlé's first experience as a frozen-food manufacturer. (Of course, freeze-dried coffee and the preparation of various ingredients used in

Nestlé's food products had necessitated the use of a certain amount of special equipment. It is also true that the manufacture of ice cream did resemble, to a certain extent, that of frozen foods. However, up to this point, Nestlé had had no opportunity to move seriously into the frozen-food industry.) The new holding company—initially established in cooperation with the Swedish company A/B Marabou—evolved from a young and rapidly developing manufacturer of frozen and canned foods. Other companies were soon to be set up in European countries where Findus products were not yet marketed.

In retrospect, it is obvious that Nestlé's merger with Maggi—whose products complemented those of Nestlé—had been beneficial to the group as a whole. Acquiring Crosse & Blackwell enabled Nestlé to enlarge its range of food products and—with the fish factory in Scotland—make its first foray into the field of seafood. The creation of the Findus Company added a whole new dimension to Nestlé's activities.

As early as 1961, it was only natural that Nestlé's management should attempt to enlarge its range of products by adding to it a line of frozen foods. The firm learned, about this time, that the Findus Company of Sweden was looking for a means of expanding its business to include all of Europe and the entire world. Before discussing the first negotiations, we shall take a somewhat closer look at the history of the Findus Company.

Poster from the 1950s advertising a traditional infant food produced by Locatelli

WITH A VIEW TO EXPANSION, FINDUS AGREED TO JOIN THE NESTLÉ GROUP IN 1962.

The Scandinavian Company Findus Joins Forces with Nestlé in 1962

☐ Although World War II was limiting its activities, in 1941, Marabou decided to enter new fields. And as soon as the opportunity arose, it bought a fruit and vegetable canning firm at Bjuv in southern Sweden, which operated under the name Findus (short for Frukt Industri, its full Swedish name). Soon afterward, Findus began to experiment with deep-freezing techniques, applying them to fruits and vegetables. In the autumn of 1945, Findus frozen products began to appear in the frozen foods sections of Stockholm grocery stores. Spinach and peas were the first frozen products that Findus launched. And they enjoyed immediate success.

A milestone in the development of Findus products was achieved with the introduction, in 1949, of boneless frozen fish fillets. Norway offered certain obvious advantages as a center for the production of frozen fish. And this led the Marabou-Freia group (Freia, as the reader will recall, was the Norwegian chocolate company that had founded Marabou in Sweden) to set up a deep-freezing facility for Findus in 1952 at Hammerfest in northern Norway, where fishing grounds were extremely rich. (This is one of the most northerly industrial plants in Europe.) The Findus factory at Hammerfest possesses a fleet of ultramodern trawlers, capable, thanks to state-of-the-art equipment, of detecting the presence of large schools of fish, of rapidly moving to the richest fishing areas during all seasons of the year, as well as of processing catches of fish right on board. Findus soon extended its activities to Denmark, where it acquired the Jalco deep-freezing plant at Frederikshaven. Since the original factory at Bjuv was unable to keep pace with the demand for frozen foods, three new Findus plants were set up in Sweden: the first two at Hälsingborg (one producing the same types of products as Bjuv, the other specializing in ready-to-eat dishes, frozen pastry, and a whole series of other precooked foods [some meat-based] for the housewife as well as large institutions). The firm's fourth Swedish factory was located at Karlskrona. At Grimsby, in Great Britain, Findus had a deep-freezing facility that also packaged products imported in bulk from Sweden.

It is easy to understand the interest of Nestlé's management in Findus. As Enrico Bignami himself was to write: "As soon as I received more detailed information on Findus, I took a plane and phoned from Copenhagen one of the two Thornton-Holst brothers, who ran the company. I said: 'I am

"Picking Oranges," a poster created by Sven Erixson for Findus jam, 1944

BY 1962, NESTLÉ HAD EXPANDED ITS NETWORK OF FACTORIES IN THE DEVELOPING COUNTRIES AND MOVED INTO AFRICA AS WELL.

Enrico Bignami from Nestlé. We don't know anything about frozen foods, but we could become your competitors one day. So, if you would be kind enough to invite me as a tourist, it would be a pleasure to get to know each other.' They replied that, as I had been honest enough to talk like that, they would be delighted to show me around their Bjuv factory. Two weeks later, we again met in Amsterdam to talk about the business and, little by little, about a possible rapprochement."

Talks continued for several months, and, in 1962, an agreement was reached that satisfied both parties. Nestlé acquired a majority interest (80 percent) in Findus, with the option of acquiring the remaining 20 percent at a future date—an option the company would take advantage of a few years later in complete agreement with the former owners. Moreover, Nestlé retained the management of Findus; and its chief executive, Lars Anderfelt, and Karl Evert Flink, head of its technical department, were subsequently to move to Vevey. This provided a satisfactory solution to the problem of ensuring the cooperation of all concerned. During the following four years, Findus extended its range of activities throughout Europe: to Belguim, France, Switzerland, Germany, and Italy. Factories were opened at Gross Reken, in Germany, and at Cisterna, near Rome, in Italy. As a result of this, Nestlé acquired know-how in a completely new field that was to prove extremely important to the company.

Of course, as Nestlé's regular operations continued to prosper in a favorable economic climate, the company was careful to maintain all of its traditional activities in the field of milk products, coffee, chocolate, and food products. This resulted in a constantly increasing level of capital investment and a growing number of new manufacturing plants being opened in several countries in Europe, America, Oceania, Asia, and Africa—where the Abidjan factory in the Ivory Coast began production early in 1962. The various Nestlé companies, in accordance with one of the firm's unvarying principles, owned none of their own cows for the supply of fresh milk nor their own sources of coffee or cocoa, and no sugar beet or sugar cane plantations. Rather, they obtained their raw

A Norwegian trawler belonging to Findus, 1960

materials via traditional suppliers, i.e., import companies dealing in foreign produce located near areas of highest demand. This saved the Nestlé companies from having to make the substantial investments that would have been otherwise necessary. A herd of cattle large enough to have produced all the milk used by Nestlé's factories throughout the world in the 1960s would have required pastureland almost the size of Switzerland! Moreover, as stated in one of Nestlé's reports to shareholders, the land needed to grow the coffee, cocoa, and sugar utilized annually by the Nestlé group would cover an area nearly eight times the size of Lake Geneva. This same report pointed out that, if one took into account the combined investment in livestock, processing plants, and equipment required, it would be "no exaggeration to state that vertical expansion of this kind would swallow up tens of billions of Swiss francs."

Chapter VII

1962–1974

A Golden Age Draws to a Close

Mergers and Alliances: Ursina-Franck and Stouffer; An Agreement with L'Oréal

THE COMMON DREAD OF ATOMIC WEAPONS BROUGHT THE AMERICANS AND SOVIETS CLOSER TOGETHER. THE WORLD ECONOMY EXPANDED RAPIDLY FROM 1945 TO 1973. THE NUMBER OF FARMS DECREASED.

1962–1974: A Time of Plenty Draws to a Close

☐ *Looking back from the vantage point of 1974, 1962 stands out clearly as a turning point in East-West relations; the agreement between Washington and Moscow over Cuba resulted in a tapering off of diplomatic jockeying. From that point on, the American and Soviet governments continued to confront each other both indirectly and, in some cases, directly, but never did they—and, in the view of optimists, never will they—confront each other in a third world war. By 1974, the Berlin, Korean, and Cuban crises were things of the past. Yet, East-West rivalry, no longer as acute in Europe and Latin America, still reared its ugly head in other parts of the world, in particular: the Middle East, Vietnam, the Persian Gulf, and southern Africa.*

Yet while a new political era was dawning in 1962, the same cannot be said for the economic situation. In fact, economically speaking, the postwar period might be seen as extending right up to the oil crisis of 1973 and its aftermath.

The postwar period, from 1945 to 1973, was marked by economic growth—strong in the industrialized countries, somewhat weaker in the developing countries. Growth was swift but sustained. Indeed, despite the unevenness of development, this may be considered a truly golden age of economic progress.

During this period, even though the U.S. economy did not grow as rapidly as Japan's or Mexico's, for example, its gross national product was far greater.

Postwar progress was most visible in the industrial sector. The automobile, television, electronics, chemistry, synthetic fabrics, nuclear energy, and exploration of outer space all began playing important roles in modern life. The use of coal as the main source of energy was, to a great extent, eclipsed by electricity, oil, and natural gas.

The economic situation in the developing countries was also improving. Yet the rift separating them from the industrialized world continued to widen, in part because of their sharply rising populations (owing to lower infant mortality rates and improved hygiene).

Throughout the world—but especially in the industrialized countries—a dramatic drop in the number of farms was accompanied, ironically, by a surge in agricultural production, thanks to technological advances. The service sector, too, grew considerably during this thirty-year postwar period—a trend which has continued unabated until the present.

During this period, the world's affluent countries steadily amassed huge amounts of capital. And money circulated freely. Although savings was still an essential part of the economic system, its importance was soon displaced by an increasing focus on consumerism, especially in poorer countries, where a greater and greater part of personal income had to be used for meeting basic needs. Moreover, the banking systems of those countries often failed to provide their customers with attractive personal savings plans, causing the wealthy to invest their money abroad. Finally, many countries, in the name of national security, embarked on expensive weapons procurement programs, and these required continual modernization.

Economic growth became a factor in the rivalry between East and West. This fact points up the extent to which political considerations were being eclipsed by economic ones, a trend that would intensify over time. Growth occurred sporadically, thereby destabilizing prices; this, in turn, stimulated inflation, which reached its peak in 1974.

During the period from 1962 to 1974, a number of significant events in the political, social, and military spheres merit special attention. It is important to note here that mass communication—be it via radio and television broadcasts or the written word—was bringing people ever more information about world events, while not necessarily providing deeper insight into the underlying forces behind those events.

The gentlemen's agreement between Kennedy and Khrushchev in 1962 led to the Moscow Agreement of 1963, which outlawed nuclear testing above the ground. It was indicative of the changing world political climate that virtually every country in the world was to ratify the agreement (except China and France). The nuclear arms race, for years the principal barometer of the cold war, was soon supplanted by the ostensibly more peaceful Soviet-American race to conquer outer space. The violent death of John F. Kennedy, assassinated in Dallas, in November, 1963, could easily have destroyed the fragile edifice built by his bold policies. Fortunately, it did not; and even when Nikita Khrushchev was removed from power in 1964, the understanding born of the Cuban crisis endured.

CAPITAL BECAME HIGHLY MOBILE. THE MASS MEDIA TOOK ON INCREASING IMPORTANCE. THE FIRST NUCLEAR ARMS AGREEMENT WAS SIGNED . . .

BUT LOCAL CONFLICTS CONTINUED TO PROLIFERATE. VIETNAM WAS THE FOCAL POINT OF ATTENTION. NEVERTHELESS, THESE WERE POSITIVE YEARS...

Still, 1964 was not without its share of conflict. In Panama, anti-American riots momentarily threatened the security of the canal. In Cyprus, a civil war between the Turkish and Greek communities required the intervention of U.N. peacekeeping forces. In the Congo, the rebellion of the so-called Congolese People's Republic, led by the pro-Chinese Christophe Gbenye, was thwarted by President Tschombe's mercenary troops equipped with American arms. In all three cases, the Soviet Union adopted an attitude of watchful restraint; even when the Americans began building up troops in South Vietnam, the Soviets remained silent. In October, 1964, three important events took place in rapid succession: Wilson's Labour cabinet defeated the conservatives and took control of the British government; Khrushchev was unexpectedly replaced by Leonid Brezhnev as secretary of the Communist Party and by Alexei Kosygin as premier; and, on October 16, China exploded its first atomic bomb.

In 1965, relations between President Johnson and the Kremlin were still so stable that even the direct intervention of American combat troops and the U.S. bombing of North Vietnam did not cause major diplomatic clashes between the two powers. China, however, seized this opportunity to step up its criticism of the Soviet Union. Neither the landing of American marines in Santo Domingo in the spring, nor the short-lived war between India and Pakistan provoked conflict between Washington and Moscow. On the contrary, the two superpowers used their influence to prevent the conflict in the Indian Peninsula from escalating into full-scale war. In 1966, thanks to the Soviets' intervention, an agreement was signed between Indian and Pakistani leaders in the Russian city of Tashkent. The American and Soviet governments also avoided direct intervention in the numerous conflicts arising between Third World countries. Two examples of this were the abortive conference at Algiers (where Colonel Boumedienne had just replaced President Ben Bella) and the pro-Western coup in Indonesia. In Europe, Ludwig Erhard carried the West German elections, and Charles de Gaulle was re-elected as president of France.

In 1966, despite general concern about escalating events in Vietnam, the world was nonetheless enjoying rapid growth. The new industrial revolution made possible by atomic energy and automation required larger economic units, more long-term and large-scale planning, and a

DURING WHICH GREAT MILITARY AND ECONOMIC ALLIANCES WERE FORMED.

higher degree of flexibility. These requirements have not changed. Indeed, the enormous scale of this scientific and technical revolution has brought about political, economic, and social changes that have affected the daily lives of people throughout the world. Yet, the concentration of economic power into larger and larger forms did not lessen the centrifugal force of international political disputes, as trivial as these might seem when measured against the fantastic opportunities that presented themselves to humanity.

Since 1966 marked Nestle's centenary, it makes sense to stop for a moment and look at the world from that vantage point. Taking into account all the various gains and losses, considerable economic progress had been achieved since World War II. This growth had been made possible by a series of economic (and sometimes military) agreements that were established slowly but surely after the war.

In Western Europe, the consolidation of economic power in the industrialized nations was embodied in the Common Market, and its counterpart, the European Free Trade Association (EFTA). In order to understand the origins of these organizations, we must search backward, through a torrent of dates and acronyms, and record the founding of these and other international organizations that came into being following World War II.

The first European customs union, Benelux, was formed in 1944 between Belgium, the Netherlands, and Luxembourg. In 1948, the Western European Union (WEU) was established as a result of the Treaty of Brussels. In that same year, the Organization for European Economic Cooperation (OEEC) was founded, with sixteen original member states, to serve as an interface between aid from the Marshall Plan—officially known as the European Recovery Program—and the beneficiary countries. The Eastern European bloc responded to the Marshall Plan with COMECON, the Council for Mutual Economic Aid, which brought together all the communist countries of Eastern Europe. In 1949, at the same time that NATO was coming into being, the Council of Europe was set up in Strasbourg, with the objective of encouraging non-military cooperation among Western European countries. In 1951, six European nations—the three Benelux countries, France, West Germany, and Italy—accepted the Schuman plan and signed the treaty establishing the European Coal and Steel Community (ECSC), which set up a regulatory

AMONG THESE: THE EUROPEAN COMMUNITY . . .

body, with headquarters in Luxembourg, to oversee coal and steel production in the member countries.

In 1954, following France's refusal to ratify the treaty establishing the European Defense Community (EDC), the Brussels Treaty of 1948 and the accompanying Western European Union were reinvoked, with Germany and Italy as new members. The Eastern European countries, unwilling to agree to the rearming of Germany, responded by forming their own military alliance, which paralleled that of NATO. In 1955, the Warsaw Pact was signed by the U.S.S.R., Poland, Czechoslovakia, East Germany, Hungary, Romania, Bulgaria, and, for a time, Albania.

Once these military alliances had been established, it was again economic problems which recaptured the attention of journalists. On March 25, 1957, the Six—Belgium, France, Italy, Luxembourg, the Netherlands, and West Germany—signed the Treaty of Rome establishing the European Economic Community (EEC) and the European Atomic Energy Commission (Euratom). Both these alliances took effect on January 1, 1958. Since then, the EEC has regulated goods, services, labor, capital, and tax issues. Its primary objective as a customs union was to promote comprehensive economic cooperation among its members in the areas of trade, finance, and social policy, and to establish a common trade policy toward non-member nations.

Over the twenty-five years following the establishment of the EEC, its membership grew to twelve countries, with the admission of Britain, Ireland, and Denmark in 1973, Greece in 1981, and Spain and Portugal in 1986. Today, the Community is about to take the next logical step and move toward complete harmonization in 1993, with its governing body, the European Commission, based in Brussels (as has been the case since 1958). Later we shall pick up the thread of the history of the EEC once again, for, in 1966, it was as yet a long way off. In 1960, Great Britain, having failed in a plan to organize a large European free-trade area including the six Common Market countries, had just signed the Stockholm Convention with two Nordic members of NATO (Denmark and Norway), three neutral countries (Austria, Sweden, and Switzerland), and Portugal. That pact, which took effect on May 3, 1960, and mandated the establishment of the European Free Trade Association (EFTA), with its headquarters in Geneva, enabled member states to adopt their own trade policies with non-members. Today, the European Free

Trade Association comprises only Austria, Iceland (since 1971), Norway, Sweden, Switzerland, and Finland (since 1985).

AND THE OECD.

In 1961, Canada and the United States entered the Organization for European Economic Cooperation (OEEC), transforming it into the Organization for Economic Cooperation and Development (OECD). This group has grown over the years to include Finland (1969), Australia (1971), and New Zealand (1973); Yugoslavia was later admitted as an associate member. The European Commission has worked in close cooperation with the OECD, whose members comprised, by 1987, 17 percent of the world's population, 45 percent of its food production, 67 percent of its industrial output, 67 percent of international trade, and 73 percent of all aid to developing countries.

Thus, by 1966 all the countries of Western Europe were already united in the OECD; unlike today, however, six of them belonged to the Common Market and seven to EFTA at that time. From 1961 on, Britain, then Denmark, Norway, Ireland, and Spain became members of the EEC; Austria and Sweden requested associate status. However, in 1963, opposition from General de Gaulle slowed the development of these organizations.

The 1957 Treaty of Rome had already paved the way for countries overseas to become associated with the EEC. In 1961, the OECD created a committee on development aid consisting of representatives from ten memberstates: Belgium, Canada, France, West Germany, Italy, the Netherlands, Norway, Portugal, the United Kingdom, and the United States. The committee, which Japan subsequently joined, was given responsibility for gathering information on the needs of the Third World, that burgeoning Afro-Asian political force twenty-nine of whose members had gathered at the 1955 Bandung Conference to adopt a policy of nonalignment with respect to the superpowers. In 1960 and 1961, the group's membership was suddenly expanded to include eighteen new African countries, including the former Belgian Congo, where bloody unrest following the secession of Katanga had necessitated the intervention of United Nations peacekeeping forces. By 1962, these nonaligned countries were making their presence felt at the United Nations. Europe, soon to lose the last of its colonies, sought ways of helping these developing countries economically without dominating them, introducing its technological advances and spreading its culture without imposing it upon them.

IN LATIN AMERICA, REGIONAL AGREEMENTS WERE ESTABLISHED. THE PRINCIPAL AGENCIES OF THE U.N. BEGAN THEIR ACTIVITIES.

In 1966, Latin America already had regional economic organizations such as the Organization of Central American States and the Latin American Free Trade Association; this latter group had established a free trade zone between Argentina, Brazil, Chili, Mexico, Peru, Paraguay, and Uruguay in Montevideo, in 1960; Colombia, Ecuador, and Venezuela subsequently became members as well. In Central America, the General Treaty of Central American Economic Integration was signed on December 13, 1960, with the objective of forming a common market between El Salvador, Guatemala, Nicaragua, Honduras, and Costa Rica. At the international level, the United Nations already had more than a hundred members and was active in a variety of areas. The organization had spawned many specialized agencies, including the International Atomic Energy Agency (IAEA), the International Labor Organization (ILO), the United Nations Educational, Scientific and Cultural Organization (UNESCO), the World Health Organization (WHO), the International Monetary Fund (IMF), the Universal Postal Union (UPU), the International Telecommunications Union (ITU), the United Nations Conference on Trade and Development (UNCTAD), the United Nations International Children's Emergency Fund (UNICEF), and the United Nations Food and Agriculture Organization, better known as the FAO.

Since its inception, the FAO has been grappling with the problem of world hunger, a problem which has only intensified over the years. Even today, more than one-third of the world's population suffers from hunger, malnutrition, or both; ridding the planet of this scourge, which is likely to worsen in the future, should be one of man's chief priorities. Indeed, the world population grew from 2,000,000,000 in 1930 to 3,000,000,000 in 1960; in 1974, it had reached 4,000,000,000 and in 1987, 5,000,000,000. In July, 1987, for example, nine out of ten children were born in the Third World. The work of the FAO and of numerous other international organizations addressing this problem has been centered on four basic tasks: understanding specific food requirements in each region of the world; making use of local resources; improving food distribution; and combating cultural taboos which, through the ages, have prevented people from satisfying their basic nutritional requirements.

Another international instrument worthy of note is the GATT, or General Agreement on Tariffs and Trade, which was signed by twenty-

A NUMBER OF SIGNIFICANT EVENTS CHARACTERIZED THE PERIOD FROM 1966 TO 1974.

three countries on October 23, 1947, in Geneva, and which took effect on January 1, 1948. This organization, too, has experienced tremendous growth since its inception; in 1987, there were ninety full members, and thirty-two countries with associate status. GATT agreements focus primarily on eliminating trade restrictions in the form of quotas, reducing customs duties, and developing international trade. These goals will be ever more difficult to achieve in a world where the gulf continues to widen between highly industrialized and less industrialized countries, between countries with limited natural resources but booming populations and others which are rich in oil reserves but sparcely populated. Indeed, these are only a few of the problems we must face in the years ahead in a world increasingly divided by huge disparities in average per capita income. And, in this area, economists from countries rich in natural resources and from consumer countries still fail to see eye to eye.

The period extending from mid-1966 to 1974 is quite rich historically. Though the list of important events is long, it is perhaps worth mentioning (though not necessarily in chronological order) some of the most outstanding of these: the conquest of the moon; the Arab-Israeli conflicts in the Middle East; the end of the Vietnam War; the Cultural Revolution in China; disturbances in the Congo; a military coup in Greece; civil war in Nigeria; social unrest in France, in May, 1968; the Soviet military intervention in Prague in August of that same year; the death, in September, of President Salazar of Portugal; serious conflicts between Catholics and Protestants in Ireland; the election of President Allende in Chili, the beginning of the conflict in Lebanon between Palestinians and the Christian Army; the 1969 takeover of power in Libya by Colonel Qaddafi; the consolidation of power by the shah of Iran; the rise to power in Syria, in November, 1969, of General Hafez el Assad; riots in Poland, in January, 1971; an armed conflict in the Indian peninsula following the secession from eastern Pakistan of Bengal, which subsequently became Bangladesh; the return of Okinawa to Japan, in June, 1970; the addition to the European Community, in January, 1972, of the United Kingdom, Ireland, Denmark, and Norway; the signing, by the U.S. and the U.S.S.R., in May of that year, of the SALT accords limiting strategic nuclear arms; the bloody Palestinian terrorist attack at the Olympic Games in Munich, in September; the return of ex-President Peron to Argentina, in November; the unfolding of the Watergate scandal, in

AMONG THESE: THE SPACE RACE BETWEEN THE SOVIETS AND THE AMERICANS; THE END OF THE VIETNAM WAR;

April, 1973; the opening, in July, in Helsinki, of the first Conference on European Security and Cooperation, which lasted until August, 1975; the first oil crisis in October, 1973; the Yom Kippur War, in October, 1973, between Israel and neighboring Arab states; a military coup in Chile , in November, in which President Allende was assassinated; an attempted coup in Spain, in December, against the government of Luis Carrero Blanco; the dismissal of the negus in Ethiopia, in September, 1974. We shall now take a somewhat closer look at some of these events.

The space race between the Americans and the Soviets was well under way, when, on April 12, 1961, the Russian, Yuri Gagarin, scored a point for his country by accomplishing the first manned flight around the earth at an altitude of approximately 180 miles. Shortly afterward, President Kennedy decided to send a manned mission to the moon; five years later, in June, 1966, the American space probe, Surveyor I, *touched down on the moon after a three-day voyage. In December, 1968, three American astronauts traveled around the moon. One month later, the Soviets accomplished the first in-flight docking between two manned spacecraft. Then, on July 16, 1969, to the delight and wonder of hundreds of millions of television viewers, Neil Armstrong and Edwin Aldrin became the first men to set foot on the moon. Four months later, another American team touched down on the moon, and, on February 5, 1971, with the help of a small vehicle, two Americans took the first samples of the moon's surface. Four months later, American astronauts took a "jeep" tour of the moon. In November of that same year, the* Mariner IX *probe transmitted the first pictures of the surface of Mars. On February 25, 1972, another American probe set out to explore Jupiter. As for the Soviets, they had launched a probe that reached Venus as early as 1966. Despite the tremendous risks involved, this remarkable series of successes in space greatly enhanced the prospects for man's comprehension of the universe.*

But even the euphoria of "conquering" outer space could not make Americans forget the continuing drama of the Vietnam War. Military units of the Democratic Republic, seconded in South Vietnam by their Vietcong partisans, were waging fierce opposition against American troops, and eventually showed the world that their grassroots effort to expel the foreign presence and confront South Vietnamese troops could destabilize a powerful regular army. In August, 1967, spurred on by a

Senate vote that granted an additional $24,000,000,000 to the war effort, President Johnson raised the number of American troops stationed in Vietnam to 525,000.

Under American protection, South Vietnamese generals carried the presidential and senatorial elections held in September; despite charges by the civilian coalition that the elections had been rigged, General Thieu assumed power as president. Meanwhile, American bombers continued blasting Vietcong positions in the southern part of the country and in the river port city of Haiphong. In December, 1968, a protracted peace process began in Paris that would last until January 27, 1973.

During those years, President Nixon worked out a troop reduction schedule; the first troops were withdrawn in October, 1969, just a month after the death of the legendary Ho Chi Minh, president, since 1954, of the Democratic Republic of Vietnam. At the same time, the U.S. decided to intervene militarily in Cambodia. In May, 1970, U.S. troops landed in Cambodia in order, according to President Nixon, "to protect their soldiers and those of their allies." This turned out to be a limited military operation whose chief objective was to install South Vietnamese troops in Cambodia. The Americans withdrew in June of 1970, while the South Vietnamese remained until January, 1971. In order to stimulate peace talks, the American government declared a blockade against North Vietnam while continuing its bombardment until December, 1972, a month before the Paris cease-fire. In March, 1973, the last American marines left Vietnam.

Though the war was over for the Americans, it dragged on for the Vietnamese until April, 1975, when the South was definitively defeated by the North. The losses were heavy: more than 200,000 South Vietnamese soldiers and nearly 500,000 civilians died; more than 56,000 American soldiers were killed out of a total of 500,000 who took part in the war. Moreover, the war cost the United States $123,000,000,000. The domestic consequences of the war were felt not only in Vietnam, where 12,000,000 people were displaced, but also in the United States, where returning soldiers encountered serious problems readapting themselves to civilian life. Moreover, the defeat left a deep psychological scar on the entire American nation.

In China, a revolution broke out in August, 1966. It began in Beijing with student demonstrations in support of the Central Committee's call

THE CULTURAL REVOLUTION IN CHINA, AND ACCORDS BETWEEN CHINA AND THE U.S.; BLOODY CONFLICTS IN ZAIRE AND IN NIGERIA;

for a "great proletarian cultural revolution." They demanded a return to the peasant communes of 1958, thereby repudiating Mao's Great Leap Forward. At this time, the Red Guards made their first appearance, and their leaders were soon calling for the resignation of President Liu Shaoqi. In February, 1967, the regular army regained control of the capital, but only two months later Liu Shaoqi was accused of having organized a coup against Mao Zedong in February of 1966.

Despite such domestic turmoil, China was conducting secret negotiations with the United States designed to improve relations between the two countries. However, in late November, the United Nations refused mainland China's request for membership in that organization. In April, 1970, China launched its first satellite; in July of that year, diplomatic relations with the U.S.S.R., which had been broken off since 1959, were partially restored. (They were not fully restored until 1989.) In September, 1971, Lin Piao, leader of the opposition to Mao Zedong, died in an airplane crash in Mongolia while attempting to flee to the Soviet Union. A month later, the People's Republic was admitted to the U.N. as the sole official representative of China, thus making impossible Taiwan's continued participation. This event marked the end of a more than twenty-year dispute. On February 21, 1972 , President Nixon went to Beijing on an official visit that had been carefully prepared by his special advisor, Henry Kissinger. This new, more pragmatic policy on the part of the head of the Chinese government, Zhou Enlai, had won out over opposition from the army and disapproval from Moscow. The United States withdrew its troops from Taiwan.

The former Belgian Congo, now independent, changed its name to Zaire. Joseph Mobutu came to power in 1966, and changed the name of the capital from Leopoldville to Kinshasa. The former prime minister, Moïse Tschombe, from the province of Katanga—which had seceded for two years and resisted United Nations peacekeeping forces with mercenaries brought in from Europe and local police—died in 1969. On November 3, 1969, General Mobutu was officially received in Brussels as president of the Democratic Republic of the Congo by King Baudouin I, whose great great uncle, Leopold II, had claimed the Congo for Belgium in 1885. Notwithstanding the guerilla activity that continued in the province of Shaba until 1978, this marked the end of a bloody regional conflict.

A MILITARY PUTSCH IN GREECE; IN 1967, THE SIX-DAY WAR IN THE MIDDLE EAST;

South of Zaire, in Nigeria, the most heavily populated country in Africa, the military seized power in 1966. In May, 1967, the province of Biafra made moves toward secession; a state of emergency was declared throughout the country, but in September, the west-central region declared its independence. The Nigerian government quelled the insurrection, setting off a civil war in Biafra. A year later, 8,000 to 10,000 civilians were dying daily in refugee camps there, most of them of hunger. Though people throughout the world were moved by the terrible suffering of children in that land, the humanitarian aid effort on the part of the International Red Cross was continually thwarted due to fighting in the area. The bloodbath lasted two and a half years, until January 12, 1970. By that date, more than 2,000,000 people had died. Especially hard hit was the Ibo tribe, with 14,000,000 people living in the eastern part of Nigeria, where the secession movement had begun. The state of emergency was lifted in September, 1978.

In Greece, a group of army colonels staged a coup, in April, 1967, under the pretext of staving off a takeover by the Left. Scores of political figures from every party were deported. The leader of the coup, Colonel Papadopoulos, was as fiercely anti-communist as he was nationalistic. At first, King Constantine accepted the situation, but in December, after trying in vain to impose a democratic government, he went into voluntary exile. In August, 1971, the military leaders, plagued by both domestic and foreign opposition, attempted to set up a new civilian government while in fact maintaining political power. Georges Papadopoulos became prime minister, minister of foreign affairs, and minister of defense. Four years later, in June, 1973, the junta proclaimed a republic; on August 19, Papadopoulos addressed the nation as president. But the regime was overthrown in November, following protests in Athens by tens of thousands of people voicing their hostility toward the new president. On July 23, 1974, the former prime minister, Constantine Caramanlis, was reinstated and democracy restored to the country.

The regional conflict that posed the most far-reaching and serious threat to world peace was incontestably in the Middle East, that strategic link between Europe and Asia. There had already been two wars between Israel and the surrounding Arab countries, one at the moment of Israel's creation in 1948, and another following the Suez affair of 1956. On June 5, 1967, following Egyptian President Nasser's call in May for

IN 1973, THE YOM KIPPUR WAR;

the withdrawal of U.N. peacekeeping forces from the Israeli-Egyptian border, Israel unleashed the third Arab-Israeli conflict. As a result of its offensive, Israel acquired three strategic territories: the Gaza Strip, along the Egyptian border; the Golan Heights, in northern Syria; and the west bank of the Jordan River. In addition, nearly all of the Sinai came under Israeli domination. The Six-Day War, as it became known, transformed the Middle East. The Arab countries, refusing to admit defeat, plotted their revenge. But only the Palestinians carried on the fighting. The Palestinian National Congress, whose task it was to coordinate the resistance, named Yasser Arafat, founder, in 1963, of the Al Fatah resistance movement, head of the Palestine Liberation Organization. In 1974, as head of the Palestinian resistance movement, Arafat delivered his famous speech to the United Nations. Various Palestinian combat groups began staging operations whose express purpose it was to bring their cause to the public's attention. One such attack, at the Olympic Games in Munich, in September, 1972, left eleven Israeli athletes dead; five terrorists were killed by German police, but the three survivors were freed after an Arab commando hijacked a Lufthansa plane and demanded their release.

In 1969, Anwar Sadat became vice-president of Egypt. In September, 1970, President Nasser died of a heart attack; and on October 15, Sadat became president. Only a month earlier, King Hussein of Jordan had ordered the brutal repression of Palestinians living in Jordan, an event which soon became known as Black September. In 1971, Sadat confirmed the presence of Soviet advisors in Egypt. Shortly thereafter, he began a purge of political adversaries suspected of plotting against him. However, he was unable to prevent the assassination, in Cairo, in November, 1971, of the prime minister of Jordan by members of the Palestinian organization Black September. In July, 1972, Sadat dismissed his Soviet military advisors.

In August, 1973, Sadat met with Colonel Qaddafi, but subsequently canceled a plan to unite Egypt with Libya. On October 6, during Yom Kippur, the most important Jewish holiday, Egypt and Syria, equipped with Soviet arms, attacked Israel. They seized the Suez Canal. But the Israelis stood firm on the Golan Heights. With the help of American military equipment, they rebounded, taking back territory they had lost, reclaiming the canal, and taking the Sinai, at least temporarily. A cease-

fire, negotiated by Henry Kissinger and Alexei Kosygin, took effect on October 25. This agreement was a prelude to a historic accord leading to the normalization of relations between Egypt and Israel and the reopening of the Suez Canal, in June, 1975. The tension that had been building up between the U.S. and the Soviet Union (both of which had put military forces on maximum alert) soon dissipated. In that same month, the solidarity of Arab nations (apart from Egypt) culminated in the first oil crisis, which we will later discuss in further detail.

MAY '68 IN FRANCE;

The 1960s were not only marked by confrontation of a military nature; indeed, the youth of the industrialized world began voicing its opposition to the values of a consumer society. In March, 1966, numerous incidents took place following demands for reform in several French universities, in particular at Paris-Nanterre. The malaise, caused by young people's disaffection with what they perceived as an inhumane capitalist system preoccupied by material gain, culminated in the historic events of May '68.

As disturbing as the university demonstrations were, few observers realized that they were, in fact, the outward manifestation of a far deeper psychological malaise affecting young people all across Europe. On May 2, classes were suspended at the University of Nanterre; two days later, the Sorbonne was closed. Police barricades were erected in the Latin Quarter in reaction to threats by a few ringleaders.

During the days that followed, university authorities hardened their position, closing more colleges. The students' anger toward the government escalated. On May 6, more than 50,000 students on vacation broke through the barricades and met head-on with about 20,000 police. What had begun as peaceful demonstrations mushroomed into processions of young people, many of whom were now singing the Internationale and shouting Maoist slogans.

The demonstrations quickly spread to other universities; in Lyon, workers joined in with the students. On May 10, in Paris, confrontations with police intensified. Workers' unions joined in the melee by calling for a general strike on Monday, May 13, in which 200,000 people marched behind leftist leaders, including Pierre Mendès-France and François Mitterrand. The movement continued to spread, affecting some theaters, the Renault automobile factories, and eventually the national railroads. On May 18, more than 2,000,000 people were on strike in Paris alone.

General de Gaulle, traveling in Romania, cut short his trip and returned to the capital. The unrest had already spread to the national radio and television network, as well as to the textile and chemical industries; by May 21, the strike was affecting 8,000,000 workers throughout France. The franc was plummeting, which caused a serious flight of capital from the country. People began hoarding food. The government, caught off guard, struggled to formulate a response. On May 24, President de Gaulle announced a referendum, and the next day, agreements were concluded between management and textile workers. But on the 29th, the unrest was still such that the president, after spending one day visiting French troops stationed in Germany, had to take his case to the people, and the next day dissolved parliament. Tensions abated; May '68 was over.

On June 30, general elections confirmed de Gaulle's wager: the Gaullist party won an absolute majority of seats in the National Assembly. The Left was defeated, and it seemed de Gaulle was more powerful than ever. Georges Pompidou was replaced by Maurice Couve de Murville as prime minister. Yes, May '68 was over; however, its impact was long felt, both within France and well beyond its borders. France's political and economic stability was so undermined that the franc was devalued in 1969. There were far-reaching sociological effects as well, ranging from an acceleration of the women's liberation movement to a new relationship between superiors and their subordinates in both the public and private sector, in education, and in the mass media.

By July, student unrest, which had spread to universities in Dakar, Germany, Belgium, and Poland, had calmed. But the political situation in France was far from stable: on April 28, 1969, voters roundly rejected de Gaulle's referendum on regionalization and Senate reform. De Gaulle, devastated, interpreted the referendum as a vote of no confidence, and stepped down from the presidency. Georges Pompidou was elected president. Eighteen months later, de Gaulle died suddenly at his home in Colombey-les-Deux-Eglises.

1968 was also a fateful year in the United States: both Martin Luther King and Robert Kennedy, the brother of John F. Kennedy, were assassinated. World attention was also focused on Czechoslovakia—and more particularly on Prague—where, in the spring of that year, Czechoslovakia attempted, in vain, to free itself from Soviet domination. A central player in the tragic events there was Alexander Dubček, who, on January 5, had become head of the Czech Communist party following the Central Committee's decision to separate the functions of chief of state from those of party chief.

While students in Paris were chanting the slogans of the far Left, young Czechs saw Alexander Dubček as a champion of a more democratic form of Marxism. Many intellectuals began raising their voices against the secret police, and the tone of state-run newspapers, hitherto strongly pro-government, changed completely. Though foreign observers contended that there were no signs of an anti-Soviet revolution like the one brutally put down by the Red Army twelve years earlier in Hungary, the Soviet government decided to take no chances. On August 20, after weeks of discussions between the Czech government and leaders of East Germany, Romania, and Yugoslavia, Soviet tanks, seconded by units from Bulgaria, East Germany,[1] Poland, and Hungary, rolled into Czechoslovakia. Unlike what had happened in Budapest in 1956, where the chief executive Imre Nagy was immediately deposed and later executed, Dubček and the reformists remained in power for a short time. In October, an accord was signed with the Soviet Union according to which it was stated that the presence of Russian tanks in Czechoslovakia was not a violation of that country's sovereignty. By the end of the month, foreign troops from countries other than the U.S.S.R. were withdrawn. In April, 1969, Alexander Dubček was stripped of all official functions and began twenty years of exclusion from public life. He was succeeded by Gustav Husak.

IN EASTERN EUROPE, THE SPRINGTIME EVENTS IN PRAGUE; A COUP IN CHILE IN 1973;

While diplomatic circles were preoccupied in 1968 by the return of democracy to Portugal after the death of the authoritarian leader, Salazar, and the rise to power of Marcello Caetano in 1969, attention was focused on another Latin (albeit overseas) country: Chile. In March, 1969, the Christian-Democratic party of President Edoardo Frei lost its majority in parliamentary elections. A coalition of leftist parties, headed by Salvador Allende, was gaining momentum.

At the end of Frei's term of office, in September, 1970, while Allende did not win an absolute majority of the votes, his party managed to edge out its conservative and Christian-Democratic rivals. On October 24, 1970, thanks to limited Christian-Democratic support, the Chilean congress confirmed the election of Allende to the presidency. Two months

IN 1971, A CONFLICT BETWEEN INDIA AND PAKISTAN;

later, the new government began nationalizing large properties, taking over the copper mines in July, 1971. However, Allende's forces were not able to carry congressional elections. Shortly afterward, the United States cut off credit to Chile. In December, demonstrators protesting against food shortages took to the streets of Santiago. Allende responded by declaring a state of emergency and by suspending the convertibility of Chilean currency.

In the autumn of 1972, the opposition issued accusations against four ministers on constitutional charges, forcing the government to step down. During the year that followed Allende was plagued by crises for which he was forced to form ministerial task forces with military and civilian members. In June, 1973, he once again declared a state of emergency, but was still unable to secure full power.

Meanwhile, the economic situation continued to deteriorate: inflation exceeded 1,000 percent, the government was completely out of money, and food and supplies were scarce. The public as well as some of the labor unions were in a state of extreme agitation. In early September, tens of thousands of women took to the streets banging pots and pans and demanding Allende's resignation. A week later, on September 11, a military putsch took place. The army insurgents, led by General Augusto Pinochet, took over Santiago, and then surrounded and bombarded the presidential palace, where Allende was later found dead. A junta made up of army, navy, air force, and police commanders came to power. Chile's popular front, communist, socialist, radical, and Christian Left parties were disbanded. In the purge that followed, more than 4,000 people died, 30,000 were arrested, and close to 10,000 were exiled. A year later, in June, General Pinochet was named chief of state and was to remain so until 1989.

In early 1971, Asia, which was soon to become the world's new economic pole of attraction, was once again in the limelight because of events on the Indian peninsula. As previously mentioned, India and Pakistan had signed an accord, in 1965, in Tashkent. Yet the rivalry between the two countries raged on. In India, maharadjas had lost their privileged status, in September, 1970, without incident. All seemed calm until, in March, 1971, during the first direct parliamentary elections in Pakistan since its independence in 1947, a government could not be formed.

Mujibur Rahman, the pro-autonomy candidate, had carried the eastern part of the country, while Zulfikar Ali Bhutto was the overwhelming victor in western Pakistan. The president, Yahya Khan, hoping to press his opponents into forming a coalition government, called out the army. This offensive against eastern Pakistan caused India to come to the aid of the autonomists and China to intervene on behalf of the Pakistani government, which was already preoccupied by the secession of Bengal. On December 3, the Indian Army attacked Pakistan, destroyed its air force, and initiated a total blockade of the latter's eastern coast. On the 14th, Indian forces took Dacca, the capital, and on the 17th, a victorious India called for an end to the fighting. During that same month, Yahya Khan announced his resignation and was succeeded by Ali Bhutto. On January 10, Bangladesh broke off diplomatic relations with Pakistan and Rahman became the head of the new country.

IN 1973, THE WATERGATE AFFAIR IN THE U.S.

A veritable bolt of lightning struck the American press in April, 1973. The Washington Post *discovered the implication of President Nixon—who had been comfortably reelected only six months earlier—in a break-in at the Democratic party headquarters in the Watergate building on June 17, 1972. This discovery quickly evolved into a serious political scandal. The journalists' investigations revealed that several men from the president's immediate entourage had been involved in the break-in. The attorney general, the secretary of commerce, and several key members of the president's cabinet, accused of having staged a cover-up, were forced to resign.*

Richard Nixon's role in the affair became the subject of passionate debate in a country where the president is a figure who is almost larger than life. Despite Nixon's television appeal for restraint, this did nothing to calm public furor. In July, the scandal took on a more drastic tone when Nixon refused to hand over tapes of presidential conversations to the Department of Justice. In August, Nixon decided to appoint Henry Kissinger, who had been successful in achieving a cease-fire in Vietnam, as well as in improving relations between Washington and Beijing, to the position of secretary of state. The resignation, in October, of Vice-President Spiro Agnew, accused of tax evasion and misappropriation of public funds, did not exactly help the situation. Nixon named Gerald Ford vice-president. In January, 1974, experts confirmed that one of the key presidential tapes had been tampered with, further undermining

IN SWITZERLAND, ALL SEEMED PEACEFUL . . .

Nixon's credibility. In July, the House of Representatives accused Nixon of obstruction of justice, abuse of power, and giving false testimony. On August 8, the thirty-seventh president of the United States submitted his resignation. Gerald Ford became president and Nelson Rockefeller became vice-president. The affair, which initially had seemed insignificant when the guilty parties were arrested during the presidential campaign two years earlier, coupled with the actions of a press confident in its role as a watchdog over political and social affairs, ultimately resulted in the downfall of a man whose role as moderator in Vietnam, with Moscow, and with Beijing was impressive, but whose arrogant style had won him critics on the domestic front.

For quiet, prosperous Switzerland, the period which we have just discussed was not what one might call historically significant. Worth mentioning, though, was the Swiss decision, on September 14, 1969, to grant women the right to vote in federal elections. A year and a month later, in a public referendum, the Swiss people rejected a proposal that would have severely limited the number of foreign workers allowed into the country. But even prosperous Switzerland could not remain invulnerable to the oil crisis of October, 1973; indeed, that phenomenon deserves closer attention, for it marked the end of a period of exceptional prosperity. No one could have predicted that, to support their interests in the Yom Kippur War, the Arab countries belonging to OPEC (Organization of Petroleum Exporting Countries) would suddenly decide to raise the price of crude oil.

Indeed, ever since World War II, the price of oil had been a topic of much discussion. Before 1939, payment of a relatively small fee enabled large oil companies to carry out the exploration of vast regions (sometimes of entire countries) in search of oil. In 1948, Venezuela was the first country to demand a share in the concessionary companies' profits. In 1949, one American company raised the level of its payments to Saudi Arabia; the other large companies soon followed suit. In that same year, Venezuela proposed to six oil-producing countries in the Middle East—in particular those located in the Persian Gulf—to band together to demand a greater share of oil profits. Shortly afterward, Iran demanded 50 percent of all profits; when the British concessionary company refused, the Mossadeq government nationalized the oil wells and refineries in the spring of 1951.

Despite the fall of the Iranian government and the subsequent exile of the shah, a precedent had been set. Nationalization was no longer challenged in principle; the only question was the form it should take. Five years later, an advisory commission was established in Cairo to assist oil-producing countries to determine prices. To the displeasure of the oil companies, in September, 1960, Venezuela, Iran, Iraq, Saudi Arabia, and Kuwait decided to formalize their position by creating OPEC. Eventually, Qatar, Indonesia, Libya, Abu-Dabi, Algeria, Nigeria, Ecuador, and Gabon were to join the organization.

YET IT, TOO, WAS SOON AFFECTED BY THE OIL CRISIS . . .

By 1973, Saudi Arabia, the United Arab Emirates, Kuwait, and Qatar were enjoying revenues of $22,000 000,000 per year; in 1971, the entire Persian Gulf—including Iran—was producing a third of the world's crude oil, of which 60 percent was being sold to Europe. A much smaller percentage was needed by the United States; moreover, the U.S. had welcomed the price increase insofar as it benefited its Iranian and Saudi allies, guaranteed production, and made the exploitation of North American crude oil reserves more profitable. On October 17, 1973, OPEC staged a major coup: it resolved to progressively reduce its oil export, for as long as the Israelis occupied Arab territory. This decision, ratified in Kuwait, not only catapulted the issue of oil production to center stage in the political arena, but had the secondary effect of highlighting the weak position of the non-oil-producing countries, in particular, those of Western Europe. OPEC declared a total embargo against those countries it deemed allies of Israel, which included the U.S., the Netherlands, Portugal, Rhodesia, and South Africa. Reductions to countries less openly supportive of Israel's policies—which included the majority of European countries—were less drastic: from November 5 on, exports of crude oil were reduced by 5 percent per month. Neutral countries were treated somewhat more favorably. Oil-poor countries found themselves obliged to take drastic measures to limit consumption—some even had to ration gasoline for automobiles. Some countries, like Austria, decided to require motorists to leave their cars at home one day per week; Switzerland prohibited driving on Sundays. Other countries, such as Denmark, Italy, Japan, Luxembourg, and Norway, prohibited all weekend driving. Most countries adopted lower speed limits.

These were some of the effects of what was subsequently dubbed the first oil crisis; the second took place in March, 1979. It is true that

MARKED BY ARAB OIL EMBARGOES AND SEVERE CONSERVATION MEASURES IN EUROPE. THE ENERGY CRISIS BECAME A CRITICAL ISSUE THROUGHOUT THE WORLD.

Nasser's closing of the Suez Canal in 1956 had served as a warning shot, as it were, in the general direction of the oil-poor countries. But the problem became much more serious in 1973. Indeed, in December of that year, in Tehran, the six members of OPEC agreed to double the price of a barrel of crude oil, which leaped from six to nearly twelve dollars.

Fortunatley, however, the world economy was not completely at the mercy of OPEC; fortunately for the oil-poor countries, a slight economic slowdown, an unusually mild winter, and restrictions on individual consumption enabled most of them to reduce their oil needs. The U.S., Japan, and Britain reduced consumption by 4 percent; France by 5 percent; West Germany by 10 percent; the Netherlands by 15 percent; and Belgium by 17 percent. These reductions were the result of limited individual consumption, restrictions on home heating temperatures, and a transition to daylight saving time. In addition, the use of coal was encouraged, as was oil exploration in virtually untapped areas such as the North Sea.

In the final analysis, the energy crisis had the positive effect of fostering a keen awareness of the energy problem. But there is no question that the West, with its seemingly unquenchable thirst for oil—for home heating, for the ubiquitous automobile, for fuel-guzzling industries and the development of plastics, for mechanized armies, and for air travel and transport—had been severely shaken. The effects of the oil crisis were felt for several years. Together with the monetary crisis of the early 1970s, the oil crisis gave rise to a long period of high inflation as well as a general and pervasive rise in unemployment.

Chapter VII – Nestlé

1962–1974

Mergers and Alliances in Rapid Succession

NESTLÉ WAS CONCERNED ABOVE ALL WITH CONSOLIDATING ITS ACQUISITIONS: MAGGI AND CROSSE & BLACKWELL. NESTLÉ CELEBRATED ITS CENTENNIAL IN 1966...

☐ From 1962 to 1974, Nestlé's activities gradually took on a more international character. A multinational must have a turnover big enough to enable it to contend with economic struggle at a global level. Until this point, Nestlé had increased its turnover by concentrating on three areas: products (improving old products and creating new ones), technology, and know-how obtained after acquiring firms that operated in fields new to Nestlé. From 1962 on, the quality of the company's milk products, chocolate, Nescafé, and frozen and nonfrozen food products were the best guarantee of its promising future. Therefore, the firm persevered in its efforts to produce high-quality products. It also devoted a lot of effort to adjusting its sales strategy to changing commercial practices that resulted from the growing importance of marketing and the appearance of big chain stores, which soon became widespread. Nestlé began selling massively to large groups of stores and no longer exclusively to a multitude of individual wholesalers or shop owners, with whom the personal influence of Nestlé's sales representatives had been the determining factor.

Moreover, whenever appropriate, the company continued integrating the firms it had acquired; it consolidated its merger with Maggi and completed the one with Crosse & Blackwell. Nestlé pushed the sale of Maggi products in their traditional European markets and introduced them in Latin America, Africa, and Asia. The company continued to pursue this policy, as we shall see in this chapter, applying it to natural mineral water in 1969, to Libby and its affiliates in 1970, to its catering service working with European restaurants, and to Roustang cheeses in France. Nestlé's 1973 acquisition of the Stouffer Corporation in the U.S., with its frozen foods and hotel chain, and the company's special agreement with L'Oréal, the French and international cosmetic giant, resulted in different types of cooperation. A vast field of activity opened up for Nestlé, which, until then, had been a large but relatively undiversified multinational. This second wind would enable Nestlé to achieve a position, once again, that was to prove all the more necessary now that competition was so fierce and the giant multinationals of the food industry had, during the same period, considerably extended the scope of their activities. Thus, following its centennial, Nestlé would increasingly expand its activities.

Nestlé celebrated its centennial in Switzerland and throughout the world in the summer of 1966. For the occasion, the company invited officials, employees, and customers to several special events. The main attraction, held in Lausanne on July 1, was preceded by speeches by Hans Schaffner, the president of Switzerland; Max Petitpierre, chairman of Nestlé Alimentana S.A. (and former president of Switzerland); Edouard Debétaz, president of the State Council of the canton of Vaud; and Hans Hürlimann, *Landamann* (cantonal president) of the canton of Zug and a future member of the Federal Council of Switzerland. (The reader will recall that Nestlé's holding company had two headquarters: at Cham in the canton of Zug and Vevey in the canton of Vaud.) Hürlimann gave a speech, following which Arthur Honegger's oratorio *Nicolas de Flue* was performed; the narrator was Pierre Fresnay, and Pierre Colombo conducted an orchestra of Swiss musicians brought together especially for the occasion.

Also attending this ceremony, which attracted nearly a thousand people, were the Federal Councilor Paul Chaudet, Pierre Graber, president of the National Council of Switzerland (and future Swiss president), Fritz Häberlin, the chief justice of Switzerland, the Swiss chancellor, officials representing the military and the church, as well as the civil administration of the cantons and cities where the company had its headquarters and factories, the president of the Federal Polytechnic Institute, the chancellors and vice-chancellors of the universities of Lausanne, Geneva, Bern, Zurich, Neuchâtel, and Saint Gall.

This celebration was also attended, as stated by Max Petitpierre, by "representatives of the Swiss and international organizations and institutions with which Nestlé maintains relationships of mutual trust and who are engaged in activities similar to our own . . . as well as by many prominent Swiss citizens and foreigners playing a prominent role in [the country's] cultural, scientific, and economic life, and with whom we have contacts or who represent business affiliates or competitors (competition need not exclude friendship); representatives of the trade unions with whom we discuss interesting—often personal—questions; the chairmen of our partners or affiliates, whose cooperation in the countries in which they operate is invaluable to us; representatives of the press; descendants of the families that founded our company; present and

Celebrating Nestlé's centennial (from left to right): Max Labenski, Jean Heer, Max Petitpierre, Yvonne Printemps

DURING WHICH ITS DIRECTORS REVIEWED ITS ACTIVITIES UP TO THAT TIME AS A DYNAMIC COMPANY RESPONSIVE TO CHANGING CONSUMER NEEDS AND UTILIZING STATE-OF-THE-ART TECHNIQUES TO MEET THE CHALLENGES OF A CONSTANTLY CHANGING WORLD.

former employees, especially those who defend our interests abroad, both in neighboring and distant countries."

In addition to such events, which took place wherever Nestlé operated, the company made available—in Switzerland and abroad—a movie about the firm's activities and a book covering its history.

What was Nestlé's position in 1966, after a century of activity throughout the world? Max Petitpierre ventured a brief evaluation, and the centennial book—which is the primary source for this one—has sketched a rough picture for us. The depiction of the firm and of the business world provided by certain speakers at Nestlé's centennial remains generally true, even today. Therefore, it is useful to recall several of their statements.

In his centennial speech, the chairman summarized his views as follows: "The two original companies evolved into what they have become today through a succession of often eventful steps. They expanded by entering into partnerships and by merging, at first with Swiss companies and then, over the years, with foreign firms. Their development was justified by the need not to depend on a single product, which was becoming increasingly subject to political considerations everywhere. They also needed to make use of the opportunities created in several countries by their bold yet circumspect sales and production policies. Research also contributed to company expansion by creating entirely new products. Finally, as the pace of modern life grew faster, it was no longer a matter of simply producing new food products or of applying to existing products the results of discoveries in the fields of medicine and hygiene. Life had to be made easier for the consumer, so that food could be prepared as rapidly as possible. Nestlé has always been careful to avoid stagnation, to avoid being too satisfied with its positive results; its greatest concern has always been to meet the challenge of changing life-styles by seeking to diversify its products and to widen the scope of its distribution by continually utilizing the most modern techniques. In order to do this, it must make an effort to understand not only the customs and tastes of each region, of each country in which it is active, but also the requirements for opening plants, training executives, and developing team spirit as well as a sense of duty among all those representing Nestlé and working for it in almost every part of the world. Today, the firm possesses factories in thirty-six countries throughout the world, and it markets its products almost everywhere. This has been achieved thanks, above all, to the perseverance, initiative, and courage of the men—in the past and the present—shouldering the considerable responsibility of managing the company, but also thanks to the relentless efforts of Nestlé employees of every nationality, who have put their energy and talent at the company's disposal." Next, Petitpierre emphasized that, during the 1950s and most notably during the previous twenty years, the world had experienced changes and upheavals that "have completely changed the business environment for multinationals as well as their position in the world in the face of new global problems that, while they are not of their own making, must also be resolved by them." Turning to challenges in the future, he went on to say: "Entering the second century of its existence, our company must stress its commitment to pursuing the policies it has pursued hitherto. Since it has always tried, throughout its long history, to keep abreast of progress, it will seek to play an increasingly active part in the development of the countries in which it operates."

NESTLÉ: A SWISS MULTINATIONAL, WITH EMPLOYEES FROM COUNTRIES ALL OVER THE WORLD.

The president of Switzerland, Hans Schaffner, pointed out:"almost uninterrupted economic growth following World War II has also had favorable effects in many respects on the expansion of individual companies. As a general rule, the bigger the company the more funds it has been able to devote to industrial research and, consequently, the better it has been able to reinforce its competitive edge. It has often been maintained that only companies with headquarters in a big market such as the United States or the EEC reap benefits when conditions for economic growth are favorable and that Swiss companies do particularly poorly under such conditions. As Nestlé and other Swiss companies demonstrate, a handicap of this kind is not insuperable. Moreover, it would be wrong to maintain that henceforth there is only room [in the marketplace] for big [companies]. Small and medium-sized firms can continue to make a name for themselves, owing to their flexibility and adaptability. Be that as it may, the example of Nestlé shows that our country's restricted economic scope is not incompatible with growth on a global scale. If Nestlé's turnover is bigger than that of any other Swiss company, it is not because it has a monopoly on the [world's] major markets, but rather because its products are widely distributed and it has a wide range of them."

After pointing out that the management and supervision of Nestlé's 214 factories meant that it employed many more managers than a company with a strongly centralized management, Hans Schaffner declared: "It would probably not have been possible to recrute such a great number of

THE NESTLÉ FOUNDATION WAS CREATED TO STUDY PROBLEMS OF GLOBAL NUTRITION. IN 1968, THERE WAS A CHANGE IN THE COMPANY'S DIRECTORS...

qualified personnel in Switzerland without jeopardizing the rest of the nation's economy. There is, therefore, every reason to be pleased that Nestlé has been able to attract many nationals of other countries. The fact that promotion into the uppermost echelons of [Nestlé's] management is open [to all], is beneficial not only to the company but to the entire Swiss economy as well. High-caliber individuals such as Maurice Paternot and Enrico Bignami underscore the extent to which we are indebted to such men." This passage reminds us that, from 1947 to 1952, Maurice Paternot—of French origin—and, after 1952, the Italian Enrico Bignami each shared, along with a Swiss colleague, the highest position in the company. (André Perrochet worked with Paternot, and Jean-Constant Corthésy with Bignami.)

Edouard Debétaz, the president of the State Council of the canton of Vaud, called attention to "the spirit of [community] service shown in the establishment of the Nestlé Foundation for the study of nutrition in the world...." That foundation began its work in the year of Nestlé's centennial. Founded with an initial endowment of SFr. 20,000,000, it continues to work toward its goals even today, without a lot of unnecessary fanfare but with endless perseverance.

After pointing out how well the economies of the industrialized countries were functioning, Hans Hürlimann, *Landamann* of the canton of Zug at the time, declared: "We also know that human beings on the other side of the globe are suffering from poverty and hunger. Faced with such suffering, an individual is helpless, but a company like yours, utilizing the latest processes to manufacture food products known for their high quality the world over, is destined just now to cooperate in the fight against hunger."

Pierre Liotard-Vogt (1909–1987)

Nestlé's sales figures were not published in 1966, but were published two years later in its report covering the period 1958 to 1968. According to that report, 1966 sales totaled SFr. 7,447,000,000, more than twice the 1959 figure.

An important change in the company's top managers took place in 1968: Jean-Constant Corthésy and Enrico Bignami retired and were replaced by Pierre Liotard-Vogt. This appointment was in keeping with two Nestlé traditions: first, that of choosing as top executives persons from within the company (Louis Dapples, from 1921 to 1936, being the only exception) and second—since 1952—that of choosing former market heads to manage the firm. Corthésy had previously been in charge of the Philippine and Latin

American markets, and Bignami of the Italian market; while Liotard-Vogt had been in charge of the French market. Liotard-Vogt joined the company in 1934 and had been in charge of Nestlé's activities in that country both during and after World War II. Thus, the new chief executive was a man well acquainted with the various aspects of Nestlé's activities. Unlike his predecessors, Pierre Liotard-Vogt took over as sole chief executive; and for a time he was even to hold the positions of both chairman and chief executive.

AND, FOR THE FIRST TIME, ITS CONSOLIDATED BALANCE SHEET WAS MADE PUBLIC, ALONG WITH OTHER COMPANY INFORMATION; NESTLÉ'S CHAIRMAN STATED ITS POLICY REGARDING SELF-FINANCING.

Earlier we mentioned that Pierre Liotard-Vogt was the son of Alfred Liotard-Vogt, one of Nestlé's four executive vice-presidents following World War I. Alfred Liotard-Vogt had married the daughter of Chairman Aguet and had remarried after her death. Pierre was the fruit of Liotard-Vogt's second marriage and had heard about Nestlé since he was a child—even though his father had resigned shortly before Louis Dapples took over. The new manager moved upward in Nestlé's hierarchy on the basis of his own merits. His appointment confirmed one of the company's basic principles: namely, to choose the best man available as chief executive. A hard worker (his capacity for work rivaled that of his two predecessors, whose prosperous company he had inherited), Liotard-Vogt soon showed the same excellent qualities as chief executive that had ensured his success with the French Nestlé Company. Under the chairmanship of Max Petitpierre, J.C. Corthésy and E. Bignami were appointed vice-chairmen of the board of directors. However, in keeping with Nestlé tradition, the actual responsibility for running the company was entrusted to the new chief executive.

Pierre Liotard-Vogt had hardly moved to Vevey when the board decided to publish the company's consolidated sales figures, which had been kept secret until then. Sales totaled SFr.8,478,000,000 in 1968. Chairman Petitpierre explained to the 1969 annual shareholders' meeting that "self-financing would continue to be guaranteed by the reinvestment of certain sources of income and an increase in reserves." He stated that this policy of self-financing, which the company had been pursuing for half a century, was justified by four factors: first, an increasingly transnational development involved risks accentuated

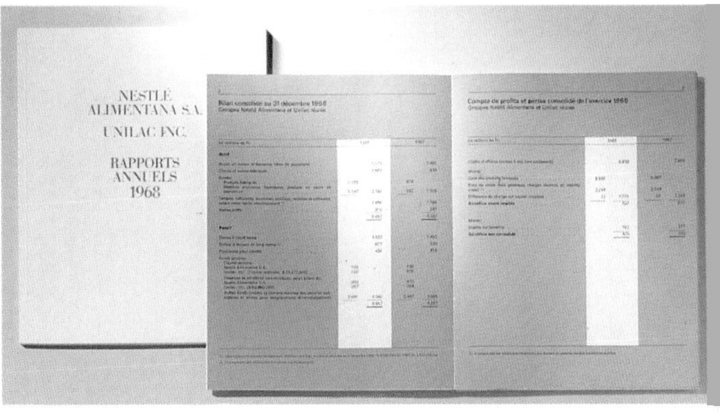

First publication of Nestlé's consolidated sales, 1968

THE IMPORTANCE OF THE HUMAN FACTOR CONTINUED TO BE STRESSED AT NESTLÉ.

by political, economic, and social instability the world over,"particularly in developing countries, which account for 22 percent of Nestlé's sales, where [it] possesses fifty-seven of the nearly two hundred factories manufacturing its products, and where 22 percent of its employees work"; second, the growing rate of scientific and technical progress meant that there was a need for increased research and investment in production facilities and modernization thereof. From 1961 to 1966, expenditures for land, buildings, machines, and equipment doubled, along with the amount devoted to research "in the last four years;" third, was the factor of increasingly fierce competition: "that can be explained by companies becoming more powerful through a concentration of financial resources resulting from mergers and take-overs, from new distribution methods, and from international price wars waged by big companies prepared to invest within the framework of their long-term policy—even when there is a risk of losses during a certain period of time—in order to conquer new markets"; and, fourth, during periods of international instability, "the search for necessary financing encounters difficulties and can be expensive. Therefore, it is important to have extensive funds available."

Between 1969 and 1974, Nestlé's acquisitions were the most conspicuous aspect of its activities. Over the course of the preceding decades, the company had acquired the experience and achieved the critical mass required for such an expansion. By 1968, Nestlé was a company with a solid foundation, good prospects for the future, and a staff of high caliber. Indeed, Liotard-Vogt constantly stressed the importance to the company of its human resources. Like his predecessors and successors, Liotard-Vogt felt that the company's most valuable assets were its employees, followed by its products, and finally its production processes.

Of course, top-quality employees are of no use unless a company's products are also top sellers in their field. Management and sales can only be decentralized if the staff in charge is extremely capable; however, finances, know-how, technology, and research must still be centralized. Nestlé's structure in 1969, which was being continually improved, had to meet these challenges. The chief executive was in charge of the general management, which was divided into departments according to function (finances, production and research, product management, personnel, etc.) and geographic location, which we shall discuss first.

THE OPERATION OF A DECENTRALIZED COMPANY SUCH AS NESTLÉ REQUIRES CONSTANT SUPERVISION AND FREQUENT CONTACTS AMONG ITS TOP MANAGERS...

There exists no ideal blueprint, universally applicable to every company; however, a few rules apply to every multinational. Nestlé's policy of relying on a decentralized form of management was easy to carry out, as its staff soon made it a habit to "think Nestlé" in international as much as national terms. Decentralization ensured that those in charge of each market had a great deal of freedom. The market head worked for one of the four regional managers, at that time, who lived in Vevey and supervised the group's activities in each geographic zone. Each of these managers reported to the chief executive and was responsible for all of Nestlé's subsidiaries in his zone.

A permanent system of control is of the utmost importance to the company, given its highly decentralized structure. At regular intervals, documents, statistics, and figures arrive in Vevey, enabling management to follow the development of company business closely and to detect any weak points. Moreover, contacts between headquarters and its affiliates are frequent: either the person in charge of the locally based company visits Vevey regularly, or managers and advisers from Vevey pay systematic visits to the company's affiliates. Foremost in the minds of Nestlé's top managers is a desire to understand the viewpoint of the various market heads. Generally, the latter are left to choose what they feel to be the best course of action, except in the case of gross errors or when too much is at stake. This kind of system obviously requires a certain amount of give-and-take and an open mind when it comes to the ideas of others. But this can be achieved over time. Of course, headquarters does indeed intervene when necessary; i.e., whenever work is badly done, mistakes made, or necessary measures fail to be taken automatically.

This form of management is the inevitable result of having chosen Switzerland as the location of the company's headquarters, a country with a population of only 6,000,000 and generating only 2.5 percent of Nestlé's sales. This is exactly the opposite of the policy pursued by big American companies, whose most important operations are generally located within the U.S., where their state-of-the-art factories and top executives are located and where they make most of their profits. Thus, managers of big

Meeting of market heads in Vevey, 1989

AS WELL AS A HIERARCHICAL STRUCTURE BASED ON CLOSE PERSONAL RELATIONSHIPS. BUDGETS ARE EXAMINED WITH THE MARKET HEADS RESPONSIBLE FOR RESPECTING THEM. THREE STAFF DIVISIONS EXIST AT HEADQUARTERS: PRODUCTION, FINANCE AND CONTROL, AND MARKETING.

American companies consider—quite legitimately—high earnings to be the proof of their excellent management methods. However, since these earnings are generated primarily in the U.S., their success proves little more than the fact that American management methods work well in America. These executives have a natural tendency, of course, to want to export their methods, applying them to all of their foreign subsidiaries, thus causing them to resemble the American head office (which serves as a model to be emulated as much as possible). It is obviously impossible for a company whose headquarters are located in a small country to act in the same manner. In this connection, Liotard-Vogt even went so far as to declare with regard to Nestlé: "many of the company's best men are not at the head office, but rather [they are working] abroad."

How are the various locally based Nestlé companies supervised? First, we must stress the fact that, from the point of view of the Nestlé Company, it is a single individual, rather than a committee, that usually has the best overall grasp of his firm's organization. It is also easier for a single individual to establish strong personal ties between Nestlé's global management and that of its locally based companies around the world. There have actually been periods in Nestlé's history when the cohesion of the group depended primarily on such relationships rather than on other factors.

One of the pillars of Nestlé's method of supervision is its system of individual budgets. Budgets from every division of the firm (production, marketing, administration and investments, maintenance and repairs, cash-flow forecasting) are incorporated into a master budget, making it possible to forecast profits and losses on the company's balance sheet. The regional managers and the various divisions at headquarters (which we shall discuss in detail later on) examine all the individual budgets in the presence of the head of the local market concerned. Apart from the master budget, the head office at Vevey also receives revised budgets throughout the year, enabling it to ensure that all the firm's markets are properly managed.

In addition to its regional management, the Nestlé Company has three traditional staff divisions: production, finance and control, and marketing (later renamed "product management").

The production division is responsible for factory construction, manufacturing processes, quality control, and factory management. The division does not have full responsibility, however, for the firm's production centers; it shares this responsibility with the regional management, which

One of the many mechanical draftsmen working at Nestlé headquarters in Vevey

RESEARCH IS AN INDISPENSABLE ASPECT OF ANY FOOD COMPANY...

makes the final decision whenever it might have serious economic repercussions.

The finance and control division does the company's accounting, draws up its balance sheet, and maintains the complex profit-and-loss accounts that a multinational requires. This division is also responsible for company financing, cash-flow management, fund allocation to Nestlé's subsidiaries, and thus Nestlé's financial policy with regard to its affiliates. Another important function of this division is auditing the results of Nestlé's holding company and its subsidiaries.

At headquarters, the marketing division's role is to assist markets too small to have their own marketing department. Marketing must be planned on a national level for big markets. If it is not effective, the headquarters' marketing division does not step in directly, but sees to it that ineffective marketing methods are changed. This division does, however, play an important role in distributing marketing information within the group. It is of primary importance that markets be informed of pilot projects being carried out in specific countries, that they be kept up to date on the latest news from Nestlé companies throughout the world, and that they be informed of the analyses of their successes as well as their failures. Finally, the marketing policy of Nestlé companies must have a certain common goal in order to be effective on an international scale. Though variations in tastes and aesthetic values must, of course, be taken into account (resulting in a certain diversity in publicity approaches), a common corporate identity must be preserved throughout the world to prevent the total distortion of the company's image. From the standpoint of Nestlé's managers, the role of the marketing division at headquarters was initially to ensure that there was some unified concept underlying the way in which Nestlé products were marketed and sold. The international success of a certain number of leading products is important, for it helps ensure their penetration into a still wider range of markets around the world.

Nestlé employees are constantly trained in all major fields

Initially, there existed a certain number of administrative staff responsible—within the framework of the production division—for research; these dealt with such questions as the choice of the direction research should follow, the planning of research programs, the hiring of personnel, and budget supervision.

In 1969, Nestec S.A. was set up at Vevey, with a view to advancing the technology applied to every sector of the food industry. Nestec is also in charge of transferring know-how in marketing, organization, management, and employee training to the companies producing and marketing Nestlé products all over the world.

AS IS STAFF TRAINING. A SINGLE INDIVIDUAL IS AT THE HEAD OF NESTLÉ.

Any company must pay constant attention to the training of its top executives. And Nestlé is no exception. There are on-the-job training seminars organized in cooperation with the personnel department. The career guidance offered employees takes not only the firm's needs but also the employees' continuing education into account. This means that an executive may be chosen to head a department or market, at times, even if there is no pressing need for him in that position, merely because it is felt that the job might be a useful part of his training. Thus, it is important not to label a particular employee—an engineer or executive, for example—in such a way that he will remain limited throughout his career to a certain number of precisely defined tasks. As early as 1969, Nestlé's chief executive was to state: "We have many people who started their career as engineers and who later proved to be extremely capable of company management."

At a lecture in Paris, in reply to a question about the links between the various parts of the company, Liotard-Vogt answered that managerial power was not exercised by a committee. Nevertheless, Nestlé has made it a point to convey important information to all its general managers, for vital decisions require an exchange of views among top managers. In a big company, there are those who feel it is important that a single individual at the top not be solely responsible for its operation. However, in the opinion of Liotard-Vogt, the best system is still to place exclusive authority in the hands of one person, provided he is capable of listening to the views of others and accepting certain ideas that are contrary to his own. Above all, he must not be opposed to the opinion of the majority of his colleagues in important matters.

As Liotard-Vogt told shareholders at the annual meeting, Nestlé's management is of the opinion that "the conductor must know not only the score but also, as far as possible, the instruments [performing it]." It is essential for the person in charge to understand the specialist so that he can judge

LONG-TERM PLANS WERE WORKED OUT. FROM 1969 ON, NESTLÉ EMBARKED ON A NEW SERIES OF ACQUISITIONS. AN AGREEMENT ON FROZEN FOOD PRODUCTS WAS REACHED WITH UNILEVER OF GERMANY.

whether or not the latter is committing an error. Sound judgment is the important thing.

1969 was also the year in which Nestlé first introduced a system of long-term planning. Forecasts were drawn up for the company's major markets as well as for the activities of the group as a whole. These ten-year forecasts were worked out in a period of economic growth that seemed destined to continue and which, in fact, was rarely perturbed. This was reflected in Nestlé's policies at that time.

Strengthened by its success, its strong financial position, and its experience in 1969, Nestlé embarked on new series of moves to acquire an interest in various companies—the first of these being Société Générale des Eaux Minérales de Vittel.

In the same year—in the field of chocolates—Nestlé purchased the shares of the minority shareholders of Sarotti AG, based in Hattersheim, Germany.

In the field of frozen foods, Nestlé remained faithful to the policy it had begun to pursue in Great Britain in 1967 in order to increase efficiency there, especially in terms of distribution. Nestlé and Unilever N.V. of Rotterdam signed an agreement covering frozen food and ice-cream in Germany, Austria, and Italy that went into effect in January, 1970, with Nestlé limiting itself to a 25 percent interest in the companies concerned by the agreement. At the time, it was felt that this pooling of interests would strengthen the position of frozen foods in the overall food market and stimulate the sale of frozen foods in the German, Austrian, and Italian marketplace. In 1986, however, Nestlé was to sell its interest back to Unilever. Also in the field of frozen foods, Nestlé, in keeping with its 1962 agreement, exercised its option to acquire the shares of its partners in Findus International S.A., thus becoming exclusive owner of that company.

Vittel bottling plant in the French city of the same name

At the same time, the Nestlé Company was careful not to neglect its other activities throughout the world, as shown by the fact that it was given responsibility for managing a locally based instant coffee factory in Tanzania that was to supply instant coffee to the Nestlé affiliate—among other companies—in charge of distributing Nescafé to various African markets. Also in Africa, Nestlé had built its first factory at Abidjan in the Ivory Coast in 1962. The government of the Ivory Coast, which had achieved independence in 1960, wished to industrialize, considering industrialization to be a necessary precondition for its development and future prosperity. Thanks to Nestlé's reputation, the French Nestlé Company was able to sign an agreement with the government of the Ivory Coast to build a factory there. As it was highly successful, this factory was enlarged several times.

NESTLÉ'S ACTIVITIES EXPANDED IN AFRICA.

VITTEL, A WELL-ESTABLISHED COMPANY IN THE VOSGES REGION OF FRANCE FOR MORE THAN 100 YEARS,

1969: A Cooperation Agreement with Société Générale des Eaux Minérales de Vittel

☐ In 1969, in an effort to its continue diversification, Nestlé entered the mineral water field. The ever-increasing consumption of mineral water in all the countries of Europe as well as the U.S. encouraged Nestlé to become involved in this sector of the food industry. A number of consumers were turning away from alcoholic beverages and beginning to prefer nonalcoholic ones—among these: mineral water. Nestlé thus acquired a 30 percent interest in Société Générale des Eaux Minérales de Vittel, a rapidly growing firm and the third largest bottler of mineral water in France.

Nestlé entered this area of the food industry, with which it had no experience, in the belief—later proved to be well-founded—that a top-quality bottled water could eventually carve out a growing share of the beverage market.

Vittel, the county seat of a canton of 7,000 inhabitants, is located about 230 miles from Paris, on what is known as the Lorraine Plateau of the Department of the Vosges, France. The town, located at an altitude of approximately 1,100 feet above sea level, was founded by the Celts. Though the Romans were aware of the medicinal properties of the region's springs, their settlement at Vittel was completely demolished during the Barbarian invasions of the fourth and fifth centuries. In 1852, when Louis Bouloumié, a lawyer from Toulouse who had been exiled to Spain for protesting against Napoleon III's coup d'etat on December 2, 1851, was authorized to spend a month in the Vosges region, under police supervision, to treat a painful kidney-stone attack, the beneficial qualities of Vittel's springs had been long forgotten by everyone but the inhabitants of the region. Bouloumié's doctor advised him to go to Vittel, where the salutary effects of the waters at Geremoy Fountain could be immediately felt by him. Having received permission to reside permanently at Vittel, Bouloumié purchased the property on which the spring was located and, on receiving a favorable analysis of its waters by the French Medical Academy, he opened a spa at the site on April 24, 1855. In spite of difficulties of every sort, the popularity of this spa was to increase by leaps and bounds, thanks to the perseverance and unflagging efforts of Louis Bouloumié and his successors (namely, his eldest son Ambroise, assisted by his youngest son, Dr. Pierre Bouloumié, and his grandson Jean). As late as 1969, the Bouloumié family was still active in perpetuating the

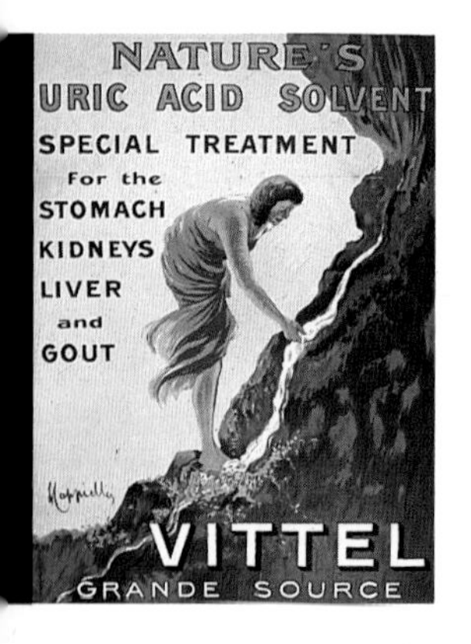

1915 poster for Vittel Grande Source mineral water

Entrance hall to hydropathic establishment at spa in Vittel

WAS SEEKING A PARTNER; NESTLÉ ACQUIRED A CONSIDERABLE INTEREST IN VITTEL AS WELL AS OTHER MINERAL-WATER FIRMS, SUCH AS BLAUE QUELLEN IN GERMANY.

family tradition, with Mrs. Germaine Bouloumié serving as chairman of the Société Générale des Eaux Minérales de Vittel, founded by her ancestor more than a century earlier. Mrs. Bouloumié's nephew, Guy de la Motte, mayor of Vittel and a county councilor for the Department of the Vosges, was the firm's chief executive officer. The number of people under a doctor's care taking the waters at Vittel grew from year to year, and the amount of bottled water exported was also constantly increasing. Soon, Vittel was to become one of France's foremost hot water spas. (It still is today.)

As in the case of most family businesses, the managers wished to secure the financial backing of a strong partner. And so, Guy de la Motte was to contact Nestlé. The markets for the most popular brands of mineral water are rather stable; and the potential for expanding them depends primarily on the length of the summer and its average temperature. Nestlé had noticed that, in many countries, either no mineral water producers existed or the industry was in its infancy. Therefore, Nestlé thought it wise to explore the possibility of developing a mineral-water firm outside of France.

The economic climate was favorable when Nestlé became the largest shareholder of Société Générale des Eaux Minérales de Vittel. Natural mineral water was not in great demand in a country such as England, for example, but the situation was very different in Germany. (It was for that reason that Nestlé took over the second biggest German bottler of mineral water, Blaue Quellen AG, in 1974.) That family business, together with its subsidiary, Trinks, had an annual turnover of approximately 100,000,000 marks. Blaue Quellen AG owned five natural mineral water springs in western and northern Germany: at Hamburg, Goslar, Lippstadt, Koblenz, and Wetzlar. In 1973, it produced approximately 220,000,000 bottles (soft drinks made with mineral water accounting for two-thirds of total sales). The principal shareholder and owner of Blaue Quellen was Fritz Meyer, the grandson of the man who had founded the company nearly a hundred years earlier. The firm's headquarters were in Rhens, on the Rhine, and it employed 1,000 persons. Meyer, who had been with the company since 1941 and had no one in his family capable of succeeding him, wished to find a buyer for his firm but to continue working for it nonetheless. Therefore, he and his associates sold their shares to Nestlé, with Meyer staying on as one of the firm's executives for many years thereafter.

We should be careful not to overestimate the importance of Nestlé's mineral-water sales. Of course, they were an important part of the company's business; however, Nestlé preferred to make brief forays, now and then, into this field rather than an all-out effort to develop it, since it was obvious that the company's future did not depend on its mineral-water division. This was clearly considered an area of long-term growth for the company, insofar as it was useless to try changing, from one day to the next, the habits of people not used to drinking mineral water. There was, however, always the distinct possibility that those who had not been among the first to firmly establish themselves in the marketplace would not be able to take advantage one day of increasing consumer interest in mineral water. Nestlé knew that it must seize the opportunity of acquiring an interest in Société Générale des Eaux Minérales de Vittel, with its modern equipment, and thus enter a new field of the food industry (in the broad sense of the term), even if it was not directly related to Nestlé's main activities. As both Nestlé and Vittel take an active interest in maintaining people's health, the two companies cooperate well together as they strive to achieve this goal. Indeed, it is far easier for two companies to complement each other's activity when both have a similar philosophy. Nestlé was to acquire a majority interest in Société Générale des Eaux Minérales de Vittel in 1987.

NESTLÉ AND VITTEL COOPERATED HARMONIOUSLY WITH ONE ANOTHER.

Founded in 1868, the U.S. firm Libby, McNeill & Libby began by producing canned corned beef...

1970: The Acquisition of Libby, McNeill & Libby

☐ In 1970, Nestlé acquired a majority interest in Libby, McNeill & Libby, a company with products ranging from canned fruit and vegetables to meat products, evaporated milk, frozen foods, and nonalcoholic beverages. Libby owned nineteen factories in the U.S., two in Canada, and one in Puerto Rico, Germany, France, Spain, Great Britain, and Swaziland. In addition, it owned three tinplate factories in the U.S., one in Canada, and one in Puerto Rico, supplying part of Libby's tin-can requirements. In 1970, Libby's turnover totaled to $350,000,000.

Nestlé's management did not try to conceal the difficulties this hundred-year-old firm was experiencing, due primarily to a very high degree of short-term indebtedness with heavy interest payments.

The reader may wonder why Nestlé decided to acquire an interest in Libby under such circumstances. First of all, as any manager knows, some of the decisions a company must make involve certain risks. What is important, of course, is for one to win more often than lose. There are no sure means, however, of forecasting the outcome of a specific decision. Every acquisition is made in the belief that it is a good risk, otherwise none would be made. And it is true that not all decisions turn out to be wise ones. However, experienced executives ultimately acquire a certain degree of equanimity in this area. The acquisition of Libby shows that, at times, the decision is made to acquire a company more for historical reasons than for any financial advantage one expects to gain from it.

Poster advertising Libby's canned corned beef, with a new invention—a key to open the can, ca. 1900

Libby was established in 1868 by Arthur A. Libby, his brother Charles, and Archibald McNeill, who had joined forces to produce corned beef in large packages and, from 1885 on, in cans. (Four years later, this firm was the first to provide the customer with a key to open their cans.) Libby began exporting its products to England in 1876, and since then, the company has become famous throughout the world. By 1904, the company had begun diversifying its range of products: canned sauerkraut was added in 1904, pickles and seasonings in 1905, Hawaiian pineapple in 1910, salmon in 1912, tomato juice in 1923, and pumpkin and squash in 1929. Libby acquired the Florida Citrus Growers Corporation in 1954; and, in 1958, it built a canned-meat factory in Illinois, which was the world's biggest and most modern one at the time.

AND, LATER, OTHER FOOD PRODUCTS, INCLUDING CANNED MILK AND FRUIT JUICES. IN 1967, NESTLÉ BECAME LIBBY'S LARGEST SHAREHOLDER;

Meanwhile, the Chicago-based firm had started producing a variety of milk products, which is what caused Nestlé to become interested in Libby in the 1930s. It had become impossible to import condensed milk into Cuba, where there was substantial demand for the product; as a result, it had to be manufactured locally. Nestlé, Libby, and Carnation, the three manufacturers who supplied canned milk to Cuba, realized that, if each company built its own factory on the island, the resulting surplus production would be detrimental to their activities there. And so, an agreement was reached between the three companies, permitting them to cooperate in the production of canned milk. Having thus established these ties with Libby, Nestlé joined forces with Libby, in the 1950s, in the operation of a large fruit and fruit-juice cannery in Cuba; and it signed contracts with Libby for the production of specific products for several other markets. When Nestlé acquired Crosse & Blackwell in 1960, it acquired a minor interest in Libby as well. When a European banking group acquired a considerable interest in Libby in 1963, Nestlé increased its own to 20 percent.

Since the banking group in question had as big an interest in Libby as did Nestlé, they decided to jointly manage their nearly 40 percent interest in the firm. In 1964, the banking group realized that Nestlé was better equipped to manage their common interest and entrusted Nestlé both with keeping abreast of developments at Libby and keeping the representatives of the banking group informed thereof. The American firm was not doing very well. In 1967, Nestlé thought it wise to acquire the shares of the banking group, thereby becoming Libby's majority shareholder. Libby continued to perform poorly; and, in 1967, Nestlé considered selling its shares. However, in 1968, when Nestlé changed chief executive officers, the board of directors decided to decline offers to purchase its interest in Libby.

In a speech at the shareholders' meeting on May 25, 1972, Karl Obrecht, Nestlé's vice-chairman, explained the reasons behind the board's decision: "In the first place, our company has not yet secured the leading position on the American market that it has in practically all the other countries of the world. In the face of fierce competition from other big companies [and] the obstacles that the [U.S.] Anti-Trust Law puts in the way of any large acquisi-

IN 1970, IT WAS TO ACQUIRE THE MAJORITY OF THE COMPANY'S SHARES; AND, IN 1975, IT ACQUIRED THE REMAINING ONES.

tions in the food industry, it seemed a shame to reduce our presence on the American market when there is so little chance of rapidly offsetting this loss. Furthermore, we have remained faithful to a Nestlé tradition: not to operate like a conglomerate, buying and selling companies for purely financial reasons. We believe that if we retain control of a firm operating in the red, it is up to us—even if this takes much time and effort—to help turn it around so it may look forward to a better future. This is what we are trying to do at Libby. We should not forget that there is little likelihood of rapid improvement. Before Libby can be in the black again, a range of new—hopefully more profitable—products will have to be developed and introduced on the market; and, initially, this will mean additional costs for the company. Also, certain losses cannot be quickly remedied." A forceful, yet nuanced statement, for it became immediately clear to Nestlé that Libby was really not in good shape. In addition, in March, 1970, the American banks that had made loans to Libby threatened to cut off those funds; and Nestlé felt obliged, as a result, to acquire a majority interest in Libby. Libby increased its capital, and Nestlé subscribed for the greater part of its new shares. By November, 1970, Nestlé possessed the majority of Libby shares.

This explains the reasons underlying Nestlé's decision to acquire Libby. The company continued to lose money as late as 1972; but business began to pick up in 1973, thanks to the new managers Nestlé had chosen to head the American company. In 1974, Nestlé increased its interest in Libby to 62 percent. It soon became evident, however, that Nestlé's freedom to make managerial decisions would be considerably limited until it had acquired all, and that it would be impossible to integrate Libby's subsidiaries outside the U.S. into the Nestlé group. Therefore, in 1975, Nestlé decided to acquire all through a take-over bid.

It is important to emphasize that it was not the fact that Libby was an attractive company which motivated Nestlé to enter the rather unprofitable field of canned foods, but rather very special circumstances. Until 1976, when it became a subsidiary of Nestlé Enterprises, Inc. of White Plains, New York, Libby was operated directly by Nestlé headquarters at Vevey.

Although losses continued, Libby's sales began to improve, thanks to its traditional range of products for the U.S. market. In 1972, the annual report noted cautiously that "subsequent improvements will depend on availability of these products, for in certain parts of the U.S., last summer's bad weather has adversely affected harvests." It went on to point out: "the high cost of the raw materials used in canned meat products will limit the growth of Libby's profits unless the government helps the company out in this area by imposing price controls [on those raw materials]."

LIBBY'S EMPLOYEES WERE EASILY INTEGRATED INTO THE NESTLÉ GROUP.

For a time, Libby's earnings from its activities abroad continued to improve, despite losses due to declining sales in Great Britain. In 1972, for example, sustained cooperation between Nestlé and Libby resulted in new products and the wide-scale introduction of technological advances. Libby and Nestlé signed a technical assistance agreement, which enabled Libby to increase its contribution to the development of new products. In order to make its operations more efficient, Libby once again thoroughly reorganized several of its divisions.

It must also be pointed out that Libby owned large pineapple plantations in Hawaii in 1970. This was not to the liking of Nestlé, which continued to remain faithful to the principle of owning very little agricultural land. Thus, Nestlé soon sold Libby's plantations, insisting, all the while that Libby continue its reorganization.

The individuals Nestlé had put in charge of Libby took great pains to solve the problems the company was facing. And some of them became extremely well integrated into the Nestlé group. Libby's general manager, for instance, was named head of Nestlé Enterprises, Inc. In spite of the risks involved, the Libby deal shows that, as early as 1970, Nestlé was already set on strengthening its position on the huge U.S. market.

Libby's fruit- and vegetable-canning divisions were sold in 1986, after a licensing agreement had been signed to use the Libby trademark. Libby's Chicago headquarters and its big Morgan Park factory were shut down; Libby's foreign companies were transformed into locally based Nestlé companies. (Canned fruit juice and sausage, for example, continued to be produced in the U.S.)

Libby's range of products, 1977

Libby's 450 workers at its factory south of Chicago as well as the 250 at headquarters became employees of either Carnation (which Nestlé acquired in 1985) or of Nestlé Foods. All canned-meat production was transferred to Carnation's Missouri plant, and beverage production to either New York or

1970: THE BEGINNING OF NESTLÉ'S COOPERATION, FOR SEVERAL YEARS, WITH COMPAGNIE INTERNATIONALE DES WAGONS-LITS ET DU TOURISME. NESTLÉ CEASED ITS ACTIVITIES IN THE CATERING FIELD—EXCEPT IN THE U.S.—AFTER 1984.

1970: NESTLÉ'S FIRST EFFORTS TO REINFORCE ITS PRESENCE IN THE FIELD OF CHEESES IN FRANCE.

the West Coast. Only products made with squash continued to be produced by Libby's factory in Morton, Illinois. The Libby trademark and those of its affiliates continued to be used on Libby products, which were now produced under the joint management of Carnation and Nestlé's Food Company. These included canned meat, salmon, squash, and Libby fruit juices, as well as the products of Crosse & Blackwell and Maggi that Libby had previously been marketing in the U.S.

☐ In 1970, Nestlé entered the catering business for a time, as it seemed that there was a growing tendency for people in the industrialized countries to eat out. The company was primarily interested in obtaining a deeper understanding of the requirements of that business so that it could develop, under the best possible conditions, a range of appealing products for restaurant owners.

Therefore, Nestlé searched for a top-quality associate, which it found in Compagnie Internationale des Wagons-Lits et du Tourisme. Until 1984, the two companies worked together developing their activities in several European countries. Theirs was an example of cooperation with a view to reconciling high-quality products and service with profitability, while, at the same time, aiming for individual growth. Nestlé, did not consider the service-oriented catering business as one of its main areas of activity, however; whereas Compagnie Internationale des Wagon-Lits et du Tourisme wished to strengthen its position in this area. The two companies cooperated for ten years in Eurest, the European Restaurant Company.

Over the years, after acquiring restaurant chains in Australia, Finland, South Africa, and Brazil, Nestlé was to realize that, although the company was increasing its know-how in a new field, its catering activities were competing directly for Nestlé's own traditional clients. Thus, the company decided to limit its activities to the manufacture and marketing of its own products. (It made a single exception, which we shall discuss later, by maintaining its control of the Stouffer hotel chain in the U.S.) In 1989, Nestlé also gave up its share of Swissair Nestlé Swissôtel S.A., managed by Swissair. Nestlé strongly wished to continue to supply restaurants with the industrially processed food they required. The Nestlé Food Service generates a considerable amount of the firm's total sales.

In 1970, Nestlé took an important step in the manufacture of cheeses, a field in which it had long been active in Holland, in France since 1947, and in

Italy since 1961. Its approach in France resembled its approach nine years earlier in Italy with its acquisition of Locatelli. Nestlé took over a local company in order to consolidate its position in an area closely related to its dairy operations. It had recently acquired Roustang, to which it now added several firms that were to be run by the same management under the name Roustang. Among these were Dupont-d'Isigny, which specialized in the production of butter and cheese (especially Camembert); Fromageries de la Blanche Côte-Antoine Jaillon, Fromageries Grosjean S.A., in which Nestlé had had a majority interest since 1969, and Société des Fromages Gerber S.A. of Pontarlier.

AWARE OF THE PROSPECTS FOR DEVELOPMENT OFFERED BY THE COMMON MARKET, NESTLÉ INCREASED ACTIVITIES THIS AREA, ACQUIRING ROUSTANG...

It must be stressed that a move as important as this requires time and a unified approach. Indeed, the first discussions with Roustang took place as far back as 1967. Moreover, Pierre Liotard-Vogt, Nestlé's chief executive who took over in 1968, carried to a successful conclusion the negotiations started by his predecessors Jean-Constant Corthésy and Enrico Bignami.

The reason that Nestlé decided to expand its activities in 1967 to include cheese making can be explained by the fact that it owned Locatelli in Milan, indirectly owned Dupont-d'Isigny at Neuilly, in the French Department of Hauts-de-Seine, as well as the processed-cheese manufacturer Société des Fromages Gerber S.A. in Pontarlier. (It must be kept in mind that this was a time when the Common Market seemed to promise better times ahead for cheese manufacturers.)

Nestlé's cheese-manufacturing activities had reached the point where it had to decide whether it wanted to follow up its foray into the international marketplace by keeping and developing them (although they were on a small scale in relation to the foreseeable economic strength of Europe) or whether it should simply cease its cheese-making activities altogether. In 1967, Nestlé's decision to step up these activities was helped along by the growing consumer interest in processed cheeses in the Old World. The company thought it advisable to concentrate its main effort in France, a country blessed with many varieties of cheese, and to link that effort to the one Nestlé would have to make in Italy. Its goal was to sell Italian cheese in France and French cheese in Italy, and, possibly, to export French and Italian cheese to other countries—particularly Germany and England.

Since a great number of small cheese makers were present on the soft-cheese market in France, there was room there for Nestlé too, provided it could find a firm capable of benefiting by a shot in the arm. It so happened

AS WELL AS FROBLANC AND GROSJEAN.

that Liotard-Vogt was well acquainted with Joseph Roustang, head of a family firm established in 1920 at Loisy, in the Department of the Meuse. As early as 1967, Roustang had considered working more closely with Nestlé. This firm possessed three factories of its own and had three others manufacturing cheeses for it. It employed a total of 900 persons (including both office and factory workers) and had a turnover of 55,700,000 French francs in 1966. Eighty-seven agents handled Roustang's marketing, principally in France, but also in Germany, Italy, Belgium, England, Switzerland, and Spain. The firm manufactured various kinds of soft cheese, including the well-known Petit Pâtre. And Roustang had signed contracts closely linking his company with Froblanc (Fromageries de la Blanche Côte-Antoine Jaillon), which also specialized in producing soft cheeses.

The acquisition of Roustang, with its highly qualified personnel, served as the basis for a merger that took place in December, 1967, once Nestlé had acquired all of Roustang's and Froblanc's shares of stock, as well as those of Grosjean, whose head, Henri Grosjean, had decided to retire. Joseph Roustang was named chairman of the new company.

We shall go into greater detail concerning Nestlé's cheese-making activities later on—paying particular attention to its cream cheese and yogurt production—when we discuss Nestlé's acquisition of the French company Chambourcy in 1978. This will make it easier to understand how Nestlé, after its initial moves into the field of fresh dairy products, in 1961, and again in 1970, became particularly active in this field from 1978 on. Nearly a decade later, after acquiring Herta of Germany in 1986—at the urging of Helmut Maucher, Nestlé's chief executive officer—the company was to strengthen its activities in the related field of cold cuts as well as other refrigerated items.

1971: Ursina-Franck's Entry into the Nestlé Group

FROM FRIENDLY MEETINGS TO DISCUSS THE ACQUISITION OF A FRENCH COMPANY...

☐ In 1971, Nestlé acquired the Swiss group Ursina, which had originally specialized primarily in milk products. (In January, 1970, after acquiring the Franck group, the firm's name was changed to Ursina-Franck.) The merger with Ursina-Franck resulted from the latter's wish to join forces with Nestlé for a specific venture in France and from its subsequent decision to opt for the pooling of all the interests of both companies.

Jean-Constant Corthésy, who had been executive vice-president of Nestlé Alimentana S.A. together with Enrico Bignami from 1952 until 1968, and who had shared the vice-chairmanship of the company with his Italian colleague until 1969, was named chairman of the board in that year. During a trip in 1970, Corthésy met Hans R. Schwarzenbach, chairman of the board of Ursina-Franck. A few years earlier, Bignami had made the acquaintance of Alfred E. Sulzer, Ursina-Franck's chief executive, but they had not discussed the prospect of working together in any way.

Schwarzenbach happened to mention to Corthésy that Ursina-Franck was interested in production facilities in France to manufacture its jars of baby food. Ursina-Franck had already been approached about purchasing the company that had been producing baby food for it up to this point. In the course of a conversation, Schwarzenbach told Corthésy about the proposal and asked him whether it would be possible for his company to acquire this company jointly with Nestlé. As Nestlé's chairman—which meant that he was not directly involved in business matters—Corthésy suggested that Schwarzenbach contact Liotard-Vogt, Nestlé's chief executive officer. The two men scheduled a meeting in Paris to get to know each other. Ursina-Franck's chairman explained that the cost of the acquisition they were considering was relatively high, and he wondered whether Nestlé might be interested in participating in the acquisition. Liotard-Vogt replied that, since their two companies were competitors, the question of which of them was to manage the new company would inevitably arise. And, in the course of their discussions, it soon became clear that they would not be able to come to an agreement on this point. Fortunately, neither man had ever considered a merger between the two rival companies until then. Without committing themselves, they agreed that perhaps the best way to acquire the French company would be first to merge into a single entity. They also decided to study what the ramifications of such an association would be, as well as the

TO MORE SERIOUS TALKS CONCERNING A MERGER BETWEEN URSINA AND NESTLÉ, DECIDED IN 1971 AND OF BENEFIT TO BOTH COMPANIES.

consequences for shareholders, and whether such a merger would ultimately prove to be advantageous.

Another meeting took place some time later at which it was pointed out that Ursina-Franck, like Nestlé, already possessed a company in France and that the two groups were also in competition in Germany. The two men felt that it was important to proceed in the same manner in the case of all of their activities. To quote Liotard-Vogt, the headquarters of both companies should investigate "how they could merge, what the likely outcome would be, which people should be kept on, what effect the merger would have, what the impact on business would be if they pooled all their resources." An outside company was asked to look into the question of how to merge the companies' sales and product-transport departments, as well as their staff departments. As its work proceeded, it became apparent that merging the two companies' shares at then current stock market prices would be to the advantage of all concerned, particularly Ursina-Franck's shareholders, who, after receiving Nestlé shares in exchange for theirs, would be paid a higher dividend than before.

Nestlé learned that the new company created by the merger would generate more funds than Nestlé would have to pay out to shareholders. Once the projected figures were verified, the two men decided to proceed with the merger. Each later declared that everything had gone as planned. Naturally, Ursina-Franck's shareholders were disconcerted by the disappearance of their firm; a few groups of shareholders of the Bernese firm engaged in a behind-the-scene attempt to try and prevent the merger. The official merger was delayed from January until September, 1971, due to such opposition. This was overcome by taking a series of steps that were ultimately to satisfy everyone; and Ursina-Franck's shareholders finally realized that they were getting a very good deal indeed. (Incidentally, after the merger, the acquisition of the French baby-food manufacturer became unnecessary.)

The clearsightedness of those responsible for the merger proved to be highly beneficial. And the experience Nestlé acquired in its merger with Maggi was very useful in the case of Ursina-Franck.

The Ursina-Franck group was created in January, 1970, with the take-over by Ursina AG, Bern, of Interfranck Holding AG, Zurich. The group was chiefly active in four areas of the food industry: dairy products, baby foods, coffee, and fine foods. Ursina-Franck controlled about seventy manufacturers, sales organizations, etc.

End of the production line for individual portions of Bären Marke coffee cream, Biessenhofen, Germany

URSINA EVOLVED FROM BERNERALPEN-MILCHGESELLSCHAFT, FOUNDED IN 1892. QUICKLY BRANCHING OUT IN EUROPE, IT BECAME A HOLDING COMPANY IN 1926. URSINA HAD AFFILIATES...

There was a certain resemblance between the early days of Ursina and those of the Anglo-Swiss Condensed Milk Company, described in the opening chapters of this work. In 1892, César Ritz, the famous Swiss hotelkeeper (who operated the Savoy Hotel in London at the time), and his friends set up the Improved Patent Sterilized Syndicate, Ltd., with a view to implementing a new process for sterilizing milk. Like the Page brothers before him, Ritz was convinced that there would be a big market for Swiss milk overseas if new canning techniques could enable stores to keep milk longer. Ritz won a friend from Lucerne, Hans Pfyffer von Altishofen, over to his view and, together with a group of Bernese businessmen, set up Berneralpen-Milchgesellschaft with a capital of SFr.400,000. Its headquarters were at Stalden in the heart of the Emmental region of Switzerland.

The aim of the Bernese company was to manufacture "canned milk and other products that are related to the milk industry or that involve canning or sterilization in one way or another." For technical, commercial, and psychological reasons, the company's first years were very difficult. In 1894, it began manufacturing sterilized canned milk. Production of cans of condensed milk and evaporated milk followed in 1895. In 1898, the company began to produce drum-dried powdered milk. The company really began to expand at the beginning of this century when the evaporated milk that the company had been manufacturing since 1895 began to enjoy considerable popularity in Switzerland, France, England, and on various export markets. The advantages of this kind of milk became immediately apparent in the tropical countries to which it was exported. In 1903, the company began producing chocolate pudding. In 1905, the company set up a factory in Germany; then, in 1917, it established another in France in cooperation with Compagnie Générale du Lait.

Poster in Paris advertising new products from Berneralpen-Milchgesellschaft, ca. 1900

By the end of World War I, the company had demonstrated to its competitors that high-quality products could successfully compete with cheap ones. To facilitate its financing of various firms, the parent company was itself transformed into a holding company in 1926, adopting the name Ursina; its initial headquarters were in Geneva, then Stans, and finally Konolfingen, in the canton of Bern. Berneralpen-Milchgesellschaft thus became an operating and sales company. New companies were set up, and Ursina AG thus became the center of a global group with administrative headquarters in Bern. In 1954, Berneralpen-Milchgesellschaft started producing instant pastry icings. By acquiring an interest in certain companies and establishing new ones, the Ursina holding company expanded from three to twenty-five firms; and, by 1970, it was present, in one way or another, in a great many areas.

IN SWITZERLAND, WHERE IT HAD TAKEN OVER GUIGOZ, PRODUCER OF A VARIETY OF MILK PRODUCTS, DISCH, PRODUCING CONFECTIONERY ITEMS...

The main dairy products sold in Switzerland under the Ursina trademark were standard and instant powdered milk, condensed milk and evaporated milk, sterilized milk, pudding, coffee cream, and various ingredients used in the manufacture of ice cream. Besides its affiliate Berneralpen-Milchgesellschaft, in Switzerland, Ursina also possessed Guigoz S.A. of Vuadens, in the canton of Fribourg, which mainly manufactured various types of infant formula, special food products to prevent diarrhea in infants, as well as milk for babies on salt-free diets; Guigoz also marketed instant infant cereal and porridge, and standard infant cereal, biscuits, baby food and fruit juice for babies, as well as such items as baby bottles and nipples.

Maurice Guigoz founded Guigoz S.A. in 1908, after purchasing a powdered-milk factory at Châtel-Saint-Denis, in the canton of Fribourg. He established Fabrique Suisse des Produits au Lait Guigoz in the neighboring town of Vuadens in 1915, to manufacture a wide range of food products. (Vuadens is located only a few miles from Broc, where Alexandre Cailler had built the large chocolate-making factory that joined the Nestlé group in 1929.) In 1921, Guigoz launched his first major campaign to promote dietetic baby food. At the same time, thanks to the efforts of Louis Guigoz, son of the company's founder, Guigoz products, manufactured in Switzerland, France, Holland, Italy, and Venezuela, were marketed by locally based Guigoz companies in Paris, Brussels, Turin, Algiers, Casablanca, and Caracas. As the company needed a considerable amount of funds to expand abroad, Guigoz's cooperation with Ursina, begun in 1931, eventually developed into a full-fledged merger in 1937.

Ever since 1961, Ursina also owned another Swiss company, Disch AG at Othmarsingen, in the canton of Aargau. Disch was founded in 1903 to manufacture and market a whole range of confectionery items: candies, toffee, gumdrops, and sugarless candies, as well as Disch brand cookies (manufactured for Disch by another company).

AND DYNA, A MANUFACTURER OF SANDWICH SPREADS; IN FRANCE, WITH LAIT MONT-BLANC AND CLAUDEL;

Dyna S.A., Fribourg, was another Swiss affiliate of Ursina; it was founded in 1938 by Claude Blancpain and Erwin Haag, who had met at the Institut Pasteur in Paris and decided to invent a range of high-protein yeast-based food products. Production of Tartex brand products and Dyna sandwich spreads began in 1942 in the company's Fribourg plant, and these items were to perform well. Dyna was incorporated in 1945; in 1949, it launched Le Parfait, a liver-based sandwich spread containing truffles. In 1959, Dyna began producing Tartex brand prepared dishes. In 1962, Dyna GmbH was set up in Germany and opened a factory in that country at Freiburg im Breisgau. M. Dünner, a specialist in sesame-based products, took control of the German company in 1967, and two years later, R.A. Jewison, Dyna's distributor in the United Kingdom, was to assume control of the company. The Ursina-Franck group acquired the Swiss Dyna Company early in 1971.

Finally, Alpura Koreco AG, Bern, founded in 1951 to apply the patented uperization process to milk and other beverages, must also be mentioned.

In France, Ursina manufactured pudding, condensed and evaporated milk, instant powdered milk, infant formula, instant infant cereal, slightly salted cheeses, and Tonimalt, a breakfast drink, at the Rumilly factory, opened in 1922. We mentioned earlier that Compagnie Générale du Lait was founded by Ursina in 1917. Originally located in Bordeaux, this company was eventually transferred to Haute-Savoie, where production methods closely resemble those of Switzerland. In 1965, the company's name was changed to Lait Mont-Blanc, the trademark under which its main line of products had made a name for itself in France. Lait Mont-Blanc was to become an important French dairy company. In 1946, Compagnie Générale du Lait acquired an interest in Claudel S.A. (known, until 1964, as Société des Laiteries de la Vire et du Cotentin) with a view to obtaining additional plants to produce Guigoz brand milk. Claudel's headquarters were in Paris. It possessed several factories at Pont Herbert, Villedieu-les-Poëles, La Chapelle d'Andaine, Pont-Tardif, Chef-du-Pont, and Rémilly/Loson. It did not take long for Claudel to become one of the main suppliers of Lait Mont-Blanc as well as one of the largest manufacturers of Guigoz

Lait Mont-Blanc factory at Rumilly, France, 1964

Poster used from 1962–1975: this baby appeared on every can of Guigoz milk

IN GERMANY, WITH ALLGÄUER ALPENMILCH, ALETE, AND A WINE PRODUCER; IN HOLLAND...

brand powdered milk. Claudel's main products were Beurre d'Isigny, Normand cheeses, fresh cream, infant formula, powdered milk, and feed for livestock. Claudel owned shares in Etablissements Avenel, Le Havre, a sales company involved mainly in exporting to Great Britain, Africa, Lebanon, and Oceania.

Duchesse de Bourgogne S.A., which Ursina AG and Compagnie Générale du Lait founded in 1932, had its headquarters at Gevrey-Chambertin in the Côte d'Or Department of France. The company operated a factory producing Duchesse de Bourgogne, Bon Vigneron, and Colomas brand fruit jelly, fruit in syrup, and jam.

Berneralpen-Milchgesellschaft had established an affiliate at Biessenhofen, Germany, in 1905. It was incorporated in 1917, becoming the independent company, Alpursa AG. In 1931, Alpursa AG became Allgäuer Alpenmilch AG, with headquarters in Munich. From the start, this company specialized in the manufacture of Bären Marke brand evaporated milk, which was still the leading brand of evaporated milk on the West German market in 1970. Produced by two factories—at Biessenhofen and Weiding—the company's main products consisted of evaporated milk and pudding. Allgäuer Alpenmilch owned Alpursa GmbH, a company that marketed other brands of evaporated milk in Germany. Alete GmbH, another member of the Ursina group, was also located in Munich; it was established in 1934 to distribute baby food, powdered milk, and Alete, a highly nutritious form of enriched sugar. The company's R&D department was actively engaged in developing new products for children: infant formula, infant cereal, milk-based and standard porridge, twenty-four varieties of baby food, as well as enriched sugar, and salt-free powdered milk. In Germany, Ursina also owned St. Ursula Weingut und Weinkellerei GmbH in Bingen on the Rhine, which had been set up in 1963 by Allgäuer Alpenmilch; it cellared and bottled the Goldener Oktober wines distributed by Allgäuer Alpenmilch's sales organization. Goldener Oktober included wines from the Rhine, the Moselle, and the Palatinate, as well as red wines from France and the Italian Tirol. St. Ursula Weingut had been established to permit Ursina's diversification. And following Nestlé's merger with Ursina-Franck, it was to contribute to Nestlé's success in the field of wine (in which it had had little previous experience). St. Ursula Weingut und Weinkellerei GmbH was finally sold in 1987.

At Nunspeet, Holland, Ursina owned Vereenigde Veluwsche Melkproductenfabrieken N.V., which specialized mainly in the production of Bear

Brand condensed milk and Guigoz powdered milk. It exported condensed milk to several countries and Guigoz milk to the Middle East and North Africa. Founded in 1938, following the take-over of J.E. Schaap & Co. as well as some smaller local dairy companies, the firm also supplied fresh dairy products for the Dutch market. P. Molenaar & Co's Meelfabrieken N.V., located at Westzaan, produced mainly infant cereal, sold primarily in Holland.

ITALY, SPAIN, AND AUSTRALIA.

In 1955, the Italian distributor, Società Anonima Italiana Prodotti Guigoz, founded in 1941, became Orsina S.p.A. of Milan. Simultaneously, Mario Rigat di A of Fossano (Cuneo) was acquired. In addition to Guigoz products, the latter firm manufactured Parmesan cheese and condensed milk for institutions and the food industry. In addition, it supplied a large portion of its fresh milk and butter to Italy's Riviera dei Fiori.

In 1963, Ursina became the majority shareholder in Massanes y Grau at San Justo Desvern (Barcelona), Spain, the oldest of the companies in this group, dating back to 1919. Massanes y Grau manufactured and marketed such milk-based products as powdered milk, condensed milk, cheeses, butter, cream, and various milk by-products. In 1971, Massanes y Grau absorbed Sociedad Anonima de Industria y Derivados Alimenticios (S.A.I.D.A.), with headquarters in Barcelona. Founded jointly in 1957 by the Franck group (to be discussed later) and Potax S.A., a Spanish company, with each partner having a 50 percent interest, S.A.I.D.A. manufactured and distributed instant coffee substitutes in Spain. Later it was to manufacture Thomy brand products (also to be discussed later), adapting them to Spanish tastes. By 1965, Thomy brand mayonnaise was performing very well there. In 1968, S.A.I.D.A. founded a new affiliate, Queserias del Noroeste, to manufacture cheeses and other dairy products. Thus, it is clear that, in Spain, the Ursina and Franck groups maintained close ties even before joining forces with one another.

In Australia, Ursina owned Tongala Milk Products Pty. Ltd., with headquarters at Tongola, a company founded originally in 1948, to supply the Far East and Pacific markets previously supplied by Berneralpen-Milchgesellschaft. In the meantime, Tongala began to focus its attention primarily on the Australian market. Ever since 1963, Tongala had a surplus of milk, owing to its acquisition of Northern Dairy Company, Ltd., which collected milk used in the manufacture of Tongala brand products. Three other Australian companies owned by Ursina were all located in Melbourne: Barnes Honey Co. Pty. Ltd. & Medallion Products Pty. Ltd., which produced confectionery items

INTERFRANCK JOINED FORCES WITH URSINA IN 1970, THE FORMER EVOLVING FROM A FIRM FOUNDED IN GERMANY IN 1828 TO PRODUCE CHICORY. AN AGREEMENT BETWEEN INTERFRANCK AND A SWISS COMPANY LED TO THE CREATION OF THOMI+FRANCK AG.

and honey; Girgarre Cheese Co. Pty. Ltd., which produced various kinds of cheese; and Halliwell Cold Storage Pty. Ltd., which specialized in building refrigeration systems for perishable items.

Ursina (Thailand) Ltd., Bangkok, manufactured Dawn Brand condensed milk, a brand owned jointly by Nestlé, General Milk, and Ursina.

The history of Interfranck, too, is that of a company that evolved during more than a century through partnerships and acquisitions. In 1828, the year it was founded, the firm Heinrich Franck's Söhne began manufacturing chicory at Wurttemberg in southern Germany. Later, in 1893, a Heinrich Franck's Söhne Company was founded in Basel. These two companies expanded vigorously throughout the Austro-Hungarian Empire until World War I. In 1913, the firm set up a holding company in Schaffhausen, Switzerland, together with Kathreiner Malzkaffee-Fabriken, which had been established in Munich in 1892 and produced mainly malt-based coffee substitutes. The name of the holding company was Internationale Nahrungs- und Genussmittel Aktiengesellschaft (I.N.G.A.). The two companies finally merged in 1943 and worked out a diversification scheme in 1954. The holding company's name was changed from I.N.G.A. to Unifranck Lebensmittelwerke GmbH in 1966; it was active in the field of coffee subtitutes, instant coffee and its substitutes, seasonings, and products for clients purchasing in large quantities.

In 1929, Heinrich Franck's Söhne AG (Interfranck) signed an agreement with Helvetia Langenthal, founded in 1884 by the Thomi family. Both companies produced chicory and were therefore in direct competition with one another. Ever since 1907, Helvetia had been producing Thomy brand mustard, introducing on the market soft metal tubes for its mustard in 1930. This agreement resulted in the creation of the firm of Thomi + Franck AG. (In 1970, the Thomi family still maintained a 49 percent interest in this company, which it was to sell to Nestlé in 1989.)

In 1957, the headquarters of I.N.G.A. were transferred to Zurich; and in 1966, the firm changed its name to Interfranck Holding AG. This was the group that Ursina acquired in January, 1970.

Thus, Thomi + Franck AG, with headquarters in Basel, was a part of the Interfranck group. Ever since 1951, the firm had been pursuing an active policy of diversification; and, as a result of that policy, it began manufacturing mayonnaise in 1951, instant coffee in 1957, tomato-paste concentrate in 1960, and vinegar in 1966. Thomi + Franck had two Swiss affiliates: Leisi AG, Wangen, near Olten, and Essigfabrik Berna AG, Bern. Founded in 1935, Leisi

Label dating from 1881, used by Heinrich Franck's Söhne, Ludwigsburg, Germany

IN FRANCE, INTERFRANCK PRODUCED VARIOUS COFFEE PRODUCTS AND SEASONINGS; IN GERMANY, IT PRODUCED, IN ADDITION TO THESE, FRUIT JUICE AND NATURAL MINERAL WATER. IN ITALY, ITS MAIN PRODUCTS WERE COFFEE SUBSTITUTES, VINEGAR, SPICES, ETC....

became a subsidiary of Thomi + Franck in 1970. It manufactured biscuit dough, puff pastry, as well as various kinds of cakes; while Essigfabrik Berna AG was acquired with a view to strengthening the market presence of Thomy brand products and to provide a foothold in the field of salad dressings.

In France, I.N.G.A. holding company, the forerunner of Interfranck, had acquired a 25 percent interest in Compagnie Française de l'Industrie Alimentaire S.A., with headquarters at Juvisy-sur-Orge, which producted Kneipp brand malt. In 1951, I.N.G.A. acquired a majority interest in the company, which was to grow over the years. Compagnie Française was active in three main areas: roasted items (malt and its derivatives, coffee substitutes), instant coffee substitutes, salad dressings and condiments. Another company, Maxime Delrue S.A., Aubervilliers (Seine-St-Denis), was also part of the Interfranck group. Since it was founded in 1893, this company had been involved solely in the field of imported food products. Until 1965, it focused its activity essentially on a range of approximately three hundred products divided into four main groups: canned fruit and vegetables, canned fish, canned salmon and shellfish, as well as dried fruit. In 1965, Maxime Delrue S.A. was the first company to import citrus fruit juice in glass bottles to France and the rest of Europe. Later, it was to market precooked American rice under the Tante Caroline trademark and, in 1969, an instant freeze-dried fruit juice.

The German operating company, Unifranck Lebensmittelwerke GmbH, Ludwigsburg, Wurttemberg, evolved from a merger between Heinrich Franck's Söhne and Kathreiner Malzkaffee-Fabriken. Unifranck possessed subsidiaries such as Tino Lebensmittel GmbH, Ludwigsburg (specialized in dietetic products, meat-based products, and various canned items, as well as instant beverages), and Helvetia Conserven GmbH, Gross Gerau, manufacturer of canned fruit juice, a wide range of canned vegetables, and frozen foods. Unifranck had entered the natural mineral-water field by acquiring Rietenauer Mineralquellen und Getränke GmbH, Rietenau, which owned five nonsaline mineral water springs. The company's bottling plants were located in Rietenau, Hamburg, Berlin, and Bad-Wildungen. Its other products included: fruit juices, dietetic beer, liquors, and wine.

Franck Alimentare Italiana S.p.A. (F.A.I.), Milan, Italy, operated two factories, one in Milan, the other in Vercelli and, from 1961 on, included several others, the oldest of which was founded in 1882. Until 1963, F.A.I. had been the leading producer of coffee substitutes—its sole product—for the Italian market. By 1970, it was producing coffee substitutes in its two plants and packaging both regular and camomile tea. The company had six subsidiaries in the food industry, including Aromateria Italiana Radaelli S.p.A. (A.I.R.), Milan, which manufactured mustard and Louit Frères brand pickles, and SAMER (Samaja Mercantile S.p.A), Florence, whose products included three brands of coffee, a range of liquors, and various products for bakeries. SAMER was acquired in 1964. Before World War II, when it was still known as Firma Nonzi, SAMER was the biggest Italian importer of pepper, paprika, and other spices. Nonzi also imported coffee, which was subsequently sold to coffee bean roasters. After the war, Nonzi decided to open its own coffee bean roasting plant—Mercantile.

IN ADDITION, IT WAS ALSO ACTIVE IN PORTUGAL. THE RAPPROCHEMENT BETWEEN NESTLÉ AND URSINA-FRANCK WAS A LOGICAL ONE; HOWEVER, NESTLÉ DID NOT INTEND TO PURSUE ALL OF URSINA'S ACTIVITIES.

At Linda-a-Velha, Portugal, Tofa S.A. manufactured coffee, instant coffee, coffee substitutes, and instant-coffee substitutes.

In this section, we have described in detail the firms founded or acquired by Ursina and Interfranck during the course of over a hundred years of activity in order to enable the reader to gain some insight into the complex structure of the groups of companies with which Nestlé was to merge in 1971.

In 1971, when it merged with Nestlé, the Ursina-Franck group had existed for only a year, meaning that, had negotiations between Hans R. Schwarzenbach and Pierre Liotard-Vogt not gone so well, the Bernese group would never have dreamed of pooling its interests with Nestlé. Fortunately, this move was beneficial to both companies; and the mutual understanding between the two parties to the merger contributed greatly to the success of their negotiations. Nestlé's merger with Ursina-Franck—its competitor in many areas—did not necessarily mean that it intended to maintain all of the latter's activities. To be sure, Ursina's firms in Australia, Belgium, France, Germany, Holland, Italy, Morocco, Portugal, Spain, Switzerland, Thailand, and Tunisia were indeed absorbed by Nestlé. However, real estate companies in France, printers, manufacturers of measuring devices, small computers, varnish, and packaging materials in Switzerland, publishers and wine companies in Germany, as well as ink and varnish manufacturers in Italy were involved in activities of no interest to Nestlé's holding company; and these were gradually dropped. Nestlé also felt no desire to become a banker, or to possess a bank that would be too small, in any case, to enable it to meet its financial requirements. Consequently, in 1976, Nestlé sold almost

Heinrich Franck's Söhne label, 1879

THE MERGER WAS ANNOUNCED AT A PRESS CONFERENCE IN JANUARY, 1971. MANAGERS FROM BOTH FIRMS EXPRESSED THEIR SATISFACTION...

all its interest in Handelsbank, Zurich, which it acquired as a result of the Ursina-Franck merger.

This merger was announced in Bern on January 12, 1971, at a press conference held by both companies—one of the first of Nestlé's encounters with the media. Until that time, the motto at Nestlé had always been, as Chairman Muller succinctly put it: "he who lives discreetly lives happily," for Swiss companies were under no legal obligation to organize such events with the press. From 1971 on, Nestlé's chief executive was to meet annually with the press and, as of 1979, biannually—at a spring press conference in Zurich and an autumn press conference in Vevey. Of course, both Swiss and foreign reporters had published the results of interviews with Nestlé's chief executive prior to 1971, but such interviews were exceptional. The Nestlé tradition was that those attending the annual shareholders' meeting (to which the press was also invited) should be the first to hear whatever information management provided apart from the company's annual report—published since 1866. Given its scope and suddenness, Nestlé's merger with Ursina-Franck caused an understandable stir in public opinion; it also provided an opportunity for the company to adopt a more open stance vis-à-vis the media.

At this press conference, Ursina-Franck's chairman, Hans R. Schwarzenbach, outlined the advantages of its merger with Nestlé. Jean-Constant Corthésy, Nestlé's chairman, made the point that his company had no intention of growing in size in order to form a monopoly. The press was to echo the major points of interest of the press conference, one of these being that the sales figure of Nestlé Alimentana S.A. for 1969 was SFr.9,379,000,000 making it the thirty-eighth largest firm in the world. Nestlé had been the biggest company in Switzerland for a long time, and Ursina-Franck was the ninth biggest one.

Hans R. Schwarzenbach

Schwarzenbach stated that the SFr.1,730,000,000 turnover of his company was chiefly generated in a single, well-defined area, and that diversification in itself could not ensure a bright future for the firm. Sixty percent of the company's sales were from dairy products; however, the price of milk was subject to political issues. Moreover, until that time, Ursina-Franck had earned 60 percent of its profits in Germany. The firm intended to enlarge its range of products and expand into other countries. It was interested in a new associate "that shows understanding for its staff and will also keep in mind its commitments to the country."

WHILE STATING THAT THEY HAD NO INTENTION OF MOVING TOWARD GIGANTISM. IT WAS POSSIBLE TO EXCHANGE SHARES ONLY WITH ANOTHER SWISS COMPANY.

Corthésy emphasized that when Nestlé first considered the possibility of a rapprochement and eventual merger with Ursina-Franck, it had initially feared that it might be criticized for attempting to move toward gigantism. As Corthésy stated: "in the world today, being big is sometimes considered to be a defect, or at least a negative point, although no one really knows why." Nestlé decided finally to pursue this path, for "whether one likes it or not, whether it is good or bad, this is a period of business mergers." With each passing day, they are growing in size. And Corthésy added: "if we want to survive amid the world's big companies engaged in permanent competition, we must grow as fast as our competitors: in other words, we must maintain a high rate of expansion." Even when it has a large amount of available funds, there is a limit to how much a company can acquire through the exchange of securities, and this fact handicapped Nestlé. The reader has already seen how important it was to the firm to maintain its Swiss identity. And, as mentioned earlier, Nestlé had taken steps, in 1956, to make sure that the majority of its share capital would be in the form of registered shares reserved primarily for Swiss citizens.

It was this concern to retain its Swiss identity that prevented Nestlé from acquiring foreign companies through exchanging securities. Corthésy went so far as to state: "The only mergers we can consider are with other Swiss companies; and, since we are a small country, our chances are extremely limited. That is why Ursina is one of the few big Swiss firms whose activities are similar enough to our own to make a merger possible, and we felt that we could not overlook this almost unique opportunity to strengthen our position by merging with a Swiss company." Revealing the motives underlying the decision of Nestlé's management, the speaker concluded: "We would really never have forgiven ourselves if, failing to agree to this move today, we had later learned that our friends had sought a rapprochement with another big international group."

Toward the end of the press conference, Pierre Liotard-Vogt, the chief executive of Nestlé Alimentana S.A., mentioned the advantages for management resulting from the merger of the two firms in such countries as Germany, France, and Switzerland. During the press conference, it was announced that, at the next annual shareholders' meeting, the board of directors of Nestlé Alimentana S.A. would propose, from 1970 on, paying the same dividend for new registered shares resulting from planned increases in the company's share capital as for old Nestlé shares. Ursina-

AT THE ANNUAL SHAREHOLDERS' MEETINGS OF THE TWO COMPANIES—ONE IN BERN, THE OTHER IN LAUSANNE—THE MERGER WAS APPROVED ON MAY 5 AND 6, 1971. NESTLÉ ABSORBED URSINA-FRANCK, EXCHANGING TWO URSINA SHARES FOR ONE NESTLÉ BEARER SHARE.

Franck planned to pay a bonus of SFr. 6 per share in addition to its dividend, which was forecast at SFr. 16.

All of the above information was communicated to and discussed once again by those present at the annual shareholders' meeting held by Ursina-Franck on May 5, 1971, in Bern, and at the annual meeting of Nestlé the following day in Lausanne. The proposals were accepted by the majority of the shareholders. Comments made by Nestlé's managers in Lausanne showed clearly what was at stake. The chairman and chief executive went into great detail during these meetings; and it might be useful to quote extensively from their statements. "Our proposal for a merger with Ursina-Franck might surprise you. Indeed, you might ask why we feel the need to increase our activity in an area—that of milk—that has hardly any growth potential and that is faced with many problems, such as the intervention of political authorities to set raw materials prices and the continuing rise in milk prices in the industrialized countries, where farmers are, quite properly, demanding an income equal to that of other classes of society. This merger is justified, however, by the substantial savings it will make possible in the production and distribution of our respective products. It also seemed advisable to combine the efforts of two Swiss companies faced with foreign competition in markets where both are present. These two issues have been carefully examined, and we have decided that we can recommend this merger to you, even though it does not open up a [new] area of growth."

Explaining how the operation would be carried out, Corthésy stated that Nestlé would absorb Ursina-Franck S.A. by exchanging one Nestlé bearer share for two Ursina-Franck shares. It was not easy to establish the rate of exchange, for Nestlé shares had been undervalued on the stock market for quite some time; while this was not true in the case of Ursina-Franck shares. This resulted from the fact that some newspapers had spread false information about Nestlé's expansion; it can also be explained by the fact that the large number of Nestlé shares on the market did not always find buyers, for Nestlé had been forced to adopt a very restrictive policy concerning the purchase of registered shares of stock by investment funds. Under the circumstances, Nestlé's management could obviously not take as its point of reference share prices as quoted on the stock exchange; rather, it had to take into account the value of both companies in terms of their ultimate profitability. Ursina-Franck's directors, on the other hand, were convinced of the importance of the market price in determining the value of shares. There was no other alternative but to exchange Ursina-Franck shares for Nestlé bearer shares insofar as the latter were quoted at a higher price than its registered shares. In the same speech, Corthésy stated: "We finally agreed to a rate of exchange of two to one, not only because of Ursina's [financial] strength, but also because of the savings this merger will make possible. However, this rate of exchange is not entirely satisfactory if profitability and future prospects are taken into account, for, clearly, both are far greater in the case of our company. This explains why we propose, ladies and gentlemen, that our capital be increased prior to the exchange of shares."

NESTLÉ INCREASED ITS CAPITALIZATION FROM SFR. 195,600,000 TO SFR. 259,920,000 BY ISSUING NEW REGISTERED SHARES WITH A VIEW TO STRENGTHENING NESTLÉ'S SWISS IDENTITY. NESTLÉ'S MANAGEMENT INSISTED ON THE IMPORTANCE OF REMAINING A GLOBAL FIRM...

Nestlé's capitalization thus increased from SFr. 195,600,000 to SFr. 259,920,000, an increase obtained by issuing against cash one new registered Nestlé share for every five original shares (bearer or registered), for a total of SFr. 39,120,000, as well as by exchanging two Ursina-Franck shares (bearer or registered) for one new Nestlé Alimentana bearer share, for a total of SFr. 25,200,000. That this merger was widely accepted is shown by the fact that, on the date of the official deadline for the exchange of shares, December 31, 1971, less than 1 percent of the original Ursina-Franck shares had not been exchanged. At the same time, the share capital of Unilac, Inc. was increased by $7,718,400, with $4,694,400 of that amount resulting from an issue of 391,200 new shares of Unilac common stock at the rate of one new share for five original ones. The rest of the increase ($3,024,000) resulted from the issue of 250,000 new shares of common stock following the merger of Nestlé and Ursina-Franck.

With a view to restoring the balance between bearer shares and registered shares, all new shares issued were registered ones. Nestlé pointed out that it had no wish to place its foreign shareholders at a disadvantage; and these were granted the same right as the Swiss to register the new shares in their possession. Explaining these somewhat complicated measures, Chairman Corthésy repeated to the annual meeting of May 6, 1971, that, under the circumstances, the firm was obliged to issue only registered shares, for it was in the interest not only of Nestlé's Swiss shareholders but also of its foreign ones that the company's Swiss identity be maintained.

Nestlé's management could not ignore the reservations of certain journalists concerning the creation of an even bigger company; and it decided that it would discuss the issue in the presence of the company's shareholders. Indeed, there was an urgent need for Nestlé to eliminate certain misconceptions on the part of the public as to its intentions. To quote Chairman

AND DEFENDED THE RAISON D'ETRE OF BIG MULTINATIONALS THAT ALSO ASSIST IN THE DEVELOPMENT OF THE THIRD WORLD...

Corthésy: "No one denies that economic realities force companies to continually seek means of streamlining, and this has made us realize that the merging of firms results in much better performance than one can obtain from a large number of small, isolated firms. This development has been underway for centuries, ever since olden times when the unit of production consisted of the master craftsman aided by a few journeymen, right up to the present, when industries are so big that their activity extends far beyond their borders, encompassing the entire planet."

Corthésy pointed out that, as one of the biggest companies in the world, Nestlé considered any attacks against multinationals to be directed against it. He admitted that "the individual craftsman, maintaining family traditions passed on from father to son, is easier to like than a completely anonymous corporation that no longer has ties to a [particular] man or family." No one can deny, however, that big corporations, owing to the funds they have at their disposal, are capable of financing the advanced research on which progress depends. Thanks to technical advances and improvements in mass production, these big companies contribute to lowering costs, thus enabling a greater number of people to buy products that were previously luxury items reserved only for the rich. "Only huge companies, for example, can produce automobiles [priced] within everyone's reach." Furthermore, owing to its power and resources, a big multinational is in a better position to help fight unemployment. Big companies also pay more taxes, thus lowering the high taxes individuals would otherwise have to pay. Both Corthésy and Liotard-Vogt emphasized the importance of the contribution of multinationals to expanding the economies of the developing countries. The merger between Nestlé and Ursina-Franck had no adverse effect on Nestlé's penetration into other world markets, especially those of the Third World. On the contrary, it was helped by the merger.

Local cereal crops being developed at a Nestlé technological development center

Aid to developing countries was—and still is—a most important issue. And spokesmen devoted many of their speeches to this problem in response to the growing number of people wishing to diminish the shocking disparity between rich and poor countries. Although grants are essential in the event of a crisis, they do not provide long-term solutions to the problems of developing countries; rather, the way to solve such problems is, as Chairman Corthésy stated: "to provide the inhabitants of developing countries with the training they lack and which will enable them to expand both their agriculture and their industry, the only true sources of wealth." Only big multinationals have sufficient funds at their disposal to set up an industry where none has existed before, and such an industry cannot flourish without proper training for all personnel.

Thus, Nestlé's management was not afraid of broaching this subject, a subject of concern to many people during the close of our century. Initially, the public had little knowledge of the many services provided by multinationals. It was far more common to hear criticism of their power, which they were accused of misusing. As management pointed out, the economic power of big companies is often discussed, and their annual sales figures are often compared with the smaller budgets of a certain number of nations. But what practical conclusions can be drawn from such comparisons? First of all, a company has no military and no political power. And it cannot make use of its financial power beyond the scope of its normal range of activities. To be sure, a multinational strives for profitability, but its activities are subject to rules and regulations that it certainly obeys far more scrupulously than other institutions.

Corthésy's remarks were even more direct: "Far be it from me to claim that the people who manage such firms are saints, more virtuous than other categories of citizens, but the innocuous nature of big companies and their scrupulous respect for the law can easily be explained by their vulnerability—even in the case of a powerful international trust vis-à-vis a small defenceless country. What happens, for example, when a disagreement occurs between an oil company, which is always very big, and a relatively poor nation? Have you never heard of nationalization or dispossession carried out with the stroke of a pen? In such cases, a company is virtually powerless to safeguard its interests and has to seek the support if its own government—which cannot completely disregard the national interest. Believe me, the power of big companies is nothing more than a myth. They are subjected to constant scrutiny and must constantly justify their actions. People accept this myth simply because there is something suspicious about every large entity, but it does not stand up to objective examination."

WHERE NESTLÉ'S PRESENCE WAS VISIBLE IN 1971, IN THE FORM OF 54 FACTORIES IN SOUTH AND CENTRAL AMERICA;

Outlining the specific activities of Nestlé in the Third World, Liotard-Vogt went about defining the company's international character. Having been obliged, very rapidly, to go beyond the narrow confines of Switzerland to ensure its expansion, Nestlé found itself in contact with the developing world sooner than other firms. "Perhaps, we are pioneers in this regard and of all the multinationals in the world the one that has contributed the most to the economic development of the so-called Third World—and this, of course, within the scope of our activities. . . . At present, there is not one country in the world—apart from those whose political system prevents it—where Nestlé products are not marketed. Whenever conditions permit, we produce locally all or part of the products we market. Except in the case of very small countries, where setting up an industry is as yet economically unfeasible, our goal has always been not to sell imported products, which means the tapping of already meager [local] resources, but rather to create local industry that will generate wealth."

Liotard-Vogt went on to point out that, in 1971, there were fifty-four factories producing Nestlé products in South and Central America, and thirteen operating in Africa. Once created, these factories can neither be moved nor destroyed. Such production centers were usually set up in areas where there was nothing of the kind. Obviously, their products were not always intended for export, for production generally depended on domestic demand. (The only exception to this was the Nescafé factory in the capital of the Ivory Coast, Abidjan, which exported 80 percent of its production.) As far as employment was concerned, the initially large European staff necessary to start up production gradually diminished, eventually becoming insignificant. For example, in Colombia there were only twenty-five foreigners out of a total staff of 1,507 in 1971. In Argentina, thirty-seven of the 2,528 employees were foreigners; in Brazil, sixty-three out of 5,155; in Malaysia, thirteen out of 538; in Singapore, five out of 144; in the Philippines, nine out of 782; and in India, seven out of 708. In reference to these figures, Liotard-Vogt added that Nestlé did not limit its training efforts to employees alone, but made it available to other population

Checking the weight of bouillon cubes at the Maggi factory in Ghana

groups within a country as well. Of course, as Liotard-Vogt reminded his listeners, the company was not a philanthropic organization, but it did not intend to grow rich by exploiting the poor. The bigger Nestlé became, the greater its economic impact and the more aware it became of its responsibilities vis-à-vis the public.

In the final analysis, a company such as Nestlé contributes far more to the Third World than it takes from it. "Which explains," said Liotard-Vogt, "why we are so shocked when certain people, who I can only assume are acting in good faith, denounce the activities of big companies—ours in particular—as nothing more and nothing less than exploitation of the developing countries. . . . Fortunately. it is those primarily concerned who show such assertions to be false." Liotard-Vogt next mentioned that Nestlé purchased more than SFr. 1,500,000,000 worth of raw materials from developing countries, "a sum far in excess of the total profits we can earn in those countries; and yet it has been our consistant policy to try and set the highest prices for commodities that we undoubtedly utilize more of than anyone else in the world."

Forty-nine percent of Nestlé's 1970 turnover of SFr. 10,205,000,000 was generated in Europe. In 1972, after its merger with Ursina-Franck, Nestlé's turnover rose to SFr. 14,651,000,000, 52.9 percent of which was generated in Europe. The company's turnover had tripled within a decade. (In 1961, it was only SFr. 4 455,000,000.) In 1971, twenty thousand employees were added to Nestlé's payroll, increasing its number of employees from 91,173 on December 31, 1970, to 111,821 at the end of 1971.

Two other issues concerned Nestlé's management at the time: the high market price of Nestlé shares and having those shares listed on European stock exchanges.

As for the distribution of shares, Nestlé was pleased, in 1972, with its large number of shareholders—61,000 owners of registered shares—which, at the time, was greater than any other Swiss company. Nevertheless, the firm did not believe that this was sufficient. As mentioned earlier, for over fifty years, Nestlé had pursued a policy of self-financing. Profits reinvested in the company increased the value of its shares. Consequently, Nestlé's registered and bearer shares reached such high prices on the stock exchange that only institutional investors and the very wealthy could afford them. The company regretted this state of affairs. In an era of rapid technological advances and growing financial strength, resulting in an increasing

NESTLÉ ALSO ANNUALLY PURCHASES SFR. 1,500,000,000 WORTH OF RAW MATERIALS FROM DEVELOPING COUNTRIES.

IN 1971, NESTLÉ EMPLOYED MORE THAN 100,000 PERSONS.

CONCERNED ABOUT THE DISTRIBUTION OF NESTLÉ SHARES...

MANAGEMENT SAW TO IT THAT THE COMPANY WAS LISTED ON FOREIGN STOCK EXCHANGES; IN ADDITION, AN EFFORT WAS MADE TO LOWER THE HIGH PRICE OF NESTLÉ SHARES.

number of mergers, Nestlé felt it was absolutely essential for big firms evolving from such mergers to belong not only to the wealthy but to a wide cross-section of the population. This was particularly important in the case of a small country such as Switzerland, whose major companies "might someday appear too big, having failed to give the entire population the possibility of investing in them," as the vice-chairman of Nestlé's board of directors, Karl Obrecht, declared in 1972.

As for having its shares listed on foreign stock exchanges, Nestlé felt that it was highly desirable for the citizens of countries in which the firm played an important economic role to have a much greater opportunity of becoming co-owners of the company. Thus, in the final months of 1972, Nestlé looked into the possibility of having its bearer shares listed on stock exchanges abroad. At that time, its shares were listed only in Paris, and Nestlé's management requested that shares be quoted on the cash market in addition to the term market. The company wished to be listed at least on the stock exchanges of the countries where its products were manufactured and in which it had a large share of the market. Unfortunately, this proved impossible in many countries, owing to listing regulations, which required that the firms provide certain information that Nestlé, "already generous in this respect—from the Swiss point of view—was not ready to furnish, or at least not as yet." The high price of Nestlé shares was another obstacle to the company's being listed abroad as well as an additional reason for it to split its shares. Until it was legally possible to do so, Nestlé had to be satisfied with having its high-priced shares listed wherever this was feasible. After Paris, Nestlé was authorized to trade its bearer shares on the Frankfurt and Düsseldorf exchanges and later on the Vienna Stock Exchange.

Former Lactogen packaging line at Nestlé's factory in Moga, India: adding the measuring cups

All of these changes took place while Nestlé remained faithful to its policy of maintaining the majority of its shares in Swiss hands. At the time, this policy appeared to be necessary due to the threat of war and, in the long term, to the problems involved in reaching bilateral agreements on double taxation. Since Swiss law allowed the firm no possibility of issuing lower-priced shares by reducing their par value below the legal minimun of SFr. 100, the company studied the possibility of issuing additional shares in order to bring down the price of each share. Unfortunately, Swiss federal tax laws as well as several cantonal laws precluded the possibility of a bonus issue by taxing such shares as income. Issuing shares at par, as had been done in the past, was also considered. However, in order to bring down the share price significantly in this way, the issue would have had to be much too large for the Swiss market. In any case, it seemed unrealistic to expect to bring down the price of Nestlé shares to a tenth or a hundredth of their value for several years to come.

Thus, Nestlé searched for an interim solution. The company issued a partial share certificate at the rate of ten certificates per share. This, however, was only a temporary solution until the law could be changed. From 1973 until 1984, Nestlé would attempt to issue, on a long-term basis, a SFr. 10 partial share certificate within the means of a greater number of people, especially Nestlé's employees. But this was a complicated procedure, particularly for banking institutions; thus, after eleven years, Nestlé had to renounce its dream of instituting this form of "everyman's capitalism," to which it was so deeply committed.

This was an example of an attempt on the part of Nestlé's management to distribute the company's capital among such a great number of citizens that it might one day have been possible to consider the company as having become the property of a large percentage of the Swiss population. Nestlé's efforts in this area did not meet with success, however.

STOUFFER, FOUNDED IN 1924, WAS ORIGINALLY A FAMILY BUSINESS PRODUCING FROZEN FOODS.

1973: Nestlé Acquires the Stouffer Corporation

☐ At the end of 1972, Nestlé's management felt that it needed to expand the company's presence on the U.S. market—the largest in the world. When Pierre Liotard-Vogt took over as c.e.o. in 1968, he inherited from his predecessors the idea that Nestlé should establish itself more firmly in the United States, not only in terms of such traditional non-dairy products as coffee, chocolates, wine, etc., but also in the area of frozen foods. The majority interest Nestlé had acquired in Libby had certainly laid the foundation for this endeavor. In the opinion of company experts in Vevey, however, Libby's frozen-food division would not be ready to expand in this field until 1977 at the earliest. Nestlé had the choice, therefore, of increasing Libby's sphere of influence or of purchasing a well-known U.S. frozen-food manufacturer.

In the autumn of 1972, while searching for possible acquisitions, Libby's management heard a rumor that Litton Industries, Inc. might be interested in selling Stouffer Corporation, an excellent frozen-food manufacturer located in Cleveland, Ohio. Libby took an immediate interest in such a promising acquisition, but it lacked the financial backing to carry it out. Thus, Nestlé's chief executive in Vevey thought it preferable for Nestlé Alimentana S.A. to acquire Stouffer directly, rather than through Libby or the U.S. Nestlé Company.

Founded in Ohio in 1924, Stouffer was a small family restaurant business managed by Vernon Stouffer and his father. The firm came into being the day people living in an apartment building in the suburbs of Cleveland asked the Stouffer restaurant to prepare some takeout dishes for them. In an initial attempt to satisfy this new demand, entrées and appetizers were put in the freezer, ready to be served on the premises or sold as carryout orders. By 1954, the restaurant's business was so great that the family had to acquire a factory and begin operating on an industrial scale. Stouffer next set up its own R&D facilities, as well as a state-of-the-art center producing packaging for Stouffer products—and handling them using a nearly fully automated system.

Litton Industries, Inc., California, had acquired all of Stouffer's shares in 1967. Litton was a conglomerate whose core activities were the manufacture of machines and electrical devices, electronics, etc. Litton was of the view at the time that it might benefit from owning a frozen-food manufacturer, as one of its subsidiaries produced microwave ovens that heated frozen dishes quickly. After some time, however, Litton noticed that less than 2 percent of the Stouffer products it sold were heated in Litton microwave ovens, whereas these ovens had a variety of other uses. Thus, it seemed wise for there to be no link between Stouffer's activities and those of Litton's microwave-oven subsidiary. Moreover, Charles B. Thornton, chairman of Litton Industries, Inc. had determined that it would be financially advantageous to Litton for it to sell Stouffer. Around thirty firms had shown varying degrees of interest in acquiring the company; most of these, however, could not be considered, owing to the danger of infringing U.S. antitrust laws or because they had insufficient financial resources. This left four big companies in the running, including the Nestlé group. It quickly became apparent that, while Stouffer's management understood why Litton wished to sell it, the former was determined to become independent once again; and, in order to do so, Stouffer's management preferred to offer its shares to the public. Such a solution would have enabled Litton to fetch a far better price, while ensuring the independence sought by Stouffer's highly capable management.

WITH QUALITY MANAGERS, STOUFFER WOULD HAVE PREFERRED TO REMAIN INDEPENDENT, FOR IT WAS FIRMLY ESTABLISHED IN THE AREA OF FOOD PRODUCTS, RESTAURANTS, AND HOTELS IN THE U.S.

In agreement with Nestlé's board of directors, Liotard-Vogt initiated negotiations with Litton after informing Libby's management that the firm would be acquired directly by Nestlé in Vevey. Preliminary contacts by letter and telephone marked the start of a real adventure that brought Nestlé's chief executive to the U.S. five times in as many months. The negotiations were characterized by rapid decisions and by respect for the desire of Stouffer's management to remain independent.

By the end of 1972, the Stouffer Corporation was a solidly established U.S. firm, with three distinct divisions: frozen foods, restaurants and hotels, and institutional cafeterias. Its annual sales totaled $124,500,000, almost half of which was generated by the manufacture and sale of frozen food, the remainder being earned by some fifty hotels and restaurants and the five institutional cafeterias operated by Stouffer. Stouffer's precooked frozen dishes consisted of entrées (where Stouffer was a leader), main courses, as well as frozen bakery items, thanks

The Stouffer restaurant on Shelby Street in Detroit, Michigan, opened in 1924

NESTLÉ MANAGED TO BE CONVINCING; AND AFTER CONTACTS, VISITS AND HESITATION ON THE PART OF STOUFFER'S MANAGEMENT...

to Stouffer's acquisition of Hanscom Bros., Inc. in 1969. Stouffer's main operational center was located at Solon, a suburb of Cleveland, near major interstate highways and railway networks.

Stouffer's executives—in particular, its chairman, James M. Biggar, son-in-law of the last heir of the firm's founders—were fully conscious of the company's value, especially that of its frozen food division.

Nestlé was faced with a twofold task: to convince Charles B. Thornton, head of Litton Industries, Inc., Beverley Hills, California, to sell Stouffer to Nestlé; and to convince Stouffer's management in Cleveland, whose cooperation was essential to the firm's future success, to stay with the company. Nestlé accomplished both these tasks in a very short time.

While these negotiations could be related in purely technical and financial terms, we would run the risk of minimizing the important human side; this can best be conveyed by citing an interview between the actors in this event.

As for Litton Industries, Inc., everything began with a series of telephone conversations, followed by a meeting in California in early January, 1973. These exploratory contacts soon made it clear that Nestlé had the serious intention to acquire Stouffer. Pierre Liotard-Vogt wished to visit the company in Cleveland.

Rather than merely relating the events, let us listen in, as it were, on Liotard-Vogt's own words: "I said to Mr. Thornton, 'I should like to go there, see the staff, see the products, and thus get a first impression; then, in the second stage, I would like my technical staff and experts to undertake a more detailed study.' 'Out of the question,' he replied. 'Just imagine,' he added, 'if an outsider were to show up, the staff would panic; it absolutely must not become known that we might sell.' I insisted on seeing the firm, and we continued our discussions, that is, I politely obtained more and more information from Mr. Thornton. That was during the morning. Suddenly, at the beginning of the afternoon, he said to me: 'You must go to Cleveland as soon as possible.'

"'Why? You said that you didn't want me to go.'

"'Yes, that's right; there are so many people hounding us over the sale of this firm, I don't want a crowd [of visitors]. I realize, however, that I can't expect you to purchase the company if I keep you from seeing it. We are now convinced that you have not just come to get information, but are really interested in the company. So you must go immediately.'

Esmeralda Resort, Stouffer's luxurious hotel complex near Palm Springs, California, opened in 1989

WHICH WAS NOT PARTICULARLY OPPOSED TO NESTLÉ...

"'Why immediately?'

"'Because the situation is very delicate; you may not be welcomed very enthusiastically by Mr. Biggar and his associates. Making contact is going to be difficult; I won't try and hide that from you, and I want you to be the one who initiates it. If you don't go immediately, while you are in the United States, you will return to Europe and send someone in your place. But I want you to be the one who goes. It must be you.' And he added: 'Listen, there's a plane that leaves in forty-five minutes; I'll reserve a seat for you. I'll send someone to your hotel for your luggage; go directly to the airport, and I'll call Jim Biggar so he can be waiting for you tonight when you arrive. He'll take you to the hotel, and tomorrow morning you can visit the factory and talk to the senior executives.'

"I was put on the plane and arrived late (owing to the time difference) in Cleveland; at the airport, I saw a man who noticed that I seemed to be looking for someone and who asked, 'Mr. Liotard-Vogt?'

"'Yes.'

"'Jim Biggar. Mr. Thornton told me to come and meet you. I'll take you to your hotel, and tomorrow I'll come and get you to take you through the factory. You'll [be able to] talk to my associates.' While driving to the hotel, he said to me: 'You know, I must warn you that we are absolutely opposed to being controlled by another firm.... We do not wish to be controlled by Nestlé any more than by an American company. I can tell you that all of my associates are of exactly the same opinion. And, above all, there are only three of us who are aware of your plans [to acquire Stouffer]. I'll show you through the factory, but very quickly so that no one will notice you.'

"The next day, I met the managers and explained to them that I wanted to get to know their company and that I was pleased to make their acquaintance.... I was given a rather chilly reception. As time passed, however, the atmosphere warmed up as we began to establish personal contact. So that by the time I left in the afternoon [I was flying to New York the same evening], I was able to sense that the people I had been talking to had nothing against me personally and nothing against the Nestlé Company; they just had no desire to work for another company, be it Nestlé or any other firm. Jim Biggar stressed this fact on our way to the airport: 'We know Litton's plans to sell. But we are the ones who are going to buy them out. We are going to go public. The firm will belong to a great number of shareholders, with us managing it....'

AN AGREEMENT WAS REACHED.

"Stouffer's management was so determined to carry out this plan that it even flew to Europe—London, Zurich, and Paris—looking for potential shareholders. It was at this point—one evening at the end of February—that Mr. Thornton, whom I had met again in Los Angeles on February 13, let me know that our bid of $105,000,000 was accepted. That clinched the deal. This was after many long private conversations and telephone calls. We agreed to meet for breakfast in a New York hotel on March 5. Meanwhile, Litton's lawyer came to Vevey to work out the sales agreement. At eight a.m., I had breakfast with Charles Thornton; together, we wrote out a press release to be issued the same day and congratulated each other on the successful conclusion of our negotiations."

At this point in the account related by Liotard-Vogt to this author in 1984, we must emphasize that Stouffer's management was still trying to have their firm go public. Thus, it became necessary to inform Stouffer's executives as to what had taken place.

To continue with the account by Nestlé's chief executive: "During our breakfast at my hotel in New York, Mr. Thornton told me that, earlier, he had phoned Jim Biggar so that he could immediately come to New York, where they were waiting for him. Biggar did not wish to come, as he had a very important appointment. 'I told him,' Thornton continued, 'that what I had to say was even more important: cancel everything, including extremely important things; take the first plane, and be in my New York office by ten or eleven o'clock.' Then he said to me: 'I'm going to have to leave you to meet privately with Jim Biggar and tell him that the company has been sold to Nestlé; I suggest that you join us in about a quarter of an hour. It will be your turn then; I will already have done my part.'

Stouffer factory at Current-Solon, Ohio

"So," said Liotard-Vogt, "I let Litton's boss go; I waited, as agreed; then, I, too, left for Litton's New York offices. I arrived at Charles Thornton's office only to be informed that Jim Biggar had not yet arrived. He had probably not been able to get on the first plane, and so we waited for him. Suddenly, the door opened, and Jim Biggar came in. He was shocked when he saw me, for he obviously sensed

HESITANT AT FIRST, STOUFFER'S MANAGEMENT...

that something was up. Thornton tapped him cordially on the shoulder, American style, saying: 'Well, Jim, I told you to come to break the news to you that Stouffer has been sold to Nestlé.' Jim Biggar asked, 'Has it been finalized?' Thornton replied, 'Yes, it has; everything's done.'

"'Fine, sir, please accept my resignation.'

"'Oh!' his former boss said, laughing, 'that's no longer any concern of mine. You can work that out with Mr. Liotard. If you want to resign, give him your resignation. I am leaving; my job is over. Good-bye.'

"He shook hands with us and left. We talked alone in Litton's reception room. Jim Biggar, still flabbergasted, told me he had to call Cleveland immediately: 'Just think, this very morning I was supposed to meet with the directors of the new company we were going to set up in a few days. When Mr. Thornton told me I had to drop everything and come, I changed the meeting to this afternoon. Now there is no reason for the meeting. I'm going to call and cancel it.' And he added: 'Do you realize we were about to go public; we already had subscribers for our shares and were within a few minutes of our goal.' Then he continued: 'What do you want to do now?' I replied: 'I thought that, following the deal, the right thing to do would be to go to Cleveland and meet with you. I had no idea that I would meet you here. And I wanted to get to know your senior executives too.' He agreed: 'I am going to phone and replace the board meeting by a meeting of our senior executives.' I said: 'I know that this has come as a shock to you, and I'm sorry that things happened this way. But you mustn't hold that against me. I decided that your company was an excellent deal, and I'm paying a reasonable price for it.' 'Yes,' he replied, 'it's true, in fact, that you've only done your job; you can't be accused of having acted improperly.'

"At this point we decided to go to Cleveland, and, late that morning, we took a taxi to New York airport. We arrived at the airport about 1 p.m., without eating lunch. We boarded the plane for the two-hour trip and sat next to each other. During the flight, we discussed business and many other topics; I asked about his family, his children. He told me that he was exhausted and was just about to leave for two weeks' vacation with his family in Hawaii, a vacation he had been putting off for a long time. I said to him, 'But you *should* take your vacation. What's to prevent you from doing so? Don't feel that because of Nestlé you can no longer take your vacation.' Finally, we arrived. We went directly to the office of Jim Biggar's father-in-law, the venerable Mr. Stouffer. Jim introduced me, saying: 'This is Mr. Liotard.' And he added, sadly: 'I was summoned to New York; we've been sold to Nestlé, and Mr. Liotard here is its president.'

"'Ah,' sighed Mr. Stouffer, and I said: 'Hello, sir; I am terribly sorry to be meeting you under these circumstances.' At this point, we convened meeting.

"This is what I saw: a kind of lecture hall with forty people seated around an enormous table. They looked at me as though I were some kind of strange beast. Biggar came in and said: 'This morning, Mr. Thornton, the chairman of Litton, called me to New York and informed me that our company had just been sold to Nestlé. I am pleased to introduce Mr. Liotard-Vogt, Nestlé's president.' He then sat down. No one said a word; everyone had his eyes riveted on me. There was some activity and whispering. I said: 'Put yourselves in my place—a poor Frenchman whose English isn't very good, while you're recovering from the shock, for I realize that you are not pleased with this news. This is not a very pleasant way for me to meet you for the first time. On the other hand, you are now a part of Nestlé, and you are unaware of what that means. I believe that I must first introduce Nestlé to you, tell you about our management philosophy, how we operate, and what kind of company we are.'

"I then described Nestlé and talked about our turnover; I especially stressed the fact that we were a very decentralized company. I gave a certain number of specific examples to enable them to understand how this functioned. Then I said: 'Listen, you are intelligent people. Intelligent people make decisions and form opinions based on complete knowledge. You're lost and don't know how things will continue; so don't think that things will not necessarily work out. Wait a while, and you'll see.' The meeting went on for over two hours until someone finally said: 'Sir, could we discuss this issue alone for just a while? ' I replied, 'Of course; take your time.' Whereupon I left with Jim Biggar, and both of us entered the office of Mr. Stouffer, who had attended the meeting. He tapped me on the shoulder, saying: 'I think you won; I know my people. I think you will do the job.' Stouffer had been won over rather quickly.

"I returned to the meeting. Two or three supposedly awkward questions had been prepared, which I answered very naturally. Then, at 7:30 p.m., it was time for me to catch the plane I planned on taking, and one of the executives was supposed to take me to the airport. As I left, I said to Jim Biggar, 'Do you like Stouffer Corporation?' He replied: 'How can you ask such a

FINALLY ACCEPTED THE ARRANGEMENT, AFTER LENGTHY DISCUSSIONS.

James M. Biggar

STOUFFER REMAINED AN INDEPENDENT COMPANY WITHIN THE NESTLÉ GROUP.

question?' I continued: 'You feel extremely attached to this company, which your father-in-law founded. You have been at Stouffer your whole life. You don't want to jeopardize it. So, no matter what decision you may later make, you would never do anything to endanger the company?' He replied: 'Oh, no, sir; I am a faithful person. And I like Stouffer very much and the people who work for it.' Then I explained: 'Listen, Jim, I want to ask you to do two things: first of all, take your vacation, and that's really the first order I am giving you as your boss. Go to Hawaii for two weeks. Forget everything. From what you've told me and from what I've seen, you have very capable associates. The company will be O.K. Leave instructions before you go, but then go and relax. The second thing I ask is that you realize that you're not chained to the company. You're a free man; you can leave at any time. So wait and see what happens. If you should decide that you can't get along with us, that we are an impossible firm to work for, it won't be too late for you to resign.' He said to me: 'Yes, you're probably right,' adding that it wasn't possible for people who had fought the idea of being taken over by another company to suddenly change their opinion."

Back in Switzerland, Liotard-Vogt at once eased Stouffer's cash-flow problems by having Nestlé take over in this area. Then he gave instructions that no one from Vevey was to go to Cleveland without his express permission. At first, it was Nestlé's chief executive alone who maintained contact with Jim Biggar. But, in less than a year, things were gradually to fall into place: the top executives of the company in Ohio stayed at their jobs; and, a few years later, Jim Biggar was even to take over as head of all the U.S. Nestlé companies—including Libby and Stouffer.

Our account would be incomplete if we did not point out that, by taking over Stouffer, Nestlé also acquired catering services and restaurants, which, as mentioned earlier, it would abandon elsewhere in the world. Even though Stouffer's operational divisions were quite independent of one another, they formed a unified whole. Thus, Nestlé had no alternative: interested primarily in Stouffer's frozen foods, it also had to take over all the latter's hotel-catering and restaurant activities—prepared to sell them at a later date if need be.

On March 7, 1973, the two companies announced the acquisition of Stouffer by Nestlé in a joint press release, which stated the former's 1971-72 sales had reached $124,000,000. Frozen foods accounted for $53,000,000 of that amount, and catering and restaurants $71,000,000. Both of these activities were quite successful, and Stouffer's net profits for the same year totaled more than $3,750,000.

AT THE SAME TIME, NESTLÉ STRENGTHENED ITS SHARE OF THE U.S. MARKET.

Nestlé Alimentana S.A. thus obtained a solid share of the U.S. frozen-food market, especially in the area of high-quality precooked dishes. This acquisition reconfirmed the group's confidence in what it considered to be one of its core areas of diversification. In addition, Stouffer Corporation possessed a chain of fifty-two restaurants and motels, and investment made in that area was meant to boost sales considerably in the following years. At Nestlé's annual shareholders' meeting of June 6, 1973, the chairman of the board of directors pointed out that this acquisition opened the way to extensive development: "We believe that this has enabled us to fill an important gap, for we possessed no restaurants in the U.S. until now, and Libby, having only a small share of the frozen food market, was incapable of providing us with the foothold we needed in this area—one in which we have been very successful in other countries of the world."

Nestlé possessed vineyards in California, but it could not sell its wine in Stouffer restaurants without infringing the laws of several states. Therefore, an independent company was created to market its wine production. Certain steps were taken to avoid possible infringement of U.S. antitrust laws, such as the cessation of Libby's frozen food production.

The future would show that Nestlé's decision to acquire Stouffer was a wise one. In 1974, a year after succeeding Jean-Constant Corthésy as chairman of the board of directors, Pierre Liotard-Vogt, who remained chief executive of Nestlé Alimentana S.A., was able to announce that Nestlé's 1973 sales figure totaled SFr. 16,420,000,000.

At that time, shortly after the 1973 oil shock, Nestlé began to examine the question of what effect the Common Market might have on company development. Studies were also carried out on the possibility of consolidating its production centers.

NOTHING CAME OF INITIAL CONTACTS WITH L'ORÉAL IN 1967.

1974: Nestlé's Rapprochement with L'Oréal

☐ Like men and women, companies, too, often choose to cohabit; sometimes, however, they prefer a freer form of relationship. Nestle's association with L'Oréal is an example of this freer form of union, in which two companies are bound financially to one another, while operating totally independently, with no consolidation being planned at any level. This is precisely the kind of successful relationship that Nestlé and L'Oréal of Paris initiated in 1974. This relationship deserves our attention, for it is still in the news today; moreover, it is the first time that Nestlé entered a field outside the food industry. (Of course, from a certain point of view, L'Oréal was active in an area quite familiar to Nestlé: i.e., the sale of consumer items to retail outlets.)

It was only logical for L'Oréal and Nestlé to cooperate with one another. The former was attempting to take advantage of the fact that Nestlé was better established in countries where its own share of the market was not big enough; while Nestlé was attempting to diversify its interests in a rapidly growing field that seemed both promising and close enough to its own activities to allow a certain amount of combined research as well as marketing.

The adventure of Nestlé and L'Oréal in the areas of finance and cooperation began after a long series of preliminary contacts. Nestlé had been attempting to diversify its activities by entering the related field of cosmetics for a long time. L'Oréal seized the opportunity of remaining independent while reaping the benefits of forming an alliance with a company that was strong financially and industrially and that was likely to become a faithful partner with which it could cooperate harmoniously.

In the 1960s, Enrico Bignami and Jean-Constant Corthésy had felt that Nestlé should diversify through the manufacture and sale of consumer items besides food products. They had become interested in cosmetics and had even hired an expert to perform a study of big cosmetic companies, particularly in the United States, England, and Germany. However, nothing came of the study, for the firms that interested Nestlé were either not for sale or were over-priced, and those that were available did not seem worth purchasing. As François Dalle, chairman and c.e.o. of L'Oréal, was acquainted with Pierre Liotard-Vogt (who, at that time, headed the French company that manufactured and sold Nestlé products), Nestlé's management asked Liotard-Vogt to contact Dalle in 1967.

One of L'Oréal's first posters, early twentieth century

FOUNDED IN 1907, L'ORÉAL WAS ALREADY A TOP-QUALITY COSMETICS FIRM, WHOSE PRINCIPAL SHAREHOLDER WAS THE DAUGHTER OF EUGÈNE SCHUELLER, THE COMPANY'S FOUNDER.

L'Oréal was already a flourishing cosmetics company at that time. Founded in 1907 by Eugène Schueller to market the first hair dyes, L'Oréal had become an important global group with a number of subsidiaries in France and elsewhere. Indeed, it was the world's leading manufacturer of hair-care products. Starting out as a joint-stock company, L'Oréal became a corporation in 1939. In 1950, it took over Monsavon, selling its soaps division in 1961. In December, 1962, the new L'Oréal company that evolved through spin-off acquired the assets and operations of the former company. Next, pursuing its policy of diversification, the group went about securing a controlling interest in several firms: it acquired a majority interest in Société Cadoricin in 1961; in 1965, it absorbed Société des Vallières, and acquired a majority interest in Lancôme S.A. (fine perfumes and cosmetics). L'Oréal thus possessed an extensive range of products for beauticians (hair dyes, permanent and hair-setting lotions, and various types of special hair treatments), for targeted distribution (hair sprays, special shampoos, deodorants, sun-tan lotions), and for large-scale distribution to department stores, luxury shops, drugstores, etc.

L'Oréal's principal shareholder was the founder's daughter, Mrs. Liliane Schueller Bettencourt. In 1967, Liotard-Vogt approached François Dalle, asking him whether Mrs. Bettencourt (whose husband was in the French government) might be willing to consider creating a partnership or any other form of cooperative arrangement with Nestlé. Many conversations ensued, and the Bettencourt family agreed to look into the matter. Enrico Bignami even met with L'Oréal's owners, but nothing came of their meeting.

L'Oréal's founder, Eugène Schueller, in his office in Paris

After being named c.e.o. of Nestlé, Liotard-Vogt happened to meet Dalle, and the two men agreed to first determine whether the French government had any objection to L'Oréal's cooperating more closely with Nestlé. The reactions of L'Oréal's employees and, especially, French public opinion had to be taken into account, for it was not at all certain that the latter would gladly accept such cooperation. Meetings between experts from both companies took place; and their firms' management met with one another on several occasions. Until 1970, when regular talks began to be held, there were few tangible results. These private talks were kept strictly confidential. "I want to state explicitly that we never tried to argue over the prices. We agreed to use the traditional method of valuation," said Liotard-Vogt.

TALKS WITH, NESTLÉ RESUMED IN 1970, RESULTING IN AN AGREEMENT IN 1974.

The political aspect of the issue and the problem of obtaining government authorization were causing the owners and management of the French firm to hesitate. Owing to the experience he had gained in the Stouffer acquisition, Nestle's new chief executive suddenly decided to have a discussion with L'Oréal's top four executives in the presence of Dalle. Liotard-Vogt explained to them the type of company Nestlé was, how it operated, and how it was organized; and Dalle asked them what their reaction would be if Nestlé should one day acquire an interest in L'Oréal; Mrs. Bettencourt would naturally remain the principal shareholder, and there would be no changes in the way the firm was run; however, Nestlé would become the second biggest shareholder after Mrs. Bettencourt. The executives' replies were cautious, but by no means negative. Commenting on the interview, Liotard-Vogt explained to this author: "Everything went well, but don't think that I consider myself exceptional; I am convinced that a number of other persons could have done as well as I."

Early in 1969, Dalle and Liotard-Vogt met privately, and, as a result, talks resumed. Toward the end of 1969, the two men began to discuss in greater detail the type of cooperation they had in mind for the two companies. When they reached the valuation stage (Mrs. Bettencourt was to be paid mainly by exchanging her L'Oréal shares for Nestlé shares), the two men felt they must determine the ratio of one stock to the other, for the official share price was just one among many other criteria. Serious political obstacles had to be overcome, which required special authorization by the French government. After a great amount of difficulty and lengthy negotiations, these obstacles were finally overcome; and the agreement between the two companies was signed in 1974.

The method of exchanging shares meant that Nestlé did not have to disburse any funds in the deal; while Mrs. Bettencourt was able to diversify her financial interests rather than "keeping all her eggs in one basket," as the saying goes. With her initial 4 percent interest in Nestle, Mrs. Bettencourt was the principal shareholder of Nestlé Alimentana S.A.

Nestlé acquired 25 percent of L'Oréal's capital; its shares were transferred to a holding company, Gesparal, set up jointly by both firms, together

A DETAILED PRESS RELEASE EXPLAINED THE BENEFITS OF COOPERATION BETWEEN NESTLÉ AND L'ORÉAL.

with Mrs. Bettencourt, who already possessed 51 percent of Gesparal (Nestlé possessed the remaining 49 percent). The daughter of L'Oréal's founder thus remained the majority shareholder of Gesparal, which, in turn, controlled L'Oréal. This, then, was the basis of the agreement, which stipulated that Mrs. Bettencourt, during her lifetime, would retain control of L'Oréal. It was also decided that L'Oréal's management would be turned over to François Dalle, the firm's particularly gifted and efficient chairman and c.e.o.

The planned agreement between L'Oréal and Nestlé was published on March 7, 1974. The press reacted favorably to the announcement. A long press release concerning the agreement (which was awaiting the approval of the French government), outlined the way in which Nestlé Alimentana and L'Oréal would cooperate, pointing out that no form of merger was planned between the two firms, which meant that the structure of the two companies would not change as a result of the agreement. Each group wished to retain its freedom of action and its own identity.

The press release read as follows: "...by enabling it to acquire a considerable interest in a dynamic company, operating, moreover, in fields in which it has not been active up to the present, Nestlé Alimentana is engaging in a promising form of diversification. Both L'Oréal and Nestlé Alimentana will discover new horizons of scientific research. For example, the study of aging, which is essential for nutrition in the future, has a close connection with L'Oréal's desire to increase its understanding of the skin's aging process.

"Furthermore, Nestlé Alimentana has long been present in Asia, Australia, North and South America, a fact that L'Oréal may want to take advantage of, if it should wish to rapidly implement its plans for expansion in those parts of the world."

The project was approved by the French authorities on March 22, 1974. At the time, L'Oréal was already the second biggest cosmetics firm in the world. Its products were manufactured in around fifteen countries and distributed through its licensees in another seventy-five. Approximately half of L'Oréal's l973 turnover of FF2,700,000,000 was generated in France. In the same year, the firm's sales were up 33 percent. L'Oréal's growth can be explained, to a great extent, by its outstanding marketing techniques, designed to increase the group's share of the various cosmetics and body-care markets.

Ad for Loulou, the famous L'Oréal perfume created by Cacharel

L'Oréal was present throughout the world. Both parties were quite satisfied with their agreement. Both companies had a similar international perspective and R&D orientation...

The L'Oréal group possessed numerous factories and product-shipping facilities: twelve in France, eleven in Europe (in West Germany, Belgium, Denmark, Great Britain, Greece, Holland, Portugal, and Sweden), six in America, two in Africa, etc. In short, L'Oréal was present, in one form or another, in sixty-five countries and/or territories around the world.

In addition to its core products already mentioned, L'Oréal was also active in the area of fashion design (André Courrèges) and perfume (Guy La Roche and Jacques Fath).

Nestlé had every reason to be pleased with its cooperation agreement with this prestigious French firm. The press was fully aware that Nestlé had no intention of forming a conglomerate, and Parisian newspapers expressed their satisfaction that L'Oréal would remain in French hands.

As for the financial details of Nestlé Alimentana's acquisition of a minority interest in the registered capital of the L'Oréal Corporation of Paris, it must be stressed that they were handled by the French holding company, Gesparal, through an exchange of Nestle-Unilac bearer shares. For Nestle, this transaction was a promising one from the standpoint of diversification, and it would permit both companies to get a foothold in new areas of scientific research. In the long run, given L'Oréal's dynamism, such an arrangement could only have a positive effect on the Swiss group's earnings.

At the annual shareholders' meeting in Zurich in 1974, Pierre Liotard-Vogt outlined Nestle's situation. The company had long felt that it would be wise, in terms of future growth, for it to become active in a field outside the food industry. However, it did not wish to enter an area that was entirely new to it; rather, it preferred to remain within that of consumer goods sold primarily through retail channels or by hairdressers, perfume shops, and drugstores (selling Vichy products). Cosmetic items appeared to be the perfect complement to Nestle's core products.

François Dalle

The chairman of Nestlé Alimentana added, in connection with L'Oréal: "Its international nature is in keeping with our own policies, and since we are probably the multinational with the greatest foreign presence, we believe that we can be of considerable help in facilitating our associate's expansion on an international scale. From an R&D point of view, we have discovered that the research departments of our two firms often work in areas very closely related to one another, which augurs well for both companies. Aware that, as a result of the large interest we have acquired, our company has been considerably strengthened, we must stress that the type of cooperation chosen has permitted a rapprochement between our two big companies, while allowing each to retain its own identity. This is a far cry from the traditional scenario, in which the larger of two companies merely absorbs the smaller one. Now and in the future, both companies will remain independent. I have just mentioned the main areas in which fruitful cooperation is possible, and this cooperation will be made easier by certain affinities between our two companies from the standpoint of their ethical and management concepts, as well as their striving to base success on high quality alone. From a purely practical point of view, we believe that our investment in a top-quality company will ultimately prove to be an excellent one for the shareholder we have become."

BUT EACH REMAINED INDEPENDENT. THEIR DECISION TO COOPERATE WITH ONE ANOTHER PROVED TO BE A VERY WISE MOVE.

Two Nestlé representatives (including Nestle's c.e.o.) joined L'Oréal's board of directors, while André Bettencourt and François Dalle became members of Nestlé's. In 1986, Dalle became one of the two vice-chairmen of Nestlé S.A.

The financial agreement reached in 1974, for a period of at least twenty years, provided for a right of first refusal for both parties, at its conclusion, should the situation require it.

Time has shown this to be an advantageous agreement, for L'Oréal is a firm that is continually expanding. Indeed, it has become the biggest cosmetics firm in the world, with sales for 1989 totaling FF9,000,000,000. Cooperation between the two companies has kept pace with this development. In the 1980s, Nestlé and L'Oréal began manufacturing dermatological products together. In addition, 50 percent of the Sophia Antipolis dermatological research center, in the Alpes Maritimes region of France, belongs to Nestlé, and 50 percent to L'Oréal.

Cooperation on a systematic basis between the research teams of Nestlé and L'Oréal in areas of interest to the latter have made possible the development of unique ingredients for a number of successful new L'Oréal products. Experience has shown that Nestle's discoveries concerning what might be termed "internal assaults" on our skin (caused by the food we eat) and L'Oréal's discoveries concerning "external assaults" on our skin (due to the sun, cold, humidity, etc.) perfectly complement one another. And, thus, the type of assistance that Nestlé provides L'Oréal is ultimately of benefit to itself as well.

Cooperation between the two companies has proven to be highly effective. And in 1987, shortly before his death, Liotard-Vogt told this author: "The development of L'Oréal has even exceeded our expectations thirteen years ago. It is a top performer, with less than half its earnings now being generated in France. L'Oréal has become increasingly international and less and less dependent on sales in France, though they are still very important to it."

CHAPTER VIII

1974–1980

Asia Becomes the World's New Trouble Spot

Nestlé Turns Its Attention to America (Alcon) and France (Chambourcy)

1974: A YEAR OF RECORD WORLD INFLATION.

1974–1980: From the First Oil Shock to the Invasion of Afghanistan

☐ *The world entered a period of economic instability in the wake of the 1973 oil crisis, which resulted in an increase in the price of oil, across-the-board inflation, as well as hard times for industrialized nations and for the non-oil-producing countries of the Third World. This situation had far-reaching social and political effects the world over, particularly in the Middle East, with its vast petroleum reserves. During this troubled period, Lebanon, Iran, and, in 1979, Afghanistan were constantly in the news. America's relative weakness during the Carter era ended with the advent of Ronald Reagan, who promised that America would assume its role once again as the premier power that it had been prior to the Vietnam tragedy—whose final act was the fall of Saigon to North Vietnamese troops on April 30, 1975.*

This was also the heyday for both national and international terrorism, be it anti-Semitic, anti-capitalist, anti-German, anti-Spanish, anti-French, or anti-Italian in nature. Northern Ireland was hit particularly hard by its devastating effects. From 1974 until 1980, more than 150 murderous acts took place, including hijackings, kidnappings, and assassinations. And this violence was not something that could be stopped overnight.

In 1974, in the wake of the first oil shock, inflation—a scourge that has plagued mankind ever since it began engaging in trade countless centuries ago—reached its apogee: an average of 16 percent throughout the world, according to statistics of the International Monetary Fund. (The actual figures for this period were: 11.9 percent for the industrialized world—9 percent in the United States—and 35 percent for the developing countries; whereas the figures for 1972 were 6.9 percent throughout the world, with 5.7 percent in the industrialized countries and 13 percent in the developing countries.) Until 1980, inflation was to remain at a very high level, and this was the principal cause of concern to governments throughout the world, not only during that period, but later on as well. Though considerable, the effects of the second oil crisis in 1979 were less devastating than those caused by the initial one in 1973. Of course, both of these violently shook the economies of the non-oil-producing countries of the Third World. As for the industrialized nati-

ons, these were to attempt—with a certain degree of success—to lessen the blow of the oil shock by adopting a certain number of conservation measures, by revamping their system of distribution, by developing new, energy-saving machines, and, above all, by drilling for oil in both North and South America, as well as in the North Sea from 1975 on.

In the Middle East, the Israeli-Egyptian cease-fire of 1974 would, in other circumstances, have produced only bitterness on the part of the nations of the Arab League, originally founded in 1945 by Saudi Arabia, Egypt, Iraq, Jordan, Lebanon, Syria, and the Arab Republic of Yemen, and later joined by Libya, Sudan, Tunisia, Kuwait, Morocco, and Algeria, followed by the People's Republic of Yemen, Bahrain, the United Arab Emirates, Oman, Qatar, Mauritania, Somalia, and Djibouti. The Palestine Liberation Organization (PLO) was also accepted as a member of the Arab League in 1976. With each passing year, the Arab League—displeased, of course, with Cairo's signing of a peace treaty with Jerusalem—was to become increasingly furious with Egypt for its act. In November, 1977, Anwar Sadat decided suddenly to accept the invitation of Israeli Prime Minister Menachem Begin and to travel to Jerusalem, despite opposition to this visit on the part of other Arab nations. This historic encounter was to pave the way for the drawing up of a set of documents that were to serve as the basis for an agreement, signed at Camp David in October of the following year, under the auspices of the United States. It was at this presidential country retreat that the leaders of Egypt and Israel—with President Carter as witness—put their signature to an agreement in principle to establish peaceful relations between the two countries. Peace was to come to that area immediately after the evacuation by the Israeli Army of two-thirds of the Sinai (with the last third returning to Egyptian sovereignty in 1982) and the establishment of diplomatic relations between the two nations. A second agreement provided for a comprehensive Middle East peace plan involving autonomy within a period of five years for the inhabitants of the Israeli- occupied west bank of the Jordan River and Gaza Strip. This plan was never implemented, however. In the wake of Camp David, Sadat was viewed more than ever by his former allies as a traitor, and Egypt soon found itself excluded from the Arab League (from which it remained barred until 1989). Ultimately, hatred of the Egyptian leader led to Sadat's assassination in 1981.

SADAT TRAVELED TO JERUSALEM, AND THE ISRAELI-EGYPTIAN PEACE TREATY WAS SIGNED AT CAMP DAVID IN 1977.

LEBANON BECAME A VERITABLE BATTLEFIELD.

These were not the only events of significance to the countries located between the eastern Mediterranean and the Persian Gulf. Indeed, Lebanon was the scene of bloody unrest as early as 1968. Nearly 500,000 Palestinians, who had fled the territory occupied by the Israeli Army after the Six Day War, had flocked to refugee camps set up by the United Nations in that country. These Palestinians were soon to set up military training camps wherever possible in an attempt to regain possession of the lands they had lost. In 1971, Lebanon was still one of the few Arab countries in which the fedayeen (Palestinian commandos) enjoyed freedom of action. In 1973, Palestinian leaders were assassinated in Beirut by Israeli commandos. And a series of bloody battles broke out between Palestinians and the Lebanese Army.

Owing to its financial strength—and despite the fact that the political influence of Lebanese Christians was becoming increasingly irreconcilable with the demographic weight of its Muslim population—the tiny country of Lebanon was often referred to as the Switzerland of the Middle East. However, it was not long before this country was to fall prey to violent civil strife that was to transform it into a giant battlefield. First came clashes due to the presence of armed Palestinians, the reaction of government troops, and ceaseless guerrilla warfare between Israelis and Palestinians in southern Lebanon. The Lebanese government—comprised of a Maronite Christian president, a Sunni Muslim prime minister, and a Shiite Muslim head of parliament—was incapable of dealing effectively with unrest caused by the arrival of a wave of armed Palestinians that had been chased out of Jordan by King Hussein's army during the Black September incident of 1970. Lebanon's religious problems were further exacerbated by antagonism between its poor Muslim population—in the majority—and its minority Christian population, who were generally in a better financial position.

The situation went from bad to worse from 1975 on, with the massacre of Palestinians, the destruction of a Christian village, and the siege of refugee camps. Lebanese Christians requested Syrian assistance in 1976. And a civil war and international conflict ensued. Arab countries sent a so-called deterrent force to the area. A considerable number of fedayeen retreated toward Tripoli, in the north, and especially toward the south of the country, where their presence was disquieting to the Israelis, who intervened militarily for the first time in Lebanon in 1978. The U.N. sent peacekeeping forces to the area, and the army of the Jewish state returned to within its borders. Hostilities flared up once again between the various parties to the conflict, however, each holding its piece of the Lebanese puzzle. There was bloodshed even within the Christian community, depending on whether one happened to be a friend or foe of Syria. In 1980, Lebanese troops held Beirut as well as the eastern and western part of the country; Syrian troops were in control of the Bekaa Valley along the road between the Lebanese capital and Damascus; and the PLO controlled a certain number of towns in southern Lebanon such as Sidon and Tyre. Given this totally chaotic situation, it was not hard to foresee the Israeli offensive that came on June 6, 1982, and which we shall discuss in greater detail later on. In any case, the destruction of Lebanon was already well underway as early as 1980, although cannonades and aerial bombardment had not yet reached the murderous intensity that they were later to reach in that war-torn country.

THE ISLAMIC REVOLUTION SWEPT THROUGH IRAN IN 1979.

As if the situation in the Mediterranean part of the Middle East were not enough, an explosive situation was also brewing in the Persian Gulf region, where Iran's social and religious problems came to a head during the Islamic revolution of 1978. The following year, the shah was forced to flee his country forever. Of course, this was not the first time that the shah, enthroned in 1941, was forced to flee the country, for as early as 1953 he had been forced to leave as a result of the activity of Mohammad Mossadeq, who was to nationalize Iran's oil industry. Reinstated by the army, the shah pursued a policy of strict authoritarianism: a policy made possible thanks to the immense wealth his country accumulated through the sale of petroleum products. Relying heavily on his army and secret police—both of which he used to supress opposition to his regime—the shah had set in motion the so-called White Revolution designed to transform Iran from an underdeveloped country to a great power in Asia. Ardently in favor of maintaining close ties with the West, the king of kings failed to take into account the discontent of his country's impoverished masses, who enjoyed none of the fruits of economic development, and that of fundamentalist religious leaders, who vehemently opposed his attempt to rapidly transform the way life of Iran's population. Opposition to the shah's regime became increasingly great from 1970 on, when certain political figures who had been barred from public life also joined forces with it. However, it was not before the mid

1970s that these opponents were to find a spokesman capable of expressing their opposition to the shah. That spokesman was Ayatollah Khomeini. At the holy city of Qum, violent demonstrations in support of the Shiite spiritual leader—living in exile in Iraq—degenerated into rioting directed against the imperial power of the shah. In October, 1978, Ayatollah Khomeini, who had been driven out of Iraq, was offered asylum in France. Disseminating his message by means of cassette recordings, this implacable opponent of the shah was increasingly successful, despite intervention by the Iranian Army (still loyal to the shah), in encouraging the revolutionary fervor of the masses as well as a certain number of storekeepers in the bazaar of Tehran. Workers in the oil industry soon joined the movement, which resulted in shortages in certain areas and a dramatic drop in exports.

Iran's mass movements soon took on an increasingly anti-American character, insofar as it was the U.S. which had always been a staunch supporter of the imperial regime. In January, 1979, the shah made a vain attempt to reshuffle his government, naming to key positions certain political figures—among these Shahpur Bakhtiar—who were not necessarily of his political persuasion. By the end of January, however, the shah was forced to step down, and he fled to Egypt, where his friend Anwar Sadat welcomed him even before Khomeini had returned to Iran from exile. Strikes were paralyzing the country, and the head offices of foreign airline companies were routinely ransacked. The faltering regime finally collapsed on February 1, when Ayatollah Khomeini made his triumphant entry into Tehran, and then Qum. It was at this point that the execution of the former members of the shah's entourage began. The provisional fundamentalist government was soon officially recognized by both the U.S.S.R. and the United States; however, this did nothing to appease angry crowds, whose revolutionary fervor was directed particularly at the U.S. In November, Revolutionary Guards occupied the embassy of the United States, where the shah was also given asylum after fleeing Iran. Damage was done to the premises and more than fifty members of the staff were held hostage by the Iranians. In April, 1980, an attempt to free them by military means failed, and in July of the same year, the shah died in Egypt. Tehran did not agree to release the American hostages until January, 1981.

The Iranian revolution against the Pahlavi dynasty was both anti-American and anti-Soviet in nature; it sought, moreover, not only to eliminate Israel, but also to spread its fundamentalist religious view throughout the Islamic world. This would most likely have remained a circumscribed phenomenon, plagued by internal struggles for power, had it not been for Iran's dispute with neighboring Arab states. On September 22, 1980, latent tension between Iran and Iraq suddenly erupted into open hostility. In Baghdad, President Saddam Hussein ordered his troops to retake former Iraqi territory east of the Shatt-al-Arab Waterway—consisting of the united waters of the Tigris and Euphrates rivers—that had been occupied by the militarily superior army of the shah in 1971. (A flimsy agreement was signed between the two countries in March, 1975.) Thus began an eight-year conflict that was to result in the death of thousands on both sides and an exacerbation of the deep-seated hatred between the two nations.

THE IRAN-IRAQ CONFLICT BROKE OUT IN 1980. THE SOVIETS MOVED INTO AFGHANISTAN AT THE END OF DECEMBER, 1979.

Later on we shall discuss this pitiless war in greater detail; it not only destroyed the area between these two oil-rich nations, but struck at their capitals as well. Fortunately, this conflict did not lead to the oil shock that many feared; however, it was particularly significant geopolitically, as the crisis following the Soviet invasion of Iran's eastern neighbor, Afghanistan, had recently increased tensions between Moscow and its allies, on the one hand, and the Western world and China on the other.

Like any other large-scale military operation, the Soviet intervention in Afghanistan, on December 24, 1979, was politically motivated. Afghanistan, nestled in the mountains between the U.S.S.R., Iran, Pakistan, and China, has always been of considerable strategic importance, for it lies at the crossroads between Soviet Russia and the warm waters of the Persian Gulf and Indian Ocean. In the nineteenth century, the British had already grasped the strategic importance of Afghanistan, while controlling the entire Indian peninsula. From the standpoint of the U.S.S.R., it was essential that this nonaligned country fall neither under the West's influence nor that of China. And this was undoubtedly an important factor leading to the military coup which, following the dismissal of King Zahir in 1973, got rid of his successor, President Daud, and helped set up a pro-Soviet government headed by Mohammad Taraki in April, 1978. Taraki, who espoused agrarian reform,

THIS CAUSED STRAINED RELATIONS BETWEEN WASHINGTON AND MOSCOW. THERE WAS ANXIETY IN CHINA, WHERE MAO ZEDONG AND ZHOU ENLAI DIED IN 1976.

was executed in September, 1979, by his Marxist rival, Hafizullah Amin; he, in turn, was deposed in December of the same year by Babrak Karmal, following the Soviets' intervention (which Karmal had requested). While rival communist leaders of this quasi-feudal country engaged in a pitiless struggle for power, many of its 14,000,000 inhabitants were strongly opposed to the Marxist economic policies favored by Taraki and his successors. Prior to the Soviet intervention, some 500,000 refugees had already crossed the border into Iran and Pakistan, and this number was to increase tenfold after the entry of Soviet troops into Kabul on Christmas Eve of 1979.

This Soviet military action led to a resurgence of tensions between the White House and the Kremlin. President Carter took various measures against the U.S.S.R. and its allies. He stopped the shipment of 17,000,000 tons of wheat to the Soviet Union and froze the shipment of important high-tech items to that country—particularly those required in the oil industry—at the very moment when the U.S.S.R. was laying its pipeline from Siberia to Western Europe. In addition, Washington stepped up its supply of arms to Pakistan; and both China and Iran lent their support to Afghanistan's nationalist and religious resistance movement.

Thus, a new hot spot had flared up near the oil fields of the Persian Gulf—which were the source of much of Western Europe's oil. And these tensions resulted in a deadlock in arms negotiations between the two superpowers. They were also have an impact on the Olympic Games of 1980, since, for the first time in their history, the games—held in Moscow that year—would have to take place in the absence of more than half the industrialized nations of the world. The Afghan crisis was to continue to dominate the news for more than a decade. It marked the beginning of a five-year period of deep mistrust between East and West, sparked by the U.S.S.R.'s attempt to go beyond its traditional sphere of influence for the first time since World War II. As the Soviet intervention took place at the end of December, 1979, it was quite fitting that 1980 should be dubbed the Year of Afghanistan.

The Soviet military presence in Kabul was a source of particular concern to China, which had already become anxious in the wake of Taraki's communist coup d'etat in 1978. And the arrival of Russian troop divisions in the valleys of Afghanistan worsened relations between Moscow and Beijing. The leaders of the world's most densely populated country remained opposed to both U.S. and Soviet hegemony. In China's view, the world was divided into three areas: that of the two nuclear superpowers, namely, imperialist America and socialist-imperialist Russia, the countries of the Second World (including Europe), threatened by these two great powers, and, finally, the exploited nations of the Third World.

China's great communist neighbor to the north and west worried it more than the United States, with which it had renewed diplomatic relations during the 1970s. Moreover, the Russians' entry into Afghanistan occurred three years after the death of the two men who had contributed so much to modern China: Mao Zedong and his right-hand man Zhou Enlai, who died in January, 1976. A communist party leader since 1924, Zhou had weathered— owing to his sense of political pragmatism—all of the party's crises and perfectly complemented Mao's activities in the field of foreign affairs. As prime minister of the Republic of China from 1949 on, Zhou Enlai had been the driving force behind his country's opening up to the West. Mao Zedong was to pass away in September. Following his Long March and the communist victory during the civil war, Mao proclaimed the establishment of the Peoples' Republic of China in 1949. A firm believer in the necessity of mobilizing the masses, Mao felt no misgivings over the final outcome of the Cultural Revolution, which he had launched during the winter of 1965-66. The personality of this remarkable revolutionary leader has already been examined in the excellent works of the American author Edgar Snow, the Chinese Han Suyin, and the French Henry Bauchau; thus, we do not intend to discuss it here in great detail. Suffice it to say that the importance of Mao's thought was such that it continued to have a lasting influence on the foreign policy of his principal successor, Deng Xiaoping. Through boundless personal energy, Mao Zedong had succeeded in reestablishing Chinese sovereignty over the entire country—particularly over China's extensive border areas. For Mao, modern China was an indivisible socialist member of the Third World, which, while nonexpansionist, was not content to concentrate merely on the domestic problems of its hundreds of millions of inhabitants. It was a country in the midst of great economic change, whose leader was confident that it was destined not only to endure, but to play an important role in the world as well. A veritable continent, in the words of the historian Jacques Freymond,

SOCIAL UPHEAVAL ROCKED POLAND IN 1980.

steeped in a civilization several thousand years old, China was "founded with a desire to live as one nation, [a desire] that has asserted itself above and beyond the specific characteristics of individual provinces or periods of weak central authority, which at times characterized its dynasties." Faithful to this doctrine, China refused to allow its economic and social achievements to be jeopardized, in 1979, by the presence of Russian tanks in Afghanistan. (It already felt threatened by the West, which, in its view, had long been intent on keeping it encircled.) Thus, the Afghan conflict was as important to China as it was to the Islamic world (which backed the Afghan resistance movement), Europe, and China's Asian neighbors (owing to their anxiety over Russia's expansionist tendencies), as well as to the United States, which had only recently seen its influence wane—owing to the Iranian revolution—in a region stretching from the Himalayas to the Mediterranean.

If, during the final quarter of this century, Asia had become the center of attention of heads of state, economic and military experts, and those in charge of the media, other areas of the globe were the scene of equally important events, whose effects can still be felt today. In Europe, for example, Poland was already in turmoil, and the spotlight was on Nicaragua as well.

In 1978, Poland saw one of its own sons, Pope John Paul II, go to St. Peter's in Rome to succeed the Italian Pope John Paul I, whose pontificate—following Paul VI's—lasted only thirty-three days. Poland was to give John Paul II a triumphal welcome during his visit in 1979. In the socialist countries of Eastern Europe, Poland was a special case, for while it was controlled by a communist regime, the role of the Catholic Church was extremely important in that country. Taking advantage of the poor economic situation there, Polish workers' associations sought to achieve increased independence from an all-powerful state through strikes. From 1980 on, repeated demonstrations were held throughout the country. At first sporadic, these became increasingly well-organized; and on August 14, a strike broke out in the heretofore model Lenin Shipyard in Gdansk (formerly Danzig) that lasted until the end of the month.

A previous strike had already taken place in the same shipyard in February, and social tension caused by it had influenced the makeup of the government at that time (though without threatening as yet the

NICARAGUA FREED ITSELF FROM SOMOZA'S DICTATORIAL YOKE IN 1979.

authority of Edward Gierek, first secretary of the communist party, who had taken the place of Wladyslaw Gomulka in 1970).

In August, at the outset of the work stoppage at the Baltic port—a movement that was to spread to other cities—the workers decided to form an association designed to band the workers of various enterprises together in a single group. On August 30, the association's principal leader, Lech Walesa, signed an agreement with a representative of the government concerning the establishment of "self-managed" trade unions. This appeared to be an important victory for the workers. On September 5, Gierek was replaced by Stanislaw Kania, who met with Walesa in November. The situation soon deteriorated once again, however, for opposition leaders felt that the Gdansk agreement was not being implemented rapidly enough. As this grass roots movement continued to gain momentum, General Wojciech Jaruzelski, then minister of defense, was appointed prime minister in February, 1981. In July, Jaruzelski traveled to the Crimea to meet with Leonid Brezhnev, whose concept of limited independence of the socialist countries of Eastern Europe—formulated in 1968 in connection with Czechoslovakia—seemed to be in jeopardy at the beginning of Poland's unrest. On September 22, 1980, Walesa was elected president of the Solidarity trade union (comprised of workers' committees from a total of thirty-eight enterprises); he attended a meeting in November, 1981, between Monsignor Glemp (who had just replaced the late Cardinal Wyszinski as Primate of Poland) and General Jaruzelski, who, in addition to being prime minister and minister of defense, had recently been appointed to the all-important position of party first secretary as well. Despite continued unrest, the situation did not deteriorate any further; but the period when things were as they had been prior to the government's declaration of martial law on December 13, 1981 was over.

Central America came into the international spotlight with the end of U.S. influence in Nicaragua, following the fall of the dictator Anastasio Somoza in 1979. The U.S. has a vital interest in this region of the world, of course, owing to its proximity to the strategically important Panama Canal. Any change in the balance of power in favor of communist Cuba would be unacceptable to it. This, however, did not stop Nicaragua, located in a key area between Honduras and Costa Rica, from setting up its Sandinista government (in memory of General Augusto Sandino,

CIVIL WAR PLAGUED ANGOLA, TOO, FROM 1976 ON.

who had dared to openly oppose the influence of the all-powerful United States in Central America and was assassinated as a result in 1934). The Sandinistas continued the struggle after the death of their leader, directing their attacks against the Somoza family in particular. In 1936, they killed Tacho Somoza, Nicaragua's first president from this family, and fought against his son Luis, president in 1957. A decade later, they continued their struggle against President Anastasio (Tachito) Somoza, who, in 1972, abolished the constitution with a view to repressing all opposition to his rule. From 1974 to 1978, virtually the entire country was plagued by bloody riots, hostage-taking, vicious attacks by members of the resistance, and continual uprisings. In 1978, civil war broke out following the assassination of the director of an important nongovernment newspaper.

Some eighteen months after violent clashes between the national guard and the Sandinista Front, in which tens of thousands of persons lost their lives, the fabulously wealthy President Somozo was forced to leave the country. A provisional government—which already included Daniel Ortega—was set up; it consisted of representatives of the various movements that had helped bring about the downfall of the former dictator. The immense wealth of the Somoza family was confiscated. Initially, the junta in power included men and women representing the entire political spectrum: communists, socialists, moderates, etc. While reaffirming its special relationship with Cuba, Nicaragua welcomed Western assistance in rebuilding the country. The effects of the new situation created in 1979 in a burst of patriotic fervor (that would soon be redirected, however) was to be felt for years to come.

Thus, 1974 to 1980 was not what one might call a period of total peace; indeed, the tranquillity of both the world's developing and developed countries was disturbed by all kinds of unrest. It was terrorism that frightened Europe, with aircraft hijackings, assassinations, and hostage-taking becoming commonplace occurrences. Not until a decade later was the situation to return to normal. Moreover, serious environmental problems, such as maritime and coastal pollution, exacerbated the general feeling of insecurity.

In southern Africa, the world's attention shifted to two former Portuguese colonies: Mozambique and Angola, which had gained their independence in 1974 and 1975 respectively. Portugal, where an authoritarian regime ceased to exist in 1974, four years after the death of Antonio de Oliveira Salazar, was incapable of preventing the rise to power in its former possessions of Marxist-oriented resistance leaders. Moreover, Portugal's military leaders were in the throes of intense domestic political strife that would not be resolved until 1976, when a civilian socialist government was set up with the support of the communists. The social-democratic party of Mario Soares received more than 33 percent of the vote in parliamentary elections—the first in at least three decades. The influence of communism in southern Africa was particularly strong as of February, 1976, following the arrival in Angola of Cuban troops and Eastern European military advisors. American diplomats sought, in vain, to obtain the withdrawal of these forces. Angola remained the scene of bitter struggle between the government that evolved from the MPLA and such resistance groups as UNITA, backed by both South Africa and the United States. Latent war began in this region of the world from that point on. In South Africa, uprisings of blacks, deprived of their basic human rights, were proof that considerable tension already existed there as a result of apartheid.

IN 1980, PRESIDENT CARTER WAS NOT REELECTED.

In 1980, Africa was not yet experiencing the misery that it would experience only a few years later, but already the climatic conditions in certain areas of the continent were such that men, women, and children there were already facing the scourge of famine. Particularly hard hit was the Sahel region and, later, Ethiopia, both of which would experience much greater misery within a few years.

From the political and economic point of view, the Carter era was a time of diminished American influence in the world. To be sure, the U.S. had retained its economic strength domestically, but it was no longer the economic giant it had been only a few years earlier. Though traumatized by their experience during the Vietnam War, Americans soon put this period out of their mind and refused to reelect Jimmy Carter to a second term of office. Rather, they preferred the former governor of California, Ronald Reagan, who promised to make America strong and self-confident once again. Reagan's election took place at the end of 1980; and that event, coupled with the freeze in U.S.-Soviet relations brought on by the Soviet invasion of Afghanistan, serves as an excellent moment to end this portion of our study.

THE EUROPEAN COMMUNITY GREW STRONGER. THE HELSINKI AGREEMENT WAS SIGNED IN 1975.

Prior to that date, constant but slow progress had been made in transforming the European Community into a viable political and economic entity. Great Britain, which became a member of the Community in 1973 (a decision reaffirmed by 62 percent of British voters in a referendum held in June, 1975), has been led by Margaret Thatcher since May, 1979. Since that time, it has proven to be rather hardheaded in its dealings with the European Community—careful, however, not to cause any irremediable damage to its institutions. In 1979, the Community spectacularly asserted itself as a full-fledged actor in world affairs: in June of that year, it elected 410 members of the European Parliament by direct suffrage; representatives from all the major political parties—socialists, liberals, christian-democrats, conservatives—were present there. (The communists occupied no more than 10 percent of the parliament's seats.)

As for East-West relations, the Helsinki Agreement, signed on August 1, 1975, by thirty-five European countries and the United States, settled the problem of relations between countries with widely differing types of regimes. This agreement underscored the equal sovereignty of all states, the need to settle disputes by peaceful means, the territorial integrity of each state, noninterference in the internal affairs of another state, respect for human rights and fundamental freedoms, the right of peoples to self-determination, the need for international cooperation, and the right of each nation to satisfy its basic needs. The signatories also agreed to permit representatives from foreign states to be present during military maneuvers, to work toward facilitating travel between all European countries, and to improve the working conditions of journalists. It was decided that, from 1977 on, conferences would take place to pursue negotiations dealing with the problem of security and cooperation and to outline the way in which the Helsinki Agreement should be implemented. It is easy to see why, for several years after 1979, the Soviet intervention in Afghanistan damaged relations between countries that had placed so much hope in the Helsinki Conference—which to some seemed to be a reaffirmation of agreements reached decades earlier at Yalta, and to others, a takeoff point for better understanding between Western-style democracies and the peoples' democracies of Eastern Europe.

CHAPTER VIII – NESTLÉ

1975–1981

Nestlé's Growth in America and Consolidation in Europe

☐ In 1975, Arthur Fürer became Nestlé's chief executive officer. Fürer, a Swiss, had started working for Nestlé in 1954. As a financial expert and executive vice-president, he contributed to developing the group's finances during the monetary crisis preceding and following the first oil shock in 1973. (Fürer was to be chairman of Nestlé's board of directors from 1982 to 1984.) Nestlé's consolidated profit reached SFr. 799,000,000 in 1975, a 4.4 percent increase over its profits in 1974, a year characterized by inflation. The number of Nestlé's employees dropped from 138,809 to 135,431, and the number of factories the firm possessed (299) decreased by four. Nestlé adhered to two of its original aims: first, to maintain the maximum number of jobs for its employees throughout the world (from time to time, however, the company failed to replace employees who left; and, in very exceptional cases, some factories, which lacked markets for their products, were closed down). Then, at a time when the world economy was experiencing difficulties, Nestlé limited investments that had become unnecessary in a depressed market, while maintaining an organization capable of relaunching the firm's development at the right time.

All these steps were taken in order to give Nestlé a more economical management without jeopardizing its efficiency. Production needed to be more strictly controlled, and production increases had to be voluntarily limited. Profit increases depended on the success of Nestlé products during the economic crisis, for at such times consumers turned to brands they had been faithfully purchasing for years. This was shown especially by the rise in sales of instant coffee. However, Nestlé's careful managers realized that the postwar period of exceptional prosperity, characterized by needed reconstruction and cheap energy, would not reoccur soon. To fight inflation, governments had to take steps that prevented extensive industrial expansion. A certain amount of protectionism resurfaced, casting its shadow, too, over future economic activities. Lack of stable exchange rates was an additional obstacle. Nestlé intended to earn its profits exclusively from its industrial role. "Which means," Nestlé's chairman stated forcefully in a speech, "that we never, even for a minute, thought of earning profits [by engaging in] financial operations involving differences in exchange rates. However, we do have a basic obligation to protect our funds by avoiding, as far as possible, the losses to which we have too often been subject, owing to various official or de facto devaluations, which successively affected too many currencies ... that must be changed into Swiss francs before they figure in our balance

Arthur Fürer

sheet." The systematic deficit in the balance of payments of a very great number of countries confirmed the impression that the fate of several nations had taken a dangerous turn for the worse. "International solidarity has its limits." This remark on the dangers of debt is still valid today.

NESTLÉ SET UP A CENTER PROVIDING INFORMATION ON MULTINATIONALS. IN 1977, THE TURNOVER OF NESTLÉ ALIMENTANA EXCEEDED SFR.20,000,000,000, BUT PROFITS WERE DOWN SOMEWHAT.

At the time, various campaigns against multinationals were in full swing. Convinced that these attacks were often accepted by sincere people who felt that there was some truth in them, Nestlé created the Centre européen d'études et d'informations sur les sociétés multinationales in Brussels in 1975. Rather than acting like an advertiser praising multinationals, its goal was to inform the public. For years, it was responsible for obtaining and distributing objective information on the activities of multinationals, as well as for organizing debates that enabled the participants to judge for themselves the arguments for and against multinationals' working methods. The center was to live up to expectations and perform the task assigned to it. In 1986, having moved to Geneva and changed its name to Institut de Recherche et d'Information sur les Multinationales, it was to stop its activities, for, by that time, the public had lost interest in the topic; and the multinationals' severest critics had toned down their criticism.

Because of Nestlé's size—by 1977, its sales already exceeded SFr. 20,000,000,000—it is not possible for us to describe every one of the company's operations throughout the world. At this stage in Nestlé's history, therefore, we can no longer list the new companies that were founded, the factories that were set up, nor the events in firm's history that are not of prime importance to our story. From this point on, we shall only describe the highlights in the development of Nestlé, one of the world's leading food companies.

Observers whose hopes had been raised by a strengthening of the American economy in late 1975 were disappointed by the results of the world's major industrialized countries (especially the nonoil-producing countries) in 1976 and 1977. Although, admittedly, the worst was over, the global economy seemed to be stagnating. On the other hand, many economically weaker oil-producing countries were enjoying an exceptional economic boom; whereas developing countries with no oil reserves were finding it increasingly difficult just to survive, becoming more and more dependent on aid from abroad. Nestlé, which was present all over the world, had to take these widely divergent situations into account. In addition, though the price of coffee beans and cocoa had risen spectacularly, owing to frost damage in

NESTLÉ ALIMENTANA S.A. BECAME NESTLÉ S.A. IN 1977.

Brazil. Within twelve months, the price of coffee beans quadrupled, and the price of cocoa tripled, then rapidly dropped. The price increases now justified passing them on to consumers by raising prices; however, such increases were frequently blocked by official measures. In such circumstances, it was extremely hard to keep earning a legitimate profit. This explains why, for example, Nestlé's profits declined from SFr.872,000,000 in 1976 to SFr. 830,000,000 in 1977, in spite of an increase of SFr. 1,000,000,000 in sales.

On May 12, 1977, the annual shareholders' meeting of Nestlé Alimentana S.A. decided to change the company's name to Nestlé S.A. The same year Arthur Fürer conducted the negotiations that led to the acquisition of Alcon in the U.S.A., thus bringing a manufacturer of pharmaceutical and ophthalmological products into the Nestlé group. Despite unstable economic conditions worldwide, Nestlé did not hesitate to take that important step for two reasons: namely, because Alcon was located in the U.S. and because of the attractive opportunities offered by an industry in which Alcon was, and remains, successful in its native land and abroad.

Bags of coffee being loaded on ships in the port of Santos, Brazil, 1972

1977: The Acquisition of Alcon

NESTLÉ WISHED TO STRENGTHEN ITS POSITION IN A PROMISING FIELD IN THE U.S.A.:

On October 17, 1977, a press release announced that, under certain conditions, Nestlé S.A. proposed to make a cash take-over bid, through one of its American subsidiaries, for all the common stock of Alcon Laboratories, Inc., whose headquarters were in Fort Worth, Texas. The proposal had been accepted by Alcon's board of directors on October 15.

According to the press release, "the contemplated bid would amount to approximately $276,500,000, if all the shares are purchased. It will be launched as soon as Nestlé has finished examining Alcon's finances and operations, and the administrative formalities have been completed." On January 11, 1978, the press was given additional information: "Delaware Bay Co., an American affiliate of Nestlé S.A., has announced in New York the conclusion of its take-over bid, at $42 per share, of Alcon Laboratories, [which was] launched last November. The deadline for the take-over bid had been extended until January 6." Spokesmen in Vevey stated that Nestlé S.A. was now in possession, via the Delaware Bay Co., of 97.4 percent of the 6,370,000 shares of Alcon Laboratories stock.

Publication of that information created something of a stir; this was the first time Nestlé had acquired a firm operating completely outside the food industry. Actually, this acquisition was easy to explain: it was in keeping with Nestlé's policy of strengthening its position in the U.S.A., not only by expanding its own companies there but also by acquiring others. It was hard to carry out a policy of acquiring food companies in the U.S., however, for antitrust laws prevented Nestlé from following up on a number of projects that interested the company. Furthermore, Nestlé did not wish to enter areas too far afield from its traditional activities.

In the past, Nestlé had made some small forays into fields closely related to pharmaceuticals: for example, with the creation of Nestrovit (a vitamin-enriched preparation, based on condensed milk in liquid form or on cocoa-butter in tablet form) in 1936, an operation carried out in cooperation with Hoffmann-La Roche of Basel. Nestlé's 1974 agreement with L'Oréal—in which it acquired a 25 percent interest in the firm—had been fundamentally financial, as we have seen; nevertheless, the cooperation that grew out of the excellent relations between the Swiss and French companies had increasingly drawn Nestlé toward the cosmetics and pharmaceutical fields. Moreover, a part of Nestlé's special dietetic food products were sold in drugstores, since they were too specialized for supermarkets to handle. Thus, Nestlé had links with the pharmaceutical field through its R&D and through the network that distributed part of its products.

THAT OF OPHTHALMOLOGIC PHARMACEUTICALS. ALCON LABORATORIES, INC. WAS FOUNDED IN TEXAS IN 1947.

This explains why Nestlé was interested in that field. However, since it was not specialized in cosmetics or pharmaceuticals, Nestlé decided to make acquisitions in those fields. One result of acquiring an interest in L'Oréal was that it enabled Nestlé to thereby acquire an interest in the French pharmaceutical company, Synthélabo. An acquisition in America would enable Synthélabo to enter the marketplace of other countries. In the long term, acquiring Alcon was to open up not only the U.S. market to Nestlé but also the other markets in which Alcon was present either as a manufacturer or as a sales company that owned land on which factories could be built. Attempts to set up a pharmaceutical company from scratch in Germany and Brazil had shown that this slow, unreliable approach was very expensive. Consequently, it was better to acquire a top quality company already in possession of reliable means of production and distribution in both the U.S. and approximately ten other countries, and which had a solid scientific reputation.

In L'Oréal's view (the reader will remember that François Dalle, the head of L'Oréal, was a member of Nestlé's board), Alcon seemed to fit the bill perfectly. Alcon was the leading U.S. manufacturer in the field of ophthalmological products; it had subsidiaries in Europe and Latin America, as well as a joint-venture with a local Japanese company in Japan. Alcon had an excellent reputation as a technologically sound company, which promised to cooperate well with the manufacturer of dermatological and cosmetic products. Finally, Nestlé's food products and cosmetics divisions would benefit from the scientific research of a strong pharmaceutical division, particularly in the field of toxicology and, more generally, from studies of the effects of food and cosmetics on the human body.

Alcon's drive-in drugstore in 1945, before it became the company's first laboratory

Alcon Laboratories, Inc. was founded in Fort Worth, Texas, in 1947. By 1977, it had been specializing for 30 years in a range of products conceived especially for ophthalmologists and eye surgeons. In addition, it

IT REMAINED AN INDEPENDENT COMPANY, AFTER BEING WARMLY WELCOMED INTO THE NESTLÉ GROUP IN 1977.

manufactured and marketed dermatological products for skin, hair, and scalp care, as well as special products for children, decongestants, and products to treat various allergies. Some Alcon products, such as contact-lens cleaning solutions, etc., were sold in supermarkets. Its hair-care products were only sold to professional hairdressers. Alcon had branch offices in about 10 countries. Its turnover as of April 30, 1977, was $81,000,000, 43 percent of which was generated outside the U.S.A. Alcon's net profits totaled $8,900,000, or 11 percent of its turnover.

We shall not go into more detail here about this acquisition, which was conducted by Nestlé's c.e.o., Arthur Fürer. Alcon remained an independent company within the Nestlé group. All 2,024 of Alcon's employees in 1977—nearly 260 of whom were engaged in research—kept their jobs. And Alcon's president, E.H. Schollmaier, remained head of the company, along with his principal associates. When Nestlé acquired Alcon the latter possessed a factory in Fort Worth, Texas, and another one in Port Washington, New York. Alcon's foreign markets were Belgium (with a production center in Brussels), Italy, Brazil (with a factory in São Paulo), Canada, Mexico (with a factory in Mexico City), Argentina, and West Germany. Alcon was also building a factory in Puerto Rico. Management had chosen Alcon's fields of specialization very carefully and placed a lot of emphasis on making its organization as effective and profitable as possible.

Alcon was warmly welcomed into the Nestlé group. Chairman Liotard-Vogt, addressing the annual shareholders' meeting of May 18, 1978, in Lausanne, stated that Nestlé was looking for areas in which innovation was possible, even if such areas were not particularly large. Alcon—whose chairman, William C. Conner, was also the company's founder—was a middle-sized company in comparison with the major European and American pharmaceutical firms; but, for several years, its shares on the New York Stock Exchange had shown some of the best performance trends in the pharmaceutical field. Alcon sales had doubled from 1973 to 1977, as had its after-tax profits. Liotard-Vogt pointed out that Alcon's growth was due to the quality of its products which enjoyed secure positions in specific niches, "and to its management, which was unanimous in welcoming this rapprochement with us."

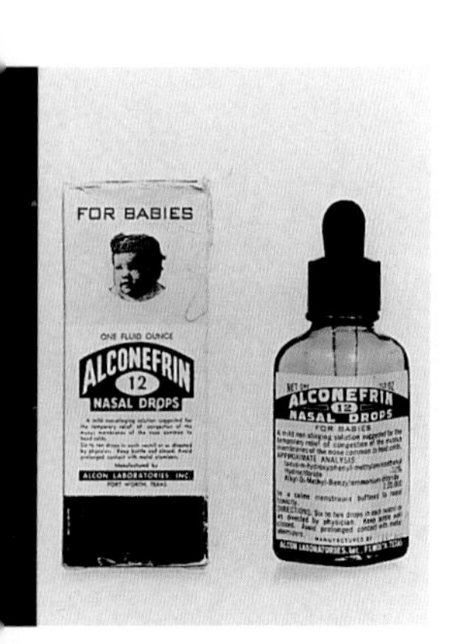

Alconefrin nose drops for babies, one of the first products Alcon launched shortly after it was founded.

Summarizing Nestlé's views, Liotard-Vogt said: "Today we find ourselves with a very wide range of activities, all of which have one thing in common: they all contribute to satisfying the requirements of the human body in various ways." As for the future, he explained that, while Nestlé had to abide by its carefully thought-out policy of diversification, which excluded any improvisation, it still felt it must remain sufficiently flexible to seize upon particularly attractive opportunities when they occurred rather than letting them slip away because the firm was a victim of its own policies. "However," Liotard-Vogt continued,"except in very special cases, we are not searching in any other direction, and [we] feel that we have more than enough to do during the next few years, developing the traditional and new fields in which we are now active, whether in the food industry or elsewhere."

IN 1978, ALCON WAS THE BIGGEST PRODUCER OF OPHTHALMIC MEDICINE AND EYE-CARE INSTRUMENTS IN THE WORLD. NESTLÉ'S ACQUISITION OF ALCON PAVED THE WAY FOR THAT OF BURTON & PARSONS IN 1979.

The annual report devoted to the 1978 fiscal year noted, for its part, that, by choosing to focus its efforts on very specific areas—drugs to fight glaucoma, infection, and inflammation, as well as emollients—Alcon not only now included some fifty different ophthalmologic drugs among its products but had also become the world's biggest manufacturer of ophthalmic and eye-care instruments, with products marketed in more than eighty countries.

Alcon was not to be any less dynamic in 1979, as a new Nestlé subsidiary. Through Alcon, Nestlé was to acquire the big U.S. pharmaceutical company Burton & Parsons, as well as three smaller American firms: two manufacturers of dermatological products, Texas Pharmacal and Allercreme Dubarry, and another pharmaceutical company, Person & Covey. It also acquired Biosynthetica, a pharmaceutical laboratory in Brazil.

Since 1977, Nestlé has continually backed Alcon's policy of strategic acquisitions in order to strengthen its leadership in the ophthalmological field and to carry on in its R & D efforts. This enabled Alcon to achieve a sales figure of SFr.1,300,000,000 in 1989, with 10 percent of that sum being invested in R & D. Today, with its activities focused on ophthalmic drugs, contact-lens cleaning solutions, and products and instruments for eye surgery, Alcon is the leader in this very specialized pharmaceutical domain.

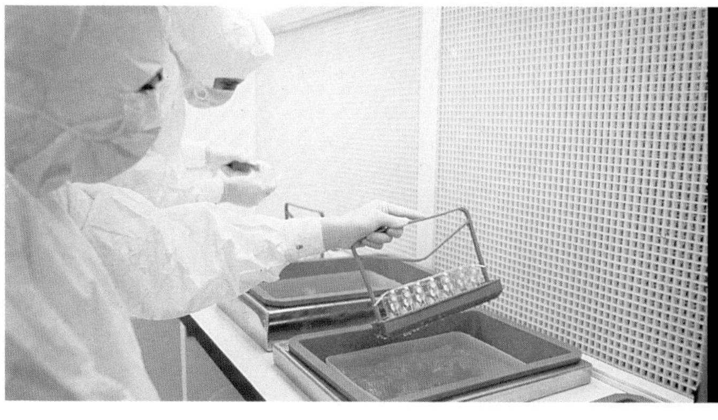

Rinsing Alcon intra-ocular implants used in cataract surgery

As for its traditional line of products, Nestlé, which had neither produced nor marketed baby food in the U.S.A. up to that point, purchased the

1979: ACQUISITION OF THE BEECH-NUT CORPORATION, A MANUFACTURER OF DIETETIC FOODS, FOUNDED IN 1973 IN THE U.S.A.

American Beech-Nut Corporation, which marketed a wide range of baby foods. Since Beech-Nut's headquarters are in the U.S.A. we shall now discuss this acquisition, although it took place in 1979, whereas Nestlé acquired its majority interest in Chambourcy (which we will discuss in the next section) in 1978.

☐ In November, 1979, Nestlé acquired the American baby foods specialist Beech-Nut Corporation. This was an important transaction, since it once again gave Nestlé a foothold in the field of infant nutrition in the U.S.A., a field that had contributed to Nestlé's reputation when it first started out in the U.S. by setting up a factory in Fulton, New York, in 1900. (Afterward, Nestlé stopped manufacturing and marketing its baby foods in the U.S.) In 1979, at the height of a boycott (discussed later) that various American groups had launched against it, Nestlé was marketing no baby foods in the U.S., where it was being viciously attacked for selling infant formula in the Third World. Almost half of all working mothers in the U.S. work outside their homes and go back to work a few weeks after giving birth. Thus, in addition to breast milk, there was a high potential demand in America for industrially produced infant formula and baby foods.

In order to enter the American baby food market, however, Nestlé had to find a company that produced and marketed a line of products for children, designed to be eaten before, during, and after their schooling. It so happened that Beech-Nut Corporation, whose headquarters are in Fort Washington, Pennsylvania, was looking for a bigger company to provide it with backing while it expanded.

Alcon general headquarters in Fort Worth, Texas

Beech-Nut Corporation was founded in March, 1973, after Frank Nicholas and two associates acquired the Beech-Nut Baby Food division of Squibb Corporation, a pharmaceutical and cosmetics company. By 1979, Beech-Nut, which employed 1,000 persons and possessed two factories (one in New York and the other in California), had enjoyed a good reputation for its baby foods for six years. Beech-Nut's range of products consisted primarily of small jars of baby food containing either fruit, vegetables, meat, or juice (mainly apple juice). Beech-Nut's management had made a certain name for the company by deciding not to put sugar or salt in its baby food, since it felt that a baby's needs should be the determining factor when preparing baby food and not the taste that appealed to its mother or adults. With sales of $65,200,000, Beech-Nut Corporation was the second biggest U.S.company in this branch. (Nestlé was to sell Beech-Nut in 1989.)

IN 1979, NESTLÉ ACQUIRED A MAJORITY INTEREST IN CONSERVES ROCO, A SWISS COMPANY.

☐ At the same time that it was acquiring Beech-Nut in the U.S., and in order to counterbalance its interests in the developing countries with those in the industrialized world, Nestlé reached an agreement with the principal shareholders of a Swiss company, Conserves Roco S.A., and acquired a majority interest in that firm. In 1970, the two companies had already agreed to set up a frozen food company together, Frisco-Findus S.A. In 1978, Roco's sales totaled SFr. 143,490,000, SFr. 52,000,000 of which was generated by Frisco-Findus. Within the framework of their 1970 agreement, the two firms had agreed to give the principal shareholders an option to sell their shares to Nestlé. And, in 1979, the shareholders made use of their option. By acquiring the majority of Roco's shares, Nestlé thereby acquired all the remaining shares of Frisco-Findus S.A. (It originally owned 50 percent.) However, as the company immediately stated, the canned foods division of Roco was not of interest to Nestlé. (It was sold soon afterward.)

IN 1978, THE YOGURT MANUFACTURER CHAMBOURCY BECAME A FULL-FLEDGED MEMBER OF THE NESTLÉ GROUP. CHAMBOURCY WAS A FRENCH COMPANY THAT EVOLVED PRIMARILY FROM A FIRM FOUNDED IN 1946.

1978: Chambourcy and Its Line of Fresh Food Products Permanently Join the Nestlé Group

In 1978, Nestlé acquired a majority interest in the French firm Chambourcy S.A., as well as responsibility for operating that firm. The reader may remember that, in 1970, Nestlé had expanded its cheese manufacturing activities in France, after also expanding its activities in Italy in that area by acquiring Locatelli of Milan in 1961. Gains in this area had been consolidated by putting all Nestlé's French cheese manufacturers under the management of a single firm: Roustang. The acquisition of Chambourcy in 1978 put the finishing touch to Nestlé's eight-year restructuring program in France.

For ten years, Chambourcy had actually been linked to Nestlé to a certain extent. In 1968, Nestlé realized that it was most desirable for the company to promote sales of fresh dairy products, especially yogurt, whose popularity dated from the end of the war. The principal yogurt-eaters, though still few in number, were students and the elderly. Eating yogurt (i.e., fermented milk) is the equivalent of drinking pasteurized milk, which is harder to digest. In the late 1940s, yogurt consumption was very low; it was produced mainly by small local manufacturers, since refrigerated vehicles for the transport of such perishable items were almost nonexistent. Yogurt originated in Bulgaria as a means of preserving milk. (It is mixed with strains of two lactic acid bacteria and then left to curdle.) Demand for yogurt soon increased considerably, for penicillin (discovered during the war) had become a commonly prescribed medicine, and, at that time, doctors recommended that patients take lactic acid bacteria to protect their intestinal flora. Demand for yogurt seemed certain to increase. Therefore, Nestlé wished to acquire an interest in a company that would enable it to enter this field and, considering its growth potential, that of soft white cheese, which professionals term fresh cheese, as well. During talks with Joseph Roustang, Nestlé learned that Chambourcy was looking for a partner abroad. Nestlé began negotiations with the head of Chambourcy, Jacques Benoit, with a view to possibly acquiring an interest in his company.

Jacques Benoit

Chambourcy S.A. was founded to manufacture, transport, and market milk and all its by-products, both in France and abroad—in particular, yogurt, fresh cheese, as well as milk-based desserts such as pudding, custard, and flans. Chambourcy had evolved from the J.A. Benoit dairy company, founded in 1949 by two brothers, Jacques and André Benoit. Later, that company was incorporated and then merged with Chambourcy-Paris on January 1, 1966, at which time its name was changed to Chambourcy S.A.

THIS RAPPROCHEMENT ENABLED NESTLÉ TO IMPROVE ITS POSITION IN THE FIELD OF REFRIGERATED FOOD PRODUCTS AND DESSERTS.

In 1968, Chambourcy's parent company was active around Paris and in southeastern France. It possessed two factories—one in Paris, the other in Marseille—as well as three subsidiaries: Chambourcy-Acquitaine, with production facilities in Bordeaux; Chambourcy-Est, with production facilities in Strasbourg; and Chambourcy-Rhône-Alpes, with a distribution company. Its two affiliated sales companies abroad were Chambourcy Italia in Turin, Genoa, and Milan; and Chambourcy Dairy Products in London. The company produced 300,000,000 jars of yogurt (13 percent of the market) 200,000,000 desserts, and 6,600 tons of fresh cheese (4 to 5 percent of the market). Chambourcy's turnover was around 89,000,000 new French francs. It adopted a policy of promoting its yogurts and desserts, while its fresh cheese was usually manufactured by other producers. When Chambourcy first got in touch with Nestlé, three possible avenues of development were open to it: to continue expanding without the help of a backer, but this would mean financial problems in the foreseeable future; to sell to a big company, which meant, however, that Chambourcy's managers would be absorbed by one of their direct competitors; to reach an agreement with Nestlé. Chambourcy's sales organization could help Nestlé sell its other cheese products and, perhaps, help it introduce into France certain varieties of Italian fresh cheese produced by Locatelli in Italy.

The third biggest manufacturer of yogurts in Italy, Chambourcy was a sound, dynamic company, well-managed by the Benoit family and utilizing state-of-the-art production methods. In addition to traditional assets such as buildings and machinery, Chambourcy's main contribution to Nestlé was its well-known name and trademarks, know-how, and distribution network for fresh food products. Late in 1968, following talks with Jacques Benoit, Nestlé Alimentana S.A. acquired a 20 percent interest in Chambourcy.

J.A. Benoit delivery van in Marseille, France, 1955

In 1978, the French and Swiss companies increased their already close cooperation when Nestlé became the principal shareholder of Chambourcy. This progressively close cooperation between the two firms went smoothly; and, from January 1 to the end of November, sales of yogurt and desserts had already exceeded 1,000,000,000 items, with Chambourcy France supplying more than half of these. Compared to the preceding year, when tonnage was already in the same range, the increase was 14 percent.

INTEGRATION OF PERSONNEL WENT VERY SMOOTHLY, AND CHAMBOURCY PRODUCTS EARNED A FINE REPUTATION THE WORLD OVER.

By 1978, Chambourcy products were already available on three continents. They could be found in most Western European countries, in South Africa, and in Latin America (notably in Brazil, Colombia, and Mexico). The advent of refrigerated transport right after the war considerably stimulated sales of yogurt, which has a high nutritional value. (Yogurt is as nutritious as milk and possesses the property of encouraging a proper balance of intestinal flora, for it activates, among other things, the vitamins B and C contained in our food.)

Just as Chambourcy and Nestlé cooperated well in the area of production and sales, the staff of the two firms were to work closely with one another as well. Jacques Benoit went to work for Nestlé. That company had made considerable progress since 1968, for it was now working with food products that were even more perishable than canned milk. Originally, selling yogurt had meant working on a short-term basis. Little by little, however, with the help of new techniques for keeping food fresh, it became increasingly possible to supply products with a longer shelf life. Of course, the company was faced with new distribution problems, but Chambourcy's experienced personnel knew how to solve them.

In his speech to the shareholders discussing company results for 1978, Nestlé's chairman was able to state: "The yogurts and desserts sold under the Chambourcy trademark are continually improving their already excellent position in France, their native country, and making substantial progress in several European and overseas countries where they were launched [on the market] just a few years ago."

Thanks to Nestlé, Chambourcy was able to become a more European and then a global company. This development was aided by good personal contact. As mentioned when discussing Nestlé's 1970 foray into the field of fresh cheese in France, the emphasis Pierre Liotard-Vogt placed on refrigerated food products was strengthened by Helmut Maucher, Nestlé's present c.e.o., upon the acquisition of Herta in 1986. Maucher was also aware of the two main areas in which demand for such products was growing: that of yogurt, milk-based desserts, and fresh cheese, etc.; and that of cold cuts and related items, and pastry dough, etc.

Nestlé, which was to control Chambourcy as of 1984, had given that company all its know-how, its extensive distribution network, and its ability to generate business, for when individuals with the same ideas come together, virtually anything is possible. The managers of the twenty-year-old French

French Chambourcy poster, 1973

GLOBAL RECESSION CAUSED NESTLÉ'S PROFITS TO DROP IN 1980.

company, which, in 1968, contacted a hundred-year-old Swiss firm receptive to its aims, were to prove to the heads of the locally based Nestlé companies that what had been achieved in France could also be achieved in their respective countries. Indeed, this was possible even starting from scratch, for apart from the acquisition of two small firms (one of which was South African), companies to produce yogurt and fresh cheese were built from the ground up in several countries.

This shows that, usually, companies are not acquired for their own sake but rather in order to found yet other firms. The strength of a brand name contributes a great deal to company development, which, in turn, serves to encourage the founding of new firms. Thus, over the next ten years, Nestlé was to set up two entirely new firms in Germany, two in Brazil, and one each in Colombia, Spain, Great Britain, Italy, and Mexico.

Now that yogurt has become a staple food product synonymous with good health, the foresight of Nestlé's management is clearly apparent. It chose the right moment to put its faith in fresh food products with considerable consumer appeal. Little by little, fresh Nestlé brand products also began to make their appearance in various countries. By 1988, the activities of Nestlé's Fresh Food Division already accounted for 7.9 percent of the company's total sales figure.

☐ 1980, the year of Afghanistan discussed earlier, was an inauspicious one for Nestlé. Although its turnover increased from SFr. 21,639,000,000 to SFr. 24,479,000,000, while its operating profit (profit before taxes and interest) exceeded the previous year's; and despite the fact that the firm's cash-flow remained at the 1979 level, Nestlé's net profit dropped from SFr. 816,000,000 to SFr. 683,000,000, which represented only 2.8 percent of total sales as compared with 3.8 percent in the previous year. The recession following the second oil shock in 1979, inflation, unemployment, and financial system difficulties were the reasons for this sad state of affairs. In addition to this, from time to time, the company had to face the results of its miscalculations with respect to certain extremely deflationary government policies. Furthermore, some of Nestlé's affiliates failed to react—or did not do so quickly enough—so that Nestlé suffered the repercussions of a global economic slump resulting from the contractual policy of various governments, from certain customers' difficulties in meeting their payments, from wars, and from currency shortages and the time required for bank transfers in several countries. It would be more accurate to say that growing inflation caused a spectacular rise in interest rates, which in turn increased Nestlé's interest rate charges from 2 to 2.5 percent of its turnover. Therefore, in 1981, Chairman Liotard-Vogt expressed his regret over the fact that 1980 had not been a better year, even though, all things considered, business had gone rather well.

THE DRASTIC MEASURES TAKEN WERE TO BEAR FRUIT, AND NESTLÉ IS NOW ONE OF THE WORLD'S LEADING FIRMS.

To prevent mismanagement and other errors, Nestlé took several drastic measures; and the beneficial effect of these measures was felt immediately. In 1981, Nestlé S.A.'s chairman could declare, with some satisfaction: "Only the 1980 balance sheet will be affected by these problems; and everything leads me to believe that, although we may not immediately be able to bring profitability back up to previous levels in the countries experiencing difficulties, this year we are at least completely sure of avoiding the heavy losses experienced in 1980. It is often possible to turn a misfortune to one's advantage, and it is now possible to state that, at present, we have done our utmost everywhere to whip the company into shape, while strengthening its organizational structure so as to infuse it with new vigor." Another aim of the internal reorganization at Nestlé was to increase the efficiency of its top management; jobs and responsibilities were redistributed. Helmut Maucher, Nestlé's future c.e.o., was about to leave Germany, where he had shaped the destiny of the German Nestlé Company. In 1981, he was to assume the position of chief executive.

While Nestlé's management was hardly enthusiastic about its 1980 results, there was no reason for pessimism. Indeed, Nestlé's top managers were not at all pessimistic; rather, they were cautious. They merely noted that business could have been better in 1980. The leadership qualities of Nestlé's new chief executive were to make it apparent quickly that the company would soon get moving once again. Nestlé's turnover had just reached SFr. 25,000,000,000. Of that amount, 46.3 percent was generated in Europe, 18.3 percent in North America, 16.1 percent in Latin America and the Caribbean, 12.1 percent in Asia, 5.1 percent in Africa, and 2.1 percent in Oceania. Nestlé employed more than 150,000 persons; it possessed 309 factories and had fixed assets totaling SFr. 1,208,000,000—a sum that had doubled since 1976. Sales of products all across the board were continuing to grow. In addition, Nestlé's entry into a new field, by way of its minority interest in L'Oréal, had yielded satisfactory results as well.

Chapter IX

1981–1988

Poor at First, Relations Between Nations Were Later to Improve

Nestlé Makes Great Strides with Carnation, Buitoni, and Rowntree

RONALD REAGAN WAS INAUGURATED IN 1981.

Soviet-American Coexistence After a Period of Considerable Tension

☐ *Until the end of 1985, difficulties in East-West coexistence after the Soviet intervention in Afghanistan marred international politics. Ronald Reagan and Mikhail Gorbachev met with each other in Geneva, in November, 1985, giving the international diplomacy of the two superpowers a human face at long last. The last meeting of this kind (between President Carter and the all-powerful Leonid Brezhnev) had taken place a mere six months before the latter sent Russian troops across the border into Afghanistan. As mentioned earlier, this move considerably damaged relations between the two countries and, in 1980, led to an American embargo on wheat sales to the U.S.S.R., a boycott of the Olympic Games in Moscow by many of America's allies, and the refusal of the countries of the Warsaw Pact to participate in the Olympic Games in Los Angeles in 1984. But most important was the fact that this straining of relations was to put talks between the two countries on nuclear disarmament on hold. Indeed, this increase in tension led to a new arms buildup, particularly on the part of the United States, which feared the possibility of a Soviet invasion of Europe. (One must recall that the U.S.S.R. continued to provide its troops with increasingly sophisticated weapons during this period.) In a word, relations between the two superpowers was characterized by mutual mistrust until 1985.*

Shortly after coming to power in January, 1981, Ronald Reagan accused the U.S.S.R. of encouraging Soviet-style revolution throughout the world. In April, Reagan lifted the embargo on grain sales to the Soviet Union. However, when martial law was declared in Poland, in December, Reagan decided to impose sanctions on any country supplying to the Russians equipment considered vital to the construction of their gas pipeline, designed to transport natural gas from Siberia to Western Europe. Reagan canceled these sanctions in November, 1982, but came up with his famous Strategic Defense Initiative—immediately dubbed "Star Wars" by the media—in March, 1983.

The soured relations between the two countries became quite evident when a Korean passenger plane was shot down by Russian fighters at the outermost bounds of Siberia in September, 1983. As a result, in November, 1983, nuclear arms talks being held in Geneva at the time were broken off. Changes in the makeup of the Soviet hierarchy—the death of Leonid Brezhnev, in November, 1982; followed by that of Yuri Andropov in February of the following year; the rise to power of Konstantin Chernenko, who died in 1985—had no decisive influence on Soviet-American relations. The U.S. secretary of state and his Soviet counterpart met at the beginning of 1984 to resume arms talks between the two nations.

In April, 1985, the nomination of Mikhail Gorbachev as leader of the U.S.S.R. came as a refreshing breeze that put an end to a monopoly on that post by the country's septuagenarians. It was decided that Gorbachev would meet with Reagan (who had won a landslide victory in his 1984 bid for a second term of office) in Geneva in November. After six years of tension, the climate of U.S.-Soviet relations began to improve. At last, the world could stop holding its breath. Each of the two leaders was helped politically by this promising meeting, which was really little more than a beginning. In October, 1986, their encounter in Reykjavik was a failure (due essentially to strong Russian opposition to Reagan's Strategic Defense Initiative—a project that Gorbachev demanded be canceled). A certain momentum was maintained, however, in Soviet-American arms negotiations, particularly with respect to the issue of intermediate-range missiles. The complexity of these talks had become clear in previous years. The presence of Soviet intermediate-range missiles pointed at Western Europe had been a source of concern to the NATO countries, which had agreed to station similar types of American-made missiles on their soil so long as a treaty to do away with such weapons could not be signed between the U.S. and Soviet Union. Moreover, the fact that certain Western European governments were so eager to accept the stationing of these weapons gave rise to a spate of demonstrations—particularly in Germany—thus adding an important political dimension to purely military questions.

A document signed by Reagan and Gorbachev in Washington in December, 1987, provided for the dismantling of a total of 1,200 missiles with a range of approximately 600 to 3,400 miles within a period of three years, and eighteen months for those with a range of 300 to 600 miles. This agreement was not yet a historic one, as it dealt with only a small portion of the superpowers' stockpile of weapons. Nevertheless, its very existence served to reduce the risk of nuclear war and paved the way for more in-depth talks on eliminating strategic arms capable of hitting U.S.

AND MIKHAIL GORBACHEV CAME TO POWER IN 1985. IN 1987, REAGAN AND GORBACHEV REACHED AN AGREEMENT ON INTERMEDIATE-RANGE NUCLEAR MISSILES.

EAST-WEST RELATIONS BEGAN TO IMPROVE. ECONOMIC PROBLEMS TOOK ON SOMEWHAT GREATER IMPORTANCE.

targets from bases in the U.S.S.R. and vice versa. For the first time, the path had been cleared for talks on an actual reduction in the number of U.S. and Soviet nuclear weapons and not merely their limitation.

At this point, a real era of detente began between the two nations most capable of destroying the entire planet. It was as if a better understanding between the U.S. and the U.S.S.R. on the question of nuclear arms helped to resolve other outstanding issues dividing the two nations. In April, 1988, for example, the Soviets decided to begin withdrawing their military divisions from Afghanistan. (This was completed in February, 1989.) In addition, the parties to the Angolan conflict started discussions with a view to ironing out their differences over the withdrawal of Cuban troops and the independence of Namibia. The Vietnamese announced their intention to pull out of Cambodia if talks on this issue seemed likely to bear fruit. Given this more relaxed international atmosphere, Iran was to agree to an armistice with Iraq put forward by the United Nations. Even in Central America—in Nicaragua, for example—guerrilla groups were to accept the idea of laying down their arms and sitting down at the negotiating table.

While contemporary history cannot be reduced merely to the actions and attitudes of the United States and the Soviet Union, relations between these two countries were, nonetheless, to have a profound effect on international politics as well as on the global economic situation. The nations of the world—particularly those that were the closest allies of the two heavily armed nuclear superpowers—were strongly affected by whether the U.S. and the Soviet Union happened to see eye to eye or to be at odds with one another at any given moment. Meanwhile, the other great power, China, realized that it could not remain on the sidelines during this period of rapid change; and, in 1989, it accepted the idea of a summit between the leaders of the Kremlin and Beijing, which Deng Xiaoping attended. The world was to gain an increased peace dividend from this meeting, despite the fact that China was to be the scene of brutal military repression in June, 1989, when students demanding greater democratic freedom were attacked by the army at Tiananmen Square.

Of course, this peace was precarious; and, during the period covered in this chapter, a variety of worrisome issues were to arise. In the modern world, political and sociological questions no longer take precedence

PEACE REMAINED FRAGILE, HOWEVER.

over economic ones, for economic events and problems are an integral part of international affairs. This must be borne in mind when attempting to sketch a general overview of our continually evolving world. Indeed, it is impossible to examine in detail the many problems raised by this situation. Thus, we shall merely mention them briefly in the pages that follow, without concerning ourselves too greatly about the order in which they are presented. These are problems that have been completely ignored or hidden in the shadows for a long time. As Jacques Freymond wrote in La paix dangereuse *(Editions de la Baconnière, Neuchâtel), history, like nature, flows and changes at every instant; it is in continual movement. There are periods, of course, when—against a background of ever-changing events—patterns may come into view (only to disappear a moment later), like the blinking lights of an instrument panel.*

During the period 1981–88, a veritable kaleidoscope of current events shimmered in the background: the population explosion (1988 global population was 5,000,000,000, two-thirds hailing from the Third World), the depletion of traditional energy sources, air and water pollution, chronic unemployment in the developed and, especially, in the developing countries (alternating with periods of inflation and recession), a world economy subject to constant fluctuations in foreign exchange rates and erratic stock market trends, and the expansion of political and religious ideologies claiming to be universally valid. This was a situation tending to generate friction between nations, between the state and individuals, and between the members of a particular society as well.

Terrorism—be it of a state-sponsored sort or merely the desperate acts of a marginal group of fanatics—is clearly an outgrowth of this sad situation. In addition to a few traditional wars, there is the constant thread of indirect war, with its panoply of espionage, foreign-sponsored subversion, blackmail, hostage-taking, etc. In the span of a mere twenty years, more than two hundred armed conflicts and as many coups have taken place around the world. Thus, ours is far from a tranquil world; it is, in fact, quite turbulent, and is accompanied by unprecedented technological advances in a variety of fields: aerospace, weapons systems, computer science, transportation, telecommunications, medicine, physics, chemistry, and particulary in the field of electronic journalism, which has benefited from technological advances to such an extent that

THE END OF THE MILLENNIUM LOOMED LARGE ON THE HORIZON. THE ISLAMIC REVOLUTION TRANSFORMED IRAN.

nowadays news is able to penetrate virtually everywhere. Unlike in past eras, today's society suffers much more from being overinformed than it does from being underinformed. Important secrets remain secrets for a while, only to be revealed in often scathing publications only a short time later. Moreover, there are the increasingly worrisome problems—on a global level—of refugees, poverty, hunger, and health. The great nations of the world must pool their efforts to combat crime, drugs, and a new form of drug-related terrorism now plaguing the streets of many of the world's major cities.

Those who follow these trends closely are quite concerned over their development; while others continue to go about their business without paying much attention to them. The reasons for this are varied. Some people are so concerned about their own survival that they cannot afford to let themselves become conscious of these problems; others feel powerless to do anything to change the situation; while others have learned to accept the fact that, as we approach the third millennium, our world is simply not an ideal place to live.

We shall now continue our brief overview of world events between 1981 and 1988, bearing in mind that we have not yet achieved the historical perspective necessary to determine their precise importance.

At the beginning of 1981, the spotlight turned to Iran once again, where, in January of that year, the fifty-two Americans taken hostage in November, 1979, were finally released. The lifting of U.S. economic sanctions against the Islamic Republic had little effect on the course of Iran's war with Iraq and the extent to which it jeopardized the entire region of the Persian Gulf. The American government—under its new president, Ronald Reagan—refused to take sides in a conflict in which Iraq enjoyed the backing not only of other Gulf states, but also of the U.S.S.R., and even of France, which had just elected François Mitterrand as its president.

The war between these two neighboring Islamic states continued to rage: in August, 1982, it appeared that Iraq would soon be overwhelmed by a massive Iranian offensive, but Iraqi armored divisions in the vicinity of Basra withstood the blow while retreating in good order. From this point on, the Iran-Iraq War—in which hundreds of thousands were killed or maimed—became bogged down for a time, only to flare up once again, in 1986, following the arrival of the Iranian Army on the

ISRAEL INVADED LEBANON IN 1982.

Fao peninsula. Iraq held its ground, however, and the Iranian offensive ended. But the battle continued at sea and in the air, endangering oil tankers operating in the Persian Gulf. The United States directed its warships to the area to protect Kuwaiti shipping, and the British, French and Italians soon followed suit. Despite the shooting down of an Iranian airliner by a U.S. ship in 1988, fears of an incident with serious consequences for the region proved to be unfounded.

Meanwhile, as aerial bombardment and missile attacks on the belligerents' capitals dragged on, a decisive turn of events occurred: Iraq launched an offensive to retake the Fao peninsula toward the end of 1987.

It is unclear whether, by accepting the terms of a cease-fire in 1988, Iran and Iraq were really ready to sign a treaty putting an end to a conflict that had lasted eight long years, had resulted in the slaughter of soldiers and civilians by the thousands, had caused widespread destruction of property near the battlefront, had depleted munitions, and had virtually wiped out the naval fleet of the two belligerents. This treaty remained unsigned as late as 1989, the year Ayatollah Khomeini died—at the height of his popularity.

The Israeli invasion of Lebanon, in June, 1982, served to exacerbate a critical situation created by nearly ten years of civil war between Christians and Muslims and between pro- and anti-Syrian Muslims. But here, too, the outbreak of hostilities was not enough to spark a global conflict (though Soviet-American relations did experience some turbulence during this period). In August, Palestinian fighters left Beirut as a result of Israeli pressure. (The Israelis had sealed off the western sector of the Lebanese capital and repelled the Syrians.) The fifth and longest Middle East war since 1948 lasted more than six weeks, further aggravating the suffering of the Lebanese population. In 1983, the American Embassy and a French military post were attacked as symbols of the Western powers that had sent troops into Lebanon to ensure order there. This resulted in the departure of the American, French, and British troops stationed in Lebanon. Prior to this, the Israeli Army had also withdrawn from most of Lebanon; while Menachem Begin stepped down in August, 1983.

Though victorious in Lebanon, Israel was to undergo a period of economic and psychological hardship, during which it could do little, from

IN 1987, AN UPRISING BROKE OUT IN THE ISRAELI OCCUPIED TERRITORIES.

its side of the border, except closely monitor events in southern Lebanon (from which it finally withdrew in 1985). Lebanese Christians maintained control of the eastern sector of Beirut; while the Syrians, who had already forced Palestinians out of the northern Lebanese town of Tripoli, in December, 1983, regained control of West Beirut in 1988. Lebanon was seriously shaken by the assassination of President Bachir Gemayel on September 14, 1982. (The post of Lebanese president was filled several days later by Bachir's brother, Amin.) The Lebanese nation was to remain in a state of perpetual turmoil from this point on, plagued by massacres in the refugee camps of Sabra and Chatila in 1985, by battles between Lebanese Christians and Palestinians, as well as Christian and Muslim factions, and by the tragic death of the Sunnite prime minister, Rachid Karami, in 1987. Alternating between calm one minute and a car bombing the next, the country was unable to elect a new president in 1988. A united Lebanon was a thing of the past. The country's small Christian enclave, led by General Michel Awn—chosen by President Gemayel to succeed him in 1988—and backed by Iraq, struggled to survive bombardment and blockade by Syria's allies in Lebanon in 1989.

Toward the end of 1987, there was a new factor in the Middle East equation: for the first time since 1967, there was now widespread Palestinian unrest over Israel's continued occupation of the West Bank and Gaza Strip. To express their opposition to the Israeli military presence, the inhabitants of these territories began to organize strikes and throw stones. In response to this new proof of the Palestinians' desire for a homeland, King Hussein of Jordan decided, in August, 1988, to sever all legal and administrative ties with the region of his country to the west of the Jordan River (territory that had been granted to the Hashemite Kingdom in 1950). From the point of view of the Arab states, the Palestine Liberation Organization (PLO) was now responsible for administering these territories. (The PLO had sought the liberation of these territories for years.) In November, 1988, the PLO proclaimed the independence of Palestinian territories under Israeli control. Some fifty countries were to recognize this new state even though it had no government and no precise borders. The Arab world and its allies were piqued by the U.S. refusal to allow the Palestinian leader, Yasir Arafat, to speak before the General Assembly of the United Nations in New York. As a result—for the first time in U.N. history—the December meeting of the General Assembly

HOSTILITIES FLARED UP BETWEEN GREAT BRITAIN AND ARGENTINA IN 1982.

was transferred temporarily to Geneva. Toward the end of December, the U.S. was to accept the idea of starting official talks with the PLO—talks that were broken off in 1990. The subtle equilibrium the world had achieved was not to be disturbed by local conflicts—however violent in nature. This was made clear in 1982 during the brief war between Great Britain and Argentina over the Falkland (Malvinas) Islands, where two Western nations confronted each other off the coast of Latin America in a very contentious area. The establishment of a revolutionary regime in Nicaragua and increased opposition to the Salvadoran and Guatemalan governments created a general climate of civil war in that part of the world. This same climate prevailed on the border of Honduras and Nicaragua, where the so-called contras were fighting against the regular army of Nicaragua.

Given the intense struggle between rival government factions—pro-communists in Nicaragua, pro-Americans in Guatemala and El Salvador—and their respective opponents in these countries, there was a danger that the occupation of the Falkland Islands by the Argentine Army and the tough reaction of Great Britain might serve to destabilize the entire Latin American subcontinent. But despite a series of particularly fierce naval battles, this did not occur. Though the Falkland Islands had been a British colony since 1832, the Argentineans had always considered them to be an inseparable part of their country. On April 2, 1982, the military government of Buenos Aires airlifted by helicopter thousands of soldiers to the outskirts of Stanley, the capital of the Falkland Islands. The British garrison there surrendered the next day, as did that of South Georgia, about 1,000 miles away. Deeply shocked by these events, Britain moved quickly: it severed diplomatic relations with Argentina and sent a large naval force from Portsmouth to the South Atlantic. Approximately 12,000 Argentine soldiers, equipped with armored vehicles and missiles, had already dug in on the islands. At sea, forty British ships, accompanied by nuclear submarines of the Royal Navy, arrived off the coast of the islands. On May 1, the British began shelling the airport at Stanley. The next day, the Argentine cruiser, General Belgrano, *was sunk by the British. On May 4, the state-of-the-art British destroyer,* Sheffield, *was, in turn, hit and sunk by an Argentine missile made by France. On May 15, British special forces attacked Pebbel Island, located just over 100 miles from Stanley. One week later,*

THERE WAS UNREST IN POLAND FROM 1981 ON.

BLOODY CONFLICT PLAGUED AFRICA.

British troops landed on the eastern part of the largest island, and on June 14, after considerable resistance, the Argentine troops finally surrendered to the British.

Meanwhile, NATO solidarity proved effective: EC countries imposed an embargo on imports from Argentina, and the U.S. halted economic and military assistance to that country. From the outset, the U.N. Security Council demanded an end to hostilities and called for negotiations to resolve the conflict. The war was soon to take its toll on the Argentine military government. It was swept from power following elections held toward the end of 1983, and Raul Alfonsin was chosen as Argentina's new civilian president. Toward the end of Alfonsin's term of office, he was to transfer power democratically to the Peronist Carlos Menem in 1989. (Diplomatic relations between London and Buenos Aires were finally restored in 1990.)

In Poland, the state of martial law, imposed in December, 1981, was lifted the following year. In November, 1982, the former president of the outlawed Solidarity trade union, Lech Walesa, was released after eleven months in prison. In Oslo, in December, 1983, Walesa's wife accepted the Nobel Peace Prize on his behalf. Clearly, peace was not in the offing for Poland, as demonstrated by the assassination of Father Popieluszko in 1984. Nevertheless, the country was able to overcome its internal difficulties, and General Jaruzelski and the communist party were able to remain in control of the state. (This no doubt helped to make Mikhail Gorbachev's trip to Poland, in 1988, a smooth one.)

In 1989, Solidarity was legalized as a result of the pressure of events in Poland. Shortly thereafter, in September, 1989, elections in Poland placed Tadeusz Mazowiecki, a jurist and journalist—and close friend of Walesa—at the head of the first Polish government since World War II that was not led by a communist majority. (At the same time, General Jaruzelski was elected president of Poland.)

Thus, the nations of the world were doing their best to maintain a policy of peaceful coexistence. The 1983 invasion of Grenada by American troops, for example, had no international ramifications. This was also the case in the Chadian conflict, where sporadic fighting occurred between French-backed government troops and Libyan-backed Chadian factions. The names Hissène Habré and Goukouni Oueddei, his rival, were continually in the headlines during this period, as the battle turned in favor of one or the other party to this conflict. In 1986, aerial combat took place between French and Libyan fighter aircraft; and shortly thereafter, the two rival factions in Chad came to an agreement, enabling them to confront their common enemy—Libya. At the beginning of 1987, Chad's armed forces retook important positions on the border, only to lose them once again in the summer. Tension between Tripoli and Ndjamena relaxed in 1988, following preliminary steps toward reconciliation between Libya and Chad—a process that would be completed the following year. Similarly, the ramifications of Britain's severing of diplomatic relations with Libya, in 1984, as well as skirmishes between the American and Libyan navy—foreshadowing the U.S. air strike on Libya in the spring of 1986—had few ramifications of international importance. Moreover, the nations of the Mahgreb were to make peace with each other in Algiers, in 1988, despite the rivalry between Algeria and Morocco, and the Algerian-backed Saharan rebel movement's opposition to a Moroccan military presence in the northwest part of Africa. For the first time in twelve years, the sultan of Morocco agreed to meet with the Algerian president. In 1987, President Ben Ali replaced Habib Bourguiba as the president of Tunisia.

Meanwhile, drought caused widespread famine that decimated the inhabitants of the Sahel as well as Ethiopia, where war continued to rage. The scale of their suffering gave rise to a remarkable show of solidarity in the Western world. Armed struggle continued in Angola between Cuban-backed government troops and UNITA forces supported by South Africa. Here, too, the thaw in East-West relations was to give new impetus to diplomatic talks that attempted—in vain—to find a solution to the complex problems of Angola. Though the intensity of racial violence in South Africa had diminished somewhat, the problem of racial discrimination in that country remained an explosive one, both within South Africa itself and elsewhere in the world. However, significant changes were not to take place there before late 1989 and early 1990: the transfer of power from Pieter Botha to Frederik de Klerk, the abolition of a law prohibiting the creation of an anti-apartheid party, and, in February, 1990, the freeing of Nelson Mandela, leader of the African National Congress (ANC), the main group opposed to South Africa's white government.

THE PHILIPPINES AND HAITI FREED THEMSELVES OF DICTATORIAL REGIMES. ASSASSINATION PLOTS AGAINST WORLD LEADERS INCREASED AROUND THE GLOBE.

This, then, was a period of thought-provoking diplomatic and political change, characterized, for instance, by the 1984 Sino-British negotiations over the return of Hong Kong to China after the expiration, on June 30, 1997, of the lease signed by China and Great Britain in 1898. A bloodless revolution took place in the Philippines in 1986; it brought to power Corazon Aquino, widow of that country's principal opposition leader, assassinated in Manila on his return from the United States in 1983. The election of Corazon Aquino put an end to twenty-one years of Ferdinand Marcos's dictatorship. Also in 1986, Haiti was to shake off more than three decades of oppression by the Duvalier clan, forcing the son of Papa Doc to seek asylum in France. During this period, Argentina and the Philippines were not the only countries that reestablished a civilian regime after years of dictatorship. Brazil went through a similar—albeit less dramatic—transformation when Tancredo de Almeida Neves was elected president at the beginning of 1985. Unfortunately, the new president died only a few months later, in April, and his post was immediately filled by Jose Sarney, who had been vice-president up to that time. In 1990, the Brazilian people elected Fernando Collor de Mello as their president.

The riskiness of being a major world figure was underscored by attempts to assassinate President Reagan and Jean Paul II in 1981, as well as the assassination attempt on the British prime minister, Margaret Thatcher, in 1984. It was brought home even more forcefully by the murder of President Anwar Sadat of Egypt in 1981, and Indira Gandhi, the Indian prime minister, in 1984. These flare-ups of violence—in certain cases, the isolated acts of madmen, in others, the carefully planned attacks of implacable political foes—took place against a background of relative peace, however. This peace would be strengthened at the end of 1988 by a reduction in tension throughout Europe, a relaxed social climate in China (though not for long), peaceful coexistence around the world, the prospect of a withdrawal of Vietnamese troops from Cambodia and of Cuban forces from Angola, and—after eight years of international disagreement—the holding of the Olympic Games in South Korea with all countries present.

The death of Pakistan's president, Muhammad Zia ul-Hag, in a mysterious airplane accident, in 1988, was not to affect the stability of that

THE SPACE RACE CONTINUED.

THE ENVIRONMENT WAS THREATENED.

country. In the Middle East, however, there was still considerable concern over the Palestinian uprising in the occupied territories. And peace in Central America would still have to wait, in spite of the the peace plan President Arias of Costa Rica worked out for the area.

In the second half of the 1980s, the United States was to lose its lead over the Soviet Union in the aerospace field. On January 28, 1986, the Challenger *spacecraft, which previously had been totally reliable, burst into flames after being launched off the coast of Cape Canaveral, Florida, killing everyone aboard. The psychological shock caused by this incident affected the entire nation, resulting in a three-year moratorium on American space flights. During this period, the Soviet space program moved ahead, Europe's* Ariane *rocket placed a number of satellites into orbit from its launch pad in French Guyana, and China pursued its own research in this field. The conquest of space continued without a hitch, and it came as no surprise when in December, 1988, two Soviet cosmonauts, Titov and Manarov, set a space endurance record of 365 days, 22 hours. In 1989, after traveling twelve years in space, the American space probe,* Voyager 2, *reached the planet Neptune, its final destination before leaving our solar system.*

The amazing technological progress made in modern times was having certain negative effects on man and his environment, however. In 1984, for example, an explosion at a chemical plant in Bhopal, India, resulted in the death of nearly 2,000 persons. Moreover, a fire and explosion at a nuclear power plant at Chernobyl in the U.S.S.R. caused a number of deaths and released radioactive substances into the atmosphere, causing considerable anxiety throughout Europe, particularly in Scandinavia. Finally, a fire at a chemical warehouse in Basel polluted the waters of the Rhine in November of the same year. The fears of environmentalists—but not just of environmentalists—over the destruction of the environment gave rise to demonstrations designed to underscore the need for stricter local ordinances and closer international cooperation in this important area. More than ever, an increasing number of individuals—particularly in the industrialized world—were now concerned with protecting the environment. (We must not forget that the American public had already been quite shaken by the accident at the Three Mile Island nuclear power plant in Pennsylvania.)

THE DREAM OF A EUROPEAN ECONOMIC COMMUNITY WAS ON THE VERGE OF BECOMING A REALITY.

It would be a mistake to exclude economic questions from this brief survey of world events. Among these was the increase in the number of members of the European Common Market on January 1, 1986, to twelve—twice the original number, that had been actively working toward European unification since 1957. The population of the European Community, including Spain and Portugal, was now 320,000,000, and it covered nearly 775,000 square miles. The European Single Act, adopted in December, 1985, stipulated that any remaining questions concerning the creation of an internal European market should be resolved by January 1, 1993. This was an extremely important decision, for it meant that the borders separating the EC countries would be completely abolished as of that date to facilitate the movement of individuals, goods, services, and capital. At first, this might appear to be a simple task. However, it requires a considerable change in the European mentality. Doing away with customs offices means that the many barriers separating Europe's differing economic, political, social security, and tax systems will simply cease to exist. At least on paper, this appears to be a great leap forward for Europe; and, indeed, corporations and trade unions on the Continent have been busy preparing for this historic event. However, the abolition of customs inspections also means that all the EC countries will have to harmonize their social security and economic policies. This huge task requires a comprehensive set of EC regulations to replace the national legislation of each individual state. Thus, certain EC members are understandably anxious over the need to renounce national sovereignty in areas such as food and health, motor vehicles, chemical and pharmaceutical products, environmental and consumer protection, security and the fight against terrorism—to name but a few. Because these common EC policies must be worked out within six short years, it is only natural that the meetings between prime ministers and presidents of the EC countries should be marked by a certain degree of friction at times. Nevertheless, their desire "to make Europe a reality despite all obstacles" has consistently won out over other considerations.

On the international level, suffice it to say that the economies of the majority of Western nations have proven to be much stronger than anticipated. This strength helped them to ride out the stock market crash of October, 1987, during which share prices dropped sharply within a few days. That crisis was but a warning signal, however.

Chapter IX – Nestlé

1981–1988

Nestlé's Dynamic Growth Places It in the Forefront of the Food Industry

THE LONG-TERM STRATEGY OF NESTLÉ'S NEW C.E.O, HELMUT MAUCHER, WAS EXTREMELY FLEXIBLE.

☐ At the end of 1981, Helmut Maucher, Nestlé's new chief executive, settled in Vevey; and, in May, 1982, Arthur Fürer took over from Pierre Liotard-Vogt (who had reached the age limit) as chairman of Nestlé S.A. Like his predecessors, Helmut Maucher had worked his way up within the company. Helmut Oswald Maucher was born in 1927, and after completing a commercial apprenticeship, he began working at Nestlé's factory in his hometown, Eisenharz, Germany, in 1948. Maucher transferred to Nestlé in Frankfort on the Main in 1951 and, parallel to his work, continued studying economics and business administration at Frankfort University, from which he obtained a B.A. in Business Administration in 1958. Maucher began climbing the rungs of the company's hierarchy at the German Nestlé Company in Frankfort. And, in 1963, he was appointed head of marketing for Germany. During the same period—from 1960–61 to be exact—he took nearly a year of courses at the International Management Development Institute (I.M.E.D.E.), a foundation that Nestlé had set up in Lausanne in 1957. In 1964, Maucher was named executive vice-president of Findus-Jopa GmbH in Frankfort. When Nestlé relinquished its German frozen foods division to Unilever, temporarily keeping only a financial interest, Maucher left Nestlé to become executive vice-president of a cooperative in Hamburg, Grosseinkaufsgesellschaft Deutscher Konsumgenossenschaften, and a member of the executive committee of the central organization of West German cooperative societies (B.D.K.). He remained in that position for two years. In 1972, Nestlé named Maucher executive vice-president of Allgäuer Alpenmilch AG in Munich. Three years later, Maucher was president and c.e.o. of Nestlé Gruppe Deutschland GmbH, the group's German subsidiary, with headquarters in Frankfort. In October, 1980, he was appointed executive vice-president of Nestlé S.A. in Vevey and became a member of the executive committee—the triumvirate that was Nestlé's highest executive body. (Maucher's two colleagues on the executive committee—José Daniel and Carl L. Angst, the committee's spokesman—were also executive vice-presidents.) In November, 1981, when Maucher was named chief executive of Nestlé S.A., the two other members of the executive committee acted as his assistants. (The committee continued to exist until the beginning of 1986, when C.L. Angst retired and was appointed to the executive committee of the board of directors.)

Helmut Maucher

Under the impetus of its new c.e.o., Nestlé resumed its brilliant upward course. For two years, in keeping with Helmut Maucher's principles, the company concentrated on strengthening its internal organization. Maucher had always felt that, while short-term measures may make it possible to win a battle, they can never win a war. "Now, I," he wrote when he was still in charge of Nestlé's German company, "am a man who intends to win the war."

AS NESTLÉ GREW STRONGER, IT CONTINUED TO PURSUE ITS POLICY OF ACQUIRING OTHER COMPANIES...

Applying a flexible long-term strategy, Nestlé relinquished firms that showed little promise or did not correspond to its orientation. At every level, working methods were streamlined, which reduced working capital while improving the profitability of company operations. Nestlé's liquid assets grew, and this led to a decision to increase the company's capital once again. Looking ahead with confidence, Nestlé's management simultaneously increased spending on research, marketing, and management training; and, thus, Nestlé's 1983 profit (SFr. 1,261,000,000) was almost double that of 1980 (SFr. 683,000,000). Nestlé's sales figure, while not as great, went from SFr. 24,500,000,000 in 1980 to SFr. 27,900,000,000 in 1983, meaning that profits as a percentage of sales rose from 2.6 percent to 4.5 percent. The early 1980s were a stormy period for the global economy, however. People were buying less; inflation was on the rise; unemployment was growing worse; interest rates were high; developing countries were accumulating a big deficit; while the Eastern European countries were suffering from slow, zero, or, in some cases, even negative growth.

Consequently, Nestlé devoted nearly four years to becoming a sounder company, paying particular attention to controlling its capital resources, its circulating funds, and its choice of financing. A stringent management policy enabled Nestlé to greatly increase its liquid assets within three to four years. The speeches that Nestlé's chairman—Pierre Liotard-Vogt until 1982, Arthur Fürer from 1983 to 1984—made at each year's annual shareholders' meeting bear witness to the company's efforts to be prepared to again acquire companies at the right moment, as soon as attractive opportunities presented themselves. As the reader will recall, acquisitions were a strategic tool for Nestlé, enabling it to expand and compete effectively with other companies. Nestlé placed particular emphasis on internal growth rather than acquisitions, which were only a means to an end and not an end in itself. Since the close of World War I, each successive chairman of Nestlé's board of directors had, under varying conditions, strongly stressed in his speeches the fact that Nestlé should not become an unwieldy conglomerate, but rather should remain a food company active in the

PARTICULARLY IN GERMANY AND OVERSEAS.

related areas of dietetic foods, ophthalmological pharmaceuticals, and cosmetics.

In 1983, Nestlé began a series of acquisitions by purchasing Auer, a West German manufacturer of food products, dietetic foods, and baby-care products. The following year, Nestlé acquired Warner Cosmetics, a U.S. company composed of the perfume and cosmetics division of Warner Commmunications, for SFr.315,000,000; Warner Cosmetics marketed Paloma Picasso, Gloria Vanderbilt, and Paulo and Ralph Lauren perfume. Nestlé combined this activity with that of Cosmair, Inc., L'Oréal's exclusive agent in the U.S.

In 1984, Nestlé also acquired Paul F. Beich Co., Inc., Bloomington, Illinois, a manufacturer of high-quality chocolate and confectionery items. Beich's products were supplied to various institutions that subsequently sold them under their own names to raise money for charity events. In 1984, Nestlé also acquired Ward Johnston, a U.S. chocolate manufacturer, for SFr.75,000,000. Determined to increase its sales of roasted coffee beans, Nestlé acquired two Canadian companies, Goodhost Foods (for SFr.35,000,000) and Hayhoe Foods, both active in producing and distributing roasted coffee to food services and institutional customers. At the same time, Nestlé came to an agreement with Hills Brothers, Coffee, Inc., San Francisco, California, a manufacturer of roasted coffee beans, on an option to purchase the firm for SFr.200,000,000. (Hills Brothers, which produced roasted and instant coffee, was to finally join the Nestlé group in 1985.) Nestlé also acquired two other manufacturers of roasted coffee in 1984: Brasilia in Spain, and Kaffeboenans in Sweden. And after acquiring the U.S. firm Fruitcrest, Nestlé added the latter's products to its own range of fruit juices.

Carnation headquarters, Los Angeles, California

The most outstanding acquisition made by Nestlé S.A. in 1984 was, however, its friendly take-over bid of $3,000,000,000 for Carnation Company, Los Angeles, California—at the time, the most expensive acquisition ever made in the food industry. Since this acquisition did not take effect until 1985, we shall discuss it in the section devoted to that year. Here we merely wish to point out that, Nestlé—far from actively seeking the Carnation acquisition—decided to seriously study the possibility of a take-over bid only after it learned that a member of the family that owned Carnation wished to sell his interest. It was Carl L. Angst who was chiefly responsible for the merger of these two big Swiss and U.S. food companies.

AN ELEVEN-YEAR DISPUTE ENDED, TO ALL INTENTS AND PURPOSES, IN 1984.

Since we are still relating events that took place in 1984, the year the U.S. consumer boycott of Nestlé products came to an end, we shall now turn to that famous eleven-year controversy over infant feeding in the Third World.

The Controversy over Infant Feeding in the Third World

☐ Nestlé's trading results for 1973 to 1984 were quite remarkable, for, during those years, its management was faced with an important controversy that stirred up the press all over the world—particularly in the U.S.—owing to the boycott launched against Nestlé by various lay and religious organizations. This long controversy was about infant feeding in the Third World. The subject set people at variance and was the cause of attacks on the food industry—essentially on Nestlé, the biggest producer and supplier of infant formula to the Third World. The dilemma stirred up passions, and, for eleven years, Nestlé was accused of engaging in promotional practices detrimental to breast-feeding in the non-communist Third World, where its products were marketed. The debate died down in 1984, but flamed up again in 1988, despite everything Nestlé was doing to conform to the World Health Organization's (W.H.O.) International Code on Marketing of Breast-Milk Substitutes.

On October 4, 1984, Nestlé and the International Nestlé Boycott Committee (I.N.B.C.) held a joint press conference in Washington, D.C. The statement issued by the company and that committee recalled that the boycott of Nestlé products was suspended in January, 1984, after the two parties reached an agreement on the way the W.H.O. code should be applied. The agreement not only put an end to the seven-year boycott of Nestlé products in the U.S., it also opened a new chapter in a latent controversy that was centuries old: what circumstances warrant feeding a baby with milk other than his own mother's breast milk? How can firms promote the use of breast-milk substitutes without discouraging mothers from breast-feeding? These are important questions. For a long time, they stirred up strong feelings—and continue to do so today. The problem is extremely complex, and

INFANT FEEDING IS AN AGE-OLD PROBLEM. IN THE THIRD WORLD, HOWEVER, IT IS A PARTICULARLY THORNY PROBLEM.

it gave rise to serious accusations against Nestlé. Therefore, we shall examine it here in some detail.

First, the controversy must be put in the proper context. To do so, we shall summarize *The Dilemma of Third World Nutrition: Nestlé and the Role of Infant Formula.* This report, written and published in 1985 by experts on breast-milk substitutes, was prepared for Nestlé by Maggie McComas, Geoffrey Fookes, and George Taucher; while the concluding section was written by Richard L. Worsnop. The medical facts were reviewed for accuracy by Professor Frank T. Falkner, M.D., chairman of the Maternal and Child Health Program at the School of Public Health, University of California, Berkeley. These experts studied the question of "Nestlé's role [as a producer of] breast-milk substitutes" at great length. The subject requires in-depth knowledge of extremely controversial material, so we shall not delve into it further than the report does during our discussion of this period—a period when several activist groups in Europe and America were attacking Nestlé in a highly critical and determined manner.

The earliest search for breast-milk substitutes is lost in the mists of time. There have always been mothers who were either unable or unwilling to breast-feed their babies, or who could not provide their infants with enough natural milk—in particular, because of working outside the home. Moreover, to ensue optimal growth, an infant often requires supplementary foods or alternatives to breast milk.

Human ingenuity, therefore, provided more or less satisfactory solutions to these vital needs throughout the ages: the wet nurse, who replaced the natural mother; milk from domestic animals; and, finally, all sorts of composite foods. However, an adequate solution was not found until a "preparation for infants," i.e., commercial infant formula, was discovered in modern times.

We must point out here that, in the first *Mothers' Guide* he published a century before the cause of babies was put forward so vehemently, Nestlé's founder wrote: "Breast milk will always be the most natural food during the first months [of life], and every mother who can should breast-feed her baby herself."

During the public controversy in the 1970s, the quality of most industrially produced infant formula was usually not in question. The controversy was over the utilization of infant formula; or, to be more precise, criticism was directed at certain means of promoting and marketing infant formula in Third World countries. Groups of critics, or activists, launched a global campaign

Leaflet with advice for mothers on feeding babies, Switzerland, 1927

THE U.N.'S PROTEIN-CALORIE ADVISORY GROUP EXAMINED THIS PROBLEM AS EARLY AS 1969. HOWEVER, THE MEMBERS OF THE P.A.G, WERE NOT OF ONE MIND,

against the baby-food industry, claiming that companies like Nestlé indulged in aggressive promotion of dietetic products and infant formula in the developing countries. These activists maintained that, as a result, Third World mothers came to believe (and wrongly so) that they could stop breast-feeding their babies, and that the often unhygienic surroundings in which those mothers lived made it impossible for them to prepare and use a breast-milk substitute safely. Again, according to the activists, the business practices of the companies in question contributed to the illness of approximately 10,000,000 babies each year, resulting in malnutrition, disease, and even death.

Among the international organizations devoted to studying and improving the world's food supply, one of the most active during the 1960s was the United Nations' Protein-Calorie Advisory Group (P.A.G.). Before the group was disbanded in 1977, its principal task was to coordinate the nutrition research and food aid programs that fell under the jurisdiction of major U.N. agencies such as the World Health Organization, the Food and Agricultural Organization (F.A.O.), and the United Nations International Children's Emergency Fund (U.N.I.C.E.F.).

In December, 1969, a P.A.G. study group decided to examine nutrition *in utero* (i.e., prior to birth) and in the first months of life. Its preliminary action program was addressed to members of the U.N., health professionals, and representatives of the baby-food industry. The inaugural session of the interdisciplinary study group was held in Bogotá, the capital of Colombia, in November, 1970, and lasted two days.

Underlying the discussions was the concern many of the experts present felt about the worldwide decline in breast-feeding. Since the causes of the phenomenon could not be pinpointed exactly, it was natural to suspect commercial baby food sold in areas showing the most spectacular decline in breast-feeding. The experts assembled in Bogotá tried, therefore, to ensure the cooperation of the baby-food industry in eliminating aggressive marketing of breast-milk substitutes and in suppressing any exacerbation of a trend for which it might be responsible. While expressing such reservations, however, many of the specialists present acknowledged that the baby-food industry's dietetic products and infant formula had a positive impact on infant nutrition in Third World settings.

Not all the participants were of that opinion, however. Dr. Derrick B. Jelliffe was among the most violent opponents of the baby-food industry;

Jelliffe, a P.A.G. consultant expert, was head of the Caribbean Food and Nutrition Institute at the time. He asserted, in particular, that the marketing methods of the baby-food industry were the *major factor* in the decline in breast-feeding. The meeting's final, diplomatically worded press release stated that, as knowledge stood at the time, no constructive purpose would be served by linking the global decline in breast-feeding to any single factor, including processed infant foods.

After this confrontation among experts, the participants decided to meet again in order to draw up a more detailed program of action.

The P.A.G.'s study group met in Paris in June, 1972, and published a general policy statement, which was to be known as "Statement 23" after it was revised and put into final form in New York in November, 1973. A long series of discussions, negotiations, and agreements were required to produce this statement. The actual program of action was very well-defined: "It is certainly important to avoid everything that would accelerate the trend away from breast-feeding; at the same time, it is essential to make formulas, foods, and instructions available to those mothers who do not breast-feed for various reasons." In July, 1973, when the final revision of "Statement 23" was nearly finished, Dr. Jelliffe stated that applying such guidelines would change nothing, adding: "Some other group may have to take a more aggressive Nader-like stance in this regard."

It did not take long for various groups of activists to follow Jelliffe's advice. *New Internationalist,* a British publication sponsored by three charities (Oxfam, Christian Aid, and Third World First), fired the first volley in August, 1973, by publishing a "report," consisting chiefly of an interview with two British child-health specialists experienced in Third World nutrition issues. Sprinkled throughout the report were assumptions about how and why dietetic products and infant formula were used and about the business practices of baby-food manufacturers—Nestlé in particular—but it supplied no proof to back up any of its claims.

To clear up the misunderstanding, Nestlé's management felt that a thorough discussion was called for; therefore, it invited the editorial staff of *New International* to visit Nestlé in Switzerland.

New International refused the proposed meeting with Nestlé; but it was accepted by Mike Muller, a free-lance journalist on assignment for War on Want, another British charity. For two days, Nestlé's experts were subjected to tough, yet constructive questioning. Within a few weeks, Muller's

AND THE RESULTS OF ITS MEETING IN PARIS IN MAY, 1972, WERE INCONCLUSIVE. A BRITISH PUBLICATION, *NEW INTERNATIONALIST,* BECAME INVOLVED IN THE CONTROVERSY. AFTER ITS MARKETING METHODS WERE ATTACKED, NESTLÉ SOUGHT AN IN-DEPTH REVIEW OF THE ISSUE. MIKE MULLER, A JOURNALIST, WENT TO VEVEY...

AND SEVERELY CRITICIZED NESTLÉ'S MARKETING PRACTICES. MULLER'S REPORT WAS DISTORTED BY A SWISS PUBLICATION TO SUCH AN EXTENT THAT NESTLÉ WAS ACCUSED OF KILLING BABIES.

report was published and released at a London press conference that rivaled the sensationalist title of Muller's report: "The Baby Killer." In his report, Muller called for nothing short of the elimination of "all promotional material" targeted at consumers or the health profession. In addition, he defined "promotional material" so as to encompass educational information essential to ensuring the proper utilization of dietetic products and infant formula.

Faced with such assertions, Nestlé's management realized it would have to provide factual proof that its business practices did not deserve such criticism. Consequently, Nestlé decided to adhere more strictly than ever to the guidelines of P.A.G. "Statement 23," ensuring that its promotional campaigns were in accordance with the most stringent ethical standards.

Yet even as Nestlé was carrying out this policy review, the campaign against it was approaching the company's headquarters in Vevey. "The Baby Killer" had been translated into German by a Swiss activist group; and the errors and lack of precision that characterized the original text were greatly exaggerated in the German translation. All the allegations of overly aggressive product promotion and the unproven assumption that commercial formula contributed to malnutrition were reduced to their simplest—libelous—expression in the title of the German translation: *Nestlé tötet Babies* ("Nestlé Kills Babies").

Before the German booklet was published in June, 1974, Nestlé had known nothing about its existence and had never heard of its authors. The company's management and employees felt they were being slandered. Nestlé had no other choice but to resort to legal action, and the company filed a libel suit against "persons as yet unknown." The hearing took place in Bern.

Almost as soon as the libel suit was filed, it became a media event. It was a natural for the front page. Recognizing this, the Swiss advocacy groups played their role to the hilt, using the traditional tools of propaganda—press conferences, letter writing campaigns, requests for support, etc.—at each stage of the trial.

Who were these activists? The publishers of the booklet were identified only as Arbeitsgruppe Dritte Welt ("Third World Working Group"); the report itself was attributed to War on Want and the German translation to yet another Swiss group, Schweizerische Arbeitsgruppen für Entwicklungspolitik ("Swiss Working Groups for a Policy of Development"). The orientation of these groups was summed up in an editorial sympathetic to the activists' cause: "...more lives can be saved by controlling or preventing the activities of multinationals than by financing aid projects...."

In accordance with Swiss legal procedure in such cases, the judge hearing the case called the adversaries together to attempt to reach a settlement on October 9, 1974. But the defendants' spokesman categorically refused an out-of-court settlement. As the hearings progressed, the defendants' testimony seemed not so much a defense of their own actions as a renewal of their attacks on Nestlé. Their avowed objective was to bring the company's marketing policies under close public scrutiny. As a result, it appeared that the company, not its critics, was on trial. The wheels of justice ground at their usual slow pace; the first hearing in the case—which took place without a jury—was not held until November, 1975, nearly a year and a half after charges had first been filed.

NESTLÉ TOOK LEGAL ACTION; THE CASE WAS HEARD IN BERN. THE AUTHORS OF THE SWISS BOOKLET WERE FOUND GUILTY, BUT NESTLÉ'S PROMOTIONAL PRACTICES WERE INDIRECTLY CRITICIZED IN THE JUDGE'S VERDICT.

Nestlé's two spokesmen, stating the company's case in a straightforward and concise manner befitting their legal and scientific backgrounds, introduced samples of the company's promotional and educational materials—tangible evidence that Nestlé did not discourage breast-feeding. The defendants' courtroom statements were as dramatically different in style as in content. Each contributed another chapter in the saga of alleged misuse of infant formula in the Third World, a saga related through anecdotes, for the most part, and frequently in quite emotional tones. Most of these unverifiable statements could have been refuted or at least severely discredited by cross-examination. But because trial procedures did not allow this, such statements went unchallenged, and Nestlé's case suffered as a consequence.

In February and June, 1976, two more courtroom sessions were devoted to hearing two witnesses for each side. The judge's swift verdict—described by the press as a "Pyrrhic Victory"—did not come as a complete surprise. From a strictly technical and legal point of view, Nestlé was the winner. The defendants were found guilty and fined a small amount. The title *Nestlé tötet Babies* was indeed libelous, said the judge, but he added: "If the company wishes to avoid charges of immoral and unethical behavior in the future, it must change its promotional practices." Although the judge's criticism was not legally binding, it would later be used by other advocacy groups as ammunition against Nestlé.

Away from the heat of Nestlé's legal battle, the infant-food industry as a whole had not abandoned efforts to find a solution to the real problem of

THE CONTROVERSY SHIFTED TO THE U.S., WHERE A CONSUMER BOYCOTT OF NESTLÉ PRODUCTS WAS LAUNCHED IN 1977.

feeding Third World infants, in particular by acting upon the recommendations spelled out in P.A.G. "Statement 23". Thus, at the end of 1975, the International Council of Infant Food Industries (I.C.I.F.I.) was formally organized in Zurich, bringing together eight of the biggest infant-formula producers in the U.S., Europe, and Japan, and including Nestlé. One of its first actions was to develop a voluntary code of marketing ethics embodying the principles of P.A.G. "Statement 23".

Just as industry was about to accept the principle of self-regulation, the campaign against it was gathering momentum in the U.S. As the Nestlé Company, Inc., White Plains, New York, Nestlé's U.S. subsidiary, was wholly owned by the Swiss parent firm and not publicly quoted or listed on any U.S. stock exchange, it seemed to be spared the kind of attacks that had plagued other American manufacturers of infant formula. Moreover, Nestlé's U.S. subsidiary neither manufactured nor distributed infant formula on either the domestic or the export market.

The company was about to experience even harsher attacks than those orchestrated by the press. In 1975, a German film director, W. Gladitz, who used the pseudonym Peter Krieg ("Peter War"), produced a propaganda film entitled *Bottle Babies,* shot primarily on location in Kenya. According to the promotional material distributed to groups showing the film, *Bottle Babies* was "not merely a documentary," but a "subjective, emotional, unequivocal ...polemic against the manufacturers of infant formula...." The film's commentary made infant formula practically synonymous with genocide and pointed to Nestlé as the principal culprit of the infant-formula industry. The film's wide distribution was largely the result of the organizational efforts of the Infant Formula Action Coalition (INFACT)—a group comprised of individuals from existing advocacy organizations already committed to the campaign against infant formula—and Nestlé was its main target.

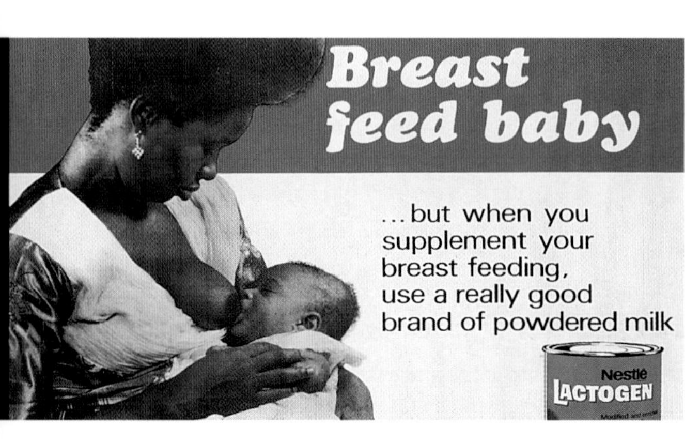

Nigerian poster encouraging breast-feeding, ca. 1968

On July 4, 1977 (American Independence Day), INFACT announced a consumer boycott of all Nestlé products sold in the U.S.

THE COMPANY'S CONTACTS WITH THE LEADERS OF THE BOYCOTT FAILED TO RESOLVE THE DISPUTE. INFLUENTIAL U.S. SENATORS ORGANIZED A SENATE HEARING ON THE ISSUE.

Nestlé's first encounter with representatives of INFACT in October, 1977, went surprisingly well. Some of the INFACT representatives requested material on Nestlé policies and on the changes already made in the company's marketing practices—which were at the center of the controversy. A great majority of the more militant activists, however, had no intention of staying within the bounds of constructive criticism. Demonstrations were held throughout the country at company facilities and retail outlets carrying Nestlé products.

INFACT also called upon nationally prominent politicians to further arouse public opinion. At the time, the marketing of infant formula in the Third World was a subject that was newsworthy enough to be debated in that typically American forum—televised congressional hearings.

As the chairman of the Senate Subcommittee on Health and Scientific Research, Senator Edward Kennedy headed the subcommittee's hearings, scheduled for May, 1978. Nestlé thought it had found the ideal spokesman, Dr. Oswaldo Ballarin, chairman of Nestlé's Brazilian subsidiary. Ballarin, a Third World citizen living in a country where Nestlé had pioneered the dairy industry and also a consultant to the U.N.'s Protein-Calorie Advisory Group, had excellent qualifications; and he had agreed to accept this difficult mission.

Owing, however, to Ballarin's statement that the authors of the boycott were spearheading a campaign "with the stated purpose of undermining the free enterprise system," the outcome of these hearings was very detrimental to Nestlé. Ballarin's statement, as everyone agrees today, was a tactical error.

As was to be expected, the results of the senate hearings were as paradoxical as the hearings themselves. They provided the activists with a treasure trove of new quotes to fuel their propaganda campaign. Among these was the claim by Dr. Jelliffe that "some 10,000,000 cases of marasmus and diarrhea occur annually in infants in developing countries, related in part to inadequate bottle-feeding." In one of its direct mail campaigns for funds to use in its battle against Nestlé, INFACT immediately exaggerated Jelliffe's claim and stated: "Ten million Third World babies are starving because of the heartless, money-hungry actions of powerful multinational corporations."

Though Senator Kennedy did not prepare draft legislation (which would, indeed, be hard to imagine) as a result of the hearings, he did encourage development of voluntary controls for appropriate marketing practices in

THE ISSUE WAS FINALLY BROUGHT BEFORE THE WORLD HEALTH ORGANIZATION. THE FIRST W.H.O. CONFERENCE ON INFANT FEEDING TOOK PLACE IN 1979, THE SECOND IN 1980,

developing countries, starting with U.S.-based firms. Self-regulation had always been the raison d'être for I.C.I.F.I., the industry council to which Nestlé belonged. The I.C.I.F.I. president therefore suggested to the senator that discussions take place within a forum of international cooperation such as the World Health Organization, for the question was within its competence. Senator Kennedy eagerly endorsed this proposal and wrote to the director-general of W.H.O., asking him to set a date for a conference at which a "uniform [and] ethical" international marketing code would be formulated. W.H.O. agreed to the proposal in September, 1978.

In the meantime, INFACT continued its boycott campaign, which was not very successful, as it had no significant impact in terms of sales.

At the October 9–12, 1979 conference on infant feeding, sponsored jointly by W.H.O. and U.N.I.C.E.F., various forces and objectives neatly converged. The industry felt it was important to transfer responsibility for the discussion of infant-formula marketing to the appropriate government authorities, health professionals, and industry experts. As for W.H.O., this new project meshed perfectly with its ongoing programs for "promoting better health for mothers and children, combating malnutrition, procuring potable water, and training health professionals" in the Third World.

Although the meeting's conclusions were termed a "consensus," this was something of a misnomer, given that strong differences still existed over precisely what should be considered "appropriate" marketing practices. On the whole, however, Nestlé was satisfied with the outcome. For one thing, many of the marketing reforms suggested in the final document echoed policy changes that the company had already put into effect. Nestlé now hoped that all parties concerned—including, naturally, the infant-formula industry—would develop more precise marketing guidelines. No sooner had the meeting been adjourned than representatives from various activist groups announced the formation of the International Baby Food Action Network (I.B.F.A.N.), which, in reality, was no more than a regrouping of the forces of INFACT, with the addition of some European and Asian advocacy groups. To increase its importance perhaps, this group, too, wished to negotiate with Nestlé. But, after its experience with INFACT, Nestlé had no desire to sit down with another such group at the bargaining table.

In 1980, the World Health Assembly confirmed the mandate given to the secretariat of W.H.O. and U.N.I.C.E.F. in October, 1979, to draft an official marketing code. Unfortunately, the text's final version left much to be desired. It was quite general—a vice as well as its primary virtue—with many ambiguous provisions and very loosely defined terms. This meant that companies implementing the code could claim compliance with it, while critics of those companies, following their own interpretation of the code's provisions, could continue to consider them as violating the code. Nevertheless, the aim of the code was clearly and completely expressed. As stated in Article 1, the code was designed to "contribute to providing safe and adequate nutrition for infants," not only through the "protection and promotion of breast-feeding" but also through the "proper use" of breast-milk substitutes, ensured through "adequate information" and "appropriate marketing and distribution."

AND THE THIRD IN 1981. AS THE U.S. BOYCOTT CONTINUED, AND NESTLÉ WENT ON THE OFFENSIVE.

This solution was approved almost unanimously by the World Health Assembly in May, 1981: with 118 votes in favor of the code, 1 opposed to it, and 3 abstentions. The negative vote was cast by the U.S. delegation, which cited conflicts with the U.S. Constitution.

Of course, this important effort at reaching a consensus in no way reduced the level of activist campaigning. At the 1980 World Health Assembly, I.B.F.A.N. used a new tactic, denouncing some two hundred alleged instances of industry marketing abuse throughout the world. The large majority of the reported infractions were either totally wrong, unconfirmed, or involved companies other than those of the I.C.I.F.I. group (whose members marketed about 85 percent of the infant formula sold in developing countries).

Nestlé's policy of replying quietly to its critics (when it chose to reply at all) puzzled many who followed the development of the infant-formula controversy. Company managers responsible for press and public relations were accustomed to handling inquiries that were modest in terms of volume and generally uncontroversial in nature. As the debate over infant-formula marketing techniques gathered momentum, however, it became evident that what the company said about the issue was as important a factor in resolving the controversy as what it actually did to ensure that the product was used in the proper manner only by those who really needed it. If the company was

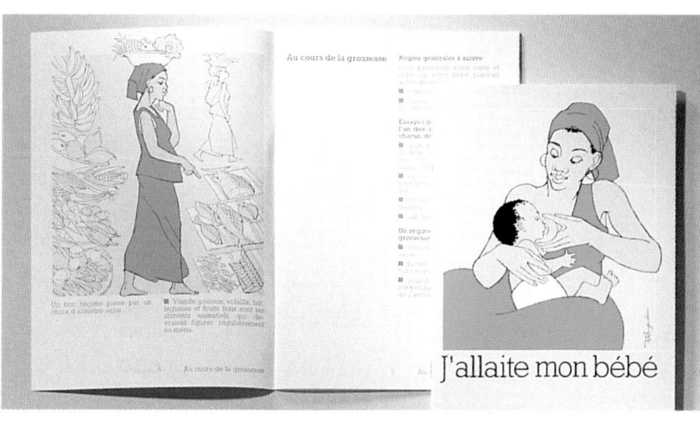

Leaflet with advice on breast-feeding

NESTLÉ DECIDED TO MODIFY ITS POLICY OF PROMOTING INFANT FORMULA.

to be blamed for anything, it was for having done too little too late in the way of public relations, failing to inform the public at large of the steps it had taken over the years to ensure that dietetic products and infant formula were being made available to women on a selective basis and that Third World consumers were being educated as to its proper use.

Faced with a dearth of knowledge about Third World nutrition and infant feeding, Nestlé decided to determine, once and for all, whether there was any scientific basis to the activists' claims, according to which only 2 percent of all mothers are physiologically incapable of breast-feeding. They also claimed that less than 6 percent of mothers are unable to breast-feed because of such factors as working outside the home and that even an undernourished mother can "adequately feed" her child during its first four months of life. If all these claims were true, Nestlé would have been required to rethink not only its specific marketing practices, but also the more important question of whether infant formula is really needed.

For that reason, Nestlé undertook a review of the existing scientific literature on the subject of infant feeding and discovered that it failed to provide scientifically satisfactory replies to its questions. Therefore, the company commissioned an independent research institute to investigate the problem of infant feeding in three developing countries—Kenya, Mexico, and Malaysia—on the basis of a significant sample of some 6,000 mothers. Completed in 1981, this research showed that, in the countries studied more than 50 percent of the mothers questioned had used supplementary foods before their infants were four months old, regardless of whether commercially produced infant formula was available or not. Moreover, many of the foods used as breast-milk substitutes and supplements (the majority of these being traditional local foods) were not recommended for this purpose; and, in general, infant-feeding patterns varied greatly among the countries and social classes studied—which served as further evidence that the Third World was far from being the homogeneous entity anti-industry activists supposed it to be when making their sweeping generalizations.

Following a marketing policy review, Nestlé nonetheless began to wonder whether, it was doing enough to encourage breast-feeding after World War II and decided to modify its promotional and educational materials at this point so as to place greater emphasis on breast-feeding. By taking this initiative, Nestlé was a step ahead of international policy in this area. Indeed, by 1979, when W.H.O. considered the question of the food industry's role in emphasizing the importance of breast-feeding, Nestlé's new policy was already in effect. In 1978, for example, Nestlé decided to end its use of the media, notably for advertising infant formula on Third World markets but also for disseminating educational information related to nutrition.

THE INTERNATIONAL CODE OF MARKETING OF BREAST-MILK SUBSTITUTES WAS ADOPTED IN 1981.

Despite these steps, criticism continued unabated, leading Nestlé to conclude, toward the end of 1980, that a new and more assertive approach should be considered. In January, 1981, the company therefore decided to establish its own strategy planning center, the Nestlé Coordination Center for Nutrition, Inc. (N.C.C.N.), in Washington, D.C.

This more assertive policy enabled Nestlé to present its position to important persons—academics, church leaders, politicians, and so on—who had previously been unaware of the well-foundedness of the company's case This established the basis for a meaningful dialogue between what had heretofore been wary and often hostile adversaries.

As mentioned earlier, in May, 1981, the World Health Assembly adopted an International Code of Marketing of Breast-Milk Substitutes. While harboring certain reservations about some of the code's provisions, Nestlé was quick to become a signatory to the document. After all, the code established an internationally agreed-upon set of procedures by which the marketing policies and practices of companies could be evaluated. Moreover, many of the code's provisions were in accordance with Nestlé's marketing policies for developing countries. For instance, Nestlé had issued instructions to its subsidiaries to cooperate with governments in developing national codes that would implement W.H.O. recommendations within the context of the social and economic situation of each country.

Nestlé's critics were still not satisfied, however. Noting that few governments had formally adopted the W.H.O. guidelines, these critics directed their attention to Article 11.3, which suggested that infant-formula producers should bear the primary responsibility for ascertaining that marketing practices were "in accordance with the principles and aims" of the code. Thus, Nestlé came under pressure to abide by the code as a whole, even in the absence of action by individual governments.

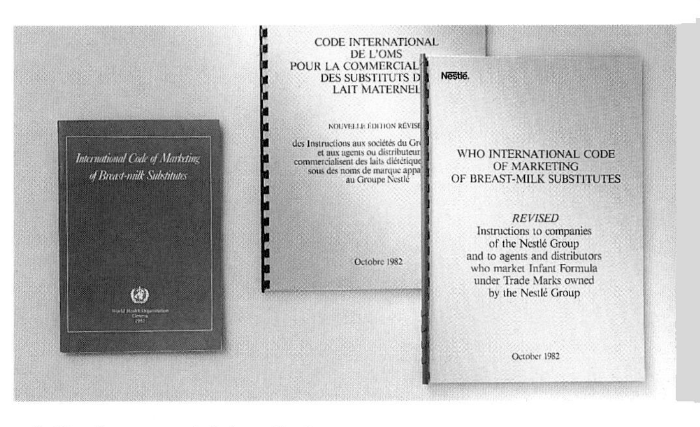

Official edition of the W.H.O. code and "Nestlé Instructions" on applying its provisions

A DIALOGUE WAS ESTABLISHED BETWEEN NESTLÉ AND THE TASK FORCE OF THE UNITED METHODIST CHURCH IN THE U.S. A LIST OF "NESTLÉ INSTRUCTIONS" WAS SENT TO EACH OF THE COMPANY'S SUBSIDIARIES.

At about this time, a dialogue was developing between Nestlé and the infant-formula task force set up in the U.S. in 1980 by the United Methodist Church (U.M.C.). Nestlé's discussions and exchanges of information with U.M.C. representatives were to prove crucial in ending the boycott of Nestlé products in North America.

Meanwhile, Nestlé was taking additional steps of its own. In view of the lack of government action, Nestlé decided to unilaterally implement the W.H.O. code in all developing countries. Accordingly, detailed "Nestlé instructions" on each of the code's provisions were sent to company subsidiaries and agents in February, 1982. Nestlé also took another, more important step: it decided to initiate personal contacts with influential religious groups, activists, and other organizations. As a result of this new policy, a meeting took place in Dayton, Ohio, between the U.M.C. task force and Helmut Maucher, assisted by Carl Angst, who was in charge of Nestlé's task force on the infant-formula controversy.

By issuing "Nestlé instructions," the company went on the offensive in the infant-formula debate for the first time. Nestlé had put its critics in a position forcing them to make the next move. And, indeed, some organizations that had been part of the boycott announced that they were abandoning it, while others indicated that they were considering similar action. As before, however, Nestlé's motives were soon questioned: INFACT and the Interfaith Center on Corporate Responsibility issued a list of more than one hundred detailed criticisms of the "Nestlé instructions" and went so far as to assert that Nestlé was trying to "rewrite" the W.H.O. code.

Of course, at least to a certain degree, such criticism resulted from the ambiguity of certain sections of the code and the difficulty of arriving at a correct interpretation of those sections. Since only the World Health Assembly or individual W.H.O. member states had the authority to put forward an official interpretation, the staff of W.H.O. and U.N.I.C.E.F. could do no more than offer their unofficial advice to companies wishing to implement the code. This, however, did nothing to prevent Nestlé's critics from insisting that it conform to their own highly restrictive interpretation of the code. While admitting that Nestlé's decision to abide by the W.H.O. code provided "the basis for settling" the boycott, Douglas Johnson, INFACT's chairman, declared: "The Nestlé boycott is continuing and shall continue until the International Nestlé Boycott Committee determines that it is no longer necessary."

In view of the ongoing stalemate, the Nestlé Coordination Center for Nutrition (N.C.C.N.) recommended to Nestlé's management in Switzerland that an independent body be established to monitor the company's code-implementation record and to investigate complaints. The creation of a panel composed of church leaders, medical experts, and scientists was announced at a news conference in Washington, D.C., on May 3, 1982. Edmund S. Muskie was to be chairman of the Nestlé Infant Formula Audit Commission (N.I.F.A.C.); Muskie, a former senator from Maine and former secretary of state, had been the Democratic vice-presidential nominee in 1968 and a candidate for the Democratic presidential nomination in 1972.

The primary task of Muskie and N.I.F.A.C. at the outset was to review the "Nestlé instructions" and to consult with W.H.O., U.N.I.C.E.F., and the scores of other organizations and individuals involved in the controversy. This process resulted in a set of N.I.F.A.C. recommendations aimed at clarifying and strengthening the original "Nestlé instructions." Most of the commission's proposals were accepted by Nestlé, and the revised instructions were jointly announced by the company and N.I.F.A.C. representatives in October, 1982.

In the same month, the United Methodist task force recommended that the church's ruling body elect to refrain from joining the boycott.

Other groups abandoned of the boycott in 1983, thus paving the way for a possible resolution of the controversy. Several leaders of the National Council of Churches, as well as leaders of churches that had called off their boycott, such as the United Methodist task force, began to apply pressure to the boycott's leadership to seek an agreement with Nestlé. As a result, activists now limited their criticism to four areas: educational materials, hazard warnings on labels, gifts to health professionals, and free supplies to hospitals. These four areas of concern raised genuine and highly complex issues with regard to the interpretation and implementation of the code.

Nestlé finally suggested requesting informal guidance from W.H.O. and U.N.I.C.E.F. on the four areas of concern to the International Nestlé Boycott Committee. Nestlé then outlined its position in a discussion paper. Nestlé's position was clarified in the course of an intensive series of joint Nestlé/I.N.B.C. meetings with U.N.I.C.E.F., held in New York in January, 1984, in the presence of representatives of the Muskie Commission. U.N.I.C.E.F. was asked to give its opinion on Nestlé's replies to each of the four points and on questions raised by I.N.B.C. (with W.H.O. also being

MOST IMPORTANT, IT SET UP A SPECIAL MONITORING COMMISSION IN WASHINGTON, D.C., HEADED BY SENATOR EDWARD MUSKIE, WHICH SOON PREPARED A SERIES OF RECOMMENDATIONS. SUPPORT FOR THE BOYCOTT BEGAN TO WANE IN 1983; ITS LEADERS LIMITED THEIR DEMANDS TO FOUR AREAS. THE ADVICE OF U.N.I.C.E.F. AND W.H.O. WAS SOUGHT.

AN AGREEMENT WAS REACHED WITH THE LEADERS OF THE BOYCOTT, WHO CALLED IT OFF IN OCTOBER, 1984. HOWEVER, THIS DID NOT PUT AN END TO THE ISSUE...

consulted at all stages of the discussions). These meetings resulted in the drafting of a statement of understanding, detailing Nestlé's proposed method of dealing with the four points at issue on the basis of its interpretation of the W.H.O. code. In view of this statement, which took into consideration the views of W.H.O., U.N.I.C.E.F., and the Muskie Commission, I.N.B.C. had to admit that Nestlé had responded positively to its concerns. Thus, on January 26, 1984, Nestlé and the leaders of I.N.B.C. announced in New York that a decision had been reached to suspend the boycott for six months, pending a final review of Nestlé's compliance with the code.

The final stage of this prolonged dispute was somewhat anti-climactic. On October 4, 1984, a news conference was held in Washington, D.C. to announce that the Nestlé boycott was officially over. Despite the fact that baby food comprises only a tiny share of Nestlé's total activities (a mere 2.5 percent to be exact), the company remains convinced that there is a real need for high-quality dietetic products and infant formula. The problem, of course, is how to make these products available to those who really need them, and at an affordable price, while ensuring that they are used correctly under widely varying conditions.

A passage in the 1985 booklet to which the main sections of this account may be attributed states that Nestlé now "hopes that the international guidelines will be followed in such a way that those truly in need are not denied either infant formula or the help of support personnel trained to give assistance in its proper use. But there is a more daunting task in improving Third World nutrition, and this is to break the destructive cycle of poverty, ignorance, and inadequate health services that all too often produce malnutrition and disease. The task necessarily requires a massive commitment of financial and human resources by international health and development agencies and governments. It is up to industry, religious organizations, organized consumer groups, and concerned individuals to contribute to this task."

The Washington Times

FRIDAY, JANUARY 27, 1984

Nestle boycott ends, firm revises tactics

By Susan Jenks
WASHINGTON TIMES STAFF

An international boycott against the Nestle Co. was suspended yesterday, as protestors and company officials broke candy together — Nestle's chocolate, of course — and celebrated the end of a 6½-year conflict. In announcing the truce, Douglas A. Johnson, national chairman of the Infant Formula Action Coalition, praised the Swiss-based company for "moving forward to become a model for the entire infant formula industry" by complying with the World Health Organization's marketing code formula worldwide, and the protesters came over the past two weeks, as both sides came to terms in four areas of concern.

These focused on Nestle's methods of marketing its powdered-milk formula, especially in Third World nations.

Mr. Johnson's group, sponsor of the U.S. boycott, and 100 other religious and health organizations, charged the company with aggressive marketing tactics that persuaded mothers in underdeveloped nations to switch from breast-feeding to bottle-feeding — thus contributing to high infant mortality rates in these areas.

Sen. Edmund Muskie, to monitor its compliance with the code and also announced several changes in its controversial marketing practices overseas, including halting distribution of free samples and outdated product information.

Yesterday, both sides indicated there had been no sudden breakthrough, but rather a coming together out of mutual concern on the issues that divided them.

"The chemistry and timing were right for intensifying our discussions," said Rafael Pagan Jr., president of the Nestle Coordination Center for Nutrition.

Mr. Pagan said this will cost the company $10 million to $20 million.

Mr. Johnson said the boycott groups spent $3.5 million to reach "this rare and unprecedented day." He also announced the intention of the coalition and the International Nestle Boycott Commission to shift attention to Nestle's competitors.

"These companies have relished sitting on the sidelines . . . and the responsible commitments won from Nestle have been unfairly exploited to expand their market share," Mr. Johnson said. "Today, we are serving notice on these companies; now they move to center

January 27, 1984 issue of The Washington Times announcing the end of the Nestlé boycott

Only four years after the ending of the boycott, a new campaign against Nestlé was under way in the U.S., with activists claiming that Nestlé had failed to live up to its 1984 commitments. These claims were firmly rejected in November, 1988, however, by the Muskie Commission. And ten days after the announcement of a new Nestlé boycott, W.H.O. put out a press release that concluded: "W.H.O. seriously hopes that the productive cooperation carefully initiated during the last decade will continue and be strengthened. Conscientiously concerted action by all groups involved in the feeding of infants and small children is, therefore, highly desirable."

FOR INFANT NUTRITION REMAINS A PROBLEM IN THE THIRD WORLD.

Nestlé reaffirmed that it has always been prepared to enter into discussion and cooperate with any group concerned with this important problem, including the leaders of international consumer movements.

1985: Carnation Joins the Nestlé Group

☐ Carnation Company had been in existence for over seventy-five years when it became an integral part of the Nestlé group, following the latter's September, 1984 take-over bid, at the beginning of 1985. Elbridge Amos Stuart, a forty-three-year-old merchant in the grocery business, had founded Carnation in September, 1899. Stuart's first factory began production at Kent, Washington, not far from Seattle; and, for thirty-three years, E.A. Stuart's company bore the stamp of his strong personality. Stuart was blessed with a keen business sense and was acutely aware of the importance of high-quality products in his line of business. At the end of the nineteenth century, he started up in an industry he knew nothing about—evaporated milk. Stuart's Pacific Coast Condensed Milk Company, incorporated in the state of Delaware, launched Carnation brand evaporated milk. In 1916, the company adopted Carnation Milk Products Company as its official name, shortening it to Carnation Company in 1929. Company headquarters are in Los Angeles, California.

From the outset, Carnation worked with a patent granted to John Meyenberg, an inventor of Swiss origin. The first two years were difficult for the young firm. Stuart first formed a partnership with Thomas E. Yerxa, but bought back Yerxa's share of the company in 1901 in order to retain control of Carnation. A second factory was opened in Oregon in 1902, with Harry Stuart, the founder's nephew, in charge. By 1903, company profits—generated by Carnation evaporated milk and cream—exceeded $100,000. Carnation grew rapidly after 1906, when it opened three new condensed milk factories in the state of Washington.

The official opening of Carnation's factory at Kent, Washington, September 6, 1899

In 1932, health problems forced E.A. Stuart to relinquish the day-to-day management of the company. (He was to serve as chairman of the board until his death in 1944.) Stuart was succeeded by his son Elbridge Hadley Stuart, who headed the company until 1957, when he took over as chairman (1957–71). A long-time colleague of Stuart's, Alfred Mills Ghormley, succeeded the founder's son as Carnation's c.e.o. in 1957; in 1963, Ghormley stepped aside to be replaced by H. Everett Olson, who had been working for Carnation since 1931. Olson was to serve as chairman from 1971 on, and as c.e.o. from 1968 on. Dwight Lyman Stuart, the founder's grandson, became company president in 1973. Chairman H.E. Olson, head of Carnation, assisted by Timm F. Crull, was to negotiate the 1984 merger with Nestlé.

CARNATION HAD BEEN IN EXISTENCE FOR 85 YEARS WHEN IT WAS ACQUIRED BY NESTLÉ. CARNATION WAS A THRIVING FIRM, BOTH IN THE U.S. AND ABROAD.

Throughout its eighty-five-year existence, Carnation was a thriving firm. Originally a dairy company, it gradually widened its range of products to include powdered milk and various malt-based beverages, later entering the field of food services and also producing dry food for dogs and cats. (Carnation's Friskies brand pet food soon enjoyed a worldwide reputation.) Carnation began making canned pet foods at the end of World War I. The company became one of the leading suppliers of the American pet-food market, as well as a well-established pet-food supplier in Europe and the Middle East. In the 1960s, after acquiring the large Albers flour mills, Carnation also began manufacturing cattle feed. None of this prevented Carnation from expanding its range of flavored, malted, and chocolate powdered milk, nor from starting production of instant dairy products, including Carnation powdered skimmed milk (which accounted for 35 percent of the American market in 1983) and Coffee-mate, a vegetable-fat-based cream substitute, with a 40-percent share of the U.S. market. A revolutionary beverage, Carnation Instant Breakfast enjoyed phenomenal success as early as 1965, for there was a real need for a practical breakfast that was both quick and nourishing. Hot Cocoa Mix, a chocolate-flavored powdered milk product to which one simply added water, was launched in 1971. Finally, following the success of its instant breakfast, the company launched Carnation Breakfast Bar. (1 cup of milk and the Carnation Breakfast Bar are the equivalent of a nourishing meal.)

Carnation gained a solid foothold in the area of culinary products in 1963 by acquiring Contadina Foods, another U.S. company, producing and marketing a wide range of canned tomato-based products used in Italian cooking, which was rapidly becoming very popular in North America.

Carnation's first farm, near Seattle, Washington, 1909

By 1984, Carnation had been active in the field of food services for about fifty years. With its range of nearly two hundred top-quality products, Carnation enjoyed a strong position in that field. After acquiring its first potato-processing factory in 1971, Carnation also became one of the four leaders in the U.S. in this area. (At the beginning of the 1980s, this industry utilized two-thirds of all the potatoes consumed in the U.S.)

IT POSSESSED 111 FACTORIES AND WAS WELL WORTH THE $3,000,000,000 NESTLÉ PAID FOR IT.

Carnation's European subsidiaries produced Glücksklee evaporated milk and yogurt in Germany; Gloria brand milk and Friskies dog and cat food in France; Carnation evaporated milk, Coffee-mate, and Go Cat cat food in Great Britain; and milk for export in the Netherlands. In the Far East and Oceania, Carnation's two major markets were the Philippines (milk) and Australia (milk and pet foods). In Canada, the company sold milk, various instant products, and frozen as well as dried potato-based products for food services. In South Africa, Carnation was active in the field of dairy products and coffee-cream substitutes made from vegetable fat. Carnation acquired a stake in companies in Peru, the Dominican Republic, and Mexico. (Carnation had previously cooperated with Nestlé in Latin America, in Cuba and the Dominican Republic.)

As for its R & D efforts, Carnation possessed a laboratory in California that engaged in research in the field of food technology and the development of new products. Carnation's experimental farm in the state of Washington carried out research aimed at improving cat and dog foods.

Carnation possessed thirty-nine factories in seventeen countries abroad; it owned seventy-two factories in the U.S., with company headquarters in Los Angeles. Carnation employed 21,800 persons, 60 percent of whom (13,000) were based in the U.S. Carnation marketed its products in 150 countries. Its 1983 turnover totaled $3,400,000,000.

After hearing, through an investment bank, that certain members of the Stuart family had decided to sell their shares, Nestlé contacted Carnation's management in Los Angeles. The Stuarts' asking price for Carnation and Nestlé's idea of a suitable price were initially far apart; however, after several meetings within a relatively short time, both parties agreed on a price per share of $83, or a total of $3,000,000,000 (SFr. 7,500,000,000).

H.E. Olson, Carnation's chairman, and T.F. Crull, its president, got along well with Nestlé's C.L. Angst. And, owing to the celebrity of the Nestlé name and its handling of previous acquisitions (that of Stouffer, for instance), Carnation's management preferred to merge with it rather than with any other firm.

Nestlé guaranteed that Carnation would remain an independent company in the U.S. Olson retired in 1985, and Timm Crull became the key man at Carnation, which was controlled directly by Nestlé headquarters in Vevey rather than being absorbed by the U.S. Nestlé Company. Olson had been both chairman and president of Carnation; Crull assumed the latter

Historic poster advertising delivery of Carnation condensed milk

IN THE U.S., NESTLÉ ESTABLISHED ITSELF EVEN MORE SOLIDLY IN THE FIELD OF FOOD PRODUCTS. NESTLÉ DID NOT WISH TO BECOME A CONGLOMERATE;

function; while Carl Angst became chairman of the board of the Carnation Company.

Nestlé had good reasons for wishing to acquire Carnation. It wanted to gain a foothold once again in the stable and free U.S. market in a traditional Nestlé field—that of dairy products. And Nestlé was pleased to be able to do this through one of the foremost food companies in the U.S. Carnation was a company with a strong tradition of excellence: it had been profitable for decades and was strengthened by solid financial reserves. In addition, Carnation's management was in favor of the acquisition. Nestlé also wished to use this acquisition to strengthen its position as a manufacturer of food products in order to gain access to U.S. food services, to enlarge its traditional range of products with other top-performing brands, and to enter the dog- and cat-food markets. This acquisition also provided Nestlé with an opportunity to gradually integrate Carnation's activities outside the U.S. into those of locally based Nestlé companies.

While extending its activities in the field of culinary products and chocolate drinks, Nestlé also counted on profiting from cooperation in other markets, which would make its activities much more efficient. Not to have accepted the challenge would have meant forgoing a golden opportunity, for Nestlé had obtained the funds needed to finance its acquisition of Carnation under very favorable terms.

After a brilliant career in the diplomatic service of Switzerland (from Swiss ambassador, he had gone on to become Swiss secretary of state for foreign economic affairs), Paul R. Jolles succeeded Arthur Fürer as chairman of Nestlé's board of directors. At the annual shareholders' meeting in May, 1985, Jolles expressed Nestlé's satisfaction with the take-over. He also pointed out that, despite its many acquisitions, Nestlé had always been opposed to hostile take-over bids, which tarnished the image of those who proposed them.

Carnation truck selling ice cream at Disneyland

Unwilling to become a conglomerate, Nestlé sold Herff Jones Company, a manufacturer of appointment calendars and school supplies, which Carnation had acquired in 1973. It also sold the various divisions of Carnation specializing in cattle, poultry, and horse feed as well as agricultural machinery.

Carnation's president, Timm Crull, stressed the excellent manner in which his firm had been integrated into Nestlé following the latter's acquisition of it. During an interview in April, 1989, Crull declared: "I believe that all of Carnation's employees are proud of belonging to the big Nestlé family. They know that this name is synonymous with quality—not just in the U.S., but all over the world as well. I would say that their main problem was getting used to such a big company and also, perhaps, no longer having as much freedom [of action] as when we were an independent company. We have to cooperate closely with headquarters in Switzerland and ensure that our activities are profitable. Our contacts with Nestlé's management are excellent. Moreover, [Nestlé] was marvelous during the acquisition; it gave us its support and encouraged [us in] what we tried to do. I don't think one could imagine a better merger."

HOWEVER, IT CONTINUED ITS EFFORTS IN THE FIELDS OF COSMETICS AND OPHTHALMOLOGICAL PRODUCTS.

IN 1985, A SHIFT OCCURRED IN THE GEOGRAPHIC DISTRIBUTION OF NESTLÉ'S TURNOVER.

Acquiring Carnation did not prevent Nestlé from engaging in expansion—through new acquisitions—in the fields of cosmetics and ophthalmological products, but it was always careful to maintain food products at the center of its activities. At the beginning of this chapter, we discussed the 1984 acquisition of Warner Cosmetics. Not all of Nestlé's take-over bids in this field were successful, however. In the spring of 1984, for example, Nestlé made a $500,000,000 take-over bid for Coopervision in the U.S. The Federal Trade Commission imposed certain conditions on its approval of the merger that the Swiss firm was not prepared to accept; and Nestlé decided to forgo it as a result. Nevertheless, between 1983 and 1985, Nestlé devoted a total of SFr. 9,000,000,000 to acquisitions. During the same period, the company's sales figure increased from SFr. 27,900,000,000 to SFr. 42,200,000,000 (due in part to the rise in value of the U.S. dollar), and its net profit rose from SFr. 1,200,000,000 to SFr. 1,750,000,000.

Timm F. Crull

In 1985, the company's rapidly growing sales throughout the world went hand in hand with a degree of geographic redistribution of Nestlé's facilities. The rate of development was most striking on the U.S. market—because of acquisitions Nestlé had made in America—followed by that of Europe and Japan. The majority of the company's activities were centered more than ever in the world's highly industrialized countries. This did not mean, however, that Nestlé had lost all interest in the Third World; for while the contribution of the developing countries to its consolidated sales figure—though

NESTLÉ CONTINUED TO ACQUIRE COMPANIES IN EUROPE AND OVERSEAS.

increasing 8.8 percent—had dropped from 28 to 22 percent, the number of factories built in the Third World continued to increase. Economic conditions in the industrialized countries had made a marked improvement, owing to a greater balance between Europe, on the one hand, and the U.S. and Japan on the other; to the overall drop in the rate of inflation; and, finally, to the fact that governments were trying harder to take into account the relationship between the various areas of economic policy, such as trade, investment incentives, and the process of debt reduction. However, this did not eliminate certain risk factors: high unemployment rates, widely varying exchange rates, a marked slump on most raw materials markets, and, above all, a high level of international debt.

After the considerable amounts it had devoted in previous years to acquisitions and on acquiring a stake in other companies, in 1986, Nestlé placed a limit of SFr. 825,000,000 on the level of funds devoted to new acquisitions. In the field of refrigerated dairy products in Europe, Chambourcy's activities were grouped together with those of La Roche aux Fées in France and Jacky in Belgium. More important, in the area of refrigerated cold cuts, Nestlé acquired a minority interest in the German Herta group in 1985. (Herta was also present on other European markets, notably in France.) Nestlé increased its interest in Herta once again in 1986, becoming its principal shareholder; then, early in 1987, it acquired 100 percent of all Herta's shares. In the field of dairy products, Nestlé acquired part of the capital of Granja Castello, a Spanish firm. It continued to expand in the field of roasted coffee beans by acquiring an interest in Zoegas in Sweden (top-quality coffee) and by acquiring Heimbs in Germany (coffee for institutional customers) through Dallmayr, a German firm. In 1989, Nestlé terminated a cooperation agreement, which it had concluded in 1981 with Swissair, the Swiss airline company, concerning the creation of a Swissôtel chain of hotels. Except for Stouffer hotels in the U.S., which were completely under its own control, Nestlé no longer wished to remain globally active in this area.

In the U.S., the Nestlé group acquired L.J. Minor, a manufacturer of sauce bases (for restaurants in particular). Via Carnation, Nestlé acquired Pasta & Cheese (refrigerated products, such as fresh pasta and high-quality sauces). Stouffer continued to expand its hotel business by acquiring an interest in companies that owned hotels in the U.S. Alcon acquired Sharpoint's line of ophthalmic products (needles, surgical threads and instruments) as well as related production facilities. Acquiring Dr. Ballard's Pet Foods in Canada en-

NESTLÉ'S PARTICIPATION CAPITAL, CREATED IN 1984, WAS INCREASED IN 1987.

abled the Nestlé group to enter the pet-food market in that country. In 1986, Nestlé in creased its interest in Life Savers, an Australian candy and chocolate company. Early in 1987, Nestlé reached an agreement on a joint venture with Life Savers and Allen's Confectionery, a chocolate and candy manufacturer and subsidiary of Rothman's Holdings (with the Nestlé group holding 50 percent of the capital of the new company, Allen Life Savers). Elsewhere in Australia, Nestlé acquired the assets and trademarks of Blenders, a company marketing, among other items, Andronicus roasted coffee beans.

In 1986, Nestlé realized Sfr. 435,000,000 through disvestiture. First, Nestlé turned over to Unilever, with which it had been associated since 1970, its 25 percent interest in the field of frozen foods in Germany, Austria, and Italy. The company preferred to utilize its funds in operations it managed itself. It transferred control of the North American and European contact-lens divisions of Alcon to Ciba-Geigy, for Alcon had decided to concentrate its activities in the areas of ophthalmic products, products for eye surgeons, and contact-lens cleaning solution. Following a decree by the president of Peru, Nestlé was to sell its 60 percent interest in the locally based Gloria Company to Peruvian shareholders, who were already in possession of 40 percent of the firm's capital.

In 1987, a change in company financing took place with regard to the bearer participation certificates (B.P.C.s) Nestlé introduced in 1984. Nestlé's shareholders had agreed to add a new article to the company articles of association in 1984, providing for the issuing of B.P.C.s up to a maximum of one-tenth of Nestlé's share capital. The 1984 annual shareholders' meeting had also voted to give the board the right to issue one or more series of B.P.C.s up to that limit. By virtue of that authority, the board of directors decided to issue 1,050,000 certificates with a par value of SFr. 20 between October, 1984 and January, 1987, thus creating a Nestlé participation capital totaling SFr. 21,000,000. B.P.C.s were issued in six series, five being offered to the Swiss public as well as to foreigners and one being reserved for options linked to a U.S. subsidiary's bond issue. After deduction of taxes and administrative charges, the company generated a total of approximately SFr.1,300,000,000 in fresh funds by issuing these B.P.C.s.

Although the board still had the right (granted it in 1984) to issue 600,000 more B.P.C.s, it felt that there might be an insufficient number of certificates available should opportunities to acquire big, attractive firms arise in the future. As B.P.C.s were a flexible form of ensuring financing at a reasonable

COMPANY PROFITS GREW IN 1987. THE COMPANY ADOPTED A GLOBAL STRATEGY. IN 1987, NESTLÉ INAUGURATED ITS RESEARCH CENTER IN SWITZERLAND, ON THE OUTSKIRTS OF LAUSANNE.

cost, Nestlé's board of directors suggested raising the limit of the company's participation capital from 10 to 20 percent of its share capital. The board's proposal was approved at the annual shareholders' meeting on May 21, 1987.

Under the combined effect of fluctuations in exchange rates and the price of coffee beans, Nestlé's turnover dropped from its 1986 level of SFr. 38,050,000,000 to SFr. 35,241,000,000 in 1987. However, Nestlé's profits increased from SFr. 1,789,000,000 in 1986 to SFr. 1,827,000,000 in 1987.

This satisfactory performance—a result of Nestlé's strong internal growth—was the result of the strategy the Nestlé group had adopted since Helmut Maucher had been placed at the head of the company in 1981. There had been no break with Nestlé's traditional policy during previous decades; however, it now took on a new dimension. Earlier we pointed out that Nestlé's long-term policy has always been extremely flexible, enabling the company to adapt to constantly changing economic conditions.

The global strategy of the company requires that Nestlé's production and marketing be highly decentralized, thus enabling it to adapt to local conditions and to better resist erratic business trends. As a result, the Nestlé group has always tried to maintain a very wide geographic base and granted a high degree of independence to its locally based firms—two factors that have increased Nestlé's ability to adapt to new situations. The necessity of maintaining a single corporate culture in all the Nestlé companies, of ensuring that they regularly exchange information on their activities, and of offering employees training, refresher, or job reclassification courses is the third important element in Nestlé's strategy. Finally, R & D has always played a decisive role in the group's development. The Nestlé Research Center, which was opened in 1986 at Vers-chez-les-Blanc, in the suburbs of Lausanne, engages in basic research. In addition, Nestlé possesses eighteen centers throughout the world that develop new products and new production processes.

Aerial view of the Nestlé Research Center (N.R.C.) at Vers-chez-les-Blanc, Switzerland

The official inauguration of the Nestlé Research Center (N.R.C.) at Vers-chez-les-Blanc, approximately 12 1/2 miles from Vevey, within the Lausanne

Plant-tissue culture at the N.R.C.

DIFFERENT BRANCHES OF RESEARCH WERE GROUPED TOGETHER UNDER ONE ROOF.

city limits, took place on June 4, 1987. It is the company's only laboratory complex where scientists are engaged in basic research. The SFr.200,000,000 laboratories and facilities at Vers-chez-les-Blanc serve as the main hub in Nestlé's research network. In addition to this complex, Nestlé also possesses an international network of eighteen development centers situated in ten countries throughout the world: Ecuador, the Federal Republic of Germany, France, Italy, Great Britain, Singapore, Spain, Sweden, Switzerland, and the United States. Besides basic research for long-term projects—often with no clear commercial application at the outset—the N.R.C. develops new scientific concepts, while the eighteen development centers have clearly defined commercial objectives: to prepare new products and new technologies, and to constantly improve existing ones. This type of applied research may require scientific support—which is also the job of the N.R.C., since not all Nestlé development centers throughout the world are equipped with the specialized laboratories needed to carry out such research.

For years, Nestlé has oriented its research toward the study of food and nutrition, in which major progress has been made. (This tendency was already mentioned when we discussed the inauguration of Nestlé's laboratories at La Tour-de-Peilz, near Vevey, in 1950.) In 1987, all those facilities as well as new, improved ones were transferred to Vers-chez-les-Blanc. Consequently, the construction of the N.R.C. was an important step, enabling the company to make new efforts to meet its future needs. Nestlé's management felt that establishing the new nutritional research laboratories was "not only important for Nestlé's future, but also contributed to better nutrition for [all] mankind."

Because basic research is both universal and interdisciplinary, grouping specialists in chemistry, physics, biology, electronics, bacteriology, physiology, immunology, experimental medicine, toxicology, psychobiology, mathematics, etc. under one roof makes it possible for the scientists engaged in this on-going and necessary work to cooperate actively with one another.

Today, the usefulness of such an institution is even more obvious: for there is still not enough food available in certain regions of the world; and, in the world's richest countries, the nutritional value of food often leaves much to be desired. At the opening of the N.R.C., Carl Angst, Nestlé's executive vice-president in charge—among other things—of the company's technical and scientific departments, pointed out: "The lack of nutritious food, on the one hand, and overeating, on the other, means that millions of men and women [have] an unbalanced diet." And Angst continued: "Detailed knowledge of the requirements of the human body is necessary to correct this hardly satisfactory—often unacceptable—situation." Indeed, when diseases caused or exacerbated by poor nutrition are taken into consideration, nutritional research becomes both essential and urgent.

MORE THAN 1 PERCENT OF NESTLÉ'S TURNOVER IS DEVOTED TO RESEARCH.

This is why the N.R.C.'s almost four hundred research scientists are attempting to determine the effects of food on the state and function of the human body so as to determine its nutritional requirements. Since the concept of the "average man" is a myth that simply does not exist in reality, these scientists are trying to discover the particular requirements of children, teenagers, adults, the elderly, as well as healthy and unhealthy men and women. They are studying the transformation that occurs in the food we eat and also seeking to achieve a thorough understanding of the characteristics and behavior of living organisms. The problem is a huge one; therefore, any contribution to its solution, no matter how small, is desirable.

Operating on a worldwide scale, the N.R.C. brings together, under one roof, several scientific branches engaged in the study of food science; Nestlé's staff concentrates particularly on the main building blocks of food—carbohydrates, proteins, and fats—and on nutrition, the major area of study at the center. Nutrition is not a separate branch of science, but rather a coming together of several different scientific branches. Nor does Nestlé's research program ignore the developing countries: utilization of locally available raw materials in certain Third World countries is also taken into account. In addition, diseases of modern civilization are being studied from the standpoint of eating habits. Finally, an entire department of the center pursues studies in the field of food science, i.e., applying the various regulations relating to food so as to ensure that the food we buy contains nothing harmful to human beings or detrimental to their development.

Latinreco, Nestlé's technological development center in Ecuador, studies different varieties of local plants such as quinoa

To sum up, the N.R.C. determines the requirements of the Nestlé group in the area of scientific research, develops and transmits the knowledge and

IN 1988,
NESTLÉ CONTINUED
TO PREPARE ITSELF
FOR CHANGES
IN THE COMMON
MARKET ANNOUNCED
FOR 1993.

experience it acquires, and offers technical assistance to various divisions of the company. Owing to the high quality of its technical assistance, the center also plays an important part in Nestlé's inventions and in the constantly improving quality of Nestlé products and the techniques used to produce them (food value, organoleptic quality, etc.). At the same time, the center improves existing Nestlé products and, mainly on the basis of analytical and nutritional studies, evaluates new products and processes. The N.R.C. is not an ivory tower; it cannot achieve its objectives unless it interacts constantly with the various divisions and development centers of the Nestlé group. In addition, the center is also be in constant contact with certain universities and research institutes working on these same problems.

In short, the N.R.C. concept of food research is a deeply human one, for all the effort of this scientific division is directed toward helping mankind. In 1989, Nestlé spent SFr.500,000,000 on research—a considerable amount for the food industry.

Nestle's acquisitions and sales of companies more or less offset each other in 1987. Internal company growth increased by 4 to 5 percent, owing, in particular, to bigger market shares. The fruit of improvements obtained as the result of considerable efforts, this growth and comfortable increase in profits may be attributed to a specifically industrial type of management. We should also point out that Nestlé was able to increase its profits from 4.7 to 5.2 percent, in spite of an average decline of more than 7 percent in its sales figure, primarily through the numerous improvements the company had managed to make at every level and through cooperation between various branches of the company resulting from previous acquisitions.

In the spring of 1988, Nestlé's decision to acquire Buitoni in Italy and its take-over bid for Rowntree in Great Britain were in keeping with the same industrial strategy: increasing Nestlé's presence in Europe in preparation for 1993, strengthening one of the firm's traditional products—chocolate—through geographic and product diversification (expanding its range of confectionery products with chocolate bars and related items), particularly in countries in which the market share of such products had been too small in comparison with other Nestlé products. None of this, however, was to affect Nestlé's desire to maintain proper geographic distribution of its worldwide sales.

1988: An Exceptional Year—Nestlé Acquires Buitoni-Perugina and Rowntree, and Permits Foreigners to Own Registered Nestlé Shares

THE PASTA MANUFACTURER BUITONI JOINS THE NESTLÉ GROUP. BUITONI, AN ITALIAN MULTINATIONAL,

☐ Three important events stand out in 1988. Nestlé's acquisition of Buitoni-Perugina (manufacturers of pasta, olive oil, cold cuts, and chocolates in Italy, as well as ready-to-eat canned goods and frozen food in France); its acquisition of the British chocolate and candy manufacturer, Rowntree; and its decision to facilitate the owning of registered shares by foreigners (up to a maximum of 3 percent per shareholder).

Nestlé paid SFr. 6,600,000,000 to acquire Rowntree and SFr. 1,800,000,000 for Buitoni-Perugina. The company's 1988 turnover increased by 15 percent, reaching SFr. 40,685,000,000; while consolidated net profits totaled SFr. 2,038,000,000 (including Buitoni-Perugina and Rowntree sales for the second half of 1988). With production facilities in sixty countries throughout the world, the number of Nestlé's factories increased from 373 to 428. In addition to its acquisitions, the company's rate of internal growth—nearly 4 percent—was proof of its soundness. This performance was made possible by Nestlé's efforts in the areas of R & D and marketing, resulting in the success of a number of its products on new markets. The company also increased the number of its employees, from 163,030 at the end of 1987, to 197,722 in 1988. These figures prove that 1988 was indeed an exceptional year for Nestlé; and, thus, it might be worthwhile to focus our attention, for a moment, on the major transactions that took place in 1988.

Nestlé's acquisition of Buitoni-Perugina, Italy's third biggest food company, with headquarters in Perugia, took place in July, 1988. From Nestlé's point of view, there were clearly defined policy considerations underlying this acquisition. After having ensured its presence in North America by acquiring Carnation in 1985, Nestlé, which was strengthening its position on the European market to prepare for the enlarged Common Market in 1993, achieved a prominent position in Italy and in France—which generated 43 and 34 percent of Buitoni's consolidated sales respectively. Merging with Nestlé provided an opportunity to emphasize both the European and global appeal of its range of the Italian group's products.

Nestlé acquired an Italian multinational with a turnover of 2,082,000,000,000 lira (SFr. 2,300,000,000), half generated by foreign

WAS FOUNDED IN 1827. BUITONI BEGAN PRODUCTION IN THE U.S. IN 1941.

subsidiaries. Of Buitoni-Perugina's 7,903 employees, 4,942 worked in Italy. (Seventeen of the Italian firm's twenty-five production facilities were located in Italy.) This acquisition also enabled Nestlé to make the best use of the growth potential of Buitoni's products for Italian cooking, which was rapidly becoming increasingly popular throughout the world.

Buitoni had long enjoyed an excellent reputation both in Italy and abroad. The company was founded by Giovan Battista Buitoni and his wife, Giulia Boninsegni. In 1827, they opened a small pasta factory at Sansepolcro in the Arezzo province of Tuscany, and then two other factories: one at Città del Castello in 1856, and the other at Perugia in 1878. Giovanni Buitoni, the founder's son, left the firm to his children. In 1907, one of these—Francesco Buitoni—founded a jam and chocolate company, La Perugina.

Before going into more detail about La Perugina, we shall first trace the development of Buitoni S.p.A. At the turn of the century, the name Buitoni was synonymous with high-quality products all over Italy and abroad. (The company had won several awards at international food competitions.) In 1922, Buitoni opened its new pasta factory in Rome. In 1930, under Giovanni Buitoni, the founder's great grandson, the firm went into the field of packaging, with the establishment of Buitoni Poligrafico. In 1935, a French subsidiary, Buitoni S.A., opened a pasta and canned goods factory at Saint-Maur-des-Fossés, near Paris. The French Buitoni Company's start was difficult: the French still ate very little pasta at the time; and, in Rome, the Italian government was preventing Buitoni's parent company from transferring funds to its subsidiary. Moreover, strikes halted production at the French firm's factory for months in 1936. Sales finally began to increase during the Paris World's Fair in 1937.

Giulia Boninsegni, known as "Mamma Buitoni" (1791–1877)

In 1941, Buitoni Foods Corporation was founded in the U.S., where Giovanni Buitoni and his wife resided. Overcoming initial difficulties—contacts between Italy and the U.S. were interrupted from the outbreak of World War II until the end of 1941—the company strengthened its position. It possessed a pasta factory in Jersey City, New Jersey, a sauce factory in Brooklyn, New York (the first to market sauces in glass jars), a restaurant on Times Square in New York City (in business from 1939 to 1960), as well as a Perugina deluxe chocolate shop on Fifth Avenue. All of these activities were controlled by Buitoni's New York City management. Contacts with Europe were rapidly reestablished in 1945.

Cover of the 1906 Buitoni catalog

AFTER THE WAR, THE BUITONI GROUP CONTINUED EXPANDING, PARTICULARLY IN EUROPE. OVER THE YEARS, PERUGINA, FOUNDED BY F. BUITONI IN 1907, BECAME A WELL-KNOWN CHOCOLATE MANUFACTURER.

At the end of the war, the European Buitoni group began a period of reconstruction and rapid expansion: factories were built at Sansepolcro in 1946, at Aprilla and at Foggia in 1961, and at Camaret, France, in 1966. During the 1950s, in order to become more competitive, the group centralized control of its European activities, putting Giovanni Buitoni in charge of Internazionale Buitoni Organizzazione (I.B.O.). After its U.S. subsidiary was incorporated in 1966, Buitoni combined with La Perugina in 1969, forming Industrie Buitoni Perugina S.p.A. (I.B.P.), in order to maximize the combined benefits of Perugina's financial resources and Buitoni's industrial and commercial potential. In 1972, I.B.P. was listed on the Milan and Rome stock exchanges. In the late 1960s and early 1970s, the group expanded into Great Britain (notably thanks to its Prince brand, following the acquisition of Bibby's), Holland, and Sweden, and continued expanding in France, where new trade and production facilities were set up. The group was also present in Brazil.

Companies with headquarters in Italy suffered seriously from the economic crisis of the 1970s, however. Increasing interest rates, inflation, and a lack of flexibility in the labor market had a much stronger impact on these firms than on foreign firms. Once market conditions had returned to normal, Buitoni held a public sale of a part of La Perugina in order to increase the liquid assets of the group, for, lacking resources, the division of nonconfectionery items found it hard to remain competitive with big national and international companies.

Buitoni pasta factory at Sansepolcro, Italy, ca. 1930

Before continuing with the story of Buitoni, let us trace the development of La Perugina. La Perugina was founded in 1907 by Francesco Buitoni and three partners, who left the company in 1921. Fabbrica Perugina per la produzione dei confetti, the firm's original name, started production in Umbria, Italy. In 1909, Giovanni Buitoni, Francesco's eighteen-year-old son, took control of the firm (which was doing very badly) and began to put it back on its feet. (It showed a profit for the first time in 1910.) In 1914, the company moved from its cramped, uncomfortable quarters in the Via Alessi in Perugia to a spacious, new factory with modern equipment at Fontivegge, near the railway station of Perugia. La Perugina was already an industrial firm operating on a national scale; its range of products included sugar-coated almonds, chocolates, caramels and toffee, and powdered cocoa. Among Giovanni Buitoni's various assistants was Luisa Spagnoli, who had founded a firm that manufactured angora wool and, later, a chain of fashionable shops, which were to acquire an international reputation. By 1917, La Perugina was a very well-known firm, which outperformed virtually all its major competitors in northern Italy. Its reputation was based on the high quality of Perugina products.

IN 1969, BUITONI MERGED WITH PERUGINA.

La Perugina, a joint-stock company up to that point, was incorporated in 1921, with Francesco Buitoni as chairman, Giovanni Buitoni as c.e.o., and Luisa Spagnoli on the board of directors. (Mario Spagnoli, Luisa's son, also actively contributed to the company's success for many years.) In 1922, Giovanni Buitoni and Luisa Spagnoli created Baci Perugina, deluxe chocolate kisses (ground-hazelnut pralines, covered with dark chocolate). The phenomenal success of Baci Perugina, with their popular flavor and very carefully designed packaging, was the main reason for the company's enormous success in Italy. La Perugina changed its name to Perugina Cioccolato e Confetture in 1923.

In the 1930s, Perugina was one of the first Italian companies to sponsor popular radio programs. This had a great impact on general Italian culture at the time and showed that Perugina knew how to fully exploit the potential of advertising. In the same decade, the company also set up a chain of shops that sold the entire range of Perugina products. (Perugina's shops were sold in 1980, except for the one located on Lexington Avenue in New York.) When television was introduced in the 1950s, Perugina, which sold 20 percent of all chocolate marketed in Italy, launched a large-scale television advertising campaign. By associating them with two holidays of English-speaking countries—Mother's Day and Valentine's Day—the company strengthened the appeal of its beautifully wrapped deluxe Baci Perugina. Early in the 1960s, Perugina, a thriving firm thanks to new products and excellent publicity campaigns, launched several more new items, including Carrarmato, Bonheur, and Flippers chocolates. It built a new factory at Perugia in 1963, and another at Castiglione del Lago in 1975.

First box of Baci, Perugina's chocolate kisses, 1922

As for Buitoni, it merged with Perugina in 1969, forming the multinational company Industrie Buitoni Perugina (I.B.P.). Later on, Perugina was to enter the field of cakes and fruitcakes—Pannettone, Pandoro, and Colomba in

IN 1985, BUITONI-PERUGINA WAS ACQUIRED BY CIR, WHICH SUBSEQUENTLY SOLD THE FIRM TO NESTLÉ IN 1988. ALL PARTIES TO THE TRANSACTION WERE IN TOTAL AGREEMENT CONCERNING THIS ACQUISITION.

particular—using chocolate to give them a novel touch. The company also began to sell packaged pastries.

On February 4, 1985, CIR S.p.A. (the holding company of Carlo de Benedetti's industrial group) took control of the entire I.B.P. group. The company's name was immediately changed from I.B.P. to Buitoni S.p.A. Its balance sheet was consolidated, and the holding company injected fresh funds into its new acquisition. Buitoni's management was rejuvenated; various departments (especially marketing) were reorganized, making the firm competitive once again not only within the context of EC countries but also on an international scale. The group's performance improved; and, between 1985 and 1987, sales doubled.

When the firm was acquired by Nestlé, Buitoni pasta had a solid foothold on many European markets, as well as that of Japan and Saudi Arabia. For several years, Buitoni had been expanding its range of deluxe-quality pasta, launching Rasagnole in 1985, and Preziose and Bella Napoli brand pasta in 1987. By 1988, Buitoni was the market leader in the sale of ready-to-eat sauces and canned items (ravioli, cannelloni, couscous, and paella) in France. The company's sauces and ravioli were also available in a certain number of other European countries. Primarily in France, Buitoni was in the process of expanding its line of frozen foods within the context of the Nestlé Food Service, thanks to Davigel products (acquired in 1986), distributed to restaurants, hotels, and institutional clients. In the field of dried breads, Buitoni was present on the Italian market with its traditional round rusks, its wholewheat Linea integrale products, and Il cestino di Buitoni, varieties of toast. The group also became one of the main Italian producers of olive oil (after acquiring P. Sasso e Figli in 1987), cold cuts (after absorbing Vismara the same year—which, in turn, absorbed King's in 1988), Berni bottled condiments (acquired in 1986), and Curtiriso rice (acquired in 1985). The pasta manufacturer Pezzullo was to join the Buitoni group in 1987.

In the meantime, Perugina improved its sales network, increasing its range of products and expanding even further on Europe's markets. In June, 1987, the company acquired Bouquet d'Or, a French firm with headquarters in Lille, giving it access to the latter's large share of the French market for boxed high-quality chocolates.

How did Nestlé happen to purchase the flourishing Buitoni-Perugina group from Carlo de Benedetti? Benedetti, who needed liquid assets for various transactions in Europe, had decided to sell Buitoni, a company active in

Buitoni pasta factory at Sansepolcro: machine producing nest-shaped rasagnole

WHICH PAVED THE WAY TO A PROMISING FUTURE IN THE FIELD OF ITALIAN COOKING.

a field in which the primarily communications-oriented Italian industrialist felt no desire to expand. With his foray into the food industry, Benedetti discovered its particular nature, requiring state-of-the-art technology in specific areas and offering only meager profit margins. Furthermore, Benedetti did not plan to acquire big food companies in Italy. As a result, he only wished to retain certain branches of his food company.

It so happened that Carlo de Benedetti and Helmut Maucher were already acquainted with one another, having met at several important meetings such as the European Round Table, a forum of European industrialists with a keen interest in European economic issues. Both men had participated in the Round Table ever since it was established. Moreover, Benedetti had confidence in Nestlé's overall reputation and the solidity of the group's financial situation. Once contacts had been made and the basis for an understanding worked out, the acquisition took place rather quickly.

Acquisitions cannot be described solely in terms of figures. Indeed, the overall situation of a company, its strategic potential, and the advantages offered by cooperation are all highly important—often even more important—factors. At least 50 percent of the ultimate success of an acquisition depends on the particular steps a company takes after deciding to make it. It is necessary to determine how the senior executives of the company acquired can be properly motivated and their participation encouraged. In the view of Helmut Maucher, they must be convinced, from the outset, that they are on an equal footing with the senior executives in the company acquiring them. For this reason, the chief executive must visit each newly acquired company, not in order to make promises he is unable to keep, but rather to establish personal contact with his new associates as soon as possible. Therefore, as he would later do following Nestlé's acquisition of Rowntree, Maucher went to Buitoni-Perugina's headquarters in Perugia and introduced himself to the managers of the company Nestlé was about to acquire.

Nestlé set up a "strategic Buitoni pasta unit" in Italy and at Vevey in order to ensure the best use of the new skills it now possessed as a result of the acquisition as well as that of the acquired company's products for Italian cooking. The new unit, part of the Culinary Products Division at Vevey, consisted of experts from both Buitoni and Nestlé. This unit was actually a center for Italian cooking and for information on the Italian way of life. In acquiring Buitoni, Nestlé had more than merely business or pasta in mind: "I also purchased a concept, the Italian manner of living and cooking," explained

Helmut Maucher. Clearly, in Maucher's view, the multinational for which he is responsible is capable of making the Italian way of life and Italian eating habits known throughout the world. And, in this connection, it is only natural that a small strategic unit should be deeply rooted in Buitoni's homeland—Italy. This unit, under the control of the division manager of Culinary Products at Vevey, serves to keep the Buitoni philosophy alive.

NESTLE'S 1988 ACQUISITION OF ROWNTREE, A BRITISH FIRM MORE THAN ONE HUNDRED YEARS OLD, CAUSED CONSIDERABLE UPROAR.

☐ Nestle's second acquisition in 1988—that of Rowntree—was less tranquil than that of Buitoni. Rowntree, with headquarters in York in northeastern England, had always been proud of being an independent company and, since its inception, had deep roots in its city of origin. (The inhabitants of York were deeply attached to Rowntree as well.) People in York could not imagine Rowntree's being purchased by a Swiss multinational. (Of course, nowhere are people happy to see a hundred-year-old firm in their locality absorbed by a bigger company—and a foreign one at that!)

Rowntree was one of Britain's foremost companies, with fifty of its Kit Kat bars—Rowntree's leading product—being consumed in that country every second, making its acquisition by a non-British group even harder to accept. In the city of York and in the nearby village of New Earswick (built by Joseph Rowntree to allow a sample population of blue-collar and white-collar workers to live together), Rowntree's approximately 5,500 employees, who lived with their families in an urban center of 100,000 inhabitants, began fearing for their jobs as soon as they heard talk of a merger. In addition, Rowntree had social commitments to York that were quite beneficial to the city: training for many young boys and girls; a one-year training course for school principals, enabling them to learn more about the business world and to pass that knowledge on to their students; sponsorship of the arts and charity events relating to health, education, and aid to children; paying company employees up to one or two years for work on public welfare projects, etc. These factors, together with the fact that Rowntree had always been well able to ensure its own expansion, gave rise to a great deal of discontent as soon as it became known that Nestlé might acquire the company. In order to better understand this reaction, we must take a closer look at the Rowntree saga.

Like many other companies involved in the food industry, Rowntree began as a simple grocery store. In 1725, a Quaker named Mary Tuke opened a store at Walmgate in York. Under the name William Tuke and Sons,

FOR FORTY YEARS, THE COMPANY BORE THE STAMP OF JOSEPH ROWNTREE, WHO PURSUED QUITE BOLD SOCIAL POLICIES.

she expanded her business, specializing in the sale of tea, chocolate, and roasted coffee beans. In 1862, the owners sold their interest in chocolate and cocoa to another Quaker, Henry Isaac Rowntree, who purchased a foundry in York in 1864 and transformed it into a production facility. In 1869, when Henry Rowntree went into business with his brother Joseph, H.I. Rowntree & Co. came into existence. It produced and marketed two main products: Superior Rock Cocoa and Homeopathic Cocoa. By 1879, nearly one hundred persons were employed by the company. In 1881, the firm began selling fruit-flavored gumdrops (a French specialty up to that time); these were a success from the very start. In 1887, the firm was also successful with its Elect Cocoa, a powdered dark chocolate that it manufactured and marketed.

When Henry I. Rowntree died in 1883, Joseph Rowntree retained sole control of the company. John Wilhelm Rowntree, Joseph's son, began working with his father in 1885, as did his brother, Seebohm Rowntree, somewhat later. The family firm was incorporated in 1897 as Rowntree & Company, Ltd., with Joseph Rowntree as its first chairman. Shortly afterward, the company moved its remaining production facilities from the old factory on Haxby Road to a large piece of land just outside the York city limits, where it had built a new factory in 1890. The group's headquarters are still there today, as are its biggest production facility for the products that made Rowntree so famous.

Henry Isaac Rowntree (1838–1883)

Rowntree's sales soon increased, as did the number of its employees, which reached 1,200 at the turn of the century. As a Quaker, Joseph Rowntree could hardly fail to encourage the well-being of his employees. In 1902, for example, he started the *Cocoa Works Magazine,* precursor of the 1969 company newspaper, *Rowntree Mackintosh News;* in 1904, he hired a physician and a dentist to provide his employees with free medical care. He started a pension fund in 1906—one of the first in the United Kingdom. Joseph Rowntree was not only a philanthropist, but also an excellent businessman, who knew how to combine the efficiency required for success with a concern for his associates' needs. That was one of his reasons for building a model village at New Earswick, on the outskirts of York, on land near Rowntree's factory. It also strengthened the esprit de corps of the company's employees. This resulted in great pride in the company's accomplishments and products—a pride characteristic of every Rowntree community, in Great Britain and abroad.

ROWNTREE MERGED WITH MACKINTOSH IN 1969.

Joseph Rowntree died in 1925. In the years following his death, the company (which employed more than 7,000 persons) gradually began to prosper under Seebohm Rowntree's leadership. Subsidiaries were set up in South Africa, Ireland, Australia, and Canada. An innovative policy for choosing brand names was initiated and new products launched. Among these were Black Magic (an assortment of dark chocolates), Aero (aerated milk-chocolate bar), Kit Kat bars (chocolate-covered wafers), and Smarties (sugar-coated chocolate drops). Each of these brands soon made a name for itself the world over. Seebohm Rowntree stepped down as chairman in 1941. (He died in 1954.) His successor was George James Harris. While Rowntree's marketing director in the 1930s, Harris had laid the foundations of the company's commercial strategy, thus ensuring its future success. He introduced products customers wanted, gave those products a unique identity and distinctive brand name, and provided the advertising needed to attract consumers. Harris had been instrumental in putting the company back on its feet in the 1930s, and he had married a member of the Rowntree family. When Harris stepped down in 1952, he was succeeded by William Wallace. Lloyd Owen became chairman in 1957, and Donald Barron took over from Owen in 1966. In an effort to expand further in Europe, Rowntree began production in Germany in 1964, and in Belgium, Holland, and Italy in 1965.

In 1969, General Foods, a U.S. giant in the food industry, made a £37,000,000 take-over bid for Rowntree; but this bid was rejected. Soon afterward, Rowntree merged with John Mackintosh & Sons, Ltd., a company already linked to Rowntree owing to various regional agreements. By 1970, the new firm exported its products to more than 120 countries.

Model village of New Earswick, near York, England

Like Rowntree, Mackintosh, too, began as a single store. In 1890, John Mackintosh and his wife Violet opened a pastry shop in Halifax. Interested in finding a speciality to attract customers, they thought of creating a mixture of English toffee and American soft toffee. Quite naturally, they named their new product—the basis of modern toffee—Mackintosh's Celebrated Toffee.

IN 1988, ROWNTREE WAS THE WORLD'S FOURTH BIGGEST MANUFACTURER OF CHOCOLATES AND OTHER CONFECTIONERY ITEMS.

Incorporated in 1899 under the name John Mackintosh, Ltd., the company was already exporting to Italy, Spain, and China by 1903. It opened its first U.S. factory in 1904 and began marketing its first chocolate in 1912. John Mackintosh died in 1920; he was succeeded by his son, Harold Mackintosh, who was knighted in 1935, became Lord Mackintosh of Halifax in 1948, and viscount in 1957. He died in 1964 and was succeeded by his brother, Eric Mackintosh, the following year. In 1921, the company, which already employed 1,000 persons, changed its name to John Mackintosh & Sons, Ltd. In 1932, it acquired the Caley chocolate company, founded at Norwich in 1860. This acquisition enabled Mackintosh to develop products that combined chocolate and toffee. Quality Street and Rolo candies quickly became Mackintosh's most important brands. After it merged with Rowntree, the company's name was changed to Rowntree Mackintosh, Ltd. The group, which employed 28,800 persons in 1971, possessed twenty-two factories.

Now an even stronger company, Rowntree was to widen the scope of its activities. During the next eighteen years, it made several acquisitions, especially in Europe, pursuing a policy it had initiated in 1964. Among its acquisitions were the French companies Chocolat-Menier S.A. (1971), Chocolat Ibled S.A. (1973), and Chocolaterie Lanvin S.A., Dijon (1977); the Dutch company Nuts Chocoladefabriek BV (1979); and—elsewhere in the world—the Australian firm James Stedman, Ltd., Australia (1971); the Canadian firm Laura Secord (1983); and the U.S. firm Sunmark (1986). In 1982, the company again changed its name to Rowntree Mackintosh plc; and it became Rowntree plc in 1987.

By the beginning of 1988, Rowntree had become the world's fourth biggest manufacturer of confectionery items and chocolates (after the U.S. firms Mars and Hershey, and the British firm, Cadbury). Rowntree's sales accounted for 37 percent of all sales in this area in Great Britain. The company marketed its products in Europe, the U.S., and Oceania and owed its comfortable share of the market to a remarkable group of brand-name products, including Kit Kat bars, Quality Street candies and chocolates, Rolo mints, multicolored Smarties (sugar-coated chocolate drops), chocolate-covered After Eight mints, Nuts (a chocolate-coated hazelnut bar), and Lion bars. Rowntree's 1987 turnover was £1,400,000,000 (more than SFr. 3,600,000,000), and it employed 33,000 persons at company headquarters and at its more than twenty-five subsidiaries. It possessed eleven

Corporate advertisement in Great Britain for Rowntree Kit Kat bars, 1987

ITS ACTIVITIES COMPLEMENTED THOSE OF NESTLÉ. NESTLE'S TAKE-OVER BID WAS DISCUSSED IN THE FINANCIAL SECTION OF NEWSPAPERS AROUND THE WORLD;

factories in the United Kingdom, as well as nineteen abroad (in South Africa, Australia, Canada, the U.S., Ireland, Holland, France, and West Germany). In 1989, Rowntree plc became Rowntree, Ltd.

Nestlé was understandably attracted by the prospect of acquiring Rowntree, whose range of confectionery items and chocolates was the perfect complement to its own products. Nestlé's own activity in this field was concentrated mainly in the area of chocolate bars; while Rowntree specialized in chocolate-covered bars and various other confectionery items.

Because of its presence the world over and its financial strength, Nestlé felt it would be able to promote Rowntree products on markets such as that of South Africa, where they were hardly—if at all—available. Moreover, for several years, Nestlé had been convinced that it must expand its range of chocolates and other confectionery items. Company managers never lost sight of the fact that, since 1929, when it merged with P.C.K., Nestlé had always been active in the field of chocolates. In addition to the fact that both Nestlé's and Rowntree's products and geographic distribution complemented each other very well, a merger with the British firm would enable Nestlé to increase its sales of chocolates and other confectionery items, which accounted for only 8 percent of its turnover at the time (but was to reach 15 percent in 1989, following the merger). Nestlé was attempting to increase its market presence in Britain in any case.

In view of these developments, it is not surprising, then, that great secrecy was to surround contacts between the heads of both companies—Helmut Maucher and Kenneth H.M. Dixon, chairman of Rowntree since 1981. The two men did not discuss a take-over, but rather the possibility of cooperating financially with one another (with Nestlé possibly purchasing a 25 percent interest in Rowntree). Nothing was decided, however. Nestlé restricted itself to considering the possibility of future cooperation with the British firm, and it acquired none of Rowntree's shares at the time, as Rowntree wished to remain independent. On April 13, 1988, another big Swiss manufacturer of chocolates and roasted coffee, the Jacobs-Suchard group, acquired 15 percent of Rowntree's shares and announced its intention to increase its interest in Rowntree to 25 percent.

Kenneth H.M. Dixon

Circumstances now forced Nestlé to break with a 122-year-old tradition and make a hostile take-over bid for Rowntree—a weapon, as we have seen, that Nestlé had never employed previously. On April 26, Nestlé offered Rowntree shareholders 890 pence per share. On May 5, Jacobs-Suchard acquired an additional 15 per cent of Rowntree's shares, bringing its stake in the company up to 30 percent. (In the meantime, Nestlé had acquired a 15.8 percent interest in the British firm.) On May 25, after an impassioned battle involving political parties, trade unions, and the media in Britain, the British government decided that, in keeping with the laws of its free enterprise system, a foreign group should be allowed to take over Rowntree. On May 26, Jacobs-Suchard offered a take-over bid of 950 pence per share for all of Rowntree's share capital. This was the opening move in a battle for control of the English company. Helmut Maucher (who successfully negotiated this acquisition) was correct in stating that it was no longer a question of Rowntree's remaining independent (as it wished) but rather of discovering which firm would acquire it.

HOWEVER, A FRIENDLY AGREEMENT WAS FINALLY REACHED. AFTER THE TAKE-OVER, NESTLÉ SET UP A SPECIAL UNIT IN YORK.

Nestlé's bid—due to expire on June 8—was extended until June 20. Three days later, the board of directors of Nestlé S.A. and of Rowntree, Ltd. reached an agreement after Nestlé raised its offer to 1,075 pence per share (i.e., £10.75 cash). Nestlé's bid, which was 129 percent above the asking price for Rowntree shares on April 12, (i.e., the day before Jacobs-Suchard's "dawn raid") was £2,500,000,000 (SFr.6,600,000,000). Rowntree's board recommended that shareholders accept Nestlé's offer, thus transforming Nestlé's hostile take-over bid into a friendly one. On June 24, Klaus Jacobs, the head of Jacobs-Suchard, decided to sell his 30 percent interest in Rowntree to Nestlé. As a result, Nestlé now gained a controlling interest in Rowntree. Given the continued production of the Swiss company and the English firm, it was clear that, after acquiring Rowntree, the Nestlé group would become one of world's leading manufacturers of chocolates.

Rowntree factory in York, England: the library in the foreground is one of Rowntree's contributions to the cultural life of York

Nestlé set up a special "strategic unit for chocolates, candy, and cookies" to prepare for the more important role confectionery items and chocolates were to play within the Nestlé group in the future and to formalize cooperation between the two companies. While it does not replace Nestlé's geographically based management structure, the new unit does play an important role in the group's development. The "strategic unit for chocolates, candy, and cookies" is based in

ROWNTREE'S EMPLOYEES EASILY ACCEPTED THE TAKE-OVER.

York. In 1988, this unit was placed under the control of Rowntree's chairman, Kenneth Dixon, who became an executive vice-president of Nestlé after the merger (residing in York and Vevey).

This was the first time in Nestlé's history that one of its product divisions, having direct links with nearby production facilities, was managed outside of Vevey. Nestlé's management made this strategic decision in order to continue to motivate an important group of employees devoting all their energy to a single field—that of confectionery items and chocolates. It was important to safeguard the single-minded pursuit of that goal, one of Rowntree's great strengths. This strategic unit, which coordinates activities relating to these products on a worldwide scale, also comprises staff divisions such as marketing, research, technology, etc.

How did Rowntree employees in York react to their company's merger with Nestlé? In November, 1988, Kenneth Dixon answered a question on this subject in an issue of both companies' newspapers printed in French and English in Vevey and York: "Once it became clear that Rowntree could not stay independent, the board was keen to recommend to our shareholders the best partner for the future." Dixon pointed out that the negotiations were very hard on a great many Rowntree's employees, especially in the United Kingdom, where everyone felt concerned. But he added: "Now that that period of uncertainty is over, there is, I believe, a sense of relief that if Rowntree could not remain independent and somebody had to win, that the winner was Nestlé. Now, although obviously there are many questions still to be answered, there are already positive signs." Dixon continued: "Nevertheless, we all still need time to accept fully this new and different situation. But already I think I can say that those...who have had contacts with Nestlé people are finding that your ways of tackling problems, like the problems themselves, are very similar to ours. This is helping to create confidence in each other...."

Asked what Rowntree employees thought of Nestlé, Dixon said: "For the vast majority of our employees, the most important point is job security. Nestlé has brought changes, of course, but provided that these do not affect job security—and in certain cases jobs will be even safer than in the past—confidence will revive. While it is clear that this will take time, I detect signs showing not only that the employees accept the situation, but that they are taking it as something very positive." In August, 1989, Kenneth Dixon reached retirement age and passed his job on to Peter Blackburn, who had played an important role as Rowntree's representative in the merger discussions with Nestlé.

At the 1989 annual shareholders' meeting, Paul Jolles, chairman of the board, expressed Nestlé's satisfaction with the acquisitions of Buitoni-Perugina and Rowntree as follows: "The good relations that exist [between Nestlé and] the managers of Buitoni and Rowntree have made it easy to integrate them [into our firm], and the effects of [our] cooperation will soon be visible."

IN 1988, NESTLÉ DECIDED TO MAKE ITS REGISTERED SHARES AVAILABLE TO FOREIGNERS. NESTLÉ WISHED TO REMAIN AN INDEPENDENT, PUBLICLY OWNED COMPANY...

☐ The third important event in 1988 was announced in a press release that caused quite a stir on Swiss stock exchanges. It stated that Nestlé's board of directors, under authority granted by the company's articles of association, decided at its November 17, 1988 meeting to henceforth allow foreigners to acquire registered shares. Formerly, these shares—first issued in 1956—had been reserved solely for Swiss citizens. (Registered shares accounted for two-thirds of Nestlé's share capital.) When registered shares were initially issued by Nestlé, it was felt that this restriction would ensure that the firm would remain a Swiss entity.

The board was well aware both of the risks to which it was exposing the company and the uproar that would be caused by its sudden decision to make registered shares available to foreigners. Therefore, Nestlé took steps to ensure that it would remain an independent, publicly owned company, while remaining faithful to a fundamental principle: Nestlé's annual shareholders' meeting "is and must remain the supreme authority of the company." While relinquishing its right to stop the transfer of registered shares at will, the board restricted the number of registered shares owned or acquired by a Swiss or foreign individual, or by institutional buyers, to 3 percent of the company's share capital. To ensure that the 3 percent limit would be respected, the board asked the annual shareholders' meeting of May 25, 1989, to modify a part of the articles of association of Nestlé S.A. as follows: "Legal entities that are linked to one another through shareholding, voting rights, management, or in any other manner, as well as all natural persons or legal entities achieving an understanding, or forming a syndicate, or otherwise acting in concert for the acquisition of shares, shall be counted as one person."

Paul R. Jolles

Among other things, the board stated that no one could exceed the 3 percent limit by acquiring or exercising subscription rights, options, or conver-

AND ENSURE THAT DECISIONS REACHED AT THE ANNUAL SHAREHOLDERS' MEETING WOULD CONTINUE TO REFLECT THE CHOICE OF A MAJORITY OF THE COMPANY'S SHAREHOLDERS.

sion rights attached to registered or bearer shares, B.P.C.s, or other securities issued by the company or by third parties. The board also reserved the right to waive the 3 percent limit in specific cases—when issuing reserve shares or exchanging shares with a company it was acquiring, for example. As a general rule, trustees may neither own nor acquire registered Nestlé shares; however, the board of directors has the authority to allow fiduciary registrations by means of regulations or within the framework of agreements with stock exchange or financial institutions, for such exceptions are necessary to facilitate the trading of registered shares on the stock exchange. Finally, the board was given the authority to retroactively cancel the registration of shares owned in violation of the regulations contained in Nestlé's articles of association.

To guard against covert acquisitions, the amendments the board proposed to shareholders stipulated that no shareholder may possess, either directly or indirectly, more than 3 percent of the firm's share capital in the form of registered shares. The 3 percent limit on the ownership of shares applies to registered shares only, since it is impossible to determine the ownership of bearer shares; whereas, it is possible to limit voting rights to a percentage of the company's share capital. This rule is designed to prevent any person or group from carrying too much weight at annual shareholders' meetings by accumulating bearer shares or proxies. Two exceptions to this rule are mentioned in the articles of association, however: shares an individual might have obtained through an exchange of securities following an acquisition, or shares deposited with banks.

In order to further ensure Nestlé's independence, an attendance quorum of two-thirds of the company's share capital is required to modify articles concerning the transfer of registered shares, the 3 percent limit on voting rights at annual shareholders' meetings, the number of board members (a minimum of seven and a maximum of nineteen according to the amendments), their term of office (five years), as well as rules relating to the transfer of company headquarters abroad, to the dissolution of the company, to revoking the mandate of more than one-third of the company's board members, and to modifying any of these articles of association. Decisions on any of these matters must be reached with a qualified majority consisting of three-fourths of the shares represented at the meeting (equivalent to 50 percent of Nestlé's share capital whenever less than two-thirds of the company's capital is represented at the annual shareholders' meeting). Stating its intentions in a special report distributed to shareholders along with the company's annual report, the board wrote: "It is not asking too much of raiders bent on taking control of the company, on fundamentally altering its course of business, and even on breaking it up or liquidating it, after having acquired its securities at a speculation price, that they should, at the very least, rely on such a majority." It was not a matter, then, of protecting a minority of shareholders from the majority, nor, according to the board, of "protecting current board members. On the contrary, our purpose is to ensure that a minority cannot suddenly dictate a fundamental change in the company." That the transfer of company headquarters abroad should require the presence at annual shareholders' meetings of two-thirds of the shareholders and a qualified majority of three-fourths of the shares represented, "shows the board of director's concern to uphold the Swiss character of the company."

NESTLÉ INTENDED TO REMAIN A SWISS COMPANY, HOWEVER. THE PURPOSE OF THE MEASURES TAKEN WAS NOT TO ERECT AN INSURMOUNTABLE PROTECTION AROUND THE COMPANY AND ITS MANAGEMENT.

It is important that the Swiss character of Nestlé be maintained in other ways than by limiting ownership of registered shares to Swiss citizens. Certain of the company's articles of association also enable it to avoid being at a disadvantage due to the limited potential of the Swiss capital market and to counter the charge that Nestlé is an "untouchable" company intent on limiting ownership of the majority of its shares (i.e., registered) to Swiss citizens alone.

The board felt that the amended articles "form a coherent whole." They instituted foreign ownership of the company's registered shares as well as the means necessary to safeguard Nestlé as an independent company with a broad public base. In conclusion, the board declared: "The objective is not to erect an insurmountable protection around your company and its management. Such protection does not exist today and would not be desirable for the future either." These modifications force raiders, who think only in terms of speculative short-term profits, to ensure that they have the support of the majority of the company's shareholders. The board ended its comments by pointing out that these measures were all the more necessary, as there were no

Annual meeting of Nestlé shareholders in Lausanne, Switzerland, 1989

regulations in Switzerland governing take-over bids or stock exchange transactions.

Those present at the annual shareholders' meeting adopted the amended articles on May 25, 1989; they also voted to increase the company's capitalization from SFr. 330,000,000 to SFr. 364,000,000 (3,640,000 shares at a par value of SFr. 100). The company issued 1,130,000 bearer shares and 2,510,000 registered shares—or approximately twice the number of bearer shares.

The amended articles of association were adopted in spite of opposition by CANES, a small group of shareholders who maintained that they limited shareholders' rights. Replying to this criticism (which he rejected), Chairman Jolles underscored the fact that the purpose of these amendments was to safeguard the independence of the Nestlé group.

The Swiss character of the company is, moreover, deeply reflected in Nestlé's corporate philosophy and in the composition of its various executive bodies.

The small CANES group was nonetheless successful in preventing the amended articles from being registered at the commercial registry. But as the board of directors still retained its authority, it decided to implement the decisions of the 1989 annual shareholders' meeting and allow registered Nestlé shares to be transferred to foreigners.

The Swiss Supreme Court, to which the case has been referred, will make the final decision in this matter.

Chapter X

1989–1990

The Dawn of a New Era

Nestlé Approaches the Twenty-First Century

1989 MARKED A TURNING POINT IN EUROPE AND THE END OF AN IDEOLOGICAL CONFLICT.

1989: Changes in Eastern Europe
1990: The Persian Gulf Crisis

☐ *1989 was such an important year that it truly deserves to be considered a turning point in contemporary history owing to the large-scale changes that took place that year in Eastern Europe, where communist regimes crumbled following changes within the various communist-bloc countries.*

The end of the ideological war between the two superpowers resulted in a complete change in relations between the countries of continental Europe. Emphasis was no longer placed on the antagonism between Marxism and capitalism, but rather on the possibility of finding areas of harmony between the two systems. Of course, it was the democratic form of government and the market economy characteristic of capitalism that were to win out. In previous years, many leftist intellectuals—particularly in France—had already abandoned Marxism, for their idea of freedom was in total opposition to the intransigent position of die-hard communist leaders, who, throughout Eastern Europe were unable to give their people the economic benefits they had been promising for years. Gradually, the masses were to lose faith in their communist leaders; and finally, social unrest became so great that it toppled the communist regimes of Eastern Europe one after another.

The leaders of the Soviet Union played a decisive role in these developments. They had already envisaged a certain degree of political reform as early as 1982, during the Andropov regime. But with Andropov's death in 1984 and Konstantin Chernenko's rise to power, the question of reform was put on the back burner for one year. In 1985, when Mikhail Gorbachev came to power, things began to change slowly but surely. Armed with the concepts of glasnost *(transparency) and* perestroika *(restructuring), Gorbachev took on the arduous task of transforming the U.S.S.R. little by little, while striving to reach an understanding with other nations of the world—the U.S. in particular—with the result that political realism ultimately won out in the U.S.S.R. over ideological concerns.*

Given the weakening appeal of Marxist theory and the Kremlin's new policy, Eastern Europe suddenly realized that, if it was ever going to try and pry open the prison bars oppressing it, now was the time to act.

And act it did: first in Poland and Hungary, later in the heart of Europe (in East Germany and Czechoslovakia), and finally in Bulgaria and Romania.

In Asia, the situation was far less encouraging, however. From April to June, 1989, the world was to witness China's use of military force to combat a movement that the central government interpreted as a threat to its existence. We shall now trace these events in China during 1989.

CHINA BRUTALLY REPRESSED A STUDENT MOVEMENT, FOLLOWING THE SIT-IN AT BEIJING'S TIANANMEN SQUARE.

The death of Hu Yaobang on April 15, sparked demonstrations six days later by some 200,000 persons—most of whom were students—in Beijing's Tiananmen Square. The death of Hu Yaobang, who had been secretary general of the communist party from 1982 until his dismissal in 1987 for espousing a certain form of "bourgeois liberalism," deeply affected the young generation in China, who saw him as one of the few advocates of increased freedom and democracy among Chinese political leaders. Initially, the authorities adopted a rather moderate approach to the student demonstrators in an attempt to avoid violent confrontations. But while the student rebels did not directly threaten the government, their activity had the potential to incite other groups to violence.

By honoring Hu Yaobang, the demonstrators were actually showing their disapproval of Mao Zedong's successor, Deng Xiaoping. It was Deng who had rejected the Cultural Revolution in 1978, and who had vehemently fought against the Gang of Four, led by Mao's widow. It was also Deng who was responsible for the modernization of China. However, the demonstrators felt that political change was too slow in coming. They decided to stage a sit-in at Tiananmen Square for several weeks, punctuating it with a series of hunger strikes. They succeeded in modifying the itinerary of Mikhail Gorbachev's trip to Beijing in May—the first visit to China by a Soviet head of state in more than a decade and a half.

When it became apparent that the demonstrators, who had been gathering by the hundreds of thousands since May 7, had no intention of leaving Tiananmen Square, China's prime minister, Li Peng, called out the army on May 19. A state of emergency was proclaimed on May 20, and the first clashes between demonstrators and the army occurred soon thereafter. On May 22, thousands of inhabitants of Beijing blocked the roads of the capital to prevent tanks from reaching the city center. On

EASTERN EUROPE'S COMMUNIST LEADERS WERE TO ACCEDE TO THE PEOPLE'S DEMANDS IN POLAND. . .

May 25, Li Peng appeared on television to justify the steps taken by the government. On June 1, government troops were in control of all of the capital's strategic points, including the main train station (which until then had served to ensure the influx of fresh groups of demonstrators into the capital), the airport, and telegraph offices. On June 3–4, government authorities ordered armed troops to forcibly evacuate the demonstrators at Tiananmen Square. A number of students were killed during this two-day period. (There was considerable disagreement between Chinese authorities and foreign observers over the exact number of casualties.) Though the Chinese government finally managed to regain control of the situation, the cost was high: chilly relations with other nations—Western nations in particular—and the situation was to drag on for months, although China reestablished relations with Japan—mainly in the economic sphere—and held meetings with American envoys. On June 25, the central committee named Jiang Zemin, the former mayor of Shanghai, head of the Chinese communist party.

In short, although the student unrest in Beijing did nothing to bring about the political reforms the demonstrators demanded, China continued to pursue its policy of economic modernization. Transferring power to Jiang Zemin, Deng Xiaoping stepped down as head of the all-powerful Chinese Military Commission in November, 1989, yet he was to retain a certain degree of political clout in his country nonetheless.

Whereas student unrest had failed to weaken the Chinese government's authority during the spring of 1989, this was not the case in Eastern Europe, where mass movements ultimately forced governments either to share their power with political opponents or to agree to radical changes to certain political institutions.

The events in Poland marked the beginning of the end of communist rule in Eastern Europe. Negotiations that had been going on for several weeks between General Kiszczak, minister of the interior, and Lech Walesa, leader of the outlawed Solidarity trade union, led to an agreement in April, 1989, which was to legalize Solidarity to all intents and purposes. It was also agreed that free elections would be held—the first in a communist-bloc country since the end of World War II. These elections were a major victory for opposition leaders; and, in August, the Polish National Assembly voted 378 to 4 in favor of a proposal to nominate Solidarity leader Tadeusz Mazowiecki prime minister. This was the first time that a communist-bloc country was led by anyone other than a member of the communist party. Thus, the party's monopoly over Poland's political landscape was finished, despite the fact that General Jaruzelski, a communist, was to remain president of Poland. When Moscow learned of the results of the election, it merely noted that Poland was taking the measures necessary to ensure the success of its transformation into a constitutional democracy with a market economy. In September, 1990, the original duration of President Jaruzelski's term of office was shortened, and new presidential elections were set for November 25. Both Lech Walesa and Tadeusz Mazowiecki announced their intention to run for this most prestigious post.

IN HUNGARY,

In Hungary, the central committee of the communist party began to promote a multiparty policy as of February, 1989. In March, a new constitution went into effect. On March 15, tens of thousands of demonstrators protested against the police state in Hungary and demanded that Soviet troops leave the country. On May 9, János Kádár, who had been in power since 1956, was replaced by an advocate of political reform. During mid-June, 300,000 persons attended a ceremony to officially rehabilitate Imre Nagy, held at a cemetery in Budapest. (Nagy had led the Hungarian revolution of 1956 and was executed several months after the massive entry of Soviet tanks into the Hungarian capital.)

At the end of July, 1989, 100 miles of the network of barbed wire separating Hungary from Austria was torn down. Meanwhile, the Hungarian authorities had witnessed the arrival of thousands of East German refugees attempting to cross over into the Federal Republic of Germany. On September 11, the Hungarian government made the decision to open up the border—much to the dismay of the East German authorities—thereby permitting thousands of East Germans to cross into West Germany via Austria. The number of refugees was soon to increase as it became clear that this was a much more convenient way to escape East Germany than trying to scale the Berlin Wall. On October 7, forty years of communist rule ended in Hungary. And the elections of March and April, 1990 clearly confirmed the Hungarians' desire to totally reject Marxist-Leninist doctrine. At the polls, various opposition groups—in particular the Democratic Forum—won out over the new social-democratic party (the new name of the former Hungarian communist party). Józef Antall was elected prime minister of Hungary; while

IN EAST GERMANY, WHERE THE BERLIN WALL CAME TUMBLING DOWN,

Arpad Goncz was named president of Hungary by the parliament. Thus, Hungary became a Western-style democracy—although participation during summer and autumn elections was low, owing, perhaps, to the frequency with which the voters were called to the polls.

East Germany was soon to follow suit. The mass exodus of East Germans toward West Germany—via Hungary or the West German embassies in Poland and Czechoslovakia—soon began to have serious repercussions within East Germany itself. Huge demonstrations took place in many of its larger cities, particularly in Leipzig, where tens of thousands of people shouted anti-communist slogans and demanded that East and West Germany be reunified. In October, the president of the German Democratic Republic, Erich Honecker—the once all-powerful communist party secretary, now an ailing old man—was compelled to resign. (This was just shortly after the celebration of the fortieth anniversary of the G.D.R., which Mikhail Gorbachev had attended.) Honecker's successor, Egon Krenz, under pressure by protesters, was forced to open the Berlin Wall on November 9.

This was a decisive step for East Germany toward freeing itself of the communist yoke. Thousands of East Germans crossed the border to spend a day in West Germany in a festive atmosphere. A week later, the flood of "visitors" began to get out of control (eventually, more than two thousand East German citizens wishing to settle in West Germany were arriving per day). Since the beginning of the year, the total number of refugees exceeded a quarter of a million. In November, 1989, in an attempt to reduce the influx of new refugees, Chancellor Helmut Kohl worked out a scheme to gradually unify Germany; however, the pace of the initial timetable was not rapid enough to stop the stream of East German refugees—young people for the most part—causing Germany's Western allies and the Soviet Union to agree that the issue of German reunification should no longer be a taboo subject. An advocate of reform, the new head of the East Berlin government, Hans Modrow, met several times with Chancellor Kohl with a view to mapping out future developments—despite the fact that Modrow would obviously no longer be in power after the elections scheduled for March, 1990. During those elections, the anti-communist parties (mainly the Center Right) did indeed score a total victory over their communist rivals. In April, Lothar de Maizière, leader of the East German Christian

Democratic Union (the East German equivalent of the dominant political party in the Bonn coalition), was elected prime minister of the G.D.R. From that point on, the reunification movement made rapid strides in East Germany.

The economic, social, and monetary integration of the two Germanies was achieved in early July, 1990; while political unification had to wait until October 3, 1990 (i.e., two months before the December 2 elections, which were held throughout East and West Germany). In a very real sense, October 3 marked the end of the postwar period. The German-Polish border was once and for all established at the Oder-Neisse line. The constitution of the German Federal Republic became valid in the territory of the former German Democratic Republic. The German Army—limited to 370,000 men—was prohibited from possessing nuclear, bacteriological, or chemical weapons. Owing to an agreement between Germany and the four victors of World War II, Germany regained complete sovereignty over its territory. Moreover, the newly unified Germany, with a population of 78,000,000, remained a member of both NATO and the European Economic Community.

IN CZECHOSLOVAKIA,

Czechoslovakia initially took somewhat longer to throw off the yoke of communist rule. Czech police had brutally repressed a group of protesters attending an antigovernment rally on January 15; however, by mid-November, Czechoslovakia, too, was racing down the path to democracy. Within the short space of one month, during the so-called Velvet Revolution, that country was to be totally transformed. On January 19, thousands of Czechs assembled on Wenceslas Square in Prague to demand the resignation of their communist leaders and free elections. Meanwhile, the antigovernment Civic Forum, formed under the leadership of the writer Václav Havel, demanded the beginning of negotiations with Czechoslovakia's leaders. On December 7, Prime Minister Ladislav Adamec resigned, as did President Hušak shortly thereafter. At the end of the month, Václav Havel—who had been serving a prison sentence for anticommunist activities only months before—was elected president of the Czech republic. Alexander Dubček (famous as Czechoslovakia's prime minister during the 1968 Prague Spring, prior to the brutal intervention of Warsaw Pact troops) was named president of the Czech parliament. The people of Czechoslovakia reaffirmed their confidence in these men in the 1990 elections.

IN BULGARIA, AND IN ROMANIA, WHERE BLOOD WAS SHED.

Bulgaria, too, was affected by the new wave of democracy sweeping over Eastern Europe. On November 10, 1989, Todor Zhivkov, was forced to step down after three and a half decades as head of the Bulgarian communist party. Since the summer of 1989, when Zhivkov introduced his policy of forcefully Bulgarizing the country's Turkish minority, more than 300,000 Bulgarian Muslims had fled to Turkey. Zhivkov's successor was Petur Mladenov, a communist, who had served as Bulgaria's minister of foreign affairs for eighteen years. In spite of widespread demonstrations, change took place very slowly in Bulgaria, and its communist regime remained essentially unshaken. Preferring peaceful evolution to violent revolution, the new Bulgarian leader worked quietly to ensure that communism would no longer dominate the political landscape of Bulgaria. General elections took place in May, 1990; their outcome showed that Bulgaria was not yet ripe for democracy (a majority of former communists were reelected). In the summer of 1990, student strikes forced Petur Mladenov out of office; in the aftermath, the leader of the coalition of opposition parties, Zhelyu Zhelev, replaced him. Nevertheless, the fact that many members of the former communist party remained in power continued to spark antigovernment protests.

While the political upheavals in Poland, East Germany, Hungary, Czechoslovakia, and Bulgaria in the autumn of 1989 occurred without bloodshed, Romania was not as fortunate. There, the revolution resulted in the execution of Nicolae Ceausescu and his wife Elena. For several years, the Romanian dictator had pursued highly unpopular policies: rationing and the systematic destruction of Romanian villages to acquire more arable land—during which Ceausescu forced the rural population to move to the cities. (Some twenty thousand Romanians—particularly ethnic Hungarians—sought asylum in Hungary.) Nevertheless, at the beginning of December, 1989, the Ceausescu regime appeared to be strong—despite harsh antigovernment criticism by dissidents within the country and the isolation of Romania internationally. At the end of November, Nicolae Ceausescu apparently scored a total victory during the Fourteenth Romanian Communist Party Congress, when, amidst loud applause, he praised the merits of Romanian socialism. The good fortune of the Romanian dictator began to take a dramatic turn for the worse about mid-December, however; and he and his wife were executed on Christmas Day.

At Timisoara, in western Romania, a Transylvanian minister—one of Romania's approximately two million ethnic Hungarians—was arrested on December 16; his ethnic Hungarian congregation, as well as many local Romanians, expressed their opposition to this arrest. Rumors of a massacre began to spread; and, two days later, a state of emergency was declared in Romania. On December 21, during a rally in Bucharest, organized by Ceausescu's special units, the dictator, who had just returned from an official visit to Iran, was heckled by the crowd, which prevented him from continuing his speech. The next day, the departure of Nicolae and Elena Ceausescu from the capital was announced. Meanwhile, riots broke out throughout the country, and there was shooting in the streets of Bucharest. The army—which had joined forces with the rebels—now clashed with the Securitate, *or Romanian secret police, and many people died in street fighting. On the evening of December 23, Romanian television—which had been taken over by the rebels—announced the arrest of Nicolae and Elena Ceausescu. On December 25, it announced that the Ceausescus had been tried and executed. A preliminary film of the trial and execution was broadcast on Romanian television, but fighting continued to rage, killing a great number of people.*

Western nations felt a sense of solidarity with the Romanian people—whose plight viewers in the West could see on their television screens—and were soon to send food, medical supplies, and rescue teams to the troubled country.

On December 27, Ion Iliescu, spokesman for the National Salvation Front, was elected interim president of Romania, and elections were scheduled for May, 1990. Though things began to calm down somewhat during the months preceding the elections, demonstrators continued to fill the streets and express their support of current leaders and to demand the dismissal of all of those previously associated with the communist party. The election results were not completely unfavorable to the communists, however. Some, indeed, retained their posts. The Romanian people chose Ion Iliescu as Romania's president. But the elections failed to put an end to protests in 1990—in Romania's capital and in the provinces—against the continued presence of former communist party members in the government. In June, the government brought truckloads of miners into the capital, who brutally put down the remaining social unrest there.

IN THE U.S.S.R., THE ISSUE OF NATIONALITIES AS WELL AS SERIOUS ECONOMIC PROBLEMS WERE IN THE FOREFRONT OF THE NEWS. SOVIET-AMERICAN RELATIONS BECAME INCREASINGLY SOLID.

In the preceding pages, we have merely sketched a few of the more important events that ultimately led to the demise of communism in Eastern Europe. While all of the countries of this region of the world were to seek closer ties with the West, they maintained their links with the U.S.S.R. nonetheless, continuing to be members of the Warsaw Pact or of Comecon (the communist Council for Mutual Economic Assistance, established in 1949, with a view to improving cooperation, encouraging economic coordination, ensuring economic growth, and reducing disparities in the development of its member states). The economic situation prevailing in all the countries of Eastern Europe was uniformly disastrous and required radical solutions. As a result of a series of economic, monetary, and social agreements it signed with the Federal Republic of Germany, East Germany was the first of the former "democratic republics" to attempt to make the difficult transition from a planned to a market economy—and it managed this transition without experiencing any major shocks.

In the Soviet Union itself, changes wrought by the Kremlin's new policy of perestroika *were soon to bring the nationalities issue to the forefront. Economic difficulties continued to plague the Soviet Union, leading a number of regions—ranging from the Baltic countries to such republics as the Ukraine, Georgia, Uzbekistan, Moldavia, Armenia, and Azerbaijan—to become the stage of proautonomy demonstrations in 1989. Repression of some of these resulted in bloodshed; at the same time, advocates of reform made spectacular advances during elections to the Congress of People's Deputies. In July, the U.S.S.R. experienced serious economic difficulties in the wake of miners' strikes in Siberia and the Ukraine. Despite the fact that he had been granted a great deal of power as president of the U.S.S.R., Mikhail Gorbachev found it very hard to resolve the economic problems plaguing his country. Gorbachev's popularity within the U.S.S.R. was waning—in marked contrast to the monumental success he was enjoying in Western nations. In September, 1990, the Supreme Soviet, or parliament of the U.S.S.R., accepted the notion of a market economy and declared itself in favor of a double reform plan. The Supreme Soviet also granted President Gorbachev special authority to make it easier for the U.S.S.R. to abandon its planned economy.*

Aware of Mikhail Gorbachev's difficult predicament—as both Soviet president and head of the Communist party—leaders of Western democ-

racies (especially President Bush, whom Gorbachev met in Malta at the end of 1989, in Washington in May, 1990, and in Helsinki in September of the same year) were careful to avoid taking any action that might jeopardize the Soviet leader's chances of success. During the meeting of NATO in July, 1990, its members decided that they would make a peace overture to the U.S.S.R. and the other Warsaw Pact nations in order to end the threat of armed conflict and open a new age of cooperation.

YUGOSLAVIA WAS SHAKEN. THE RAPPROCHEMENT BETWEEN THE U.S. AND U.S.S.R. HAD A POSITIVE EFFECT IN THE CASE OF ANGOLA,

The West felt it important to give Gorbachev the time he required to overcome the enormous difficulties with which he was faced. This was striking proof that the ideological war, which had strained East-West relations for so many years, was now at an end. Indeed, it had become clear that the problems between East and West were problems both blocs shared, and Gorbachev's difficulties were liable to weaken one of the men responsible—along with President Reagan and President Bush—for the rapprochement between the two superpowers, thus preventing the world's two most important leaders from turning their attention to much more important global issues, such as disarmament, the Third World's debt, the global economy, the environment, hunger, drug addiction, AIDS, human rights, etc.

Another European communist country—Yugoslavia—was also being affected by the many changes taking place in the rest of the communist bloc. The events affecting Yugoslavia not only caused it to distance itself still further from the Tito era, but also brought to the surface latent nationalist sentiment in the six republics that comprised the Yugoslav federation. In the spring of 1990, Slovenia and Croatia held free elections. (The dominant role of the communist party had already been rejected in February.) Serbia continued to advocate a form of nationalism that did not call the country's unity into question; it, too, rejected the preeminence of the communist party in September, 1990. Serbia's attempt to make the autonomous provinces of Vojvodina and especially Kosovo (where the majority of the population is of Albanian origin) toe the line resulted in bloody clashes in the latter region. For a time, it was feared that this unrest might destroy the unity of Yugoslavia, where economic difficulties are more acute in Montenegro, Macedonia, Bosnia-Herzegovina, and Serbia than in Slovenia or Croatia.

The rapprochement between the superpowers affected other parts of the world as well, for the days when the struggle between East and West

IN NAMIBIA,

IN SOUTH AFRICA...

served to fuel local conflicts were over. This was the case in Angola, for instance, where the officially recognized Marxist regime and UNITA rebels agreed to a cease-fire on June 24, 1989. This conflict between government troops in Luanda, seconded by thousands of Cuban soldiers, and UNITA, which was supported by South Africa and the United States, had been going on ever since Angola became independent in 1975, resulting in the death of tens of thousands of persons. President Mobutu of Zaire served as the mediator in talks that led to the signing of a peace treaty on June 22, 1989, in Gbadolite, Zaire. Fighting continued, however; and direct, secret talks began in Portugal between the Angolan government and UNITA rebels in April, 1990.

At the same time, an agreement was signed in April, 1989 between Angola, South Africa, and Cuba, paving the way for the immediate withdrawal of South African troops from Namibia (which had been administered since World War I by South Africa) and the gradual withdrawal of Cuban troops from Angola. Namibian elections, supervised by the U.N., were held during November 7-11, 1989. The South-West African Peoples Organization (SWAPO), the main independence movement, received 57 percent of the votes, winning forty-one out of a total of seventy-two seats in the constituent assembly. This assembly adopted one of the most liberal constitutions in all of Africa on February 9, 1990. At Windhoek, on March 21, the last remaining colony on the African continent—Namibia—celebrated its independence, electing the SWAPO leader Sam Nujoma as its first president.

In neighboring South Africa, where the effects of international sanctions imposed against it in 1985 continued to be felt, Frederick de Klerk replaced Pieter Botha as president in August, 1989. Following elections in September, de Klerk was successful in effecting a gradual change in South Africa's apartheid policy. In October, the government freed eight leaders of the African National Congress (ANC), who had been given heavy prison sentences for their active opposition to the notion of white supremacy in South Africa. This move served to reduce tension between blacks and whites in the country, and it was followed by the ANC's legalization in February, 1990, and by the freeing, a few days later, of its vice-president, Nelson Mandela, who had been imprisoned for more than a quarter of a century.

IN LATIN AMERICA...

In May, 1990, Nelson Mandela and President de Klerk chaired preliminary direct talks between the ANC and the South African government. In an agreement reached in August, 1990, the ANC formally renounced its policy of armed struggle—a policy that it had pursued for three decades. In return, the South African government promised to release all political prisoners. Thus, the path was cleared for an irreversible process of negotiation between hitherto bitter enemies leading to the drafting of a new constitution. But despite such positive developments, from August, 1990 on, bloody clashes between the two largest black communities in South Africa—the Zulus, led by Buthelezi, and the ANC, led by Mandela—left hundreds dead. For a time, these sad events threatened to call into question negotiations between the South African government and the ANC; and Frederick de Klerk had to take strict measures to restore order (following which it remained possible to cancel the state of emergency in Natal, the last province in which it remained in effect after June).

In Latin America, as they both embarked on the road to democracy, Panama and Nicaragua were often in the news in 1989. Through military force, the United States succeeded in arresting Panama's leader, General Noriega, and transferring him to Florida to stand trial on charges of drug-trafficking. In May, General Noriega declared the results of Panama's democratic elections (that had been lost by the candidates he supported) to be null and void. Eventually, however, the civilian winners of these elections were able to take office. In Nicaragua, ten years of Sandinista rule came to an end following free elections on February 25, 1990. A coalition of opposition parties worked to ensure the election of Violeta Barrios de Chamorro—to the great surprise of the government of Daniel Ortega, which had accepted the peace scheme worked out by the president of Costa Rica, Oscar Arias. The new president of Nicaragua took office on April 25, after reaching an agreement with Humberto Ortega (Daniel Ortega's brother), allowing him to retain his post as the country's defense minister. The problem of the U.S.-backed contras—based primarily in Honduras—who had taken up arms in an attempt to topple the Sandinista government, was apparently resolved after an agreement was reached concerning the disbanding of these forces.

Also in Latin America—in Chili this time—a civilian political leader, Patricio Aylwin, replaced General Augusto Pinochet, following free

AS WELL AS IN ASIA. LEBANON, HOWEVER, REMAINED PREY TO INTERNECINE STRUGGLE.

elections held in 1989. (Pinochet, Chili's leader ever since the coup d'etat of 1973, was to remain head of the Chilean Army nonetheless.) Mexico's president, Carlos Salinas de Gortari, had been in office since July, 1988; while Alberto Fujimori—of Japanese origin—was elected president of Peru.

The wave of social unrest sweeping through Eastern Europe was having serious consequences in Asia as well. The Mongolian People's Republic had rejected the idea of a one-party political system in the autumn of 1989; and in Nepal in early in 1990, a multiparty system had replaced the existing absolute monarchy.

Lebanon was to remain the stage of armed conflict and assassinations, punctuated by rapidly violated cease-fires. Syria continued to maintain its troops throughout most of the country—with the exception of the small Christian-held area of East Beirut and southern Lebanon, where Israel's influence was felt. Meeting at Taif, Saudi Arabia, in October, 1989, members of Lebanon's parliament accepted a peace plan put forward by the Arab League. The agreement provided for modifying Lebanon's constitution, which up to that point had greatly favored the country's Christian community. This agreement referred explicitly to Syrian interests in Lebanon; as a result, General Michel Awn (who controlled a 115-square-mile area of Beirut's Christian sector from his presidential palace—transformed into a kind of mini-fortress—along with an army of about 15,000 men) refused to ratify it.

In November,, 1989, only a few days after the Lebanese parliament chose him to serve as the country's president, René Moawad was assassinated. His post was immediately filled by Elias Hrawi, who was unable to get a hold on the situation for some time due to Awn's resistance. In early 1990, armed conflict broke out between General Awn and the Christian Lebanese Forces, led by Samir Geagea; this bloody inter-Christian fighting dragged on for many months, despite repeated attempts to achieve a lasting cease-fire. The conflict between General Awn and Samir Geagea was due to the former's total opposition to the Taif peace plan, which President Hrawi had signed and which was somewhat less unpalatable to Geagea. In the autumn of 1990, Lebanese Army troops—which had remained faithful to President Hrawi—succeeded in blockading the area controlled by General Awn. With military support from Syria, the Lebanese president's action was successful, and the rebel

Christian general was obliged to lay down his arms and take refuge at the French Embassy in Beirut. With the elimination of General Awn, Syria was finally able to extend its influence throughout virtually all of Lebanon.

In the Far East, the reduction in East-West tension also affected even the most die-hard communist states. The leaders of both North Korea and Vietnam tried to put an end to their countries' extreme isolation. Kim Il Sung, North Korea's leader, sought closer ties with Japan in response to Soviet contacts with South Korea. Of course, normalization of relations between North Korea, Japan, and the U.S., on the one hand, and South Korea, the U.S.S.R., and China, on the other, was still a long way off. An important step in this direction had been taken, however. At the same time, relations between North and South Korea continued to improve, thanks to meetings between the leaders of those countries in Seoul, in September, and in Pyongyang, in October, 1990. Yet, despite these contacts, little progress was made toward reunification of the two countries.

GENERAL MICHEL AWN, A CHRISTIAN, CAPITULATED. IN THE FAR EAST, KOREA REMAINED DIVIDED; THE CAMBODIAN ISSUE BECAME SOMEWHAT LESS OF A PROBLEM.

The withdrawal of Vietnamese troops from Cambodia in the summer of 1990, as well as the desire of the permanent members of the U.N. Security Council to put an end to a war that had raged in Cambodia for nearly twenty years, had a beneficial effect on Vietnam's relations with both the United States and China. The U.N. was granted extensive authority to put an end to the Cambodian conflict and to organize democratic elections there. A Supreme National Council (S.N.C.) was formed until these elections could be held; it was comprised of an equal number of representatives from the Vietnamese-backed government and from the three resistance groups involved in the conflict, and was headed by Prince Sihanouk. Despite sporadic fighting in Cambodia, the prospects of finding a diplomatic solution began to brighten with America's decision in the summer of 1990 to end its support of the Chinese-backed Khmer Rouge (one of several factions in the coalition opposed to the Phnom Penh government). A very faint glimmer of hope appeared in the Cambodian conflict.

Not until May, 1990, was the last European communist country—Albania—affected, at least to a certain extent, by the steps taken a year earlier by former communist-bloc countries—from Poland to Bulgaria—to no longer resist Western influences. As in the case of the

THE GULF CRISIS ERUPTED IN AUGUST, 1990, FOLLOWING IRAQ'S INVASION OF KUWAIT.

other "people's democracies," television played a major role in developments in Albania. Bombarded day after day by broadcasts on Yugoslav television, which reached northern Albania and Tirane, by Italian television, which reached the Albanian coast, and by Greek television, which reached southern Albania, Albanians were unable to be totally insensitive to what was going on in neighboring communist countries. As a result, the government of Albania decided to reestablish diplomatic relations with the United States and U.S.S.R. and to participate in Vienna in the meetings of the Conference on Security and Cooperation in Europe, which were attended by thirty-five nations. In the summer of 1990, nearly five thousand Albanians scaled the walls of various embassies in Tirane and, after several days of negotiations, were allowed to leave Albania for the country of their choice.

At first, it appeared as if the rapprochement between the United States and the Soviet Union, and its repercussions in Eastern Europe as well as in other areas of the world, might also have a positive effect on problems in the Persian Gulf. This was not to be the case, however, despite the fact that the cease-fire between Tehran and Baghdad continued be respected.

On August 2, 1990, approximately 100,000 troops of the Iraqi Army crossed the border into Kuwait. Two days later, the tiny emirate was totally overrun by Iraqi troops. The well-planned Iraqi attack caught both Arab countries and the international community off guard. Initially, the Arab countries reacted with considerable caution, fearing for their own safety in the face of Iraq's might; while the international community—with the U.S. in the lead—decided to impose economic sanctions on Iraq so as to isolate its leaders. On August 6, the five permanent members of the U.N. Security Council—China, the United States, France, the United Kingdom, and the Soviet Union—and the ten elected members of that body voted 13 to 0, with 2 abstentions, to impose economic, financial, and military sanctions against Iraq until it withdrew its troops from Kuwait and reestablished the officially recognized Kuwaiti government. Iraq set up a puppet government in Kuwait for several days; it consisted of opponents of the emir of Kuwait (who, meanwhile, had been given asylum in Saudi Arabia). On August 8, Iraq's Revolutionary Command Council decided to up the ante by proclaiming the "complete and irreversible fusion" of Iraq and Kuwait, a measure that was immediately declared null and void by the U.N. Security Council.

OIL PRICES SOARED, WHILE SHARE PRIÇES PLUMMETED ON THE WORLD'S STOCK EXCHANGES. SAUDI ARABIA REQUESTED U.S. MILITARY ASSISTANCE.

Iraq's decision to invade and annex Kuwait was all the more surprising insofar as the emirate had provided its northern neighbor with financial support from 1980 until 1988 during Saddam Hussein's war against Iran. Talks between Iraqi representatives and envoys from Kuwait were broken off on the eve of the invasion, after the delegations failed to reach an agreement on the precise location of the border between the two countries and on financial compensation which Iraq claimed it was owed by Kuwait as a result of the latter's having pumped oil from an underground oil deposit, located in the disputed border area that Iraq considered to be its own territory. Thus, a serious crisis—which deserves to be discussed in some depth in light of its extreme complexity—suddenly developed, much to the amazement of a world that had been concerned up to that time mainly with the political and economic situation in Eastern Europe.

The Iraqi move played havoc with the stock exchanges of the Western world; and, as a result, the price of oil rose sharply. While Arab states such as Egypt and Jordan tried in vain to act as mediators, Western nations—led by the United States—took steps to freeze not only Iraqi assets, but also Kuwaiti assets in order to prevent Iraq from gaining access to the huge amount of funds the emirate had invested abroad. Moreover, Turkey and Saudi Arabia shut off Iraqi oil flowing through the pipelines running across their territory.

Meanwhile, sensing the threat of a buildup of Iraqi troops along the Saudi border, King Fahd of Saudi Arabia called for American assistance. Troops from the United States took up positions on Saudi territory, while the American fleet steamed toward the Persian Gulf. The American moves caused the Iraqis to call on all Muslims to defend the holy places in Saudi Arabia "threatened by the presence of foreigners."

On August 12, Saddam Hussein televised a proposal for a comprehensive solution to the problems of the Middle East, suggesting that all foreign troops be withdrawn from territory that did not belong to them and be replaced by Arab forces. (Nothing came of this proposal, however.) This scheme would require that Israel leave the West Bank, the Gaza Strip, the Golan Heights and southern Lebanon; Syria would have to give up the territory it controlled in Lebanon; the United States would have to pull its troops out of the Persian Gulf area (where they would be replaced by Arab forces); and Iraq would withdraw both from territory along the

SADDAM HUSSEIN RESTORED LINKS WITH IRAN. THE UNITED STATES ENFORCED THE INITIAL U.N. EMBARGO AGAINST IRAQ.

Iranian border and Kuwait. On August 15, Saddam Hussein decided to unilaterally carry out his part of this proposal—of direct interest to Iran—by not only withdrawing his troops from Iranian territory (which had been under Iraqi occupation since an armistice was signed with Iran), but also accepting the terms of the 1975 Algiers Treaty (which established the middle of the Shatt-al-Arab Waterway as the Iran-Iraq border) and arranging for an immediate exchange of prisoners. (This last measure went into immediate effect.) Saddam Hussein's proposal was significant, for it meant that he was now accepting Tehran's conditions for a peace treaty between the two countries without reserve. In effect, Saddam Hussein was proposing to forget all the reasons that had compelled him to take up arms against Iran in 1980.

Meanwhile, a conference of all Arab states—with the exception of Tunisia—took place in Cairo. It soon became clear that there were two distinct blocs: the majority of those present, who would not tolerate Iraq's invasion of Kuwait, and those who did not wish to create an inter-Arab force for the defense of Saudi Arabia. In the end, the Arab troops sent to Saudi Arabia came mainly from Egypt, Syria, and Morocco; while Great Britain, Australia, and Canada—among other countries—sent ships to second the U.S. vessels already in the area. France also sent warships to the region.

The situation in the Gulf became particularly tense after the U.S. government ordered its naval fleet to step up surveillance in the region and to stop and board all foreign ships carrying cargo to or from Iraq. In response to this action, Iraq refused to grant exit visas to the thousands of Americans and Europeans stranded in Kuwait and Iraq.

On August 19, a U.N. Security Council vote condemned Iraq's decision to bar the citizens of countries with a military presence in the Gulf from leaving Iraq and to send a certain number of them to military or nonmilitary facilities to be used as human shields against foreign attack. On August 25, the Security Council authorized the use of force to ensure the embargo against Iraq. Things calmed down for a while after this vote, for it demonstrated clearly to Iraq the extent to which the international community was united against it. Soon thereafter, Iraq accepted U.N. Secretary General Pérez de Cuéllar's offer to discuss the Gulf crisis in Amman, the Jordanian capital. For a time, it appeared as if a diplomatic solution to the Gulf crisis might be possible. King Hussein of Jordan had also been visiting a number of Arab and European nations in an attempt to find an Arab solution to the crisis. And although the U.S.S.R. had condemned the position of Iraq, it also preferred a political solution.

On August 25, Saddam Hussein declared his readiness to release the women and children of countries whose naval vessels had been given the task of maintaining the U.N. embargo against Iraq. On August 29, the Iraqi dictator said he would release all foreigners held in Iraq in return for a nonaggression pact with the international community. This proposal was rejected, however, because it made no mention of the problem of Kuwait.

During these tense days, the price of oil fluctuated wildly on world markets, depending on the degree of optimism or pessimism the Persian Gulf crisis caused at any particular moment. Soon the price of oil had doubled; however, the Organization of Petroleum Exporting Countries (O.P.E.C.) succeeded—despite opposition by certain of its members—in voting to authorize countries such as Saudi Arabia, the United Arab Emirates, and Venezuela to offset the loss of Iraqi and Kuwaiti oil supplies by increasing their own production.

On August 30, U.N. Secretary General Pérez de Cuéllar met with the Iraqi minister of foreign affairs in Amman. Nothing came of their discussions, however; and, despite Iraq's decision to allow several hundred Western and Japanese women and children to leave the country at the beginning of September, the die seemed to be cast when George Bush's September 9 meeting with Mikhail Gorbachev in Helsinki was announced.

The meeting between U.S. and Soviet leaders took place after a series of fruitless talks at the Kremlin, four days earlier, between Tariq Aziz, the Iraqi minister of foreign affairs, and Mikhail Gorbachev. In Helsinki, the leaders of the two superpowers agreed to pursue their cooperation. These talks clearly demonstrated the Soviet Union's firm desire to find a diplomatic solution to the Gulf crisis; but President Bush did not entirely rule out the possibility of military intervention. For the time being, however, both leaders agreed to ensure that U.N. sanctions against Iraq were respected. In the wake of the Bush-Gorbachev meetings, the threat of war seemed to dissipate, and this was reflected in a certain optimism on Western stock exchanges.

AFTER A SERIES OF FRUITLESS TALKS BETWEEN THE U.N. SECRETARY GENERAL AND THE IRAQI MINISTER OF FOREIGN AFFAIRS, THE TWO SUPERPOWERS REAFFIRMED THEIR COOPERATION IN HELSINKI.

DURING THIS TIME, THERE WAS A BUILDUP OF FORCES OF THE ANTI-IRAQ COALITION IN THE PERSIAN GULF. BOTH SIDES TOUGHENED THEIR STANCE.

In mid-October, following Tariq Aziz's visit to the Iranian capital on September 9, Iraq and Iran decided to normalize diplomatic relations. The next day, Saddam Hussein offered to supply free oil to Third World countries particularly hard hit by the sharp increase in oil prices, providing they agreed to take delivery of the oil in Iraq. This proposal was unfeasible, however, for the countries concerned had no way of running the U.N. embargo.

International tensions relaxed somewhat at this point, as the world braced for a dispute that was likely to last for a considerable period of time. Saudi Arabia, the United Arab Emirates, and Kuwait agreed to help pay for sending troops to defend them against Iraq and stationing those troops in the region, while the NATO countries announced their readiness to provide the U.S. with an increased transport capability.

For weeks and weeks, military forces continued to arrive in the Gulf region. The international community was counting on the effectiveness of its military and economic embargo to make Iraq reconsider its position. However, the Iraqi government merely pursued its policy of transforming Saddam Hussein into a hero for dissatisfied Arabs in the Gulf and elsewhere, who were opposed to wealthy kings and emirs. Saddam Hussein then announced that he would no longer recognize the legal status of foreign embassies in Kuwait, and he soon took steps to cut off their water, electricity, and food supplies.

Meanwhile, on the border between Iraq and Jordan, great crowds of Egyptian and Asian refugees waited weeks for humanitarian organizations and Jordanian authorities to begin their repatriation. (Most of them were foreign workers who had chosen to settle in Kuwait.) In stifling heat, thousands thronged the refugee camps that were set up in the desert—one of the most heartbreaking aspects of the Gulf crisis, for these refugees were to encounter enormous difficulties once they had returned to their countries of origin.

Tension suddenly increased once again on September 14, 1990, when Iraqi soldiers entered the residence of the French ambassador to Kuwait and ordered three French citizens to leave with them. President François Mitterrand immediately announced a series of diplomatic and military reprisals to counter the Iraqi move and strengthen the U.N. embargo. In New York, the U.N. Security Council strongly condemned Iraq's violation of the diplomatic status of embassies in Kuwait. Meanwhile, in Iran,

Ayatollah Khamenei, successor to Ayatollah Khomeini, called on all Muslims to wage a holy war against the United States.

The anti-Iraq front began to toughen its stand against Saddam Hussein: Iraqi military attachés were expelled from EC countries; the military maneuvers of the nine members of the Western European Union (WEU) were coordinated; and the Soviet Union took a firm stance vis-à-vis the Iraqi government, reserving the right—if need be—to send Soviet troops to the Persian Gulf under U.N. command. During this time, King Hussein of Jordan went on television in the U.S. to explain the dangers of war in the Persian Gulf—a war, in his view, that would quickly spread beyond the Middle East. As for Iraq, its leaders let it be known that in case of a military conflict, Iraq was determined to destroy all of the region's oil fields. These threats had no effect on the outcome of the debate within the Security Council, however. On September 25, it voted 14 to 1 to extend the land and sea blockade against Iraq to air traffic as well. (Cuba was the only member of the Security Council opposed to this decision.) Two days earlier, before the U.N. General Assembly in New York, President Mitterrand had spelled out his conditions for a settlement of the crisis: as a precondition to possible talks on Middle East issues, Mitterrand insisted on Iraq's withdrawal from Kuwait and the freeing of all foreigners held against their will in Iraq. On October 1, President Bush stated that a political settlement was still possible if Iraqi troops would withdraw from Kuwait; he announced that he would even be ready to participate in an international conference on the Middle East to discuss the issue of the Arab-Israeli conflict if Iraq agreed to his conditions.

THE U.N. SECURITY COUNCIL VOTED AN AIR EMBARGO AGAINST IRAQ. BLOOD WAS SHED IN JERUSALEM.

Despite this narrow ray of hope, the "logic of war," in François Mitterrand's words, seemed to be forcing men and machines toward inevitable confrontation in the Persian Gulf. Though no clashes had yet occurred, the extent of the military buildup in the area—one of the largest since World War II—reflected the international community's firm intention to force Iraq to back down. Tens of thousands of combat-ready fighting men—mainly from the United States, Europe, and certain Arab nations—were at their battle stations.

In this explosive context, bloodshed occurred in Jerusalem on October 8, 1990. Israeli police opened fire on groups of Palestinians on the Temple Mount—one of Islam's and Judaism's holiest places. By the time

THERE WAS CONCERN OVER THE POSSIBILITY OF A WAR IN THE MIDDLE EAST. CIVIL WAR BROKE OUT IN LIBERIA...

the shooting had stopped, 20 Palestinians were dead and nearly 140 lay wounded at the holy site. The Arabs claimed that the Israelis had deliberately shot at the Palestinians; while the Israelis accused the Palestinians of having provoked police by throwing stones on Jews praying at the Wailing Wall. With the Arab-Israeli conflict again taking center stage, tension in the area suddenly mounted even higher. The next day, Saddam Hussein demanded that Israel withdraw from the occupied territories, that the U.S. withdraw its troops from Saudi Arabia, and threatened to attack the Jewish state with a new missile capable of reaching targets hundreds of miles away. Oil prices shot upward once again; share prices on the world's stock exchanges fell, and the dollar lost further ground against most foreign currencies. Following five days of debate, the U.N. Security Council voted a unanimous resolution condemning the violence of the Israeli police, and it decided to send the U.N. secretary general to the area to prepare a report on the killings on the Temple Mount by the end of October. But the Israeli government categorically refused to cooperate with the mission of Pérez de Cuéllar, insofar as the U.N. "did not recognize Israel's sovereignty over Jerusalem, the sovereign and unified capital of Israel."

This incident caused grave concern the world over. Would Saddam Hussein be tempted to resort to the use of chemical weapons in the event of a war in the Gulf? Might he direct terrorist attacks against those countries present in the region?

□ *Given the fact that public opinion during the summer of 1990 was focused essentially on the Gulf crisis, the veritable bloodbath that occurred in Liberia was not given the media coverage it would have received under normal circumstances. Nevertheless, that small African republic was shaken by events serious and atrocious enough to require the presence of American ships, carrying some two thousand marines.*

For more than 130 years, Liberia was governed by the descendants of American slaves, who founded the country in 1847. In 1980, Sergeant Samuel Doe seized power after murdering President William Richard Tolbert. Doe—who represented the inhabitants of Liberia who had no ties with the American-Liberian faction, but who enjoyed U.S. financial backing—remained in power for nine years and survived several coup attempts. In December, 1989, Charles Taylor, one of Doe's assistants, led a rebellion against him. During the months that followed, Taylor was able to gradually conquer the entire country; and by summer he was on the outskirts of Monrovia. The civil war unleashed by Taylor eventually degenerated into a battle along ethnic lines—with each protagonist at the head of rival groups. The situation became even more complicated in the spring of 1990. Another rebel leader, Prince Johnston—one of Taylor's former supporters—decided to take up arms against both Doe and Taylor. Deserted by his ministers and the majority of his former supporters (who had sought asylum abroad), Doe barricaded himself in the presidential palace and refused to yield to opponents calling for his resignation.

AND CONTINUED TO RAGE, EVEN AFTER THE DEATH OF PRESIDENT DOE.

Foreigners were caught in the crossfire of this tribal warfare. Therefore, the U.S. ordered two hundred marines to land in Liberia in August. Their job was to evacuate the Americans, Europeans, and Asians stranded there. The marines were completely successful and avoided the danger of themselves becoming involved in the civil war.

During this same period, five of the sixteen members of the Economic Community of West African States succeeded in setting up a peacekeeping force to intervene in the Liberian conflict. In August, some six thousand soldiers from Gambia, Ghana, Guinea, Nigeria, and Sierra Leone also took up positions in the port of Monrovia, despite the opposition of Charles Taylor's forces. The death of President Doe in September—killed during an attack by Prince Johnston's followers—failed to put an immediate end to the fighting in the city of Monrovia, which was in ruins. And, during this troubled period, thousands of Liberians continued to flee the country.

☐ *As the final lines of this work are being written—in October, 1990—preparations for a meeting of the thirty-four members of the Conference on Security and Cooperation in Europe are under way in Paris. (East Germany, having been absorbed by the Federal Republic, is no longer a member.) This summit, proposed by Mikhail Gorbachev in 1989, will be held from November 19-21, 1990, in Paris. It will take place under the most favorable of circumstances. A treaty on the reduction of conventional forces in Europe is due to be signed prior to the summit, which will serve to establish a new order in Europe and provide a lighter administrative structure, comprised of a perma-*

IMPORTANT TALKS TOOK PLACE WITHIN THE FRAMEWORK OF GATT. . .

nent secretariat and a Center for the Prevention and Resolution of Conflicts.

From the standpoint of the world economy, 1990 was an important year insofar as it was during that year that important multilateral trade negotiations within the framework of the General Agreement on Tariffs and Trade (GATT) took place, as well as talks between the European Economic Community (EEC) and the European Free Trade Association (EFTA) on future relations between the two organizations.

As mentioned earlier, the GATT agreement went into effect on January 1, 1948. With its fifty-three members, GATT soon became the perfect forum for multilateral trade talks. The aim of GATT is to liberalize world trade by reducing or eliminating tariff barriers. Whereas most-favored-nation status is a trade privilege usually restricted to bilateral trade relations, GATT works to ensure that this status is granted on a multilateral basis to all its members (except where special customs unions or free-trade zones exist).

Several rounds of special GATT trade negotiations have taken place since the organization was created. The first, held in May, 1961, was termed the Dillon Round; it was rather modest in terms of the number of its participants and tangible results. The second series of meetings, known as the Kennedy Round, lasted from 1964 until 1967, and resulted in the removal of tariff barriers in the fields of steel, chemicals, and grains. The third round of negotiations, known as the Nixon Round, and the later Tokyo Round, began in 1973. These served to strengthen world trade in the area of industrial products, while, at the same time, achieving a certain number of breakthroughs in the agricultural field, through the setting up of international trade mechanisms for dairy products. On September 25, 1986, the fourth round of GATT talks—the so-called Uruguay Round—got under way in Punta del Este. Fifteen negotiating committees attended the first session of the Uruguay Round, which has taken on the important task of trying to reach agreements in such highly important areas as: services, intellectual property, barriers to investment, and the reduction of domestic subsidies granted to farmers by certain countries (as well as the effect of these subsidies on international trade). As these lines are being written, the ninety-eight countries participating in this essential round of discussions are nearing the completion of their work in Brussels. The results of the Uruguay Round (due to con-

tinue in Brussels, in December, 1990) will certainly have a strong impact on world trade for years to come.

AS WELL AS BETWEEN THE EEC AND EFTA.

Relations between the European Economic Community (EEC), founded in 1957, and the European Free Trade Association (EFTA), founded in 1960, have always been defined by a series of bilateral agreements. In 1973, similar agreements went into effect between the EEC and Austria, the EEC and Sweden, the EEC and Switzerland, the EEC and Iceland, and the EEC and Finland in 1974. (Austria, Sweden, Switzerland, Iceland, and Finland are all members of EFTA.) These bilateral agreements have gradually resulted in the creation of a tightly knit free-trade zone for industrial goods. Moreover, the agreements have been reinforced by three hundred trade agreements in specific areas.

Over the years, however, the very success of EEC-EFTA cooperation has underscored its limits. For example, during the EEC-EFTA summits, held in Luxembourg in 1984 and at Interlaken in 1987, the EEC gave priority to preparing its own internal market for 1993; greater clarity was required with respect to the decision-making capacity of the various member states and to equitable sharing of advantages and special exceptions for particular member states.

For this reason, rather than continuing to pursue the development of these relations in a haphazard manner, the president of the EC Commission, Jacques Delors, proposed to EFTA members on January 17, 1989, the creation of the European Economic Space. In Mr. Delors's opinion, the creation of this European Economic Space would require that all EFTA members accept such major EEC achievements as the free circulation of goods, persons, capital, and services, and would necessitate a unified policy in regard to competition, subsidies, environmental and consumer protection. It would also require that an ad hoc decision-making body be set up to ensure the preservation and development of such achievements. In the future, there might be a need to agree on additional measures with respect to education, research and development, and even monetary cooperation.

Preliminary diplomatic contacts between the EEC and EFTA took place in 1989. The actual negotiations began on June 20, 1990; these should enable the nineteen European nations involved to sign a multilateral treaty leading to the establishment of the European Economic Space by January 1, 1993.

THE COUNCIL OF EUROPE RECEIVED REQUESTS FOR MEMBERSHIP FROM SEVERAL EASTERN EUROPEAN NATIONS.

Before ending this section on the various international organizations that were often in the news during 1990—owing to the importance of the decisions they were called on to make—we should say a few words about the Council of Europe. Conceived at the same time and within the same framework as the Western European Union (WEU) and the Organization for European Economic Cooperation (OEEC), the Council of Europe was the concrete expression of a certain current of thought first expressed by Winston Churchill in his famous speech at the University of Zurich in 1946 and further developed at the Congress of European Movements held in The Hague in 1948.

The Congress of The Hague (at which such eminent political figures as Winston Churchill, Robert Schuman, Alcide de Gasperi, and Paul-Henri Spaak were present) was the scene of a clash between two opposing views: on the one hand, there were those who wished to see the immediate creation of a "United States of Europe"; on the other, those who wished to work toward gradual unification by increasing cooperation between the various countries of Europe.

The Council of Europe was a compromise between these two opposing tendencies. On May 5, 1949, a European Assembly was created in Strasbourg; its members were elected by the national parliaments of member states and by a council of ministers. The European Assembly was composed of the five participants at the Convention of Brussels that had formed the Western European Union (France, the United Kingdom, Belgium, the Netherlands, and Luxembourg) and was later joined by Italy, Denmark, Norway, Sweden, and Ireland. Germany eventually became a member, followed by all of the other noncommunist nations of Europe. (In 1990, several Eastern European nations also applied for membership.)

Such, then, is a rough sketch of today's world on October 15, 1990, as this work is about to go to press.

Chapter X – Nestlé

Nestlé Looks Ahead to the Year 2000

AFTER TRACING THE FIRST THREE PERIODS IN NESTLÉ'S RECENT HISTORY. . .

☐ Nestlé's future development, after 1990, must be considered in terms of the way the company evolved after World War II. Earlier, when discussing this period of nearly fifty years, we described the main events in the story of Nestlé. Without wishing to repeat ourselves, it might be worthwhile to summarize them here in order to emphasize those aspects of its recent history on which Nestlé plans to base its future development. According to Helmut Maucher, the Nestlé story may be divided into roughly four main periods following Nestlé's merger with Maggi in 1947.

The first period, which lasted until the end of the 1950s, was characterized by rapid internal growth. Nestlé made no important acquisitions during that decade; nevertheless, its turnover in constant Swiss francs practically doubled within ten years. Moreover, Nestlé's geographic expansion on all four continents was constant and wide-ranging. The growth rate differed from one product category to another, however. Sales of the firm's two newest products—culinary products, which it acquired after the merger with Maggi in 1947, and, especially, instant drinks, including Nescafé, invented in 1938—grew the most rapidly. (Between 1950 and 1959, sales of instant coffee practically tripled.)

During the second period, from 1960 to 1974, Nestlé took steps to diversify its field of activities, while sales of instant coffee continued to grow rapidly. Nestlé's sales increased from SFr.1,146,000,000 in 1960 to SFr. 16,624,000,000 in 1974. External growth occurred in the following areas: 1) canned foods: Nestlé's take-over of Crosse & Blackwell in 1960 and its interest in Libby, McNeill & Libby acquired in 1963; 2) ice cream: France-Glace, set up with French partners in 1960, the acquisition in 1960 of Jopa in Germany and of Delasa in Spain in 1963; 3) frozen foods: acquisition of a controlling (80 percent) interest in Findus International, Sweden, in 1962 (reaching 100 percent in 1969), and of Stouffer Corporation in the U.S. in 1973; 4) refrigerated products: initially, acquisition of a minority interest in Chambourcy, France, in 1968; 5) mineral water: acquisition of a minority interest in Vittel, France, in 1968 (reaching 100 percent less than twenty years later), acquisition of Deer Park in the U.S. in 1969, and of Blaue Quellen, Germany, in 1974; 6) restaurants: establishment of the Eurest organization in Europe with Compagnie Internationale des Wagons-Lits in 1970 and acquisition of a majority interest in Cahills restaurant chain in Australia in 1971; 7) California wines: acquisition of the Beringer vineyards and trademark in 1971. Moreover, the company expanded its traditional range of activities in 1971 by merging with Ursina-Franck, a Swiss company. Lastly, Nestlé diversified its activities, moving into a non-food area in 1974 through an agreement with the French cosmetics firm, L'Oréal. During the fourteen-year period extending from 1960 to 1974, Nestlé's internal growth was considerable, especially in the area of instant coffee (sales of which quadrupled, in terms of tonnage, within that period of time).

IT IS CLEAR THAT THE FOURTH PERIOD. . .

The third period lasted six years—from 1975 to 1980—and was characterized by the difficulties encountered in the face of a rapidly changing environment. Nestlé's growth rate slowed down, as reflected in the company's sales figure, which rose from SFr.18,286,000,000 in 1975 to SFr.21,639,000,000 in 1979. The first oil shock in 1973 put an end to this rapid and constant economic growth; in OECD countries, the unemployment rate rose from 3.5 percent of the working population in 1974 to 5.7 percent in 1980. The industrialized countries experienced double-digit inflation, and galloping inflation plagued the developing countries as well. Currency exchange rates fluctuated widely, and all foreign currencies lost value in relation to the Swiss franc. Finally, the price of the two raw materials used in greatest quantity by Nestlé—coffee and cocoa—skyrocketed between 1975 and 1977, with coffee prices quadrupling, and cocoa prices tripling.

The internal growth of the Nestlé group continued nonetheless, particularly in the developing countries. External growth played a more or less secondary role during this period. In 1977, Nestlé's acquisition policy was pursued in the purchase of Alcon Laboratories, a U.S. ophthalmological firm. In the second half of the 1970s, Nestlé was forced to tackle the difficult problems of a long-term trend toward reduced consumer demand in the industrialized countries and the increased risk of overly rapid growth in the countries of the Third World.

Beringer wine from Napa Valley, California: wine label for Private Reserve Cabernet Sauvignon

The fourth period began in 1981, when Nestlé emphasized its strong points to help ensure future development. The first stage in this process was internal in nature, with Nestlé turning its attention to increasing its profits and improving its financial situation. Nestlé decided to end its involve-

WAS CHARACTERIZED BY CHANGES IN THE COMPANY'S STRUCTURE AND FURTHER EFFORTS WITHIN THE FRAMEWORK OF NESTLÉ'S GLOBAL STRATEGY,

ment with products having very little added value (for example, Libby, McNeill & Libby's fruit and vegetable canning operations, which were sold in 1982). The company also eliminated sources of persistent loss (for example, in 1985, Nestlé handed over control of Claudel-Roustang cheeses in France to Besnier in exchange for a 20 percent interest in the latter—which Nestlé was to relinquish to Besnier a few years later). Starting in 1981, Nestlé gradually sold the interests it had acquired in various restaurant businesses—except for its stake in Stouffer; however, the company tried hard to increase sales of its special products for restaurants and catering services. Lastly, in a number of countries, Nestlé was to reevaluate its existing product range, concentrating its efforts on items that were very popular with consumers and eliminating peripheral and marginal ones.

It is not surprising that, for a time, the cessation or disposal of certain of Nestlé's activities slightly slowed the growth of sales (SFr. 24,479,000,000 in 1980, and SFr. 27,943,000,000 in 1983). As Nestlé streamlined its structure and adopted new methods, company profits improved. Among the measures taken were a 10 percent reduction in the firm's total staff from 1980 to 1984; increased flexibility and less dogmatism on the part of management; a reduction in the company's net interest burden from 2.5 percent of its turnover in 1980 to only 0.2 percent in 1984; measures to reduce inventory and the number of debtors; a limited outlay of capital for fixed assets between 1981 and 1983; a reduction in the level of funds earmarked for acquisitions during that time; and, lastly, an improvement in Nestlé's cash situation.

These decisions all contributed to an increase in the company's net profit, which rose from SFr. 683,000,000 in 1980 (2.8 percent of sales) to SFr. 1,487,000,000 in 1984 (4.8 percent of sales). The liquid funds of the Nestlé group doubled between 1980 and 1984; and, in 1984, the group had a net positive balance, compared with a net negative one at the end of 1980. In order to strengthen its competitive edge, Nestlé increased its marketing budget from 1982 on—with increased advertising being substituted for product promotion—as well as its expenditures on R & D so as to improve existing product ranges and create new ones for the future.

As for the company's products, at this time Nestlé made decisions that proved to be of great help to it later on. It decided, for example, to enter the roasted coffee market, thanks to certain acquisitions as well as in-house efforts. (Nestlé introduced roasted coffee under its own trademark in Great

There is now a whole range of special food products to help catering specialists in their work

MAKING IT POSSIBLE TO CONSIDER NEW ACQUISITIONS.

Britain and Japan.) It needed to become far more active in the field of chocolates and to further develop its food-service business in the future—especially products specifically designed for caterers and group-catering organizations. Simultaneously, certain aspects of Nestlé's structure and methods were modified to improve the manner in which the company's development strategies were conceived and implemented. At Nestlé headquarters, some departments were reinforced, while the task of certain others was modified to prepare for future projects rather than immediate concerns (mainly the task of Nestlé's locally based companies).

"In addition," to quote Helmut Maucher, "long-term plan procedures were significantly changed by reducing their formal aspects—fewer detailed forecasts with figures—to foster a climate of innovation among those responsible for markets, to develop discussions, to study the possible alternatives in greater detail, etc." Indeed, it is from the English off-print of Maucher's "The Nestlé Group's Development Strategy over the Last Forty Years" (published in 1986 by Editions universitaires de Fribourg [Suisse] in *Diversification, intégration et concentration*) that we have taken most of our remarks on Nestlé's activity during the forty years since the end of World War II.

Having increased its profits and improved its financial situation, toward the middle of 1983 Nestlé was able to begin considering acquisitions once again. (These have been discussed in detail in the preceding chapter.) The company's acquisition policy had several objectives: to increase Nestlé's presence in the U.S.; to acquire small or medium-sized firms with a capacity for innovation and specific know-how that Nestlé did not yet possess; to acquire food companies with very good brands, capable of being introduced onto other markets; to reinforce the two non-food fields (ophthalmological and cosmetic items) in which Nestlé was active by acquiring companies specialized in these areas.

Nestlé's acquisitions after 1983 were usually made in accordance with several of these objectives. As stated earlier, up to 1986, Nestlé spent almost SFr.9,000,000,000 on acquisitions. Among these were the 1983 purchase of Auer, a German manufacturer of infant foods and baby-care products, and the 1984 acquisition of the Ward Johnston chocolate company in the U.S., as well as two firms specializing in sales to caterers, Paul F. Beich in the U.S. and Goodhost in Canada. In 1985, two U.S. coffee roasters, Hills Brothers and M.J.B., joined the Nestlé group; and an interest was acquired in firms of coffee roasters in Germany (Dallmayr) and in Spain. In 1984, in the field of cosmetics, Nestlé acquired a U.S. firm, Warner Cosmetics, which subsequently merged with Cosmair, Inc., L'Oréal's agent in the U.S., thereby transforming Nestlé's minority interest in Cosmair into a majority interest. Moreover, Nestlé signed a contract with L'Oréal, placing it in control of Cosmair.

NEW PRODUCTS WERE CREATED AND EXISTING ONES IMPROVED.

Mainly to strengthen its presence in the U.S., Nestlé purchased the Carnation Corporation in 1985. Carnation was attractive owing to the fact that it had a large market share, that it was profitable, that its main fields of activity were ones with which Nestlé was already very familiar, that it was active in the new and interesting field of pet foods, that it had a strong presence in the field of catering products, that its acquisition would enable Nestlé to become active once again on the U.S. milk market, that it was managed according to principles fairly similar to Nestlé's own, that its activities outside the U.S. could easily be incorporated into those of locally based Nestlé companies, and, finally, that Carnation's management was also in favor of the acquisition.

The acquisition of Carnation was fully in keeping with the principles of Nestlé's development strategies. The 1988 acquisitions of Buitoni-Perugina, an Italian manufacturer of pasta and chocolates, and of the British chocolate manufacturer Rowntree were also in keeping with those basic principles of developing and making proper use of company know-how, acting with a view to long-term results, and keeping the human factor in mind at all times.

In order to develop and make proper use of company know-how, new products must be invented and existing ones improved. This is why Nestlé considers R & D to be so important. Innovation plays an essential role in the company's growth. The invention of Nescafé in 1938 and the continual improvement of its quality are significant in this regard: in the early 1950s, pure instant coffee (without additional carbohydrates) was developed; then, in the early 1960s, new aroma extraction methods were devised; shortly afterward, popular freeze-dried coffee was invented. Moreover, industrial production of instant pow-

Nestlé also markets pet foods

NESTLÉ ALSO ADAPTED ITS PRODUCTS TO LOCAL TASTES. NESTLÉ TAKES A LONG-TERM VIEW OF BUSINESS...

dered milk in the early 1960s proved that innovations can also lead a firm to reevaluate the importance of a certain number of its activities. (Powdered milk, for example, has taken the place of condensed milk, a traditional Nestlé specialty.) Between 1974 and 1984, sales of powdered milk increased by 50 percent, whereas those of condensed milk dropped by over 20 percent.

Once it has successfully launched a product on a given market, one of Nestlé's basic strategies has always been to extend the sale of that product—and often its production as well—to many other countries and, if necessary, to adapt that product to local conditions and tastes. This was the case with Nescafé, which originally was only produced in Switzerland, France, Great Britain, and the U.S. By 1986, however, Nestlé was producing Nescafé in twenty-nine countries (ten in Europe and North America, nine in America, eight in Asia and Oceania, and two in Africa). Although at first Nescafé was mainly targeted at industrialized countries with a long coffee-drinking tradition, it soon became enormously popular in coffee-producing countries as well. When Maggi joined the Nestlé group in 1947, culinary products were produced mainly in Europe; by 1986, the group was producing these in forty-two countries (twelve of which were in Europe).

During the course of this work, we have repeatedly stressed the fact that Nestlé, unlike a typical conglomerate, does not consider its acquisitions in purely financial terms. Acquisitions are meant to help Nestlé penetrate into new fields and to enhance its existing market presence in order to ensure proper geographic or product-based balance, as well as the distribution of products on a variety of markets. Nestlé's acquisitions must also contribute to the profitability of the group as a whole. Though the group's activities range from the purchase of raw materials and shipping of finished products to the operation of distribution networks, these are carried out by locally based companies rather than by Nestlé in Vevey. Thus, Nestlé itself is not directly involved in agricultural production, cattle-raising, or distribution to consumers.

One of the company's other basic principles is to take a long-term view of things. There can be no question of Nestlé's trying to maximize short-term performance at the expense of long-term goals. Being a Swiss company (and thus under no legal obligation to publish its accounts every three months) is a definite advantage when it comes to applying this principle, for Nestlé is not forced to publish favorable quarterly results at all times. Nestlé has been publishing its annual reports for a long time. And, since 1989, it also publishes a semi-annual one.

It is important for a company like Nestlé to maintain a certain degree of balance in its activities and in its efforts to minimize risk. First of all, Nestlé tries to keep its product range balanced. To avoid being excessively dependent on instant coffee sales, other product categories are strongly encouraged. There have also been efforts made to ensure a sort of geographic distribution, not in terms of individual countries but rather in terms of larger areas: Europe, North America and Latin America, Asia, Oceania, Africa, or industrialized and developing countries.

AND ATTEMPTS TO MINIMIZE RISKS BY REFUSING TO PUT ALL ITS EGGS IN ONE BASKET. THE HUMAN FACTOR PLAYS A DECISIVE ROLE AT NESTLÉ.

The company, which first began its development in Europe, is now firmly established there. Unlike Europe—at least at present—the U.S. constitutes one vast unified market. The other continents consist of a certain number of developed countries (such as Japan and Australia) and others that are less developed. Today, the developing countries, which were initially fast-growing markets, are suffering the effects of harsh austerity policies. In addition to the risk of full or partial nationalization in certain countries, there are now a whole new series of other uncertainties due to economic difficulties: the possibility of import restrictions, restrictions on the transfer of funds, significant currency devaluation, frozen or strictly controlled prices, continually rising costs, etc. As a result, Nestlé must constantly strive to achieve a certain degree of balance in its activities—which, in 1984, was the reason that it decided to increase its hitherto inadequate presence in the U.S.

The ability of a company to act depends largely on its financial situation; in order for Nestlé to act, it must have sufficient funds available to do so. Nestlé must not only avoid too great an increase in its working capital through strict control of inventory and debtors, it must also do its best to centralize funds so that they are readily available to management rather than scattered haphazardly throughout the Nestlé group. However, to quote Helmut Maucher again, "...being concerned about a sound financial situation does not mean becoming set in ultraconservatism. A sound financial situation is a means of action rather than an end in itself."

The human factor plays a central role in Nestlé's strategy. It is essential for a firm like Nestlé to place emphasis on men and products rather than on systems. Our account of the history of the Nestlé Company has limited itself, up to this point, to a description of the decisions of Nestlé's managers

EMPLOYEES REQUIRE AN ATMOSPHERE CONDUCIVE TO THE PERFORMANCE OF THEIR TASKS, AND NESTLÉ PLACES CONSIDERABLE EMPHASIS ON THE TRAINING OF ITS EMPLOYEES.

and their complex responsibilities; it has not directly touched on the important moral obligations of a private firm. A company like Nestlé must be prepared for risks and disappointments as well as success in the conduct of its business. No firm can expand or avoid the dangers inherent in all business activities without a staff sure of in its own future and capable of making the individual and group efforts needed to ensure its continuing growth.

Those dedicated to reaching a common goal should be provided with a working atmosphere properly adapted to that goal. No matter what size company they work for, no matter what their job, employees must be convinced that they are part of something larger than themselves. Nestlé provides a vital service in the field of nutrition, but the company would be unable fulfill its obligation to millions of consumers without the unflagging efforts of the men and women working in Nestlé's many factories, offices, laboratories, and sales organizations. These men and women are fully aware of the importance of their task, which in difficult times can require practically superhuman commitment. Thus, each Nestlé employee must feel secure in his job and be perfectly aware of his assigned task.

Such an approach is essential in order to ensure employee self-development. Nestlé must provide not only accident insurance, an understanding attitude when employees happen to fall ill, and the opportunity for each employee to realize his full potential, but it must also assist its retired employees as well as the survivors of employees who have died.

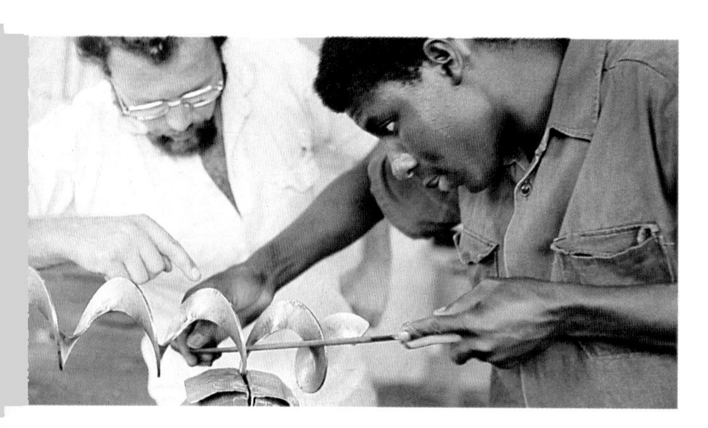

Foreman advising an apprentice in the Ivory Coast

Besides the company's social security benefits, Nestlé has always considered employee training to be as essential as the assistance it provides to retired employees. By assigning each employee a particular place in the company, Nestlé endeavors to give everyone the chance to make the most of his potential, his desire to learn, and his ambition. Thus, providing he is capable and has gained sufficient job experience, each Nestlé employee can hope to move up within the company. Nestlé encourages the development of employees with a general education, a keen mind, and a solid character no less than it does those possessing outstanding professional diplomas.

THE RIVE-REINE TRAINING CENTER WAS ENLARGED.

Nestlé trains its employees itself. We have already mentioned Nestlé's training schools for salesmen in various countries; it has also set up a variety of other training programs. Staff training is a basic obligation vis-à-vis society. In today's world, merely giving employees the opportunity to broaden their professional horizon with sporadic—often improvised—individual training is inadequate. Employee training must be systematic, constant, and must involve staff at all levels of a company. This is just as important as scientific research or technological development. Of course, this problem is not new. For a long time, Nestlé has been training qualified employees capable of solving the problems confronting it. However, constant scientific advances, technological development, and changes in the global economy as well as company structure (whose specialized activities multiply rapidly as the firm develops) make it necessary for a company like Nestlé to adopt a comprehensive approach to training.

A distinction is made between training programs for new employees (at headquarters in Vevey as well as at companies that produce and market Nestlé products) and training programs for future executives (in Switzerland and abroad). New employees attend special courses designed to inform them about the company. After these introductory courses, many new employees enter one- or two-year training programs.

Development programs are provided for men and women who need to improve their general knowledge. Employees with proven track records at the company can take advantage of courses that teach new methods of personnel management or business administration. Those who have attended previous courses also have the opportunity to attend refresher courses to keep them abreast of advances made in the meantime.

In today's fast-paced world, no one can ever rest on his laurels; rather, he must constantly try to broaden his knowledge. This applies especially to highly specialized personnel and business executives. At the Nestlé training center, created in 1963, comfortable rooms, abundant documentation, and simultaneous translation facilities are available to those attending courses. The International Center of Rive-Reine, situated in La Tour-de-Peilz, near Vevey, serves as a model for other locally based Nestlé training centers and helps ensure a unified approach for all of the company's training centers.

In 1989, at the urging of Helmut Maucher, the company decided to enlarge the International Center of Rive-Reine, which already comprised a group of classrooms and a dormitory to house those attending courses.

EXECUTIVE TRAINING IS AN ON-GOING PROCESS.

Nestlé has recently invested more than SFr.30,000,000 to enlarge its training center, thus enhancing its ability to fulfill the task of constantly improving the know-how of Nestlé's employees and executives. The important thing is for Nestlé's employees to be encouraged to perform to the best of their ability at every level of the company: indeed, this has always been at the heart of the company's training philosophy.

It is not enough for the company to work toward improving the professional capacities of its staff; it is essential that they be imbued with the Nestlé spirit. To achieve this, the Nestlé Company has established its own educational institution in Switzerland. German-born Helmut Maucher, Nestlé's chairman and c.e.o., explained to this author the motivations for doing so. First of all, in such an institution students can learn much more than marketing and working methods; such a school can nurture a deep sense of company spirit, commitment, and enthusiasm. Secondly, Nestlé chose to locate its school in Switzerland because the same results simply cannot be obtained elsewhere; students in Switzerland obtain first-hand knowledge about the country, its civilization, and its environment, thus making it easier for them to grasp the importance of the Nestlé Company's Swiss origins. Moreover, with the company school being located in Switzerland, employees are able to get acquainted with company headquarters and also with the firm's top executives, insofar as they—along with company specialists—attend seminars, give speeches, form personal relationships, and attend meetings and functions outside the classroom. Thus, attending these courses permits students to get a good idea of company headquarters, its various executive bodies, and the role of the latter. Finally, while attending their training courses in Switzerland, Nestlé employees from all over the world have a chance to meet and share their experiences.

It must be stressed that, despite Nestlé's emphasis on group training, individual training is important as well. "Hands-on" courses, supervised by the employees' direct superior, are essential, as are the regular training periods organized by the company, periods during which employees temporarily replace their colleagues assigned to carry out special tasks, or perform a variety of jobs within the firm.

A sense of initiative within the framework of a flexible yet well-defined training system, understanding of each person's task, and detailed technical know-how—all these qualities, which the company's training courses endeavor to develop in its students, are even more necessary in the case of

Rive-Reine, Nestlé's international employee training center in La Tour-de-Peilz, Switzerland

FOUNDED IN 1957, THE EXECUTIVE TRAINING SCHOOL, IMEDE...

top executives working for an international corporation. Executives of that caliber must be particularly capable of moving from jobs at headquarters to top posts in markets around the world, and vice-versa. They must also be capable of fully assimilating the technical and practical instruction they have received. Top company executives are not created out of thin air. Careful selection can help talented employees acquire the essential theoretical knowledge required to highlight their personality, dynamism, and intelligence through a healthy atmosphere of competition.

It is important to prepare Nestlé's top executives for the key posts that they will one day be called on to fill within the Nestlé group. This requires that decisions with regard to selection and training be made sufficiently in advance. Moreover, as far as possible, Nestlé tries to fill its top posts through in-house promotion rather than by recruiting people from outside the company. This helps both to maintain unity and to permit a choice of candidates as quickly as possible.

It is also important to consider the human factor in company acquisitions. Integration has a better chance of success if the firms that are merging have a similar philosophy. As Helmut Maucher has written, "Success also depends on the good or bad grace with which the acquisition is accepted by the top people of the company concerned." This is why Nestlé tries to reach an agreement with the management of all companies it wishes to acquire and has never made a hostile take-over bid. (The case of Rowntree in 1988 was a special one; and, even then, Nestlé's initially hostile take-over bid was rapidly transformed into a friendly one, as stated earlier.) Nestlé's sensitivity to the human factor during company acquisitions has always resulted in excellent subsequent cooperation.

Similar reasoning, applied on a broader level, was behind the creation of the International Management Development Institute (IMEDE) in Lausanne, which Nestlé set up together with Lausanne University. IMEDE provides training for people from the entire business community, not just Nestlé employees. Founded in 1957, IMEDE is normally open only to students with a university degree and quite a few years of practical experience; however, it will accept anyone who meets certain basic requirements, regardless of nationality or the type of firm for which they work—be it in the field of industry, trade, finance, administration, etc. Nestlé employees attending IMEDE courses mix in their classes with experts from many other areas of the food industry. During the months they study and live together, students are taught using the case-study approach originally devised by the Harvard Business School. (Additional case studies prepared by IMEDE are also used to teach students to analyse and solve concrete problems dealing with the specific business environment in which they will work as well as the international situation they are likely to encounter at the conclusion of their studies.)

WAS ENLARGED IN 1989.

In May, 1989, IMEDE merged with the International Management Institute (I.M.I.) of Geneva, founded by Alcan Aluminium of Canada. Although both business schools were originally sponsored by private companies, the statutes of each describe them as providing a public service. The new school in Lausanne, the Institute for Management Development (I.M.D.), has retained strong links with industry; indeed, its annual budget (SFr.30,000,000) is provided in part by donations, primarily from Swiss and foreign companies. It is normal for two Swiss business schools, located less than 40 miles away from each other, to have joined forces in an attempt to become one of the world's leading training centers for high-level executives. Moreover, it is logical for such an institution to have several sponsors rather than being sponsored by a single company. (This is a question of company philosophy, rather than a financial one.) Moreover, the creation of a business school in Switzerland, which offers an excellent environment for learning, clearly underscores the European and extra-European outlook of its founders. Along with the Institut européen d'administration des affaires (INSEAD) at Fontainebleau, France, I.M.D. is now one of the two most important business schools in Europe.

Obviously, I.M.D. will have an increasingly crucial role to play within the framework of a unified Europe facing more intense global competition. Indeed, Europe today has the unique opportunity to provide the rest of the world with highly trained businessmen, trained in accordance with European standards of excellence and traditions. As global competition becomes ever more fierce, Europe must begin to tap its great potential. Indeed, Europe is now in a position to offer its top-quality products, services, and businessmen to the rest of the world; and, thus, a Swiss-based multinational like Nestlé has an important role to play in this connection.

Institute for Management Development (I.M.D.), Lausanne, Switzerland

NESTLE INTENDS TO MAINTAIN ITS LEAD IN THE AREA OF ENVIRONMENTAL AND EMPLOYEE PROTECTION. THE COMPANY WILL CONTINUE TO FOCUS ITS ENERGY ON THE DEVELOPMENT OF FOOD PRODUCTS.

Nestlé, together with about a dozen other companies—companies such as Anova, Ciba-Geigy, and I.B.M.—is in a position to contribute to the continued development of this vitally necessary institution. As a multinational corporation, Nestlé's global view of the food industry is reflected in its approach to training, which the company's chief executive, Helmut Maucher, considers to be of particular importance to Nestlé.

It is Nestlé's firm intention to remain a leader in the social and environmental fields, making a maximum effort in these areas, while being careful to protect Nestlé's competitive edge.

Nestlé's future will be a bright one as long as the economic situation of the industrial countries remains relatively sound and stable, as the countries in Latin America, the Middle and the Far East can avoid serious economic and political problems, and as there is not too much upheaval in African countries. Of course, exchange rates will continue to fluctuate in the future, which may influence company strategy to a certain extent. The relatively weak Swiss franc—the currency into which Nestlé's earnings are converted—may adversely affect the company's financial situation, since its debts are contracted principally in foreign currencies; however, the effect on Nestlé's consolidated profit and loss account (in Swiss francs) may also be beneficial.

Nestlé will most probably continue concentrating its future activities in the fields of food products and beverages, for Nestlé is first and foremost a food company. Twenty years ago, Nestlé's best-known food products included such items as Nescafé, bouillon cubes, dietetic products, milk products, chocolates, etc. Today, with the company's expansion into the fields of frozen foods, culinary products, and catering products, with Nestlé's acquisition of Carnation and its lines of food products, Buitoni and its lines of Italian foods as well as Rowntree and its lines of chocolates, the Nestlé group has developed into one of the biggest food companies in the world. This situation has vastly increased Nestlé's know-how in a variety of fields. At the same time, the company has become a leader in a variety of food-industry fields. In order to remain strong in the face of stiff competition, Nestlé must retain its leading edge in one, two, three—often as many as four—areas of food products. Nestlé's competitors may deem it sufficient to concentrate solely on the specific items they manufacture and market; however, product specialists at Nestlé, which is active in several fields of the food industry, must have a greater degree of motivation and be able to concentrate their efforts on the items for which they are responsible. For Nestlé's managers, therefore, expertise in a particular area goes hand in hand with broad general knowledge. Such a philosophy is essential for a firm of Nestlé's size (whose current turnover in constant Swiss francs is sixteen times greater than that following the end of World War II).

NESTLE IS ENGAGED IN ACTIVITIES IN THE FIELD OF CLINICAL NUTRITION. A JOINT VENTURE WITH GENERAL MILLS IS STRENGTHENING NESTLÉ'S SHARE OF THE BREAKFAST CEREAL MARKET.

Nestlé's role as one of the world's foremost food companies was confirmed by the joint venture it undertook with a U.S. firm in 1989 in the field of clinical nutrition. In the spring of 1989, Nestlé and Baxter Healthcare Corporations, Deerfield, Illinois, announced their intention to create a network of companies (in which each would have a 50 percent interest) to develop, market, and distribute products on an international scale. Clinical nutrition is a rapidly growing health-care field, catering for patients unable to feed themselves normally as well as for those in need of nutritional supplements. In the U.S., the company is known as Clintec Nutrition Company (operating as a Baxter subsidiary since 1986). Clintec served as the distributor of Baxter products and services for parenteral feeding (the administering of nutrients directly into the bloodstream) as well as of Nestlé and Carnation products for enteral feeding (the administering of foods orally or by tube-feeding). In 1988, Clintec's sales in the U.S. already exceeded $100,000,000.

The success of their U.S. venture encouraged Nestlé and Baxter to set up similar companies in other parts of the world. All of these joint ventures (except for the one in the U.S.) are given their orientation, are supervised, and controlled by a central unit—Clintec International Operations in Vevey. Coordinating the activities of these companies as well as their R & D programs is the responsibility of the chief executive of Clintec International, Inc. in Deerfield, Illinois. An advisory board, composed of one representative from Nestlé, one representative from Baxter, and one representative from Clintec, with the c.e.o. of Nestlé S.A. as its chairman, coordinates the activities of the two partners.

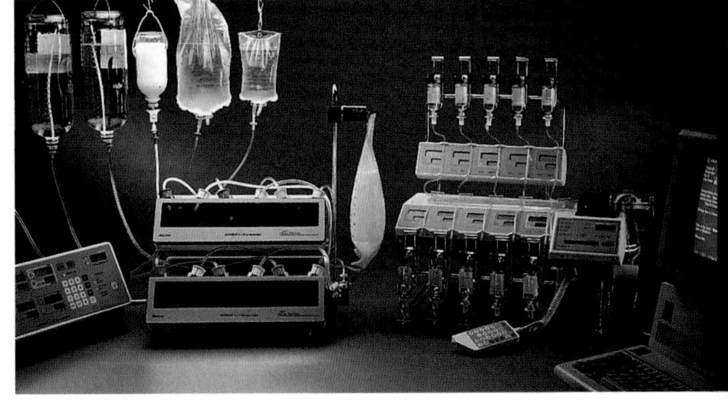

Clintec automatic parenteral feeding units

That Nestlé considers itself to be a food company above all was underscored in November, 1989, when it announced its decision to create a joint

NESTLÉ SIGNED AN AGREEMENT WITH THE WALT DISNEY GROUP.

venture in the field of breakfast cereals with the U.S. firm, General Mills. In their press release, Nestlé S.A. and General Mills stated that they planned to develop the market for breakfast cereals together all over the world, with the exception of the U.S. and Canada. Both companies expressed their conviction that this strategic alliance would enable them to quickly become a top performer in this rapidly expanding market. (It is estimated that breakfast cereal sales will reach several billion Swiss francs before the end of the century.) The press release further stated that products marketed under the General Mills and Nestlé trademark would bear Nestlé's trademark as their principal one. Each of the partners would possess 50 percent of the capital of their joint venture and provide 50 percent of the funds required for investment. Moreover, the two companies agreed that neither partner would attempt to take over the other.

At the beginning of 1990, Nestlé's joint venture with General Mills took on concrete form with the establishment of a Swiss company, Cereal Partners Worldwide S.A., Morges, Switzerland. Cereal Partners is responsible for developing a big, international breakfast cereal company. In the summer of 1990, it acquired the breakfast cereal division of the British firm, Ranks Hovis McDougall. The acquisition (SFr. 240,000,000) was handled through a new company set up by General Mills and Nestlé—Cereal Partners U.K. This company is the third biggest breakfast cereal company in the United Kingdom. This acquisition was an important step toward the goal Nestlé and General Mills had set for themselves, i.e., that Cereal Partners Worldwide's turnover should reach $1,000,000,000 (SFr. 1,400,000,000) by the year 2000.

The press release published at the time provided other details. This acquisition enabled Cereal Partners Worldwide S.A. "to penetrate the world's second biggest breakfast cereal market [i.e., the market with the world's highest per capita consumption] at once and in depth." In addition, the former Rank Hovis McDougall's factories were, at a later stage, to contribute to supplying overseas markets; and this division sustained growth by introducing the company's new brands of cereal.

In 1990, Nestlé reached an agreement with the Walt Disney group concerning a long-term partnership in Europe, thus making Nestlé the exclusive food supplier of Euro-Disneyland's Magic Kingdom park near Paris (due to open in 1992). Nestlé products will be present in the park's restaurants and shops (which 11,000,000 persons are expected to visit each year). Nestlé and Euro-Disneyland plan to develop joint marketing programs throughout

Europe, as well as in North Africa and the Middle East. Furthermore, as of 1991, Nestlé will be the only company in Europe and the Middle East authorized to use Walt Disney characters on the packaging and advertising of its food products.

IN 1989, FUNDS EARMARKED FOR ACQUISITIONS TOTALED SFR. 1,600,000,000; SFR. 700,000,000 WAS REALIZED THROUGH DIVESTITURES.

It is also worth mentioning that, during the past two years, Nestlé has devoted large sums to acquisitions (though not as large as in 1988). Thus, in 1989, Nestlé allocated SFr. 1,600,000,000 to either increasing its interest in firms in which it was already the majority shareholder or acquiring new ones. Such figures would have made headlines a decade earlier, as would the SFr. 700,000,000 Nestlé realized through divestitures; however, now, this was not the case, since the size of the company easily justified such expenditures. (Nestlé's 1989 turnover was SFr. 48,000,000,000.) The firms in which Nestlé increased its stake were Allen Life Savers (from 50 to 100 percent), Australian manufacturers of chocolates and confectionery items, with a turnover of SFr. 210,000,000; Thomi & Franck (from 51 to 92 percent), Swiss producers of culinary products, with a turnover of SFr. 150,000,000; and Davigel (from 70 to 100 percent), French manufacturers of frozen foods, with a turnover of SFr. 530,000,000.

Among Nestlé's more important acquisitions were Cooper Surgical, manufacturers of instruments for eye surgery, with a turnover of SFr. 450,000,000, and Curtiss Brands (the chocolate division of R.J.R. Nabisco, Inc.), U.S. manufacturers of Baby Ruth and Butterfinger candy bars, with a turnover of SFr. 450,000,000. These acquisitions enabled Nestlé to double its market share in the U.S. Other important acquisitions were Arnott-Harper, manufacturers of pet foods in Australia and New Zealand, with a turnover of SFr. 100,000,000; Savoy, a Venezuelan producer of chocolates and confectionery items; and Dr. Thilo, a West German manufacturer of ophthalmic products, with a turnover of SFr. 25,000,000.

As stated earlier, divestitures brought in SFr. 700,000,000. Among the firms involved were the U.S. retailers Original Cookie, Gorant Candies, and Hot Sam; Princes & Trex, British manufacturers of canned meat and fish; Poligrafico, the Italian printer and packaging manufacturer; Beech-Nut, U.S. manufacturers of baby foods, as well as Swissôtel.

Helmut Maucher

In 1990, a change took place on Nestlé's board of directors: at the age of seventy, Paul R. Jolles stepped down as chairman, a post he had held since 1984, and Helmut Maucher assumed the chairmanship, while retaining the post of chief executive officer.

NESTLÉ'S SIZE IS NOT A HANDICAP. NESTLÉ WILL CONTINUE ITS DEVELOPMENT IN OTHER AREAS.

Over the past three decades, Nestlé's size has often been the subject of considerable discussion. According to Helmut Maucher, Nestlé's size would indeed present a problem if it caused the group to become unmanageable (which is far from the case, thanks to Nestlé's highly decentralized structure). It would also be a problem if the group became too gigantic for its environment. But the origin of Nestlé's turnover, its activities, and its factories are distributed throughout the world. The biggest Nestlé unit employs only about 2,000 persons; and most of the others have, on average, a staff of only a few hundred. There would also be a problem if Nestlé's size caused it to monopolize the market. There is no danger of this, however. Indeed, the Nestlé group faces keen, often fierce competition on the markets where it is present. And this has a beneficial effect, for competition brings consumer and company interests into line with one another.

Thus, it is quite possible that Nestlé's sales will reach SFr.100,000,000,000 in the year 2000. Its size will continue to be an asset to it in terms of R & D and will also allow it to take advantage of its sound position on all its markets. What is essential is for Nestlé to retain a leading edge on every market for each specific group of its products. Reaching that goal will require, among other things, unflagging efforts in terms of know-how and staff training.

The company must also pursue its efforts over the past few years to encourage progress in other areas. For example, Nestlé's top management has been reorganized and the responsibility of top executives increased. R & D is now represented within the framework of the company's top management. Nestlé's management has also streamlined its organizational structure, eliminated a number of unnecessary administrative positions, accelerated its decision-making process, and reduced the number of hierarchical levels in the company. Nestlé's legal structure has also been streamlined, decentralization stepped up, and the role of company headquarters in Vevey modified to emphasize its strategic and coordinating function, while delegating more responsibility for day-to-day operations to locally based companies. Executive training has been intensified and an effort made to judge the value of executives according to of criteria other than merely professional ones. An overall effort has been made to improve public relations. And the reintroduction of the company logo—the Nestlé nest—as well as a closer association between the Nestlé name and its products has improved public relations considerably. The importance of brand names has been

Nestlé headquarters in Vevey, Switzerland

NESTLÉ IS HELPING TO MEET THE NUTRITIONAL NEEDS OF THE WORLD'S POPULATION.

stressed anew, and company policy concerning trademarks has changed. Nestlé's financial policy is now more flexible and pragmatic, and the level of its circulating capital has been reduced. In a very important move, the company has also opened its capital to the international investment community, thus gaining access to international capital markets; it has also increased its efforts to provide information to investors throughout the world. Finally, the group's data-processing system has been upgraded at regular intervals.

It is very likely that Nestlé will continue pursuing its strategy adopted in the 1980s; namely, marketing traditional, locally manufactured products in the countries of the Third World and creating products specifically for those countries using locally produced raw materials adapted to local tastes, thus permitting the consumers of the Third World to find food products they like at prices they can afford. Nestlé has already launched dozens of new products in Latin America, sub-Saharan Africa, and Asia.

These developments in the food industry must be considered in the larger context of feeding the world's population (more than 6,000,000,000 by the year 2000 and sure to reach 10,000,000,000 in the not-too-distant future). Such a great number of people could never be fed on a diet consisting primarily of meat products. People will eventually have to turn to vegetable protein such as that contained in soja, rice, corn, wheat, etc., which is significantly cheaper than animal protein. Considerable progress has been made in improving the taste of vegetable protein and in making it easier to prepare. There is no danger involved in applying genetic engineering techniques to increasing the nutritional value of plants. Plants can also be adapted to local climatic conditions. Thus, the food industry can contribute greatly to providing a more economical means of feeding people in the future—especially in Third World countries.

Fully mature soysprout

It was with these long-range goals in mind that Nestlé decided to acquire Buitoni, for example, a company manufacturing a variety of meatless products, to enter the field of breakfast cereals, and to form an alliance with General Mills. This is how Nestlé is preparing for the future, to be capable of supplying a significant amount of the food that will one day be required.

It is also with these goals in mind that Nestlé decided to establish an industrial presence in countries in which it was not previously active in this way. In the last few years, Nestlé has signed contracts with consortiums or created joint ventures in such countries as Pakistan, Egypt, Saudi

Arabia, and China. Indeed, Nestlé is now present in almost all the world's countries, and there is a good chance that it will soon sign agreements in Eastern Europe, too, following the spectacular social and economic changes that occurred there at the end of 1989 and in 1990. (A certain number of Nestlé products are already manufactured under license in Yugoslavia and Hungary.) As this work goes to press, there are encouraging signs that Nestlé sales will progress not only in the eastern part of Germany, now that it has been united with the Federal Republic, but will also expand throughout most of Eastern Europe before the end of the century.

THE COMPANY IS RESPONSIVE TO CHANGES IN EATING HABITS, IN THE THIRD WORLD AS WELL.

In the industrialized countries, Nestlé will have to make a constant effort to adapt its products to changing tastes and life-styles. The growing number of the elderly, an increase in the number of households made up of one or two persons, changing eating habits within the family, a growing degree of health consciousness, and the consumer's desire to purchase quality brand-name products are all subjects of importance to Nestlé. If Europe is successful in creating a unified supranational market, this will have repercussions on the company's production network, which will have to be modified. There will be fewer, more specialized factories and an increase in deliveries across borders. In all the industrialized countries, a concerted effort will continue to be made in the retail trade, which will progressively become international. Therefore, innovation must be encouraged, and new products regularly launched. In addition, the cost price of products will have to remain competitive, and advertising and trademark policies adapted to follow ever-changing market trends.

In the developing countries, the role played by private firms and multinationals has now been recognized; and there is now a trend for these to encourage foreign investment—thus serving to stimulate trade there. Soon the average annual growth rate of the developing countries is likely to be even higher than that of the industrialized nations. Thus, the relative importance of Nestlé's sales in the Third World is certain to increase.

Helmut Maucher and his associates have estimated that, in 1989, more than 80 percent of Nestlé's turnover was generated by 16 percent of the world's population, living in the industrialized nations of the free world; while 52 percent of the world's population, living in the developing countries, accounted for only 18 percent of the company's total sales. It is the developing countries, however, that have the world's highest birth rates. Thus,

RESEARCH IS ONE OF NESTLÉ'S MAIN PRIORITIES.

Nestlé should pursue its policy of encouraging the sale of traditional products, at the same time creating the infrastructure required to ensure their success. This will contribute to increasing the value added produced locally. The company must also endeavor to increase the number of its products adapted to local tastes, by using locally available raw materials (which is often the most economically advantageous approach).

The reader will recall that Nestlé purchases 11 percent of all the world's coffee beans and 10 percent of its cocoa. The company will pursue its policy of encouraging international agreements with Third World producers of commodities such as coffee or cocoa. In Nestlé's view, such agreements are important politically; furthermore, they are in the best interest of all concerned, since they make it possible to avoid erratic price fluctuations.

As mentioned several times during the course of this work, Nestlé places great emphasis on R & D. Its R & D units must be increasingly aware of the close link between proper eating habits and good health. They must also be sensitive to the increasing popularity of fresh food products. Moreover, they must work to develop food products for specific needs. (Once again, these must be high-quality, good-tasting products.)

One of R & D's tasks is to contribute to reducing costs while maintaining product quality. As far as raw materials for food products are concerned, researchers can help developing countries to learn to process these and to employ genetic engineering to produce new types of plants, which can be used in the manufacture of traditional products. Nestlé has already set up two technological development centers in the Third World: one in Asia, the other in Latin America. (An African center will soon be opened in the Ivory Coast as well.) These are involved in the study of locally available raw materials and the eating habits of local populations. In addition, research is also carried out to improve ways of maintaining the natural qualities of foods: sterile filling procedures, fermentation, etc. Environmental problems, changes in consumer habits and modern production methods continually pesent R & D with new challenges in the area of product safety. Lastly, a company must constantly strive to increase the

Experimental farm in Malaysia, a branch of Eastreco, Nestlé's technological development center in Singapore

efficiency of its R & D programs by cooperating with specialized institutes, universities, and even other firms.

In a completely different area, the Nestlé group is conscious of its increasingly important role as a patron of the arts.

NESTLÉ MUST MAINTAIN A LEADING EDGE OVER ITS COMPETITORS.

Keenly aware of the importance of environmental protection, Nestlé decided to strengthen and coordinate its activities in this area in 1990 and to let its efforts be known outside the group. With this in mind, the company created the position of corporate environment officer in Vevey. A female executive was the first person chosen for this position. Working directly under the c.e.o., the corporate environment officer concentrates on all environmental problems related to company activities. She keeps both headquarters and markets outside Switzerland abreast of the latest developments in this area and is also responsible for drawing up recommendations concerning internal company policy. She also sees to it that staff adheres to these recommendations. It is the corporate environment officer who represents Nestlé at the national and international level during meetings to work out environmental regulations; and it is also she who is the company's spokesperson for all environmental questions. In addition, a multidisciplinary group of environmental experts has been created to assist her at Nestlé headquarters in Vevey.

Thus, Nestlé's future will certainly continue to depend on the company's ability to compete with certain very large firms simultaneously on several fronts throughout the world and on its ability to compete in specific areas with its smaller competitors determined to strengthen their market position. Nestlé ranks first or second in terms of sales of several important categories of products in the world's major nations: industrially processed milk, infant formula and baby cereal, chocolate bars, instant coffee, cocoa-based beverages, various categories of culinary products, and frozen foods. On the other hand, Nestlé faces stiff competition in such areas as roasted coffee, mineral water, nonalcoholic beverages, refrigerated food products, pet foods, and various food ingredients and flavorings.

☐ 125 years ago, a few enterprising men decided—almost simultaneously—to found food companies on the shores of Lake Geneva and the Lake of Zug in Switzerland, which were eventually to evolve into today's Nestlé group. During this period, working conditions for blue- and white-collar employees and executives, political, economic, demographic, and social

NESTLÉ HAS KEPT ALL ITS VITALITY.

conditions throughout the world, science and technology as well as consumer habits and human behavior have changed considerably. However, one thing has not changed during the course of this century and a quarter of revolutionary ideas and ever-changing life-styles, and that is Nestlé's vitality. Aware of the challenge posed by three major industrial revolutions, two terrible world wars, dozens of bloody local conflicts, several economic crises, and the extraordinary development of new energy sources, means of transport, and ways of storing and retrieving information, Nestlé constantly seeks to prepare for the future with both pragmatism and boldness, drawing upon its wealth of experience to make the right choice in the present. Despite its size, Nestlé has always remained flexible; improving its working methods year after year, the company has succeeded in continually reshaping its structure in response to strong competition in all the fields in which it is active.

It is being in constant competition with firms similar to itself (though sometimes more highly specialized in certain product areas) that has helped Nestlé to keep its leading edge today as in the past. In our work published for Nestlé's centennial in 1966, we wrote: "If an athlete is to win his race, he must be at the peak of fitness, confident in himself and his judgment; he must time his effort wisely, and, at the decisive moment of challenge, give it all he has got. Similarly, Nestlé has to keep its financial strength and its structure intact, look ahead, act with proper deliberation, keep pace with changing trends in distribution, the steady progress of automation, and the changes in international economic groupings such as the Common Market." "In short," we wrote, "Nestlé has to keep constantly on the alert. The secret of the firm's past and present success is its vitality." Twenty-five years later, this vitality is still the best guarantee of Nestlé's future.

Three statistics illustrate Nestlé's vitality in 1991: more than 400 production centers throughout the world; 100,000 Swiss and foreign shareholders; and nearly 200,000 employees, manufacturing and marketing Nestlé products.

Although it has always remained faithful to its Swiss origins, Nestlé has evolved over the years into the most internationally oriented multinational in the world. Thanks to the efforts of management and staff at every level of the company, today, as in the past, Nestlé can face the future with confidence. Nestlé has come a long way since its founding in the age of oil lamps. But this is only the beginning, and the future still holds much in store for the company.

In this rapidly changing world, in which ideologies come and go, a new wind is blowing: virtually everywhere free markets are being introduced in countries that only a short time ago were languishing under planned economies. Realism has triumphed over utopianism. These are exceptional times. International cooperation is now global in nature; many countries have opened their doors to world trade. The coming era will be one of increased solidarity. There are many new opportunities on the horizon for multinationals, which have gained acceptance virtually everywhere. Nestlé's prospects for continued growth in the coming years are promising and exciting.

Index

This index includes only the names of the persons mentioned in the sections of each chapter devoted to the Nestlé Company.

L

M

N

O

P

ACKNOWLEDGMENTS
We are extremely grateful to everyone who helped us with the photographic research, in particular Mrs. Irène Décombaz, Mr. Robert Lorenz, and Dr. René Koenig.

PHOTO CREDITS
Nestlé Archives
Private collections: pp. 54, 71, 109, 254, 306
Musée historique du Vieux-Vevey: pp. 53, 135
Pierre Izard, Pully, Switzerland: p. 195

ICONOGRAPHY
Nestec S.A., Visual Communications-CI/IE, Lydia de Burlet and Colette Vurlod.

CONCEPT AND DESIGN
Nestec S.A., Visual Communications-CI.
Art Director and Designer: René Ciocca.

FILM SETTING
Stämpfli + Cie AG, Bern, Switzerland.

PHOTOLITHOGRAPHS
Berger et Fatio, Denges, Switzerland.

PRINTING AND BINDING
Stämpfli + Cie AG, Bern, Switzerland.

Original title: *Nestlé: Cent vingt-cinq ans de 1866 à 1991*

TRANSLATION
B.J. Benson with Constance Devanthéry-Lewis

This work, originally written in French, is also being published in English, German, Italian, and Spanish.